REPAIR MANUAL

FORD TAURUS MERCURY SABLE 1986-92

Covers all U.S. and Canadian models

President, Chilton Enterprises	David S. Loewith
Senior Vice President	Ronald A. Hoxter
Publisher and Editor-In-Chief	Kerry A. Freeman, S.A.E.
Managing Editors	Peter M. Conti, Jr. □ W. Calvin Settle, Jr., S.A.E.
Assistant Managing Editor	Nick D'Andrea
Senior Editors	Debra Gaffney □ Ken Grabowski, A.S.E., S.A.E.
	Michael L. Grady □ Richard J. Rivele, S.A.E.
	Richard T. Smith □ Jim Taylor
	Ron Webb
Director of Manufacturing	Mike D'Imperio

CHILTON BOOK COMPANY

ONE OF THE DIVERSIFIED PUBLISHING COMPANIES,
A PART OF CAPITAL CITIES/ABC, INC.

SAFETY NOTICE

Proper service and repair procedures are vital to the safe, reliable operation of all motor vehicles, as well as the safety of those performing repairs. This book outlines procedures for servicing and repairing vehicles using safe effective methods. The procedures contain many NOTES, CAUTIONS and WARNINGS which should be followed along with standard safety procedures to eliminate the possibility of personal injury or improper service which could damage the vehicle or compromise its safety.

It is important to note that repair procedures and techniques, tools and parts for servicing motor vehicles, as well as the skill and experience of the individual performing the work vary widely. It is not possible to anticipate all of the conceivable ways or conditions under which vehicles may be serviced, or to provide cautions as to all of the possible hazards that may result. Standard and accepted safety precautions and equipment should be used during cutting, grinding, chiseling, prying, or any other process that can cause material removal or projectiles.

Some procedures require the use of tools specially designed for a specific purpose. Before substituting another tool or procedure, you must be completely satisfied that neither your personal safety, nor the performance of the vehicle will be endangered.

Although the information in this guide is based on industry sources and is as complete as possible at the time of publication, the possibility exists that the manufacturer made later changes which could not be included here. While striving for total accuracy, Chilton Book Company cannot assume responsibilty for any errors, changes, or omissions that may occur in the compilation of this data.

PART NUMBERS

Part numbers listed in the reference are not recommendations by Chilton for any product by brand name. They are references that can be used with interchange manuals and aftermarket supplier catalogs to locate each brand supplier's discrete part number.

SPECIAL TOOLS

Special tools are recommended by the vehicle manufacturer to perform their specific job. Use has been kept to a minimum, but where absolutely necessary, they are referred to in the text by the part number of the tool manufacturer. These tools can be purchased, under the appropriate part number, from your Ford or Mercury dealer or regional distributor, or an equivalent tool can be purchased locally from a tool supplier or parts outlet. Before substituting any tool for the one recommended, read the SAFETY NOTICE at the top of this page.

ACKNOWLEDGEMENTS

Chilton Book Company expresses appreciation to Ford Motor Company; Ford Parts and Service Division, Service Technical Communications Department, Dearborn, Michigan for their generous assistance

Chilton's Repair Manual: Ford Taurus/Mercury Sable 1986–92
ISBN 0–8019–8297–9 pbk.
Library of Congress Catalog Card No. 91–058852

CONTENTS

GENERAL INFORMATION and MAINTENANCE

1 How to use this book
2 Tools and Equipment
7 Routine Maintenance

ENGINE PERFORMANCE and TUNE-UP

50 Tune-Up Performance
51 Tune-Up Specifications

ENGINE and ENGINE OVERHAUL

65 Engine Electrical System
72 Engine Service
77 Engine Specifications

EMISSION CONTROLS

153 Emission Controls System and Service

FUEL SYSTEM

170 Fuel Injection System
192 Fuel Tank

CHASSIS ELECTRICAL

195 Heating and Air Conditioning
210 Instruments and Switches
217 Lighting
222 Circuit Protection

7  DRIVE TRAIN

227 Manual Transaxle
235 Clutch
239 Automatic Transaxle
246 Halfshafts

8  SUSPENSION and STEERING

254 Front Suspension
262 Rear Suspension
274 Steering

9  BRAKES

291 Brake Systems
296 Front Disc Brakes
299 Rear Drum Brakes
302 Rear Disc Brakes

10  BODY

315 Exterior
330 Interior

11 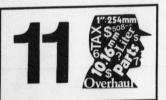 MECHANIC'S DATA

348 Mechanic's Data
350 Glossary
356 Abbreviations
358 Index

173 Chilton's Fuel Economy
and Tune-Up Tips

333 Chilton's Body Repair Tips

General Information and Maintenance

1

HOW TO USE THIS BOOK

Chilton's Repair Manual for Ford Taurus and Mercury Sable is intended to teach you more about the inner workings of your car and save you money on its upkeep. The first two Chapters will be used the most, since they contain maintenance and tune-up information and procedures. The following Chapters concern themselves with the more complex systems. Operating systems from engine through brakes are covered to the extent that we feel the average do-it-yourselfer should get involved as well as more complex procedures that will benefit both the advanced do-it-yourselfer mechanic as well as the professional.

A secondary purpose of this book is as a reference for owners who want to understand their car and/or their mechanics better. In this case, no tools at all are required.

Before attempting any repairs or service on your car, read through the entire procedure outlined in the appropriate Chapter. This will give you the overall view of what tools and supplies will be required. There is nothing more frustrating than having to walk to the bus stop on Monday morning because you were short one gasket on Sunday afternoon. So read ahead and plan ahead. Each operation should be approached logically and all procedures thoroughly understood before attempting any work. Some special tools that may be required can often be rented from local automotive jobbers or places specializing in renting tools and equipment. Check the yellow pages of your phone book.

All Chapters contain adjustments, maintenance, removal and installation procedures, and overhaul procedures. When overhaul is not considered practical, we tell you how to remove the failed part and then how to install the new or rebuilt replacement. In this way, you at least save the labor costs. Backyard overhaul of some components is just not practical, but the removal and installation procedure is often simple and well within the capabilities of the average car owner.

Two basic mechanic's rules should be mentioned here. First, whenever the LEFT side of the car or engine is referred to, it is meant to specify the DRIVER'S side of the car. Conversely, the RIGHT side of the car means the PASSENGER'S side. Second, all screws and bolts are removed by turning counterclockwise, and tightened by turning clockwise, unless otherwise noted.

Safety is always the most important rule. Constantly be aware of the dangers involved in working on or around an automobile and take proper precautions to avoid the risk of personal injury or damage to the vehicle. See the section in this Chapter, Servicing Your Vehicle Safely, and the SAFETY NOTICE on the acknowledgment page before attempting any service procedures and pay attention to the instructions provided. There are 3 common mistakes in mechanical work:

1. Incorrect order of assembly, disassembly or adjustment. When taking something apart or putting it together, doing things in the wrong order usually just costs you extra time; however it CAN break something. Read the entire procedure before beginning disassembly. Do everything in the order in which the instructions say you should do it, even if you can't immediately see a reason for it. When you're taking apart something that is very intricate, you might want to draw a picture of how it looks when assembled at one point in order to make sure you get everything back in its proper position. We will supply exploded views whenever possible, but sometimes the job requires more attention to detail than an illustration provides. When making adjustments (especially

tune-up adjustments), do them in order. One adjustment often affects another and you cannot expect satisfactory results unless each adjustment is made only when it cannot be changed by any other.

2. Overtorquing (or undertorquing) nuts and bolts. While it is more common for over-torquing to cause damage, undertorquing can cause a fastener to vibrate loose and cause serious damage, especially when dealing with aluminum parts. Pay attention to torque specifications and utilize a torque wrench in assembly. If a torque figure is not available remember that, if you are using the right tool to do the job, you will probably not have to strain yourself to get a fastener tight enough. The pitch of most threads is so slight that the tension you put on the wrench will be multiplied many times in actual force on what you are tightening. A good example of how critical torque is can be seen in the case of spark plug installation, especially where you are putting the plug into an aluminum cylinder head. Too little torque can fail to crush the gasket, causing leakage of combustion gases and consequent overheating of the plug and engine parts. Too much torque can damage the threads or distort the plug, which changes the spark gap at the electrode. Since more and more manufacturers are using aluminum in their engine and chassis parts to save weight, a torque wrench should be in any serious do-it-yourselfer's tool box.

There are many commercial chemical products available for ensuring that fasteners won't come loose, even if they are not torqued just right (a very common brand is Loctite®). If you're worried about getting something together tight enough to hold, but loose enough to avoid mechanical damage during assembly, one of these products might offer substantial insurance. Read the label on the package and make sure the product is compatible with the materials, fluids, etc. involved before choosing one.

3. Crossthreading. This occurs when a part such as a bolt is screwed into a nut or casting at the wrong angle and forced, causing the threads to become damaged. Crossthreading is more likely to occur if access is difficult. It helps to clean and lubricate fasteners, and to start threading with the part to be installed going straight in, using your fingers. If you encounter resistance, unscrew the part and start over again at a different angle until it can be inserted and turned several times without much effort. Keep in mind that many parts, especially spark plugs, use tapered threads so that gentle turning will automatically bring the part you're threading to the proper angle if you don't force it or resist a change in angle. Don't

put a wrench on the part until it's been turned in a couple of times by hand. If you suddenly encounter resistance and the part has not seated fully, don't force it. Pull it back out and make sure it's clean and threading properly.

Always take your time and be patient; once you have some experience, working on your car will become an enjoyable hobby.

TOOLS AND EQUIPMENT

Naturally, without the proper tools and equipment it is impossible to properly service your vehicle. It would be impossible to catalog each tool that you would need to perform each or every operation in this book. It would also be unwise for the amateur to rush out and buy an expensive set of tools an the theory that he may need one or more of them at sometime.

The best approach is to proceed slowly, gathering together a good quality set of those tools that are used most frequently. Don't be misled by the low cost of bargain tools. It is far better to spend a little more for better quality. Forged wrenches, 6- or 12-point sockets and fine tooth ratchets are by far preferable to their less expensive counterparts. As any good mechanic can tell you, there are few worse experiences than trying to work on a truck with bad tools. Your monetary savings will be far outweighed by frustration and mangled knuckles.

Certain tools, plus a basic ability to handle tools, are required to get started. A basic mechanics tool set, a torque wrench, and a Torx bits set. Torx bits are hexlobular drivers which fit both inside and outside on special Torx head fasteners used in various places on your vehicle.

Begin accumulating those tools that are used most frequently; those associated with routine maintenance and tune-up.

In addition to the normal assortment of screwdrivers and pliers you should have the following tools for routine maintenance jobs (your vehicle, depending on the model year, uses both SAE and metric fasteners):

1. SAE/Metric wrenches, sockets and combination open end/box end wrenches in sizes from $1/8$ in. (3mm) to $3/4$ in. (19mm); and a spark plug socket ($13/16$ in.) If possible, buy various length socket drive extensions. One break in this department is that the metric sockets available in the U.S. will all fit the ratchet handles and extensions you may already have ($1/4$ in., $3/8$ in., and $1/2$ in. drive).

2. Jackstands for support
3. Oil filter wrench
4. Oil filter spout for pouring oil

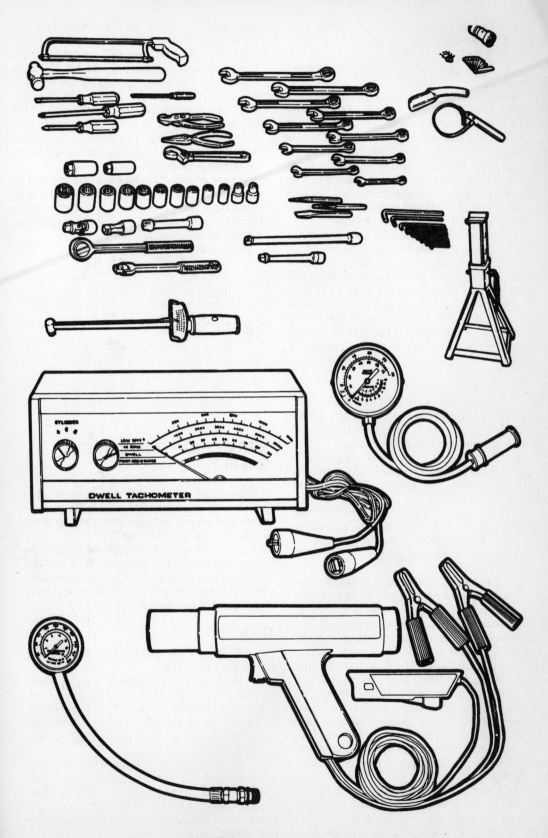

Typical tools needed for vehicle repairs

5. Grease gun for chassis lubrication
6. Hydrometer for checking the battery
7. A container for draining oil
8. Many rags for wiping up the inevitable mess.

In addition to the above items there are several others that are not absolutely necessary, but handy to have around. These include oil-dry (cat box litter works just as well and may be cheaper), a transmission funnel and the usual supply of lubricants, antifreeze and fluids, although these can be purchased as needed. This is a basic list for routine maintenance, but only your personal needs and desires can accurately determine your list of necessary tools.

The second list of tools is for tune-ups. While the tools involved here are slightly more sophisticated, they need not be outrageously expensive. There are several inexpensive tach/dwell meters on the market that are every bit as good for the average mechanic as a $100.00 professional model. Just be sure that it goes to at least 1,200–1,500 rpm on the tach scale and that it works on 4, 6 and 8 cylinder engines. A basic list of tune-up equipment could include:

1. Tach-dwell meter
2. Spark plug wrench
3. Timing light (a DC light that works from the vehicle's battery is best, although an AC light that plugs into 110V house current will suffice at some sacrifice in brightness)
4. Wire spark plug gauge/adjusting tools

In addition to these basic tools, there are several other tools and gauges you may find useful. These include:

1. A compression gauge. The screw-in type is slower to use, but eliminates the possibility of a faulty reading due to escaping pressure
2. A manifold vacuum gauge
3. A test light
4. An induction meter. This is used for determining whether or not there is current in a wire. These are handy for use if a wire is broken somewhere in a wiring harness.

Normally, the use of special factory tools is avoided for repair procedures, since these are not readily available for the do-it-yourself mechanic. When it is possible to perform the job with more commonly available tools, it will be pointed out, but occasionally, a special tool was designed to perform a specific function and should be used. Before substituting another tool, you should be convinced that neither your safety nor the performance of the vehicle will be compromised.

When a special tool is indicated, it will be referred to by the manufacturer's part number. Some special tools are available commercially from major tool manufacturers. Others for your car can be purchased from your Ford/Mercury dealer or from the Owatonna Tool Co., Owatonna, Minnesota 55060.

As a final note, you will probably find a torque wrench necessary for all but the most basic work. The beam type models are perfectly adequate, although the newer click (breakaway) type are more precise, and you don't have to crane your neck to see a torque reading in awkward situations. The breakaway torque wrenches are more expensive and should be recalibrated periodically.

Torque specification for each fastener will be given in the procedure in any case that a specific torque value is required. If no torque specifications are given, use the following values as a guide, based upon fastener size:

Bolts marked 6T
6mm bolt/nut — 5–7 ft. lbs.
8mm bolt/nut — 12–17 ft. lbs.
10mm bolt/nut — 23–34 ft. lbs.
12mm bolt/nut — 41–59 ft. lbs.
14mm bolt/nut — 56–76 ft. lbs.

Bolts marked 8T
6mm bolt/nut — 6–9 ft. lbs.
8mm bolt/nut — 13–20 ft. lbs.
10mm bolt/nut — 27–40 ft. lbs.
12mm bolt/nut — 46–69 ft. lbs.
14mm bolt/nut — 75–101 ft. lbs.

SERVICING YOUR VEHICLE SAFELY

It is virtually impossible to anticipate all of the hazards involved with automotive maintenance and service but care and common sense will prevent most accidents.

The rules of safety for mechanics range from "don't smoke around gasoline," to "use the proper tool for the job." The trick to avoid injuries is to develop safe work habits and take every possible precaution.

Do's

• Do keep a fire extinguisher and first aid kit within easy reach.
• Do wear safety glasses or goggles when cutting, drilling, grinding or prying. If you wear glasses for the sake of vision, then they should be made of hardened glass that can serve also as safety glasses, or wear safety goggles over your regular glasses.
• Do wear safety glasses whenever you work around the battery. Batteries contain sulphuric acid. In case of contact with the eyes or skin, flush the area with water or a mixture of water and baking soda and get medical attention immediately.
• Do use safety stands for any under-car

service. Jacks are for raising vehicles; safety stands are for making sure the vehicle stays raised until you want it to come down. Whenever the vehicle is raised, block the wheels remaining on the ground and set the parking brake.

• Do use adequate ventilation when working with any chemicals. Asbestos dust resulting from brake lining wear can cause cancer.

• Do disconnect the negative battery cable when working on the electrical system. The primary ignition system can contain up to 40,000 volts.

• Do follow manufacturer's directions whenever working with potentially hazardous materials. Both brake fluid and antifreeze are poisonous if taken internally.

• Do properly maintain your tools. Loose hammerheads, mushroomed punches and chisels, frayed or poorly grounded electrical cords, excessively worn screwdriver, spread wrenches (open end), cracked sockets can cause accidents.

• Do use the proper size and type of tool for the job being done.

• Do when possible, pull on a wrench handle rather than push on it, and adjust your stance to prevent a fall.

• Do be sure that adjustable wrenches are tightly adjusted on the nut or bolt and pulled so that the face is on the side of the fixed jaw.

• Do select a wrench or socket that fits the nut or bolt. The wrench or socket should sit straight, not cocked.

• Do strike squarely with a hammer to avoid glancing blows.

• Do set the parking brake and block the drive wheels if the work requires that the engine is running.

Don'ts

• Don't run an engine in a garage or anywhere else without proper ventilation — EVER! Carbon monoxide is poisonous. It is absorbed by the body 400 times faster than oxygen. It takes a long time to leave the human body and you can build up a deadly supply of it in you system by simply breathing in a little every day. You may not realize you are slowly poisoning yourself. Always use power vents, windows, fans or open the garage doors.

• Don't work around moving parts while wearing a necktie or other loose clothing. Short sleeves are much safer than long, loose sleeves. Hard-toed shoes with neoprene soles protect your toes and give a better grip on slippery surfaces. Jewelry such as watches, fancy belt buckles, beads or body adornment of any kind is not safe working around a car. Long hair should be hidden under a hat or cap.

• Don't use pockets for tool boxes. A fall or bump can drive a screwdriver deep into you body. Even a wiping cloth hanging from the back pocket can wrap around a spinning shaft or fan.

• Don't smoke when working around gasoline, cleaning solvent or other flammable material.

• Don't smoke when working around the battery. When the battery is being charged, it gives off explosive hydrogen gas.

• Don't use gasoline to wash your hands. There are excellent soaps available. Gasoline may contain lead, and lead can enter the body through a cut, accumulating in the body until you are very ill. Gasoline also removes all the natural oils from the skin so that bone dry hands will suck up oil and grease.

• Don't service the air conditioning system unless you are equipped with the necessary tools and training. Do wear safety glasses, the refrigerant, is extremely cold and when exposed to the air, will instantly freeze any surface it comes in contact with, including your eyes. Although the refrigerant is normally nontoxic, it becomes a deadly poisonous gas in the presence of an open flame. One good whiff of the vapors from burning refrigerant can be fatal.

MODEL IDENTIFICATION

The vehicle model year identification can be confirmed by locating the 10th position of the

SERIAL NUMBER IDENTIFICATION

Vehicle

The official vehicle identification (serial) number (used for title and registration purposes) is stamped on a metal tab fastened to the instrument panel and visible through the driver's side of the windshield from the outside. The vehicle identification (serial) number contains a 17 digit number. The number is used for warranty identification of the vehicle and indicates: manufacturer, type of restraint system, line, series, body type, engine, model year, and consecutive unit number.

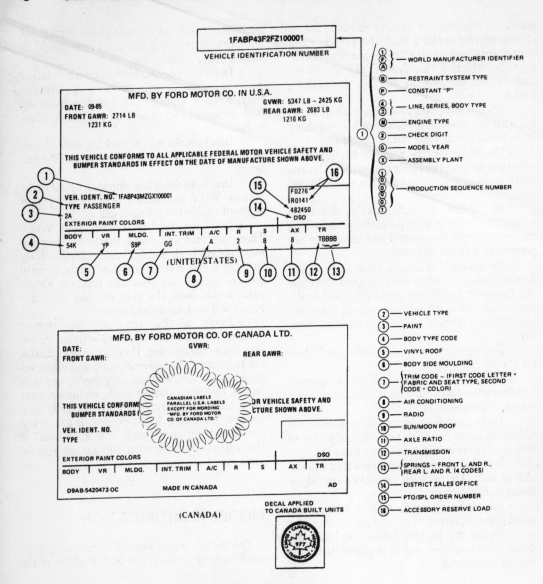

1FABP43F2FZ100001

VEHICLE IDENTIFICATION NUMBER

① F — WORLD MANUFACTURER IDENTIFIER
① A
⑧ B — RESTRAINT SYSTEM TYPE
⑨ P — CONSTANT "P"
④ 3 — LINE, SERIES, BODY TYPE
③
⑩ M — ENGINE TYPE
② — CHECK DIGIT
G — MODEL YEAR
X — ASSEMBLY PLANT
1
0
0
0
0
1 — PRODUCTION SEQUENCE NUMBER

MFD. BY FORD MOTOR CO. IN U.S.A.

DATE: 09-85
FRONT GAWR: 2714 LB
1231 KG

GVWR: 5347 LB – 2425 KG
REAR GAWR: 2683 LB
1216 KG

THIS VEHICLE CONFORMS TO ALL APPLICABLE FEDERAL MOTOR VEHICLE SAFETY AND BUMPER STANDARDS IN EFFECT ON THE DATE OF MANUFACTURE SHOWN ABOVE.

① VEH. IDENT. NO. 1FABP43MZGX100001
② TYPE PASSENGER
③ 2A
EXTERIOR PAINT COLORS

⑮ F0276 ⑯
R0141
⑭ 482450
DSO

④ BODY	VR	MLDG.	INT. TRIM	A/C	R	S	AX	TR
54K	YP	S9P	GG	A	2	B	8	TBBBB

(UNITED STATES)
⑤ ⑥ ⑦ ⑧ ⑨ ⑩ ⑪ ⑫ ⑬

MFD. BY FORD MOTOR CO. OF CANADA LTD.

DATE:
FRONT GAWR:

GVWR:
REAR GAWR:

CANADIAN LABELS PARALLEL U.S.A. LABELS EXCEPT FOR WORDING "MFD. BY FORD MOTOR CO. OF CANADA LTD."

THIS VEHICLE CONFORMS ... OR VEHICLE SAFETY AND BUMPER STANDARDS I ...CTURE SHOWN ABOVE.

VEH. IDENT. NO.
TYPE

EXTERIOR PAINT COLORS
DSO

BODY	VR	MLDG.	INT. TRIM	A/C	R	S	AX	TR

D9AB-5420472-0C

MADE IN CANADA

AD

(CANADA)

DECAL APPLIED TO CANADA BUILT UNITS

CANADA 977

② — VEHICLE TYPE
③ — PAINT
④ — BODY TYPE CODE
⑤ — VINYL ROOF
⑥ — BODY SIDE MOULDING
⑦ — TRIM CODE – (FIRST CODE LETTER = FABRIC AND SEAT TYPE, SECOND CODE = COLOR)
⑧ — AIR CONDITIONING
⑨ — RADIO
⑩ — SUN/MOON ROOF
⑪ — AXLE RATIO
⑫ — TRANSMISSION
⑬ — SPRINGS – FRONT L. AND R., REAR L. AND R. (4 CODES)
⑭ — DISTRICT SALES OFFICE
⑮ — PTO/SPL ORDER NUMBER
⑯ — ACCESSORY RESERVE LOAD

Vehicle certification lable

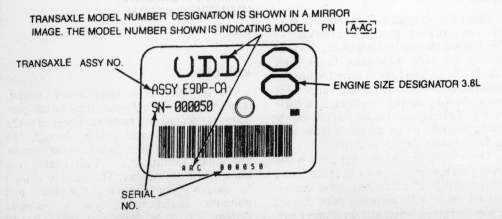

TRANSAXLE MODEL NUMBER DESIGNATION IS SHOWN IN A MIRROR IMAGE. THE MODEL NUMBER SHOWN IS INDICATING MODEL PN [A-AC]

TRANSAXLE ASSY NO.

UDD 8

ASSY E9DP-CA
SN- 000050

ENGINE SIZE DESIGNATOR 3.8L

ARC 000050

SERIAL NO.

Identification tag — AXOD and AXOD-E automatic transaxles

VEHICLE IDENTIFICATION CHART

It is important for servicing and ordering parts to be certain of the vehicle and engine identification. The VIN (vehicle identification number) is a 17 digit number visible through the windshield on the driver's side of the dash and contains the vehicle and engine identification codes. The tenth digit indicates model year and the eighth digit indicates engine code. It can be interpreted as follows:

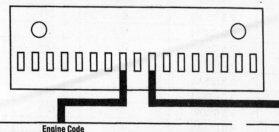

Engine Code							Model Year	
Code	Liter	Cu. In. (cc)	Cyl.	Fuel Sys.	Eng. Mfg.		Code	Year
D (86–90)	2.5	153	4	CEFI	FMCO		H	1986
D (1991)	2.5	153	4	SEFI	FMCO		I	1987
U (86–90)	3.0	182	6	EFI	FMCO		J	1988
U (91–92)	3.0	182	6	SEFI	FMCO		K	1989
Y	3.0	182	6	SEFI	Yamaha		L	1990
4 (88)	3.8	232	6	EFI	FMCO		M	1991
4 (89–92)	3.8	232	6	SEFI	FMCO		N	1992

CFI—Central fuel injection
EFI—Electronic fuel injection
SEFI—Sequential electronic fuel injection
FMCO—Ford Motor Company

Certification Label

The Vehicle Certification Label is found on the left door lock face panel or door pillar. The upper half of the label contains the name of the manufacturer, month and year of manufacture, gross weight rating, gross axle weight, and the certification statements pertinent. The certification also repeats the VIN number and gives the color code and the accessories found on the car.

Engine

The vehicle engine identification can be located on the 8th position of the VIN code.

Transaxle

The transaxle code is located on the bottom edge of the Vehicle Certification Label for vehicles equipped with the manual transaxle. The identification tag for vehicles equipped with the ATX automatic transaxle is located under one of the valve body cover retaining bolts. The identification tag for vehicles equipped with the AXOD and AXOD-E automatic transaxles is located on top of the coverter housing.

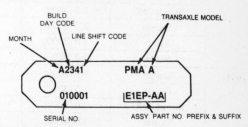

Identification tag — ATX automatic transaxle

ROUTINE MAINTENANCE

Air Cleaner

The air cleaner element should be replaced every 30 months or 30,000 miles. More frequent changes are necessary if the car is operated in dusty conditions.

REMOVAL AND INSTALLATION

1. Loosen the air cleaner outlet tube clamp and disconnect the tube.
2. Disconnect the hot air tube (2.5L engine only), PCV inlet tube and the zip tube.
3. Disconnect the cold weather modulator vacuum hose at the temperature sensor (2.5L engine only).

ENGINE IDENTIFICATION

Year	Model	Engine Displacement Liters (cc)	Engine Series (VIN)	Fuel System	No. of Cylinders	Engine Type
1986	Taurus	2.5 (2500)	D	CFI	4	OHV
	Taurus	3.0 (3000)	U	EFI	6	OHV
	Sable	2.5 (2500)	D	CFI	4	OHV
	Sable	3.0 (3000)	U	EFI	6	OHV
1987	Taurus	2.5 (2500)	D	CFI	4	OHV
	Taurus	3.0 (3000)	U	EFI	6	OHV
	Sable	2.5 (2500)	D	CFI	4	OHV
	Sable	3.0 (3000)	U	EFI	6	OHV
1988	Taurus	2.5 (2500)	D	CFI	4	OHV
	Taurus	3.0 (3000)	U	EFI	6	OHV
	Taurus	3.8 (3800)	4	EFI	6	OHV
	Sable	2.5 (2500)	D	CFI	4	OHV
	Sable	3.0 (3000)	U	EFI	6	OHV
	Sable	3.8 (3800)	4	EFI	6	OHV
1989	Taurus	2.5 (2500)	D	CFI	4	OHV
	Taurus	3.0 (3000)	U	EFI	6	OHV
	Taurus SHO	3.0 (3000)	Y	SEFI	6	DOHC
	Taurus	3.8 (3800)	4	SEFI	6	OHV
	Sable	3.0 (3000)	U	EFI	6	OHV
	Sable	3.8 (3800)	4	EFI	6	OHV
1990	Taurus	2.5 (2500)	D	CFI	4	OHV
	Taurus	3.0 (3000)	U	EFI	6	OHV
	Taurus SHO	3.0 (3000)	Y	SEFI	6	DOHC
	Taurus	3.8 (3800)	4	SEFI	6	OHV
	Sable	3.0 (3000)	U	SEFI	6	OHV
	Sable	3.8 (3800)	4	SEFI	6	OHV
1991	Taurus	2.5 (2500)	D	SEFI	4	OHV
	Taurus	3.0 (3000)	U	SEFI	6	OHV
	Taurus SHO	3.0 (3000)	Y	SEFI	6	DOHC
	Taurus	3.8 (3800)	4	SEFI	6	OHV
	Sable	3.0 (3000)	U	SEFI	6	OHV
	Sable	3.8 (3800)	4	SEFI	6	OHV
1992	Taurus	3.0 (3000)	U	SEFI	6	OHV
	Taurus SHO	3.0 (3000)	Y	SEFI	6	DOHC
	Taurus	3.8 (3800)	4	SEFI	6	OHV
	Sable	3.0 (3000)	U	SEFI	6	OHV
	Sable	3.8 (3800)	4	SEFI	6	OHV

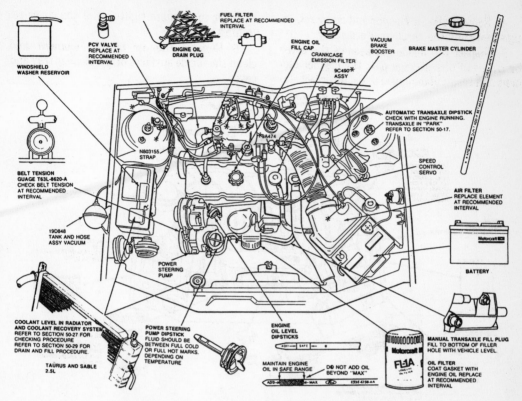

Routine maintenance component location — 2.5L engine

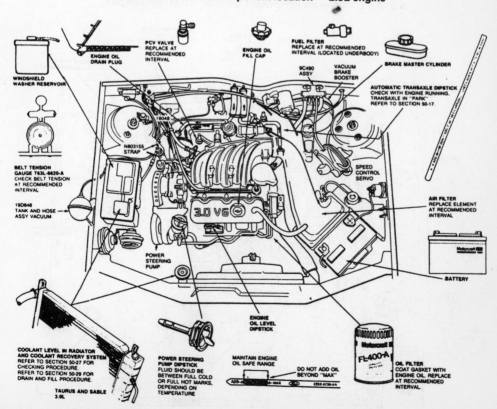

Routine maintenance component location — 3.0L engine except SHO

4. Remove the air cleaner and cover retaining screws and the air cleaner assembly.

5. Inspect the inside surfaces of the cover for traces of dirt leakage past the cleaner element as a result of damaged seals, incorrect element or inadequate tightness of the cover retaining clips.

6. Remove the air cleaner element and clean the inside surfaces of the cleaner tray and cover.

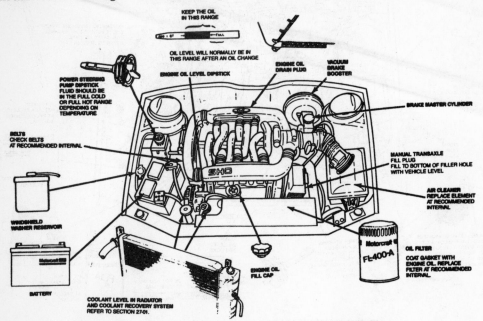

Routine maintenance component location — 3.0L SHO engine

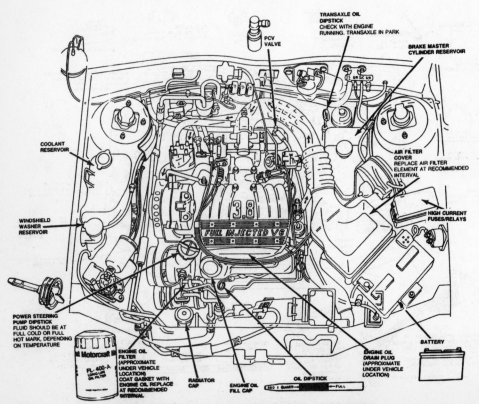

Routine maintenance component location — 3.8L engine

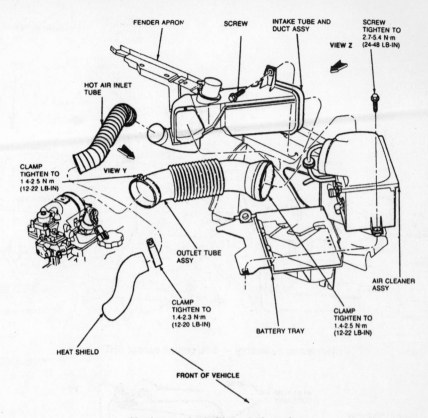

Air cleaner assembly — 2.5L engine

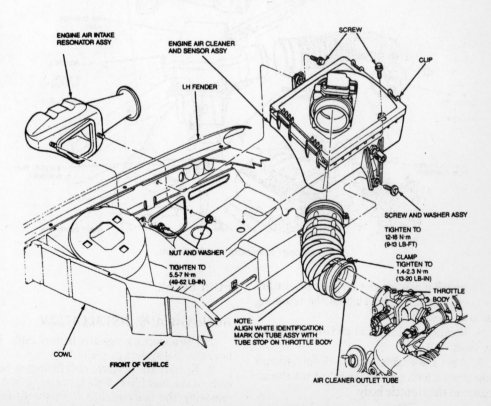

Air cleaner assembly — 3.0L SHO engine

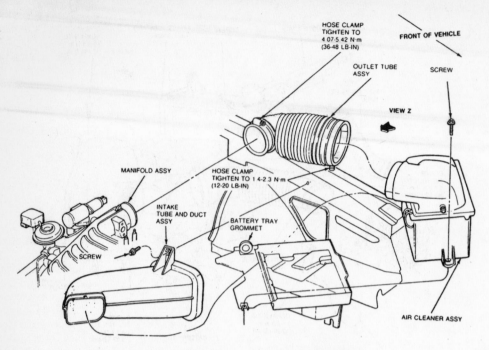

Air cleaner assembly — 3.0L engine except SHO

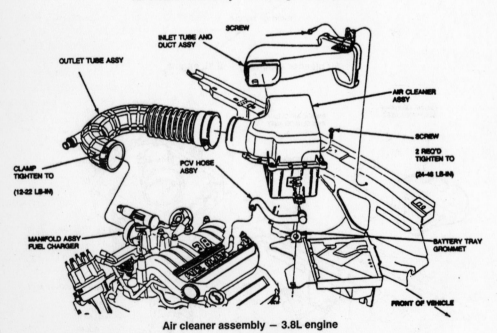

Air cleaner assembly — 3.8L engine

7. Install a new air cleaner element, install the cover and assembly. Tighten the retaining clamp to 12–20 ft. lbs.

8. Reconnect all vacuum and air duct hoses and lines.

9. Start the engine and check for vacuum leaks around both ends of the tube from the air cleaner to the throttle body.

Fuel Filter

REMOVAL AND INSTALLATION

1. Disconnect the negative battery cable. Relieve the fuel system pressure.

2. Remove the push connect fittings at both ends of the fuel filter. This is accomplished by removing the hairpin clips from the fittings. Remove the hairpin clips by first bending and

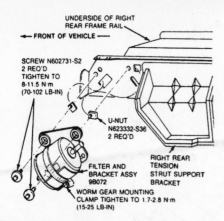

UNDERSIDE OF RIGHT
REAR FRAME RAIL

← FRONT OF VEHICLE →

SCREW N602731-S2
2 REQ'D
TIGHTEN TO
8-11.5 N·m
(70-102 LB-IN)

U-NUT
N623332-S36
2 REQ'D

FILTER AND
BRACKET ASSY
9B072

RIGHT REAR
TENSION
STRUT SUPPORT
BRACKET

WORM GEAR MOUNTING
CLAMP TIGHTEN TO 1.7-2.8 N·m
(15-25 LB-IN)

Fuel mount location

then breaking the shipping tabs on the clips. Then spread the 2 clip legs approximately ⅛ in. (3mm) to disengage the body and push the legs into the fitting. Pull on the triangular end of the clip and work it clear of the fitting.

3. Remove the filter from the mounting bracket by loosening the worm gear mounting clamp enough to allow the filter to pass through.

To install:

4. Install the filter in the mounting bracket, ensuring that the flow direction arrow is pointing forward. Locate the fuel filter against the tab at the lower end of the bracket.

5. Insert a new hairpin clip into any 2 adjacent openings on each push connect fitting, with the triangular portion of the clip pointing away from the fitting opening. Install the clip to fully engage the body of the fitting. This is indicated by the legs of the hairpin clip being locked on the outside of the fitting body. Apply a light coat of engine oil to the ends of the fuel filter and then push the fittings onto the ends of the fuel filter. When the fittings are engaged, a definite click will be heard. Pull on the fittings to ensure that they are fully engaged.

6. Tighten the worm gear mounting clamp to 15–25 inch lbs. (1.7–2.8 Nm).

7. Start the engine and check for leaks.

PCV Valve

SERVICING

1. Visually inspect the components of the PCV valve system. Check for rough idle, slow starting, high oil consumption and loose, leaking, clogged or damaged hoses.

2. Check the fresh air supply hose and the PCV hose for air leakage or flow restriction due to loose engagement, hose splitting, cracking or kinking, nipple damage, rubber grommet fit or any other damage.

3. If a component is suspected as the obvi-

ous cause of a malfunction, correct the cause before proceeding to the next Step.

4. If all checks are okay, proceed to the pinpoint tests.

PINPOINT TESTS

1. Remove the PCV valve from the valve cover grommet and shake the valve. If the valve rattles when shaken, reinstall and proceed to Step 2. If the valve does not rattle, it is sticking and should be replaced.

2. Start the engine and bring to normal operating temperature.

3. On the 2.5L engine, remove the corrugated hose from the oil separator nipple. On all other engines, disconnect the hose from the remote air cleaner or air outlet tube.

4. Place a stiff piece of paper over the nipple or hose end and wait 1 minute. If vacuum holds the paper in place, the system is okay; reconnect the hose. If the paper is not held in place, the system is plugged or the evaporative emission valve is leaking, if equipped. If the evaporative emission valve is suspected of leaking, proceed to Step 5.

5. Disconnect the evaporative hose, if equipped and cap the connector.

6. Place a stiff piece of paper over the hose/nipple, as in Step 4 and wait 1 minute. If vacuum holds the paper in place, proceed to evaporative emission system testing. If the paper is not held in place, check for vacuum leaks/obstruction in the system: oil cap, PCV valve, hoses, cut grommets, the oil separator on the 2.5L engine and valve cover for bolt torque/gasket leak.

REMOVAL AND INSTALLATION

1. Remove the PCV valve from the mounting grommet in the valve cover.

2. Disconnect the valve from the PCV hose and remove the valve from the vehicle.

3. Installation is the reverse of the removal procedure.

Evaporative Canister

To prevent gasoline vapors from being vented into the atmosphere, an evaporative emission system captures the vapors and stores them in a charcoal filled canister.

SERVICING

Since the canister is purged of fumes when the engine is operating, no real maintenance is required. However, the canister should be visually inspected for cracks, loose connections, etc. The emission canister is located on the driver's side fender near the battery. The canister should have no liquid fuel in it and if it does

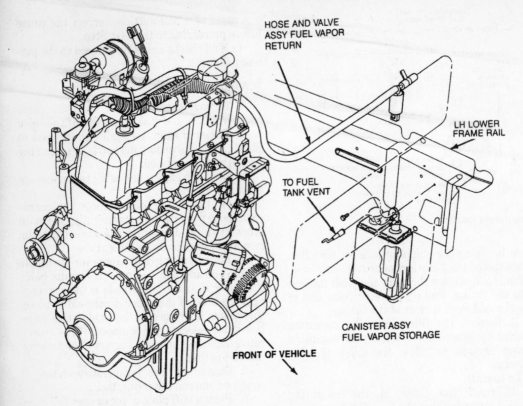

HOSE AND VALVE
ASSY FUEL VAPOR
RETURN

LH LOWER
FRAME RAIL

TO FUEL
TANK VENT

CANISTER ASSY
FUEL VAPOR STORAGE

FRONT OF VEHICLE

Evaporative emission control system and related components — 2.5L engine

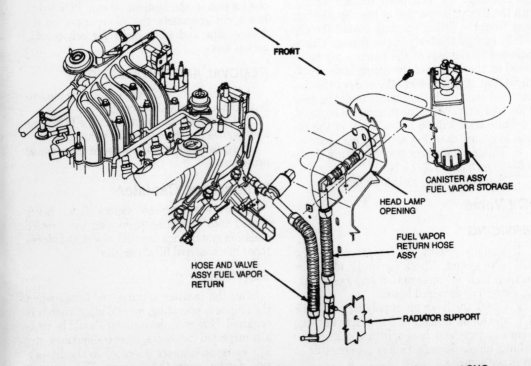

FRONT

CANISTER ASSY
FUEL VAPOR STORAGE

HEAD LAMP
OPENING

FUEL VAPOR
RETURN HOSE
ASSY

HOSE AND VALVE
ASSY FUEL VAPOR
RETURN

RADIATOR SUPPORT

Evaporative emission control system and related components — 3.0L engine except SHO

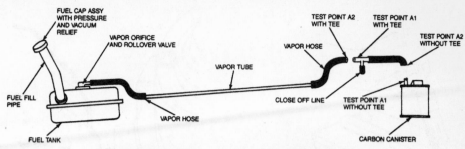

Evaporative emission control system flow schematic

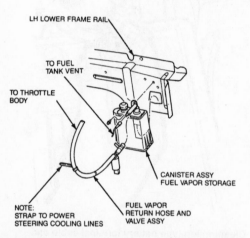

Evaporative emission control system and related components — 3.0L SHO engine

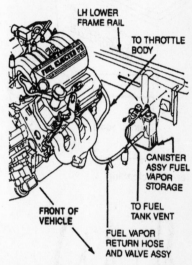

Evaporative emission control system and related components — 3.8L engine

replace it. Replacement is simply a matter of disconnecting the hoses, loosening the mount and replacing the canister.

Battery

GENERAL MAINTENANCE

Loose, dirty, or corroded battery terminals are a major cause of "no-start." Every 3 months or so, remove the battery terminals and clean them. This will help to retard corrosion.

Check the battery cables for signs of wear or chafing and replace any cable or terminal that looks marginal. Battery terminals can be easily cleaned and inexpensive terminal cleaning tools are an excellent investment that will pay for themselves many times over. They can usually be purchased from any well-equipped auto store or parts department. Side terminal batteries require a different tool to clean the threads in the battery case. The accumulated white powder and corrosion can be cleaned from the top of the battery with an old toothbrush and a solution of baking soda and water.

Unless you have a maintenance-free battery, check the electrolyte level and check the specific gravity of each cell. Be sure that the vent holes in each cell cap are not blocked by grease or dirt. The vent holes allow hydrogen gas, formed by the chemical reaction in the battery, to escape safely.

FLUID LEVEL (EXCEPT MAINTENANCE FREE BATTERIES)

Check the battery electrolyte level at least once a month, or more often in hot weather or during periods of extended car operation. The level can be checked through the case on translucent polypropylene batteries; the cell caps must be removed on other models. The electrolyte level in each cell should be kept filled to the split ring inside, or the line marked on the outside of the case.

If the level is low, add only distilled water, or colorless, odorless drinking water, through the opening until the level is correct. Each cell is completely separate from the others, so each must be checked and filled individually.

If water is added in freezing weather, the car should be driven several miles to allow the water to mix with the electrolyte. Otherwise, the battery could freeze.

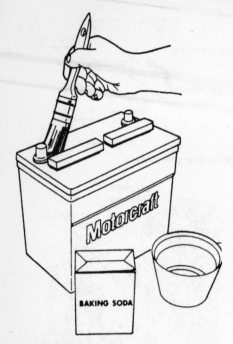

Battery terminal cleaning

Cleaning top type battery terminal cable end

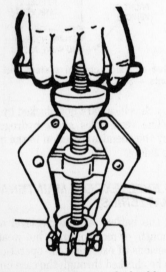

Removing top type battery terminal cable end

SPECIFIC GRAVITY (EXCEPT MAINTENANCE FREE BATTERIES)

At least once a year, check the specific gravity of the battery. It should be between 1.20 in.Hg and 1.26 in.Hg at room temperature.

The specific gravity can be check with the use of an hydrometer, an inexpensive instrument available from many sources, including auto parts stores. The hydrometer has a squeeze bulb at one end and a nozzle at the other. Bat-tery electrolyte is sucked into the hydrometer until the float is lifted from its seat. The specific gravity is then read by noting the position of the float. Generally, if after charging, the specific gravity between any two cells varies more than 50 points (0.50), the battery is bad and should be replaced.

It is not possible to check the specific gravity in this manner on sealed (maintenance free) batteries. Instead, the indicator built into the top of the case must be relied on to display any signs of battery deterioration. If the indicator is dark, the battery can be assumed to be OK. If the indicator is light, the specific gravity is low, and the battery should be charged or replaced.

CABLES

Once every 6 months, the battery terminals and the cable clamps should be cleaned. Loosen the clamps and remove the cables, negative cable first. On batteries with posts on top, the use of a puller specially made for the purpose is recommended. Damage may occur to battery if proper terminal pullers are not used. These are inexpensive, and available in auto parts stores. Side terminal battery cables are secured with a bolt.

Clean the cable clamps and the battery ter-minal with a wire brush, until all corrosion,

JUMP STARTING A DEAD BATTERY

The chemical reaction in a battery produces explosive hydrogen gas. This is the safe way to jump start a dead battery, reducing the chances of an accidental spark that could cause an explosion.

Jump Starting Precautions

1. Be sure both batteries are of the same voltage.
2. Be sure both batteries are of the same polarity (have the same grounded terminal).
3. Be sure the vehicles are not touching.
4. Be sure the vent cap holes are not obstructed.
5. Do not smoke or allow sparks around the battery.
6. In cold weather, check for frozen electrolyte in the battery. Do not jump start a frozen battery.
7. Do not allow electrolyte on your skin or clothing.
8. Be sure the electrolyte is not frozen.
CAUTION: *Make certain that the ignition key, in the vehicle with the dead battery, is in the OFF position. Connecting cables to vehicles with on-board computers will result in computer destruction if the key is not in the OFF position.*

Jump Starting Procedure

1. Determine voltages of the two batteries; they must be the same.
2. Bring the starting vehicle close (they must not touch) so that the batteries can be reached easily.
3. Turn off all accessories and both engines. Put both cars in Neutral or Park and set the handbrake.
4. Cover the cell caps with a rag—do not cover terminals.
5. If the terminals on the run-down battery are heavily corroded, clean them.
6. Identify the positive and negative posts on both batteries and connect the cables in the order shown.
7. Start the engine of the starting vehicle and run it at fast idle. Try to start the car with the dead battery. Crank it for no more than 10 seconds at a time and let it cool off for 20 seconds in between tries.
8. If it doesn't start in 3 tries, there is something else wrong.
9. Disconnect the cables in the reverse order.
10. Replace the cell covers and dispose of the rags.

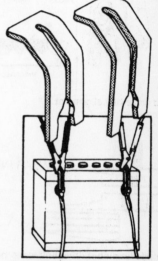

Side terminal batteries oc casionally pose a problem when connecting jumper cables. There frequently isn't enough room to clamp the cables without touching sheet metal .Side terminal adaptors are available to alleviate this problem and should be removed after use.

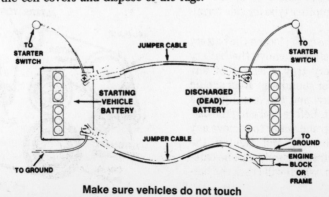

Make sure vehicles do not touch

This hook–up for negative ground cars only

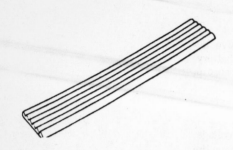

Six rib drive belt identification

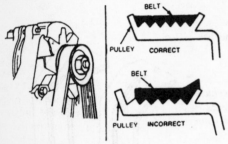

Six rib drive belt alignment

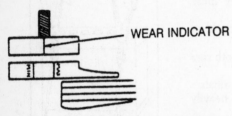

Automatic tensioner drive belt wear indicator

grease, etc. is removed and metal is shiny. It is especially important to clean the inside of the clamp thoroughly, since a small deposit of foreign material or oxidation there will prevent a sound electrical connection and inhibit either starting or charging. Special tools are available for cleaning these parts, one type of conventional batteries and another type for side terminal batteries.

Before installing the cable, loosen the battery holddown clamp or strap, remove the battery and check the battery tray. Clear it of any debris, and check it for soundness. Rust should be wire brushed away, and the metal given a coat of anti-rust paint. Before replacing the battery wash it with soap and water to remove any dirt. Replace the battery and tighten the holddown clamp or strap securely, but be careful not to overtighten, which will crack the battery case.

After the clamps and terminals are clean, reinstall the cables, negative cable last; do not

hammer on the clamps to install. Tighten the clamps securely, but do not distort them. Give the clamps and terminals a thin external coat of grease after installation, to retard corrosion.

Check the cables at the same time that the terminals are cleaned. If the cable insulation is cracked or broken, or if the ends are frayed, the cable should be replace with a new cable of the same length and gauge.

NOTE: *Keep flame or sparks away from the battery; it gives off explosive hydrogen gas. Battery electrolyte contains sulphuric acid. If you should splash any on your skin or in your eyes, flush the affected areas with plenty of clear water; if it lands in your eyes, get medical help immediately.*

REPLACEMENT

The cold power rating of a battery measures battery starting performance and provides an approximate relationship between battery size and engine size. The cold power rating of a replacement battery should match or exceed your engine size in cubic inches.

Belts

All vehicles are equipped with V-ribbed belts. Replacement belts should be of the same type as originally installed. Loose belts will result in slippage and cause improper operation of the driven accessory, power steering, air conditioning, etc. Over-tightened belts will put a severe load on accessory bearings and will almost certainly cause them to self destruct.

INSPECTION

Inspect all drive belts for excessive wear, cracks, glazed condition and frayed or broken cords. Replace any drive belt showing the above condition(s).

NOTE: *If a drive belt continually gets cut, the crankshaft pulley might have a sharp pro-*

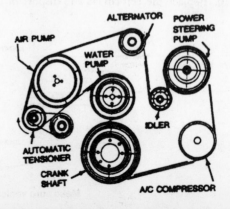

Drive belt installation — 3.8L engine

HOW TO SPOT WORN V-BELTS

V-Belts are vital to efficient engine operation—they drive the fan, water pump and other accessories. They require little maintenance (occasional tightening) but they will not last forever. Slipping or failure of the V-belt will lead to overheating. If your V-belt looks like any of these, it should be replaced.

Cracking or weathering

This belt has deep cracks, which cause it to flex. Too much flexing leads to heat build-up and premature failure. These cracks can be caused by using the belt on a pulley that is too small. Notched belts are available for small diameter pulleys.

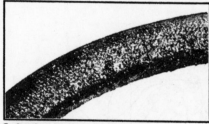

Softening (grease and oil)

Oil and grease on a belt can cause the belt's rubber compounds to soften and separate from the reinforcing cords that hold the belt together. The belt will first slip, then finally fail altogether.

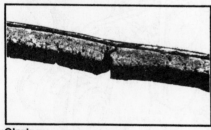

Glazing

Glazing is caused by a belt that is slipping. A slipping belt can cause a run-down battery, erratic power steering, overheating or poor accessory performance. The more the belt slips, the more glazing will be built up on the surface of the belt. The more the belt is glazed, the more it will slip. If the glazing is light, tighten the belt.

Worn cover

The cover of this belt is worn off and is peeling away. The reinforcing cords will begin to wear and the belt will shortly break. When the belt cover wears in spots or has a rough jagged appearance, check the pulley grooves for roughness.

Separation

This belt is on the verge of breaking and leaving you stranded. The layers of the belt are separating and the reinforcing cords are exposed. It's just a matter of time before it breaks completely.

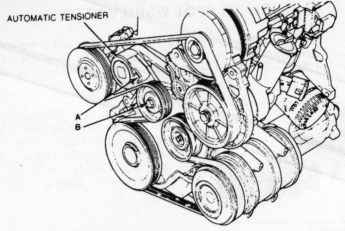

AUTOMATIC TENSIONER

A. USE 1/2-INCH FLEX HANDLE HERE.
B. USE 18mm SOCKET HERE.

Drive belt installation — 2.5L engine

jection on it. Have the pulley replaced if this condition continues.

ADJUSTMENT

Alternator Belt

2.5L AND 3.8L ENGINES

The V-ribbed belts used on these engines, utilize an automatic belt tensioner which maintains the proper belt tension for the life of the belt. The automatic belt tensioner has a belt wear indicator mark and **MIN** and **MAX** marks. If the indicator mark is not between the **MIN** and **MAX** marks, the belt is worn or an incorrect belt is installed.

3.0L ENGINE EXCEPT SHO

1. Disconnect the negative battery cable.
2. Loosen the alternator adjustment and pivot bolts.
3. Apply tension to the belt using the adjusting screw.
4. Using a belt tension gauge, set the belt to the proper tension. The tension should be 150 lbs. for a new belt or 120 lbs. for a used belt, except for 1992 vehicles. On 1992 vehicles it should be 180–210 lbs. (82–95 kg) for a new belt and 140–160 lbs. (64–73 kg) for a used belt.
5. When the belt is properly tensioned, tighten the alternator adjustment bolt to 27 ft. lbs. (37 Nm).
6. Remove the tension gauge and run the engine for 5 minutes.
7. With the engine **OFF** and the belt tension gauge in place, check that the adjusting screw is in contact with the bracket before loosening the alternator adjustment bolt. Rotate the adjustment screw until the belt is tensioned to 120 lbs.

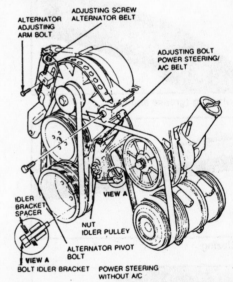

ADJUSTING SCREW
ALTERNATOR BELT
ALTERNATOR ADJUSTING ARM BOLT
ADJUSTING BOLT POWER STEERING/A/C BELT
IDLER BRACKET SPACER
NUT IDLER PULLEY
VIEW A
ALTERNATOR PIVOT BOLT
BOLT IDLER BRACKET
POWER STEERING WITHOUT A/C
VIEW A

Drive belt installation — 3.0L engine except SHO

8. Tighten the alternator adjustment bolt to 27 ft. lbs. (37 Nm) and the pivot bolt to 43 ft. lbs. (58 Nm).

3.0L SHO ENGINE

1. Disconnect the negative battery cable.
2. Loosen the idler pulley nut.
3. Turn the adjusting bolt until the belt is adjusted properly.

NOTE: *Turning the wrench to the right tightens the belt adjustment and turning the wrench to the left loosens the belt tension.*

4. Tighten the idler pulley nut to 25–37 ft. lbs. (34–50 Nm) and check the belt tension.

REMOVAL AND INSTALLATION

NOTE: *When installing belts on the pulley, ensure that all of the V-grooves are making contact with the pulleys.*

2.5L Engine

ALTERNATOR, POWER STEERING AND AIR CONDITIONING

1. Insert a 1/2 in. breaker bar in the square hole in the tensioner, rotate the tensioner counterclockwise and remove the belt from the pulleys.

NOTE: *Be careful when removing or installing belts that the tool doesn't slip!*

2. Install the belt over all pulleys except the alternator pulley.

3. Rotate the tensioner as described in Step 1 and install the belt over the alternator pulley. Check that all the V-grooves make proper contact with the pulleys.

3.0L Engine Except SHO

ALTERNATOR BELT WITHOUT AUTOMATIC TENSIONER

1. Loosen the adjusting arm and the pivot bolts.

2. Turn the alternator belt adjusting screw counterclockwise until the old belt can be removed. Remove the belt.

3. Install the new belt over the pulleys. Check that all the V-grooves make proper contact with the pulleys.

4. Adjust the belt tension.

3.0L SHO Engine

ALTERNATOR BELT

1. Loosen the nut in the center of the idler pulley.

2. Loosen the idler adjusting screw until the old belt can be removed and remove the belt.

3. Install the new belt over the pulleys in the proper contact with the pulleys.

4. Adjust the new belt to specifications as follows: Turn the idler pulley nut to the right to tighten the belt to a specification of 220–265 lbs. (100–120 kg) with a belt tension guage. Torque the idler pulley nut to 25–37 ft. lbs. (34–50 Nm).

POWER STEERING AND AIR CONDITIONING BELT

1. Remove the alternator belt.

2. Loosen the nut on the tensioner pulley.

3. Turn the belt adjusting screw on the tensioner counterclockwise until the belt can be removed.

4. To install, position the new belt over the proper pulleys making sure the V-grooves are properly seated. Install the alternator belt. Adjust the power steering and air conditioning belt to a specification of 154–198 lbs. with a belt tension gauge. Adjust the alternator belt.

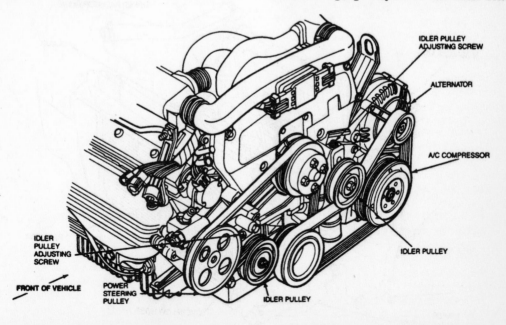

Drive belt installation – 3.0L SHO engine

3.0L Engine Except SHO and 3.8L Engine

WITH AUTOMATIC TENSIONER

1. Insert a ¹/₂ in. breaker bar in the square hole in the tensioner.

NOTE: *On the 3.8L engine the tensioner has a ¹/₂ in. square hole cast into the rear of the tension arm directly behind the pulley. On the 3.0L engine the ¹/₂ in. square hole is cast into the spring housing on the front of the tensioner.*

2. Rotate the tensioner clockwise and remove the belt.

3. Installation is the reverse of the removal procedure.

Hoses

REMOVAL AND INSTALLATION

1. Open the hood and cover the fenders to protect them from scratches.

2. Disconnect the negative (–) battery cable at the battery.

3. Place a suitable drain pan under the radiator and drain the cooling system.

NOTE: *Place a small hose on the end of the radiator petcock, this will direct the coolant into the drain pan.*

CAUTION: *The engine must be cooled down before any hoses may be replaced. If engine is hot, let it cool down for at least an hour.*

When draining the coolant, keep in mind that cats and dogs are attracted by the ethylene glycol antifreeze, and are quite likely to drink any that is left in an uncovered container or in puddles on the ground. This will prove fatal in sufficient quantity. Always drain the coolant into a sealable container. Coolant should be reused unless it is contaminated or several years old.

4. After the radiator has drained, position the drain pan under the lower hose. Loosen the lower hose clamps, disconnect the hose from the water pump inlet pipe and allow to drain. Disconnect the other end of the hose from the radiator and remove the hose.

5. Loosen the clamps retaining the upper hose, disconnect and remove the hose.

NOTE: *If only the upper hose is to be replaced, drain off enough coolant so the level is below the hose.*

6. If heater hoses need replacement, drain the coolant, loosen the clamps and remove the hose(s).

7. Installation of new hose(s) is in the reverse order of removal.

8. Tighten hoses clamps.

9. Be sure the petcock is closed. Fill the cooling system with the required protection mixture of water and permanent antifreeze. Connect the negative battery cable.

10. Run the engine until normal operating temperature is reached. Shut off the engine

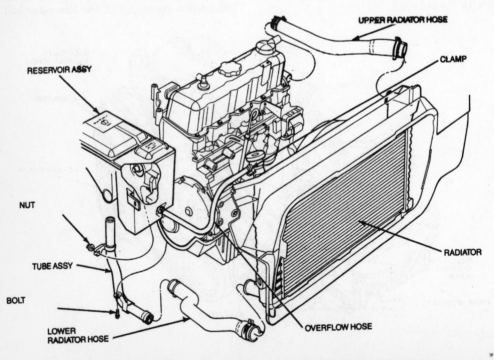

Radiator hose and related cooling system component locations — 2.5L engine

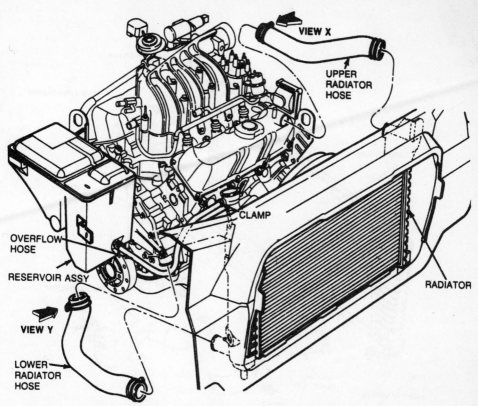

Radiator hose and related cooling system component locations — 3.0L engine except SHO

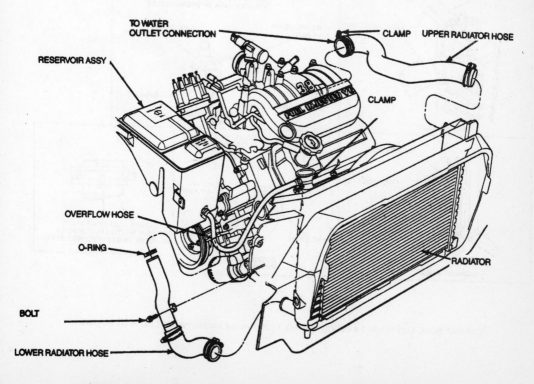

Radiator hose and related cooling system component locations — 3.8L engine

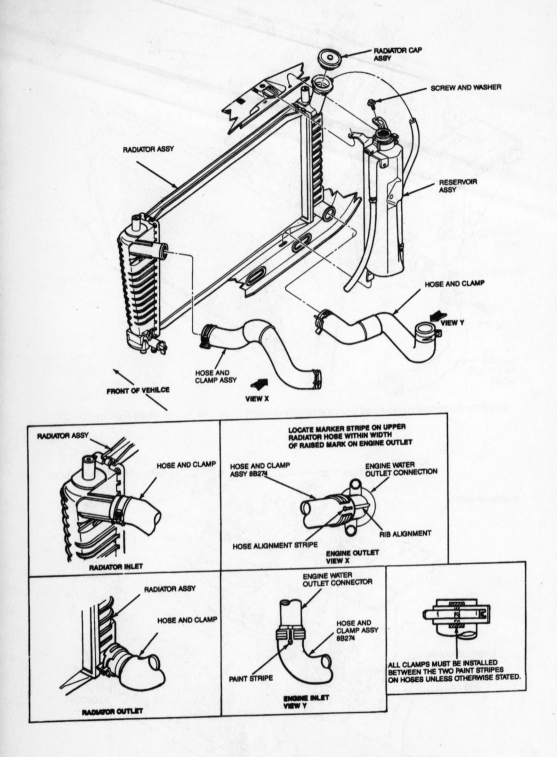

Radiator hose and related cooling system component locations — 3.0L SHO engine

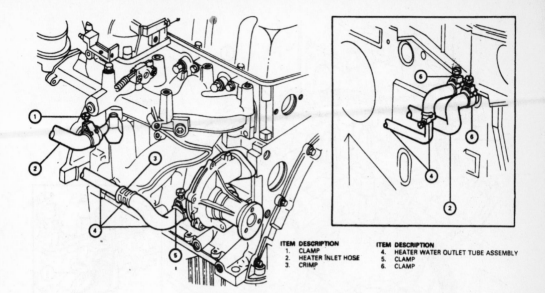

ITEM DESCRIPTION
1. CLAMP
2. HEATER INLET HOSE
3. CRIMP

ITEM DESCRIPTION
4. HEATER WATER OUTLET TUBE ASSEMBLY
5. CLAMP
6. CLAMP

Heater hose routing — 2.5L engine

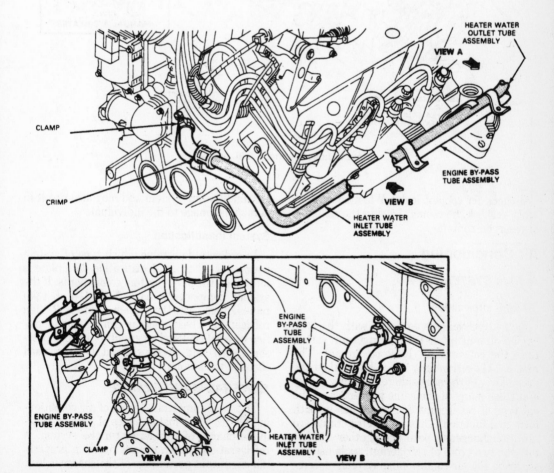

Heater hose routing — 3.0L engine except SHO

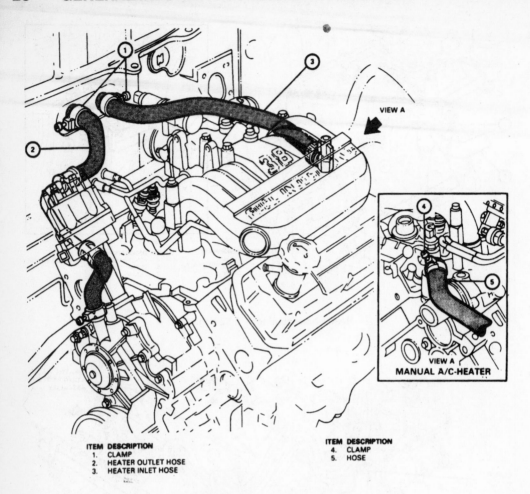

ITEM	DESCRIPTION
1.	CLAMP
2.	HEATER OUTLET HOSE
3.	HEATER INLET HOSE

ITEM	DESCRIPTION
4.	CLAMP
5.	HOSE

VIEW A
MANUAL A/C-HEATER

Heater hose routing — 3.8L engine

and check for coolant leaks. When the engine cools, recheck the coolant level in the radiator, or reservoir container.

Air Conditioning

R-134a SYSTEMS

General Information

Some 1992 vehicles equipped with the 3.0L engine are using R-134a refrigerant rather than the conventional R-12 refrigerant. The new R-134a refrigerant is not harmful to the ozone layer of the atmosphere. The new refrigerant has many of the same properties as the old type of refrigerant and is similar in both form and function. These two refrigerants are not interchangeable with one another. Do not mix the two types of refrigerant, tools used in servicing the air conditioning system, or component replacement parts from the two air conditiong systems. Failure to follow these guidlines will result in damage to the vehicle

air conditioning system and may also result in personal damage to the individual.

System Identification

In order to determine which type of system your vehicle has an identification data plate is located on the major system components. If the system components have YELLOW R-134a non-cfc tags than the system requires R-134a refrigerant. These systems can also be identified by a gold colored air conditioning compressor clutch and green colored O-rings used through the system.

GENERAL MAINTENANCE

The most important aspect of air conditioning service is the maintenance of pure and adequate charge of refrigerant in the system. A refrigeration system cannot function properly if a significant percentage of the charge is lost. Leaks are common because the severe vibration encountered in an automobile can easily cause a sufficient cracking or loosening of the

HOW TO SPOT BAD HOSES

Both the upper and lower radiator hoses are called upon to perform difficult jobs in an inhospitable enviorment. They are subject to nearly 18 psi at under hood temperature often over 280F., and must circulate an hour-3 good reasons to have good hoses.

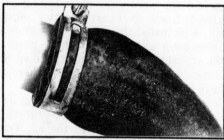

Swollen hose

A good test for any hose is to feel it for soft or spongy spots. Frequently these will appear as swollen areas of the hose. The most likely cause is oil soaking. This hose could burst at any time, when hot or under pressure.

Cracked hose

Cracked hoses can usually be seen but feel the hoses to be sure they have not hardened; a prime cause of cracking. This hose has cracked down to the reinforcing cords and could split at any of the cracks.

Frayed hose end (due to weak clamp)

Weakened clamps frequently are the cause of hose and cooling system failure. The connection between the pipe and hose has deteriorated enough to allow coolant to escape when the engine is hot.

Debris in cooling system

Debris, rust and scale in the cooling system can cause the inside of a hose to weaken. This can usually be felt on the outside of the hose as soft or thinner areas.

Identifying R-134a and R-12 Systems

In order to determine which type of A/C system a particular vehicle has, inspect the A/C system major components and refrigerant lines. If the system components have yellow R-134a NON-CFC tags as shown below, it is an R-134a system requiring the use of R-134a refrigerant.

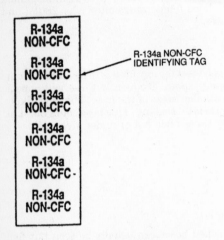

NOTE: R-134a A/C systems can also be identified by a gold colored A/C compressor clutch and green colored O-rings used throughout the system.

If the A/C system has any of the R-134a identifying characteristics outlined, R-134a refrigerant is the only type of refrigerant that can be used in the A/C system. If the A/C system is not identified as an R-134a system as previously outlined, it is an R-12 system requiring the use of R-12 refrigerant.

CAUTION: Do not add R-12 refrigerant to an A/C system that requires the use of R-134a refrigerant. Do not add R-134a refrigerant to an A/C system that requires the use of R-12 refrigerant. These two types of refrigerant should never be mixed. Doing so may cause damage to the A/C system.

R-134a identification tag and important data

air conditioning fittings. As a result, the extreme operating pressures of the system force refrigerant out.

The problem can be understood by considering what happens to the system as it is operated with a continuous leak. Because the expansion valve regulates the flow of refrigerant to the evaporator, the level of refrigerant there is fairly constant. The receiver/drier stores any excess of refrigerant, and so a loss will first appear there as a reduction in the level of liquid. As this level nears the bottom of the vessel, some refrigerant vapor bubbles will begin to appear in the stream of liquid supplied to the expansion valve. This vapor decreases the capacity of the expansion valve very little as

the valve opens to compensate for its presence. As the quantity of liquid in the condenser decreases, the operating pressure will drop there and throughout the high side of the system. As the refrigerant continues to be expelled, the pressure available to force the liquid through the expansion valve will continue to decrease, and, eventually, the valve's orifice will prove to be too much of a restriction for adequate flow even with the needle fully withdrawn.

At this point, low side pressure will start to drop, and severe reduction in cooling capacity, marked by freeze-up of the evaporator coil, will result. Eventually, the operating pressure of the evaporator will be lower than the pressure of the atmosphere surrounding it, and air will be drawn into the system wherever there are leaks in the low side.

Because all atmospheric air contains at least some moisture, water will enter the system and mix with the refrigerant and the oil. Trace amounts of moisture will cause sludging of the oil, and corrosion of the system. Saturation and clogging of the filter/drier, and freezing of the expansion valve orifice will eventually result. As air fills the system to a greater and greater extent, it will interfere more and more with the normal flows of refrigerant and heat.

SYSTEM INSPECTION

It is possible to detect possible air conditioning system problems by a visual inspection. Check for a broken air conditioning belt, dirt blocking the condenser, disconnected wires, a loose compressor clutch and oily residue around the air conditioning hose fittings. Missing service gauge port caps may also cause a leak to be present.

REFRIGERANT LEVEL CHECKS

The only way to accurately check the refrigerant level to measure the system evaporator pressures with a manifold gauge set, although rapid on/off cycling of the compressor clutch indicates that the air conditioning system is low on refrigerant. The normal refrigerant capacity is 40 oz. ± 1 oz.

R-12 refrigerent is a chlorofluorcarbon which when released into the atmosphere, can contribute to the depletion of the ozone layer in the upper atmosphere. Ozone filters out harmful radiation from the sun. For enviormental and safety reasons it is recommeneded that rigerent level checks and discharging and charging of air conditioning systems should be done by professional service technicians, equipped with SAE approved R-12 recovery/recycling machines.

Windshield Wipers

Intense heat from the sun, snow, and ice, road oils and the chemicals used in windshield washer solvent combine to deteriorate the rubber wiper refills. The refills should be replaced about twice a year or whenever the blades begin to streak or chatter.

REMOVAL AND INSTALLATION

Normally, if the wipers are not cleaning the windshield properly, only the refill has to be replaced. The blade and arm usually require replacement only in the event of damage. It is not necessary (except on new Tridon® refills) to remove the arm or the blade to replace the refill (rubber part), though you may have to position the arm higher on the glass. You can do this turning the ignition switch on and operating the wipers. When they are positioned where they are accessible, turn the ignition switch off.

There are several types of refills and your vehicle could have any kind, since aftermarket blades and arms may not use exactly the same type refill as the original equipment.

Most Anco® styles use a release button that is pushed down to allow the refill to slide out of the yoke jaws. The new refill slides in and locks in place.

Some Trico® refills are removed by locating where the metal backing strip or the refill is wider. Insert a small pry bar type tool between the frame and metal backing strip. Press down to release the refill from the retaining tab.

Other Trico® blades are unlocked at one end by squeezing 2 metal tabs, and the refill is slid out of the frame jaws. When the new refill is installed, the tabs will click into place, locking the refill.

The polycarbonate type is held in place by a locking lever that is pushed downward out of the groove in the arm to free the refill. When the new refill is installed, it will lock in place automatically.

The Tridon® refill has a plastic backing strip with a notch about 1 in. (25mm) from the end. Hold the blade (frame) on a hard surface so that the frame is tightly bowed. Grip the tip of the backing strip and pull up while twisting counterclockwise. The backing strip will snap out of the retaining tab. Do this for the remaining tabs until the refill is free of the arm. The length of these refills is molded into the end and they should be replaced with identical types.

No matter which type of refill you use, be sure that all of the frame claws engage the refill. Before operating the wipers, be sure that no part of the metal frame is contacting the windshield.

Tires And Wheels

TIRE ROTATION

Tire wear can be equalized by switching the position of the tires about every 7,500 miles. Including a conventional spare in the rotation pattern can give up to 20% more tire life. Do not include the new SpaceSaver® temporary spare tires in the rotation pattern.

TIRE DESIGN

All tires made since 1968 have 8 built-in tread wear indicator bars that show up as $1/2$ in. (13mm) wide smooth bands across the tire when $1/16$ in. (1.6mm) of tread remains. The appearance of tread wear indicators means that the tires should be replaced. In fact, many states have laws prohibiting the use of tires with less than $1/16$ in. (1.6mm) of tread remains. The appearance of tread wear indicators means that the tires should be replace. In fact, many states have laws prohibiting the use of tires with less than $1/16$ in. (1.6mm) tread. Tread thickness under $1/16$ in. (1.6mm) is very dangerous on wet road conditions due to hydroplanning.

You can check you own tread depth with an inexpensive gauge or by using a Lincoln head penny. Slip the Lincoln penny into several tread grooves. If you can see the top of Lincoln's head in 2 adjacent grooves, the tires have less than $1/16$ in. (1.6mm) tread left and should be replaced. You can measure snow tires in the same manner by using the tails side of the Lincoln penny. If you see the top of the Lincoln memorial, it's time to replace the snow tires.

NOTE: *When you replace tires, never mix radial, bias-belted or bias type tires. Use only the tire sizes listed on the tire decal attached to your vehicle on the driver's side door post. Make sure that all tires are the same size, speed rating and load carrying capacity. Use only tire and wheel combinations as recommended on the tire decal or by your dealer. Failure to follow these precautions can adversely affect the safety and handling of your vehicle.*

TIRE STORAGE

Store the tires at proper inflation pressures if they are mounted on wheels. All tires should be kept in a cool, dry place. If they are stored in the garage or basement, do not let them stand on a concrete floor; set them on strips of wood.

TIRE INFLATION

Tire inflation is the most ignored item of auto maintenance. Gasoline mileage can drop

Blade replacement
1. Cycle arm and blade assembly to a position on the windshield where removal of blade assembly can be performed without difficulty. Turn ignition key off at desired position.
2. To remove blade assembly from wiper arm, press on spring lock and pull blade assembly from pin (View A).
3. To install, push the blade assembly on the pin so that the spring lock engages the pin (View A). Be sure the blade assembly is securely attached to pin.

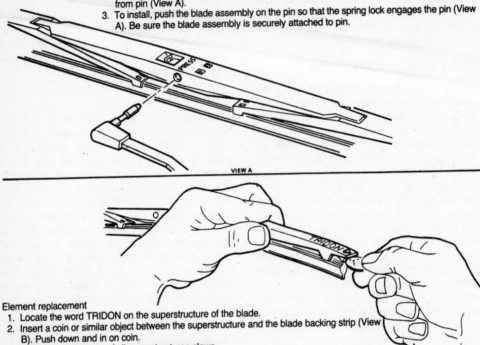

Element replacement
1. Locate the word TRIDON on the superstructure of the blade.
2. Insert a coin or similar object between the superstructure and the blade backing strip (View B). Push down and in on coin.
3. Slide the element out of all superstructures claws.
4. Locate the rectangular slot on the top/end of the element backing strip.
5. Locate the end on the blade superstructure without the word TRIDON.
6. Insert the "slot" end of the blade element into the first superstructure claw and continue to slide the blade element into all claws of the superstructure. The blade element will "snap" into place when the element is fully installed through the last superstructure claw (located at the end with the word TRIDON) (View C).
NOTE: Make sure that the element backing strip has been installed into all the superstructure claws and that the locking rib is securely engaged.

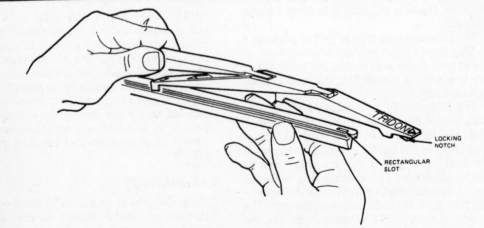

Wiper blade replacement — Tridon

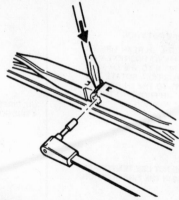

Blade replacement

1. Cycle arm and blade assembly to up position on the windshield where removal of blade assembly can be performed without difficulty. Turn ignition key off at desired position.
2. To remove blade assembly, insert screwdriver in slot, push down on spring lock and pull blade assembly from pin (View A).
3. To install, push the blade assembly on the pin so that the spring lock engages the pin (View A). Be sure the blade assembly is securely attached to pin.

VIEW A

NOTE: INSERT SCREWDRIVER
3.2mm(1/8") OR LESS PAST
THIS EDGE

TWIST CLOCKWISE

Element replacement

1. Insert screwdriver between the edge of the super structure and the blade backing drip (View B). Twist screwdriver slowly until element clears one side of the super structure claw.
2. Slide the element out of all the super structure claws.

VIEW B

4. Insert element into one side of the end claws (View D) and with a rocking motion push element upward until it snaps in (View E).

VIEW D

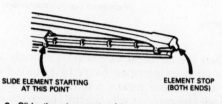

SLIDE ELEMENT STARTING
AT THIS POINT

ELEMENT STOP
(BOTH ENDS)

3. Slide the element into the super structure claws, starting with second set from either end (View C) and continue to slide the blade element into all the super structure claws to the element stop (View C).

VIEW C

VIEW E

Wiper blade replacement — Trico

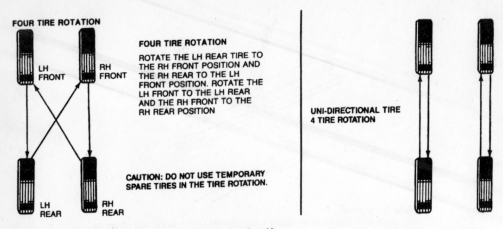

FOUR TIRE ROTATION

FOUR TIRE ROTATION
ROTATE THE LH REAR TIRE TO THE RH FRONT POSITION AND THE RH REAR TO THE LH FRONT POSITION. ROTATE THE LH FRONT TO THE LH REAR AND THE RH FRONT TO THE RH REAR POSITION

LH FRONT   RH FRONT

UNI-DIRECTIONAL TIRE 4 TIRE ROTATION

CAUTION: DO NOT USE TEMPORARY SPARE TIRES IN THE TIRE ROTATION.

LH REAR   RH REAR

CAUTION: Never use the temporary spare for tire rotation or as a regular tire.

Tire rotation patterns

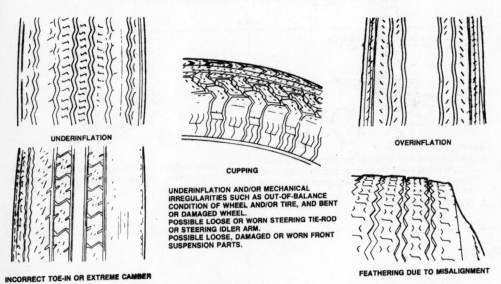

UNDERINFLATION

OVERINFLATION

CUPPING

UNDERINFLATION AND/OR MECHANICAL IRREGULARITIES SUCH AS OUT-OF-BALANCE CONDITION OF WHEEL AND/OR TIRE, AND BENT OR DAMAGED WHEEL.
POSSIBLE LOOSE OR WORN STEERING TIE-ROD OR STEERING IDLER ARM.
POSSIBLE LOOSE, DAMAGED OR WORN FRONT SUSPENSION PARTS.

INCORRECT TOE-IN OR EXTREME CAMBER

FEATHERING DUE TO MISALIGNMENT

Tire wear patterns

as much as 0.8% for every 1 pound per square inch (psi) of under inflation.

Two items should be a permanent fixture in every glove compartment: a tire pressure gauge and a tread depth gauge. Check the tire air pressure (including the spare) regularly with a pocket type gauge. Kicking the tires won't tell you a thing, and the gauge on the service station air hose is notoriously inaccurate. Also, just looking at the tire does not indicate if it underinflated.

The tire pressures recommended for you car are usually found on a label attached to the door pillar or on the glove box inner cover or in the owner's manual. Ideally, inflation pressure should be checked when the tires are cool.

When the air becomes heated it expands and the pressure increases. Every 10° rise (or drop) in temperature means a difference of 1 psi, which also explains why the tire appears to lose air on a very cold night. When it is impossible to check the tires cold, allow for pressure build-up due to heat. If the hot pressure exceeds the cold pressure by more than 15 psi, reduce your speed. Otherwise internal heat is created in the tire. When the heat approaches the temperature at which the tire was cured, during manufacture, the tread can separate from the body.

CAUTION: *Never counteract excessive pressure build-up by bleeding off air pressure (letting some air out). This will only further raise the tire operating temperature.*

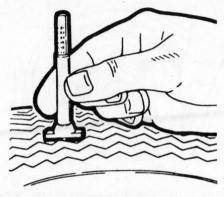

Reading tire depth with tire depth tool

Before starting a long trip with lots of luggage, you can add about 2–4 psi to the tires to make them run cooler, but never exceed the maximum inflation pressure on the side of the tire.

CARE OF SPECIAL WHEELS

To clean the wheels, wheel covers and wheel ornamentation use a mild soap solution and throughly rinse with clean water. Do not use steel wool, abrasive type cleaner or strong detergents containing high alkaline or caustic agents as damage to the protective coating and discoloration may result.

FLUIDS AND LUBRICANTS

Fuel And Engine Oil Recommendations

FUEL RECOMMENDATIONS

Unleaded gasoline having a Research Octane Number (RON) of 91, or an Antiknock Index of 87 is recommended for your car.

CAUTION: *Leaded gasoline will quickly interfere the operation of the catalytic converter and just a few tankfuls of leaded gasoline will render the converter useless. This will cause the emission of much greater amounts of hydrocarbons and carbon monoxide from the exhaust system, void your warranty and cost a considerable amount of money for converter replacement.*

OIL RECOMMENDATIONS

Oil meeting API classification SG or SG/CC or SG/CD is recommended for use in your vehicle. Ford has filled your crankcase with SAE 5W-30 and recommends that you continue to use this as long as the outside temperatures don't exceed 100°F (38°C). There are other op-

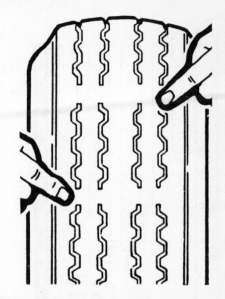

Replace tire that shows the built in bump strip

tions however, see the viscosity to temperature chart in this Chapter.

Engine

OIL LEVEL CHECK

It is a good idea to check the engine oil each time or at least every other time you fill your gas tank.

1. Be sure your car is on level ground. Shut off the engine and wait for a few minutes to allow the oil to drain back into the oil pan.

2. Remove the engine oil dipstick and wipe clean with a rag.

3. Reinsert the dipstick and push it down until it is fully seated in the tube.

4. Remove the stick and check the oil level shown. If the oil level is below the lower mark, add one quart.

5. If you wish, you may carefully fill the oil pan to the upper mark on the dipstick with less than a full quart. Do not, however, add a full quart when it would overfill the crankcase (level above the upper mark on the dipstick). The excess oil will generally be consumed at an excessive rate even if no damage to the engine seals occurs.

OIL AND FILTER CHANGE

Change the engine oil and oil filter every 3 months or 3000 miles. If the car is used in severe service or dusty conditions, change the engine oil and oil filter more frequently. Following these recommended intervals will help keep you car engine in good condition. Dirty oil loses its lubricating qualities and can cause premature wear in your engine.

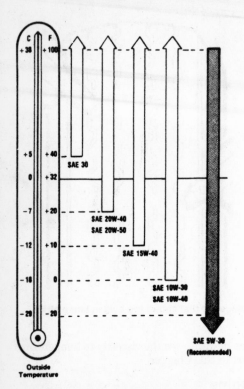

Engine oil viscosity recommendations

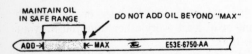

Engine oil dipstick and fill markings

1. Make sure the engine is at normal operating temperature (this promotes complete draining of the old oil).

2. Apply the parking brake and block the wheels or raise and support the car evenly on jackstands.

3. Place a drain pan of about a gallon and a half capacity under the engine oil pan drain plug. Use the proper size box or socket wrench, loosen and remove the plug. Allow all the old oil to drain. Wipe the pan and the drain plug with a clean rag. Inspect the drain plug gasket, replace if necessary.

4. Reinstall and tighten the drain plug. DO NOT OVERTIGHTEN.

5. Move the drain pan under the engine oil filter. Use a strap wrench and loosen the oil filter (do not remove), allow the oil to drain. Unscrew the filter the rest of the way by hand. Use a rag, if necessary, to keep from burning your fingers. When the filter comes loose from the engine, turn the mounting base upward to avoid spilling the remaining oil.

6. Wipe the engine filter mount clean with a rag. Coat the rubber gasket on the new oil

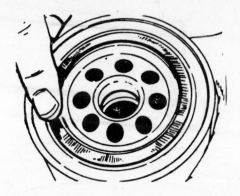

Lubricate oil filter with clean engine oil prior to installation

filter with clean engine oil, applying it with a finger. Carefully start the filter onto the threaded engine mount. Turn the filter until it touches the engine mounting surface. Tighten the filter, by hand, 1/2 turn more or as recommended by the filter manufacturer.

7. Lower the vehicle to the ground. Refill the crankcase to specification with the proper grade and type motor oil. Replace the filler cap and start the engine. Allow the engine to idle and check for oil leaks. Shut off the engine, wait for several minutes, then check the oil level with the dipstick. Oil level while drop as the filter fills up with oil, Add oil to the proper dipstick level.

Manual Transaxle

FLUID RECOMMENDATIONS AND LEVEL CHECK

Each time the engine oil is changed, the fluid level of the transaxle should be checked. The car must be resting on level ground or supported on jackstands (front and back) evenly. To check the fluid, remove the filler plug, located on the upper front (driver's side) of the transaxle with a 9/16 in. wrench.

The filler plug has a hex head, do not mistake any other bolts for the filler plug. Do not overfill the transaxle. The oil level should be even with the edge of the filler hole or within 1/4 in. (6mm) of the hole. If the oil is low, add Dexron®II or Mercon® automatic transmission fluid.

Automatic Transaxle

FLUID RECOMMENDATIONS AND LEVEL CHECK

A dipstick is provided in the engine compartment to check the level of the automatic transaxle. Check the lubrication and service charts in the beginning of this Chapter for dipstick location. Be sure the car is on level ground and that the car's engine and transaxle have reached normal operating temperatures. Start the engine, put the parking brake on the transaxle selector lever in the PARK position. Move the selector lever through all the positions and return to the PARK position. DO NOT TURN OFF THE ENGINE DURING THE FLUID LEVEL CHECK. Clean all dirt from the dipstick cap before removing the dipstick. Remove the dipstick and wipe clean. Reinsert the dipstick making sure it is fully seated. Pull the dipstick out of the tube and check the fluid level. The fluid level should be between the FULL and ADD marks.

If necessary, add enough fluid through the dipstick tube/filler to bring the level to the FULL mark on the dipstick. Use Dexron®II or Mercon® fluid in the ATX 3-speed transaxle, AXOD and AXOD-E overdrive transaxles.

Do not overfill. Can cause damage to transaxle. Make sure the dipstick is fully seated. If by chance you overfill the transaxle, Thread a small piece of rubber vacuum hose into the dipstick tube until it hits bottom. Using a large turkey baster or equivalent to pull the excess fluid out.

DRAIN AND REFILL

In normal service it should not be necessary or required to drain and refill the automatic transaxle. However, under severe operation or dusty conditions the fluid should be changed every 20 months or 20,000 miles.

1. Raise the car and safely support it on jackstands. If the pan is equipped with a drain plug, drain the fluid into a suitable conatiner.

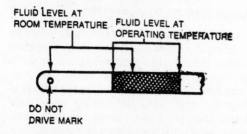

Transaxle dipstick and fill markings — ATX automatic transaxle

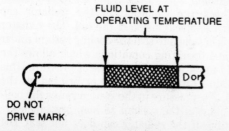

Transaxle dipstick and fill markings — AXOD and AXOD-E automatic transaxles

2. If the pan does not have a drain plug, place a suitable drain pan underneath the transaxle oil pan. Loosen the oil pan mounting bolts and allow the fluid to drain until it reaches the level of the pan flange. Remove the attaching bolts, leaving one end attached so that the pan will tip and the rest of the fluid will drain.

3. Remove the oil pan. Thoroughly clean the pan. Remove the old gasket. Make sure that the gasket mounting surfaces are clean.

4. Remove the transaxle filter screen retaining bolt. Remove the screen.

5. Install a new filter screen and O-ring. Place a new gasket on the pan to the transaxle. Torque the transaxle pan to 15–19 ft. lbs.

6. Fill the transaxle to the correct level. Remove the jackstands and lower the car to the ground.

Cooling System

FLUID RECOMMENDATIONS

This engine has an aluminum cylinder head and requires a special unique corrosion inhibited coolant formulation to avoid radiator damage. Use only a permanent type coolant that meets Ford Specifications such as Ford Cooling System Fluid, Prestone® II or other approved coolants.

LEVEL CHECK

The cooling system of your car contains, among other items, a radiator and an expansion tank. When the engine is running heat is generated. The rise in temperature causes the coolant, in the radiator, to expand and builds up internal pressure. When a certain pressure is reached, a pressure relief valve in the radiator filler cap (pressure cap) is lifted from its seat and allows coolant to flow through the radiator filler neck, down a hose, and into the expansion reservoir.

When the system temperature and pressure are reduced in the radiator, the water in the expansion reservoir is syphoned back into the radiator.

DRAIN AND REFILL

On systems without a coolant recovery tank, the engine coolant level should be maintained 1–2 in. (25–51mm) below the bottom of the radiator filler neck when the engine is at air temperature and 1 in. (25mm) below the bottom of the filler neck when the engine is hot.

On systems with a coolant recovery tank, maintain the coolant level at the level marks on the recovery bottle.

For best protection against freezing and overheating, maintain an approximate 50% water

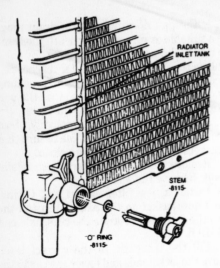

Radiator drain valve location

and 50% ethylene glycol antifreeze mixture in the cooling system. Do not mix different brands of antifreeze to avoid possible chemical damage to the cooling system.

Avoid using water that is known to have a high alkaline content or is very hard, except in emergency situations. Drain and flush the cooling system as soon as possible after using such water.

CAUTION: *Cover the radiator cap with a thick cloth before removing it from a radiator in a vehicle that is hot. Turn the cap counterclockwise slowly until pressure can be heard escaping. Allow all pressure to escape from the radiator before completely removing the radiator cap. It is best to allow the engine to cool if possible, before removing the radiator cap.*

NOTE: *Never add cold water to an overheated engine while the engine is not running.*

After filling the radiator, run the engine until it reaches normal operating temperature, to make sure that the thermostat has opened and all the air is bled from the system.

CAUTION: *The cooling fan motor is controlled by a temperature switch. The fan may come on and run when the engine is off. It will continue to run until the correct temperature is reached. Take care not to get your fingers, etc. caught in the fan blades.*

Draining Coolant

CAUTION: *When draining the coolant, keep in mind that cats and dogs are attracted by the ethylene glycol antifreeze, and are quite likely to drink any that is left in an uncovered container or in puddles on the ground. This will prove fatal in sufficient quantity.*

Always drain the coolant into a sealable container. Coolant should be reused unless it is contaminated or several years old.

To drain the coolant, connect a hose, 457mm long, with an inside diameter of 9.5mm, to the nipple on the drain valve located on the bottom left (driver side) of the radiator. With the engine cool, set the heater control to the maximum heat position, remove the radiator cap and open the drain valve or remove allen head plug ($\frac{3}{16}$ in.) allowing the coolant to drain into a container. When all of the coolant is drained, remove the 9.5mm hose and close the drain valve.

Replacing Coolant

If there is any evidence of rust or scaling in the cooling system, the system should be flushed thoroughly before refilling. With the engine OFF and COOL:

1. Using a funnel, add a 50 percent coolant and 50 percent water solution to the radiator.

2. Reinstall the radiator cap to the pressure relief position by installing the cap to the fully installed position and then backing off to the first stop.

3. Start and idle the engine until the upper radiator hose is warm.

4. Immediately shut off engine. Cautiously remove radiator cap and add water until the radiator is full. Reinstall radiator cap securely.

5. Add coolant to the ADD mark on the reservoir, then fill to the FULL HOT mark with water.

6. Check system for leaks and return the heater temperature control to normal position.

RADIATOR CAP INSPECTION

Allow the engine to cool sufficiently before attempting to remove the radiator cap. Use a rag to cover the cap, then remove by pressing down and turning counterclockwise to the first stop. If any hissing is noted (indicating the release of pressure), wait until the hissing stops completely, then press down again and turn counterclockwise until the cap can be removed.

CAUTION: *DO NOT attempt to remove the radiator cap while the engine is hot. Severe personal injury from steam burns can result.*

Check the condition of the radiator cap gasket and seal inside of the cap. The radiator cap is designed to seal the cooling system under normal operating conditions which allows the build up of a certain amount of pressure (this pressure rating is stamped or printed on the cap). The pressure in the system raises the boiling point of the coolant to help prevent overheating. If the radiator cap does not seal, the boiling point of the coolant is lowered and overheating will occur. If the cap must be replaced,

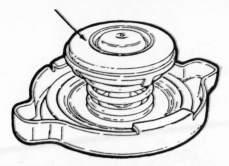

Check the radiator cap for defective gasket

purchase the new cap according to the pressure rating which is specified for your vehicle.

Prior to installing the radiator cap, inspect and clean the filler neck. If you are reusing the old cap, clean it thoroughly with clear water. After turning the cap on, make sure the arrows align with the overflow hose.

FLUSHING AND CLEANING THE SYSTEM

1. Drain the cooling system. Drain the engine block. Refill the system with water at the radiator fill neck.

2. Allow the engine to idle for about 5 minutes. Turn the engine off. Drain the cooling system.

3. Repeat the above Steps until nearly clear water is drained from the radiator. Allow the remaining water to drain and then close the draincock.

4. Disconnect the overflow hose from the radiator filler neck connection. Remove the coolant recovery reservoir from the fender apron and empty the fluid.

5. Flush the reservoir with clean water. Reinstall the component.

6. Fill the radiator and cooling system with the proper grade and type antifreeze mixture.

Master Cylinder

FLUID RECOMMENDATIONS

When adding or refilling the master cylinder be sure to use H. D. brake fluid that meets or exceeds Ford Motor Company specification ESA-M6C25-A or Ford Motor Company part number C6AZ-19542-AA or BA.

LEVEL CHECK

The brake master cylinder is located under the hood, on the left side (drivers side) of firewall. Check the lubrication and service charts for location. Before removing the master cylinder reservoir cap, make sure the vehicle is rest-

ing on level ground and clean all the dirt away from the top of the master cylinder. Remove the master cylinder cap.

Some vehicles are equipped with Anti-lock brakes. To check the fluid level in the anti-lock master cylinder reservoir.

1. Turn ignition OFF.

2. Pump the brake pedal at least 20 times or until the pedal feel becomes hard, then turn ignition key to ON position.

3. Wait at least 60 seconds to be sure the fluid level is stabilized.

4. The fluid level should be at the MAX line as indicated on the side of the reservoir. If the level is low, remove the cap and add Heavy Duty Brake Fluid (Dot 3) until the MAX line is reached.

The level of the brake fluid should be at the **MAX** mark embossed on the translucent plastic reservoir of the master cylinder. If the level is less than half the volume of the reservoir, check the brake system for leaks. Leaks in the brake system most commonly occur at the rear wheel cylinders. or at the front calipers. Leaks at brake lines or the master cylinder can also be the cause of the loss of brake fluid.

The fluid level lowers due to normal brake shoe wear. After filling the master cylinder to the proper level with brake fluid (Type DOT 3), but before replacing the cap, fold the rubber diaphragm up into the cap, then replace the cap on the reservoir and snap the retaining clip back in place.

Power Steering Pump

FLUID RECOMMENDATIONS

Use premium power steering fluid Ford Motor Company E6AZ-19582-AA (ESW-M2C33-F) or equivalent.

LEVEL CHECK

Run the engine until it reaches normal operating temperature. While the engine is idling, turn the steering wheel all the way to the right and then left several times. Shut OFF the engine. Open the hood and remove the power steering pump dipstick located on the right side (passenger side) near the front of the engine. Wipe the dipstick clean and reinstall into the pump reservoir. Withdraw the dipstick and note the fluid level shown. The level must show in the hot full range on the dipstick. Add Ford power steering fluid, if necessary, but do not overfill. Remove any excess fluid with a suction bulb or equivalent.

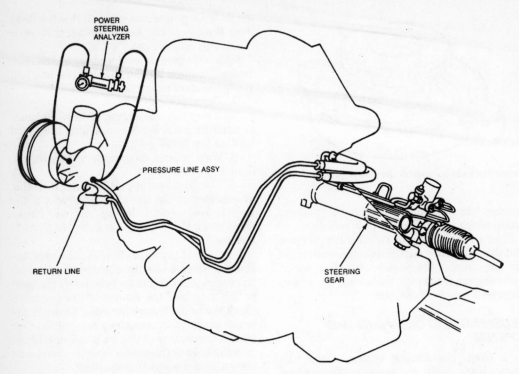

Power steering system — except SHO engine

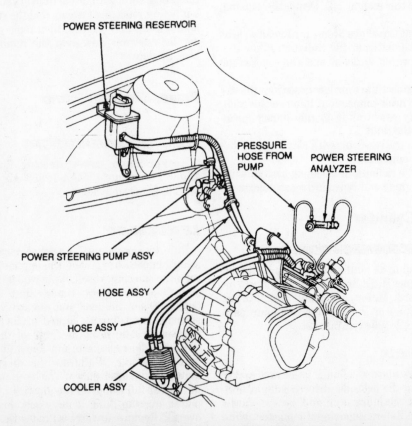

Power steering system — SHO engine

POWER STEERING PUMP MODEL IDENTIFICATION

THE POWER STEERING PUMPS HAVE A SERVICE IDENTIFICATION TAG,
TO IDENTIFY ASSEMBLIES FOR SERVICE PURPOSES. TAGS CONTAIN
INFORMATION AS SHOWN BELOW.
TAG LOCATION: ON RESERVOIR BODY

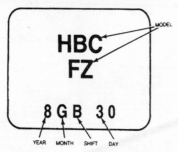

Power steering pump identification tag — except SHO engine

Power Steering Pump Model Identification
The Power Steering Pumps have a service identification tag to identify assemblies for service purposes. Tags contain the information shown.

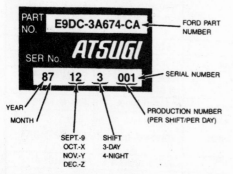

Power steering pump identification tag — SHO engine

Steering Rack

FLUID RECOMMENDATIONS

Use premium power steering fluid Ford Motor Company E6AZ–19582–AA (ESW–M2C33–F) or equivalent.

Body Maintenance

Regular body maintenance preserves the vehicles appearance during the life of the vehicle. When washing or waxing the exterior of the vehicle be sure to use products that meet or exceed Ford Motor Companys specifications. Replace all damaged weatherstrips as needed. Replace all chipped or cracked glass as needed. Drain holes are located under each rocker panel, quater panel and door, these holes should be kept open to allow water to drain.

Wheel Bearings

CAUTION: *When servicing the rear wheel bearings, brake shoes contain asbestos which*

has been determined to be a cancer causing agent. Never clean the brake surfaces with compressed air! Avoid inhaling any dust from any brake surface! When cleaning brake surfaces, use a commercially available brake cleaning fluid.

PACKING AND ADJUSTMENT

NOTE: *Sodium-based grease is not compatible with lithium-based grease. Read the package labels and be careful not to mix the two types. If there is any doubt as to the type of grease used, completely clean the old grease from the bearing and hub before replacing.*

Before handling the bearings, there are a few things that you should remember to do and not to do.

Remember to DO the following:
• Remove all outside dirt from the housing before exposing the bearing.
• Treat a used bearing as gently as you would a new one.
• Work with clean tools in clean surroundings.
• Use clean, dry canvas gloves, or at least clean, dry hands.
• Clean solvents and flushing fluids are a must.
• Use clean paper when laying out the bearings to dry.
• Protect disassembled bearings from rust and dirt. Cover them up.
• Use clean rags to wipe bearings.
• Keep the bearings in oil-proof paper when they are to be stored or are not in use.
• Clean the inside of the housing before replacing the bearing.

Do NOT do the following:
• Don't work in dirty surroundings.
• Don't use dirty, chipped or damaged tools.
• Try not to work on wooden work benches or use wooden mallets.
• Don't handle bearings with dirty or moist hands.
• Do not use gasoline for cleaning; use a safe solvent.
• Do not spin-dry bearings with compressed air. They will be damaged.
• Do not spin dirty bearings.
• Avoid using cotton waste or dirty cloths to wipe bearings.
• Try not to scratch or nick bearing surfaces.
• Do not allow the bearing to come in contact with dirt or rust at any time.

The following procedure should be performed whenever the wheel is excessively loose on the spindle or it does not rotate freely.

LUBRICATION SPECIFICATIONS

Description	Part Name	Ford Part Number	Ford Specification
Door and Deck Lid Latches	Multi-Purpose Grease Spray	D7AZ-19584-AA	ESR-M1C159-A
Hinges, Hinge Checks and Pivots			
Hood Latch and Auxiliary Catch			
Parking Brake Cable			
Disc Brake Caliper Locating Pin and Insulator	Sillicone Dielectric Compound	D7AZ-19A331-A Motorcraft WA-10	ESE-M1C171-A
Lock Cylinders	Lock Lubricant	D8AZ-19587-AA	ESB-M2C20-A
Steering Gear (Power)	Steering Gear Grease	C3AZ-19578-A	ESW-M1C87-A
Steering—Power (Pump Reservoir)	Motorcraft/Type F Auto. Trans. Fluid	XT-1-QF	ESW-M2C33-F
Transaxle AXODE (Automatic)	Motorcraft Ford MERCON® Auto. Trans. Fluid	XT-2-QDX	MERCON®
Transaxle (Manual)	Motorcraft MERCON® Auto. Trans. Fluid	XT-2-QDX	MERCON®
Oil Filter—2.5L—Automatic Transaxle	Long-Life Oil Filter FL-300	D4ZZ-6731-B	ES-E3ZE-6714-CA
Engine Oil Filter 3.0L, 3.8L and 3.0L SHO	Long-Life Oil Filter FL-400A	E4FZ-6731-AES-E4EE-6714-AA	
Engine Oil—Gasoline Engines	MOTORCRAFT: 5W30 Super Premium 10W30 Super Premium	XO-5W30-QSP XO-10W30-QSP	ESE-M2C153-E and API Category SG
Speedometer Cable	Speedometer Cable Lube	E6TZ-19581-A	ESF-M1C160-A
Engine Coolant	Premium Cooling System Fluid	E2FZ-19549-AA	ESE-M97B44-A
Brake Master Cylinder	H.D. Brake Fluid	C6AZ-19542-AA or BA	ESAM6C25-A
Drum Brake Shoe Ledges	Disc Brake Caliper Slide Grease	D7AZ-19590-A	ESA-M1C172-A
Brake Master Cylinder Push Rod and Bushing	Motorcraft SAE 10W30 Engine Oil	XO-10W30-QSP	ESE-M2C153-E
Brake Pedal Pivot Bushing			
Tire Mounting Bead (of Tire)	Tire Mounting Lube	D9AZX-19583-A	ESA-M1B6-A
Clutch Cable Connection Transaxle End	Long-Life Lubricant	XG-1-C	ESA-M1C75-B
Clutch Release Lever—At Fingers (Both Sides and Fulcrum)			
Clutch Release Bearing Retainer			
Outboard CV Joints	CV Joint Bearing Grease	E2FZ-19590-B	ESP-M1C216-A
Inboard CV Joints	CV Joint Bearing Grease	E43Z-19590-A	ESP-M1C207-A

NOTE: *The rear wheel uses a tapered roller bearing which may feel loose when properly adjusted; this feel should be considered normal.*

Adjustment

The following procedure applies only to 1986–89 vehicles. Adjustment is not possible on 1990–91 vehicles. This procedure should be performed whenever the wheel is excessively loose on the spindle or it does not rotate freely.

NOTE: *The rear wheel uses a tapered roller bearing which may feel loose when properly adjusted; this condition should be considered normal.*

1. Raise and support the rear of the vehicle until tires clear the floor.

2. Remove the wheel cover or the ornament and nut covers. Remove the hub grease cap.

NOTE: *If the vehicle is equipped with styled steel or aluminum wheels, the wheel/tire assembly must be removed to remove the dust cover.*

3. Remove the cotter pin and the nut retainer.

4. Back off the hub nut 1 full turn.

5. While rotating the hub/drum assembly, tighten the adjusting nut to 17–25 ft. lbs. (23–24 Nm). Back off the adjusting nut ½ turn, then retighten it to 24–28 inch lbs. (2.7–3.2 Nm).

6. Position the nut retainer over the adjusting nut so the slots are in line with cotter pin hole, without rotating the adjusting nut.

7. Install the cotter pin and bend the ends around the retainer flange.

8. Check the hub rotation. If the hub rotates freely, install the grease cap. If not, check the bearings for damage and replace, as necessary.

9. Install the wheel and tire assembly and the wheel cover, if necessary. Lower the vehicle.

REMOVAL AND INSTALLATION

Drum Brakes

1986–89

1. Raise the vehicle and support it safely. Remove the wheel from the hub and drum.

2. Remove the grease cap from the hub. Remove the cotter pin, nut retainer, adjusting nut and keyed flat washer from the spindle. Discard the cotter pin.

3. Pull the hub and drum assembly off of the spindle. Remove the outer bearing assembly.

4. Using seal remover tool 1175–AC or equivalent, remove and discard the grease seal. Remove the inner bearing assembly from the hub.

5. Wipe all lubricant from the spindle and inside of the hub. Cover the spindle with a clean cloth and vacuum all loose dust and dirt from the brake assembly. Carefully remove the cloth to prevent dirt from falling on the spindle.

6. Clean both bearing assemblies and cups using a suitable solvent. Inspect the bearing assemblies and cups for excessive wear, scratches, pits or other damage and replace as necessary.

7. If the cups are to be replaced, remove them with impact slide hammer T50T–100–A

and bearing cup puller T77F–1102–A or equivalent.

To install:

8. If the inner and outer bearing cups were removed, install the replacement cups using driver handle T80T–4000–W and bearing cup replacers T73T–1217–A and T77F–1217–A or equivalent. Support the drum hub on a block of wood to prevent damage. Make sure the cups are properly seated in the hub.

NOTE: *Do not use the cone and roller assembly to install the cups. This will result in damage to the bearing cup and the cone and roller assembly.*

9. Make sure all of the spindle and bearing surfaces are clean.

10. Using a bearing packer, pack the bearing assemblies with a suitable wheel bearing grease. If a packer is not available, work in as much grease as possible between the rollers and cages. Grease the cup surfaces.

NOTE: *Allow all of the cleaning solvent to dry before repacking the bearings. Do not spin-dry the bearings with air pressure.*

11. Install the inner bearing cone and roller assembly in the inner cup. Apply a light film of grease to the lips of a new grease seal and install the seal with rear hub seal replacer T56T–4676–B or equivalent. Make sure the retainer flange is seated all around.

12. Apply a light film of grease on the spindle shaft bearing surfaces. Install the hub and drum assembly on the spindle. Keep the hub centered on the spindle to prevent damage to the grease seal and spindle threads.

13. Install the outer bearing assembly and the keyed flatwasher on the spindle. Install the adjusting nut and adjust the wheel bearings. Install a new cotter pin. Install the grease cap.

14. Install the wheel and tire assembly and lower the vehicle.

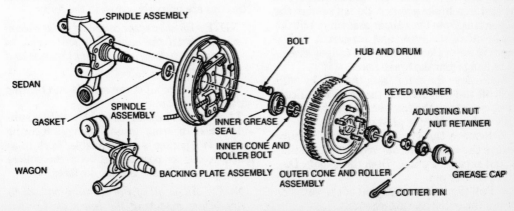

Rear hub and bearing assembly — 1988–89 vehicles with drum brakes

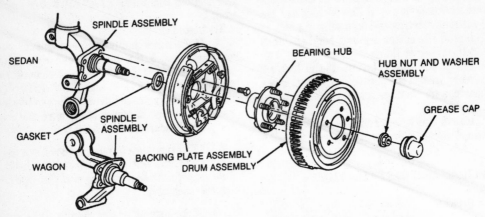

Rear hub and bearing assembly — 1990–92 vehicles with drum brakes

1990–92

1. Raise the vehicle and support it safely.
2. Remove the wheel.
3. Remove the 2 pushnuts retaining the drum to the hub and remove the drum.
4. Remove the grease cap from the bearing and hub assembly and discard it.
5. Remove the hub retaining nut and remove the bearing and hub assembly from the spindle.
6. Install in the reverse order of removal. Use coil remover T89P–19623–FH or equivalent, to install the new grease cap. Tap on the tool to make sure the grease cap is fully seated. Tighten the hub retaining nut to 188–254 ft. lbs. (255–345 Nm).

Disc Brakes

1986–89

1. Raise the vehicle and support it safely. Remove the tire and wheel assembly from the hub.
2. Remove the brake caliper by removing the 2 bolts that attach the caliper support to the cast iron brake adapter. Do not remove the caliper pins from the caliper assembly. Lift the caliper off of the rotor and support it with a length of wire. Do not allow the caliper assembly to hang from the brake hose.
3. Remove the rotor from the hub by pulling it off the hub bolts. If the rotor is difficult to remove, strike the rotor sharply between the studs with a rubber or plastic hammer.
4. Remove the grease cap from the hub. Remove the cotter pin, nut retainer, adjusting nut and keyed flat washer from the spindle. Discard the cotter pin.
5. Pull the hub assembly off of the spindle. Remove the outer bearing assembly.
6. Using seal remover tool 1175–AC or equivalent, remove and discard the grease seal. Remove the inner bearing assembly from the hub.
7. Wipe all of the lubricant from the spindle and inside of the hub. Cover the spindle with a clean cloth and vacuum all of the loose dust and dirt from the brake assembly. Carefully remove the cloth to prevent dirt from falling on the spindle.
8. Clean both bearing assemblies and cups using a suitable solvent. Inspect the bearing assemblies and cups for excessive wear, scratches, pits or other damage and replace as necessary.
9. If the cups are being replaced, remove them with impact slide hammer tool T50T–100–A and bearing cup puller tool T77F–1102–A or equivalent.

To install:

10. If the inner and outer bearing cups were removed, install the replacement cups using driver handle tool T80T–4000–W and bearing cup replacer tools T73F–1217–A and T77F–1217–B or equivalent. Support the hub on a block of wood to prevent damage. Make sure the cups are properly seated in the hub.

NOTE: *Do not use the cone and roller assembly to install the cups. This will result in damage to the bearing cup and the cone and roller assembly.*

11. Make sure all of the spindle and bearing surfaces are clean.
12. Pack the bearing assemblies with a suitable wheel bearing grease using a bearing packer. If a packer is not available, work in as much grease as possible between the rollers and the cages. Grease the cup surfaces.

NOTE: *Allow all of the cleaning solvent to dry before repacking the bearings. Do not spin-dry the bearings with air pressure.*

13. Place the inner bearing cone and roller assembly in the inner cup. Apply a light film of grease to the lips of a new grease seal and install the seal with rear hub seal replacer tool T56T–4676–B or equivalent. Make sure the retainer flange is seated all around.

14. Apply a light film of grease on the spindle shaft bearing surfaces. Install the hub assembly on the spindle. Keep the hub centered on the spindle to prevent damage to the grease seal and spindle threads.

15. Install the outer bearing assembly and keyed flat washer on the spindle. Install the adjusting nut and adjust the wheel bearings. Install a new cotter pin. Install the grease cap.

16. Install the disc brake rotor to the hub assembly. Install the disc brake caliper over the rotor.

17. Install the wheel and tire assembly and lower the vehicle.

1990–92

1. Raise the vehicle and support it safely.

2. Remove the wheel and tire assembly.

3. Remove the caliper assembly from the brake adapter. Support the caliper assembly with a length of wire.

4. Remove the push on nuts that retain the rotor to the hub and remove the rotor.

5. Remove the grease cap from the bearing and hub assembly and discard the grease cap.

6. Remove the bearing and hub assembly retaining nut and remove the bearing and hub assembly from the spindle.

7. Install in the reverse order of removal. Install a new grease cap using coil remover tool T89P–19623–FH or equivalent. Tap on the tool until the grease cap is fully seated. Tighten the hub retaining nut to 188–254 ft. lbs. (255–345 Nm).

TRAILER TOWING

General Recommendations

Towing a trailer puts additional load on your vehicles engine, drivetrain, brakes, tires and suspension. For your safety and the care of your car, make sure the trailer towing equipment is properly matched to the trailer. All towing equipment should be safely attached to the vehicle and of the proper weight class.

NOTE: *Trailer towing should only be attempted with the 3.0L or 3.8L V6 engine!*

The maximum trailer weight that your vehicle can tow is 1,000 lbs. gross trailer axle weight with a maximum tongue load of 100 lbs. and must abide to the following qualifications:

• Any model equipped with a AXOD or AXOD-E overdrive transaxle should be shifted to the "D" DRIVE position to avoid excessive shifting between the overdrive and third gears.

• Auxiliary oil coolers are recommended for the power steering system and the automatic transaxle during long distance towing (greater than 50 miles, towing in hilly terrain or frequent towing).

• Vehicle speed no higher than 55 mph is recommended while towing a trailer.

Towing Tips

Before starting on a trip, practice turning, stopping and backing up in an area away from other traffic (such as a deserted shopping center parking lot) to gain experience in handling the extra weight and length of the trailer. Take enough time to get the feel of the vehicle/trailer combination under a variety of situations.

Skillful backing requires practice. Back up slowly with an assistant acting as a guide and watching for obstructions. Use both rear view mirrors. Place your hand at the bottom of the steering wheel and move it in the direction you want the rear of the trailer to swing. Make small corrections, instead of exaggerated ones, as a slight movement of the steering wheel will result in a much larger movement of the rear of the trailer.

Allow considerable more room for stopping when a trailer is attached to the vehicle. Keep in mind, the car/trailer combination is a considerable increase in the weight that your car's brakes have to bring to a stop. If you have a manual brake controller, lead with the trailer brakes when approaching a stop. Trailer brakes are also handy for correcting side sway. So just touch them for a moment without using your vehicle brakes and the trailer should settle down and track straight again.

To assist in obtaining good handling with the car/trailer combination, it is important that the trailer tongue load be maintained at approximately 10–15% of the loaded trailer weight.

Check everything before starting out on the road, then stop after you've traveled about 50 miles and double-check the trailer hitch and electrical connections to make sure everything is still OK. Listen for sounds like chains dragging on the ground (indicating that a safety chain has come loose) and check your rear view mirrors frequently to make sure the trailer is still there and tracking properly. Check the trailer wheel lug nuts to make sure they're tight and never attempt to tow the trailer with a space saver spare installed on the car.

Remember that a car/trailer combination is

more sensitive to cross winds and slow down when crossing bridges or wide open expanses in gusty wind conditions. Exceeding the speed limit while towing a trailer is not only illegal, it is foolhardy and invites disaster. A strong gust of wind can send a speeding car/trailer combination out of control.

Because the trailer wheels are closer than the towing vehicle wheels to the inside of a turn, drive slightly beyond the normal turning point when negotiating a sharp turn at a corner. Allow extra distance for passing other vehicles and downshift if necessary for better acceleration. Allow at least the equivalent of one vehicle and trailer length combined for each 10 mph of road speed.

Finally, remember to check the height of the loaded car/trailer, allowing for luggage racks, antenna, etc. mounted on the roof and take note of low bridges or parking garage clearances.

PUSHING AND TOWING

Vehicle Towing

Whenever you are towing another vehicle, or being towed, make sure the strap or chain is sufficiently long and strong. Straps are recommended because they have more stretch then a chain. Attach the strap or chain securely at a point on the frame, shipping tie-down slots are provided on the front and rear of you car and should be used. Never attach a strap or chain to any steering or suspension part. Never try to start the vehicle when being towed, it might run into the back of the tow car. Do not allow too much slack in the tow line, the towed car could run over the line and damage to both cars could occur. If your car is being towed by a tow truck, the towing speed should be limited to 50 mph with the driving wheels off the ground. If it is necessary to tow the car with the drive wheels on the ground, speed should be limited to no more then 35 mph and the towing distance should not be greater than 50 miles. If towing distance is more than 50 miles the front of the car should be put on dollies.

NOTE: *If the car is being towed with the front (drive) wheels on the ground, never*

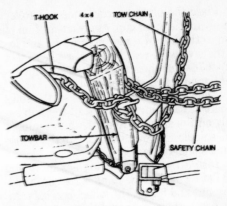

Proper vehicle tow hook up — rear SHO engine

allow the steering lock to keep the wheels straight, damage to the steering could occur. In general, don't do this! A new transaxle will cost you a lot more than a reasonable towing service. Remember the old saying, "you can pay me now, or you can pay me later".

Vehicle Pushing

Push starting is not recommended on cars with a catalytic converter. Gas accumulation in the converter will cause damage to the system. Also you can't push start a Taurus/Sable with an automatic transaxle anyway.

JACKING

The service jack that is provided with your vehicle is only intended to be used in an emergency for changing a flat tire. Never use this jack to hoist the vehicle for any other service. When servicing the vehicle use a floor jack. When using a floor jack, raise the front of the vehicle by positioning the floor jack under either the subframe or body side rail behind the engine support bracket. The rear may be lifted by positioning a floor jack under either rear suspension body bracket. Under no circumstances should the vehicle ever be lifted by the front or rear control arms, halfshafts or CV joints. Severe damage to the vehicle could result.

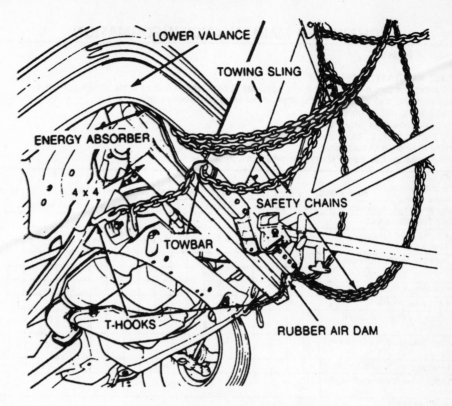

LOWER VALANCE

TOWING SLING

ENERGY ABSORBER

4 x 4

SAFETY CHAINS

TOWBAR

T-HOOKS

RUBBER AIR DAM

Proper vehicle tow hook up — front

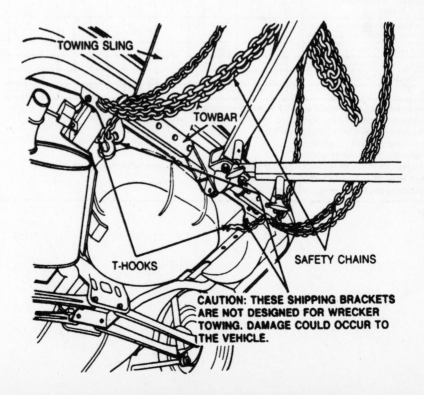

TOWING SLING

TOWBAR

T-HOOKS

SAFETY CHAINS

CAUTION: THESE SHIPPING BRACKETS ARE NOT DESIGNED FOR WRECKER TOWING. DAMAGE COULD OCCUR TO THE VEHICLE.

Proper vehicle tow hook up — rear except SHO engine

SCHEDULE A MAINTENANCE INFORMATION

Maintenance Schedules

CUSTOMER MAINTENANCE SCHEDULE A

Follow Maintenance Schedule A, if your driving habits MAINLY include one or more of the following conditions:
- Short trips of less than 16 km (10 miles) when outside temperatures remain below freezing.
- Operating during HOT WEATHER:
  —Driving in stop-and-go "rush hour" traffic.
- Towing a trailer, using a camper or car-top carrier.
- Operating in severe dust conditions.
- Extensive idling, such as police, taxi or door-to-door delivery service.

SERVICE INTERVAL Perform at the months or distances shown, whichever comes first.	Miles × 1000	3	6	9	12	15	18	21	24	27	30	33	36	39	42	45	48	51	54	57	60
	Kilometers × 1000	4.8	9.6	14.4	19.2	24	28.8	33.6	38.4	43.2	48	52.8	57.6	62.4	67.2	72	76.8	81.6	86.4	91.2	96
EMISSION CONTROL SERVICE																					
Replace Engine Oil and Oil Filter Every 3 Months OR		✓	✓	✓	✓	✓	✓	✓	✓	✓	✓	✓	✓	✓	✓	✓	✓	✓	✓	✓	✓
Spark Plugs 3.0L SHO Platinum Plugs																					✓
2.5L, 3.0L, 3.8L											✓										✓
Inspect Accessory Drive Belt(s)											✓										
Replace Air Cleaner Filter ①											✓										
Replace Crankcase Filter Four Cylinder Engines Only ①											✓										
Replace Cam Belt and Adjust Valve Lash—3.0L SHO											✓										✓
Replace Engine Coolant Every 36 Months OR																					
Check Engine Coolant Protection, Hoses and Clamps		ANNUALLY																			
GENERAL MAINTENANCE																					
Inspect Exhaust Heat Shields											✓										✓
Change Automatic Transaxle Fluid (2.5L, 3.0L, 3.8L) ②											✓										✓
Inspect Disc Brake Pads and Rotors (Front) ③ (Front and Rear—SHO)											✓										✓
Inspect Brake Linings and Drums ③											✓										
Inspect Battery Fluid Level (SHO only) ④								✓								✓					
Inspect and Repack Rear Wheel Bearings											✓										✓
Rotate Tires		✓					✓					✓					✓				

① If operating in severe dust, more frequent intervals may be required—consult your dealer.
② Change automatic transaxle fluid if your driving habits frequently include one or more of the following conditions:
  - Operating during HOT WEATHER (above 32°C (90°F)).
  - Towing a trailer or using a car top carrier.
  - Police, taxi or door-to-door delivery service.
③ If your driving includes continuous stop and go driving or driving in mountainous areas, more frequent intervals may be required.
④ If operating in temperatures above 32°C (90°F) check more often.
✓ All items designated with an "✓" must be performed in all states.

CUSTOMER MAINTENANCE SCHEDULE B

Follow this Schedule if, generally, you drive your vehicle on a daily basis for several miles and NONE OF THE UNIQUE DRIVING CONDITIONS SHOWN IN SCHEDULE A APPLY TO YOUR DRIVING HABITS.

SERVICE INTERVALS Perform at the months or distances shown, whichever comes first.		7.5	15	22.5	30	37.5	45	52.5	60
	Miles × 1000	7.5	15	22.5	30	37.5	45	52.5	60
	Kilometers × 1000	12	24	36	48	60	72	84	96
EMISSIONS CONTROL SERVICE									
Replace Engine Oil and Oil Filter Every 6 Months OR		✔	✔	✔	✔	✔	✔	✔	✔
Replace Spark Plugs 2.5L, 3.8L					✔				✔
3.0L, 3.0L SHO Platinum Plugs									✔
Replace Cam Belt and Adjust Valve Lash—3.0L SHO									✔
Replace Crankcase Filter—Four Cylinder Engine Only									✔
Inspect Accessory Drive Belt(s)					✔				✔
Replace Air Cleaner Filter ①					✔				✔
Replace Engine Coolant Every 36 Months OR					✔				✔
Check Engine Coolant Protection, Hoses and Clamps					ANNUALLY				
GENERAL MAINTENANCE									
Inspect Battery Fluid Level (SHO only) ④				✔			✔		
Check Exhaust Heat Shields									
Inspect Disc Brake Pads and Rotors (Front) (Front and Rear—SHO) ②					✔				✔
Inspect Brake Linings and Drums (Rear) ②				✔②					✔②
Inspect Brake Linings and Drums (Rear) ③				✔②					✔②
Rotate Tires		✔		✔		✔		✔	

① If operating in severe dust, more frequent intervals may be required. Consult your dealer.
② If your driving includes continuous stop-and-go driving or driving in mountainous areas, more frequent intervals may be required.
④ If operating in temperatures above 32°C (90°F) check more often.
✔ All items designated with an "✔" must be performed in all states.

CAPACITIES

Year	Model	Engine VIN	Engine Displacement Liters (cc)	Engine Crankcase with Filter	Transmission (pts.)		Drive Axle (pts.)	Fuel Tank (gal.)	Cooling System (qts.)
					5-Spd	Auto.			
1986	Taurus	D	2.5 (2500)	5.0	6.2	16.6	①	②	8.3
	Taurus	U	3.0 (3000)	4.5	6.2	21.8	①	②	③
	Sable	D	2.5 (2500)	5.0	6.2	16.6	①	②	8.3
	Sable	U	3.0 (3000)	4.5	6.2	21.8	①	②	③
1987	Taurus	D	2.5 (2500)	5.0	6.2	16.6	①	②	8.3
	Taurus	U	3.0 (3000)	4.5	6.2	21.8	①	②	③
	Sable	D	2.5 (2500)	5.0	6.2	16.6	①	②	8.3
	Sable	U	3.0 (3000)	4.5	6.2	21.8	①	②	③
1988	Taurus	D	2.5 (2500)	5.0	6.2	16.6	①	②	8.3
	Taurus	U	3.0 (3000)	4.5	6.2	21.8	①	②	③
	Taurus	4	3.8 (3800)	5.0	—	26.2	①	②	12.1
	Sable	D	2.5 (2500)	5.0	6.2	16.6	①	②	8.3
	Sable	U	3.0 (3000)	4.5	6.2	21.8	①	②	③
	Sable	4	3.8 (3800)	5.0	—	26.2	①	②	12.1
1989	Taurus	D	2.5 (2500)	5.0	6.2	16.6	①	②	8.3
	Taurus	U	3.0 (3000)	4.5	6.2	21.8	①	②	③
	Taurus SHO	Y	3.0 (3000)	4.5	6.2	21.8	①	②	11.6
	Taurus	4	3.8 (3800)	5.0	—	26.2	①	②	12.1
	Sable	D	2.5 (2500)	5.0	6.2	16.6	①	②	8.3
	Sable	U	3.0 (3000)	4.5	6.2	21.8	①	②	③
	Sable	4	3.8 (3800)	5.0	—	26.2	①	②	12.1
1990	Taurus	D	2.5 (2500)	5.0	—	16.0	①	②	8.3
	Taurus	U	3.0 (3000)	4.5	—	25.6	①	②	③
	Taurus SHO	Y	3.0 (3000)	5.0	6.2	25.6	①	②	11.6
	Taurus	4	3.8 (3800)	4.5	—	25.6	①	②	12.1
	Sable	U	3.0 (3000)	4.5	—	25.6	①	②	③
	Sable	4	3.8 (3800)	4.5	—	25.6	①	②	12.1
1991	Taurus	D	2.5 (2500)	5.0	—	16.0	①	②	8.3
	Taurus	U	3.0 (3000)	4.5	—	25.6	①	②	③
	Taurus SHO	Y	3.0 (3000)	5.0	6.2	25.6	①	②	11.6
	Taurus	4	3.8 (3800)	4.5	—	25.6	①	②	12.1
	Sable	U	3.0 (3000)	4.5	—	25.6	①	②	③
	Sable	4	3.8 (3800)	4.5	—	25.6	①	②	12.1
1992	Taurus	U	3.0 (3000)	4.5	—	25.6	①	②	③
	Taurus SHO	Y	3.0 (3000)	5.0	6.2	25.6	①	②	11.6
	Taurus	4	3.8 (3800)	4.5	—	25.6	①	②	12.1
	Sable	U	3.0 (3000)	4.5	—	25.6	①	②	③
	Sable	4	3.8 (3800)	4.5	—	25.6	①	②	12.1

① Included in transaxle capacity
② Standard 16.0
　 Optional 18.6
③ Except Wagon with air conditioning 11
　 Wagon with air conditioning 11.8

PREVENTIVE MAINTENANCE CHART

Item No.	To Be Serviced	When to Perform Miles or Months, Whichever Occurs First / Miles (000)	The services shown in this schedule up to 60,000 miles are to be performed after 60,000 miles at the same intervals							
			7.5	15	22.5	30	37.5	45	52.5	60
1	Engine Oil Change	Every 7,500 Miles or 12 Months	✔	✔	✔	✔	✔	✔	✔	✔
	Oil Filter Change	At First and Every Other Oil Change or 12 Months	✔		✔		✔		✔	
2	Chassis Lubrication	Every oil change	✔	✔	✔	✔	✔	✔	✔	✔
3	Carburetor Choke and Hoses Inspection	At 6 Months or 7,500 Miles and at 60,000 Miles	✔			✔				✔
4	Carburetor or T.B.I. Mounting Bolt Torque Check	At 6 Months or 7,500 Miles and at 60,000 Miles	✔							✔
5	Engine Idle Speed Adjustment	At 6 Months or 7,500 Miles and at 60,000 Miles	✔							✔
6	Engine Accessory Drive Belts Inspection	Every 24 Months or 30,000 Miles				✔				✔
7	Cooling System Service	Every 24 Months or 30,000 Miles				✔				✔
8	Front Wheel Bearing Repack	Every 30,000 Miles				✔				✔
9	Transmission Service	Every 30,000 Miles				✔				✔
10	Vacuum Advance System Inspection	Check at 6 Months or 7,500 Miles, then at 30,000 Miles, and then at 15,000 Mile intervals	✔			✔		✔		✔
11	Spark Plugs and Wire Service	Every 30,000 Miles				✔				✔
12	PCV System Inspection	Every 30,000 Miels				✔				✔
13	EGR System Check	Every 30,000 Miles				✔				✔
14	Air Cleaner and PCV Filter Replacement	Every 30,000 Miles				✔				✔
15	Engine Timing Check	Every 30,000 Miles				✔				✔
16	Fuel Tank, Cap and Lines Inspection	Every 24 Months or 30,000 Miles				✔				✔
17	Early Fuel Evaporation System Inspection	At 7,500 Miles and at 30,000 Miles then at 30,000 Mile intervals	✔			✔				✔
18	Evaporative Control System Inspection	Every 30,000 Miles				✔				✔
19	Fuel Filter Replacement	Every 30,000 Miles				✔				✔
20	Valve Lash Adjustment	Every 15,000 Miles		✔		✔		✔		✔
21	Thermostatically Controlled Air Cleaner Inspection	Every 30,000 Miles				✔				✔

Engine Performance and Tune-Up

2

TUNE-UP PROCEDURES

In order to extract the full measure of performance and economy from your engine it is essential that it be properly tuned at regular intervals. A regular tune-up will keep your vehicle's engine running smoothly and will prevent the annoying minor breakdowns and poor performance associated with an untuned engine.

A complete tune-up should be performed every 12,000 miles (19,300km) or twelve months, whichever comes first. This interval should be halved if the vehicle is operated under severe conditions, such as trailer towing, prolonged idling, continual stop and start driving, or if starting or running problems are noticed. It is assumed that the routine maintenance has been kept up, as this will have a decided effect on the results of a tune-up. All of the applicable steps of a tune-up should be followed in order, as the result is a cumulative one.

If the specifications on the tune-up sticker in the engine compartment disagree with the Tune-Up Specifications chart, the figures on the sticker must be used. The sticker often reflects changes made during the production run.

Spark Plugs

A typical spark plug consists of a metal shell surrounding a ceramic insulator. A metal electrode extends downward through the center of the insulator and protrudes a small distance. Located at the end of the plug and attached to the side of the outer metal shell is the side electrode. The side electrode bends in at a 90° angle so that its tip is even with, and parallel to, the tip of the center electrode. The distance between these two electrodes (measured in thousandths of an inch) is called the spark plug gap. The spark plug in no way produces a spark but merely provides a gap across which the current

can arc. The coil produces anywhere from 20,000 to 40,000 volts which travels to the distributor where it is distributed through the spark plug wires to the spark plugs. The current passes along the center electrode and jumps the gap to the side electrode, and, in do doing, ignites the air/fuel mixture in the combustion chamber.

Spark plugs ignite the air and fuel mixture in the cylinder as the piston reaches the top of the compression stroke. The controlled explosion that results forces the piston down, turning the crankshaft and the rest of the drive train.

The average life of a spark plug is dependent on a number of factors: the mechanical condition of the engine; the type of engine; the type of fuel; driving conditions; and the driver.

When you remove the spark plugs, check their condition. They are a good indicator of the condition of the engine.

A small deposit of light tan or gray material on a spark plug that has been used for any period of time is to be considered normal.

The gap between the center electrode and the side or ground electrode can be expected to increase not more than 0.001 in. (0.025mm) every 1,000 miles (1,600km) under normal conditions.

When a spark plug is functioning normally or, more accurately, when the plug is installed in an engine that is functioning properly, the plugs can be taken out, cleaned, regapped, and reinstalled in the engine without doing the engine any harm.

When, and if, a plug fouls and beings to misfire, you will have to investigate, correct the cause of the fouling, and either clean or replace the plug.

Spark plug heat range is the ability of the plug to dissipate heat. The longer the insulator (or the farther it extends into the engine), the hotter the plug will operate; the shorter the in-

GASOLINE ENGINE TUNE-UP SPECIFICATIONS

Year	Engine VIN	Engine Displacement Liters (cc)	Spark Plugs Gap (in.)	Ignition Timing ① (deg.) MT	AT	Fuel Pump (psi)	Idle Speed (rpm) MT	AT	Valve Clearance In.	Ex.
1986	D	2.5 (2500)	0.044	10	10	13–17	725	650	Hyd.	Hyd.
	U	3.0 (3000)	0.044	—	10	35–45	—	625	Hyd.	Hyd.
1987	D	2.5 (2500)	0.044	10	10	13–17	725	650	Hyd.	Hyd.
	U	3.0 (3000)	0.044	—	10	35–45	—	625	Hyd.	Hyd.
1988	D	2.5 (2500)	0.044	10	10	13–17	725	650	Hyd.	Hyd.
	U	3.0 (3000)	0.044	—	10	35–45	—	625	Hyd.	Hyd.
	4	3.8 (3800)	0.056	②	②	35–45	②	②	Hyd.	Hyd.
1989	D	2.5 (2500)	0.044	10	10	13–17	725	650	Hyd.	Hyd.
	U	3.0 (3000)	0.044	—	10	35–45	—	625	Hyd.	Hyd.
	Y	3.0 (3000)	0.044	10	—	36–39	800	—	0.008③	0.012③
	4	3.8 (3800)	0.054	②	②	35–45	②	②	Hyd.	Hyd.
1990	D	2.5 (2500)	0.044	—	②	13–17	—	②	Hyd.	Hyd.
	U	3.0 (3000)	0.044	—	②	35–45	—	②	Hyd.	Hyd.
	Y	3.0 (3000)	0.044	10	—	35–45	②	—	0.008③	0.012③
	4	3.8 (3800)	0.054	—	②	35–45	—	②	Hyd.	Hyd.
1991	D	2.5 (2500)	0.044	—	②	45–60	—	②	Hyd.	Hyd.
	U	3.0 (3000)	0.044	—	②	35–45	—	②	Hyd.	Hyd.
	Y	3.0 (3000)	0.044	10	—	35–45	②	—	0.008③	0.012③
	4	3.8 (3800)	0.054	—	②	35–45	—	②	Hyd.	Hyd.
1992	U	3.0 (3000)	0.044	—	②	35–45	—	②	Hyd.	Hyd.
	Y	3.0 (3000)	0.044	10	—	35–45	②	—	0.008③	0.012③
	4	3.8 (3800)	0.054	—	②	35–45	—	②	Hyd.	Hyd.

NOTE: The lowest cylinder pressure should be within 75% of the highest cylinder pressure reading. For example, if the highest cylinder is 134 psi, the lowest should be 101. Engine should be at normal operating temperature with throttle valve in the wide open position.

The underhood specifications sticker often reflects tune-up specifications changes in production. Sticker figures must be used if they disagree with those in this chart.

① BTDC—Before top dead center

② The Calibration levels vary from vehicle to vehicle. Refer to the Vehicle Emission Control information label for ignition timing and idle speed specifications.

③ Shim set bucket type valve lifter

sulator the cooler it will operate. A plug that absorbs little heat and remains too cool will quickly accumulate deposits of oil and carbon since it is not hot enough to burn them off. This leads to plug fouling and consequently to misfiring. A plug that absorbs too much heat will have no deposits, but, due to the excessive heat, the electrodes will burn away quickly and in some instances, preignition may result. Preignition takes place when plug tips get so hot that they glow sufficiently to ignite the fuel/air mixture before the actual spark occurs. This early ignition will usually cause a pinging during low speeds and heavy loads.

The general rule of thumb for choosing the correct heat range when picking a spark plug is: if most of your driving is long distance, high speed travel, use a colder plug; if most of your driving is stop and go, use a hotter plug. Original equipment plugs are compromise plugs, but most people never have occasion to change their plugs from the factory-recommended heat range.

Ford recommends that spark plugs be changed every 30,000 miles (48,300km) for the 2.5L, 3.0L, and 3.8L engines. The 3.0L SHO engine is equipped with Platinum spark plugs that have a recommended life of 60,000 miles (96,500km). Under severe driving conditions, those intervals should be halved (except 3.0L SHO). Severe driving conditions are:

1. Extended periods of idling or low speed operation, such as off-road or door-to-door delivery.

2. Driving short distances — less than 10 miles (16km) when the average temperature is below 10°F (−12°C) for 60 days or more.

3. Excessive dust or blowing dirt conditions.

REMOVAL AND INSTALLATION

A Set of spark plugs usually requires replacement every 30,000 miles (48,300km), − 60,000 miles (96,500km) for the 3.0L SHO engine — depending on your style of driving. In normal operation, plug gap increases about 0.025mm for every 1,000–2,500 miles (1600–4000km). As the gap increases, the plug's voltage requirement also increases. It requires greater voltage to jump the wider gap and about two to three times as much voltage to fire a plug at higher speeds than at idle.

The spark plugs used in your car require a deep spark plug socket for removal and installation. A special designed pair of plug wire removal pliers is also a good tool to have. The special pliers have cupped jaws that grip the plug wire boot and make the job of twisting and pulling the wire from the plug easier. Damage may occur to the spark plug wire if wire removal pliers are not used

NOTE: *The original spark plug wires are marked for cylinder location. If replacement wires have been installed, be sure to tag them for proper location. It is a good idea to remove the wires one at a time, service the spark plug, reinstall the wire and move onto the next cylinder.*

For easy access for servicing the spark plugs, remove the air cleaner assembly and air intake tube.

1. Twist the spark plug boot and gently pull it and the wire from the spark plug. This is where the special plug wire pliers come in handy.

NOTE: *Never pull on the wire itself, damage to the inside conductor could occur.*

Checking spark plug gap with proper tool

2. The plug wire boot has a cover which shields the plug cavity (in the head) against dirt. After removing the wire, blow out the cavity with air or clean it out with a small brush so dirt will not fall into the engine when the spark plug is removed.

3. Remove the spark plug with a spark plug socket. Turn the socket counterclockwise to remove the plug. Be sure to hold the socket straight on the plug to avoid breaking the insulator (a deep socket designed for spark plugs has a rubber cushion built-in to help prevent plug breakage).

4. Once the plug is out, check its condition to determine the engine condition. This is crucial since spark plug readings are vital signs of engine condition and pending problems.

5. If the old plugs are to be reused, clean and regap them. If new spark plugs are to be installed, always check the gap. Use a round wire feeler gauge to check plug gap. The correct size gauge should pass through the electrode gap with a slight drag. If you're in doubt, try the next smaller and one size larger. The smaller gauge should go through easily and the larger should not go through at all. If adjustment is necessary use the bending tool on the end of the gauge. When adjusting the gap, always bend the side electrode. The center electrode is non-adjustable.

6. Squirt a drop of penetrating oil or anti-seize compound on the threads of the spark plug and install it. Don't oil the threads heavily. Turn the plug in clockwise by hand until it is snug. Be careful not to cross thread the plug

7. When the plug is finger tight, tighten it to the proper torque 5–10 ft. lbs. except SHO engine and 16–20 ft. lbs. for the SHO engine. DO NOT OVERTIGHTEN.

8. Install the plug wire and boot firmly over the spark plug after coating the inside of the boot and terminal with a thin coat of dielectric compound (Motorcraft D7AZ19A331A or white lithium grease).

9. Proceed to the next spark plug.

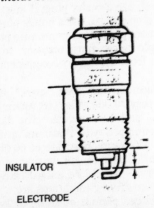

INSULATOR

ELECTRODE

Spark plug heat range measurement location

Spark Plug Wires

Your car is equipped with a electronic ignition system which utilizes 8mm wires to conduct the hotter spark produced. The boots on these wires are designed to cover the spark plug cavities on the cylinder head.

Inspect the wires without removing them from the spark plugs, distributor cap or coil. Look for visible damage such as cuts, pinches, cracks or torn boots. Replace any wires that show damage. If the boot is damaged, it may be replaced by itself. It is not necessary to replace the complete wire just for the boot.

To replace the wire, grasp and twist the boot back and forth while pulling away from the spark plug. Use a special pliers if available.

NOTE: *Always coat the terminals of any wire removed or replaced with a thin layer of dielectric compound.*

When installing a wire be sure it is firmly mounted over or on the plug, distributor cap connector or coil terminal.

REMOVAL AND INSTALLATION

1. Disconnect the negative battery cable.
2. Locate the plug wire. Tag it for reinstallation.
3. Before removing the plug wire from the distributor cap and the spark plug check and remove any retaining clamps.
4. Properly remove the spark plug wire using the proper tools, if required.
5. When reinstalling the spark plug wire be sure to route it exactly as it was removed.

FIRING ORDERS

NOTE: *To avoid confusion, remove and tag spark plug wires one at a time, for replacement*

ELECTRONIC IGNITION

Description And Operation

Your car uses an electronic ignition system. The purpose of using an electronic ignition system is: To eliminate the deterioration of spark quality which occur in the breaker point ignition system as the breaker points wore. To extend maintenance intervals. To provide a more intense and reliable spark at every firing impulse in order to ignite the leaner gas mixtures necessary to control emissions.

The breaker points, point actuating cam and the condenser have been eliminated in the solid

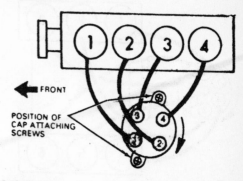

2.5L Engine
Engine Firing Order: 1–3–4–2
Distributor Rotation: Clockwise

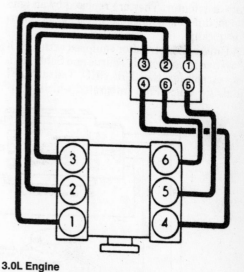

3.0L Engine
Engine Firing Order: 1–4–2–5–3–6
Distributor Rotation: Clockwise

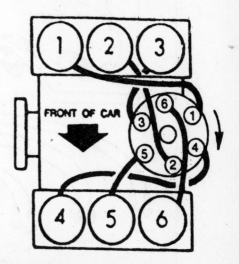

3.0L SHO Engine
Engine Firing Order: 1–4–2–5–3–6
Distributorless Ignition System

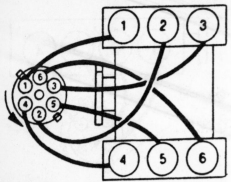

3.8L Engine
Engine Firing Order: 1–4–2–5–3–6
Distributor Rotation: Counterclockwise

state distributor. They are replaced by an ignition module and a magnetic pulse-signal generator (pickup).

A Universal Distributor equipped with a TFI-IV system is used on all Taurus and Sable vehicles, except for the 3.0L SHO Taurus. TFI stands for Thick Film Integrated which incor-

porates a molded thermoplastic module mounted on the distributor base. TFI also uses an "E" coil which replaces the oil filled design used with earlier systems.

The Universal Distributor equipped with TFI-IV uses a vane switch stator assembly which replace the coil stator. The IV system incorporates provision for fixed octane adjustment and has no centrifugal or vacuum advance mechanisms. All necessary timing requirements are handled by the EEC-IV electronic engine control system.

The 3.0L SHO Taurus is equipped with a Distributorless Ignition System (DIS). As the name implies, there is no conventional distributor assembly in the engine. The DIS system consists of: a crankshaft timing sensor that is a single hall effect magnetic switch which is activated by three vanes on the crankshaft timing pulley, a camshaft sensor that is a single hall effect magnetic switch also, but is activated by a single vane driven by the camshaft, an ignition module that receives the signal from the

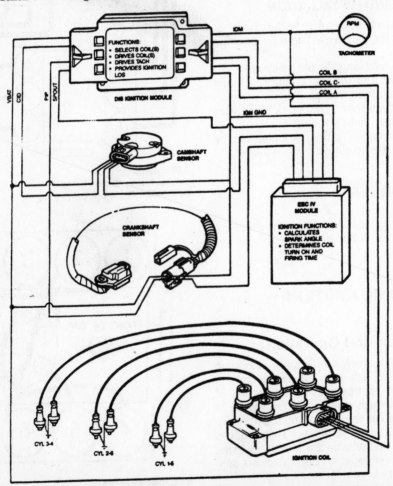

Distributorless ignition system and related components—3.0L SHO engine

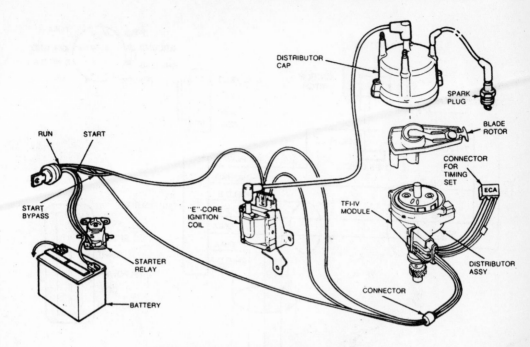

TFI-IV ignition system—except 3.0L SHO engine

crankshaft sensor, camshaft sensor, and spout information for the EEC-IV module, and an ignition coil pack that houses the spark plug wires like the conventional distributor cap.

Parts Replacement

DISTRIBUTOR SYSTEMS

REMOVAL AND INSTALLATION

IGNITION COIL

1. Disconnect the negative battery cable.
2. Disconnect the electrical connectors from the coil assembly.
3. Remove the coil retaining bolts. Remove the coil from its mounting.
4. Installation is the reverse of the removal procedure.

EXCEPT 3.8L ENGINE

1. Disconnect the negative battery cable. Remove the distributor cap and position it to the side.
2. Remove the TFI-IV harness connector. Remove the distributor from the engine.
3. Position the distributor on the work bench. Remove the module retaining screws.
4. Pull the right side of the module down the distributor mounting flange in order to disengage the module terminals from the connector in the distributor base.
5. The module can be pulled toward the flange and away from the distributor.

NOTE: *Do not attempt to lift the module from the mounting surface prior to removing the entire TFI-IV module toward the distributor flange as the pins will break at the distributor/module connector.*

6. Installation is the reverse of the removal procedure. Coat the metal base of the module with silcone compound approximately $\frac{1}{32}$ in. (0.8mm) thick prior to installing it.

3.8L ENGINE

1. Disconnect the negative battery cable
2. Remove the screws attaching the leaf screen and cowl dash extension panel in the area of the TFI module assembly. Remove the leaf screen.
3. Disconnect the harness connector from the module assembly. The connector latch is underneath the module shroud and must be pressed upward to unlatch it.
4. Remove the retaining nuts attaching the TFI/heatsink assembly to the cowl dash extension panel.
5. Remove the TFI/Heatsink assembly. The assembly is mounted with the heatsink pointed down.
6. Remove the module retaining screws and remove the module from the heatsink. While holding the module connector shroud pull the seal off the other end of the module.
7. Installation is the reverse of the removal procedure. Coat the metal base of the module

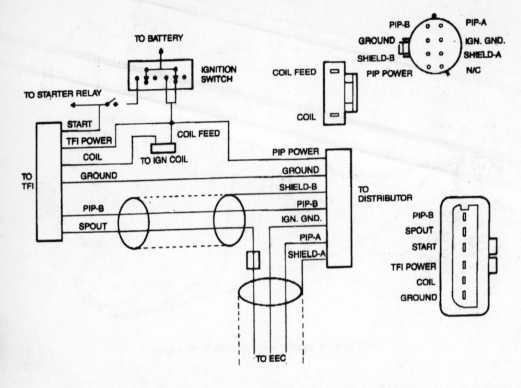

TFI ignition system and closed bowl distributor electrical schematic

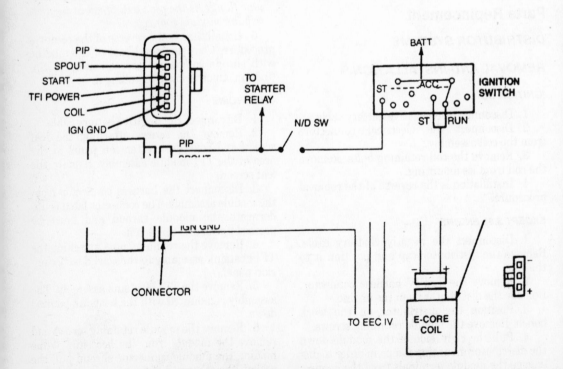

TFI ignition system and open bowl distributor electrical schematic

with silcone compound approximately $\frac{1}{32}$ in. (0.8mm) thick prior to installing it.

DISTRIBUTORLESS SYSTEMS

Removal and Installation

CRANKSHAFT SENSOR

1. Disconnect the negative battery cable.
2. Loosen the tensioner pulleys for the air conditioning compressor and power steering pump belts. Remove the belts from the crankshaft pulley.
3. Remove the upper timing belt cover.
4. Disconnect the sensor wiring harness at the connector and route the wiring harness through the belt cover.
5. Raise and safely support the vehicle.
6. Remove the right front wheel and tire assembly.
7. Remove the crankshaft pulley using a suitable puller.
8. Remove the lower timing belt cover.
9. Rotate the crankshaft by hand to position the metal vane of the shutter outside of the sensor air gap.
10. Remove the crankshaft sensor mounting screws and remove the sensor.

To install:
11. Route the sensor wiring harness through the belt cover. Install the sensor assembly on the mounting pad and install the retaining screws loosely. Do not tighten the screws at this time.
12. Set the clearance between the crankshaft sensor assembly and 1 vane on the crankshaft timing pulley and vane assembly using a 0.03 in. (8mm) feeler gauge. Tighten the screws to 22–31 inch lbs. (2.5–3.5 Nm).
13. Install the lower timing belt cover. Be careful not to damage the sensor wiring harness. Install the crankshaft pulley using a suitable installation tool. Tighten the pulley bolt to 112–127 ft. lbs. (152–172 Nm).
14. Install the remaining components in the reverse order of their removal.

CAMSHAFT SENSOR

1. Disconnect the negative battery cable.
2. Remove the engine torque strut.
3. Disconnect the camshaft sensor wiring connector.
4. Remove the camshaft sensor mounting bolts and remove the sensor.
5. Installation is the reverse of the removal procedure. Tighten the sensor mounting bolts to 22–31 inch lbs. (2.5–3.5 Nm).

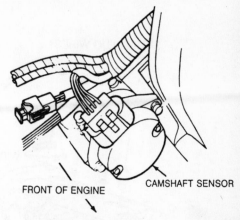

FRONT OF ENGINE   CAMSHAFT SENSOR

DIS camshaft sensor location

IGNITION MODULE

1. Disconnect the negative battery cable.
2. Disconnect the wiring connectors at the module.
3. Remove the module mounting bolts and remove the module.
4. Installation is the reverse of the removal procedure. Apply a uniform coating of heat sink grease ESF–M99G123–A or equivalent, to the mounting surface of the module prior to installation. Tighten the mounting bolts to 22–31 inch lbs. (2.5–3.5 Nm).

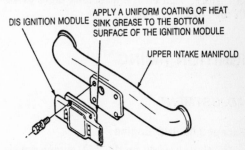

APPLY A UNIFORM COATING OF HEAT
DIS IGNITION MODULE SINK GREASE TO THE BOTTOM
SURFACE OF THE IGNITION MODULE

UPPER INTAKE MANIFOLD

DIS ignition module location

IGNITION COIL PACK

1. Disconnect the negative battery cable.
2. If equipped, remove the cover from the coil pack.
3. Disconnect the electrical connector from the coil pack.
4. Remove the spark plug wires by squeezing the locking tabs to release the coil boot retainers. Tag the wires and mark their position on the coil pack prior to removal.
5. Remove the coil pack attaching bolts and remove the coil pack.

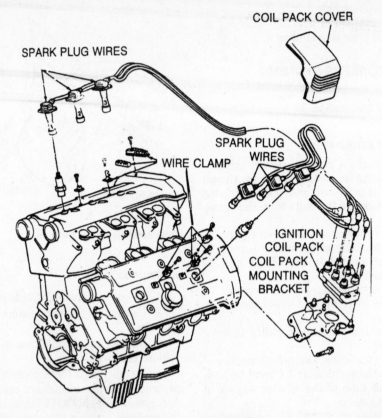

DIS ignition coil pack location

6. Installation is the reverse of the removal procedure. Tighten the attaching bolts to 40–62 inch lbs. (5–7 Nm).

IGNITION TIMING

ADJUSTMENT

Except 3.0L SHO Engine

The timing marks on the 2.5L engine are visible through a hole in the top of the transaxle case. The 3.0L and 3.8L engines have the timing marks on the crankshaft pulley and a timing pointer near the pulley.

1. Place the transaxle in the **P** or **N** position. Firmly apply the parking brake and block the wheels. The air conditioner and heater must be in the **OFF** position.

2. Open the hood, locate the timing marks and clean with a stiff brush or solvent. On vehicles with manual transaxle, it will be necessary to remove the cover plate which allows access to to the timing marks.

3. Using white chalk or paint, mark the specified timing mark and pointer.

4. Remove the inline spout connector or remove the shorting bar from the double wire

spout connector. The spout connector is the center wire between the electronic control assembly (ECA) connector and the Thick Film Ignition (TFI) module.

5. Connect a suitable inductive type timing light to the No. 1 spark plug wire. Do not, puncture and ignition wire with any type of probing device.

NOTE: *The high ignition coil charging currents generated in the EEC–IV ignition system may falsely trigger timing lights with capacitive or direct connect pickups. It is necessary that an inductive type timing light be used in this procedure.*

6. Connect a suitable tachometer to the engine. The ignition coil connector allows a test lead with an alligator clip to be connected to the

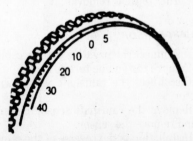

Timing mark location on flywheel – 2.5L engine with manual transaxle

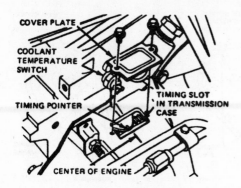

Timing mark location—2.5L engine with manual transaxle

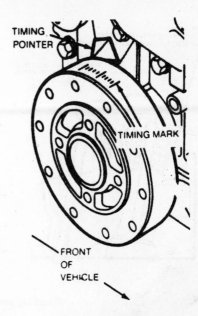

Timing mark location—3.0L engine except SHO

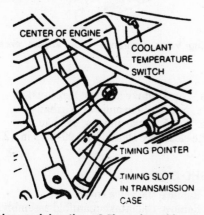

Timing mark location on flywheel—2.5L engine with automatic transaxle

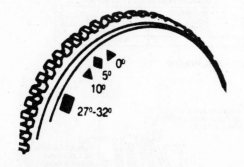

Timing mark location—2.5L engine with automatic transaxle

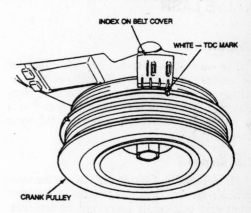

Timing mark location—3.0L SHO engine

Distributor Electronic Control (DEC) terminal without removing the connector.

7. Start the engine and let it run until it reaches normal operating temperature.

NOTE: *Only use the ignition key to start the vehicle. Do not use a remote starter, as disconnecting the start wire at the starter relay will cause the TFI module to revert to start mode timing, after the vehicle is started. Reconnecting the start wire after the vehicle is running will not correct the timing.*

8. Check the engine idle rpm, if it is not within specifications, adjust as necessary. Idle speed is not adjustable on 1991–92 vehicles. After the rpm has been adjusted or checked, aim the timing light at the timing marks. If they are not aligned, loosen the distributor clamp bolt slightly and rotate the distributor body until the marks are aligned under timing light illumination.

9. Tighten the distributor clamp bolt and recheck the ignition timing. Readjust the idle speed as necessary. Shut the engine off, remove all test equipment, reconnect the inline spout connector to the distributor and, if necessary, reinstall the cover plate on the manual transaxle vehicles.

3.0L SHO Engine

The base ignition timing is set at 10° BTDC and is not adjustable.

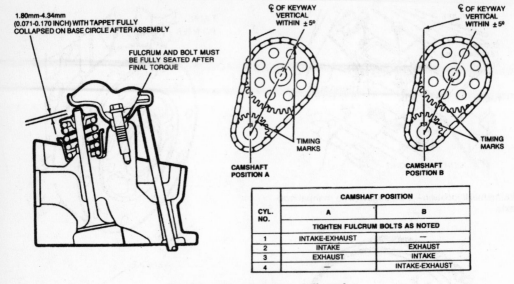

CYL. NO.	CAMSHAFT POSITION	
	A	B
	TIGHTEN FULCRUM BOLTS AS NOTED	
1	INTAKE-EXHAUST	—
2	INTAKE	EXHAUST
3	EXHAUST	INTAKE
4	—	INTAKE-EXHAUST

Checking valve clearance—2.5L engine

VALVE LASH

CHECKING

The valve stem-to-rocker arm clearance for all engines except the 3.0L SHO should be within specification with the valve lifter completely collapsed. To determine the rocker arm to valve lifter clearance, make the following checks.

2.5L Engine

1. Set the No. 1 piston on TDC on the compression stroke. The timing marks on the camshaft and crankshaft gears will be together. Check the clearance in No. 1 intake, No. 1 exhaust, No. 2 intake and No. 3 exhaust valves.

2. Rotate the crankshaft 1 complete turn, 180° for the camshaft gear. Check the clearance in No. 2 exhaust, No. 3 intake, No. 4 intake and No. 4 exhaust.

3. The clearance between the rocker arm and the valve stem tip should be 0.072–0.174 in. (1.80–4.34mm) with the lifter on the base circle of the cam.

3.0L Engine Except SHO and 3.8L Engine

1. Rotate the engine until the No. 1 cylinder is at TDC of its compression stroke and check the clearance between the rocker arm and the following valves.

    a. No. 1 intake and No. 1 exhaust
    b. No. 3 intake and No. 2 exhaust
    c. No. 6 intake and No. 4 exhaust

2. Rotate the crankshaft 360° and check the clearance between the rocker arm and the following valves.

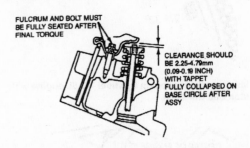

Checking valve clearance—3.0L engine except SHO

    a. No. 2 intake and No. 3 exhaust
    b. No. 4 intake and No. 5 exhaust
    c. No. 5 intake and No. 6 exhaust

3. The clearance should be 0.09–0.19 in. (2.3–4.8mm).

3.0L SHO Engine

1. Remove the valve cover.
2. Remove the intake manifold assembly.
3. Insert a feeler gauge under the cam lobe at a 90° angle to the camshaft. Clearance for the intake valves should be 0.006–0.010 in. (0.15–0.25mm). Clearance for the exhaust valves should be 0.010–0.014 in. (0.25–0.35mm).

NOTE: *The cam lobes must be directed 90° or more away from the valve lifters.*

ADJUSTMENT

3.0L SHO Engine

1. Disconnect the negative battery cable.
2. Remove the valve cover.

3. Remove the intake manifold assembly.

4. Install lifter compressor tool T89P–6500–A or equivalent, under the camshaft next to the lobe and rotate it downward to depress the valve lifter.

5. Install valve lifter holding tool T89P–6500–B or equivalent, and remove the compressor tool.

6. Using pick tool T71P–19703–C or equivalent, lift the adjusting shim and remove the shim with a magnet.

7. Determine the size of the shim by the

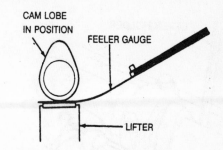

Checking valve clearance—3.0L SHO engine

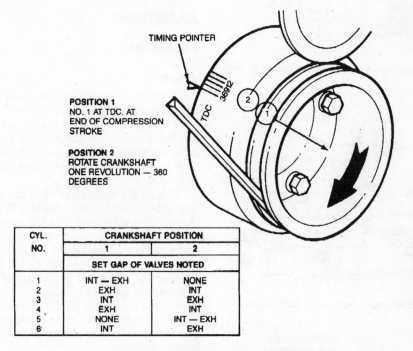

POSITION 1
NO. 1 AT TDC. AT
END OF COMPRESSION
STROKE

POSITION 2
ROTATE CRANKSHAFT
ONE REVOLUTION — 360
DEGREES

CYL.	CRANKSHAFT POSITION	
NO.	1	2
	SET GAP OF VALVES NOTED	
1	INT — EXH	NONE
2	EXH	INT
3	INT	EXH
4	EXH	INT
5	NONE	INT — EXH
6	INT	EXH

Checking valve clearance—3.8L engine

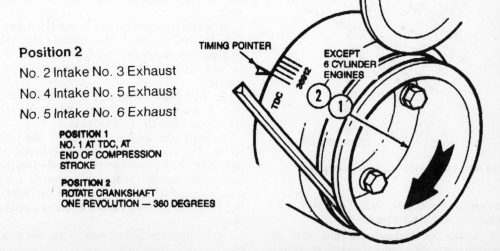

Position 2

No. 2 Intake No. 3 Exhaust

No. 4 Intake No. 5 Exhaust

No. 5 Intake No. 6 Exhaust

POSITION 1
NO. 1 AT TDC, AT
END OF COMPRESSION
STROKE

POSITION 2
ROTATE CRANKSHAFT
ONE REVOLUTION — 360 DEGREES

Valve clearance measurement at pushrod—3.0L engine except SHO

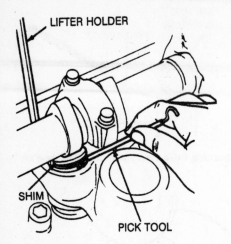

Removing the shim from the valve lifter — 3.0L SHO engine

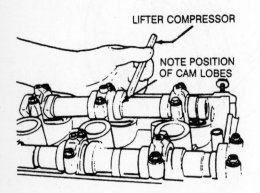

Valve lifter compressor tool — 3.0L SHO engine

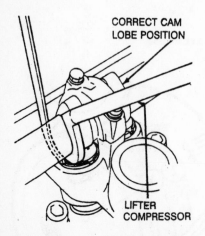

Valve lifter holding tool — 3.0L SHO engine

numbers on the bottom face of the shim or by measuring with a micrometer.

8. Install the replacement shim with the numbers down. Make sure the shim is properly seated.

9. Release the lifter holder tool by installing the compressor tool.

10. Repeat the procedure for each valve by rotating the crankshaft as necessary.

IDLE SPEED AND MIXTURE ADJUSTMENT

Idle Speed

ADJUSTMENT

2.5L ENGINE

1986–90

1. Apply the parking brake, block the drive wheels and place the vehicle in **P** or **N**.

2. Start the engine and let it run until it reaches normal operating temperature, then turn the engine **OFF**. Disconnect the negative battery cable for 5 minutes minimum, then reconnect it.

3. Start the engine and let it run at idle for 2 minutes. The idle rpm should now return to the specified idle speed. The idle specifications can be found on the calibration sticker located under the hood. Now lightly step on and off the accelerator. The engine rpm should return to the specified idle speed. If the engine does not idle properly, proceed to Step 4.

4. Shut the engine **OFF** and remove the air cleaner. Locate the self-test connector and self-test input connector in the engine compartment.

5. Connect a jumper wire between the self-test input connector and the signal return pin, the top right terminal on the self-test connector.

6. Place the ignition key in the **RUN** position but do not start the engine. The ISC plunger will retract, so wait approximately 10–15 seconds until the ISC plunger is fully retracted.

7. Turn the ignition key to the **OFF** position. Remove the jumper wire and unplug the ISC motor from the wire harness.

8. Start the engine and check the idle speed. On automatic transaxle vehicles, it should be 50 rpm less than that specified on the calibration sticker. On manual transaxle vehicles, it should be 100 rpm less than that specified on the calibration sticker. If not proceed to Step 9.

9. Remove the CFI assembly from the vehicle.

10. Use a small punch or equivalent, to

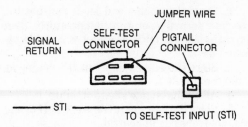

Jumper wire terminal connection points — 2.5L engine with CFI

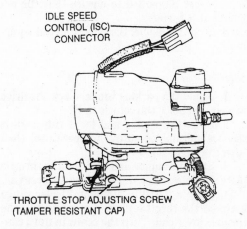

Throttle stop adjusting screw location — 2.5L engine with CFI

punch through and remove the aluminum plug which covers the throttle stop adjusting screw.

11. Remove and replace the throttle stop screw. Reinstall the CFI assembly onto the vehicle.

12. Start the engine and allow to the idle to stabilize. Set the idle rpm to the specification listed in Step 8. 13. Turn **OFF** the engine. Reconnect the ISC motor wire harness, remove all test equipment and reinstall the air cleaner assembly.

3.0L Engine Except SHO

1986–90

1. Apply the parking brake, turn the air conditioning control selector **OFF** and block the wheels.

2. Connect a tachometer and an inductive timing light to the engine. Start the engine and allow it to reach normal operating temperatures.

3. Unplug the spout line at the distributor, then check and/or adjust the ignition timing to the specification listed on the underhood emission calibration decal.

4. Stop the engine and remove the PCV hose at the PCV valve. Install a 0.200 in. (5mm) diameter orifice, tool T86P–9600–A or equivalent.

5. Disconnect the idle speed control/air bypass solenoid.

6. Start the engine and run at 2000 rpm for 30 seconds.

7. If equipped with an automatic transaxle, place the selector in **D**. If equipped with a manual transaxle, place the selector in neutral.

8. Check and/or adjust, the idle speed to 760 ± 20 rpm by turning the throttle plate stop screw.

9. After adjusting the idle speed, stop the engine and disconnect the battery for 5 minutes minimum.

10. Stop the engine and remove all test equipment. Reconnect the spout line and remove the orifice from the PCV hose. Reconnect the idle speed control/air bypass solenoid.

11. Make sure the throttle is not stuck in the bore and the linkage is not preventing the throttle from closing.

3.0L SHO Engine

1989–90

1. Apply the parking brake, turn the air conditioning control selector **OFF** and block the wheels.

2. Connect a tachometer and an inductive timing light to the engine. Start the engine and allow it to reach normal operating temperatures.

3. Unplug the spout line at the distributor,

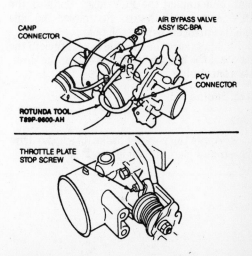

Throttle stop adjusting screw location — 3.0L SHO engine

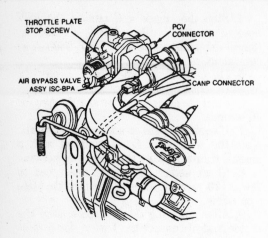

Idle stop adjusting screw—3.0L SHO engine

then check and/or adjust the ignition timing to the specification listed on the underhood emission calibration decal.

4. Stop the engine and disconnect and plug the PCV hose at the intake manifold. Remove the CANP hose from the intake manifold and connect tool T89P–9600–AH or equivalent, between the PCV and CANP ports.

5. Disconnect the idle speed control/air bypass solenoid.

6. Start the engine and let it idle. Place the transaxle selector lever in **N**.

7. Check and/or adjust the idle speed to 800 ± 30 rpm by turning the throttle plate stop screw.

8. Shut the engine off and repeat Steps 6–8.

9. Stop the engine and remove all test equipment. Remove tool T89P–9600–AH or equivalent, and unplug the PCV hose. Connect the PCV and CANP hoses. Reconnect the idle speed control/air bypass solenoid.

10. Make sure the throttle is not stuck in the bore and the linkage is not preventing the throttle from closing.

3.8L Engine

1988

1. Apply the parking brake, block the drive wheels and place the vehicle in **P** or **N**.

2. Start the engine and let it run until it reaches normal operating temperature, then turn the engine **OFF**. Connect a suitable tachometer.

3. Start the engine and run the engine at 2500 rpm for 30 seconds.

4. Allow the engine idle to stabilize.

5. Place the automatic transaxle in **D** or the manual transaxle in neutral.

6. Adjust the engine idle rpm to the specification shown on the vehicle emission control label by adjusting the throttle stop screw.

7. After the idle speed is within specification, repeat Steps 3–6 to ensure that the adjustment is correct.

8. Stop the engine. Disconnect all test equipment.

1988–90

1. Apply the parking brake, block the drive wheels and place the vehicle in **P**.

2. Start the engine and let it run until it reaches normal operating temperature, then turn the engine **OFF**.

3. Stop the engine and back out the throttle plate stop screw clear off the throttle lever pad.

4. Place a 0.010 in. (0.25mm) feeler gauge between the throttle plate stop screw and the throttle lever pad. Turn the screw in until contact is made, then turn it an additional 1½ turns. Remove the feeler gauge.

5. Start the engine and let the idle stabilize for 2 minutes. Lightly depress and release the accelerator. Let the engine idle.

2.5L, 3.0L and 3.8L Engines

1991–92

The idle speed on these engines is preset at the factory and is not adjustable in the field. In the event that adjustment is necessary, STAR tester 007–00028 or equivalent, must be used.

Idle Mixture

ADJUSTMENT

Idle mixture is controlled by the electronic control unit. No adjustment is possible.

ENGINE ELECTRICAL

Ignition Coil

TESTING

EEC-IV System

1. At the center terminal on the distributor cap, follow the coil wire to the end. This is the ignition coil "E" type. Make sure transmission is in PARK and ignition is turned OFF.

2. Separate the wiring harness connector from the ignition module at the distributor. Inspect for dirt, corrosion and damage. Reconnect harness if no problem found.

NOTE: *Push connector tabs to separate.*

3. Attach a 12 volt DC test light between coil Tach terminal and engine ground. Crank engine, if the light flashes or lights continuous.

    a. Turn ignition switch OFF

    b. Disconnect ignition coil connector on top of the coil and inspect for dirt, corrosion and damage.

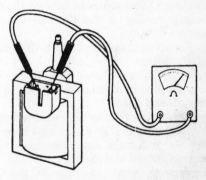

Testing ignition coil primary resistance

    c. Measure the ignition coil primary resistance, using an ohm Ω meter, from positive (+) to negative (−) terminal of ignition coil. Check coil diagram A for terminal location.

    d. The ohmmeter reading should be 0.3–1.0Ω. If the reading is less than 0.3Ω or greater than 1.0Ω, the ignition coil should be replaced.

    e. Measure the coil secondary resistance, using an ohmmeter, connect it to the negative (−) terminal and high voltage terminal.

    f. The resistance should be 6,500–11,500Ω with the ohm meter set on $\Omega \times 1000$. If the reading is less than 6,500Ω or greater than 11,500Ω, replace the coil.

REMOVAL AND INSTALLATION

EEC-IV System

1. Disconnect the negative battery cable.

2. Disconnect the electrical connectors from the coil assembly.

3. Remove the coil retaining bolts. Remove the coil from its mounting.

4. Installation is the reverse of the removal procedure.

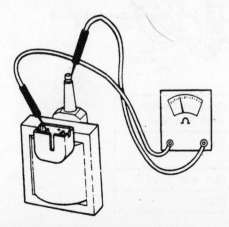

Testing ignition coil secondary resistance

Thick Film Ignition Module

TESTING

1. Make sure ignition is turned OFF.
2. Remove coil wire and ground it to car body.
3. Attach the negative (–) voltmeter lead to the distributor base.
4. Disconnect the pin in-line connector near the distributor and attach positive (+) voltmeter lead to the TFI module side of connector.
5. Turn the ignition to the ON position.
6. Bump the starter so that the engine rotates a small amount and stops. Record the voltage reading. (Allow sufficient time for the digital voltage reading to stabilize before taking measurement).
7. The voltage reading should be 70 percent of battery voltage.
8. If the voltage is less than 70 percent, remove the distributor from the engine to test the module and stator.
9. Remove the TFI module from the distributor by removing the two mounting screws. Be careful not to damage stator terminals when pulling module out of distributor.
10. Measure resistance between the TFI module by using an ohmmeter. Place one meter terminal on the ground terminal and place the second meter terminal on the PIP-IN terminal on the module. Check module testing diagram in this Chapter for terminal location and ohm specifications.

11. After recording ohm resistances, if the readings are within specifications replace the stator assembly in the distributor. If the readings are NOT within specifications replace the module assembly.

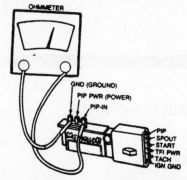

Measure Between These Terminals	Resistor Should Be
● GND - PIP In	Greater than 500 Ohms
● PIP PWR - PIP In	Less than 2K Ohms
● PIP PWR - TFI PWR	Less than 200 Ohms
● GND - IGN GND	Less than 2 Ohms
● PIP In - PIP	Less than 200 Ohms

Module testing locations

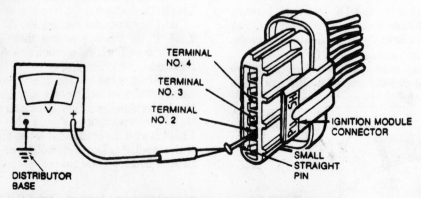

Connector Terminal	Wire/Circuit	Ignition Switch Test Position
#2	To Ignition Coil (–) Terminal	Run
#3	Run Circuit	Run and Start
#4	Start Circuit	Start

Wiring harness testing locations

REMOVAL AND INSTALLATION

Except 3.8L Engine

1. Disconnect the negative battery cable. Remove the distributor cap and position it to the side.

2. Remove the TFI-IV harness connector. Remove the distributor from the engine.

3. Position the distributor on the work bench. Remove the module retaining screws.

4. Pull the right side of the module down the distributor mounting flange in order to disengage the module terminals from the connector in the distributor base.

5. The module can be pulled toward the flange and away from the distributor.

NOTE: *Do not attempt to lift the module from the mounting surface prior to removing the entire TFI-IV module toward the distributor flange as the pins will break at the distributor/module connector.*

6. Installation is the reverse of the removal procedure. Coat the metal base of the module with silcone compound approximately $\frac{1}{32}$ in. (0.8mm) thick prior to installing it.

3.8L Engine

1. Disconnect the negative battery cable

2. Remove the screws attaching the leaf screen and cowl dash extension panel in the area of the TFI module assembly. Remove the leaf screen.

3. Disconnect the harness connector from the module assembly. The connector latch is underneath the module shroud and must be pressed upward to unlatch it.

4. Remove the retaining nuts attaching the TFI/heatsink assembly to the cowl dash extension panel.

5. Remove the TFI/Heatsink assembly. The assembly is mounted with the heatsink pointed down.

6. Remove the module retaining screws and remove the module from the heatsink. While holding the module connector shroud pull the seal off the other end of the module.

7. Installation is the reverse of the removal procedure. Coat the metal base of the module with silcone compound approximately $\frac{1}{32}$ in. (0.8mm) thick prior to installing it.

Distributor

REMOVAL AND INSTALLATION

1. Disconnect the negative battery cable.

2. Disconnect the wiring connector from the distributor.

3. Remove distributor cap and position it

and the attached wires aside, so as not to interfere with removing the distributor.

4. Mark the position of the rotor in relation to the distributor housing and mark the position of the distributor housing on the engine.

5. Remove the rotor.

6. Remove the distributor hold-down bolt and clamp and remove the distributor.

To install:

NOTE: *Before installation, inspect the distributor O-ring and drive gear for wear and/ or damage. Rotate the distributor shaft to make sure it moves freely, without binding.*

TIMING NOT DISTURBED

1. Install the distributor, aligning the distributor housing and rotor with the marks that were made during the removal procedure.

2. Install the distributor hold-down bolt and clamp. Only snug the bolt at this time.

3. Connect the distributor to the wiring harness.

4. Install the rotor and the distributor cap. Make sure the ignition wires are securely connected to the distributor cap and spark plugs. Tighten the distributor cap screws to 18–23 inch lbs. (2.0–2.6 Nm).

5. Connect a suitable timing light and set the initial timing.

6. Tighten the distributor hold-down bolt to 17–25 ft. lbs. (23–34 Nm) on the 2.5L engine, 14–21 ft. lbs. (19–28 Nm) on the 3.0L engine or 20–29 ft. lbs. (27–40 Nm) on the 3.8L engine.

7. Recheck the initial timing and adjust if necessary.

TIMING DISTURBED

1. Disconnect the spark plug wire from the No. 1 cylinder spark plug and remove the spark plug.

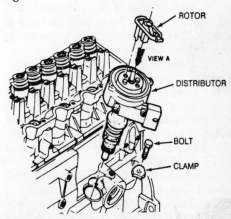

Distributor location – 2.5L engine

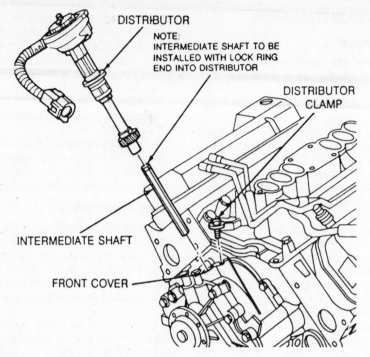

DISTRIBUTOR

NOTE:
INTERMEDIATE SHAFT TO BE
INSTALLED WITH LOCK RING
END INTO DISTRIBUTOR

DISTRIBUTOR
CLAMP

INTERMEDIATE SHAFT

FRONT COVER

Distributor location — 3.8L engine

2. Place a finger over the spark plug hole. Rotate the engine clockwise until compression is felt at the spark plug hole.

3. Align the timing pointer with the TDC mark on the crankshaft damper.

4. Install the rotor on the distributor shaft. Rotate the distributor shaft so the rotor tip is pointing to the distributor cap No. 1 spark plug tower position.

5. While installing the distributor, continue rotating the rotor slightly so the leading edge of the vane is centered in the vane switch stator assembly.

6. Rotate the distributor in the block to align the leading edge of the vane and vane switch stator assembly. Make sure the rotor is pointing to the distributor cap No. 1 spark plug tower position.

NOTE: *If the vane and vane switch stator cannot be aligned by rotating the distributor in the block, remove the distributor just enough to disengage the distributor gear from the camshaft gear. Rotate the rotor enough to engage the distributor gear on another tooth of the camshaft gear. Repeat Steps 1 and 2, if necessary.*

7. Install the distributor hold-down bolt and clamp. Only snug the bolt at this time.

8. Connect the distributor to the wiring harness and install the distributor cap. Tighten the distributor cap hold-down screws to 18–23 inch lbs. (2.0–2.6 Nm).

9. Install the No. 1 cylinder spark plug and connect the spark plug wire.

10. Connect a suitable timing light and set the initial timing.

11. Tighten the distributor hold-down bolt to 17–25 ft. lbs. (23–34 Nm) on the 2.5L engine, 14–21 ft. lbs. (19–28 Nm) on the 3.0L engine or 20–29 ft. lbs. (27–40 Nm) on the 3.8L engine.

12. Recheck the initial timing and adjust if necessary.

Distributorless Ignition

The 3.0L SHO engine is equipped with a Distributorless Ignition System (DIS) which consists of the following components:
Crankshaft timing sensor
Camshaft sensor
DIS ignition module
Ignition coil pack
The spark angle portion of the EEC–IV module

REMOVAL AND INSTALLATION

CRANKSHAFT TIMING SENSOR

1. Disconnect the negative battery cable.

2. Loosen the tensioner pulleys for the air conditioning compressor and the power steering pump belts. Remove the belts from the crankshaft pulley.

3. Disconnect the DIS module and remove the intake manifold crossover tube.

4. Remove the upper timing belt cover.

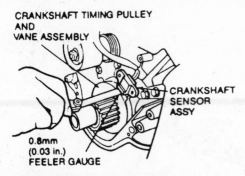

Ajusting crankshaft sensor to vane clearance — 3.0L SHO engine

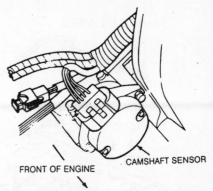

DIS camshaft sensor assembly — 3.0L SHO engine

5. Disconnect the sensor wiring harness at the connector and route the wiring harness through the belt cover.

6. Raise the vehicle and support it safely.

7. Remove the right front wheel and tire assembly.

8. Remove the crankshaft pulley using universal puller T67L–3600–A or equivalent.

9. Remove the center and lower timing belt covers.

10. Rotate the crankshaft by hand, to position the metal vane of the shutter outside of the sensor air gap.

11. Remove the crankshaft sensor mounting screws and remove the sensor.

To install:

12. Route the sensor wiring harness through the belt cover. Install the sensor assembly on the mounting pad and install but do not tighten, the retaining screws.

13. Use a 0.03 in. (0.76mm) feeler gauge to set the clearance between the crankshaft sensor assembly and 1 vane on the crankshaft timing pulley and vane assembly. Tighten the screws to 22–31 inch lbs. (2.5–3.5 Nm).

NOTE: *This is a critical torque. Overtightening can cause damage to the timing sensor.*

14. Install the lower timing belt cover. Install the crankshaft pulley using a suitable tool. Tighten the pulley bolt to 112–127 ft. lbs. (152–172 Nm).

15. Install the center timing belt cover.

16. Install the right front wheel and tire assembly. Lower the vehicle.

17. Route and connect the sensor wiring harness.

18. Install the upper timing belt cover.

19. Install the intake manifold crossover tube and connect the DIS module.

20. Install the air conditioning and power steering belts and adjust them to the proper tension.

21. Connect the negative battery cable.

CAMSHAFT SENSOR ASSEMBLY

1. Disconnect the negative battery cable.

2. Remove the engine torque strut.

3. Remove the power steering belt and the pump pulley.

4. Disconnect the camshaft sensor wiring connector.

5. Remove the mounting bolts and remove the sensor.

6. To install, reverse the removal procedure. Tighten the mounting bolts to 22–31 inch lbs. (2.5–3.5 Nm).

DIS IGNITION MODULE

1. Disconnect the negative battery cable.

2. Disconnect the wiring connectors at the module.

3. Remove the module mounting bolts and remove the module.

4. To install, reverse the removal procedure. Apply a uniform coating of heat sink grease to the mounting surface of the DIS module before it is installed. Tighten the mounting bolts to 22–31 inch lbs. (2.5–3.5 Nm).

IGNITION COIL PACK

1. Disconnect the negative battery cable.

2. Remove the cover from the coil pack and disconnect the electrical connector.

3. Remove the spark plug wires by squeez-

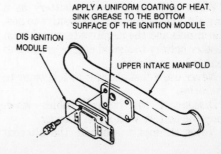

DIS ignition coil pack location — 3.0L SHO engine

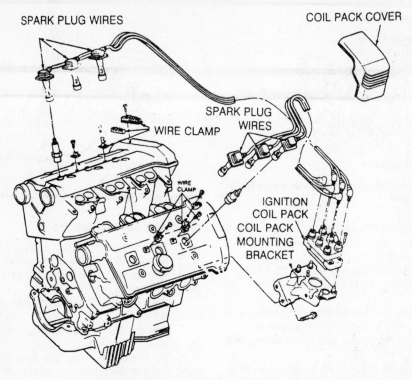

SPARK PLUG WIRES

COIL PACK COVER

SPARK PLUG WIRES

WIRE CLAMP

WIRE CLAMP

IGNITION COIL PACK
COIL PACK MOUNTING BRACKET

DIS ignition module location — 3.0L SHO engine

ing the locking tabs to release the coil boot retainers.

4. Remove the coil pack mounting screws and remove the coil pack.

5. To install, reverse the removal procedure. Tighten the mounting screws to 40–62 inch lbs. (4.5–7 Nm).

Alternator

ALTERNATOR PRECAUTIONS

Several precautions must be observed with alternator equipped vehicles to avoid damage to the unit.

• If the battery is removed for any reason, make sure it is reconnected with the correct polarity. Reversing the battery connections may result in damage to the one-way rectifiers.

• When utilizing a booster battery as a starting aid, always connect the positive to positive terminals and the negative terminal from the booster battery to a good engine ground on the vehicle being started.

• Never use a fast charger as a booster to start vehicles.

• Disconnect the battery cables when charging the battery with a fast charger.

• Never attempt to polarize the alternator.

• Do not use test lights of more than 12 volts when checking diode continuity.

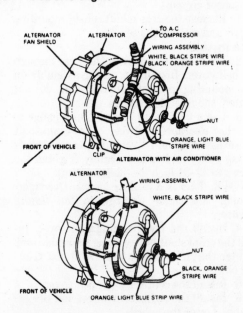

ALTERNATOR FAN SHIELD

ALTERNATOR

TO A.C COMPRESSOR

WIRING ASSEMBLY
WHITE, BLACK STRIPE WIRE
BLACK, ORANGE STRIPE WIRE

NUT

ORANGE, LIGHT BLUE STRIPE WIRE

FRONT OF VEHICLE

CLIP

ALTERNATOR WITH AIR CONDITIONER

ALTERNATOR

WIRING ASSEMBLY

WHITE, BLACK STRIPE WIRE

NUT

BLACK, ORANGE STRIPE WIRE

FRONT OF VEHICLE

ORANGE, LIGHT BLUE STRIP WIRE

Alternator harness connector locations

• Do not short across or ground any of the alternator terminals.

• The polarity of the battery, alternator and regulator must be matched and considered before making any electrical connections within the system.

• Never separate the alternator on an

open circuit. Make sure all connections within the circuit are clean and tight.

• Disconnect the battery ground terminal when performing any service on electrical components.

• Disconnect the battery if arc welding is to be done on the vehicle.

REMOVAL AND INSTALLATION

Except 3.0L SHO Engine

1. Disconnect the negative battery cable.
2. Tag and disconnect the wire harness from the alternator.
3. If equipped with an automatic belt tensioner, rotate the tensioner counterclockwise and remove the drive belt from the pulley.
4. If not equipped with an automatic tensioner, loosen the alternator pivot bolt and remove the adjustment arm bolt from the alternator. Remove the alternator belt from the pulley.
5. Remove the alternator mounting bolts or the pivot bolt, as required, and remove the alternator.
6. Installation is the reverse of the removal procedure. Torque the adjusting arm bolt to 15-22 ft. lbs. and the pivot bolt to 40-45 ft. lbs.
7. Adjust the belt tension, if not equipped with an automatic belt tensioner.

3.0L SHO Engine

1. Disconnect the battery cables and remove the battery and battery tray.
2. Tag and disconnect the wire harness from the alternator.
3. Loosen the belt tensioner and remove the alternator belt from the pulley.
4. Remove the mounting bolts and the alternator.
5. Installation is the reverse of the removal procedure. Tighten the front mounting bolt to 36–53 ft. lbs. (48–72 Nm) and the rear mounting bolts to 25–37 ft. lbs. (34–50 Nm). Adjust the belt tension.

BRUSH REPLACEMENT

1. Remove the alternator from the vehicle and position it in a suitable holding fixture.
2. As necessary, remove the alternator pulley, using the proper removal tools.
3. Remove the alternator case retaining screws. Separate the alternator halves.
4. Remove the brushes from their mountings inside the alternator.

To install:

5. Carefully position the new brushes inside the alternator case, using th proper brush retainer tool.

6. Assemble the alternator case halves together. Install the alternator pulley, if removed.
7. Install the alternator on the vehicle.

Voltage Regulator

ADJUSTMENT

The electronic voltage regulator is calibrated and preset by the manufacturer. No adjustment is required or possible.

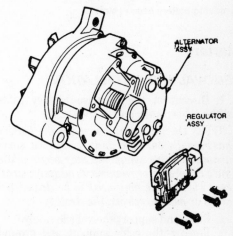

Internal regulator location

REMOVAL AND INSTALLATION

1. Disconnect the negative battery cable.
2. Disconnect the electrical connectors from the wiring harness.
3. Remove the regulator mounting screws and the regulator.
4. Installation is the reverse of the removal procedure.
5. Connect the negative battery cable. Test the system for proper voltage regulation.

Battery

REMOVAL AND INSTALLATION

1. Disconnect the negative battery cable. Disconnect the positive battery cable.
2. Remove the battery holddown bracket retaining bolt. Remove the holddown bracket.
3. Carefully lift the battery from its mounting.
4. Installation is the reverse of the removal procedure.

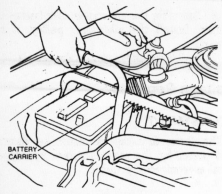

Removing battery from vehicle

Starter

REMOVAL AND INSTALLATION

1. Disconnect the negative battery cable and the cable connection at the starter.

NOTE: *On 1992 vehicles, when the battery has been disconnected and reconnected, some abnormal drive symptoms may occur while the EEC processor relearns its adaptive strategy. The vehicle may need to be driven ten miles or more to relearn the strategy.*

2. Raise and support the vehicle safely.

3. Remove the cable support and ground cable connection from the upper starter stud bolt, if necessary.

4. If equipped, remove the starter brace from the cylinder block and the starter.

5. Remove the starter-to-bell housing bolts and remove the starter.

6. Installation is the reverse of the removal procedure.

ENGINE MECHANICAL

Engine Overhaul Tips

Most engine overhaul procedures are fairly standard. In addition to specific parts replacement procedures and complete specifications for each individual engine. This Section is also a guide to acceptable rebuilding procedures. Examples of standard rebuilding practice are shown and should be used along with specific details concerning your particular engine.

Competent and accurate machine shop services will insure maximum performance, reliability and engine life. In most instances, it is more profitable for the do-it-yourself mechanic to remove, clean and inspect the component, buy the necessary parts and deliver these to a shop for actual machine work.

On the other hand, much of the rebuilding work (crankshaft, block, bearings, piston rods, and other components) is well within the scope of the do-it-yourself mechanic.

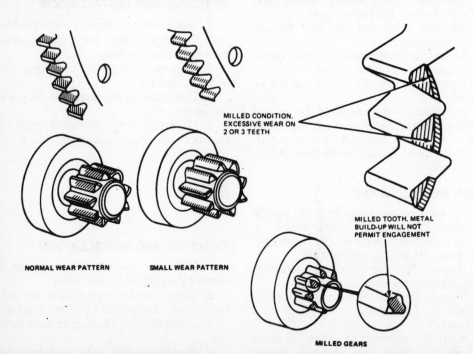

Starter drive gear wear patterns

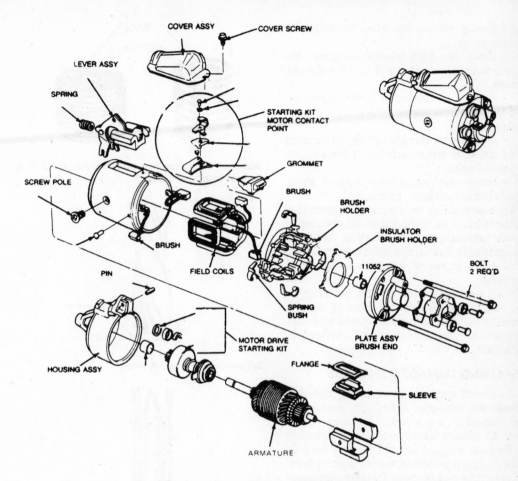

Starter motor assembly — exploded view

TOOLS

The tools required for an engine overhaul or parts replacement will depend on the depth of your involvement. With few exceptions, they will be the tools found in any mechanic's tool kit. More in-depth work will require some or all of the following:

• Dial indicator (reading in thousandths) mounted on a universal base
• Micrometers and telescope gauges
• Jaw and screw-type pullers
• Scraper
• Valve spring compressor
• Ring groove cleaner
• Piston ring expander and compressor
• Ridge reamer
• Cylinder hone or glaze breaker
• Plastigage®
• Engine hoist and stand

The use of most of these tools is illustrated in this Chapter. Many can be rented for a one-time use from a local parts jobber or tool supply house specializing in automotive work. Occasionally, the use of special tools is called for.

INSPECTION TECHNIQUES

Procedures and specifications are given in this Chapter for inspecting, cleaning and assessing the wear limits of most major components. Other procedures such as Magnaflux® and Zyglo® can be used to locate material flaws and stress cracks. Magnaflux® is a magnetic process applicable only to ferrous materials. The Zyglo® process coats the material with a fluorescent dye penetrant and can be used on any material. Checking for suspected surface cracks can be more readily made using spot check dye. The dye is sprayed onto the suspected area, wiped off and the area sprayed with a developer. Cracks will show up brightly.

OVERHAUL NOTES

Aluminum has become extremely popular for use in engines, due to its low weight. Observe the following precautions when handling aluminum parts:

• Never hot tank aluminum parts; the caustic hot-tank solution will dissolve the aluminum.

• Remove all aluminum parts (identification tag, etc.) from engine parts prior to the hot tanking.

• Always coat threads lightly with engine oil or anti-seize compounds before installation, to prevent seizure.

• Never over torque bolts or spark plugs, especially in aluminum threads.

When assembling the engine, any parts that will be in frictional contact must be prelubed to provide lubrication at initial start-up. Any product specifically formulated for this purpose can be used, but engine oil is not recommended as a prelube.

When semi-permanent (locked, but removable) installation of bolts or nuts is desired, threads should be cleaned and coated with Loctite® or other similar, commercial non-hardening sealant.

REPAIRING DAMAGED THREADS

1. Several methods of repairing damaged threads are available. Heli-Coil®, Keenserts® and Microdot® are among the most widely used. All involve basically the same principle (drilling out stripped threads, tapping the hole and installing a prewound insert), making welding, plugging and oversize fasteners unnecessary.

2. Two types of thread repair inserts are usually supplied: a standard type for most Inch Coarse, Inch Fine, Metric Course and Metric Fine thread sizes and a spark lug type to fit most spark plug port sizes. Consult the individual manufacturer's catalog to determine exact applications.

3. Typical thread repair kits will contain a

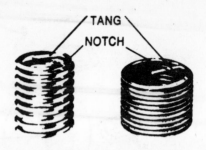

Standard thread repair insert (left) and spark plug thread repair insert (right)

Drilling out damaged threads

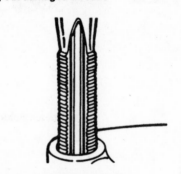

Using tap to repair damaged hole

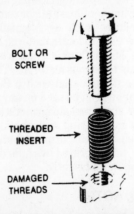

Damaged bolt holes can be repaired with thread repair inserts

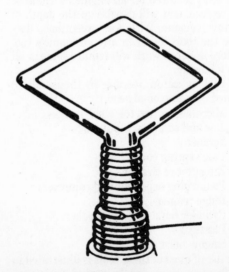

Installing new threaded insert

selection of prewound threaded inserts, a tap (corresponding to the outside diameter threads of the insert) and an installation tool. Spark plug inserts usually differ because they require a tap equipped with pilot threads and a combined reamer/tap section.

4. Most manufacturers also supply blister packed thread repair inserts separately in addition to a master kit containing a variety of taps and inserts plus installation tools.

5. Before attempting a repair to a threaded hole, remove any snapped, broken or damaged bolts or studs. Penetrating oil can be used to free frozen threads. The offending item can be removed with locking pliers or with a screw or stud extractor. After the hole is clear, the thread can be repaired.

Engine

REMOVAL AND INSTALLATION

CAUTION: *When draining the coolant, keep in mind that cats and dogs are attracted by the ethylene glycol antifreeze, and are quite likely to drink any that is left in an uncovered container or in puddles on the ground.*

This will prove fatal in sufficient quantity. Always drain the coolant into a sealable container. Coolant should be reused unless it is contaminated or several years old. *The EPA warns that prolonged contact with used engine oil may cause a number of skin disorders, including cancer! You should make every effort to minimize your exposure to used engine oil. Protective gloves should be worn when changing the oil. Wash your hands and any other exposed skin areas as soon as possible after exposure to used engine oil. Soap and water, or waterless hand cleaner should be used.*

2.5L Engine

1. Disconnect the negative battery cable and relieve the fuel system pressure.

2. If equipped with automatic transaxle, remove the transaxle timing window cover and rotate the engine until the flywheeel timing marker is aligned with the timing pointer.

3. Place a reference mark on the crankshaft pulley at the 12 o'clock position (TDC) then rotate the crankshaft pulley mark to the 6 o'clock postion (BTDC).

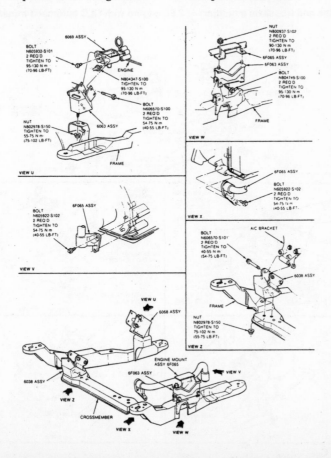

Engine and transaxle mounting — 2.5L engine with AXOD automatic transaxle

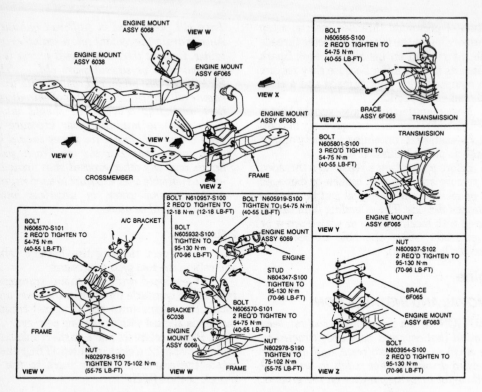

Engine and transaxle mounting — 2.5L engine with CLC automatic transaxle

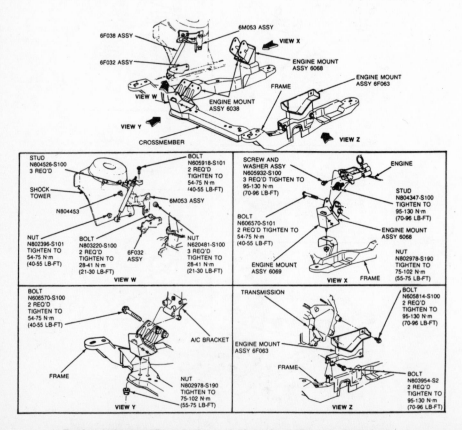

Engine and transaxle mounting — 2.5L engine with manual transaxle

GENERAL ENGINE SPECIFICATIONS

Year	Engine VIN	Engine Displacement Liters (cc)	Fuel System Type	Net Horsepower @ rpm	Net Torque @ rpm (ft. lbs.)	Bore × Stroke (in.)	Compression Ratio	Oil Pressure @ rpm
1986	D	2.5 (2500)	CFI	80 @ 4600	130 @ 2800	3.70 × 3.60	9.7:1	55–70 @ 2000
	U	3.0 (3000)	EFI	140 @ 4800	160 @ 3000	3.50 × 3.10	9.3:1	55–70 @ 2000
1987	D	2.5 (2500)	CFI	80 @ 4600	130 @ 2800	3.70 × 3.60	9.7:1	55–70 @ 2000
	U	3.0 (3000)	EFI	140 @ 4800	160 @ 3000	3.50 × 3.10	9.3:1	55–70 @ 2000
1988	D	2.5 (2500)	CFI	88 @ 4600	130 @ 2800	3.70 × 3.60	9.7:1	55–70 @ 2000
	U	3.0 (3000)	EFI	140 @ 4800	160 @ 3000	3.50 × 3.10	9.3:1	55–70 @ 2000
	4	3.8 (3800)	EFI	140 @ 3800	215 @ 2200	3.81 × 3.39	9.0:1	40–60 @ 2000
1989	D	2.5 (2500)	CFI	88 @ 4600	130 @ 2800	3.70 × 3.60	9.7:1	55–70 @ 2000
	U	3.0 (3000)	EFI	140 @ 4800	160 @ 3000	3.50 × 3.10	9.3:1	55–70 @ 2000
	Y	3.0 (3000)	SEFI	220 @ 6200	200 @ 4800	3.50 × 3.15	9.8:1	13 @ 800
	4	3.8 (3800)	SEFI	140 @ 3800	215 @ 2200	3.81 × 3.39	9.0:1	40–60 @ 2000
1990	D	2.5 (2500)	CFI	90 @ 4400	130 @ 2800	3.70 × 3.60	9.7:1	55–70 @ 2000
	U	3.0 (3000)	EFI	140 @ 4800	160 @ 3000	3.50 × 3.10	9.3:1	40–60 @ 2500
	Y	3.0 (3000)	SEFI	220 @ 6200	200 @ 4800	3.50 × 3.15	9.8:1	13 @ 800
	4	3.8 (3800)	SEFI	140 @ 3800	215 @ 2200	3.81 × 3.39	9.0:1	40–60 @ 2500
1991	D	2.5 (2500)	SEFI	105 @ 4400	140 @ 2400	3.70 × 3.60	9.0:1	55–70 @ 2000
	U	3.0 (3000)	SEFI	140 @ 4800	160 @ 3000	3.50 × 3.10	9.3:1	40–60 @ 2500
	Y	3.0 (3000)	SEFI	220 @ 6200	200 @ 4800	3.50 × 3.15	9.8:1	13 @ 800
	4	3.8 (3800)	SEFI	140 @ 3800	215 @ 2200	3.81 × 3.39	9.0:1	40–60 @ 2500
1992	U	3.0 (3000)	SEFI	140 @ 4800	160 @ 3000	3.50 × 3.10	9.3:1	40–60 @ 2500
	Y	3.0 (3000)	SEFI	220 @ 6200	200 @ 4800	3.50 × 3.15	9.8:1	13 @ 800
	4	3.8 (3800)	SEFI	140 @ 3800	215 @ 2200	3.81 × 3.39	9.0:1	40–60 @ 2500

NOTE: Horsepower and torque are SAE net figures. They are measured at the rear of the transmission with all accessories installed and operating. Since the figures vary when a given engine is installed in different models, some are representative rather than exact.
CFI—Central fuel injection
EFI—Electronic fuel injection
SEFI—Sequential electronic fuel injection

4. Mark the position of the hood hinges and remove the hood.

5. Remove the air cleaner assembly and drain the cooling system.

6. Disconnect the upper radiator hose at the engine.

7. Identify, tag and disconnect all electrical wiring and vacuum hoses as required.

8. Disconnect the crankcase ventilation hose at the valve cover and intake manifold.

9. Disconnect the fuel lines and heater hoses.

10. Disconnect the engine ground wire.

11. Disconnect the accelerator and throttle valve control cables at the throttle body.

12. Properly discharge the air conditioning system and remove the suction and discharge lines from the compressor, if equipped.

13. On manual transaxle equipped vehicles, remove the engine damper brace.

14. Remove the driver belt and water pump pulley.

15. Remove the air cleaner-to-canister hose.

16. Raise the vehicle and support safely.

17. Drain the engine oil and remove the oil filter.

18. Disconnect the starter cable and remove the starter motor.

19. On automatic transaxle equipped vehicles, remove the converter nuts and align the previously made reference mark as close to the 6 o'clock (BTDC) position as possible with the converter stud visible.

NOTE: *The flywheel timing marker must be in the 6 o'clock (BDC) position for proper engine removal and installation.*

20. Remove the engine insulator nuts.

21. Disconnect the exhaust pipe from the manifold.

22. Disconnect the canister and halfshaft brackets from the engine.

23. Remove the lower engine-to-transaxle retaining bolts.

24. Disconnect the lower radiator hose.

25. Lower the vehicle and position a floor jack under the transaxle.

CAMSHAFT SPECIFICATIONS

All measurements given in inches.

Year	Engine VIN	Engine Displacement Liters (cc)	Journal Diameter					Elevation		Bearing Clearance	Camshaft End Play
			1	2	3	4	5	In.	Ex.		
1986	D	2.5 (2500)	2.006–2.008	2.006–2.008	2.006–2.008	2.006–2.008	2.006–2.008	0.249	0.239	0.001–0.003	0.009
	U	3.0 (3000)	2.007–2.008	2.007–2.008	2.007–2.008	2.007–2.008	2.007–2.008	0.260	0.260	0.001–0.003	0.005
1987	D	2.5 (2500)	2.006–2.008	2.006–2.008	2.006–2.008	2.006–2.008	2.006–2.008	0.249	0.239	0.001–0.003	0.009
	U	3.0 (3000)	2.007–2.008	2.007–2.008	2.007–2.008	2.007–2.008	2.007–2.008	0.260	0.260	0.001–0.003	0.005
1988	D	2.5 (2500)	2.006–2.008	2.006–2.008	2.006–2.008	2.006–2.008	2.006–2.008	0.249	0.239	0.001–0.003	0.009
	U	3.0 (3000)	2.007–2.008	2.007–2.008	2.007–2.008	2.007–2.008	2.007–2.008	0.260	0.260	0.001–0.003	0.005
	4	3.8 (3800)	2.050–2.052	2.050–2.052	2.050–2.052	2.050–2.052	2.050–2.052	0.240	0.241	0.001–0.003	①
1989	D	2.5 (2500)	2.006–2.008	2.006–2.008	2.006–2.008	2.006–2.008	2.006–2.008	0.249	0.239	0.001–0.003	0.009
	U	3.0 (3000)	2.007–2.008	2.007–2.008	2.007–2.008	2.007–2.008	2.007–2.008	0.260	0.260	0.001–0.003	0.001–0.005
	Y	3.0 (3000)	1.2189–1.2195	1.2189–1.2195	1.2189–1.2195	1.2189–1.2195	1.2189–1.2195	0.335	0.315	0.001–0.003	0.012
	4	3.8 (3800)	2.050–2.052	2.050–2.052	2.050–2.052	2.050–2.052	2.050–2.052	0.240	0.241	0.001–0.003	①
1990	D	2.5 (2500)	2.006–2.008	2.006–2.008	2.006–2.008	2.006–2.008	2.006–2.008	0.249	0.239	0.001–0.003	0.009
	U	3.0 (3000)	2.007–2.008	2.007–2.008	2.007–2.008	2.007–2.008	2.007–2.008	0.260	0.260	0.001–0.003	0.001–0.005
	Y	3.0 (3000)	1.2189–1.2195	1.2189–1.2195	1.2189–1.2195	1.2189–1.2195	1.2189–1.2195	0.335	0.315	0.001–0.003	0.012
	4	3.8 (3800)	2.050–2.052	2.050–2.052	2.050–2.052	2.050–2.052	2.050–2.052	0.245	0.259	0.001–0.003	①
1991	D	2.5 (2500)	2.006–2.008	2.006–2.008	2.006–2.008	2.006–2.008	2.006–2.008	0.249	0.241	0.001–0.003	0.009
	U	3.0 (3000)	2.007–2.008	2.007–2.008	2.007–2.008	2.007–2.008	2.007–2.008	0.260	0.260	0.001–0.003	0.001–0.005
	Y	3.0 (3000)	1.2189–1.2195	1.2189–1.2195	1.2189–1.2195	1.2189–1.2195	1.2189–1.2195	0.335	0.315	0.001–0.003	0.012
	4	3.8 (3800)	2.050–2.052	2.050–2.052	2.050–2.052	2.050–2.052	2.050–2.052	0.245	0.259	0.001–0.003	①
1992	U	3.0 (3000)	2.007–2.008	2.007–2.008	2.007–2.008	2.007–2.008	2.007–2.008	0.260	0.260	0.001–0.003	0.001–0.005
	Y	3.0 (3000)	1.2189–1.2195	1.2189–1.2195	1.2189–1.2195	1.2189–1.2195	1.2189–1.2195	0.335	0.315	0.001–0.003	0.012
	4	3.8 (3800)	2.050–2.052	2.050–2.052	2.050–2.052	2.050–2.052	2.050–2.052	0.245	0.259	0.001–0.003	①

① No endplay—camshaft retained by a spring

CRANKSHAFT AND CONNECTING ROD SPECIFICATIONS

All measurements are given in inches.

Year	Engine VIN	Engine Displacement Liters (cc)	Crankshaft				Connecting Rod		
			Main Brg. Journal Dia.	Main Brg. Oil Clearance	Shaft End-play	Thrust on No.	Journal Diameter	Oil Clearance	Side Clearance
1986	D	2.5 (2500)	2.2489–2.2490	0.0008–0.0015	0.004–0.008	3	2.1232–2.1240	0.0008–0.0014	0.0035–0.0105
	U	3.0 (3000)	2.5190–2.5198	0.0010–0.0014	0.004–0.008	3	2.1253–2.1261	0.0010–0.0014	0.006–0.014
1987	D	2.5 (2500)	2.2489–2.2490	0.0008–0.0015	0.004–0.008	3	2.1232–2.1240	0.0008–0.0014	0.0035–0.0105
	U	3.0 (3000)	2.5190–2.5198	0.0010–0.0014	0.004–0.008	3	2.1253–2.1261	0.0010–0.0014	0.006–0.014
1988	D	2.5 (2500)	2.2489–2.2490	0.0008–0.0015	0.004–0.008	3	2.1232–2.1240	0.0008–0.0014	0.0035–0.0105
	U	3.0 (3000)	2.5190–2.5198	0.0010–0.0014	0.004–0.008	3	2.1253–2.1261	0.0010–0.0014	0.006–0.014
	4	3.8 (3800)	2.5190–2.5198	0.0010–0.0014	0.004–0.008	3	2.3103–2.3111	0.0010–0.0014	0.0047–0.0114
1989	D	2.5 (2500)	2.2489–2.2490	0.0008–0.0015	0.004–0.008	3	2.1232–2.1240	0.0008–0.0014	0.0035–0.0105
	U	3.0 (3000)	2.5190–2.5198	0.0010–0.0014	0.004–0.008	3	2.1253–2.1261	0.0010–0.0014	0.006–0.014
	Y	3.0 (3000)	2.5187–2.5197	0.0011–0.0022	0.0008–0.0087	3	2.0463–2.0472	0.0009–0.0022	0.0063–0.0123
	4	3.8 (3800)	2.5190–2.5198	0.0010–0.0014	0.004–0.008	3	2.3103–2.3111	0.0010–0.0014	0.0047–0.0114
1990	D	2.5 (2500)	2.2489–2.2490	0.0008–0.0015	0.004–0.008	3	2.1232–2.1240	0.0008–0.0014	0.0035–0.0105
	U	3.0 (3000)	2.5190–2.5198	0.0010–0.0014	0.004–0.008	3	2.1253–2.1261	0.0010–0.0014	0.006–0.014
	Y	3.0 (3000)	2.5187–2.5197	0.0011–0.0022	0.0008–0.0087	3	2.0463–2.0472	0.0009–0.0022	0.0063–0.0123
	4	3.8 (3800)	2.5190–2.5198	0.0010–0.0014	0.004–0.008	3	2.3103–2.3111	0.0010–0.0014	0.0047–0.0114
1991	D	2.5 (2500)	2.2489–2.2490	0.0008–0.0015	0.004–0.008	3	2.1232–2.1240	0.0008–0.0014	0.0035–0.0105
	U	3.0 (3000)	2.5190–2.5198	0.0010–0.0014	0.004–0.008	3	2.1253–2.1261	0.0010–0.0014	0.006–0.014
	Y	3.0 (3000)	2.5187–2.5197	0.0011–0.0022	0.0008–0.0087	3	2.0463–2.0472	0.0009–0.0022	0.0063–0.0123
	4	3.8 (3800)	2.5190–2.5198	0.0010–0.0014	0.004–0.008	3	2.3103–2.3111	0.0010–0.0014	0.0047–0.0114
1992	U	3.0 (3000)	2.5190–2.5198	0.0010–0.0014	0.004–0.008	3	2.1253–2.1261	0.0010–0.0014	0.006–0.014
	Y	3.0 (3000)	2.5187–2.5197	0.0011–0.0022	0.0008–0.0087	3	2.0463–2.0472	0.0009–0.0022	0.0063–0.0123
	4	3.8 (3800)	2.5190–2.5198	0.0010–0.0014	0.004–0.008	3	2.3103–2.3111	0.0010–0.0014	0.0047–0.0114

VALVE SPECIFICATIONS

Year	Engine VIN	Engine Displacement Liters (cc)	Seat Angle (deg.)	Face Angle (deg.)	Spring Test Pressure (lbs. @ in.)	Spring Installed Height (in.)	Stem-to-Guide Clearance (in.)		Stem Diameter (in.)	
							Intake	Exhaust	Intake	Exhaust
1986	D	2.5 (2500)	45	44	182 @ 1.13	1.49	0.0018	0.0023	0.3422	0.3418
	U	3.0 (3000)	45	44	185 @ 1.11	1.58	0.0010– 0.0028	0.0015– 0.0032	0.3126	0.3121
1987	D	2.5 (2500)	45	44	182 @ 1.13	1.49	0.0018	0.0023	0.3422	0.3418
	U	3.0 (3000)	45	44	185 @ 1.11	1.58	0.0010– 0.0028	0.0015– 0.0032	0.3126	0.3121
1988	D	2.5 (2500)	45	44	182 @ 1.13	1.49	0.0018	0.0023	0.3422	0.3418
	U	3.0 (3000)	45	44	185 @ 1.11	1.58	0.0010– 0.0028	0.0015– 0.0032	0.3126	0.3121
	4	3.8 (3800)	46	46	190 @ 1.28	1.70	0.0010– 0.0028	0.0015– 0.0033	0.3423– 0.0033	0.3418– 0.3410
1989	D	2.5 (2500)	45	44	182 @ 1.13	1.49	0.0018	0.0023	0.3422	0.3418
	U	3.0 (3000)	45	44	185 @ 1.11	1.58	0.0010– 0.0028	0.0015– 0.0032	0.3126	0.3121
	Y	3.0 (3000)	45	45.5	120.8 @ 1.19	1.52	0.0010– 0.0023	0.0012– 0.0025	0.2346– 0.2352	0.2344– 0.2350
	4	3.8 (3800)	46	46	220 @ 1.28	1.65	0.0010– 0.0028	0.0015– 0.0033	0.3423– 0.3415	0.3418– 0.3410
1990	D	2.5 (2500)	45	44	182 @ 1.13	1.49	0.0018	0.0023	0.3415– 0.3422	0.3411– 0.3418
	U	3.0 (3000)	45	44	180 @ 1.16	1.58	0.0010– 0.0028	0.0015– 0.0033	0.3134– 0.3126	0.3129– 0.3121
	Y	3.0 (3000)	45	45.5	120.8 @ 1.19	1.52	0.0010– 0.0023	0.0012– 0.0025	0.2346– 0.2352	0.2344– 0.2350
	4	3.8 (3800)	44.5	45.8	220 @ 1.18	1.65	0.0010– 0.0028	0.0015– 0.0033	0.3423– 0.3415	0.3418– 0.3410
1991	D	2.5 (2500)	45	44	182 @ 1.13	1.49	0.0018	0.0023	0.3415– 0.3422	0.3411– 0.3418
	U	3.0 (3000)	45	44	180 @ 1.16	1.58	0.0010– 0.0028	0.0015– 0.0033	0.3134– 0.3126	0.3129– 0.3121
	Y	3.0 (3000)	45	45.5	120.8 @ 1.19	1.52	0.0010– 0.0023	0.0012– 0.0025	0.2346– 0.2352	0.2344– 0.2350
	4	3.8 (3800)	44.5	45.8	220 @ 1.18	1.65	0.0010– 0.0028	0.0015– 0.0033	0.3423– 0.3415	0.3418– 0.3410
1992	U	3.0 (3000)	45	44	180 @ 1.16	1.58	0.0010– 0.0028	0.0015– 0.0033	0.3134– 0.3126	0.3129– 0.3121
	Y	3.0 (3000)	45	45.5	121 @ 1.19	1.52	0.0010– 0.0023	0.0012– 0.0025	0.2346– 0.2352	0.2344– 0.2350
	4	3.8 (3800)	44.5	45.8	220 @ 1.18	1.65	0.0010– 0.0028	0.0015– 0.0033	0.3423– 0.3415	0.3418– 0.3410

PISTON AND RING SPECIFICATIONS

All measurements are given in inches.

Year	Engine VIN	Engine Displacement Liters (cc)	Piston Clearance	Ring Gap			Ring Side Clearance		
				Top Compression	Bottom Compression	Oil Control	Top Compression	Bottom Compression	Oil Control
1986	D	2.5 (2500)	0.0012–0.0022	0.0080–0.0160	0.0080–0.0160	0.0150–0.0550	0.0020–0.0040	0.0020–0.0040	Snug
	U	3.0 (3000)	0.0014–0.0022	0.0100–0.0200	0.0100–0.0200	0.0100–0.0490	0.0016–0.0037	0.0016–0.0037	Snug
1987	D	2.5 (2500)	0.0012–0.0022	0.0080–0.0160	0.0080–0.0160	0.0150–0.0550	0.0020–0.0040	0.0020–0.0040	Snug
	U	3.0 (3000)	0.0014–0.0022	0.0100–0.0200	0.0100–0.0200	0.0100–0.0490	0.0016–0.0037	0.0016–0.0037	Snug
1988	D	2.5 (2500)	0.0012–0.0022	0.0080–0.0160	0.0080–0.0160	0.0150–0.0550	0.0020–0.0040	0.0020–0.0040	Snug
	U	3.0 (3000)	0.0014–0.0022	0.0100–0.0200	0.0100–0.0200	0.0100–0.0490	0.0016–0.0037	0.0016–0.0037	Snug
	4	3.8 (3800)	0.0014–0.0032	0.0100–0.0200	0.0100–0.0200	0.0150–0.0583	0.0016–0.0037	0.0016–0.0037	Snug
1989	D	2.5 (2500)	0.0012–0.0022	0.0080–0.0160	0.0080–0.0160	0.0150–0.0550	0.0020–0.0040	0.0020–0.0040	Snug
	U	3.0 (3000)	0.0014–0.0022	0.0100–0.0200	0.0100–0.0200	0.0100–0.0490	0.0016–0.0037	0.0016–0.0037	Snug
	Y	3.0 (3000)	0.0012–0.0020	0.0120–0.0180	0.0120–0.0180	0.0080–0.0200	0.0008–0.0024	0.0006–0.0022	0.0024–0.0050
	4	3.8 (3800)	0.0014–0.0032	0.0110–0.0220	0.0100–0.0200	0.0150–0.0583	0.0016–0.0037	0.0016–0.0037	Snug
1990	D	2.5 (2500)	0.0012–0.0022	0.0080–0.0160	0.0080–0.0160	0.0150–0.0550	0.0020–0.0040	0.0020–0.0040	Snug
	U	3.0 (3000)	0.0014–0.0022	0.0100–0.0200	0.0100–0.0200	0.0100–0.0490	0.0016–0.0037	0.0016–0.0037	Snug
	Y	3.0 (3000)	0.0012–0.0020	0.0120–0.0180	0.0120–0.0180	0.0080–0.0200	0.0008–0.0024	0.0006–0.0022	0.0024–0.0059
	4	3.8 (3800)	0.0014–0.0032	0.0110–0.0220	0.0100–0.0200	0.0150–0.0583	0.0016–0.0034	0.0016–0.0034	Snug
1991	D	2.5 (2500)	0.0012–0.0022	0.0080–0.0160	0.0080–0.0160	0.0150–0.0550	0.0020–0.0040	0.0020–0.0040	Snug
	U	3.0 (3000)	0.0014–0.0022	0.0100–0.0200	0.0100–0.0200	0.0100–0.0490	0.0012–0.0031	0.0012–0.0031	Snug
	Y	3.0 (3000)	0.0012–0.0020	0.0120–0.0180	0.0120–0.0180	0.0080–0.0200	0.0008–0.0024	0.0006–0.0022	0.0024–0.0059
	4	3.8 (3800)	0.0014–0.0032	0.0110–0.0220	0.0100–0.0200	0.0150–0.0583	0.0016–0.0034	0.0016–0.0034	Snug
1992	U	3.0 (3000)	0.0014–0.0022	0.0100–0.0200	0.0100–0.0200	0.0100–0.0490	0.0012–0.0031	0.0012–0.0031	Snug
	Y	3.0 (3000)	0.0012–0.0020	0.0120–0.0180	0.0120–0.0180	0.0080–0.0200	0.0008–0.0024	0.0006–0.0022	0.0024–0.0059
	4	3.8 (3800)	0.0014–0.0032	0.0110–0.0220	0.0100–0.0200	0.0150–0.0583	0.0016–0.0034	0.0016–0.0034	Snug

TORQUE SPECIFICATIONS
All readings in ft. lbs.

Year	Engine VIN	Engine Displacement Liters (cc)	Cylinder Head Bolts	Main Bearing Bolts	Rod Bearing Bolts	Crankshaft Damper Bolts	Flywheel Bolts	Manifold Intake	Manifold Exhaust	Spark Plugs	Lug Nut
1986	D	2.5 (2500)	①	51–66	21–26	140–170	54–64	15–23	②	5–10	80–105
	U	3.0 (3000)	③	65–81	26	141–169	54–64	④	19	5–10	80–105
1987	D	2.5 (2500)	①	51–66	21–26	140–170	54–64	15–23	②	5–10	80–105
	U	3.0 (3000)	③	65–81	26	141–169	54–64	④	19	5–10	80–105
1988	D	2.5 (2500)	①	51–66	21–26	140–170	54–64	15–23	②	5–10	80–105
	U	3.0 (3000)	③	65–81	26	139–169	54–64	⑨	19	5–10	80–105
	4	3.8 (3800)	⑤	65–81	31–36	93–121	54–64	⑥	16–24	5–10	80–105
1989	D	2.5 (2500)	①	51–66	21–26	140–170	54–64	15–23	②	5–10	80–105
	U	3.0 (3000)	⑦	65–81	26	141–169	54–64	④	19	5–10	80–105
	Y	3.0 (3000)	⑩	⑪	⑫	112–127	⑬	12–17	26–38	16–20	80–105
	4	3.8 (3800)	⑤	65–81	31–36	93–121	54–64	⑥	16–24	5–10	80–105
1990	D	2.5 (2500)	①	51–66	21–26	140–170	54–64	15–23	②	5–10	80–105
	U	3.0 (3000)	⑦	63–69	26	107	54–64	⑨	19	5–10	80–105
	Y	3.0 (3000)	⑩	⑪	⑫	112–127	⑬	12–17	26–38	16–20	80–105
	4	3.8 (3800)	⑤	65–81	31–36	103–132	54–64	⑥	15–22	5–10	80–105
1991	D	2.5 (2500)	①	52–66	21–26	140–170	54–64	⑧	②	5–10	80–105
	U	3.0 (3000)	⑦	55–63	26	107	59	⑨	19	5–10	80–105
	Y	3.0 (3000)	⑩	⑪	⑫	113–126	⑬	11–17	26–38	17–19	80–105
	4	3.8 (3800)	⑭	65–81	31–36	103–132	54–64	⑥	15–22	5–10	80–105
1992	U	3.0 (3000)	⑦	55–63	26	107	59	⑨	19	6–10	80–105
	Y	3.0 (3000)	⑩	⑪	⑫	113–126	⑬	11–17	26–38	12–19	80–105
	4	3.8 (3800)	⑭	65–81	31–36	103–132	54–64	⑥	15–22	5–10	80–105

① Tighten in 2 steps: 52–59 ft. lbs. and then the final torque of 70–76 ft. lbs.
② Tighten in 2 steps:
Step 1: 5–7 ft. lbs.
Step 2: 20–30 ft. lbs.
③ Tighten in 2 steps: 48–54 ft. lbs. and then the final torque of 63–80 ft. lbs.
④ Tighten in 3 steps: 11, 18 and the final torque of 24 ft. lbs.
⑤ Tighten in 4 steps:
Step 1: 37 ft. lbs.
Step 2: 45 ft. lbs.
Step 3: 52 ft. lbs.
Step 4: 59 ft. lbs.
Back off all bolts 2–3 revolutions, then repeat steps 1–4.
⑥ Tighten in 3 steps:
Step 1: 7 ft. lbs.
Step 2: 15 ft. lbs.
Step 3: 24 ft. lbs.
⑦ Tighten in 2 steps:
Step 1: 37 ft. lbs.
Step 2: 68 ft. lbs.
⑧ Tighten in 2 steps:
Step 1: 5–7 ft. lbs.
Step 2: 15–22 ft. lbs.
⑨ Tighten in 2 steps:
Step 1: 11 ft. lbs.
Step 2: 21 ft. lbs.
⑩ Tighten in 2 steps:
Step 1: 37–50 ft. lbs.
Step 2: 62–68 ft. lbs.
⑪ Tighten in 2 steps:
Step 1: 34–50 ft. lbs.
Step 2: 58–65 ft. lbs.

⑫ Tighten in 2 steps:
Step 1: 22–26 ft. lbs.
Step 2: 33–36 ft. lbs.
⑬ Tighten in 2 steps:
Step 1: 29–43 ft. lbs.
Step 2: 51–58 ft. lbs.
⑭ A. Tighten in 4 steps:
Step 1: 37 ft. lbs.
Step 2: 45 ft. lbs.
Step 3: 52 ft. lbs.
Step 4: 59 ft. lbs.
B. In sequence, loosen each bolt 2–3 revolutions
C. Tighten long bolts to 11–18 ft. lbs., then
an additional 85–105 degrees. Tighten
short bolts to 11–18 ft. lbs., then an additional
65–85 degrees.

26. Disconnect the power steering lines from the pump.

27. Install engine lifting eyes tool D81L–6001–D or equivalent and engine support tool T79P–6000–A or equivalent.

28. Connect suitable lifting equipment to support the engine and remove the upper engine-to-transaxle retaining bolts.

29. Remove the engine from the vehicle and support on a suitable holding fixture.

To install:

30. Make sure the timing marker is in the 6 o'clock (BDC) position.

31. Remove the engine from the stand and position it in the vehicle. Remove the lifting equipment.

32. Install the upper engine-to-transaxle bolts and tighten to 26–34 ft. lbs. (34–47 Nm). Use a floor jack under the transaxle to aid alignment.

33. Connect the power steering lines to the pump.

34. Raise the vehicle and support it safely.

35. Connect the lower radiator hose to the tube.

36. Install the lower engine-to-transaxle attaching bolts and tighten to 26–34 ft. lbs. (34–47 Nm).

37. Connect the halfshaft bracket to the engine and the exhaust pipe to the manifold.

38. Install the engine insulator nuts and tighten to 40–55 ft. lbs. (54–75 Nm).

39. Position the marks on the crankshaft pulley as close to 6 o'clock position (BDC) as possible and install the converter nuts. Tighten the nuts to 20–33 ft. lbs. (27–46 Nm).

40. Install the starter and connect the starter cable.

41. Install the oil filter and make sure the oil drain plug is tight.

42. Lower the vehicle.

43. Install the air cleaner-to-canister hose and the water pump pulley and drive belt.

44. Connect the air conditioning lines to the compressor, if equipped.

45. Connect the accelerator cable and throttle valve control cable at the throttle body.

46. Connect the negative battery cable at the engine and connect the heater hoses and fuel lines.

47. Connect the crankcase ventilation hose at the valve cover and the intake manifold.

48. Connect the engine control sensor wiring assembly and vacuum lines.

49. Connect the upper radiator hose at the engine and install the air cleaner assembly.

50. Connect the negative battery cable.

51. Rotate the engine until the flywheel timing marker is aligned with the timing pointer. Install the timing window cover.

52. Connect the electrical connector at the inertia switch.

53. Fill the cooling system with the proper amount and type of coolant and fill the crankcase with the proper engine oil to the required level.

54. Install the hood.

55. Charge the air conditioning system, if equipped.

56. Check all fluid levels and start the vehicle. Check for leaks.

3.0L Engine

1. Disconnect the battery cables and drain the cooling system. Mark the position of the hood on the hinges and remove the hood.

2. Evacuate the air conditioning system safely and properly. Relieve the fuel system pressure. Remove the air cleaner assembly. Remove the battery and the battery tray.

3. Remove the integrated relay controller, cooling fan and radiator with fan shroud. Remove the engine bounce damper bracket on the shock tower.

4. Remove the evaporative emission line, upper radiator hose, starter brace and lower radiator hose.

5. Remove the exhaust pipes from both exhaust manifolds. Remove and plug the power steering pump lines.

6. Remove the fuel lines and remove and tag all necessary vacuum lines.

7. Disconnect the ground strap, heater

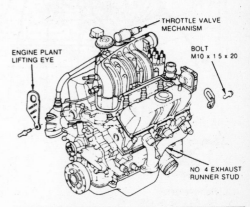

Engine support tools — 3.0L engine

lines, accelerator cable linkage, throttle valve linkage and speed control cable.

8. Disconnect and label the following wiring connectors; alternator, air conditioning clutch, oxygen sensor, ignition coil, radio frequency suppressor, cooling fan voltage resistor, engine coolant temperature sensor, Thick film ignition module, injector wiring harness, ISC motor wire, throttle position sensor, oil pressure sending switch, ground wire, block heater, if equipped, knock sensor, EGR sensor and oil level sensor.

9. Raise the vehicle and support it safely. Remove the engine mount bolts and engine mounts. Remove the transaxle to engine mounting bolts and transaxle brace assembly.

10. Lower the vehicle. Install a suitable engine lifting plate onto the engine and use a suitable engine hoist to remove the engine from the vehicle. Remove the main wiring harness from the engine.

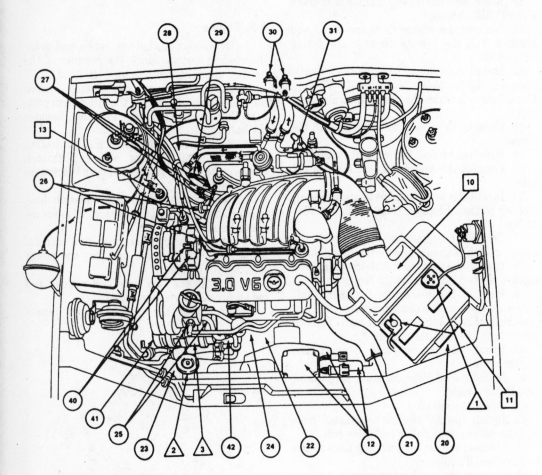

△ Service:
   1. Disconnect battery cables
   2. Drain radiator
   3. Discharge A/C

☐ Remove/install
   10. Air cleaner assembly
   11. Battery and tray
   12. Integrated relay controller, cooling fan radiator and shroud
   13. Bounce damper bracket on shock tower

◯ Disconnect/connect:
   20. Evaporative emission line
   21. Upper radiator hose
   22. Starter brace
   23. Lower radiator hose

   24. Exhaust manifold at pipe
   25. Power steering pump lines
   26. Fuel lines
   27. Vacuum lines
   28. Exhaust manifold at pipe
   29. Ground strap
   30. Heater lines
   31. Accelerator cable linkage
       Throttle valve linkage
       Speed control cable

◯ Disconnect/connect-wiring:
   40. Alternator
   41. A/C clutch
   42. EGO sensor

Engine removal/component disconnect points — 3.0L engine

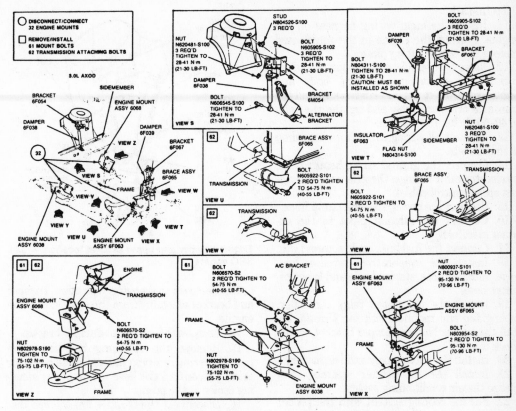

Engine and transaxle mounting — 3.0L engine except SHO

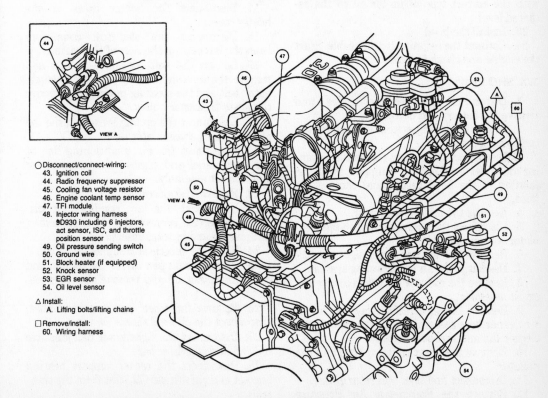

○ Disconnect/connect-wiring:
43. Ignition coil
44. Radio frequency suppressor
45. Cooling fan voltage resistor
46. Engine coolant temp sensor
47. TFI module
48. Injector wiring harness
   9D930 including 6 injectors,
   act sensor, ISC, and throttle
   position sensor
49. Oil pressure sending switch
50. Ground wire
51. Block heater (if equipped)
52. Knock sensor
53. EGR sensor
54. Oil level sensor

△ Install:
   A. Lifting bolts/lifting chains

☐ Remove/install:
   60. Wiring harness

Engine electrical wiring harness connector locations — 3.0L engine

To install:

11. Install the main wiring harness on the engine. Position the engine in the vehicle and remove the engine lifting plate.

12. Raise the vehicle and support it safely. Install the engine mounts and bolts and tighten to 40–55 ft. lbs. (54–75 Nm). Install the transaxle brace assembly and tighten the bolts to 40–55 ft. lbs. (54–75 Nm).

13. Connect all wiring connectors according to their labels.

14. Connect the ground strap, heater lines, accelerator cable linkage, throttle valve linkage and speed control cables.

15. Connect the power steering pump lines.

16. Connect the exhaust pipes to the exhaust manifolds.

17. Connect the fuel lines and vacuum lines.

18. Install the evaporative emission line, upper radiator hose, starter brace and lower radiator hose.

19. Install the integrated relay controller, cooling fan and radiator with fan shroud. Install the engine bounce damper bracket on the shock tower.

20. Install the battery tray and the battery.

21. Install the air cleaner assembly and charge the air conditioning system.

22. Fill the cooling system with the proper type and quantity of coolant. Fill the crankcase with the correct type of motor oil to the required level.

23. Install the hood.

24. Connect the negative battery cable. Start the engine and check for leaks.

3.0L SHO Engine

1. Disconnect the battery cables and remove the battery and battery tray.

2. Drain the cooling system and relieve the fuel system pressure.

3. Disconnect the wiring connector retaining the under hood light, if equipped, mark the position of the hood hinges and remove the hood.

4. Remove the oil level indicator.

5. Disconnect the alternator and voltage regulator wiring assembly.

6. Remove the radiator upper sight shield.

7. Discharge the air conditioning system.

8. Remove the radiator coolant recovery reservoir assembly.

9. Remove the integrated relay controller, air cleaner hose assembly, upper radiator hose, electric fan and shroud assembly.

10. Remove the lower radiator hose and the radiator.

11. Disconnect fuel inlet and return hose.

12. Remove the Barometric Air Pressure (BAP) sensor.

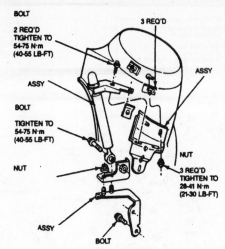

Engine damper and upper bracket location — 3.0L SHO engine

13. Remove the engine vibration damper and bracket assembly from the right side of the engine.

14. Remove the engine to damper bracket.

15. Remove the retaining bolt from the power steering reservoir and place the reservoir aside. Disconnect the hose to the power steering cooler at the pump.

16. Disconnect the throttle linkage and disconnect and tag the vacuum hoses.

17. Disconnect the heater hoses at the heater core.

18. Disconnect the electrical connectors from the harness on the rear of the engine.

19. Loosen the belt tensioner pulleys and remove the air conditioning compressor/alternator belt and the steering pump belt. Remove the lower tensioner pulley.

20. Disconnect the cycling switch on the top of the suction accumulator/drier.

21. Disconnect the air conditioning line at the dash panel and remove the accumulator and bracket assembly.

22. Remove the alternator assembly.

23. Disconnect the air conditioning discharge hose and remove the air conditioning compressor and bracket assembly.

24. Raise the vehicle and support it safely.

25. Place a drain pan under the oil pan and drain the motor oil and remove the filter element.

26. Remove the wheel and tire assemblies. Disconnect the oil level sensor switch.

27. Disconnect the right lower ball joint, tie rod end and stabilizer bar.

28. Disconnect the center support bearing bracket and right-hand CV-joint from the transaxle.

29. Disconnect the oxygen sensor assembly

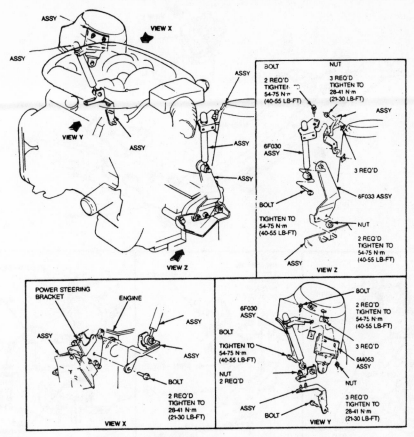

Engine damping system — 3.0L SHO engine

and the 4 exhaust catalyst to engine retaining bolts.

30. Remove the starter motor assembly.

31. Remove the lower transaxle to engine retaining bolts.

32. Remove the engine mount to sub-frame nuts.

33. Remove the crankshaft pulley assembly.

34. Lower the vehicle and remove the upper transaxle to engine retaining bolts.

35. Install engine lifting eyes.

36. Position a floor jack under the transaxle.

37. Position suitable engine lifting equipment, raise the transaxle assembly slightly and remove the engine from the vehicle.

To install:

38. Position the engine assembly in the vehicle.

39. Install the upper transaxle to engine bolts and remove the floor jack and engine lifting equipment. Remove the engine lifting eyes.

40. Raise the vehicle and support it safely.

41. Install the crankshaft pulley assembly. Tighten the retaining bolt to 113–126 ft. lbs. (152–172 Nm).

42. Install the engine mount to sub-frame nuts and the lower transaxle to engine retain-

ing bolts. Tighten the bolts to 25–35 ft. lbs. (34–47 Nm).

43. Install the starter motor assembly.

44. Install the 4 exhaust catalyst to engine retaining nuts and tighten them to 19–34 ft. lbs. (27–47 Nm). Apply anti-seize compound to the threads, then install the oxygen sensor assembly. Tighten to 27–33 ft. lbs. (37–45 Nm).

45. Connect the center support bearing bracket and install the right-hand CV-joint.

46. Connect the right lower ball joint, tie rod end and stabilizer bar.

47. Connect the oil level sensor and install the wheel and tire assemblies.

48. Install the oil filter. Install the oil drain plug and tighten to 15–24 ft. lbs. (20–33 Nm).

49. Lower the vehicle.

50. Install the air conditioning compressor and bracket assembly, tighten to 27–40 ft. lbs. (36–55 Nm) and connect the air conditioning discharge hose.

51. Install the alternator assembly and tighten to 36–53 ft. lbs. (48–72 Nm).

52. Install the accumulator and bracket assembly and connect the cycling switch to the top of the accumulator.

53. Install the lower belt tensioner. Install

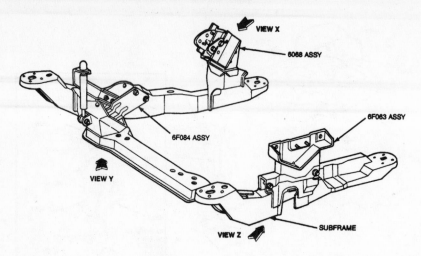

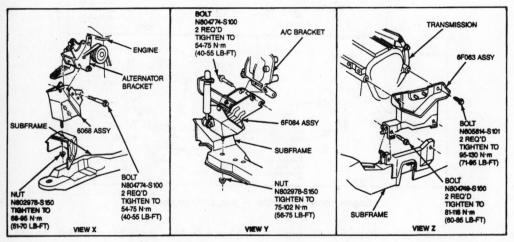

Engine and transaxle mounting — 3.0L SHO engine

the power steering and air conditioning compressor/alternator belts and tighten the tensioner pulleys.

54. Connect the electrical connectors from the harness on the rear of the engine.

55. Connect the heater hoses, vacuum hoses and throttle linkage.

56. Connect the hose from the power steering cooler at the pump and install the power steering reservoir.

57. Install the damper bracket to the engine and install the engine vibration damper and bracket assembly to the right side of the engine.

58. Install the BAP sensor.

59. Connect the fuel inlet and return hoses.

60. Install the radiator assembly and the lower radiator hose.

61. Install the electric fan and shroud assembly, upper radiator hose, air cleaner hose, integrated relay controller, radiator coolant recovery reservoir and radiator upper sight shield.

62. Connect the alternator and voltage regulator wiring.

63. Install the oil level indicator tube.

64. Install the hood and connect the under hood light wiring, if equipped.

65. Install the battery tray and the battery.

66. Install the negative battery cable.

67. Fill the cooling system with the proper type and quantity of coolant and fill the crankcase with the proper type of motor oil to the required level.

68. Drain, evacuate, pressure test and recharge the air conditioning system.

69. Start the engine and check for leaks.

3.8L Engine

1. Drain the cooling system and disconnect the battery ground cable. Properly relieve the fuel system pressure.

2. Disconnect the underhood light wiring connector. Mark position of hood hinges and remove hood.

3. Remove the oil level indicator tube.

4. Disconnect alternator to voltage regulator wiring assembly.

5. Remove the radiator upper sight shield. Remove the engine cooling fan motor relay retaining bolts and position cooling fan motor relay aside.

6. Remove the air cleaner assembly.

7. Disconnect the radiator electric fan and motor assembly. Remove fan shroud.

8. Remove upper radiator hose.

9. Disconnect the transaxle oil cooler inlet and outlet tubes and cover the openings to prevent the entry of dirt and grease. Disconnect the heater hoses.

10. Disconnect the power steering pressure hose assembly.

11. Disconnect the air conditioner compressor clutch wire assembly. Discharge the air conditioning system and disconnect the compressor-to-condenser line.

12. Remove the radiator coolant recovery reservoir assembly. Remove the wiring shield.

13. Remove accelerator cable mounting bracket.

14. Disconnect fuel inlet and return lines.

15. Disconnect power steering pump pressure and return tube brackets.

16. Disconnect the engine control sensor wiring assembly.

17. Identify, tag and disconnect all necessary vacuum hoses.

18. Disconnect the ground wire assembly. Remove the duct assembly.

19. Disconnect one end of the throttle control valve cable. Disconnect the bulkhead electrical connector and transaxle pressure switches.

20. Remove transaxle support assembly retaining bolts and remove transaxle and support assembly from vehicle.

21. Raise the vehicle and support safely. Remove the wheel and tire assemblies. Drain the engine oil and remove the filter.

22. Disconnect the oxygen sensor assembly.

23. Loosen and remove drive belt assembly. Remove the crankshaft pulley and drive belt tensioner assemblies.

24. Remove the starter motor assembly. Remove the converter housing assembly and remove the inlet pipe converter assembly.

25. Remove the engine left and right front support insulator retaining nuts.

26. Remove the converter-to-flywheel nuts.

27. Disconnect the oil level indicator sensor. Remove crankshaft pulley assembly.

28. Disconnect the lower radiator hose.

29. Remove the engine-to-transaxle bolts and partially lower engine. Remove the wheel assemblies.

30. Remove the water pump pulley retaining bolts and the water pump pulley.

31. Remove the distributor cap and position aside. Remove distributor rotor.

32. Remove the exhaust manifold bolt lock retaining bolts. Remove the thermactor air pump retaining bolts and the thermactor air pump.

33. Disconnect the oil pressure engine unit gauge assembly.

34. Install engine lifting eyes and connect suitable lifting equipment to the lifting eyes.

35. Position a suitable jack under the transaxle and raise the transaxle a small amount.

36. Remove the engine from the vehicle and position in a suitable holding fixture.

To install:

NOTE: *Lightly oil all bolt and stud threads before installation except those specifying special sealant.*

37. Remove the engine assembly from the work stand and position it in the vehicle.

38. Install the engine to transaxle bolts and remove the jack from under the transaxle and the engine lifting equipment. Remove the engine lifting eyes.

39. Tighten the engine to transaxle bolts to 41–50 ft. lbs. (55–68 Nm).

40. Connect the oil pressure engine unit gauge assembly.

41. Install the air conditioning compressor and tighten the retaining bolts to 30–45 ft. lbs. (41–61 Nm). Connect the compressor to condenser discharge line and the compressor clutch wire assembly.

42. Connect the heater hoses, vacuum hoses and the fuel tube hose and return line hose.

43. Connect the engine control module wiring assembly.

44. Connect the transaxle oil cooler inlet and outlet tubes.

45. Install the radiator assembly.

46. Partially raise the vehicle and support it safely.

47. Install the converter to flywheel bolts and tighten to 20–34 ft. lbs. (27–46 Nm).

48. Install the left and right transaxle and engine mount retaining nuts and install the converter housing cover.

49. Install the starter motor.

50. Connect the lower radiator hose.

51. Install the drive belt tensioner assembly and the crankshaft pulley assembly. Tighten the crankshaft pulley retaining bolts to 20–28 ft. lbs. (26–38 Nm).

52. Install the catalytic converter assembly

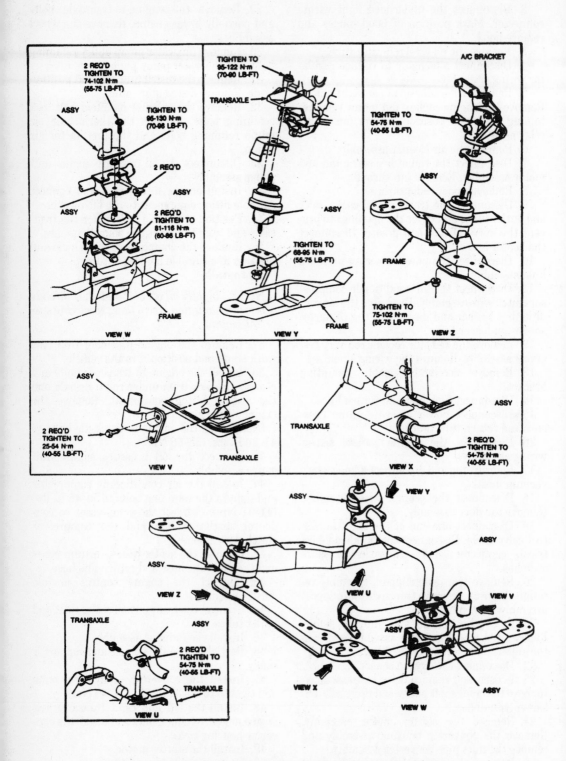

Engine and transaxle mounting — 3.8L engine with automatic transaxle

and connect the heated exhaust gas oxygen sensor.

53. Install the oil filter and connect the oil level indicator sensor.

54. Lower the vehicle.

55. Position the thermactor air supply pump and install the retaining bolts.

56. Connect the vacuum pump and install the exhaust air supply pump pulley assembly.

57. Install the wiring shield.

58. Install the distributor cap and rotor.

59. Install the radiator coolant recovery reservoir assembly, upper radiator hose and water pump pulley.

60. Connect the alternator-to-voltage regulator wiring assembly and the engine control module wiring assembly.

61. Connect the wiring asembly ground.

62. Install the accelerator cable mounting bracket.

63. Connect the power steering pressure hose assembly and the power steering line.

64. Install the fan shroud.

65. Connect the radiator electric motor assembly and install the engine cooling fan motor relay assembly.

66. Install the drive belts.

67. Position and install the transaxle support assembly.

68. Install the radiator upper sight shield.

69. Partially raise the vehicle and support it safely. Install the wheel and tire assemblies.

70. Install the hood and connect the negative battery cable.

71. Fill the cooling system with the proper type and quantity of coolant and fill the crankcase with the proper type of motor oil to the required level.

72. Drain, evacuate, pressure test and recharge the air conditioning system.

73. Start the engine and check for leaks.

Engine Mounts

REMOVAL AND INSTALLATION

2.5L and 3.0L Engines

RIGHT REAR ENGINE INSULATOR (NO. 3)

1. Disconnect the negative battery cable. Remove the lower damper nut from the right side of the engine on manual transaxle equipped vehicles. Raise and support the vehicle safely.

2. Place a suitable jack and a block of wood the engine block.

3. Remove the nut attaching the right front and rear insulators to the frame.

4. Raise the engine with the jack until enough of a load is taken off of the insulator.

5. Remove the insulator retaining bolts and remove the insulator from the engine support bracket.

6. Installation is the reverse of the removal procedure. Tighten the insulator to engine support bracket to 40–55 ft. lbs. (54–75 Nm). Tighten the nut attaching the right, front and rear insulators to frame to 55–75 ft. lbs. (75–102 Nm).

LEFT ENGINE INSULATOR AND SUPPORT ASSEMBLY – AUTOMATIC TRANSAXLE

1. Disconnect the negative battery cable. Raise and support the vehicle safely. Remove the wheel and tire assembly.

2. Place a suitable jack and a block of wood under the transaxle and support the transaxle.

3. Remove the nuts attaching the insulator to the support assembly. Remove the through bolts attaching the insulator to the frame.

4. Raise the transaxle with the jack enough to relieve the weight on the insulator.

5. Remove the bolts attaching the support assembly to the transaxle. Remove the insulator and/or transaxle support assembly.

6. .Installation is the reverse of the removal procedure. Tighten the support assembly retaining bolts to 40–55 ft. lbs. (54–75 Nm). Tighten the insulator-to-frame bolts to 60–86 ft. lbs. (81–116 Nm). Tighten the insulator to support assembly nuts to 55–75 ft. lbs. (74–102 Nm).

LEFT ENGINE INSULATOR AND SUPPORT ASSEMBLY – MANUAL TRANSAXLE

1. Disconnect the negative battery cable. Raise and support the vehicle safely. Remove the tire and wheel assembly.

2. Place a jack and a block of wood under the transaxle and support the transaxle.

3. Remove the bolts attaching the insulator to the frame.

4. Raise the transaxle with the jack enough to relieve the weight on the insulator.

5. Remove the bolts attaching the insulator to the transaxle. Remove the insulator.

6. Installation is the reverse of the removal procedure. Tighten the insulator-to-transaxle bolts to 60–86 ft. lbs. (81–116 Nm). Tighten the insulator-to-frame bolts to 60–86 ft. lbs. (81–116 Nm).

RIGHT FRONT ENGINE INSULATOR (NO. 2)

1. Disconnect the negative battery cable. Remove the lower damper nut or bolt from the right side of the engine. Raise and support the vehicle safely.

2. Place a jack and a block of wood under the engine block.

3. Remove the nuts attaching the right front and rear insulators to the frame.

4. Raise the engine with the jack until enough of a load is taken off of the insulator.

5. Remove the bolt(s) and the insulator from the engine bracket.

6. Installation is the reverse of the removal procedure. Tighten the insulator-to-engine bracket bolt(s) to 40–55 ft. lbs. (54–75 Nm) on 2.5L engine or 71–95 ft. lbs. (90–130 Nm) on 3.0L engine. Tighten the nut attaching the right front and right rear insulators to frame to 55–75 ft. lbs. (75–102 Nm).

3.0L SHO Engine

RIGHT FRONT (NO. 2) AND RIGHT REAR (No. 3)

1. Remove the lower damper bolt from the right side of the engine.

2. Raise the vehicle and support it safely.

3. Place a jack and a wood block in a suitable place under the engine.

4. Remove the roll damper to engine retaining nuts and remove the roll damper.

5. Raise the engine enough to unload the insulator.

6. Remove the 2 through bolts and remove the insulators from the engine bracket.

7. Installation is the reverse of the removal procedure. Tighten the insulator-to-engine bracket bolts to 40–55 ft. lbs. (54–75 Nm). Tighten the insulator to frame nuts to 50–70 ft. lbs. (68–95 Nm). Tighten the roll damper retaining nuts to 40–55 ft. lbs. (54–75 Nm). Tighten the engine damper to engine bolt to 40–55 ft. lbs. (54–75 Nm).

LEFT ENGINE INSULATOR AND SUPPORT ASSEMBLY

1. Remove the bolt retaining the roll damper to the lower damper bracket and place the damper shaft aside.

2. Remove the backup light switch and the energy management bracket.

3. Raise the vehicle and support it with jackstands under the vehicle body, allowing the subframe to hang.

4. Remove the left tire and wheel assembly.

5. Place a jack and wood block under the transaxle.

6. Remove the nuts retaining the lower damper bracket to engine mount and the bolts retaining the insulator to the transaxle and subframe.

7. Raise the transaxle with the jack enough to unload the insulator.

8. Remove the insulator and lower damper bracket.

9. Installation is the reverse of the removal procedure. Tighten the damper bracket to insulator nuts to 40–55 ft. lbs. (54–75 Nm). Tighten the insulator to transaxle bolts to 70–95 ft. lbs.

(95–130 Nm). Tighten the insulator to frame bolts to 60–85 ft. lbs. (81–116 Nm). Tighten the damper to damper bracket bolt to 40–55 ft. lbs. (54–75 Nm).

3.8L Engine

RIGHT FRONT ENGINE INSULATOR

1. Disconnect the negative battery cable. Remove the air conditioning compressor-to-engine mounting bracket mounting bolts and position the compressor to the side. Do not discharge the air conditioning system.

2. Raise the vehicle and support safely.

3. Remove nut attaching engine mount to air conditioning compressor bracket.

4. Temporarily attach the air conditioning compressor to the mounting bracket with the 2 lower bolts.

5. Position a jack and wood block in a convenient location under the engine block.

6. Remove the upper and lower nuts attaching the right front and left rear insulators to the frame.

7. Raise the engine with the jack enough to relieve the load on the insulator.

8. Remove insulator assembly. Remove heat shield from insulator.

9. Installation is the reverse of the removal procedure. Tighten the upper insulator stud retaining nut to 40–55 ft. lbs. (54–75 Nm) and the lower retaining nut to 50–70 ft. lbs. (68–95 Nm).

RIGHT REAR ENGINE INSULATOR (NO. 3)

1. Disconnect the negative battery cable and raise and support the vehicle safely.

2. Remove the nuts retaining the right front and right rear engine mounts to the frame.

3. Lower the vehicle.

4. Using suitable engine lifting equipment, raise the engine approximately 1 in. (25mm).

5. Loosen the retaining nut on the right rear (No. 3) mount and heat shield assembly.

6. Raise and support the vehicle safely.

7. Remove the insulator retaining nut and the insulator and heat shield assembly.

8. Installation is the reverse of the removal procedure. Tighten the top retaining nut on the insulator to 40–55 ft. lbs. (54–75 Nm). Tighten the retaining nuts on the right front and right rear engine mounts to 55–75 ft. lbs. (68–95 Nm).

LEFT ENGINE MOUNT AND SUPPORT ASSEMBLY

1. Raise the vehicle and support it safely.

2. Remove the tire and wheel assembly.

3. Place a jack and wood block under the transaxle and support the transaxle.

4. Remove the 2 bolts retaining the vertical restrictor assembly.

5. Remove the nut retaining the transaxle mount to the support assembly.

6. Remove the 2 through bolts retaining the transaxle mount to the frame.

7. Raise the transaxle with the jack enough to unload the mount.

8. Remove the bolts retaining the support assembly to the transaxle and remove the mount and/or transaxle support assembly.

9. Installation is the reverse of the removal procedure. Tighten the support assembly to transaxle bolts to 35 ft. lbs. (48 Nm). Tighten the mount to frame bolts to 60–86 ft. lbs. (81–116 Nm). Tighten the transaxle mount to support nut to 55–75 ft. lbs. (74–102 Nm). Tighten the 2 bolts retaining the vertical restrictor assembly to 40–55 ft. lbs. (54–75 Nm).

Rocker Arm Cover

REMOVAL AND INSTALLATION

2.5L Engine

1. Disconnect the negative battery cable.

2. Remove the oil fill cap and rocker arm filter and set aside. Disconnect the PCV hose and set it aside.

3. Disconnect the throttle linkage cable from the top of the rocker arm cover. Discon-nect the speed control cable from the top of the rocker arm cover, if equipped.

4. Remove the rocker arm cover bolts. Remove the rocker cover and gasket from the engine.

5. Installation is the reverse of the removal procedure. Be sure to use new gaskets or RTV sealant, as required.

3.0L Engine

1. Disconnect the negative battery cable. Disconnect and tag the spark plug wires.

2. Remove the ignition wire/separator assembly from the rocker arm attaching bolt studs. If the left rocker arm cover is being removed, remove the oil fill cap, disconnect the air cleaner closure system hose and remove the fuel injector harness from the inboard rocker arm cover studs.

3. If the right rocker arm cover is being removed, remove the PCV valve, loosen the lower EGR tube, if equipped, retaining nut and rotate the tube aside, remove the throttle body and move the fuel injection harness aside.

4. Remove the rocker arm cover attaching screws and the covers and gaskets from the vehicle.

5. Installation is the reverse of the removal procedure. Be sure to use new gaskets or RTV sealant, as required.

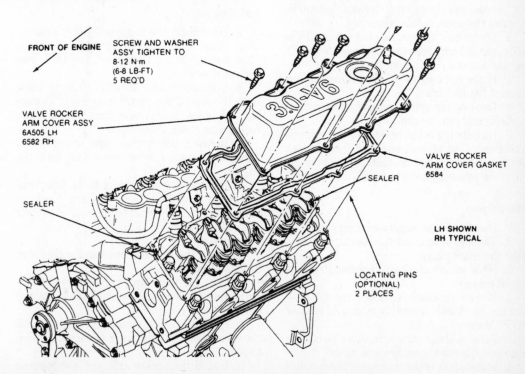

Rocker arm cover assembly–3.0L engine except SHO

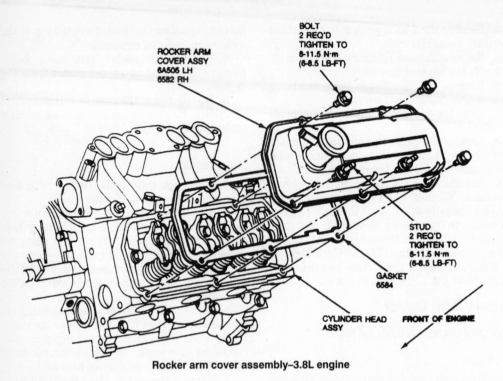

ROCKER ARM COVER ASSY 6A505 LH 6582 RH

BOLT 2 REQ'D TIGHTEN TO 8-11.5 N·m (6-8.5 LB-FT)

STUD 2 REQ'D TIGHTEN TO 8-11.5 N·m (6-8.5 LB-FT)

GASKET 6584

CYLINDER HEAD ASSY

FRONT OF ENGINE

Rocker arm cover assembly–3.8L engine

3.0L SHO Engine

1. Disconnect the negative battery cable. Relieve the fuel system pressure.
2. Disconnect all vacuum lines and electrical connectors from the intake assembly. Remove the upper intake assembly.
3. Disconnect the spark plug wires. If the left cover is being removed, remove the oil fill cap and the coil pack plastic cover.
4. If the right cover is being removed, disconnect the fuel lines.
5. Remove the cylinder head cover retaining bolts and remove the cover.
6. Installation is the reverse of the removal procedure. Coat all bolt and stud threads with clean engine oil prior to installation. Torque the cover retaining bolts to 8-11 ft. lbs.

3.8L Engine

1. Disconnect the negative battery cable.
2. Tag and disconnect the spark plug wires from the spark plugs.
3. If the left cover is being removed, remove the oil fill cap.
4. If the right cover is being removed, position the air cleaner assembly aside and remove the PCV valve.
5. Remove the rocker arm cover mounting bolts and remove the rocker arm cover.
6. Installation is the reverse of the removal procedure. Be sure to use new gaskets or RTV sealant, as required.

Rocker Arms

REMOVAL AND INSTALLATION

2.5L Engine

1. Disconnect the negative battery cable.
2. Remove the oil fill cap and rocker arm filter and set aside. Disconnect the PCV hose and set it aside.
3. Disconnect the throttle linkage cable from the top of the rocker arm cover. Disconnect the speed control cable from the top of the rocker arm cover, if equipped.
4. Remove the rocker arm cover bolts. Remove the rocker cover and gasket from the engine.
5. Remove the rocker arm bolts, fulcrums, rocker arms and fulcrum washers. Keep all parts in order so they can be reinstalled to their original position.
To install:
6. Clean the cylinder head and rocker arm cover mating surfaces.
7. Coat the valve tips, rocker arm and fulcrum contact areas with Lubriplate® or equivalent.
8. For each valve, rotate the engine until the lifter is on the base circle of the cam (valve closed).
9. Install the rocker arm and components and tighten the rocker arm bolts in 2 steps, the first to 6-8 ft. lbs. (8-12 Nm) and the second

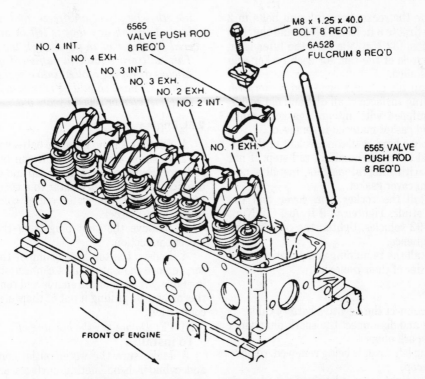

Rocker arms and related components — 2.5L engine

torque to 20–26 ft. lbs. (28–35 Nm). Be sure the lifter is on the base circle of the cam for each rocker arm as it is installed. For the final tightening, the camshaft may be in any position. Check the valve lash.

10. Install a new rocker arm cover gasket, using suitable sealer, unless the cover is equipped with a moulded-in gasket, in which case no sealer should be used.

NOTE: *If the moulded-in gasket is damaged by cuts and/or nicks less than 1/8 in. (3mm) long in a maximum of 2 places, the damaged area can be filled in with RTV sealant. If the nicks or cuts are longer than 1/8 in. (3mm) or there are more than 3 of any size, the entire rocker arm cover should be replaced.*

11. Install the rocker arm cover and tighten the bolts to 6–8 ft. lbs. (8–12 Nm).

12. Install the throttle cable(s), PCV hose and oil filler cap. Connect the negative battery cable.

3.0L Engine

1. Disconnect the negative battery cable. Disconnect and tag the spark plug wires.

2. Remove the ignition wire/separator assembly from the rocker arm attaching bolt studs. If the left rocker arm cover is being removed, remove the oil fill cap, disconnect the air cleaner closure system hose and remove the

fuel injector harness from the inboard rocker arm cover studs.

3. If the right rocker arm cover is being removed, remove the PCV valve, loosen the lower EGR tube, if equipped, retaining nut and rotate the tube aside, remove the throttle body and move the fuel injection harness aside.

4. Remove the rocker arm cover attaching screws and the covers and gaskets from the vehicle.

5. Remove the rocker arm bolts, fulcrums, rocker arms and fulcrum washers. Keep all parts in order so they can be reinstalled to their original position.

To install:

6. Coat the valve tips, rocker arm and fulcrum contact areas with Lubriplate® or equivalent. Lightly oil all the bolt and stud threads before installation.

7. Rotate the engine until the lifter is on the base circle of the cam (valve closed).

8. Install the rocker arm and components

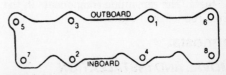

Rocker arm cover bolt torque sequence — 3.0L engine except SHO (1990–92)

and torque the rocker arm fulcrum bolts in 2 steps: the first to 8 ft. lbs. (11 Nm) and the final to 24 ft. lbs. (32 Nm). Be sure the lifter is on the base circle of the cam for each rocker arm as it is installed.

9. Clean the cylinder head and rocker arm cover sealing surfaces of all dirt and old sealer. If not equipped with integral gaskets, make sure all old gasket material is removed.

10. Apply a bead of silicone sealant at the cylinder head to intake manifold rail step. If not equipped with integral gaskets, install a new rocker arm cover gasket.

11. Install the rocker arm cover and the bolts and studs. Tighten to 9 ft. lbs. (12 Nm). On 1991–92 vehicles, tighten the cover in the proper sequence.

12. Install the remaining components in the reverse order of their removal.

3.8L Engine

1. Disconnect the negative battery cable.

2. Tag and disconnect the spark plug wires from the spark plugs.

3. If the left cover is being removed, remove the oil fill cap.

4. If the right cover is being removed, position the air cleaner assembly aside and remove the PCV valve.

5. Remove the rocker arm cover mounting bolts and remove the rocker arm cover.

6. Remove the rocker arm bolt, fulcrum and rocker arm. Keep all parts in order so they can be reinstalled in their original positions.

To install:

7. Coat the valve tips, rocker arm and fulcrum contact areas with Lubriplate® or equivalent. Install the rocker arm, fulcrum and rocker arm bolt.

8. Rotate the crankshaft until the lifter rests on the base circle of the camshaft lobe, then tighten the rocker arm bolt. Tighten in 2 steps, first to 62–132 inch lbs. (7–15 Nm) and finally to 19–25 ft. lbs. (25–35 Nm).

9. Clean the rocker arm cover and cylinder head mating surfaces of old gasket material and dirt.

10. Position a new gasket onto the cylinder head. install the rocker arm cover and the mounting bolts. Note the location of the spark plug wire routing clip stud bolts. Tighten the bolts to 80–106 inch lbs. (9–12 Nm).

11. Install the remaining components in the reverse order of their removal.

Thermostat

REMOVAL AND INSTALLATION

CAUTION: *When draining the coolant, keep in mind that cats and dogs are attracted by the ethylene glycol antifreeze, and are quite likely to drink any that is left in an uncovered container or in puddles on the ground. This will prove fatal in sufficient quantity. Always drain the coolant into a sealable container. Coolant should be reused unless it is contaminated or several years old.*

2.5L Engine

1. Disconnect the negative battery cable.

2. Position a suitable drain pan below the radiator. Remove the radiator cap and open the draincock. Drain the radiator to a corresponding level below the water outlet connection. Close the draincock.

3. Remove the vent plug from the water outlet connection.

4. Loosen the top hose clamp at the radiator, remove the water outlet connection retaining bolts, lift clear of the engine and remove the thermostat by pulling it out of the water outlet connection.

NOTE: *Do not pry the housing off.*

To install:

5. Make sure the water outlet connection and cylinder head mating surfaces are clean

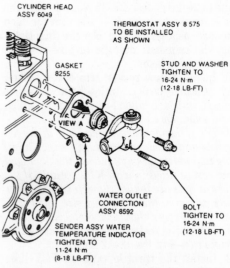

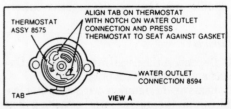

Thermostat mounting — 2.5L engine

and free from gasket material. Make sure the water outlet connection pocket and air vent passage are clean and free from rust. Clean the vent plug and gasket.

6. Place the thermostat in position, fully inserted to compress the gasket and pressed into the water outlet connection to secure. Install the water outlet connection to the cylinder head using a new gasket. Tighten the bolts to 12–18 ft. lbs. (16–24 Nm). Position the top hose to the radiator and tighten the clamps.

7. Refill the cooling system. Connect the negative battery cable. Start the engine and check for leaks. Check the coolant level and add as required.

3.0L Engine Except SHO

1. Disconnect the negative battery cable.
2. Place a suitable drain pan under the radiator.
3. Remove the radiator cap and open the draincock. Drain the cooling system.
4. Remove the upper radiator hose from the thermostat housing.
5. Remove the 3 retaining bolts from the thermostat housing.
6. Remove the housing and the thermostat as an assembly.

To install:
7. Make sure all sealing surfaces are free of old gasket material.
8. Install the thermostat into the housing.
9. Position a new gasket onto the housing using the bolts as a holding device. Install the thermostat assembly and tighten the bolts to 9 ft. lbs. (12 Nm).

10. Install the upper radiator hose and tighten the clamp.
11. Fill and bleed the cooling system. Connect the negative battery cable, start the engine and check for coolant leaks. Check the coolant level and add as required.

3.0L SHO Engine

1. Disconnect the negative battery cable.
2. Place a suitable drain pan below the radiator. Remove the radiator cap and open the draincock. Partially drain the cooling system and then close the draincock.
3. Remove the air cleaner tube.
4. Disconnect the hose from the water outlet tube.
5. Remove the 2 retaining nuts and remove the water outlet tube.
6. Remove the thermostat and seal from the water outlet housing.

To install:
7. Install the seal around the outer rim of the thermostat and install the thermostat into the water outlet housing. Align the jiggle valve of the thermostat with the upper bolt on the water outlet housing.
8. Install the water outlet tube. Tighten the 2 retaining nuts to 5–8 ft. lbs. (7–11 Nm).
9. Install the air cleaner tube.
10. Refill the cooling system. Connect the negative battery cable. Start the engine and check for leaks. Check the coolant level and add as necessary.

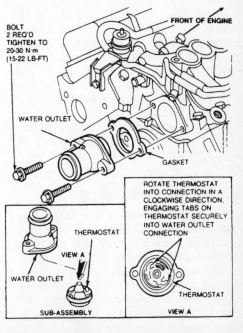

Thermostat mounting — 3.0L SHO engine

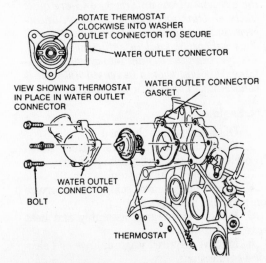

Thermostat mounting — 3.0L engine except SHO

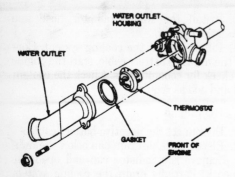

Thermostat mounting — 3.8L engine

3.8L Engine

1. Disconnect the negative battery cable.
2. Place a suitable drain pan below the radiator.
3. Remove the radiator cap and open the draincock. Drain the radiator to a level below the water outlet connection and then close the draincock.
4. Loosen the top hose clamp at the radiator, remove the water outlet connection retaining bolts and lift the water outlet clear of the engine. Remove the thermostat by rotating it counterclockwise in the water outlet connection until the thermostat becomes free to remove.

NOTE: *Do not pry the housing off.*

To install:

5. Make sure the water outlet connection pocket and all mating surfaces are clean.
6. Install the thermostat into the water outlet connection by rotating it clockwise until the engaging ramps on the thermostat are secure. Install the water outlet connection on the intake manifold with a new gasket and tighten the mounting bolts to 15–22 ft. lbs. (20–30 Nm). Position the top hose to the radiator and tighten the clamps.
7. Refill the cooling system. Connect the negative battery cable. Start the engine and check for leaks. Check the coolant level and add as required.

Cooling System Bleeding

CAUTION: *When draining the coolant, keep in mind that cats and dogs are attracted by the ethylene glycol antifreeze, and are quite likely to drink any that is left in an uncovered container or in puddles on the ground. This will prove fatal in sufficient quantity. Always drain the coolant into a sealable container. Coolant should be reused unless it is contaminated or several years old.*

When the entire cooling system is drained, the following procedure should be used to ensure a complete fill.

1. Install the block drain plug, if removed and close the draincock. With the engine off, add anti-freeze to the radiator to a level of 50 percent of the total cooling system capacity. Then add water until it reaches the radiator filler neck seat.

NOTE: *On 2.5L engine, remove the vent plug on the water connection outlet. The vent plug must be removed before the radiator is filled or the engine may not fill completely. Do not turn the plastic cap under the vent plug or the gasket may be damaged. Do not try to add coolant through the vent plug hole. Install the vent plug after filling the radiator and before starting the engine.*

2. Install the radiator cap to the first notch to keep spillage to a minimum.
3. Start the engine and let it idle until the upper radiator hose is warm. This indicates that the thermostat is open and coolant is flowing through the entire system.
4. Carefully remove the radiator cap and top off the radiator with water. Install the cap on the radiator securely.
5. Fill the coolant recovery reservoir to the FULL COLD mark with anti-freeze, then add water to the FULL HOT mark. This will ensure that a proper mixture is in the coolant recovery bottle.
6. Check for leaks at the draincock, block plug and at the vent plug on 2.5L engine.

Intake Manifold

REMOVAL AND INSTALLATION

CAUTION: *When draining the coolant, keep in mind that cats and dogs are attracted by the ethylene glycol antifreeze, and are quite likely to drink any that is left in an uncovered container or in puddles on the ground. This will prove fatal in sufficient quantity. Always drain the coolant into a sealable container. Coolant should be reused unless it is contaminated or several years old.*

2.5L Engine

1. Open and secure the hood.
2. Disconnect the negative battery cable. Properly relieve the fuel system pressure.
3. Drain the cooling system.
4. Remove accelerator cable and the cruise control cable, if equipped.
5. Remove air cleaner assembly and heat stove tube at heat shield.
6. Remove required vacuum lines and electrical connections.
7. As required on vehicles before 1990, disconnect the thermactor check valve hose at the

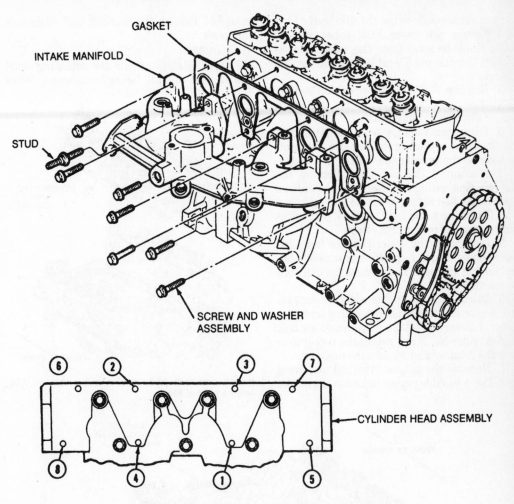

Intake manifold bolt torque sequence — 2.5L engine

tube assembly and remove the bracket to EGR valve attaching nuts.

8. Disconnect the fuel supply and return lines.

9. As required on vehicles before 1990, disconnect the water inlet tube at the intake manifold. On 1991–92 vehicles, remove the exhaust manifold heat shroud assembly.

10. Disconnect EGR tube at EGR valve.

11. Remove the intake manifold retaining bolts. Remove the intake manifold. Remove the gasket and clean the gasket contact surfaces.

To install:

12. Install intake manifold with gasket and retaining bolts. Tighten the retaining bolts to 15–22 ft. lbs. (20–30 Nm) in the proper sequence.

13. As required on vehicles before 1990, connect water inlet tube at intake manifold, connect thermactor check valve hose at tube assembly and install bracket to EGR valve attaching nuts.

14. Connect EGR tube to EGR valve.

15. Connect the fuel supply and return lines.

16. Install vacuum lines and connect electrical connectors.

17. On 1991–92 vehicles, install the heat shroud.

18. Install air cleaner assembly and heat stove tube.

19. Install accelerator cable and cruise control cable, if equipped.

20. Connect negative battery cable and fill the cooling system.

21. Start engine and check for leaks.

3.0L Except SHO Engine

1. Disconnect the negative battery cable and drain the engine cooling system. Relieve the fuel system pressure.

2. Loosen the hose clamp attaching the flex hose to the throttle body. Remove the air cleaner flex hose.

3. Identify, tag and disconnect and all

vacuum connections to the throttle body.

4. Loosen the lower EGR tube nut and rotate the tube away from the valve. Disconnect the throttle and TV cable from the throttle linkage.

5. Disconnect the throttle position sensor, air charge temperature sensor and idle speed control electrical connectors.

6. Disconnect the PCV hose and disconnect the alternator support brace. Remove the throttle body retaining bolts and the throttle body.

7. Disconnect the fuel lines. Remove the fuel injection wiring harness from the engine. Remove the fuel supply manifold and injectors.

8. Disconnect and tag the spark plug wires and remove the rocker arm covers.

9. Disconnect the upper radiator hose and heater hoses. Mark the position of the distributor housing and rotor and remove the distributor assembly.

10. Disconnect the engine coolant temperature sensor and temperature sending unit connector. Loosen the intake valve retaining bolt from cylinder No. 3 and rotate the rocker arm from the retainer and remove the pushrod.

11. Remove the intake manifold attaching bolts. Use a suitable prybar to loosen the intake

manifold. Remove the manifold and old gaskets and seals.

To install:

NOTE: *Lightly oil all the attaching bolts and stud threads before installation. When*

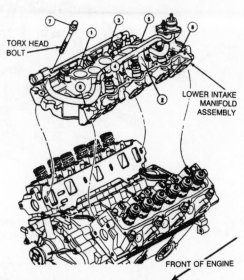

Intake manifold bolt torque sequence — 3.0L engine except SHO

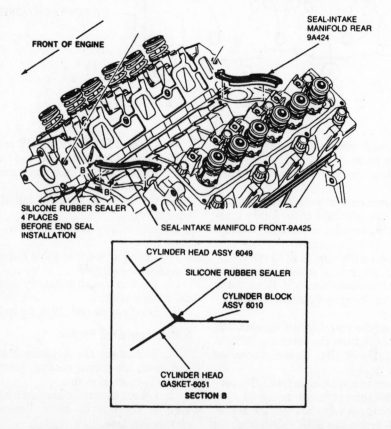

Intake manifold seal point locations — 3.0L engine except SHO

using a silcone rubber sealer, assembly must occur within 15 minutes after the sealer has been applied. After this time, the sealer may start to set-up and its sealing quality may be reduced. In high temperature/humidty conditions, the sealant will start to set up in approximately 5 minutes.

12. The intake manifold, cylinder head and cylinder block mating surfaces should be clean and free of old silicone rubber sealer. Use a suitable solvent to clean these surfaces.

13. Apply a suitable silicone rubber sealer to the intersection of the cylinder block end rails and cylinder heads.

14. Install the front and rear intake manifold end seals in place and secure. Install the intake manifold gaskets.

15. Carefully lower the intake manifold into position on the cylinder block and cylinder heads to prevent smearing the silicone sealer and causing gasket voids.

16. Install the retaining bolts and tighten the bolts, in sequence, to 11 ft. lbs. (15 Nm), then retorque to 21 ft. lbs. (28 Nm).

17. Install the fuel supply manifold and injectors. Apply lubricant to the injector holes in the intake manifold and fuel supply manifold prior to injector installation. Install the fuel supply manifold retaining bolts and tighten to 7 ft. lbs. (10 Nm).

18. Install the thermostat housing and a new gasket, if removed. Tighten the retaining bolts to 9 ft. lbs. (12 Nm).

19. Install the No. 3 cylinder intake valve pushrod. Apply Lubriplate® or equivalent to the pushrod and valve stem prior to installation. Position the lifter on the base circle of the camshaft and tighten the rocker arm bolt in 2 steps, first to 8 ft. lbs. (11 Nm) and then to 24 ft. lbs. (32 Nm).

20. Install the rocker arm covers. Install the fuel injector harness and attach to the injectors.

21. Install the throttle body with new gaskets.

22. Connect the PCV line at the PCV valve. Connect all necessary electrical connections and vacuum lines.

23. Connect the EGR tube and the fuel lines.

24. Install the distributor assembly, aligning the marks that were made during the removal procedure.

25. Install the coil and bracket. Install the upper radiator and heater hose.

26. Install and connect the air cleaner assembly and outlet tube. Fill the cooling system.

27. Reconnect the negative battery cable, start the engine and check for coolant, fuel and oil leaks.

28. Check and if necessary, adjust the engine

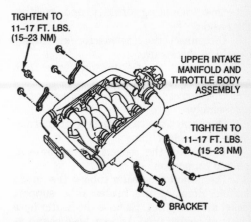

TIGHTEN TO 11–17 FT. LBS. (15–23 NM)

UPPER INTAKE MANIFOLD AND THROTTLE BODY ASSEMBLY

TIGHTEN TO 11–17 FT. LBS. (15–23 NM)

BRACKET

Intake manifold removal and installation — 3.0L SHO engine

idle speed, transaxle throttle linkage and speed control.

3.0L SHO Engine

1. Disconnect the negative battery cable. Properly relieve the fuel system pressure.

2. Partially drain the engine cooling system.

3. Disconnect all electrical connectors and vacuum lines from the intake assembly.

4. Remove the air cleaner tube.

5. Disconnect the coolant lines and cables from the throttle body.

6. Remove the bolts retaining the upper intake brackets.

7. Loosen the lower bolts and remove the brackets.

8. Remove the bolts retaining the intake to the cylinder heads.

9. Remove the intake assembly and the gaskets.

10. Installation is the reverse of the removal procedure.

11. Lightly oil the attaching bolts and stud threads before installation.

NOTE: *The intake gasket is reuseable.*

12. Install the retaining bolts and tighten to 11–17 ft. lbs. (15–23 Nm).

3.8L Engine

1. Disconnect the negative battery cable. Drain the cooling system.

2. Properly relieve the fuel system pressure. Remove the air cleaner assembly including air intake duct and heat tube.

3. Disconnect the accelerator cable at throttle body assembly. Disconnect speed control cable, if equipped.

4. Disconnect the transaxle linkage at the upper intake manifold.

5. Remove the attaching bolts from acceler-

ator cable mounting bracket and position cables aside.

6. Disconnect the thermactor air supply hose at the check valve.

7. Disconnect the flexible fuel lines from steel lines over rocker arm cover.

8. Disconnect the fuel lines at injector fuel rail assembly.

9. Disconnect the radiator hose at thermostat housing connection.

10. Disconnect the coolant bypass hose at manifold connection.

11. Disconnect the heater tube at the intake manifold. Remove the heater tube support bracket attaching nut. Remove the heater hose at rear of heater tube. Loosen hose clamp at heater elbow and remove heater tube with hose attached. Remove heater tube with fuel lines attached and set the assembly aside.

12. Disconnect vacuum lines at fuel rail assembly and intake manifold.

13. Identify, tag and disconnect all necessary electrical connectors.

14. If equipped with air conditioning, remove the air compressor support bracket.

15. Disconnect the PCV lines. One is located on upper intake manifold. The second is located at the left rocker cover and the lower intake stud.

16. Remove the throttle body assembly and remove the EGR valve assembly from the upper manifold.

17. Remove the attaching nut and remove wiring retainer bracket located at the left front of the intake manifold and set aside with the spark plug wires.

18. Remove the upper intake manifold attaching bolts/studs. Remove the upper intake manifold.

19. Remove the injectors with fuel rail assembly.

20. Remove the heater water outlet hose.

21. Remove the lower intake manifold attaching bolts/stud and remove the lower intake manifold. Remove the manifold side gaskets and end seals. Discard and replace with new.

NOTE: *The manifold is sealed at each end with RTV-type sealer. To break the seal, it may be necessary to pry on the front of the manifold with a small or medium pry bar. If it is necessary to pry on the manifold, use care to prevent damage to the machined surfaces.*

To install:

22. Lightly oil all attaching bolt and stud threads before installation.

NOTE: *When using silicone rubber sealer, assembly must occur within 15 minutes after sealer application. After this time, the sealer may start to set-up and its sealing effective-*

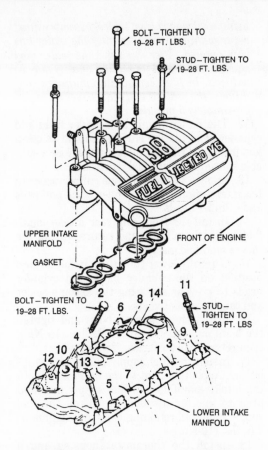

BOLT—TIGHTEN TO 19–28 FT. LBS.

STUD—TIGHTEN TO 19–28 FT. LBS.

UPPER INTAKE MANIFOLD

FRONT OF ENGINE

GASKET

BOLT—TIGHTEN TO 19–28 FT. LBS.

STUD—TIGHTEN TO 19–28 FT. LBS

LOWER INTAKE MANIFOLD

Lower intake manifold bolt torque sequence — 3.0L SHO engine

ness may be reduced. *The lower intake manifold, cylinder head and cylinder block mating surfaces should be clean and free of oil gasketing material. Use a suitable solvent to clean these surfaces.*

23. Apply a bead of contact adhesive to each cylinder head mating surface. Press the new intake manifold gaskets into place, using locating pins as necessary to aid in assembly alignment.

24. Apply a 1/8 in. (3mm) bead of silicone sealer at each corner where the cylinder head joins the cylinder block.

25. Install the front and rear intake manifold end seals.

26. Carefully lower the intake manifold into position on cylinder block and cylinder heads. Use locating pins as necessary to guide the manifold.

27. Install the retaining bolts and stud bolts in their original locations. Torque the retaining bolts in numerical sequence to the following specifications in 3 steps.

    a. Step 1 – 8 ft. lbs. (10 Nm)

    b. Step 2 – 15 ft. lbs. (20 Nm)

    c. Step 3 – 24 ft. lbs. (32 Nm)

28. Connect the rear PCV line to upper intake tube and install the front PCV tube so the mounting bracket sits over the lower intake stud.

29. Install the injectors and fuel rail assembly. Tighten the screws to 6–8 ft. lbs. (8–11 Nm).

30. Position the upper intake gasket and manifold on top of the lower intake. Use locating pins to secure position of gasket between manifolds.

31. Install bolts and studs in their original locations. Tighten the 4 center bolts, then tighten the end bolts. Repeat Step 27. 32. Install the EGR valve assembly on the manifold. Tighten the attaching bolt to 15–22 ft. lbs. (20–30 Nm).

33. Install the throttle body. Cross-tighten the retaining nuts to 15–22 ft. lbs. (20–30 Nm).

34. Connect the rear PCV line at PCV valve and upper intake manifold connections. If equipped with air conditioning, install the compressor support bracket. Tighten attaching fasteners to 15–22 ft. lbs. (20–30 Nm).

35. Connect all electrical connectors and vacuum hoses.

36. Connect the heater tube hose to the heater elbow. Position the heater tube support bracket and tighten attaching nut to 15–22 ft. lbs. (20–30 Nm). Connect the heater hose to the rear of the heater tube and tighten hose clamp.

37. Connect coolant bypass and upper radiator hoses and secure with hose clamps.

38. Connect the fuel line(s) at injector fuel rail assembly and connect the flexible fuel lines to steel lines.

39. Position the accelerator cable mounting bracket and install and tighten attaching bolts to 15–22 ft. lbs. (20–30 Nm).

40. Connect the speed control cable, if equipped. Connect the transaxle linkage at upper intake manifold.

41. Fill the cooling system to the proper level.

42. Start the engine and check for coolant or fuel leaks.

43. Check and, if necessary, adjust engine idle speed, transaxle throttle linkage and speed control.

44. Install the air cleaner assembly and air intake duct.

Exhaust Manifold

REMOVAL AND INSTALLATION

CAUTION: *When draining the coolant, keep in mind that cats and dogs are attracted by the ethylene glycol antifreeze, and are quite likely to drink any that is left in an uncovered container or in puddles on the ground. This will prove fatal in sufficient quantity. Always drain the coolant into a sealable container. Coolant should be reused unless it is contaminated or several years old.*

2.5L Engine

1. Open and secure the hood.

2. Disconnect the negative battery cable.

3. Drain the cooling system.

4. Remove the accelerator cable and the cruise control cable, if equipped.

5. Remove air cleaner assembly and heat stove tube at heat shield.

6. Identify, tag and disconnect all necessary vacuum lines and electrical connections.

7. Disconnect the exhaust pipe-to-exhaust manifold retaining nuts.

8. Remove exhaust manifold heat shroud. Disconnect the oxygen sensor wire at the connector.

9. Disconnect the fuel supply and return lines.

10. As required on vehicles before 1990, disconnect the thermactor check valve hose at tube assembly, remove bracket-to-EGR valve at-

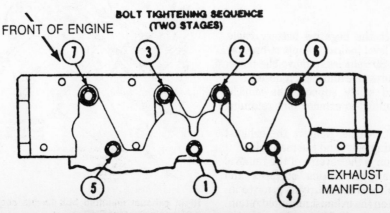

Exhaust manifold bolt torque sequence — 2.5L engine

taching nuts and disconnect water inlet tube at intake manifold.

11. Disconnect EGR tube from the EGR valve.

12. Remove the intake manifold.

13. Remove the exhaust manifold retaining nuts. Remove the exhaust manifold from the vehicle.

To install:

14. Position exhaust manifold to the cylinder head using guide bolts in holes 2 and 3.

15. Install the remaining attaching bolts.

16. Tighten the attaching bolts until snug, then remove guide bolts and install attaching bolts in holes 2 and 3.

17. Tighten all exhaust manifold bolts to specification using the following tightening procedure: torque retaining bolts, in sequence, to 5–7 ft. lbs. (7–10 Nm), then retorque, in sequence, to 20–30 ft. lbs. (27–41 Nm).

18. Install the intake manifold gasket and bolts. Tighten the intake manifold retaining bolts to 15–23 ft. lbs. (20–30 Nm).

19. As required on vehicles before 1990, connect the water inlet tube at intake manifold, connect thermactor check valve hose at tube assembly and install bracket to EGR valve attaching nuts.

20. Connect the oxygen sensor wire.

21. Connect the EGR tube to EGR valve.

22. Install exhaust manifold studs.

23. Connect exhaust pipe to exhaust manifold.

24. Install vacuum lines and electrical connectors.

25. Install air cleaner assembly and heat stove tube.

26. Install accelerator cable and cruise control cable, if equipped.

27. Connect the negative battery cable.

28. Fill the cooling system.

29. Start engine and check for leaks.

3.0L Engine

LEFT SIDE

1. Disconnect the negative battery cable. Remove the oil level indicator support bracket.

2. On 1986–89 vehicles, remove the power steering pump pressure and return hoses.

3. Raise and safely support the vehicle. Remove the manifold-to-exhaust pipe retaining nuts.

4. Lower the vehicle. Remove the exhaust manifold attaching bolts and the manifold.

5. Installation is the reverse of the removal procedure. Clean all mating surfaces and lightly oil all bolt and stud threads prior to installation. Tighten the exhaust manifold retaining bolts to 19 ft. lbs. (25 Nm) and tighten the

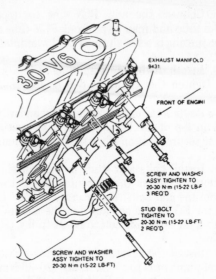

Left exhaust manifold bolt torque sequence — 3.0L engine except SHO

exhaust pipe attaching nuts to 30 ft. lbs. (41 Nm).

RIGHT SIDE

1. Disconnect the negative battery cable. Remove the heater hose support bracket.

2. Disconnect and plug the heater hoses. Remove the EGR tube from the exhaust manifold. Use a back-up wrench on the lower adapter.

3. Raise the vehicle and support it safely. Remove the manifold-to-exhaust pipe attaching nuts and remove the pipe from the manifold.

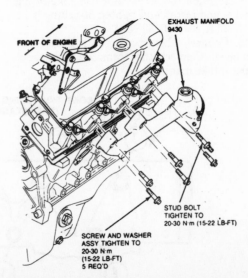

Right exhaust manifold bolt torque sequence — 3.0L engine except SHO

4. Lower the vehicle. Remove the exhaust manifold attaching bolts and remove the exhaust manifold from the vehicle.

5. Installation is the reverse of the removal procedure. Clean all mating surfaces and lightly oil all bolt and stud threads prior to installation. Tighten the exhaust manifold retaining bolts to 19 ft. lbs. (25 Nm) and tighten the exhaust pipe attaching nuts to 30 ft. lbs. (41 Nm). Tighten the EGR tube to the exhaust manifold to 31 ft. lbs. (42 Nm).

3.0L SHO Engine

LEFT SIDE

1. Disconnect the negative battery cable.
2. Remove the oil level indicator tube support bracket.
3. Remove the power steering pump pressure and return hoses.
4. Remove the manifold to exhaust pipe attaching nuts.
5. Remove the heat shield retaining bolts.
6. Remove the exhaust manifold retaining nuts and manifold.
7. Installation is the reverse of the removal procedure. Clean all mating surfaces and lightly oil all bolt and stud threads before installation. Tighten the manifold retaining nuts to 26–38 ft. lbs. (35–52 Nm), the heat shield retaining bolts to 11–17 ft. lbs. (15–23 Nm) and the exhaust pipe to manifold nuts to 16–24 ft. lbs. (21–32 Nm).

RIGHT SIDE

1. Disconnect the negative battery cable.
2. Remove the right cylinder head.
3. Remove the heat shield retaining bolts.
4. Remove the exhaust manifold retaining nuts and manifold.
5. Installation is the reverse of the removal procedure. Clean all mating surfaces and lightly oil all bolt and stud threads prior to installation. Tighten the manifold retaining nuts to 26–38 ft. lbs. (35–52 Nm). Tighten the heat shield retaining bolts to 11–17 ft. lbs. (15–23 Nm).

3.8L Engine

LEFT SIDE

1. Disconnect the negative battery cable. Remove the oil level dipstick tube support bracket.
2. Tag and disconnect the spark plug wires.
3. Raise the vehicle and support safely.
4. Remove the manifold-to-exhuast pipe attaching nuts.
5. Lower the vehicle.
6. Remove the exhaust manifold retaining bolts and remove the manifold from vehicle.
   To install:
7. Lightly oil all bolt and stud threads before installation. Clean the mating surfaces on the exhaust manifold, cylinder head and exhaust pipe.

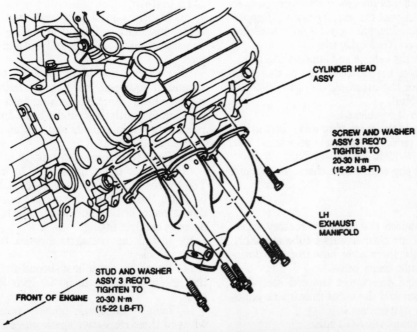

Left exhaust manifold bolt torque sequence — 3.8L engine

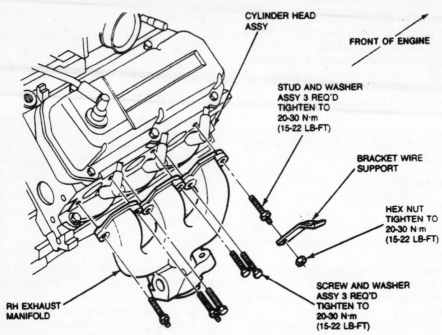

CYLINDER HEAD ASSY

FRONT OF ENGINE

STUD AND WASHER ASSY 3 REQ'D TIGHTEN TO 20-30 N·m (15-22 LB-FT)

BRACKET WIRE SUPPORT

HEX NUT TIGHTEN TO 20-30 N·m (15-22 LB-FT)

SCREW AND WASHER ASSY 3 REQ'D TIGHTEN TO 20-30 N·m (15-22 LB-FT)

RH EXHAUST MANIFOLD

Right exhaust manifold bolt torque sequence — 3.8L engine

8. Position the exhaust manifold on the cylinder head. Install the lower front bolt hole on No. 5 cylinder as a pilot bolt.

9. Install the remaining manifold retaining bolts. Tighten the bolts 15–22 ft. lbs. (20–30 Nm).

NOTE: *A slight warpage in the exhaust manifold may cause a misalignment between the bolt holes in the head and the manifold. Elongate the holes in the exhaust manifold as necessary to correct the misalignment, if apparent. Do not elongate the pilot hole, the lower front bolt on No. 5 cylinder.*

10. Raise the vehicle and support safely.

11. Connect the exhaust pipe to the manifold. Tighten the attaching nuts to 16–24 ft. lbs. (21–32 Nm).

12. Lower the vehicle.

13. Connect the spark plug wires. Install dipstick tube support bracket attaching nut. Tighten to 15–22 ft. lbs. (20–30 Nm).

14. Start the engine and check for exhaust leaks.

RIGHT SIDE

1. Disconnect the negative battery cable. Remove the air cleaner outlet tube assembly. Disconnect the thermactor hose from the downstream air tube check valve.

2. Tag and disconnect the coil secondary wire from coil and the wires from spark plugs. Remove the spark plugs.

3. Disconnect the EGR tube.

4. Raise the vehicle and support safely.

5. Remove the transaxle dipstick tube. Remove the thermactor air tube by cutting the tube clamp at the underbody catalyst fitting with a suitable cutting tool.

6. Remove the manifold-to-exhaust pipe attaching nuts.

7. Lower the vehicle.

8. Remove the exhaust manifold retaining bolts and the exhaust manifold.

To install:

9. Lightly oil all bolt and stud threads before installation. Clean the mating surfaces on exhaust manifold cylinder head and exhaust pipe.

10. Position the inner half of the heat shroud, if equipped, and exhaust manifold on cylinder head. Start 2 attaching bolts to align the manifold with the cylinder head. Install the remaining retaining bolts and tighten to 15–22 ft. lbs. (20–30 Nm).

11. Raise the vehicle and support safely.

12. Connect the exhaust pipe to manifold. Tighten the attaching nuts to 16–24 ft. lbs. (21–32 Nm). Position the thermactor hose to the downstream air tube and clamp tube to the underbody catalyst fitting.

13. Install the transaxle dipstick tube and lower vehicle.

14. Install the outer heat shroud and tighten the retaining screws to 50–70 inch lbs. (5–8 Nm).

15. Install the spark plugs. Connect the wires to their respective spark plugs and connect coil secondary wire to coil.

16. Connect the EGR tube. Connect the thermactor hose to the downstream air tube and secure with clamp. Install the air cleaner outlet tube assembly.

17. Start the engine and check for exhaust leaks.

Radiator

REMOVAL AND INSTALLATION

CAUTION: *When draining the coolant, keep in mind that cats and dogs are attracted by the ethylene glycol antifreeze, and are quite likely to drink any that is left in an uncovered container or in puddles on the ground. This will prove fatal in sufficient quantity. Always drain the coolant into a sealable container. Coolant should be reused unless it is contaminated or several years old.*

1. Disconnect the negative battery cable.

2. Drain the cooling system by removing the radiator cap and opening the draincock located at the lower rear corner of the radiator inlet tank.

3. Remove the rubber overflow tube from the coolant recovery bottle and detach it from the radiator. On Taurus SHO, disconnect the tube from the radiator and remove the recovery bottle.

4. Remove 2 upper shroud retaining screws and lift the shroud out of the lower retaining clips.

5. Disconnect the electric cooling fan motor wires and remove the fan and shroud assembly.

6. Loosen the upper and lower hose clamps at the radiator and remove the hoses from the radiator connectors.

7. If equipped with an automatic transaxle, disconnect the transmission oil cooling lines from the radiator fittings using disconnect tool T82L–9500–AH or equivalent.

8. If equipped with 3.0L and SHO engines, remove 2 radiator upper retaining screws. If equipped with the 3.8L engine, remove 2 hex nuts from the right radiator support bracket and 2 screws from the left radiator support bracket and remove the brackets.

9. Tilt the radiator rearward approximately 1 in. (25mm) and lift it directly upward, clear of the radiator support.

10. Remove the radiator lower support rubber pads, if pad replacement is necessary.

To install:

11. Position the radiator lower support rubber pads to the lower support, if removed.

12. Position the radiator into the engine compartment and to the radiator support. Insert the moulded pins at the bottom of each tank through the slotted holes in the lower support rubber pads.

13. Make sure the plastic pads on the bottom of the radiator tanks are resting on the rubber pads. Install 2 upper retaining bolts to attach the radiator to the radiator support. Tighten the bolts to 46–60 inch lbs. (5–7 Nm). If equipped with the 3.8L engine, tighten the bolts to 13–20 ft. lbs. (17–27 Nm).

14. If equipped with the 3.8L engine, fasten the left radiator support bracket to the radiator support with 2 screws. Tighten the screws to 8.7–17.7 ft. lbs. (11.8–24 Nm). Attach the right support bracket to the radiator support with 2 hex nuts. Tighten the nuts to 8.7–17.7 ft. lbs. (11.8–24 Nm).

15. Attach the radiator upper and lower hoses to the radiator. Position the hose on the radiator connector so the index arrow on the hose is in line with the mark on the connector. Tighten the clamps to 20–30 inch lbs. (2.3–3.4 Nm) if equipped with the 2.5L engine. If equipped with the 3.8L and 3.0L SHO engines, install constant tension hose clamps between the alignment marks on the hoses.

16. If equipped with automatic transaxles, connect the transmission cooler lines using oil resistant pipe sealer.

17. Install the fan and shroud assembly by connecting the fan motor wiring and positioning the assembly on the lower retainer clips. Attach the top of the shroud to the radiator with 2 screw, nut and washer assemblies. Tighten to 35 inch lbs. (4 Nm).

18. Attach the rubber overflow tube to the radiator filler neck overflow nipple and coolant recovery bottle. On Taurus SHO, install the coolant recovery bottle and connect the overflow hose.

19. Refill the cooling system. If the coolant is being replaced, refill with a 50/50 mixture of water and anti-freeze. Connect the negative battery cable. Operate the engine for 15 minutes and check for leaks. Check the coolant level and add, as required.

Engine Fan

REMOVAL AND INSTALLATION

1. Disconnect the negative battery cable.

2. Remove the radiator sight shield.

3. Disconnect the electrical connector and remove the integrated relay control assembly located on the radiator support.

4. Disconnect the fan electrical connector.

5. If necessary, remove the air bag crash sensor.

6. Unbolt the fan/shroud assembly from the radiator and remove.

7. Remove the retainer and the fan from the motor shaft and unbolt the fan motor from the shroud.

8. Installation is the reverse of the removal procedure.

Water Pump

REMOVAL AND INSTALLATION

CAUTION: *When draining the coolant, keep in mind that cats and dogs are attracted by the ethylene glycol antifreeze, and are quite likely to drink any that is left in an uncovered container or in puddles on the ground. This will prove fatal in sufficient quantity. Always drain the coolant into a sealable container. Coolant should be reused unless it is contaminated or several years old.*

2.5L Engine

1. Disconnect the negative battery cable.

2. Remove the radiator cap and position a drain pan under the bottom radiator hose.

3. Raise and support the vehicle safely. Remove the lower radiator hose from the radiator and drain the coolant into the drain pan.

4. Remove the water pump inlet tube. Loosen the belt tensioner by inserting a 1/2 in. flex handle in the square hole of the tensioner and rotate the tensioner counterclockwise and remove the belt from the pulleys.

5. Disconnect the heater hose from the water pump. Remove the water pump retaining bolts and remove the pump from the engine.

6. Installation is the reverse of the removal procedure. Torque the water pump-to-engine block retaining bolts to 15–23 ft. lbs. (20–30 Nm).

7. Refill the cooling system to the proper level. Start the engine and allow to reach normal operating temperature and check for leaks.

3.0L Engine Except SHO

1. Disconnect the negative battery cable and place a drain pan under the radiator drain cock.

2. Remove the radiator cap, open the drain cock on the radiator and drain the cooling system.

3. Loosen the 4 water pump pulley retaining bolts while the accessory drive belts are still tight.

4. Loosen the alternator belt adjuster jack screw to provide enough clearance for removal of the alternator belt.

5. Using a 1/2 in. breaker bar, rotate the automatic tensioner down and to the left. Remove the power steering/air conditioner belt.

6. Remove the 2 nuts and 1 bolt retaining the automatic tensioner to the engine.

7. Disconnect and remove the lower radiator and heater hose from the water pump.

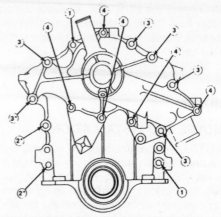

NUMBER	PART NUMBER	SIZE	QTY	N·m	LB-FT
1	N605909-S8	M8 x 1.25 x 42.0	2	20-30	15-22
2	N804113-S2	M8 x 1.25 x 43.5 (LARGE HEX)	2	20-30	15-22
3	N606547-S8	M8 x 1.25 x 70.0	6	20-30	15-22
4	N804168-S8	M6 x 1.0 x 25.0	5	8-12	6-8

NOTE: APPLY PIPE SEALANT D6AZ-19558-A TO THE THREADS OF THESE BOLTS

Water pump mounting and bolt location — 3.0L engine except SHO

8. Remove the water pump to engine retaining bolts and lift the water pump and pulley up and out of the vehicle.

To install:

9. Clean the gasket surfaces on the water pump and front cover.

10. Install the water pump with the pulley loosely positioned on the hub, using a new gasket.

11. Install and tighten the retaining bolts as indicated. Apply a suitable pipe sealant prior to installation.

12. Hand tighten the water pump pulley retaining bolts.

13. Install the automatic belt tensioner assembly. Tighten the 2 retaining nuts and bolt to 35 ft. lbs. (48 Nm).

14. Install the alternator and power steering belts. Final tighten the water pump pulley retaining bolts to 16 ft. lbs. (21 Nm).

15. Install the lower radiator and heater hoses. Fill and bleed the cooling system with the appropriate quantity and coolant type.

16. Connect the negative battery cable. Start the engine and check for leaks.

3.0L SHO Engine

1. Disconnect the battery cables and remove the battery and the battery tray.

2. Drain the cooling system and remove the accessory drive belts.

3. Remove the bolts retaining the air conditioning and alternator idler pulley and bracket assembly.

4. Disconnect the electrical connector from

the ignition module and ground strap.

5. Loosen the clamps on the upper intake connector tube, remove the retaining bolts and remove the connector tube.

6. Raise and safely support the vehicle. Remove the right wheel and tire assembly.

7. Remove the splash shield.

8. Remove the upper timing belt cover, crankshaft pulley and lower timing belt cover.

9. Remove the bolts from the center timing belt cover and position it aside.

10. Remove the water pump attaching bolts and remove the water pump.

11. To install, reverse the removal procedure. Tighten the water pump bolts to 12–16 ft. lbs. (15–23 Nm). Tighten the crankshaft pulley bolt to 113–126 ft. lbs. (152–172 Nm).

3.8L Engine

1. Disconnect the negative battery cable. Drain the cooling system.

2. Remove the lower nut on both right engine mounts. Raise and safely support the engine.

3. Loosen the accessory drive belt idler. Remove the drive belt and water pump pulley.

4. Remove the air suspension pump, if equipped.

5. Remove the power steering pump mounting bracket attaching bolts. Leaving hoses connected, place pump/bracket assembly aside in a position to prevent fluid from leaking out.

6. If equipped with air conditioning, remove the compressor front support bracket.

7. Leave the compressor in place, if removed.

8. Disconnect coolant bypass and heater hoses at the water pump.

9. Remove the water pump-to-engine block attaching bolts and remove the pump from the vehicle. Discard the gasket and replace with new.

To install:

10. Lightly oil all bolt and stud threads before installation except those that require sealant. Thoroughly clean the water pump and front cover gasket contact surfaces.

11. Apply a coating of contact adhesive to both surfaces of the new gasket. Position a new gasket on water pump sealing surface.

12. Position water pump on the front cover and install attaching bolts.

13. Tighten the attaching bolts to 15–22 ft. lbs.

14. Connect the cooling bypass hose, heater hose and radiator lower hose to water pump and tighten the clamps.

15. If equipped with air conditioning, install compressor front support bracket.

16. Install the air suspension pump, if equipped.

17. Position the accessory drive belt over the pulleys.

18. Install the water pump pulley, fan/clutch assembly and fan shroud. Cross-tighten fan/clutch assembly attaching bolts to 12–18 ft. lbs.

19. Position accessory drive belt over pump pulley and adjust drive belt tension.

20. Lower the engine.

21. Install and tighten the lower right engine mount nuts.

22. Fill cooling system to the proper level.

23. Start engine and check for coolant leaks.

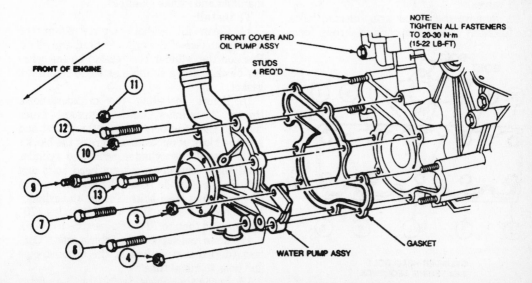

NOTE:
TIGHTEN ALL FASTENERS TO 20-30 N·m (15-22 LB-FT)

FRONT COVER AND OIL PUMP ASSY

FRONT OF ENGINE

STUDS 4 REQ'D

WATER PUMP ASSY

GASKET

Water pump mounting and bolt location — 3.8L engine

Cylinder Head

REMOVAL AND INSTALLATION

CAUTION: *When draining the coolant, keep in mind that cats and dogs are attracted by the ethylene glycol antifreeze, and are quite likely to drink any that is left in an uncovered container or in puddles on the ground. This will prove fatal in sufficient quantity. Always drain the coolant into a sealable container. Coolant should be reused unless it is contaminated or several years old.*

2.5L Engine

1. Disconnect the negative battery cable. Drain the cooling system.

2. Remove the air cleaner assembly. Properly relieve the fuel system pressure.

3. As required on vehicles before 1990, disconnect the heater hose at the fitting located under the intake manifold. On 1991–92 vehicles, disconnect the heater hose at the heater inlet tube and disconnect the adapter hose at the water outlet connector.

4. Disconnect the upper radiator hose at the cylinder head and the electric cooling fan switch at the plastic connector.

5. Disconnect distributor cap and spark plug wire and remove as an assembly.

6. Remove spark plugs, if necessary.

7. Disconnect and tag required vacuum hoses. Disconnect the accessory drive belts.

8. Remove dipstick. Disconnect the choke cap wire.

9. Remove rocker cover retaining bolts and remove cover. Disconnect the EGR tube at the EGR valve.

10. Remove the rocker arm fulcrum bolts, the fulcrums, rocker arms and pushrods. Iden-

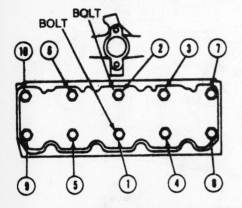

CYLINDER HEAD BOLT TIGHTENING SEQUENCE

Cylinder head bolt torque sequence — 2.5L engine

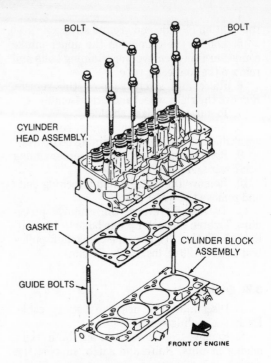

Cylinder head installation-2.5L engine

tify the location of each so they may be reinstalled in their original positions.

11. Disconnect the fuel supply and return lines at the rubber connections. Disconnect the accelerator cable and speed control cable, if equipped.

12. Raise the vehicle and support it safely. Disconnect the exhaust system at the exhaust pipe, hose and tube. Lower the vehicle.

13. Remove the cylinder head bolts. Remove the cylinder head and gasket with the exhaust manifold and intake manifold.

To install:

14. Clean all gasket material from the mating surface of the cylinder head and block. Position the cylinder head gasket on the cylinder block, using a suitable sealer to retain the gasket.

15. Before installing the cylinder head, thread 2 cylinder head alignment studs through the head bolt holes in the gasket and into the block at opposite corners of the block.

16. Install the cylinder head and cylinder head bolts. Run down several head bolts and remove the 2 guide bolts. Replace them with the remaining head bolts. Torque the cylinder head bolts in 2 steps, first to 52–59 ft. lbs. (70–80 Nm) and then to 70–76 ft. lbs. (95–103 Nm).

17. Raise and support the vehicle safely. Connect the exhaust system at the exhaust pipe and hose to metal tube.

18. Lower the vehicle. Install the thermactor pump drive belt, if equipped. Connect the accel-

erator cable and speed control cable, if equipped.

19. Connect the fuel supply and return lines. Connect the choke cap wire, if equipped.

20. Install the pushrods, rocker arms, fulcrums and fulcrum bolts in their original positions. Install the rocker arm cover.

21. Connect the EGR tube at the EGR valve. Install the distributor cap and spark plug wires as an assembly. Install the spark plugs, if removed.

22. Connect all accessory drive belts.

23. Connect the required vacuum hoses. Install the air cleaner assembly. Connect the electric cooling fan switch at the connector.

24. Connect the upper radiator hose and the heater hose. Fill the cooling system. Connect the negative battery cable.

25. Start the engine and check for leaks. After the engine has reached normal operating temperature, check and if necessary add coolant.

3.0L Except SHO Engine

1. Disconnect the negative battery cable. Properly relieve the fuel system pressure. Drain the cooling system. Remove the air cleaner assembly.

2. Loosen the accessory drive belt idler pulley, remove the drive belt.

3. If the left cylinder head is being removed, perform the following:

a. Disconnect the alternator electrical connectors.

b. Rotate the tensioner clockwise and remove the accessory drive belt.

c. Remove the automatic belt tensioner assembly.

d. Remove the alternator.

e. Remove the power steering mounting bracket retaining bolts. Leave the hoses connected and place the pump aside in a position to prevent fluid from leaking out.

f. Remove the engine oil dipstick tube from the exhaust manifold.

4. If the right head is being removed, perform the following:

a. Remove the alternator belt tensioner bracket.

b. Remove the heater supply tube retaining brackets from the exhaust manifold.

c. Remove the vehicle speed sensor cable retaining bolt and the EGR vacuum regulator sensor and bracket.

5. Remove the exhaust manifolds from both heads. Remove the PCV and the rocker arm covers. Loosen the rocker arm fulcrum attaching bolts enough to allow the rocker arm to be lifted off the pushrod and rotated to one side.

6. Remove the pushrods. Be sure to identify and label the position of each pushrod. The rods should be installed in their original position during reassembly.

7. Remove the intake manifold.

8. Remove the cylinder head attaching bolts and remove the cylinder heads from the engine. Remove and discard the old cylinder head gaskets.

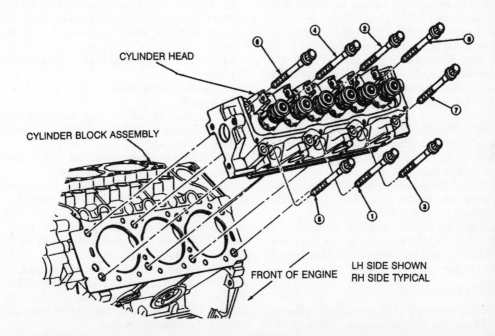

CYLINDER HEAD

CYLINDER BLOCK ASSEMBLY

FRONT OF ENGINE

LH SIDE SHOWN
RH SIDE TYPICAL

Cylinder head bolt torque sequence — 3.0L engine

To install:

9. Lightly oil all bolt and stud bolt threads before installation. Clean the cylinder head, intake manifold, rocker arm cover and cylinder head gasket contact surfaces. If the cylinder head was removed for a cylinder head gasket replacement, check the flatness of the cylinder head and block gasket surfaces.

NOTE: *If the flat surface of the cylinder head is warped, do not plane or grind off more than 0.010 in. (0.25mm). If the head is machined past its resurface limit, the head will have to be replaced with a new one.*

10. Position new head gaskets on the cylinder block using the dowels in the engine block for alignment. If the dowels are damaged, they must be replaced.

11. Position the cylinder head on the cylinder block. Tighten the cylinder head attaching bolts in 2 steps following the proper torque sequence. The first step is 37 ft. lbs. (50 Nm) and the second step is 68 ft. lbs. (92 Nm).

NOTE: *When cylinder head attaching bolts have been tightened using the above procedure, it is not necessary to retighten the bolts after extended engine operation. The bolts can be rechecked for tightness if desired.*

12. Install the intake manifold. Connect the coolant temperature sending unit connectors.

13. Dip each pushrod end in oil conditioner or heavy engine oil. Install the pushrods in their original position.

14. Before installation, coat the valve tips, rocker arm and fulcrum contact areas with Lubriplate® or equivalent. Lightly oil all the bolt and stud threads before installation.

15. Rotate the engine until the lifter is on the base circle of the cam (valve closed).

16. Install the rocker arm and components and torque the rocker arm fulcrum bolts to 24 ft. lbs. (32 Nm). Be sure the lifter is on the base circle of the cam for each rocker arm as it is installed.

NOTE: *The fulcrums must be fully seated in the cylinder head and the pushrods must be seated in the rocker arm sockets prior to the final tightening.*

17. Install the exhaust manifolds, the oil dipstick tube. Install the remaining components by reversing the removal procedure.

18. Start the engine and check for leaks.

19. Check and if necessary, adjust the transaxle throttle linkage and speed control. Install the air cleaner outlet tube duct.

3.0L SHO Engine

1. Disconnect the negative battery cable.

2. Drain the cooling system. Properly relieve the fuel system pressure.

3. Remove the air cleaner outlet tube.

4. Remove the intake manifold.

5. Loosen the accessory drive belt idlers and remove the drive belts.

6. Remove the upper timing belt cover.

7. Remove the left idler pulley and bracket assembly.

8. Raise the vehicle and support it safely.

9. Remove the right wheel and inner fender splash shield.

10. Remove the crankshaft damper pulley.

11. Remove the lower timing belt cover.

12. Align both camshaft pulley timing marks with the index marks on the upper steel belt cover.

13. Release the tension on the belt by loosening the tensioner nut and rotating the tensioner with a hex head wrench. When tension is released, tighten the nut. This will hold the tensioner in place. Lower the vehicle until the wheels touch but keep the vehicle supported.

14. Disconnect the crankshaft sensor wiring assembly.

15. Remove the center cover assembly.

16. Remove the timing belt noting the location of the letters **KOA** on the belt. The belt must be installed in the same direction.

17. Remove the cylinder head covers.

18. Remove the camshaft timing pulleys.

19. Remove the upper rear and the center rear timing belt covers.

20. If the left cylinder head is being removed, remove the DIS coil bracket and the oil dipstick tube. If the right cylinder head is being removed, remove the coolant outlet hose.

21. Remove the exhaust manifold on the left cylinder head. On the right cylinder head the exhaust manifold must be removed with the head.

22. Remove the cylinder head to block retaining bolts.

23. Remove the cylinder head.

To install:

NOTE: *Lightly oil all bolt and stud bolt threads before installation except those specifying special sealant.*

24. Clean the cylinder head and engine block mating surfaces of all gasket material.

25. Position the cylinder head and gasket on the engine block and align with the dowel pins.

26. Install the cylinder head bolts and tighten, in sequence, in 2 steps, the first to 37–50 ft. lbs. (49–69 Nm) and finally to 62–68 ft. lbs. (83–93 Nm).

27. When installing the left cylinder head, install the exhaust manifold, DIS coil bracket and oil dipstick tube. When installing the right cylinder head, install the coolant outlet hose and connect the exhaust catalyst.

28. Install the upper rear and center rear timing belt covers.

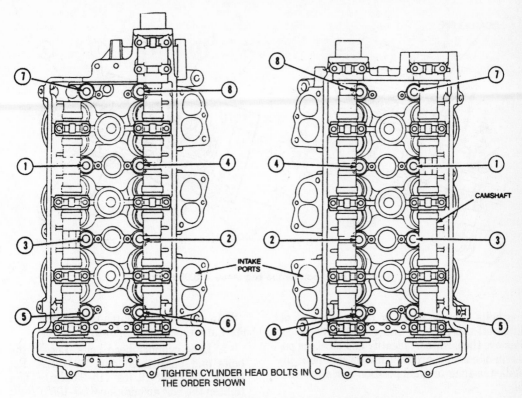

TIGHTEN CYLINDER HEAD BOLTS IN
THE ORDER SHOWN

Cylinder head bolt torque sequence — 3.0L SHO engine

29. Install the camshaft pulleys in the timed position.

30. Install the cylinder head covers.

31. Install and adjust the timing belt.

32. Install the center timing belt cover.

33. Connect the crankshaft sensor wiring assembly and install the lower timing belt cover.

34. Raise the vehicle and support it safely.

35. Install the inner fender splash shield and the right wheel and tire assembly.

36. Install the left idler pulley and bracket.

37. Install the upper timing belt cover.

38. Install the accessory drive belts.

39. Install the intake manifold.

40. Install the air cleaner oulet tube.

41. Connect the negative battery cable.

42. Fill the engine cooling system with the proper type and quantity of coolant.

43. Start the engine and check for coolant, fuel or oil leaks.

3.8L Engine

1. Drain the cooling system and disconnect the negative battery cable.

2. Properly relieve the fuel system pressure. Remove the air cleaner assembly including air intake duct and heat tube.

3. Loosen the accessory drive belt idler and remove the drive belt.

4. If the right head is being removed, pro-

ceed to Step 5. If the left cylinder head is being removed, perform the following:

a. Remove the oil fill cap.

b. Remove the power steering pump. Leave the hoses connected and place the pump/bracket assembly aside in a position to prevent fluid from leaking out.

c. If equipped with air conditioning, remove mounting bracket attaching bolts. Leaving the hoses connected, position the compressor aside.

d. Remove the alternator and bracket.

5. If the right cylinder head is being removed, perform the following:

a. Disconnect the thermactor air control valve or bypass valve hose assembly at the air pump.

b. Disconnect the thermactor tube support bracket from the rear of cylinder head.

c. Remove accessory drive idler.

d. Remove the thermactor pump pulley and thermactor pump.

e. Remove the PCV valve.

6. Remove the upper intake manifold.

7. Remove the valve rocker arm cover attaching screws.

8. Remove the injector fuel rail assembly.

9. Remove the lower intake manifold and the exhaust manifold(s).

10. Loosen the rocker arm fulcrum attach-

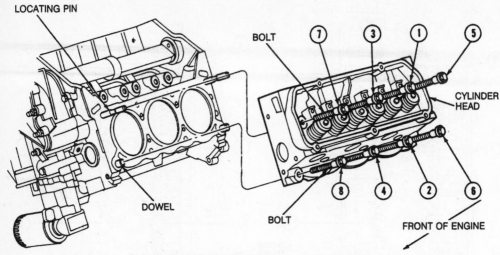

Cylinder head bolt torque sequence — 3.8L engine

ing bolts enough to allow rocker arm to be lifted off the pushrod and rotate to one side. Remove the pushrods. Identify and label the position of each pushrod. Pushrods should be installed in their original position during assembly.

11. Remove the cylinder head attaching bolts and discard. Do not reuse the old bolts.

12. Remove the cylinder head(s). Remove and discard old cylinder head gasket(s).

To install:

13. Lightly oil all bolt threads before installation.

14. Clean cylinder head, intake manifold, valve rocker arm cover and cylinder head gasket contact surfaces. If cylinder head was removed for a cylinder head gasket replacement, check flatness of cylinder head and block gasket surfaces.

15. Position the new head gasket(s) onto cylinder block using dowels for alignment. Position cylinder head(s) onto block.

16. Apply a thin coating of pipe sealant with Teflon® to the threads of the short cylinder head bolts, nearest to the exhaust manifold. Do not apply sealant to the long bolts. Install the cylinder head bolts.

NOTE: *Always use new cylinder head bolts to ensure a leak-tight assembly. Torque retention with used bolts can vary, which may result in coolant or compression leakage at the cylinder head mating surface area.*

17. Tighten the cylinder head attaching bolts, in sequence, to the following specifications:

Step 1–37 ft. lbs. (50 Nm)
Step 2–45 ft. lbs. (60 Nm)
Step 3–52 ft. lbs. (70 Nm)
Step 4–59 ft. lbs. (80 Nm)

18. In sequence, retighten the cylinder head bolts 1 at a time in the following manner:

a. Long cylinder head bolts: Loosen the bolts and back them out 2–3 turns. Retighten to 11–18 ft. lbs. (15–25 Nm). Then tighten the bolt an additional 85–105° ($^{1}/_{4}$–$^{1}/_{3}$ turn) and go to the next bolt in sequence.

b. Short cylinder head bolts: Loosen the bolts and back them out 2–3 turns. Retighten to 11–18 ft. lbs. (15–25 Nm). Then tighten the bolt an additional 65–85° ($^{3}/_{16}$–$^{1}/_{4}$ turn).

NOTE: *When cylinder head attaching bolts have been tightened using the above procedure, it is not necessary to retighten bolts after extended engine operation. However, bolts can be checked for tightness if desired.*

19. Dip each pushrod end in oil conditioner or heavy engine oil. Install pushrods in their original position.

20. For each valve, rotate crankshaft until the tappet rests on the heel (base circle) of the camshaft lobe. Torque the fulcrum attaching bolts to 43 inch lbs. maximum.

21. Lubricate all rocker arm assemblies with oil conditioner or heavy engine oil.

22. Tighten the fulcrum bolts a second time to 19–25 ft. lbs. (25–35 Nm). For final tightening, camshaft may be in any position.

NOTE: *If original valve train components are being installed, a valve clearance check is not required. If a component has been replaced, perform a valve clearance check.*

23. Install the exhaust manifold(s), lower intake manifold and injector fuel rail assembly.

24. Position the cover(s) and new gasket on cylinder head and install attaching bolts. Note location of spark plug wire routing clip stud

bolts. Tighten attaching bolts to 80–106 inch lbs. (9–12 Nm).

25. Install the upper intake manifold and connect the secondary wires to the spark plugs.

26. If the left cylinder head is being installed, perform the following: install oil fill cap, compressor mounting and support brackets, power steering pump mounting and support brackets and the alternator/support bracket.

27. If the right cylinder head is being installed, perform the following: install the PCV valve, alternator bracket, thermactor pump and pump pulley, accessory drive idler, thermactor air control valve or air bypass valve hose.

28. Install the accessory drive belt. Attach the thermactor tube(s) support bracket to the rear of the cylinder head. Tighten the attaching bolts to 30–40 ft. lbs. (40–55 Nm).

29. Connect the negative battery cable and fill the cooling system.

30. Start the engine and check for leaks.

31. Check and, if necessary, adjust curb idle speed.

32. Install the air cleaner assembly including air intake duct and heat tube.

CLEANING AND INSPECTION

Except 3.0L SHO Engine

1. Remove the cylinder head from the vehicle. Place the head on a workbench and remove any manifolds that are still connected.

2. Turn the cylinder head over so that the mounting surface is facing up and support evenly on wooden blocks.

NOTE: *If you have an aluminum cylinder head, exercise care when cleaning it.*

3. Use a scraper and remove all of the gasket material stuck to the head mounting surface. Mount a wire carbon removal brush in an electric drill and clean away the carbon on the valves and head combustion chambers.

NOTE: *When scraping or decarbonizing the cylinder head take care not to damage or nick the gasket mounting surface.*

4. Number the valve heads with a permanent felt-tip marker for cylinder location.

3.0L SHO Engine

1. Remove the cylinder head from the vehicle.

2. Place the head on a holding fixture.

NOTE: *The camshaft end play must be inspected before head disassembly. Measure the end play by using a dial indicator while moving the camshaft back and forth. Maximum end play is 0.3mm.*

3. Remove the timing chain tensioner attaching bolts.

4. Uniformly loosen and remove the bearing cap bolts.

NOTE: *If the bearing cap bolts are not removed uniformly, the camshaft may be damaged.*

5. Remove the valve shim and bucket.

6. Install a valve spring compressor tool part No. T89P-6565-A or equivalent and stand on the cylinder head.

7. Align the spring compressor squarely over the valve retainer. Attach a $1/2$ in. drive ratchet handle and apply pressure to the valve retainer. Support the valve in the head if necessary to separate the retainer from the valve stem.

8. Remove the valve keepers with a magnet and remove the valve.

RESURFACING

If the cylinder head is warped resurfacing by a machine shop is required. Place a straightedge across the gasket surface of the head. Using feeler gauges, determine the clearance at the center and along the length between the head and straightedge. Measure clearance at the center and along the lengths of both diagonals. If warpage exceeds 0.076mm in a 152mm span, or 0.15mm over the total length the cylinder head must be resurfaced.

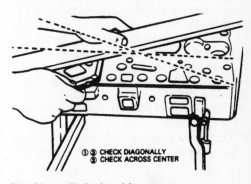

① ③ CHECK DIAGONALLY
② CHECK ACROSS CENTER

Checking cylinder head for warpage

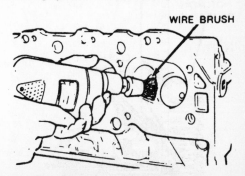

WIRE BRUSH

Removing carbon from cylinder head

Valves and Springs

REMOVAL AND INSTALLATION

1. Block the head on its side, or install a pair of head-holding brackets made especially for valve removal.

2. Use a socket slightly larger than the valve stem and keepers, place the socket over the valve stem and gently hit the socket with a plastic hammer to break loose any varnish buildup.

3. Remove the valve keepers, retainer, spring shield and valve spring using a valve spring compressor (the locking C-clamp type is the easiest kind to use).

4. Put the parts in a separate container numbered for the cylinder being worked on. Do not mix them with other parts removed.

5. Remove and discard the valve stem oil seal, a new seal will be used at assembly time.

6. Remove the valve from the cylinder head and place, in order, through numbered holes punched in a stiff piece of cardboard or wooden valve holding stick.

NOTE: *The exhaust valve stems, on some engines, are equipped with small metal caps. Take care not to lose the caps. Make sure to reinstall them at assembly time. Replace any caps that are worn.*

7. Use an electric drill and rotary wire brush to clean the intake and exhaust valve ports, combustion chamber and valve seats. In some cases, the carbon will need to be chipped away. Use a blunt pointed drift for carbon chipping, be careful around the valve seat areas.

8. Use a wire valve guide cleaning brush and safe solvent to clean the valve guides.

9. Clean the valves with a revolving wire brush. Heavy carbon deposits may be removed with the blunt drift.

NOTE: *When using a wire brush to clean carbon from the valve ports, valves etc., be sure that the deposits are actually removed, rather than burnished.*

10. Wash and clean all valve spring, keepers, retaining caps etc., in safe solvent.

11. Clean the head with a brush and some safe solvent and wipe dry.

12. Check the head for cracks. Cracks in the cylinder head usually start around an exhaust valve seat because it is the hottest part of the combustion chamber. If a crack is suspected but cannot be detected visually have the area checked with dye penetrant or other method by a machine shop.

13. After all cylinder head parts are reasonably clean, check the valve stem-to-guide clearance. If a dial indicator is not on hand, a visual inspection can give you a fairly good idea if the guide, valve stem or both are worn.

14. Insert the valve into the guide until slightly away from the valve seat. Wiggle the valve sideways. A small amount of wobble is normal, excessive wobble means a worn guide or valve stem. If a dial indicator is on hand, mount the indicator so that the stem of the valve is at 90° to the valve stem, as close to the valve guide as possible. Move the valve off the seat, and measure the valve guide-to-stem clearance by rocking the stem back and forth to actuate the dial indicator. Measure the valve stem using a micrometer and compare to specifications to determine whether stem or guide wear is causing excessive clearance.

15. The valve guide, if worn, must be repaired before the valve seats can be resurfaced. Ford supplies valves with oversize stems to fit valve guides that are reamed to oversize for repair. The machine shop will be able to handle the guide reaming for you. In some cases, if the guide is not too badly worn, knurling may be all that is required.

16. Reface, or have the valves and valve seats refaced. The valve seats should be a true

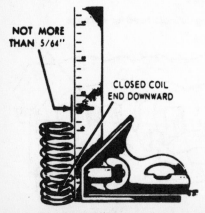

Checking Valve spring height

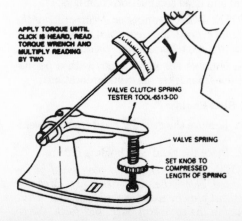

Checking valve spring pressure

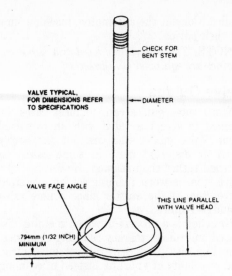

Checking valve edge

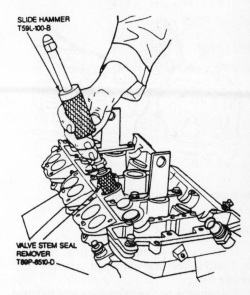

Removing valve and keepers — 3.0L SHO engine

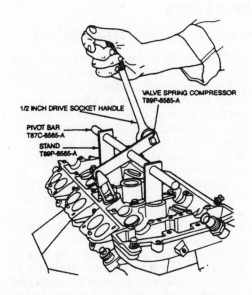

Valve spring compressor and stand — 3.0L SHO engine

45° angle for the 2.5L and 3.0L engines, and 44.5° angle for the 3.8L engine. Remove only enough material to clean up any pits or grooves. Be sure the valve seat is not too wide or narrow. Use a 60° grinding wheel to remove material from the bottom of the seat for raising and a 30° grinding wheel to remove material from the top of the seat to narrow.

17. After the valves are refaced by machine, hand lap them to the valve seat. Clean the grinding compound off and check the position of face-to-seat contact. Contact should be close to the center of the valve face. If contact is close to the top edge of the valve, narrow the seat; if too close to the bottom edge, raise the seat.

18. Valves should be refaced to a true angle of 44° for the 2.5L and 3.0L engines, and 45.8° for the 3.8L engine. Remove only enough metal to clean up the valve face or to correct runout. If the edge of the valve head, after machining, is 0.8mm or less replace the valve. The tip of the valve stem should also be dressed on the valve grinding machine, however, do not remove more than 0.25mm.

19. After all valve and valve seats have been machined, check the remaining valve train parts (springs, retainers, keepers, etc.) for wear. Check the valve springs for straightness and tension.

20. Reassemble the head in the reverse order of disassembly using new valve guide seals and lubricating the valve stems. Check the valve spring installed height, shim or replace as necessary.

Valve Stem Seals

REPLACEMENT

Most engines are equipped with a positive valve stem seal using a Teflon® insert. Teflon® seals are available for other engines but usually require valve guide machining, consult your automotive machine shop for advice on having positive valve stem oil seals installed.

When installing valve stem oil seals, ensure that a small amount of oil is able to pass the seal to lubricate the valve stems and guide walls; otherwise, excessive wear will occur.

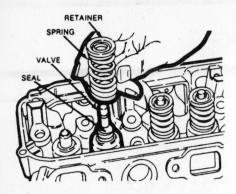

Valve stem oil seal installation

Head Off Vehicle

1. Remove the cylinder head from the vehicle. Position the assembly in a cylinder head holding fixture.

2. Using the proper valve stem seal removal tool, remove the valve keepers from the valve stem. Remove and discard the old valve stem seal.

3. As required, remove the valve from the cylinder head. Be sure to keep the valves in the proper order for reassembly.

4. Continue this process for the remaining valves.

5. Installation is the reverse of the removal procedure.

Head On Vehicle

1. Disconnect the negative battery cable. Remove the valve cover.

2. Remove the spark plug from the cylinder that you are working on.

3. Position the engine so that both the intake and exhaust valves are closed.

4. Screw the proper tool into the spark plug hole. Attach an air line to the tool and pressurize the cylinder with low pressure compressed air, just enough to hold the valves in the closed position.

NOTE: *Failure to properly compress air into the cylinder will result in the valve falling into the cylinder bore which will necessiate disassembling the engine to retrieve them.*

5. Using the proper valve stem seal removal tool, remove the valve keepers from the valve stem. Remove and discard the old valve seal.

6. Installation is the reverse of the removal procedure.

Valve Seats

If a valve seat is damaged or burnt and cannot be serviced by refacing, it may be possible to have the seat machined and an insert in-

stalled. Consult the automotive machine shop for their advice.

NOTE: *The aluminum heads on some engines are equipped with inserts.*

Valve Guides

Worn valve guides can, in most cases, be reamed to accept a valve with an oversized stem. Valve guides that are not excessively worn or distorted may, in some cases, be knurled rather than reamed. However, if the valve stem is worn reaming for an oversized valve stem is the answer since a new valve would be required.

Knurling is a process in which metal is displaced and raised, thereby reducing clearance. Knurling also produces excellent oil control. The possibility of knurling instead of reaming the valve guides should be discussed with a machinist.

Valve Lifters

REMOVAL AND INSTALLATION

CAUTION: *When draining the coolant, keep in mind that cats and dogs are attracted by the ethylene glycol antifreeze, and are quite likely to drink any that is left in an uncovered container or in puddles on the ground. This will prove fatal in sufficient quantity. Always drain the coolant into a sealable container. Coolant should be reused unless it is contaminated or several years old. The EPA warns that prolonged contact with used engine oil may cause a number of skin disorders, including cancer! You should make every effort to minimize your exposure to used engine oil. Protective gloves should be worn when changing the oil. Wash your hands and any other exposed skin areas as soon as possible after exposure to used engine oil. Soap and water, or waterless hand cleaner should be used.*

2.5L Engine

1. Disconnect the negative battery cable. Remove the cylinder head.

2. Using a magnet, remove the lifters. Identify, tag and place the lifters in a rack so they can be installed in the original positions.

3. If the lifters are stuck in their bores by excessive varnish or gum, it may be necessary to use a hydraulic lifter puller tool to remove the lifters. Rotate the lifters back and forth to loosen any gum and varnish which may have formed. Keep the assemblies intact until the are to be cleaned.

4. Install the lifters through the pushrod openings with a magnet.

5. Install the cylinder head and related parts.

3.0L Engine Except SHO

1. Disconnect the negative battery cable.

2. Drain the cooling system and relieve the fuel system pressure.

3. Disconnect the fuel lines from the fuel supply manifold and remove the throttle body.

4. Disconnect the spark plug wires from the spark plugs. Remove the ignition wire/separator assembly from the rocker cover retaining studs.

5. Mark the position of the distributor housing and rotor and remove the distributor.

6. Remove the rocker arm covers. Loosen the No. 3 intake valve rocker arm retaining bolt to allow the rocker arm to be rotated to 1 side.

7. Remove the intake manifold assembly.

8. Loosen the rocker arm fulcrum retaining bolt enough to allow the rocker arm to be lifted off the pushrod and rotated to 1 side.

9. Remove the pushrod(s). If more than 1 is removed, identify each pushrods location. The pushrods should be installed in their original position during reassembly.

10. On 1992 engines equipped with roller lifters, loosen the two roller lifter guide plate retaining bolts. Remove the guide plate retainer assembly from the lifter valley. Remove the lifter guide plate from the lifter by lifting straight up. To remove, grasp the lifter and pull it in line with the bore.

11. Remove the lifter(s) using a magnet, as required.

NOTE: *If the lifter(s) are stuck in the bore(s) due to excessive varnish or gum deposits, it may be necessary to use a claw-type tool to aid removal. Rotate the lifter back and forth to loosen it from the gum or varnish that may have formed on the lifter.*

To install:

11. Clean all gasket mating surfaces. Place a rag in the lifter valley to catch any stray gasket material.

12. Lubricate each lifter and bore with heavy engine oil. Install the lifter in the bore, checking for free fit.

13. If equipped with roller lifters align the lifter flat to the lifter guide plate. Install the plate with the word UP and or button visable. Install the guide retainer assembly over the guide plates. Tighten the bolts to 8–10 ft. lbs.

14. Install the intake manifold and new gaskets. Dip each pushrod end in oil conditioner and install in it's original position.

15. For each valve, rotate the crankshaft until the lifter rests on the base circle of the camshaft lobe. Position the rocker arms over the pushrod and valve. Tighten the retaining

bolt to 8 ft. lbs. (11 Nm) to initially seat the fulcrum into the cylinder head and onto the pushrod. Final tighten the bolt to 24 ft. lbs. (32 Nm).

16. Install the rocker arm covers and the distributor.

17. Install the throttle body and connect the fuel lines to the fuel supply manifold. Install the safety clips.

18. Install the coolant hoses. Fill and bleed the cooling system. Drain and change the crankcase oil.

19. Connect the air cleaner hoses to the throttle body and rocker cover.

20. Connect the negative battery cable, start the engine and check for leaks. Check the ignition timing.

3.8L Engine

1. Disconnect the negative battery cable. Disconnect the secondary ignition wires at the spark plugs.

2. Remove the plug wire routing clips from mounting studs on the rocker arm cover attaching bolts. Lay plug wires with routing clips toward the front of engine.

3. Remove the upper intake manifold, rocker arm covers and lower intake manifold.

4. Sufficiently loosen each rocker arm fulcrum attaching bolt to allow the rocker arm to be lifted off the pushrod and rotated to one side.

5. Remove the pushrods. The location of each pushrod should be identified and labeled. When engine is assembled, each rod should be installed in its original position.

6. If equipped with roller lifters, remove the 2 tappet guide plate retainers and 6 guide plates.

7. Remove the lifters using a magnet. The location of each lifters should be identified and labeled. When engine is assembled, each lifter should be installed in its original position.

NOTE: *If lifters are stuck in bores due to excessive varnish or gum deposits, it may be necessary to use a hydraulic lifter puller tool to aid removal. When using a remover tool, rotate lifter back and forth to loosen it from gum or varnish that may have formed on the lifter.*

To install:

8. Lightly oil all bolt and stud threads before installation. Using solvent, clean the cylinder head and valve rocker arm cover sealing surfaces.

9. Lubricate each lifter and bore with oil conditioner or heavy engine oil.

10. Install each lifter in bore from which it was removed. If a new tappet(s) is being installed, check new lifter for a free fit in bore.

11. If equipped with roller lifters, align the flats on the sides of the lifters and install the 6 guide plates between the adjacent lifters. Make sure the word "up" and/or button is showing. Install the 3 guide plate retainers and tighten the 4 bolts to 6–10 ft. lbs. (8–14 Nm).

12. Dip each pushrod end in oil conditioner or heavy engine oil. Install pushrods in their orignial positions.

13. For each valve, rotate crankshaft until lifter rests onto heel (base circle) of camshaft lobe. Position rocker arms over pushrods and install the fulcrums. Initially tighten the fulcrum attaching bolts to 44 inch lbs. maximum.

14. Lubricate all rocker arm assemblies with suitable heavy engine oil.

15. Finally tighten the fulcrum bolts to 19–25 ft. lbs. (25–35 Nm). For the final tightening, the camshaft may be in any position.

NOTE: *Fulcrums must be fully seated in the cylinder head and pushrods must be seated in rocker arm sockets prior to the final tightening.*

16. Complete the installation of the lower intake manifold, valve rocker arm covers and the upper intake manifold by reversing the removal procedure.

17. Install the plug wire routing clips and connect wires to the spark plugs.

18. Start the engine and check for oil or coolant leaks.

Oil Pan

REMOVAL AND INSTALLATION

CAUTION: *The EPA warns that prolonged contact with used engine oil may cause a number of skin disorders, including cancer! You should make every effort to minimize your exposure to used engine oil. Protective gloves should be worn when changing the oil. Wash your hands and any other exposed skin areas as soon as possible after exposure to used engine oil. Soap and water, or waterless hand cleaner should be used.*

2.5L Engine

1. Disconnect the negative battery cable. Raise the vehicle and support safely.

2. Drain the crankcase and drain the cooling system by removing the lower radiator hose.

3. Remove the roll restrictor on manual transaxle equipped vehicles.

4. Disconnect the starter cable and remove the starter.

5. Disconnect the exhaust pipe from oil pan.

6. Remove the engine coolant tube located

from the lower radiator hose, water pump and at the tabs on the oil pan. Position air conditioner line off to the side. Remove the retaining bolts and remove the oil pan.

To install:

7. Clean both mating surfaces of oil pan and cylinder block making certain all traces of RTV sealant are removed.

8. Remove and clean oil pump pick-up tube and screen assembly. After cleaning, install tube and screen assembly.

9. Fill the oil pan groove with RTV sealer; the bead should be approximately 1/8 in. (3mm) above the surface of the pan rail. Immediately (within 5 minutes) install the oil pan.

10. Install and tighten the 2 oil pan-to-transaxle bolts to 30–39 ft. lbs. (40–50 Nm) to align the pan with the transaxle then back off 1/2 turn.

11. Tighten the pan flange bolts to 6–8 ft. lbs. (8–12 Nm).

12. Tighten the 2 oil pan-to-transaxle bolts to 30–39 ft. lbs. (40–50 Nm).

13. Install the remaining components in the reverse order of their removal.

14. Fill the crankcase and cooling system to the proper level.

15. Start the engine and inspect for leaks.

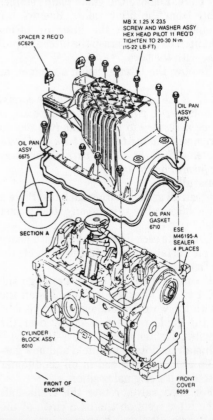

Oil pan assembly — 2.5L engine

3.0L Except SHO Engine

1. Disconnect the negative battery cable and remove the oil level dipstick.

2. Raise the vehicle and support safely. If equipped with a low level sensor, remove the retainer clip at the sensor. Remove the electrical connector from the sensor.

3. Drain the crankcase. Remove the starter motor and disconnect the electrical connector from the oxygen sensor.

4. Remove the catalyst and pipe assembly. Remove the lower engine/flywheel dust cover from the torque converter housing.

5. Remove the oil pan attaching bolts and slowly remove the oil pan from the engine block. Remove the oil pan gasket.

To install:

6. Clean the gasket surfaces on the cylinder block and oil pan. Apply a $\frac{3}{16}$ in. (5mm) bead of silicone sealer to the junction of the rear main bearing cap and cylinder block junction of the front cover assembly and cylinder block.

NOTE: *When using a silicone sealer, the assembly process should occur within 15 minutes after the sealer has been applied. After this time, the sealer may start to set-up and its sealing effectiveness may be affected.*

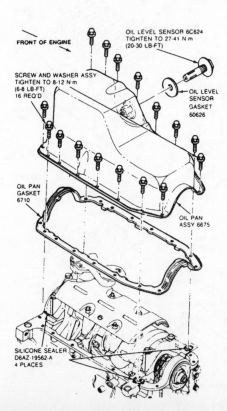

Oil pan assembly — 3.0L engine except SHO

7. Position the oil pan gasket over the oil pan and secure the gasket with a suitable sealer contact adhesive.

8. Position the oil pan on the engine block and install the oil pan attaching bolts. Torque the bolts to 8 ft. lbs. (10 Nm).

9. Install the lower engine/flywheel dust cover to the torque converter housing. Install the catalyst and pipe assembly. Connect the oxygen sensor connector.

10. Install the starter motor. Install the low oil level sensor connector to the sensor and install the retainer clip. Lower the vehicle and replace the oil level dipstick.

11. Connect the negative battery cable. Fill the crankcase. Start the engine and check for oil and exhaust leaks.

3.0L SHO Engine

1. Disconnect the negative battery cable.

2. Remove the oil level dipstick.

3. Remove the accessory drive belts.

4. Remove the timing belt.

5. Raise the vehicle and support it safely.

6. If equipped with a low oil level sensor, remove the retainer clip and the electrical connector from the sensor.

7. Drain the engine oil.

8. Remove the starter motor.

9. Disconnect the oxygen sensors.

10. Remove the catalyst and pipe assembly.

11. Remove the lower flywheel dust cover from the converter housing.

12. Remove the oil pan attaching bolts and the oil pan.

To install:

13. Clean the gasket surfaces of the cylinder block and the oil pan.

14. Position the oil pan gasket on the oil pan and secure with silicone sealer.

15. Position the oil pan and tighten the retaining bolts to 11–17 ft. lbs. (15–23 Nm).

16. Install the lower flywheel dust cover to the converter housing.

17. Install the catalyst and pipe assembly and connect the oxygen sensors.

18. Install the starter and connect the low oil level sensor connector to the sensor. Install the retainer clip.

19. Lower the vehicle and install the accessory drive belts.

20. Replace the oil level dipstick and connect the negative battery cable.

21. Fill the crankcase with the proper type and quantity of oil. Start the vehicle and check for leaks.

3.8L Engine

1. Disconnect the negative battery cable.

2. Raise the vehicle and support safely.

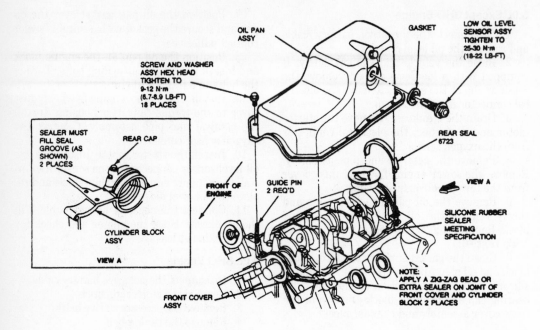

Oil pan assembly — 3.0L SHO engine

3. Drain the crankcase and remove the oil filter element.

4. Remove the converter assembly, starter motor and converter housing cover.

5. Remove the retaining bolts and remove the oil pan.

To install:

6. Clean the gasket surfaces on cylinder block, oil pan and oil pickup tube.

7. Trial fit oil pan to cylinder block. Ensure enough clearance has been provided to allow oil pan to be installed without sealant being scraped off when pan is positioned under engine.

8. Apply a bead of silicone sealer to the oil pan flange. Also apply a bead of sealer to the front cover/cylinder block joint and fill the grooves on both sides of the rear main seal cap.

NOTE: *When using silicone rubber sealer, assembly must occur within 15 minutes after sealer application. After this time, the sealer may start to harden and its sealing effectiveness may be reduced.*

9. Install the oil pan and secure to the block with the attaching screws. Tighten the screws to 7–9 ft. lbs. (9–12 Nm).

10. Install a new oil filter element. Install the converter housing cover and starter motor.

11. Install the converter assembly and lower the vehicle.

12. Fill the crankcase and connect the negative battery cable.

13. Start the engine and check for leaks.

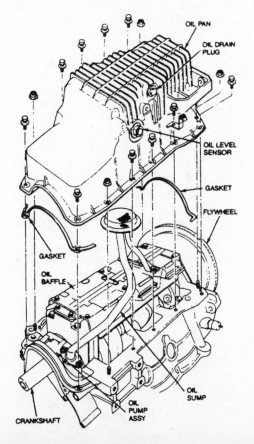

Oil pan assembly — 3.8L engine

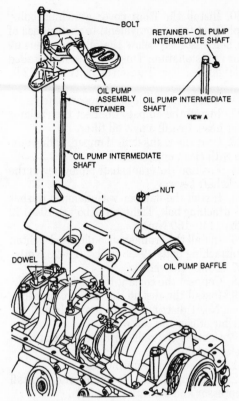

BOLT

RETAINER—OIL PUMP INTERMEDIATE SHAFT

OIL PUMP ASSEMBLY RETAINER

OIL PUMP INTERMEDIATE SHAFT

VIEW A

OIL PUMP INTERMEDIATE SHAFT

NUT

DOWEL

OIL PUMP BAFFLE

Oil pump and related components — 3.0L engine except SHO

Oil Pump

REMOVAL AND INSTALLATION

2.5L Engine

1. Remove the oil pan.
2. Remove oil pump attaching bolts and remove oil pump and intermediate driveshaft.

To install:

3. Prime oil pump by filling inlet port with engine oil. Rotate pump shaft until oil flows from outlet port.
4. If screen and cover assembly have been removed, replace gasket. Clean screen and reinstall screen and cover assembly and tighten attaching bolts.
5. Position intermediate driveshaft into distributor socket.
6. Insert intermediate driveshaft into oil pump. Install pump and shaft as an assembly.

NOTE: *Do not attempt to force the pump into position if it will not seat. The shaft hex may be mis-aligned with the distributor shaft. To align, remove the oil pump and rotate the intermediate driveshaft into a new position.*

7. Tighten the oil pump attaching bolts to 15–22 ft. lbs. (20–30 Nm).
8. Install the oil pan.
9. Fill the crankcase. Start engine and check for leaks.

3.0L Except SHO Engine

1. Remove the oil pan.
2. Remove the oil pump attaching bolts. Lift the oil pump off the engine and withdraw the oil pump driveshaft.

To install:

3. Prime the oil pump by filling either the inlet or the outlet port with engine oil. Rotate the pump shaft to distribute the oil within the oil pump body cavity.
4. Insert the oil pump intermediate shaft assembly into the hex drive hole in the oil pump assembly until the retainer "clicks" into place. Place the oil pump in the proper position with a new gasket and install the retaining bolt.
5. Torque the oil pump retaining bolt to 35 ft. lbs. (48 Nm).
6. Install the oil pan with new gasket.
7. Fill the crankcase. Start engine and check for leaks.

3.0L SHO Engine

1. Remove the oil pan.
2. Remove crankshaft timing belt pulley.
3. Remove the sump to oil pump bolts.
4. Remove the oil pump to block bolts and remove the pump.

To install:

5. Align the oil pump on the crankshaft and install the oil pump retaining bolts. Tighten the bolts to 11–17 ft. lbs. (15–23 Nm).
6. Install the oil sump to oil pump retaining bolts and tighten to 6–8 ft. lbs. (7–11 Nm).
7. Install the crankshaft timing belt pulley.
8. Install the oil pan with a new gasket.
9. Fill the crankcase with the proper type and quantity of oil.
10. Start the engine and check for leaks.

3.8L Engine

NOTE: *The oil pump, oil pressure relief valve and drive intermediate shaft are contained in the front cover assembly.*

1. Disconnect the negative battery cable. Drain the cooling system and crankcase.
2. Remove the air cleaner assembly and air intake duct.
3. Loosen the accessory drive belt idler. Remove the belt and water pump pulley.
4. Remove the power steering pump mounting bracket attaching bolts. Leaving the hoses connected, place the pump/bracket assembly in a position that will prevent the loss of power steering fluid.

5. If equipped with air conditioning, remove the compressor front support bracket. Leave the compressor in place.

6. Disconnect coolant bypass and heater hoses at the water pump. Disconnect radiator upper hose at thermostat housing.

7. Disconnect the coil wire from distributor cap and remove cap with secondary wires attached. Remove the distributor hold-down clamp and lift distributor out of the front cover.

8. Raise the vehicle and support safely.

9. Remove the crankshaft damper and pulley.

NOTE: *If the crankshaft pulley and vibration damper have to be separated, mark the damper and pulley so they may be reassembled in the same relative position. This is important as the damper and pulley are initially balanced as a unit. If the crankshaft damper is being replaced, check if the original damper has balance pins installed. If so, new balance pins (E0SZ–6A328–A or equivalent) must be installed on the new damper in the same position as the original damper. The crankshaft pulley must also be installed in original installation position.*

10. Remove the oil filter, disconnect the radiator lower hose at the water pump and remove the oil pan.

11. Lower the vehicle.

12. Remove the front cover.

NOTE: *Do not overlook the cover attaching bolt located behind the oil filter adapter. The front cover will break if pried upon if all attaching bolts are not removed.*

13. Remove the oil pump cover attaching bolts and remove the cover. Lift the pump gears off the front cover pocket. Remove the cover gasket and replace with new.

To install:

14. Clean the front cover oil pump gasket contact surface. Place a straight edge across the oil pump cover mounting surface and check for wear or warpage using a feeler gauge. If the surface is out of flat by more than 0.0016 in. (0.04mm), replace the cover.

15. Lightly pack the gear pocket with petroleum jelly or coat all pump gear surfaces with oil conditioner.

16. Install the gears in the pocket. Make certain the petroleum jelly fills the gap between the gears and the pocket.

17. Position the oil pump cover gasket and install the oil pump cover. Tighten oil pump cover retaining bolts to 18–22 ft. lbs. (25–30 Nm).

18. Clean the gasket surfaces of the front cover and cylinder block.

19. Position a new gasket and the front cover on the cylinder block.

20. Install the front cover attaching bolts. Apply Loctite® or equivalent, to the threads of the bolt installed below the oil filter housing prior to installation. This bolt is to be installed and tightened last. Tighten all bolts to 15–22 ft. lbs. (20–30 Nm).

21. Raise the vehicle and support safely.

22. Install the oil pan. Connect the radiator lower hose. Install a new oil filter.

23. Coat the crankshaft damper sealing surface with clean engine oil.

24. Position the crankshaft pulley key in the crankshaft keyway.

25. Install the damper with damper washer and attaching bolt. Tighten the bolt to 104–132 ft. lbs. (140–180 Nm).

26. Install the crankshaft pulley and tighten the attaching bolts 19–28 ft. lbs. (26–28 Nm).

27. Lower the vehicle.

28. Connect the coolant bypass hose.

29. Install the distributor with rotor pointing at No. 1 distributor cap tower. Install the distributor cap and coil wire.

30. Connect the radiator upper hose at thermostat housing.

31. Connect the heater hose.

32. If equipped with air conditioning, install compressor and mounting brackets.

33. Install the power steering pump and mounting brackets.

34. Position the accessory drive belt over the pulleys.

35. Install the water pump pulley. Position the accessory drive belt over water pump pulley and tighten the belt.

36. Connect battery ground cable. Fill the crankcase and cooling system to the proper level.

37. Start the engine and check for leaks.

38. Check the ignition timing and curb idle speed, adjust as required.

39. Install the air cleaner assembly and air intake duct.

Timing Chain Cover

REMOVAL AND INSTALLATION

CAUTION: *When draining the coolant, keep in mind that cats and dogs are attracted by the ethylene glycol antifreeze, and are quite likely to drink any that is left in an uncovered container or in puddles on the ground. This will prove fatal in sufficient quantity. Always drain the coolant into a sealable container. Coolant should be reused unless it is contaminated or several years old. The EPA warns that prolonged contact with used engine oil may cause a number of skin disorders, including cancer! You should make every effort to minimize your exposure to* used engine oil. Protective gloves should be worn when changing the oil. Wash your hands and any other exposed skin areas as soon as possible after exposure to used engine oil. Soap and water, or waterless hand cleaner should be used.

2.5L Engine

1. Disconnect the negative battery cable.
2. Remove the engine and transaxle assembly from the vehicle and position in a suitable holding fixture. Remove the dipstick.
3. Remove accessory drive pulley, if equipped. Remove the crankshaft pulley attaching bolt and washer and remove pulley.
4. Remove front cover attaching bolts from front cover. Pry the top of the front cover away from the block.
5. Remove the oil pan.
6. Clean all dirt and old gasket material from all mating surfaces.

To install:

7. Clean and inspect all parts before installation. Clean the oil pan, cylinder block and front cover of gasket material and dirt.
8. Apply oil resistant sealer to a new front cover gasket and position gasket into front cover.
9. Remove the front cover oil seal and position the front cover on the engine.
10. Position front cover alignment tool T84P–6019–C or equivalent, onto the end of the crankshaft, ensuring the crank key is aligned with the keyway in the tool. Bolt the front cover to the engine and tighten the bolts to 6–8 ft. lbs. (10–12 Nm). Remove the front cover alignment tool.
11. Install a new front cover oil seal using a suitable seal installer. Lubricate the hub of the crankshaft pulley with polyethylene grease to prevent damage to the seal during installation and initial engine start. Install crankshaft pulley.
12. Install the oil pan.

FRONT OF ENGINE | GASKET | FRONT COVER ASSEMBLY | BOLT | FRONT COVER ALIGNER TOOL | GUIDE | CYLINDER BLOCK ASSEMBLY | TIMING CHAIN DAMPER ASSEMBLY

Timing chain front cover and related components – 2.5L engine

13. Install the accessory drive pulley, if equipped.
14. Install crankshaft pulley attaching bolt and washer. Tighten to 140–170 ft. lbs. (190–230 Nm).
15. Install the engine and transaxle assembly in the vehicle. Connect the negative battery cable.

3.0L Engine Except SHO

1. Disconnect the negative battery cable.
2. Loosen the 4 water pump pulley bolts while the water pump drive belt is in place.
3. Loosen the alternator belt-adjuster jackscrew to provide enough slack in the alternator drive belt for removal.
4. Using a $1/2$ in. drive breaker bar, rotate the automatic belt tensioner down and to the left to remove the water pump drive belt.
5. Drain the cooling system.
6. Remove the lower radiator hose and the heater hose from the water pump.
7. Remove the crankshaft pulley and damper.
8. Drain and remove the oil pan.
9. Remove the retaining bolts from the timing cover to the block and remove the timing cover.

NOTE: *The timing cover and water pump may be removed as an assembly by not removing bolts 11–15.*

To install:

10. Lightly oil all bolt and stud threads except those specifying special sealant.
11. Clean all old gasket material and sealer from the timing cover, oil pan and cylinder block.
12. Inspect the timing cover seal for wear or damage and replace if necessary.
13. Align a new timing cover gasket over the cylinder block dowels.
14. Install the timing cover/water pump assembly onto the cylinder block with the water pump pulley loosely attached to the water pump hub.
15. Apply pipe sealant to bolt numbers 1, 2 and 3 and hand start them along with the rest of the cover retaining bolts. Tighten bolts 1–10 to 19 ft. lbs. (25 Nm) and 11–15 to 7 ft. lbs. (10 Nm).
16. Install the oil pan and tighten the retaining bolts to 9 ft. lbs. (12 Nm).
17. Hand tighten the water pump pulley retaining bolts.
18. Install the crankshaft damper and pulley. Torque the damper bolt to 107 ft. lbs. (145 Nm) and the 4 pulley bolts to 26 ft. lbs. (35 Nm).
19. Install the automatic belt tensioner.

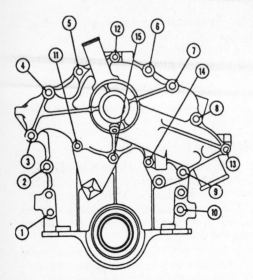

**Water pump and front cover bolt identification —
3.0L engine except SHO**

Tighten the 2 retaining nuts and bolt to 35 ft. lbs. (48 Nm).

20. Install the water pump and accessory drive belts. Torque the water pump pulley retaining bolts to 16 ft. lbs. (21 Nm).

21. Install the lower radiator hose and the heater hose and tighten the clamps.

22. Fill the crankcase with the correct amount and type of engine oil. Connect the negative battery cable. Fill and bleed the cooling system.

23. Start the engine and check for coolant and oil leaks.

3.8L Engine

1. Disconnect the negative battery cable. Drain the cooling system and crankcase.

2. Remove the air cleaner assembly and air intake duct.

3. Loosen the accessory drive belt idler. Remove the drive belt and water pump pulley.

4. Remove the power steering pump mounting bracket attaching bolts. Leaving the hoses connected, place the pump/bracket assembly in a position that will prevent the loss of power steering fluid.

5. If equipped with air conditioning, remove the compressor front support bracket. Leave the compressor in place.

6. Disconnect coolant bypass and heater hoses at the water pump. Disconnect radiator upper hose at thermostat housing.

7. Disconnect the coil wire from distributor cap and remove cap with secondary wires attached. Remove the distributor retaining clamp and lift distributor out of the front cover.

8. Raise the vehicle and support safely.

9. Remove the crankshaft damper and pulley.

NOTE: *If the crankshaft pulley and vibration damper have to be separated, mark the damper and pulley so they may be reassembled in the same relative position. This is important as the damper and pulley are initially balanced as a unit. If the crankshaft damper is being replaced, check if the original damper has balance pins installed. If so, new balance pins (E0SZ–6A328–A or equivalent) must be installed on the new damper in the same position as the original damper. The crankshaft pulley must also be installed in the original installation position.*

10. Remove the oil filter, disconnect the radiator lower hose at the water pump and remove the oil pan.

11. Lower the vehicle.

12. Remove the front cover attaching bolts.

NOTE: *Do not overlook the cover attaching bolt located behind the oil filter adapter. The front cover will break if pried upon if all attaching bolts are not removed.*

13. Remove the ignition timing indicator.

14. Remove the front cover and water pump as an assembly. Remove the cover gasket and discard.

NOTE: *The front cover houses the oil pump. If a new front cover is to be installed, remove the water pump and oil pump from the old front cover.*

To install:

15. Lightly oil all bolt and stud threads before installation. Clean all gasket surfaces on the front cover, cylinder block and fuel pump. If reusing the front cover, replace crankshaft front oil seal.

16. If a new front cover is to be installed, complete the following:

    a. Install the oil pump gears.

    b. Clean the water pump gasket surface. Position a new water pump gasket on the front cover and install the water pump. Install the pump attaching bolts and tighten to 15–22 ft. lbs.

17. Install the distributor drive gear.

18. Lubricate the crankshaft front oil seal with clean engine oil.

19. Position a new cover gasket on the cylinder block and install the front cover/water pump assembly using dowels for proper alignment. A suitable contact adhesive is recommended to hold the gasket in position while the front cover is installed.

20. Position the ignition timing indicator.

21. Install the front cover attaching bolts. Apply Loctite® or equivalent, to the threads of the bolt installed below the oil filter housing prior to installation. This bolt is to be installed

and tightened last. Tighten all bolts to 15–22 ft. lbs. (20–30 Nm).

22. Raise the vehicle and support safely.

23. Install the oil pan. Connect the radiator lower hose. Install a new oil filter.

24. Coat the crankshaft damper sealing surface with clean engine oil.

25. Position the crankshaft pulley key in the crankshaft keyway.

26. Install the damper with damper washer and attaching bolt. Tighten the bolt to 104–132 ft. lbs. (140–180 Nm).

27. Install the crankshaft pulley and tighten the attaching bolts 19–28 ft. lbs. (26–28 Nm).

28. Lower the vehicle.

29. Connect the coolant bypass hose.

30. Install the distributor with rotor pointing at No. 1 distributor cap tower. Install the distributor cap and coil wire.

31. Connect the radiator upper hose at thermostat housing.

32. Connect the heater hose.

33. If equipped with air conditioning, install compressor and mounting brackets.

34. Install the power steering pump and mounting brackets.

35. Position the accessory drive belt over the pulleys.

36. Install the water pump pulley. Position the accessory drive belt over water pump pulley and tighten the belt.

37. Connect battery ground cable. Fill the crankcase and cooling system to the proper level.

38. Start the engine and check for leaks.

39. Check the ignition timing and curb idle speed, adjust as required.

40. Install the air cleaner assembly and air intake duct.

Timing Chain Cover Oil Seal

REPLACEMENT

2.5L Engine

NOTE: *The removal and installation of the front cover oil seal on these engines can only be accomplished with the engine removed from the vehicle.*

1. Remove the engine from the vehicle and position in a suitable holding fixture.

2. Remove the bolt and washer at the crankshaft pulley.

3. Remove the crankshaft pulley.

4. Remove the front cover oil seal.

5. Coat a new seal with grease. Install and drive the seal until it is fully seated. Check the seal after installation to be sure the spring is properly positioned in the seal.

6. Install the crankshaft pulley, attaching

bolt and washer. Tighten the crankshaft pulley bolt to 140–170 ft. lbs. (190–230 Nm).

3.0L Engine Except SHO

1. Disconnect the negative battery cable and remove the accessory drive belts.

2. Raise the vehicle and support safely. Remove the right front wheel and tire assembly.

3. Remove the pulley-to-damper attaching bolts and remove the crankshaft pulley.

4. Remove the crankshaft damper retaining bolt and washer. Remove the damper from the crankshaft using a damper removal tool.

5. Pry the seal from the timing cover with a suitable tool and be careful not to damage the front cover and crankshaft.

To install:

NOTE: *Before installation, inspect the front cover and shaft seal surface of the crankshaft damper for damage, nicks, burrs or other roughness which may cause the new seal to fail. Service or replace components as necessary.*

6. Lubricate the seal lip with clean engine oil and install the seal using a seal installer tool.

7. Coat the crankshaft damper sealing surface with clean engine oil. Apply RTV to the keyway of the damper prior to installation. Install the damper using a damper seal installer tool. Install the damper retaining bolt and washer. Tighten to 107 ft. lbs. (145 Nm).

8. Position the crankshaft pulley and install the attaching bolts. Tighten the attaching bolts to 26 ft. lbs. (35 Nm).

9. Install the right front wheel and tire assembly and lower the vehicle.

10. Position the drive belt over the crankshaft pulley. Check the drive belt for proper routing and engagement in the pulleys.

11. Reconnect the negative battery cable and start the engine and check for oil leaks.

3.8L Engine

1. Disconnect the negative battery cable.

2. Loosen the accessory drive belt idler.

3. Raise the vehicle and support safely.

4. Disengage the accessory drive belt and remove crankshaft pulley.

5. Remove the crankshaft damper using a suitable removal tool.

6. Remove the seal from the front cover with a suitable prying tool. Use care to prevent damage to front cover and crankshaft.

To install:

NOTE: *Inspect the front cover and crankshaft damper for damage, nicks, burrs or other roughness which may cause the seal to fail. Service or replace components as necessary.*

7. Lubricate the seal lip with clean engine oil and install the seal using suitable seal installer.

8. Lubricate the seal surface on the damper with clean engine oil. Install damper and pulley assembly. Install the damper attaching bolt and tighten to 103–132 ft. lbs. (140–180 Nm).

9. Position the crankshaft pulley and install the retaining bolts. Tighten to 19–28 ft. lbs. (26–38 Nm).

10. Position accessory drive belt over crankshaft pulley.

11. Lower the vehicle.

12. Check accessory drive belt for proper routing and engagement in the pulleys. Adjust the drive belt tension.

13. Connect the negative battery cable. Start the engine and check for leaks.

Timing Chain And Sprockets

REMOVAL AND INSTALLATION

CAUTION: *When draining the coolant, keep in mind that cats and dogs are attracted by the ethylene glycol antifreeze, and are quite likely to drink any that is left in an uncovered container or in puddles on the ground. This will prove fatal in sufficient quantity. Always drain the coolant into a sealable container. Coolant should be reused unless it is contaminated or several years old. The*

EPA warns that prolonged contact with used engine oil may cause a number of skin disorders, including cancer! You should make every effort to minimize your exposure to used engine oil. Protective gloves should be worn when changing the oil. Wash your hands and any other exposed skin areas as soon as possible after exposure to used engine oil. Soap and water, or waterless hand cleaner should be used.

2.5L Engine

1. Remove the engine and transaxle from the vehicle as an assembly and position in a suitable holding fixture. Remove the dipstick.

2. Remove accessory drive pulley, if equipped, Remove the crankshaft pulley attaching bolt and washer and remove pulley.

3. Remove front cover attaching bolts from front cover. Pry the top of the front cover away from the block.

4. Clean any gasket material from the surfaces.

5. Check timing chain and sprockets for excessive wear. If the timing chain and sprockets are worn, replace with new.

6. Check timing chain tensioner blade for wear depth. If the wear depth exceeds specification, replace tensioner.

7. Turn engine over until the timing marks are aligned. Remove camshaft sprocket attach-

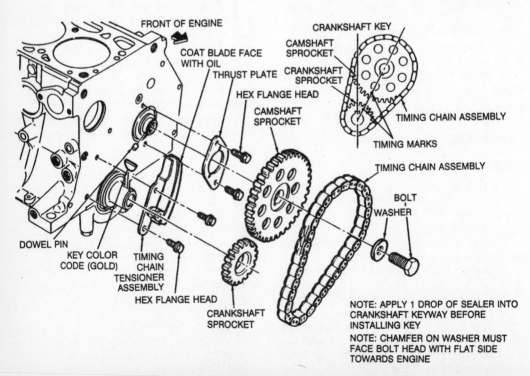

Timing chain alignment and related components — 2.5L engine

ing bolt and washer. Slide both sprockets and timing chain forward and remove as an assembly.

8. If equipped, check timing chain vibration damper for excessive wear. Replace if necessary; the damper is located inside the front cover.

9. Remove the oil pan.

To install:

10. Clean and inspect all parts before installation. Clean the oil pan, cylinder block and front cover of gasket material and dirt.

11. Slide both sprockets and timing chain onto the camshaft and crankshaft with timing marks aligned. Install camshaft bolt and washer and tighten to 41–56 ft. lbs. (55–75 Nm). Oil timing chain, sprockets and tensioner after installation with clean engine oil.

12. Apply oil resistant sealer to a new front cover gasket and position gasket into front cover.

13. Remove the front cover oil seal and position the front cover on the engine.

14. Position front cover alignment tool T84P–6019–C or equivalent, onto the end of the crankshaft, ensuring the crank key is aligned with the keyway in the tool. Bolt the front cover to the engine and tighten the bolts to 6–8 ft. lbs. (8–12 Nm). Remove the front cover alignment tool.

15. Install a new front cover oil seal using a suitable seal installer. Lubricate the hub of the crankshaft pulley with polyethylene grease to prevent damage to the seal during installation and initial engine start. Install crankshaft pulley.

16. Install the oil pan.

17. Install the accessory drive pulley, if equipped.

18. Install crankshaft pulley attaching bolt and washer. Tighten to 140–170 ft. lbs. (190–230 Nm).

19. Remove engine from work stand and install in vehicle.

3.0L Engine Except SHO

1. Disconnect the negative battery cable. Drain the cooling system and crankcase. Remove the crankshaft pulley and front cover assemblies.

2. Rotate the crankshaft until the No. 1 piston is at the TDC on its compression stroke and the timing marks are aligned.

3. Remove the camshaft sprocket attaching bolt and washer. Slide both sprockets and timing chain forward and remove as an assembly.

4. Check the timing chain and sprockets for excessive wear. Replace if necessary.

To install:

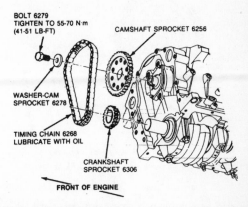

BOLT 6279 TIGHTEN TO 55–70 N·m (41–51 LB-FT)

CAMSHAFT SPROCKET 6256

WASHER-CAM SPROCKET 6278

TIMING CHAIN 6268 LUBRICATE WITH OIL

CRANKSHAFT SPROCKET 6306

FRONT OF ENGINE

Timing chain and sprocket assembly — 3.0L engine except SHO

NOTE: *Before installation, clean and inspect all parts. Clean the gasket material and dirt from the oil pan, cylinder block and front cover.*

5. Slide both sprockets and timing chain onto the camshaft and crankshaft with the timing marks aligned. Install the camshaft bolt and washer and torque to 46 ft. lbs. (63 Nm). Apply clean engine oil to the timing chain and sprockets after installation.

NOTE: *The camshaft bolt has a drilled oil passage in it for timing chain lubrication. If the bolt is damaged, do not replace it with a standard bolt.*

6. Install the timing cover and the crankshaft pulley and damper. Tighten the crankshaft damper bolt to 107 ft. lbs. (145 Nm) and the pulley bolts to 26 ft. lbs. (35 Nm).

7. Fill the crankcase with the proper type and quantity of oil and the cooling system with coolant. Connect the negative battery cable.

3.8L Engine

1. Disconnect the negative battery cable. Drain the cooling system and crankcase.

2. Remove the air cleaner assembly and air intake duct.

3. Loosen the accessory drive belt idler. Remove the drive belt and water pump pulley.

4. Remove the power steering pump mounting bracket attaching bolts. Leaving the hoses connected, place the pump/bracket assembly in a position that will prevent the loss of power steering fluid.

5. If equipped with air conditioning, remove the compressor front support bracket. Leave the compressor in place.

6. Disconnect coolant bypass and heater hoses at the water pump. Disconnect radiator upper hose at thermostat housing.

7. Disconnect the coil wire from distributor

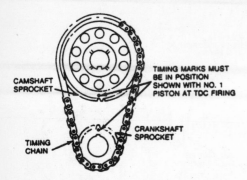

Timing chain alignment — 3.0L and 3.8L engines

cap and remove cap with secondary wires attached. Remove the distributor retaining clamp and lift distributor out of the front cover.

8. Raise the vehicle and support safely.

9. Remove the crankshaft damper and pulley.

NOTE: *If the crankshaft pulley and vibration damper have to be separated, mark the damper and pulley so they may be reassembled in the same relative position. This is important as the damper and pulley are initially balanced as a unit. If the crankshaft damper is being replaced, check if the original damper has balance pins installed. If so, new balance pins (E0SZ–6A328–A or equivalent) must be installed on the new damper in the same position as the original damper. The crankshaft pulley must also be installed in original installation position.*

10. Remove the oil filter, disconnect the radiator lower hose at the water pump and remove the oil pan.

11. Lower the vehicle.

12. Remove the front cover attaching bolts.

NOTE: *Do not overlook the cover attaching bolt located behind the oil filter adapter. The front cover will break if pried upon if all attaching bolts are not removed.*

13. Remove the ignition timing indicator.

14. Remove the front cover and water pump as an assembly. Remove the cover gasket and discard.

15. Remove the camshaft bolt and washer from end of the camshaft. Remove the distributor drive gear.

16. Remove the camshaft sprocket, crankshaft sprocket and timing chain.

17. Remove the chain tensioner assembly from the front of the cylinder block. This is accomplished by pulling back on the ratcheting mechanism and installing a pin through the hole in the bracket to relieve tension.

NOTE: *The front cover houses the oil pump. If a new front cover is to be installed, remove*

the water pump and oil pump from the old front cover.

To install:

18. Lightly oil all bolt and stud threads before installation. Clean all gasket surfaces on the front cover, cylinder block and fuel pump. If reusing the front cover, replace crankshaft front oil seal.

19. If a new front cover is to be installed, complete the following:

    a. Install the oil pump gears.

    b. Clean the water pump gasket surface. Position a new water pump gasket on the front cover and install water pump. Install the pump attaching bolts and tighten to 15–22 ft. lbs.

20. Rotate the crankshaft as necessary to position piston No. 1 at TDC and the crankshaft keyway at the 12 o' clock position.

21. Install the tensioner assembly. Make sure the ratcheting mechanism is in the retracted position with the pin pointing outward from the hole in the bracket assembly. Tighten the retaining bolts to 6–10 ft. lbs. (8–14 Nm).

22. Lubricate timing chain with clean engine oil. Install the camshaft sprocket, crankshaft sprocket and timing chain.

23. Remove the pin from the tensioner assembly. Make certain the timing marks are positioned across from each other.

24. Install the distributor drive gear.

25. Install the washer and bolt at end of camshaft and tighten to 30–37 ft. lbs. (40–50 Nm).

26. Lubricate the crankshaft front oil seal with clean engine oil.

27. Position a new cover gasket on the cylinder block and install the front cover/water pump assembly using dowels for proper alignment. A suitable contact adhesive is recommended to hold the gasket in position while the front cover is installed.

28. Position the ignition timing indicator.

29. Install the front cover attaching bolts. Apply Loctite® or equivalent, to the threads of the bolt installed below the oil filter housing prior to installation. This bolt is to be installed and tightened last. Tighten all bolts to 15–22 ft. lbs. (20–30 Nm).

30. Raise the vehicle and support safely.

31. Install the oil pan. Connect the radiator lower hose. Install a new oil filter.

32. Coat the crankshaft damper sealing surface with clean engine oil.

33. Position the crankshaft pulley key in the crankshaft keyway.

34. Install the damper with damper washer and attaching bolt. Tighten the bolt to 104–132 ft. lbs. (140–180 Nm).

35. Install the crankshaft pulley and tighten the attaching bolts 19–28 ft. lbs. (26–28 Nm).

36. Lower the vehicle.

37. Connect the coolant bypass hose.

38. Install the distributor with rotor pointing at No. 1 distributor cap tower. Install the distributor cap and coil wire.

39. Connect the radiator upper hose at thermostat housing.

40. Connect the heater hose.

41. If equipped with air conditioning, install compressor and mounting brackets.

42. Install the power steering pump and mounting brackets.

43. Position the accessory drive belt over the pulleys.

44. Install the water pump pulley. Position the accessory drive belt over water pump pulley and tighten the belt.

45. Connect battery ground cable. Fill the crankcase and cooling system to the proper level.

46. Start the engine and check for leaks.

47. Check the ignition timing and curb idle speed, adjust as required.

48. Install the air cleaner assembly and air intake duct.

Timing Belt Cover

REMOVAL AND INSTALLATION

3.0L SHO Engine

1. The front cover on the 3.0L SHO engine is made up of 3 sections. Disconnect the battery cables and remove the battery. Remove the right engine roll damper.

2. Disconnect the wiring to the ignition module. Remove the intake manifold crossover tube bolts, loosen the crossover tube clamps and remove the crossover tube.

3. Loosen the alternator/air conditioner belt tensioner pulley and relieve the tension on the belt by backing out the adjustment screw. Remove the belt.

4. Loosen the water pump/power steering belt tensioner pulley and relieve the tension on the belt by backing out the adjustment screw. Remove the belt.

5. Remove the alternator/air conditioner belt tensioner pulley and bracket assembly. Remove the water pump/power steering belt tensioner pulley only.

6. Remove the upper timing belt cover.

7. Disconnect the crankshaft sensor connectors.

8. Raise and safely support the vehicle. Remove the right front wheel and tire assembly.

9. Loosen the fender splash shield and move aside. Remove the crankshaft damper using a suitable puller.

10. Remove the center and lower timing belt covers.

11. Installation is the reverse of the removal procedure. Tighten the timing belt cover retaining bolts to 60–90 inch lbs. (7–11 Nm) and the crankshaft damper bolt to 113–126 ft. lbs. (152–172 Nm).

Timing Belt Cover Oil Seal

REPLACEMENT

3.0L SHO Engine

1. Loosen the accessory drive belts.

2. Raise the vehicle and support it safely.

3. Remove the right front wheel.

4. Remove the damper attaching bolt and the accessory drive belts from the crankshaft damper.

5. Using a suitable puller, remove the crankshaft damper from the crankshaft.

6. Remove the timing belt.

7. Remove the crankshaft timing gear using a suitable puller.

NOTE: *Be careful not to damage the crankshaft sensor or shutter.*

8. Remove the crankshaft front oil seal using a suitable puller.

To install:

9. Inspect the front cover and shaft seal surface of the crankshaft damper for damage, nicks, burrs or other roughness which may cause the new seal to fail. Repair or replace as necessary.

10. Using suitable tools, install a new crankshaft front oil seal and the crankshaft timing gear.

11. Install the timing belt.

12. Install the crankshaft damper using a suitable tool. Tighten the damper attaching bolt to 113–126 ft. lbs. (152–172 Nm).

13. Install the accessory drive belts.

14. Lower the vehicle.

15. Start the engine and check for oil leaks.

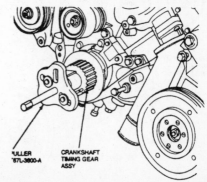

Lower timing cover removal tool — 3.0L SHO engine

Timing Belt and Tensioner

REMOVAL AND INSTALLATION

3.0L SHO Engine

1. Disconnect the battery cables.
2. Remove the battery.
3. Remove the right engine roll damper.
4. Disconnect the wiring to the ignition module.
5. Remove the intake manifold crossover tube bolts. Loosen the intake manifold tube hose clamps. Remove the intake manifold crossover tube.
6. Loosen the alternator/air conditioning belt tensioner pulley and relieve the tension on the belt by backing out the adjustment screw. Remove the alternator/air conditioning belt.
7. Loosen the water pump/power steering belt tensioner pulley and relieve the tension on the belt by backing out the adjustment screw. Remove the water pump/power steering belt.
8. Remove the alternator/air conditioning belt tensioner pulley and bracket assembly.
9. Remove the water pump/power steering belt tensioner pulley only.
10. Remove the upper timing belt cover.
11. Disconnect the crankshaft sensor connectors.
12. Place the gear selector in **N**.
13. Set the engine to the TDC on No. 1 cylinder position. Make sure the white mark on the crankshaft damper aligns with the **0** degree index mark on the lower timing belt cover and that the marks on the intake camshaft pulleys align with the index marks on the metal timing belt cover.
14. Raise the vehicle and support safely.

15. Remove the right front wheel and tire assembly.
16. Loosen the fender splash shield and place it aside.
17. Using a suitable puller, remove the crankshaft damper.
18. Remove the lower timing belt cover.
19. Remove the center timing belt cover and disconnect the crankshaft sensor wire and grommet from the slot in the cover and the stud on the water pump.
20. Loosen the timing belt tensioner, rotate the pulley 180° (¹/₂ turn) clockwise and tighten the tensioner nut to hold the pulley in the unload position.
21. Lower the vehicle and remove the timing belt.

To install:

NOTE: *Before installing the timing belt, inspect it for cracks, wear or other damage and replace, if necessary. Do not allow the timing belt to come into contact with gasoline, oil, water, coolant or steam. Do not twist or turn the belt inside out.*

22. Make sure the engine is at TDC on the No. 1 cylinder. Check that the camshaft pulley marks line up with the index marks on the upper steel belt cover and that the crankshaft pulley aligns with the idex mark on the oil pump housing. The timing belt has 3 yellow lines. Each line aligns with the index marks.
23. Install the timing belt over the crank-

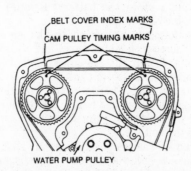

Camshaft pulley to belt cover index marks — 3.0L SHO engine

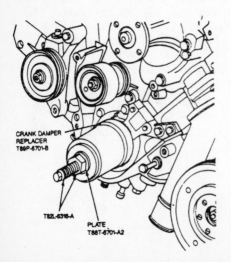

Crankshaft oil seal installation tool — 3.0L SHO engine

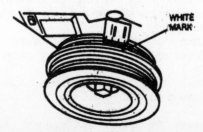

Crankshaft damper to lower timing cover index mark alignment — 3.0L SHO engine

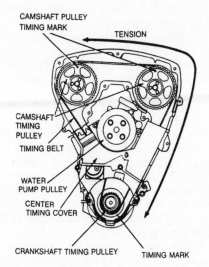

CAMSHAFT PULLEY
TIMING MARK

TENSION

CAMSHAFT
TIMING
PULLEY

TIMING BELT

WATER
PUMP PULLEY

CENTER
TIMING COVER

CRANKSHAFT TIMING PULLEY   TIMING MARK

Timing belt index marks — 3.0L SHO engine

shaft and camshaft pulleys. The lettering on the belt **KOA** should be readable from the rear of the engine; top of the lettering to the front of the engine. Make sure the yellow lines are aligned with the index marks on the pulleys.

24. Release the tensioner locknut and leave the nut loose.

25. Raise the vehicle and support safely.

26. Install the center timing belt cover. Make sure the crankshaft sensor wiring and grommet are installed and routed properly. Tighten the mounting bolts to 60–90 inch lbs. (7–11 Nm).

27. Install the lower timing belt cover. Tighten the bolts to 60–90 inch lbs. (7–11 Nm).

28. Using a suitable tool, install the crankshaft damper. Tighten the damper attaching bolt to 113–126 ft. lbs. (152–172 Nm).

29. Rotate the crankshaft 2 revolutions in the clockwise direction until the yellow mark on the damper aligns with the 0° mark on the lower timing belt cover.

30. Remove the plastic door in the lower timing belt cover. Tighten the tensioner locknut to 25–37 ft. lbs. (33–51 Nm) and install the plastic door.

31. Rotate the crankshaft 60° ($^3/_5$ turn) more in the clockwise direction until the white mark on the damper aligns with the 0° mark on the lower timing belt cover.

32. Lower the vehicle.

33. Make sure the index marks on the camshaft pulleys align with the marks on the rear metal timing belt cover.

34. Route the crankshaft sensor wiring and connect with the engine wiring harness.

35. Install the upper timing belt cover. Tighten the bolts to 60–90 inch lbs. (7–11 Nm).

36. Install the water pump/power steering tensioner pulley. Tighten the nut to 11–17 ft. lbs. (15–23 Nm).

37. Install the alternator/air conditioning tensioner pulley and bracket assembly. Tighten the bolts to 11–17 ft. lbs. (15–23 Nm).

38. Install the water pump/power steering and alternator/air conditioning belts and set the tension. Tighten the idler pulley nut to 25–36 ft. lbs. (34–50 Nm).

39. Install the intake manifold crossover tube. Tighten the bolts to 11–17 ft. lbs. (15–23 Nm).

40. Install the engine roll damper and the battery.

41. Connect the battery cables.

42. Raise the vehicle and support safely.

43. Install the splash shield and the right front wheel and tire assembly.

44. Lower the vehicle.

Timing Sprockets

REMOVAL AND INSTALLATION

3.0L SHO Engine

1. Disconnect the negative battery cable.

2. Remove the timing belt.

3. Remove the camshaft and crankshaft timing belt sprockets.

4. Install in the reverse order of removal. Tighten the camshaft timing belt sprocket bolts to 15–18 ft. lbs. (21–25 Nm) and the crankshaft pulley bolt to 113–126 ft. lbs. (152–172 Nm).

Camshaft

REMOVAL AND INSTALLATION

CAUTION: *When draining the coolant, keep in mind that cats and dogs are attracted by the ethylene glycol antifreeze, and are quite likely to drink any that is left in an uncovered container or in puddles on the ground. This will prove fatal in sufficient quantity. Always drain the coolant into a sealable container. Coolant should be reused unless it is contaminated or several years old.*

2.5L Engine

1. Drain the cooling system and the crankcase. Relieve the fuel system pressure.

2. Remove the engine from the vehicle and position in a suitable holding fixture. Remove the engine oil dipstick.

3. Remove necessary drive belts and pulleys.

4. Remove cylinder head.

5. Using a magnet, remove the hydraulic lifters and label them so they can be installed in

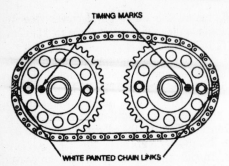

Camshaft sprocket timing marks — 3.0L SHO engine

their original positions. If the tappets are stuck in the bores by excessive varnish, etc., use a suitable claw-type puller to remove the tappets.

6. Loosen and remove the drive belt, fan and pulley and crankshaft pulley.

7. Remove the oil pan.

8. Remove the cylinder front cover and gasket.

9. Check the camshaft endplay as follows:

   a. Push the camshaft toward the rear of the engine and install a dial indicator tool, so the indicator point is on the camshaft sprocket attaching screw.

   b. Zero the dial indicator. Position a small prybar or equivalent, between the camshaft sprocket or gear and block.

   c. Pull the camshaft forward and release it. Compare the dial indicator reading with the camshaft endplay specification of 0.009 in. (0.23mm).

   d. If the camshaft endplay is over the amount specified, replace the thrust plate.

10. Remove the timing chain, sprockets and timing chain tensioner.

11. Remove camshaft thrust plate. Carefully remove the camshaft by pulling it toward the front of the engine. Use caution to avoid damaging bearings, journals and lobes.

To install:

12. Clean and inspect all parts before installation.

13. Lubricate camshaft lobes and journals with heavy engine oil. Carefully slide the camshaft through the bearings in the cylinder block.

14. Install the thrust plate. Tighten attaching bolts to 6–9 ft. lbs. (8–12 Nm).

15. Install the timing chain, sprockets and timing chain tensioner.

16. Install the cylinder front cover and crankshaft pulley.

17. Clean the oil pump inlet tube screen, oil pan and cylinder block gasket surfaces. Prime oil pump by filling the inlet opening with oil and rotate the pump shaft until oil emerges

from the outlet tube. Install oil pump, oil pump inlet tube screen and oil pan.

18. Install the accessory drive belts and pulleys.

19. Lubricate the lifters and lifter bores with heavy engine oil. Install tappets into their original bores.

20. Install cylinder head.

21. Install the engine assembly.

22. Position No. 1 piston at TDC after the compression stroke. Position distributor in the block with the rotor at the No. 1 firing position. Install distributor retaining clamp.

23. Connect engine temperature sending unit wire. Connect coil primary wire. Install distributor cap. Connect spark plug wires and the coil high tension lead.

24. Fill the cooling system and crankcase to the proper levels. Connect the negative battery cable.

25. Start the engine. Check and adjust ignition timing. Check for leaks.

3.0L Except SHO Engine

1. Drain the cooling system and crankcase. Relieve the fuel system pressure.

2. Remove the engine from the vehicle and position in a suitable holding fixture.

3. Remove the accessory drive components from the front of the engine.

4. Remove the throttle body and the fuel injector harness. Remove the distributor assembly.

5. Remove and tag the spark plug wires and rocker arm covers. Loosen the rocker arm fulcrum nuts and position the rocker arms to the side for easy access to the pushrods. Remove the pushrods and label so they may be installed in their original positions.

6. Remove the intake manifold.

7. Using a suitable magnet or lifter removal tool, remove the hydraulic lifters and keep them in order so they can be installed in their original positions. If the lifters are stuck in the bores by excessive varnish use a hydraulic lifter puller to remove the lifters.

8. Remove the crankshaft pulley and damper using a suitable removal tool. Remove the oil pan assembly.

9. Remove the front cover assembly. Align the timing marks on the camshaft and crankshaft gears. Check the camshaft endplay as follows:

   a. Push the camshaft toward the rear of the engine and install a dial indicator tool, so the indicator point is on the camshaft sprocket attaching screw.

   b. Zero the dial indicator. Position a small prybar or equivalent, between the camshaft sprocket or gear and block.

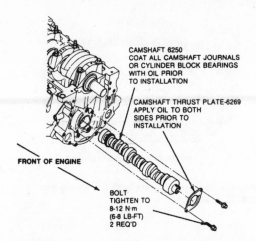

CAMSHAFT 6250
COAT ALL CAMSHAFT JOURNALS
OR CYLINDER BLOCK BEARINGS
WITH OIL PRIOR
TO INSTALLATION

CAMSHAFT THRUST PLATE-6269
APPLY OIL TO BOTH
SIDES PRIOR TO
INSTALLATION

FRONT OF ENGINE

BOLT
TIGHTEN TO
8-12 N·m
(6-8 LB-FT)
2 REQ'D

Camshaft removal — 3.0L engine except SHO engine

c. Pull the camshaft forward and release it. Compare the dial indicator reading with the camshaft endplay service limit specification of 0.005 in. (0.13mm).

d. If the camshaft endplay is over the amount specified, replace the thrust plate.

10. Remove the timing chain and sprockets.

11. Remove the camshaft thrust plate. Carefully remove the camshaft by pulling it toward the front of the engine. Remove it slowly to avoid damaging the bearings, journals and lobes.

To install:

12. Clean and inspect all parts before installation.

13. Lubricate camshaft lobes and journals with heavy engine oil. Carefully insert the camshaft through the bearings in the cylinder block.

14. Install the thrust plate. Tighten the retaining bolts to 7 ft. lbs. (10 Nm).

15. Install the timing chain and sprockets. Check the camshaft sprocket bolt for blockage of drilled oil passages prior to installation and clean, if necessary.

16. Install the front timing cover and crankshaft damper and pulley.

17. Lubricate the lifters and lifter bores with a heavy engine oil. Install the lifters into their original bores.

18. Install the intake manifold assembly.

19. Lubricate the pushrods and rocker arms with heavy engine oil. Install the pushrods and rocker arms into their original positions. Rotate the crankshaft to set each lifter on its base circle, then tighten the rocker arm bolt. Tighten the rocker arm bolts to 24 ft. lbs. (32 Nm).

20. Install the oil pan and the rocker covers.

21. Install the fuel injector harness and the throttle body. Install the distributor and connect the spark plug wires to the spark plugs.

22. Install the accessory drive components and install the engine assembly.

23. Connect the negative battery cable. Start the engine and check for leaks. Check and adjust the ignition timing.

3.0L SHO Engine

1. Disconnect the negative battery cable. Properly relieve the fuel system pressure.

2. Set the engine on TDC on No. 1 cylinder.

3. Remove the intake manifold assembly.

4. Remove the timing cover and belt.

5. Remove the cylinder head covers.

6. Remove the camshaft pulleys, noting the location of the dowel pins.

7. Remove the upper rear timing belt cover.

8. Uniformly loosen the camshaft bearing caps.

NOTE: *If the camshaft bearing caps are not uniformly loosened, camshaft damage may result.*

9. Remove the bearing caps and note their positions for installation.

10. Remove the camshaft chain tensioner mounting bolts.

11. Remove the camshafts together with chain and tensioner.

12. Remove and discard the camshaft oil seal.

13. Remove the chain sprocket from the camshaft.

To install:

14. Align the timing marks on the chain sprockets with the camshaft and install the sprockets. Tighten the bolts to 10–13 ft. lbs. (14–18 Nm).

15. Install the chain over the camshaft sprockets. Align the white painted link with the timing mark on the sprocket.

16. Rotate the camshafts 60° ($\frac{3}{5}$ turn) counterclockwise. Set the chain tensioner between the sprockets and install the camshafts on the cylinder head. The left and right chain tensioners are not interchangeable.

17. Apply a thin coat of engine oil to the camshaft journals and install bearing caps No. 2 through No. 5 and loosely install the bolts.

NOTE: *The arrows on the bearing caps point to the front of the engine when installed.*

18. Apply silicone sealer to outer diameter of the new camshaft seal and the seal seating area on the cylinder head. Install the camshaft seal.

19. Apply silicone sealer to the No. 1 bearing cap and install the bearing cap.

20. Tighten the bearing caps in sequence using a 2 step method. Tighten to 12–16 ft. lbs. (16–22 Nm). For left camshaft installation,

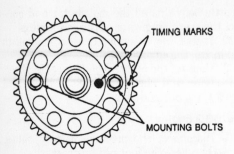

Timing chain sprocket and camshaft alignment — 3.0L SHO engine

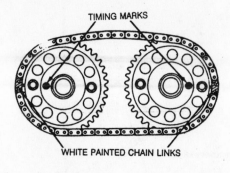

Aligning the timing chain with the timing marks — 3.0L SHO engine

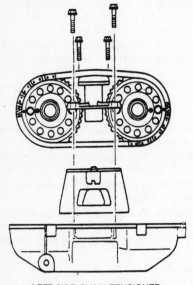

LEFT SIDE CHAIN TENSIONER

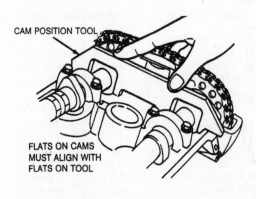

Camshaft positioning tool — 3.0L SHO engine

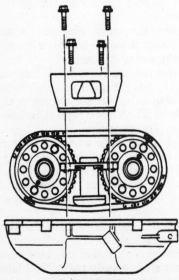

RIGHT SIDE CHAIN TENSIONER

Timing chain tensioner installation — 3.0L SHO engine

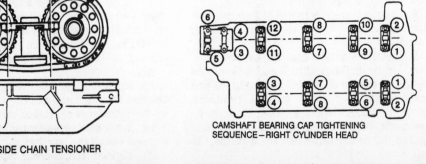

CAMSHAFT BEARING CAP TIGHTENING SEQUENCE—LEFT CYLINDER HEAD

CAMSHAFT BEARING CAP TIGHTENING SEQUENCE—RIGHT CYLINDER HEAD

Camshaft bearing cap bolt torque sequence — 3.0L SHO engine

apply pressure to the chain tensioner to avoid damage to the bearing caps.

21. Install the chain tensioner and tighten the bolts to 11–14 ft. lbs. (15–19 Nm). Rotate the camshafts 60° (⅗ turn) clockwise and check for proper alignment of the timing marks. Marks on the camshaft sprockets should align with the cylinder head cover mating surface.

22. Install the camshaft positioning tool T89P–6256–C or equivalent, on the camshafts to check for correct positioning. The flats on the tool should align with the flats on the camshaft. If the tool does not fit and/or timing marks will not line up, repeat the procedure from Step 14.

23. Install the timing belt rear cover and tighten the bolts to 70 inch lbs. (8.8 Nm).

24. Install the camshaft pulleys and tighten the bolts to 15–18 ft. lbs. (21–25 Nm).

25. Install the timing belt and cover.

26. Install the cylinder head covers and tighten the bolts to 8–11 ft. lbs. (10–16 Nm).

27. Install the intake manifold assembly.

3.8L Engine

1. Disconnect the negative battery cable.

2. Properly relieve the fuel system pressure.

3. Drain the cooling system and crankcase.

4. Remove the engine from the vehicle and position in a suitable holding fixture.

5. Remove the intake manifold.

6. Remove the rocker arm covers, rocker arms, pushrods and lifters.

7. Remove the oil pan.

8. Remove the front cover and timing chain.

9. Remove the thrust plate. Remove the camshaft through the front of the engine, being careful not to damage bearing surfaces.

To install:

10. Lightly oil all attaching bolts and stud threads before installation. Lubricate the cam lobes, thrust plate and bearing surfaces with a suitable heavy engine oil.

11. Install the camshaft being careful not to damage bearing surfaces while sliding into position. Install the thrust plate and tighten the bolts to 6–10 ft. lbs. (8–14 Nm).

12. Install the front cover and timing chain.

13. Install the oil pan.

14. Install the lifters.

15. Install the upper and lower intake manifolds.

16. Install the engine assembly.

17. Fill the cooling system and crankcase to the proper level and connect the negative battery cable.

18. Start the engine. Check and adjust the ignition timing and engine idle speed as necessary. Check for leaks.

INSPECTION

1. Remove the camshaft from the engine.

2. Check each lobe for excessive wear, flatness, pitting or other physical damage. Replace the camshaft as required.

3. Using a micrometer mic the lobes, if not within specification, replace the camshaft.

4. If replacing the camshaft be sure to check and replace the valve lifters.

Balance Shaft

REMOVAL AND INSTALLATION

CAUTION: *When draining the coolant, keep in mind that cats and dogs are attracted by the ethylene glycol antifreeze, and are quite likely to drink any that is left in an uncovered container or in puddles on the ground. This will prove fatal in sufficient quantity. Always drain the coolant into a sealable container. Coolant should be reused unless it is contaminated or several years old. The EPA warns that prolonged contact with used engine oil may cause a number of skin disorders, including cancer! You should make every effort to minimize your exposure to used engine oil. Protective gloves should be worn when changing the oil. Wash your hands and any other exposed skin areas as soon as possible after exposure to used engine oil. Soap and water, or waterless hand cleaner should be used.*

3.8L Engine

1. Remove the engine from the vehicle.

2. Remove the intake manifolds.

3. Remove the oil pan.

4. Remove the front cover and timing chain and camshaft sprocket.

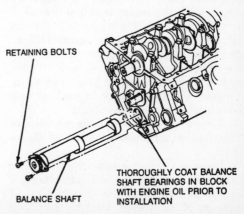

RETAINING BOLTS

THOROUGHLY COAT BALANCE SHAFT BEARINGS IN BLOCK WITH ENGINE OIL PRIOR TO INSTALLATION

BALANCE SHAFT

Balancer shaft assembly and related components – 3.8L engine

5. Remove the balance shaft drive gear and spacer.

6. Remove the balance shaft gear, thrust plate and shaft assembly.

To install:

7. Thoroughly coat the balance shaft bearings in the block with engine oil.

8. Install the balance shaft gear.

9. Install the balance shaft, thrust plate and gear and tighten the retaining bolts to 6–10 ft. lbs. (8–14 Nm).

10. Install the timing chain and camshaft sprocket.

11. Install the oil pan.

12. Install the timing cover.

13. Install the intake manifolds.

14. Install the engine in the vehicle.

Piston and Connecting Rods

REMOVAL AND INSTALLATION

CAUTION: *When draining the coolant, keep in mind that cats and dogs are attracted by the ethylene glycol antifreeze, and are quite likely to drink any that is left in an uncovered container or in puddles on the ground. This will prove fatal in sufficient quantity. Always drain the coolant into a sealable container. Coolant should be reused unless it is contaminated or several years old.   The EPA warns that prolonged contact with used engine oil may cause a number of skin disorders, including cancer! You should make every effort to minimize your exposure to used engine oil. Protective gloves should be worn when changing the oil. Wash your hands and any other exposed skin areas as soon as possible after exposure to used engine oil. Soap and water, or waterless hand cleaner should be used.*

1. Although, in most cases, the pistons and connecting rods can be removed from the engine (after the cylinder head and oil pan are removed) while the engine is still in the car, it is far easier to remove the engine from the car. If removing pistons with the engine still installed, disconnect the radiator hoses, automatic transmission cooler lines and radiator shroud. Unbolt front mounts before jacking up the engine. Block the engine in position with wooden blocks between the mounts.

2. Remove the engine from the car. Remove cylinder head(s), oil pan and front cover (if necessary).

3. Because the top piston ring does not travel to the very top of the cylinder bore, a ridge is built up between the end of the travel and the top of the cylinder. Pushing the piston and connecting rod assembly past the ridge is difficult and may cause damage to the piston. If

new rings are installed and the ridge has not been removed, ring breakage and piston damage can occur when the ridge is encountered at engine speed.

4. Turn the crankshaft to position the piston at the bottom of the cylinder bore. Cover the top of the piston with a rag. Install a cylinder ridge reamer part No. T64L-6011-EA in the bore and follow the manufacturer's instructions to remove the ridge. Use caution. Avoid cutting too deeply or into the ring travel area. Remove the rag and medal cuttings from the top of the piston. Remove the ridge from all cylinders.

5. Check the edges of the connecting rod and bearing cap for numbers or matchmarks, if none are present mark the rod and cap numerically and in sequence from front to back of engine. The numbers or marks not only tell from which cylinder the piston came from but also ensures that the rod caps are installed in the correct matching position.

6. Turn the crankshaft until the connecting rod is at the bottom of the travel. Remove the two attaching nuts and the bearing cap. Take two pieces of rubber tubing and cover the rod bolts to prevent crank or cylinder scoring. Use a wooden hammer handle to help push the piston and rod up and out of the cylinder. Reinstall the rod cap in proper position. Remove all pistons and connecting rods. Inspect cylinder walls and deglaze or hone using a cylinder hone set part No. T73L-6011-A or equivalent.

To install:

7. Lubricate each piston, rod bearing, and cylinder wall with heavy weight engine oil.

8. Take the bearing nuts and cap off connecting rod. Install rubber hoses over the connecting rod bolts to protect the block and crankshaft journal.

9. Install a ring compressor over the piston, position piston with the mark toward front of engine and carefully install.

10. Position the connecting rod with bearing insert over the crank journal. Install the rod cap with bearing in proper position. Secure with rod nuts and torque to the proper specifications. Install all of the rod and piston assemblies.

CLEANING AND INSPECTION

1. Use a piston ring expander and remove the rings from the piston.

2. Clean the ring grooves using piston ring groove cleaner part No. D81L-6002-D or equivalent. Exercise care to avoid cutting too deeply.

3. Clean all varnish and carbon from the piston with a safe solvent. Do not use a wire brush or caustic solution on the pistons.

4. Inspect the pistons for scuffing, scoring,

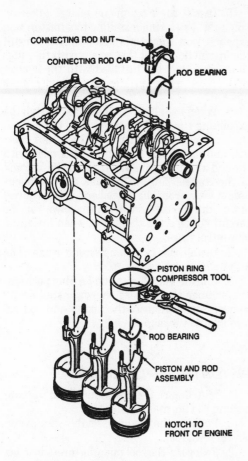

Piston and connecting rod assembly — 2.5L engine

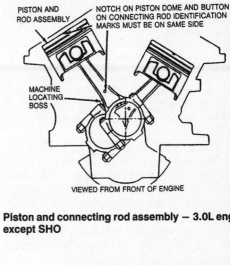

Piston and connecting rod assembly — 3.0L engine except SHO

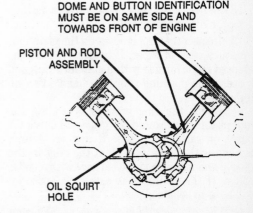

Piston and connecting rod assembly — 3.8L engine

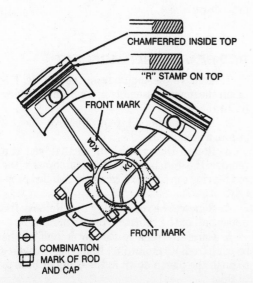

Piston and connecting rod assembly — 3.0L SHO engine

cracks, pitting or excessive ring groove wear. If wear is evident, the piston must be replaced.

5. Have the piston and connecting rod assembly checked by a machine shop for correct alignment, piston pin wear and piston diameter. If the piston has collapsed it will have to be replace or knurled to restore original diameter. Connecting rod bushing replacement, piston pin fitting and piston changing can be handled by the machine shop.

CYLINDER BORE

Check the cylinder bore for wear using a telescope gauge and a micrometer, measure the cylinder bore diameter perpendicular to the piston pin at a point 63.5mm below the top of the engine block. Measure the piston skirt perpendicular to the piston pin. The difference between the two measurements is the piston clearance. If the clearance is within specifications, finish honing or glaze breaking is all that is required. If clearance is excessive a slightly over-size piston may be required. If greatly oversize, the engine will have to be bored and oversized pistons installed.

PISTON RING REPLACEMENT

1. Take the new piston rings and compress them, one at a time into the cylinder that they will be used in. Press the ring about 25mm below the top of the cylinder block using an inverted piston.

2. Use a feeler gauge and measure the distance between the ends of the ring. This is called measuring the ring end gap. Compare the reading to the one called for in the specifications table. If the measurement is too small, when the engine heats up the ring ends will butt together and cause damage. File the ends of the ring with a fine file to obtain necessary clearance.

NOTE: *If inadequate ring end gap is utilized, ring breakage will result.*

3. Inspect the ring grooves on the piston for excessive wear or taper. If necessary, have the grooves recut for use with a standard ring and spacer. The machine shop can handle the job for you.

4. Check the ring grooves by rolling the new piston ring around the groove to check for burrs or carbon deposits. If any are found, remove with a fine file. Hold the ring in the groove and measure side clearance with a feeler gauge. If the clearance is excessive, spacer(s) will have to be added.

NOTE: *Always add spacers above the piston ring.*

5. Install the ring on the piston, lower oil ring first. Use a ring installing tool (piston ring expander) on the compression rings. Consult the instruction sheet that comes with the rings to be sure they are installed with the correct side up. A mark on the ring usually faces upward.

6. When installing oil rings, first, install the expanding ring in the groove. Hold the ends of the ring butted together (they must not overlap) and install the bottom rail (scraper) with the end about 25mm away from the butted end of the control ring. Install the top rail about 25mm away from the butted end of the control but on the opposite side from the lower rail. Be careful not to scrap the piston when installing oil control rings.

7. Install the two compression rings. The lower ring first.

8. Consult the illustration for ring positioning, arrange the rings as shown, install a ring compressor and insert the piston and rod assembly into the engine.

PISTON PIN REPLACEMENT

1. Matchmark the piston head and the connecting rod for reassembly.

2. Position the piston assembly in a piston pin removal tool.

3. Following the tool manufacturers instructions, press the piston pin from the piston.

4. Check the piston pin bore for damage, replace defective components as required. Check the piston pin for damage, replace as required.

5. Installation is the reverse of the removal procedure.

ROD BEARING REPLACEMENT

1. Remove the engine from the vehicle. Position the engine assembly in a suitable holding fixture.

2. Remove the oil pan. Remove the oil pump, as required.

3. Rotate the crankshaft so that you can remove the rod bearing cap. Matchmark the rod bearing cap so that it can be reinstalled properly.

4. Remove the rod bearing cap. Remove the upper half of the bearing from its mounting.

5. Carefully remove the lower half of the bearing from its mounting. It may be necessary to push the piston down in the cylinder bore to to this.

6. Installation is the reverse of the removal procedure.

2ND. COMP. RING
LOWER SIDE RAIL
FRONT MARK
60°
EXPANDER
30°
UPPER SIDE RAIL
1ST. COMP RING

Piston ring positioning

Rear Main Seal

REMOVAL AND INSTALLATION

1. Disconnect the negative battery cable.
2. Raise the vehicle and support it safely. Remove the transaxle.
3. Remove flywheel. Remove the cover plate, if necessary.
4. With a suitable tool, remove the oil seal.
NOTE: *Use caution to avoid damaging the oil seal surface.*
To install:
5. Inspect the crankshaft seal area for any damage which may cause the seal to leak. If damage is evident, service or replace the crankshaft as necessary.
6. Coat the crankshaft seal area and the seal lip with engine oil.
7. Using a seal installer tool, install the seal. Tighten the 2 bolts of the seal installer tool evenly so the seal is straight and seats without mis-alignment.
8. Install the flywheel. Tighten attaching bolts to 54–64 ft. lbs. (73–87 Nm) on all except the 3.0L SHO engine. On the 3.0L SHO engine, tighten the bolts to 51–58 ft. lbs. (69–78 Nm).
9. Install rear cover plate, if necessary.
10. Install the transaxle and connect the negative battery cable.

Crankshaft and Main Bearings

REMOVAL AND INSTALLATION

CAUTION: *When draining the coolant, keep in mind that cats and dogs are attracted by the ethylene glycol antifreeze, and are quite likely to drink any that is left in an uncovered container or in puddles on the ground. This will prove fatal in sufficient quantity. Always drain the coolant into a sealable container. Coolant should be reused unless it is contaminated or several years old. The EPA warns that prolonged contact with used engine oil may cause a number of skin disorders, including cancer! You should make*

Rear main bearing seal installation — 3.0L engine except SHO

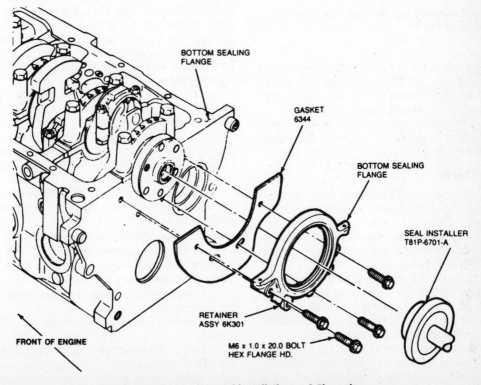

Rear main bearing seal installation — 2.5L engine

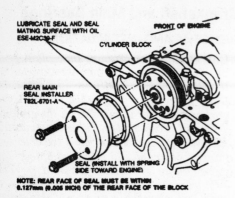

Rear main bearing seal installation — 3.8L engine

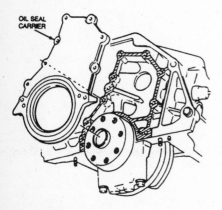

Rear main bearing seal and seal carrier installation — 3.0L SHO engine

every effort to minimize your exposure to used engine oil. Protective gloves should be worn when changing the oil. Wash your hands and any other exposed skin areas as soon as possible after exposure to used engine oil. Soap and water, or waterless hand cleaner should be used.

2.5L Engine

1. With the engine removed from the vehicle and placed on a work stand, remove the oil level dipstick.

2. Remove the accessory drive pulley, if so equipped. Remove the crankshaft pulley attaching bolts and washer.

3. Remove the cylinder front cover and the air conditioning idler pulley assembly, if so equipped. Remove cover assembly.

4. Check the timing chain deflection. Remove the timing chain and sprockets.

5. Invert the engine on work stand. Remove the flywheel and the rear seal cover. Remove the oil pan and gasket. Remove the oil pump inlet and the oil pump assembly.

6. Ensure all bearing caps (main and connecting rod) are marked so they can be installed in their original positions. Turn the crankshaft until the connecting rod from which cap is being removed is up. Remove the connecting rod cap. Install rubber hose onto the connecting rod bolts to prevent journal damage. Push the connecting rod and piston assembly up in the cylinder and install the cap and nuts in their original positions. Repeat the procedure for the remaining connecting rod assemblies.

7. Remove the main bearing caps.

8. Carefully lift crankshaft out of block so upper thrust bearing surfaces are not damaged. Reinstall the main bearing caps on the block.

NOTE: *Handle the crankshaft with care to avoid possible fracture or damage to the finished surfaces.*

To install:

NOTE: *If the bearings are to be reused they should be identified to ensure that they are installed in their original position.*

1. Remove the main bearing inserts from the block and bearing caps.

2. Remove the connecting rod bearing inserts from connecting rods and caps.

3. Install a new rear oil seal in rear seal cover.

4. Apply a thin coat of Ford Polyethylene Grease D0AZ-19584-A (ESR-M1C159-A or ESB-M1C93-A) or equivalent, to the rear crankshaft surface. Do not apply sealer to the area forward of oil sealer groove. Inspect all the machined surfaces on the crankshaft for nicks, scratches or scores which could cause premature bearing wear.

5. If the crankshaft main bearing journals have been refinished to a definite undersize, install the correct undersize bearings, usually 0.25mm, 0.50mm, 0.80mm undersize. Ensure the bearing inserts and bearing bores are clean. Foreign material under the inserts will distort the bearing and cause a failure.

6. Place the upper main bearing inserts in position in the bores with the tang fitted in the slot provided.

NOTE: *Lubricate the bearing surfaces with Oil Conditioner part No. D9AZ-19579-CF or equivalent. Conditioner is needed for lubrication at initial start up.*

7. Install the lower main bearings inserts in the bearing caps.

8. Carefully lower the crankshaft into place.

9. Check the clearance of each main bearing. Select fit the bearings for proper clearance.

10. After the bearings have been fitted, apply a light coat of oil conditioner to journals

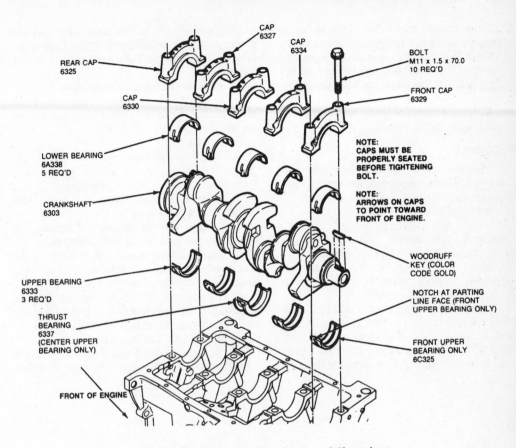

Crankshaft and related components — 2.5L engine

and bearings. Install all the bearing caps and torque to proper specifications.

NOTE: *The main bearing cap must be installed in their original positions.*

11. Align the upper thrust bearing.

12. Check the crankshaft end play, using a dial indicator mounted on the front of the engine.

13. If the end play exceeds specification, replace the upper thrust bearing. If the end play is less than the specification, inspect the thrust bearing faces for damage, dirt or improper alignment. Install the thrust bearing and align the faces. Check the end play.

14. Install the new bearing inserts in the connecting rods and caps. Install rubber hoses on the rod bolts to prevent crankshaft journal damage. Check the clearance of each bearing using a piece of Plastigage®.

15. If the bearing clearances are to specification, apply a light coat of Oil Conditioner part No. D9AZ-19579-CF to the journals and bearings.

16. Turn the crankshaft throw to the bottom of the stroke. Push the piston all the way down until the rod bearings seat on the crankshaft journal.

17. Install the connecting rod cap and nuts. Torque the nuts to specifications

18. After the piston and connecting rod assemblies have been installed, check all the connecting-rod-crankshaft journal clearances using a piece of Plastigage®.

19. Turn the engine on the work stand so the front end is up. Install the timing chain, sprockets, timing chain tensioner, front cover, oil seal and the crankshaft pulley.

20. Clean the oil pan, oil pump and the oil pump screen assembly.

21. Prime the oil pump by filling the inlet opening with oil and rotating the pump shaft until oil emerges from the outlet opening. Install the oil pump. Install the oil pan.

22. Position the flywheel on the crankshaft. Apply Pipe Sealant with Teflon D8AZ-19554-A (ESG-M4G194-A and ESR-M18P7-A) or equivalent oil resistant sealer to the flywheel attaching bolts. Torque to specification.

NOTE: *On the flywheel, if equipped with manual transmission, locate clutch disc and install pressure plate.*

23. Turn the engine on the work stand so the engine is in the normal upright position. Install the oil level dipstick. Install the accessory drive pulley, if so equipped. Install and adjust the drive belt and the accessory belts to specification.

24. Remove the engine from work stand. Install the engine in the vehicle.

3.0L Engine

1. With the engine removed from the vehicle and placed on a workstand, loosen the idler pulley and the alternator belt adjusting bolt.

2. Remove the oil pan and gasket.

3. Remove the front cover assembly.

4. Check the timing chain deflection. Remove the timing chain and sprockets.

5. Invert the engine on the workstand. Remove the flywheel. Remove the oil pump inlet and the oil pump assembly.

6. Ensure all bearing caps (main and connecting rod) are marked so that they can be installed in their original positions. Turn the crankshaft until the connecting rod from which the cap is being removed is up. Remove the con-

necting rod cap. Push the connecting rod and piston assembly up in the cylinder. Repeat the procedure for the remaining connecting rod assemblies.

7. Remove the main bearing caps.

8. Carefully lift the crankshaft out of the block so that the upper thrust bearing surfaces are not damaged.

To install:

NOTE: *If the bearings are to be reused they should be identified to ensure that they are installed in their original positions.*

1. Remove the main bearing inserts from the block and bearing caps.

2. Remove the connecting rod bearing inserts from the connecting rods and caps.

3. Inspect all the machined surfaces on the crankshaft for nicks, scratches, scores, etc., which could cause premature bearing wear.

4. If the crankshaft main bearing journals have been refinished to a definite undersize, install the correct undersize bearings, usually in 0.25mm, 0.50mm, 0.80mm undersize.

NOTE: *Ensure the bearing inserts and the bearing bores are clean. Foreign material*

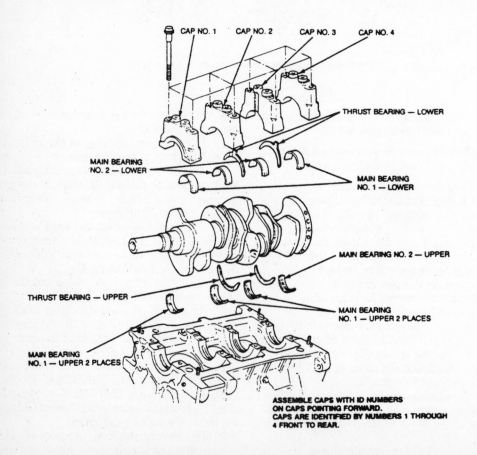

Crankshaft and related components — 3.0L SHO engine

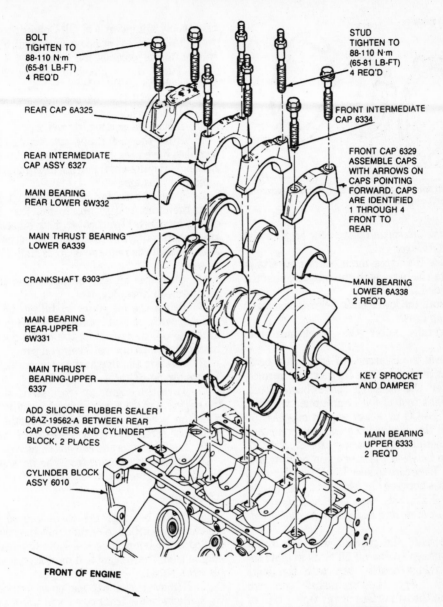

BOLT
TIGHTEN TO
88-110 N·m
(65-81 LB-FT)
4 REQ'D

STUD
TIGHTEN TO
88-110 N·m
(65-81 LB-FT)
4 REQ'D

REAR CAP 6A325

FRONT INTERMEDIATE
CAP 6334

REAR INTERMEDIATE
CAP ASSY 6327

FRONT CAP 6329
ASSEMBLE CAPS
WITH ARROWS ON
CAPS POINTING
FORWARD. CAPS
ARE IDENTIFIED
1 THROUGH 4
FRONT TO
REAR

MAIN BEARING
REAR LOWER 6W332

MAIN THRUST BEARING
LOWER 6A339

CRANKSHAFT 6303

MAIN BEARING
LOWER 6A338
2 REQ'D

MAIN BEARING
REAR-UPPER
6W331

MAIN THRUST
BEARING-UPPER
6337

KEY SPROCKET
AND DAMPER

ADD SILICONE RUBBER SEALER
D6AZ-19562-A BETWEEN REAR
CAP COVERS AND CYLINDER
BLOCK, 2 PLACES

MAIN BEARING
UPPER 6333
2 REQ'D

CYLINDER BLOCK
ASSY 6010

FRONT OF ENGINE

Crankshaft and related components — 3.0L engine except SHO

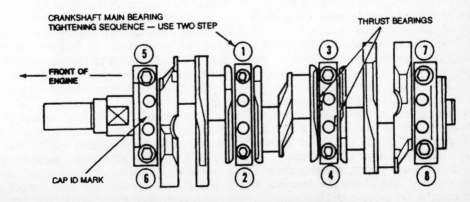

CRANKSHAFT MAIN BEARING
TIGHTENING SEQUENCE — USE TWO STEP

THRUST BEARINGS

FRONT OF
ENGINE

CAP ID MARK

Thrust bearing positioning — 3.0L SHO engine

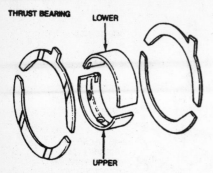

Crankshaft main bearing cap torque bolt sequence — 3.0L SHO engine

under the inserts will distort the bearing and cause a failure.

5. Place the upper main bearing inserts in position in the bores with the tang fitted in the slot provided.

6. Install the lower main bearing inserts in the bearing caps.

7. Carefully lower the crankshaft into place.

8. Check the clearance of each main bearing. Select fit the bearings for proper clearance.

9. After the bearings have been fitted, apply a light coat of Oil Conditioner part No. D9AZ-19578-CO or heavy engine oil, SAE 50 weight, to the journals bearings and rear seal surface. Install all the bearing caps. Apply RTV to the gap between the rear main bearing and the block. Take care to keep RTV from the parting surfaces between the block and the cap.

NOTE: *Ensure the main bearing caps are installed in their original positions and orientation.*

10. Lubricate the journal with oil conditioner or heavy engine oil 50 SAE weight. Install the thrust bearing cap with the bolts finger-tight. Pry the crankshaft forward against the thrust surface of the upper half of the bearing. Hold the crankshaft cap to the rear. This will align the thrust surfaces of both halves of the bearing to be positioned properly. Retain the forward pressure on the crankshaft. Tighten the cap bolts to 65-81 ft. lbs.

11. Check the crankshaft end play with a dial indicator mounted on the front of the engine.

12. If the end play exceeds specification, replace the upper and lower thrust bearings. If the end play is less than specification, inspect the thrust bearing faces for damage, dirt or improper alignment. Install the thrust bearing and align the faces. Recheck the end play.

13. Install the new bearing inserts in the connecting rods and caps. Check the clearance of each bearing by using a piece of Plastigage®.

14. If the bearing clearances are to specifica-tion, apply a light coat of Oil Conditioner part No. D9AZ-19579-C or heavy engine oil, SAE 50 weight, to the journals and bearings.

15. Turn the crankshaft throw to the bottom of the stroke. Push the piston all the way down until the rod bearings seat on the crankshaft journal.

16. Install the connecting rod cap.

17. After the piston and connecting rod assemblies have been installed, check all the connecting rod crankshaft journal clearances using a piece of Plastigage®.

18. Turn the engine on the work stand so that the front end is up. Install the timing chain, sprockets, front cover, new oil seal and crankshaft pulley. Turn the engine on the work stand so that the rear end is up. Install the rear oil seal.

19. Clean the oil pan, oil pump and the oil pump screen assembly.

20. Prime the oil pump by filling the inlet opening with oil and rotating the pump shaft until the oil emerges from the outlet opening. Install the oil pump, baffle and oil pan.

21. Position the flywheel on the crankshaft. Tighten to 54-64 ft lbs.

22. Turn the engine on work stand so that the engine is in the normal upright position. Install the accessory drive pulley. Install and adjust the accessory drive belts to specification.

23. Install the torque converter, as required.

24. Remove the engine from the work stand. Install the engine in the vehicle.

3.8L Engine

1. If the bearings are to be reused they should be identified to ensure that they are installed in their original positions. Remove the engine from the vehicle and mount on a suitable work stand.

2. Remove the oil pan and oil pickup tube.

3. Remove the front cover and water pump as an assembly.

4. Remove the distributor drive gear, timing chain assembly, and flywheel.

5. Remove the connecting rod bearing nuts and caps. Identify each bearing cap to insure that they are installed in their original positions. Push the pistons up into the cylinder and put pieces of rubber hose on the connecting rod bolts so the crankshaft journals do not get damaged.

6. Inspect all the machined surfaces on the crankshaft for nicks, scratches, scores, etc., which could cause premature bearing wear.

NOTE: *Because the engine crankshaft incorporates deep rolling of the main journal fillets, journal refinishing is limited to 0.25mm undersize. Further refinishing may result in fatigue failure of the crankshaft. Ensure*

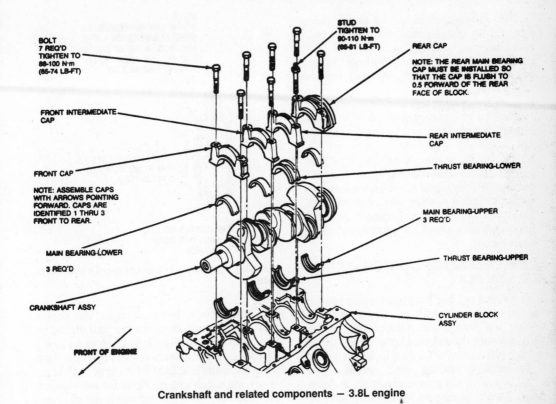

Crankshaft and related components — 3.8L engine

the bearing inserts and the bearing bores are clean. Foreign material under the inserts will distort the bearing and cause a failure.

7. Remove the main bearing caps and identify each bearing cap to insure that they are installed in their original positions.

8. Carefully lift the crankshaft out of the block to prevent damage to bearing surfaces.

To install:

1. Make sure all crankshaft bearing journals and bearing caps are clean. Contaminants under a bearing will cause distortion. Contaminants on the bearing surface will cause damage to the bearing journals.

2. If the crankshaft journals have been refinished to a definite undersize, make sure the proper undersize is being used.

3. Install the used main bearings to their original positions. If using new ones, install the tabs on the bearings into the slots in the cap and the block.

4. Carefully lower crankshaft into position in the cylinder block. Be careful not to damage the thrust bearing surfaces.

5. Apply a 3mm bead of Silicone Sealer part No. D6AZ-19562-A or equivalent to the rear main bearing cap-to-cylinder block parting line.

6. Lubricate the bearing surfaces and journals with Oil Conditioner part No. D9AZ-19579-CF or equivalent heavy engine oil 50 SAE weight.

7. Install the main bearing caps in the proper direction. Torque the bolts to the proper specifications, 65-81 ft. lbs.

8. If the end play exceeds specification, replace the upper and lower thrust bearings. If the end play is less than specification, inspect the thrust bearing faces for damage, dirt or improper alignment. Install the thrust bearing and align the faces. Recheck the end play.

9. Install the used connecting rod bearings to their original positions. If using new ones, install the tabs on the bearings into the slots in the cap and the rod.

10. Rotate the crankshaft as necessary to bring each throw to the lowest point of travel. Pull the piston downward until the connecting rod seats on the crank throw. Install the rod caps and torque to specification, 31-36 ft. lbs.

11. Install the timing chain assembly, distributor gear, oil pan, rear cover and flywheel, and spark plugs.

12. Install the engine in the vehicle.

BEARING OIL CLEARANCE

Remove the cap from the bearing to be checked. Using a clean, dry rag, thoroughly clean all oil from the crankshaft journal and bearing insert.

NOTE: *Plastigage® is soluble in oil, therefore, oil on the journal or bearing could result in erroneous readings.*

Place a piece of Plastigage® along the full width of the bearing insert, reinstall cap, and torque to specifications.

Remove the bearing cap, and determine bearing clearance by comparing width of the bearing insert, reinstall cap, and torque to specifications.

NOTE: *Do not rotate crankshaft with Plastigage® installed. If the bearing insert and journal appear intact, and are within tolerances, no further main bearing service is required. If the bearing or journal appear defective, cause of failure should be determined before replacement.*

CRANKSHAFT ENDPLAY/CONNECTING ROD SIDE PLAY

1. Place a pry bar between a main bearing cap and crankshaft casting taking care not to damage any journals. Pry backward and forward, measure the distance between the thrust bearing and crankshaft with a feeler gauge.

2. Compare reading with specifications, 0.10-0.20mm. If too great a clearance is determined, a main bearing with a larger thrust surface or crank machining may be required. Check with an automotive machine shop for their advice.

3. Connecting rod clearance between the rod and crankthrow casting can be checked with a feeler gauge. Pry the rod carefully on one side as far as possible and measure the distance on the other side of the rod. Check the crankshaft and connecting rod specification table.

CRANKSHAFT REPAIRS

If a journal is damaged on the crankshaft, repair is possible by having the crankshaft machined to a standard undersize.

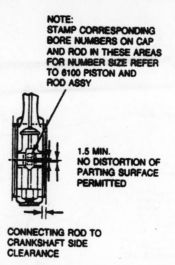

NOTE: STAMP CORRESPONDING BORE NUMBERS ON CAP AND ROD IN THESE AREAS FOR NUMBER SIZE REFER TO 6100 PISTON AND ROD ASSY

1.5 MIN. NO DISTORTION OF PARTING SURFACE PERMITTED

CONNECTING ROD TO CRANKSHAFT SIDE CLEARANCE

Checking connecting rod to crankshaft side clearance

In most cases, however, since the engine must be removed from the car and disassembled, some thought should be given to replacing the damaged crankshaft with a reground shaft kit. A reground crankshaft kit contains the necessary main and rod bearings for installation. The shaft has been ground and polished to undersize specifications and will usually hold up well if installed correctly.

Flywheel/Flexplate

REMOVAL AND INSTALLATION

1. Remove the transaxle from the vehicle.
2. Remove the flywheel/flexplate attaching bolts and the flywheel.
3. The rear cover plate can be removed (manual transmission only).

To install:

NOTE: *All major rotating components including the flexplate/flywheel are individually balance to zero. Engine assembly balanc-*

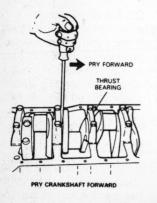

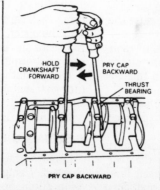

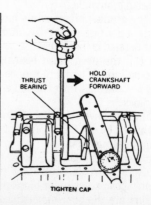

Thrust bearing alignment — 3.0L engine except SHO

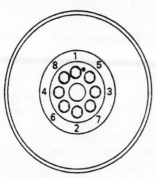

Flywheel bolt torque sequence — 3.0L SHO engine

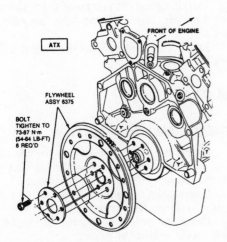

Flywheel and related components — 3.0L engine except SHO

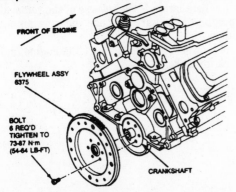

Flywheel and related components — 3.8L engine

ing is not required. Balance weights should not be installed on new flywheels.

1. Install the rear cover plate, if removed.

2. Position the flywheel on the crankshaft and install the attaching bolts. Tighten the attaching bolts to 54-64 ft. lbs., using the standard cross-tightening sequence.

EXHAUST SYSTEM

Safety Precautions

For a number of reasons, exhaust system work can be the most dangerous type of work you can do on your car. Always observe the following precautions:

• Support the car extra securely. Not only will you often be working directly under it, but you'll frequently be using a lot of force, say, heavy hammer blows, to dislodge rusted parts. This can cause a car that's improperly supported to shift and possibly fall.

• Wear goggles. Exhaust system parts are always rusty. Metal chips can be dislodged, even when you're only turning rusted bolts. Attempting to pry pipes apart with a chisel makes the chips fly even more frequently.

• If you're using a cutting torch, keep it a great distance from either the fuel tank or lines. Stop what you're doing and feel the temperature of the fuel bearing pipes on the tank frequently. Even slight heat can expand and/or vaporize fuel, resulting in accumulated vapor, or even a liquid leak, near your torch.

• Watch where your hammer blows fall and make sure you hit squarely. You could easily tap a brake or fuel line when you hit an exhaust system part with a glancing blow. Inspect all lines and hoses in the area where you've been working.

CAUTION: *Be very careful when working on or near the catalytic converter. External temperatures can reach 1,500°F (816°C) and more, causing severe burns. Removal or installation should be performed only on a cold exhaust system.*

Special Tools

A number of special exhaust system tools can be rented from auto supply houses or local stores that rent special equipment. A common one is a tail pipe expander, designed to enable you to join pipes of identical diameter.

It may also be quite helpful to use solvents designed to loosen rusted bolts or flanges. Soaking rusted parts the night before you do the job can speed the work of freeing rusted parts considerably. Remember that these solvents are often flammable. Apply only to parts after they are cool!

Inspect inlet pipes, outlet pipes and mufflers for cracked joints, broken welds and corrosion damage that would result in a leaking exhaust system. It is normal for a certain amount of moisture and staining to be present around the muffler seams. The presence of soot, light surface rust or moisture does not indicate a faulty muffler. Inspect the clamps, brackets and insulators for cracks and stripped or badly corroded bolt threads. When flat joints are loosened and/or disconnected to replace a shield pipe or muffler, replace the bolts and flange nuts if there is reasonable doubt that its service life is limited.

The exhaust system, including brush shields, must be free of leaks, binding, grounding and excessive vibrations. These conditions are usually caused by loose or broken flange bolts, shields, brackets or pipes. If any of these conditions exist, check the exhaust system components and alignment. Align or replace as necessary. Brush shields are positioned on the underside of the catalytic converter and should be free from bends which would bring any part of the shield in contact with the catalytic converter or muffler. The shield should also be clear of any combustible material such as dried grass or leaves.

Coat all of the exhaust connections and bolt threads with anti-seize compound to prevent corrosion from making the next disassembly difficult.

Muffler

REMOVAL AND INSTALLATION

1. Raise and support the vehicle safely.
2. Remove the retaining clamps that support the muffler to its mounting under the car.
3. Using the proper tools separate the muffler from the exhaust pipes.
4. Carefully slide the muffler forward, to remove it from the rear exhaust pipe. Slide the muffler backward to remove it from the other exhaust pipe. Lower the muffler to the ground.
5. Installation is the reverse of the removal procedure. Be sure to use new retaining clamps.

6. Lower the vehicle. Start the engine and check for leaks.

Catalytic Converter

REMOVAL AND INSTALLATION

1. Raise the vehicle and support the vehicle safely. As required, remove the transmission to converter support brace.
2. Remove the front catalytic converter flange fasteners at the flex joint and discard the flex joint gasket, remove the rear U-bolt connection.
3. Separate the catalytic converter inlet and outlet connections. Remove the converter.
4. Installation is the reverse of the removal procedure. Be sure to use new retaining clamps.
5. Lower the vehicle. Start the engine and check for leaks.

Tail Pipe

REMOVAL AND INSTALLATION

1. Raise the vehicle and support the vehicle safely. Remove the tail pipe retaining clamp from the tail pipe to the frame, if equipped.
2. Remove the retaining clamp holding the tail pipe to the muffler or resonator.
3. Using the proper tool separate the tail pipe from the muffler or resonator.
4. Carefully remove the tail pipe from the vehicle.
5. Installation is the reverse of the removal procedure. Be sure to use new retaining clamps.
6. Lower the vehicle. Start the engine and check for leaks.

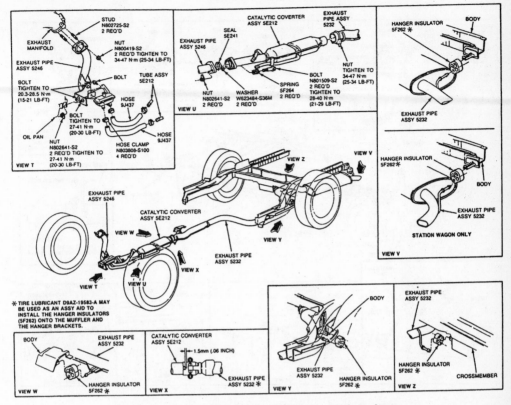

Exhaust system and related components — 2.5L engine

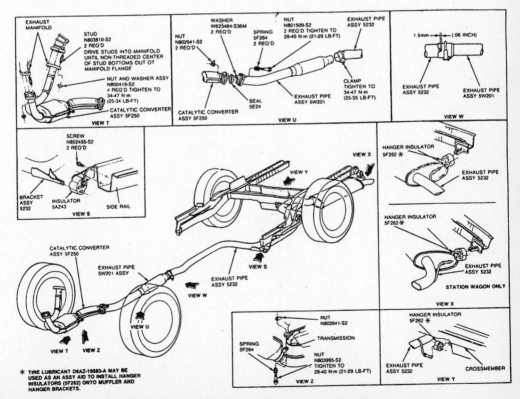

Exhaust system and related components — 3.0L engine

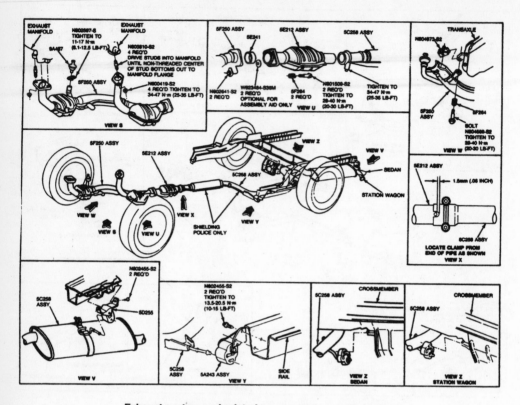

Exhaust system and related components — 3.8L engine

EMISSION CONTROLS

Crankcase Ventilation System

OPERATION

The PCV valve system is used on all vehicles. The PCV valve system vents harmful combustion blow-by fumes from the engine crankcase into the engine air intake for burning with the fuel and air mixture. The PCV valve limits the fresh air intake to suit the engine demand and also serves to prevent combustion backfiring into the crankcase. The PCV valve system maximizes oil cleanliness by venting moisture and corrosive fumes from the crankcase.

On some engine applications, the PCV valve system is connected with the evaporative emission system. Do not remove the PCV valve system from the engine, as doing so will adversely affect fuel economy and engine ventilation with resultant shortening of engine life.

The components used in the PCV valve system consist of the PCV valve, the rubber mounting grommet in the valve cover, the nipple in the air intake system and the necessary connecting hoses.

The PCV valve controls the amount of blow-by vapors pulled into the intake manifold from the crankcase. It also acts as a one-way check valve that prevents air from entering the crankcase in the opposite direction.

SERVICE

System Inspection

1. Visually inspect the components of the PCV valve system. Check for rough idle, slow starting, high oil consumption and loose, leaking, clogged or damaged hoses.
2. Check the fresh air supply hose and the PCV hose for air leakage or flow restriction due to loose engagement, hose splitting, cracking or kinking, nipple damage, rubber grommet fit or any other damage.
3. If a component is suspected as the obvious cause of a malfunction, correct the cause before proceeding to the next Step.
4. If all checks are okay, proceed to the pinpoint tests.

Pinpoint Tests

1. Remove the PCV valve from the valve cover grommet and shake the valve. If the valve rattles when shaken, reinstall and proceed to

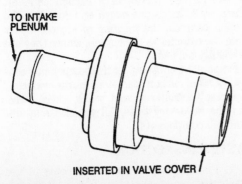

TO INTAKE PLENUM

INSERTED IN VALVE COVER

PCV valve

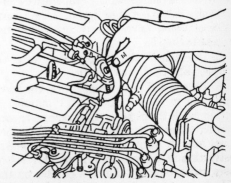

PCV system testing

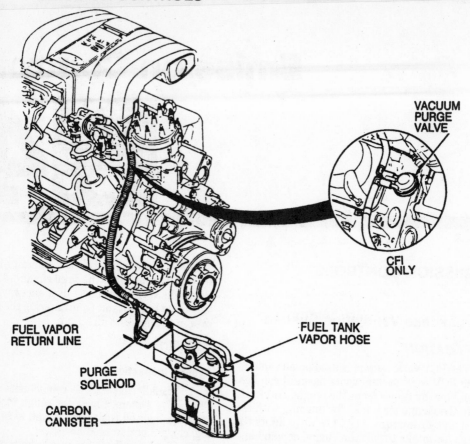

VACUUM
PURGE
VALVE

CFI
ONLY

FUEL VAPOR
RETURN LINE

FUEL TANK
VAPOR HOSE

PURGE
SOLENOID

CARBON
CANISTER

EEC-IV evaporative emission control system layout

Step 2. If the valve does not rattle, it is sticking and should be replaced.

2. Start the engine and bring to normal operating temperature.

3. On the 2.5L engine, remove the corrugated hose from the oil separator nipple. On all other engines, disconnect the hose from the remote air cleaner or air outlet tube.

4. Place a stiff piece of paper over the nipple or hose end and wait 1 minute. If vacuum holds the paper in place, the system is okay; reconnect the hose. If the paper is not held in place, the system is plugged or the evaporative emission valve is leaking, if equipped. If the evaporative emission valve is suspected of leaking, proceed to Step 5.

5. Disconnect the evaporative hose, if equipped and cap the connector.

6. Place a stiff piece of paper over the hose/nipple, as in Step 4 and wait 1 minute. If vacuum holds the paper in place, proceed to evaporative emission system testing. If the paper is not held in place, check for vacuum leaks/obstruction in the system: oil cap, PCV valve, hoses, cut grommets, the oil separator on the 2.5L engine and valve cover for bolt torque/gasket leak.

REMOVAL AND INSTALLATION

1. Remove the PCV valve from the mounting grommet in the valve cover.

2. Disconnect the valve from the PCV hose and remove the valve from the vehicle.

3. Installation is the reverse of the removal procedure.

Evaporative Emission Controls

The evaporative emission control system prevents the escape of fuel vapors to the atmosphere under hot soak and engine off conditions by storing the vapors in a carbon canister. Then, with the engine warm and running, the system controls the purging of stored vapors from the canister to the engine, where they are efficiently burned.

Evaporative emission control components consist of the carbon canister, purge valve(s), vapor valve, rollover vent valve, check valve and the necessary lines. All vehicles may not share all components.

SYSTEM INSPECTION

1. Visually inspect the components of the evaporative emission system. Check for the following, as applicable:

a. Discharged battery.
b. Damaged connectors.
c. Damaged insulation.
d. Malfunctioning ECU.
e. Damaged air flow meter or speed sensor.
f. Inoperative solenoids.
g. Fuel odor or leakage.
h. Damaged vacuum or fuel vapor lines.
i. Loose or poor line connections.
j. Poor driveability during engine warm-up.

2. Check the wiring and connectors for the solenoids, vane air flow meter, speed sensor and ECU, as applicable, for looseness, corrosion, damage or other problems. This must be done with the engine fully warmed up so as to activate the purging controls.

3. Check the fuel tank, fuel vapor lines, vacuum lines and connections for looseness, pinching, leakage, damage or other obvious cause for malfunction.

4. If fuel line, vacuum line or orifice blockage is suspected as the obvious cause of an observed malfunction, correct the cause before proceeding further.

CARBON CANISTER

The carbon canister contains vapor absorbent material to facilitate the storage of fuel vapors. Fuel vapors flow from the fuel tank to the canister, where they are stored until purged to the engine for burning.

Adjustment

There are no moving parts and nothing to wear in the canister. Check for loose, missing, cracked or broken connections and parts. There should be no liquid in the canister.

Removal and Installation

1. Disconnect the vapor hoses from the carbon canister.
2. Remove the canister mounting bolts and remove the canister.
3. Installation is the reverse of the removal procedure.

PURGE VALVES

The purge valves control the flow of fuel vapor from the carbon canister to the engine. Purge valves are either vacuum or electrically controlled. When electrically controlled, a purge valve is known as a purge solenoid. A vehicle may be equipped with a vacuum purge valve or purge solenoid or a combination of the two. Purging occurs when the engine is at operating temperature and off idle.

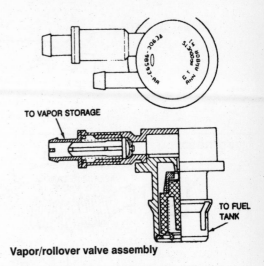

TO VAPOR STORAGE

TO FUEL TANK

Vapor/rollover valve assembly

Removal and Installation

1. Disconnect the negative battery cable.
2. Disconnect the vacuum hose or the electrical connector from the purge valve.
3. Disconnect the vapor hoses and remove the purge valve from the vehicle.
4. Installation is the reverse of the removal procedure.

VAPOR VALVE

The vapor valve is located on or near the fuel tank. It's function is to prevent fuel from flooding the carbon canister. The vapor valve incorporates the rollover valve. In the event of a vehicle rollover, the valve blocks the vapor line automatically to prevent fuel leakage.

Removal and Installation

1. Disconnect the negative battery cable.
2. Raise and safely support the vehicle. Remove the fuel tank to gain access to the vapor valve.
3. Disconnect the vapor hoses from the vapor valve.
4. Remove the vapor valve mounting screws and the vapor valve from the underside of the vehicle or remove the vapor valve from the fuel tank, as necessary.
5. Installation is the reverse of the removal procedure.

CHECK VALVE

The check valve is located in the fuel filler cap or on the underside of the vehicle. It's function is to protect the fuel tank from heat build-up rupture and cool-down collapse by allowing air to pass in or out of the tank to equalize pressure. On cool-down, air enters either at the carbon canister vent or at the check valve.

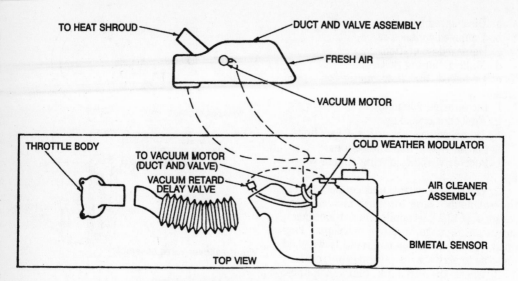

Thermostatic air inlet system—2.5L engine

Exhaust Emission Control system

The exhaust emission control system begins at the air intake and ends at the tailpipe. All vehicles are equipped with the following systems or components to manage exhaust emission control: thermostatic air inlet system, thermactor air injection system, pulse air injection system, exhaust gas recirculation system and exhaust catalyst. All vehicles do not share all systems or all components.

THERMOSTATIC AIR INLET STYSTEM

The thermostatic air inlet system is used on is used on vehicles equipped with the 2.5L engine. The thermostatic air inlet system regulates the air inlet temperature by drawing air in from a cool air source as well as heated air from a heat shroud which is mounted on the exhaust manifold. The system consists of the following components: duct and valve assembly, heat shroud, bimetal sensor, cold weather modulator, vacuum delay valve and the necessary vacuum lines and air ducts. All vehicles do not share all components.

DUCT AND VALVE ASSEMBLY

The duct and valve assembly which regulates the air flow from the cool and heated air sources is located either inside the air cleaner or mounted on the air cleaner. The flow is regulated by means of a door that is operated by a vacuum motor. The operation of the motor is controlled by delay valves, temperature sensors and other vacuum control systems. All vary with each application and engine calibration.

Testing

1. If the duct door is in the closed to fresh air position, remove the hose from the air cleaner vacuum motor.
2. The door should go to the open to fresh air position. If it sticks or binds, service or replace, as required.
3. If the door is in the open to fresh air position, check the door by applying 8 in. Hg or greater of vacuum to the vacuum motor.
4. The door should move freely to the closed to fresh air position. If it binds or sticks, service or replace, as required.

NOTE: *Make sure the vacuum motor is functional before changing the duct and valve assembly.*

Removal and Installation

1. Disconnect the vacuum hose from the vacuum motor.
2. Separate the vacuum motor from the vacuum operated door and remove the vacuum motor.
3. Installation is the reverse of the removal procedure.

BIMETAL SENSOR

The core of the bimetal sensor is made of 2 different types of metals bonded together, each having different temperature expansion rates. At a given increase in temperature, the shape of the sensor core changes, bleeding off vacuum available at the vaccum motor. This permits the vacuum motor to open the duct door to allow fresh air in while shutting off full heat. The bimetal sensor is calibrated according to the needs of each particular application.

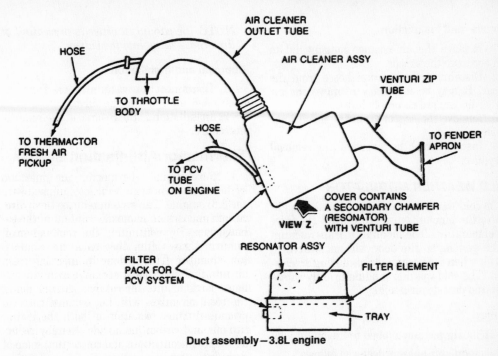

Duct assembly—3.8L engine

Testing

1. Bring the temperature of the bimetal sensor below 75°F (24°C) and apply 16 in. Hg of vacuum with a vacuum pump at the vacuum source port of the sensor.

2. The duct door should stay closed. If not, replace the bimetal sensor.

3. The sensor will bleed off vacuum to allow the duct door to open and let in fresh air at or above the following temperatures:

a. Brown—75°F (24°C)
b. Pink, black or red—90°F (32.2°C)
c. Blue, yellow or green—105°F (40.6°C)

NOTE: *Do not cool the bimetal sensor while the engine is running.*

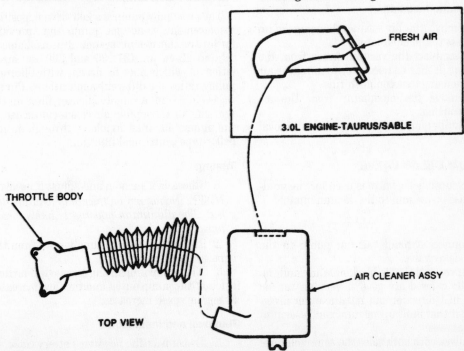

Duct assembly—3.0L engine except SHO

Removal and Installation

1. Remove the air cleaner housing lid to gain access to the sensor.
2. Disconnect the vacuum hoses from the sensor. It may be necessary to move the air cleaner housing to accomplish this.
3. Remove the sensor from the air cleaner housing.
4. Installation is the reverse of the removal procedure.

COLD WEATHER MODULATOR

The cold weather modulator is used in addition to the bimetal sensor to control the inlet air temperature. The modulator traps vacuum in the system, so the door will not switch to cold air when the vacuum drops during acceleration. The cold weather modulator only works when the outside air is cold.

Testing

A 16 in. Hg vacuum applied to the motor side of the modulator holds or leaks as follows:

Black—holds below 20°F (–6.7°C) and leaks above 35°F (1.7°C)
Blue—holds below 40°F (4.4°C) and leaks above 55°F (12.8°C)
Green—holds below 50°F (10°C) and leaks above 76°F (24.4°C)
Yellow—holds above 65°F (18.3°C) and leaks below 50°F (10°C)

Removal and Installation

1. Remove the air cleaner housing lid to gain access to the modulator.
2. Disconnect the vacuum hoses from the modulator. It may be necessary to move the air cleaner housing to accomplish this.
3. Remove the modulator from the air cleaner housing.
4. Installation is the reverse of the removal procedure.

VACUUM DELAY VALVE

The vacuum delay valve is used for the gradual release of vacuum to the vacuum motor.

Testing

1. Connect a hand vacuum pump to the vacuum delay valve.
2. Valves with 1 side black or white and the other side colored are good if vacuum can be built up in 1 direction but not the other direction and if that built up vacuum can be seen to slowly decrease.
3. Valves with both sides the same color are good if vacuum can be built up in both directions before visibly decreasing.

NOTE: *Be careful in order to prevent oil or dirt from getting into the valve.*

Removal and Installation

1. Disconnect the vacuum hoses from the delay valve and remove the valve.
2. Installation is the reverse of the removal procedure.

Thermactor Air Injection System

A conventional thermactor air injection system is used on some vehicles equipped with the 3.8L engine. The system reduces the hydrocarbon and carbon monoxide content of the exhaust gases by continuing the combustion of unburned gases after they leave the combustion chamber. This is done by injecting fresh air into the hot exhaust stream leaving the exhaust ports or into the catalyst. At this point, the fresh air mixes with hot exhaust gases to promote further oxidation of both the hydrocarbons and carbon monoxide, thereby reducing their concentration and converting some of them into harmless carbon dioxide and water. During highway cruising and WOT operation, the thermactor air is dumped to atmosphere to prevent overheating in the exhaust system.

A typical air injection system consists of an air supply pump and filter, air bypass valve, check valves, air manifold, air hoses and air control valve.

AIR SUPPLY PUMP

The air supply pump is a belt-driven, positive displacement, vane-type pump that provides air for the thermactor system. It is available in 19 and 22 cu. in. (311.35 and 360.5cc) sizes, either of which may be driven with different pulley ratios for different applications. Pumps recieve air from a remote silencer filter on the rear side of the engine air cleaner attached to the pumps' air inlet nipple or through an impeller-type centrifugal filter fan.

Testing

1. Check belt tension and adjust if needed.
NOTE: *Do not pry on the pump to adjust the belt. The aluminum housing is likely to collapse.*
2. Disconnect the air supply hose from the bypass control valve.
3. The pump is operating properly if airflow is felt at the pump outlet and the flow increases as engine speed increases.

Removal and Installation

1. Disconnect the negative battery cable.
2. Remove the drive belt from the air pump pulley.

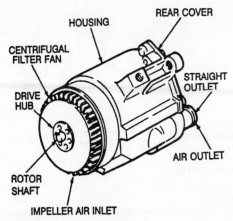

Air supply pump assembly

3. Disconnect the air hose(s) from the air pump.

4. Remove the mounting bolts and, if necessary, the mounting brackets.

5. Remove the air pump from the vehicle.

6. Installation is the reverse of the removal procedure.

AIR BYPASS VALVE

The air bypass valve supplies air to the exhaust system with medium and high applied vacuum signals when the engine is at normal operating temperature. With low or no vacuum applied, the pumped air is dumped through the silencer ports of the valve or through the dump port.

Testing

1. Disconnect the air supply hose at the valve outlet.

2. Remove the vacuum line to check that a vacuum signal is present at the vacuum nipple. There must be a vacuum present at the nipple before proceeding.

3. With the engine at 1500 rpm and the vacuum line connected to the vacuum nipple, air pump supply air should be heard and felt at the air bypass valve outlet.

4. With the engine at 1500 rpm, disconnect the vacuum line. Air at the outlet should be significantly decreased or shut off. Air pump supply air should be heard or felt at the silencer ports or at the dump port.

5. If the air bypass valve does not successfully complete these tests, check the air pump. If the air pump is operating properly, replace the air bypass valve.

Removal and Installation

1. Disconnect the negative battery cable.

2. Disconnect the air inlet and outlet hoses and the vacuum hose from the bypass valve.

3. Remove the bypass valve from the vehicle.

4. Installation is the reverse of the removal procedure.

CHECK VALVE

The air check valve is a 1-way valve that allows thermactor air to pass into the exhaust system while preventing exhaust gases from passing in the opposite direction.

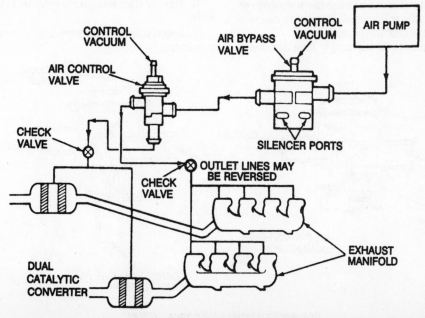

Thermactor air injection system

Testing

1. Visually inspect the thermactor system hoses, tubes, control valve(s) and check valve(s) for leaks that may be due to the backflow of exhaust gas. If holes are found and/or traces of exhaust gas products are evident, the check valve may be suspect.

2. Check valves should allow free flow of air in the incoming direction only. The valves should check or block, the free flow of exhaust gas in the opposite direction.

3. Replace the valve if air does not flow as indicated or if exhaust gas backflows in the opposite direction.

Removal and Installation

1. Disconnect the negative battery cable.
2. Disconnect the input hose from the check valve.
3. Remove the check valve from the connecting tube.
4. Installation is the reverse of the removal procedure.

AIR SUPPLY CONTROL VALVE

The air supply control valve directs air pump output to the exhaust manifold or downstream to the catalyst system depending upon the engine control strategy. It may also be used to dump air to the air cleaner or dump silencer.

Testing

1. Verify that airflow is being supplied to the valve inlet by disconnecting the air supply hose at the inlet and verifying the presensce of airflow with the engine at 1500 rpm. Reconnect the air supply hose to the valve inlet.

2. Disconnect the air supply hose at outlets

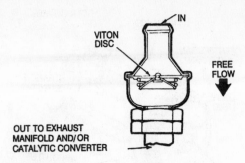

OUT TO EXHAUST
MANIFOLD AND/OR
CATALYTIC CONVERTER

Air check valve

A and B.

3. Remove the vacuum line at the vacuum nipple.

4. Accelerate the engine to 1500 rpm. Airflow should be heard and felt at outlet B with little or no airflow at outlet A.

5. With the engine at 1500 rpm, connect a direct vacuum line from any manifold vacuum fitting to the air control valve vacuum nipple. Airflow should be heard and felt at outlet A with little or no airflow at outlet B.

6. If airflow is noted in Steps 4 and 5, the valve is okay. Reinstall the clamps and hoses. If the valve does not pass Step 4 and/or 5, replace the valve.

Removal and Installation

1. Disconnect the negative battery cable.
2. Disconnect the air hoses and the vacuum line from the air control valve.
3. Remove the air control valve from the vehicle.
4. Installation is the reverse of the removal procedure.

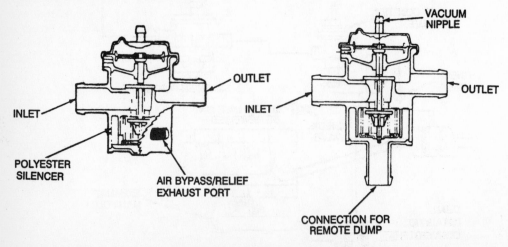

Crossectional view of air bypass valves

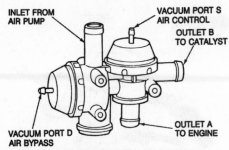

Combination air bypass/air control valve

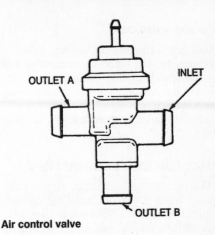

Air control valve

COMBINATION AIR BYPASS/AIR CONTROL VALVE

The combination air control/bypass valve combines the secondary air bypass and air control functions. The valve is located in the air supply line between the air pump and the upstream/downstream air supply check valves.

The air bypass portion controls the flow of thermactor air to the exhaust system or allows thermactor air to be bypassed to atmosphere. When air is not being bypassed, the air control portion of the valve switches the air injection point to either an upstream or downstream location.

Testing

1. Disconnect the hoses from outlets A and B.

2. Disconnect and plug the vacuum line to port D.

3. With the engine operating at 1500 rpm, airflow should be noted coming out of the bypass vents.

4. Reconnect the vacuum line to port D and disconnect and plug the vacuum line to port S. Make sure vacuum is present in the line to vacuum port D.

5. With the engine operating at 1500 rpm, airflow should be noted coming out of outlet B and no airflow should be detected at outlet A.

6. Apply 8–10 in. Hg of vacuum to port S. With the engine operating at 1500 rpm, airflow should be noted coming out of outlet A.

7. If the valve is the bleed type, some lesser amount of air will flow from outlet A or B and the main discharge will change when vacuum is applied to port S.

Removal and Installation

1. Disconnect the negative battery cable.

2. Disconnect the air hoses and vacuum lines from the valve.

3. Remove the valve from the vehicle.

4. Installation is the reverse of the removal procedure.

Solenoid vacuum valve assembly

SOLENOID VACUUM VALVE ASSEMBLY

The normally closed solenoid valve assembly consists of 2 vacuum ports with an atmospheric vent. The valve assembly can be with or without control bleed. The outlet port of the valve is opened to atmospheric vent and closed to the inlet port when de-energized. When energized, the outlet port is opened to the inlet port and closed to atmospheric vent. The control bleed is provided to prevent contamination entering the solenoid valve assembly from the intake manifold.

Testing

1. The ports should flow air when the solenoid is energized.

2. Check the resistance at the solenoid terminals with an ohmmeter. The resistance should be 51–108Ω.

3. If the resistance is not as specified, replace the solenoid.

NOTE: *The valve can be expected to have a very small leakage rate when energized or de-energized. This leakage is not measurable in the field and is not detrimental to valve function.*

Removal and Installation

1. Disconnect the negative battery cable.
2. Disconnect the electrical connector and the vacuum lines from the solenoid valve.
3. Remove the mounting bolts and remove the solenoid valve.
4. Installation is the reverse of the removal procedure.

THERMACTOR IDLE VACUUM VALVE

The TIV valve vents the vacuum signal to the atmosphere when the preset manifold vacuum or pressure is exceeded. It is used to divert thermactor airflow during cold starts to control exhaust backfire.

Testing

The following applies to TIV valves with the code words ASH or RED on the decal.

1. Apply the parking brake and block the drive wheels. With the engine at idle, and the transaxle selector lever in **N** on automatic transaxle equipped vehicles or neutral on manual transaxle equipped vehicles, apply vacuum to the small nipple and place fingers over the TIV valve atmospheric vent holes. If no vacuum is sensed, the TIV is damaged and must be replaced.

2. With the engine still idling and the transaxle selector lever remaining in **N** or neutral, apply 1.5–3.0 in. Hg of vacuum to the large nipple of the ASH TIV valve or 3.5–4.5 in. Hg of vacuum to the large nipple of the RED TIV valve from a test source. If vacuum is still sensed when placing fingers over the vent holes, the TIV is damaged and must be replaced.

3. If the TIV valve meets both requirements, disconnect the TIV valve small nipple from the manifold vacuum and the TIV valve large nipple from the test vacuum. Reconnect

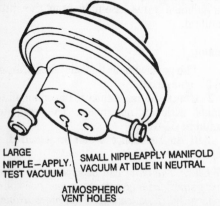

LARGE NIPPLE—APPLY TEST VACUUM   SMALL NIPPLE APPLY MANIFOLD VACUUM AT IDLE IN NEUTRAL

ATMOSPHERIC VENT HOLES

Thermactor idle vacuum valve assembly

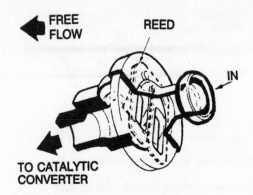

FREE FLOW   REED   IN

TO CATALYTIC CONVERTER

Pulse air valve air flow schematic

the TIV valve to the original hoses or connectors.

Removal and Installation

1. Disconnect the negative battery cable.
2. Disconnect the vacuum lines from the TIV valve and remove the valve from the vehicle.
3. Installation is the reverse of the removal procedure.

Pulse Air Injection System

The pulse air injection system is used on some vehicles equipped with the 2.5L engine.

The pulse air injection system does not use an air pump. The system uses natural pulses present in the exhaust system to pull air into the catalyst through pulse air valves. The pulse air valve is connected to the catalyst with a long tube and to the air cleaner and silencer with hoses.

PULSE AIR VALVE

The pulse air control valve is normally closed. Without a vacuum signal from the solenoid, the flow of air is blocked.

TESTING

1. Visually inspect the system hoses, tubes, control valve(s) and check valve(s) for leaks that may be due to backflow of exhaust gas. If holes are found and/or traces of exhaust gas products are evident, the check valve may be suspect.

2. The valve should allow free flow of air in 1 direction only. The valve should check or block, the free flow of exhaust gas in the opposite direction.

3. Replace the valve if air does not flow as indicated or if exhaust gas backflows in the wrong direction.

4. Remove the inlet hose.

5. Apply the parking brake and block the

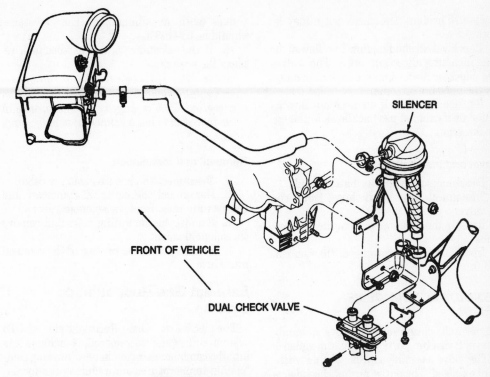

SILENCER

FRONT OF VEHICLE

DUAL CHECK VALVE

Pulse air injection system—2.5L engine

drive wheels. With the engine at normal operating temperature and idling and the transaxle selector lever in **N** on automatic transaxle equipped vehicles or neutral on manual transaxle equipped vehicles, air should be drawn into the valve.

6. Remove the vacuum line and air flow should stop.

7. If these conditions are met, the valve is operating properly.

8. If these conditions are not met, verify that vacuum is present at the valve. Check the solenoid valve if vacuum is not present.

9. If vacuum is present but no air flows, check the pulse air check valve, silencer filter and air cleaner for blocked or restricted passages.

10. If vacuum is present and no blocked or restricted passages are found, replace the valve.

Removal and Installation

1. Disconnect the negative battery cable.

2. Disconnect the air hose(s) from the pulse air valve.

3. Disconnect the vacuum line, if necessary.

4. Remove the pulse air valve.

5. Installation is the reverse of the removal procedure.

AIR SILENCER/FILTER

The air silencer is a combustion silencer and filter for the pulse air system. The air silencer is mounted in a convenient position in the engine compartment and is connected to the pulse air valve inlet by means of a flexible hose.

Testing

1. Inspect the hoses and air silencer for leaks.

2. Disconnect the hose from the air silencer outlet, remove the silencer and visually inspect for plugging.

3. The air silencer is operating properly, if no plugging or leaks are encountered.

Removal and Installation

1. Disconnect the negative battery cable.

2. Disconnect the hose from the silencer and remove the silencer.

3. Installation is the reverse of the removal procedure.

CHECK VALVE

The air check valve is a 1-way valve that allows air to pass into the exhaust system while preventing exhaust gases from passing in the opposite direction.

Testing

1. Visually inspect the system hoses, tubes, control valve(s) and check valve(s) for leaks that may be due to the backflow of exhaust gas. If holes are found and/or traces of exhaust gas

products are evident, the check valve may be suspect.

2. Check valves should allow free flow of air in the incoming direction only. The valves should check or block, the free flow of exhaust gas in the opposite direction.

3. Replace the valve if air does not flow as indicated or if exhaust gas backflows in the opposite direction.

Removal and Installation

1. Disconnect the negative battery cable.

2. Disconnect the input hose from the check valve.

3. Remove the check valve from the connecting tube.

4. Installation is the reverse of the removal procedure.

SOLENOID VACUUM VALVE ASSEMBLY

The normally closed solenoid valve assembly consists of 2 vacuum ports with an atmospheric vent. The valve assembly can be with or without control bleed. The outlet port of the valve is opened to atmospheric vent and closed to the inlet port when de-energized. When energized, the outlet port is opened to the inlet port and closed to atmospheric vent. The control bleed is provided to prevent contamination entering the solenoid valve assembly from the intake manifold.

Testing

1. The ports should flow air when the solenoid is energized.

2. Check the resistance at the solenoid ter-

minals with an ohmmeter. The resistance should be 51–108Ω.

3. If the resistance is not as specified, replace the solenoid.

NOTE: *The valve can be expected to have a very small leakage rate when energized or de-energized. This leakage is not measurable in the field and is not detrimental to valve function.*

Removal and Installation

1. Disconnect the negative battery cable.

2. Disconnect the electrical connector and the vacuum lines from the solenoid valve.

3. Remove the mounting bolts and remove the solenoid valve.

4. Installation is the reverse of the removal procedure.

Exhaust Gas Recirculation System

The Exhaust Gas Recirculation (EGR) system is designed to reintroduce exhaust gas into the combustion cycle, thereby lowering combustion temperatures and reducing the formation of nitrous oxide. There are a few different EGR systems used on front wheel drive vehicles.

The most commonly used system is the Pressure Feedback Electronic (PFE) system. The PFE is a subsonic closed loop EGR system that controls EGR flow rate by monitoring the pressure drop across a remotely located sharp-edged orifice. The system uses a pressure transducer as the feedback device and controlled pressure is varied by valve modulation using vacuum output of the EGR Vacuum Regulator (EVR) solenoid. With the PFE system,

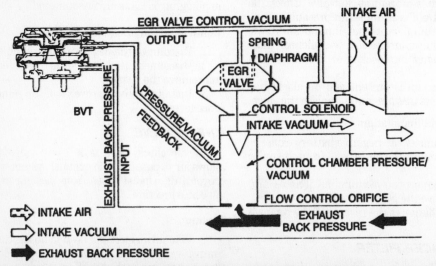

Back pressure variable transduced EGR system schematic

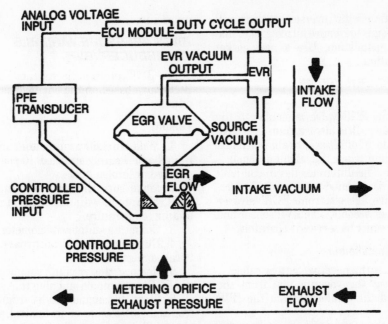

Pressure feedback electronic EGR system schematic

the EGR valve only serves as a pressure regulator rather than a flow metering device.

The Electronic EGR valve (EEGR) system is used on some vehicles equipped with the 2.5L engine. An electronic EGR valve is required in EEC systems where EGR flow is controlled according to computer demands by means of an EGR Valve Position (EVP) sensor attached to the valve. The valve is operated by a vacuum signal from the electronic vacuum regulator which actuates the valve diaphragm. As supply vacuum overcomes the spring load, the diaphragm is actuated. This lifts the pintle off of it's seat allowing exhaust gas to recirculate. The amount of flow is proportional to the pintle position. The EVP sensor mounted on the valve sends an electrical signal of it's position to the ECU.

PORTED EGR VALVE

This is the most common form of EGR valve. The ported EGR valve is operated by a vacuum signal which actuates the valve diaphragm. As the vacuum increases sufficiently to overcome the power spring, the valve is opened allowing EGR flow. The vacuum to the EGR valve is controlled using devices such as the EVR or the BVT, depending on system application.

Removal and Installation

1. Disconnect the negative battery cable.
2. Disconnect the vacuum line from the EGR valve.
3. Remove the mounting bolts and remove the EGR valve.

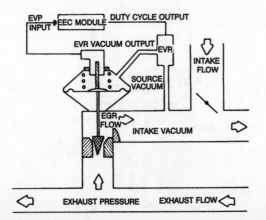

Electronic EGR system schematic

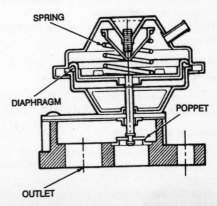

Crossectional view of a ported EGR valve assembly

4. Installation is the reverse of the removal procedure. Be sure to remove all old gasket material before installation. Use a new gasket during installation.

ELECTRONIC EGR (EEGR) VALVE

The electronic EGR valve is similar to the ported EGR valve. It is also vacuum operated, lifting the pintle off of it's seat to allow exhaust gas to recirculate when the vacuum signal is strong enough. The difference lies in the EVP sensor which is mounted on top of the electronic EGR valve. The electronic EGR valve assembly is not serviceable. The EVP sensor and the EGR valve must be serviced separately.

Removal and Installation

1. Disconnect the negative battery cable.
2. Disconnect the vacuum line from the EGR valve and the connector from the EVP sensor.
3. Remove the mounting bolts and remove the EGR valve.
4. Remove the EVP sensor from the EGR valve.
5. Installation is the reverse of the removal procedure. Be sure to remove all old gasket material before installation. Use a new gasket during installation.

PRESSURE FEEDBACK ELECTRONIC (PFE) EGR TRANSDUCER

The PFE EGR transducer converts a varying exhaust pressure signal into a proportional analog voltage which is digitized by the ECU. The ECU uses the signal recieved from the PFE transducer to complete the optimum EGR flow.

Removal and Installation

1. Disconnect the negative battery cable.
2. Disconnect the electrical connector and the exhaust pressure line from the transducer.
3. Remove the transducer.
4. Installation is the reverse of the removal procedure.

EGR VALVE POSITION (EVP) SENSOR

The EVP sensor provides the ECU with a signal indicating the position of the EGR valve.

Removal and Installation

1. Disconnect the negative battery cable.
2. Disconnect the electrical connector from the sensor.
3. Remove the sensor mounting nuts and remove the sensor from the EGR valve.
4. Installation is the reverse of the removal procedure.

BACK PRESSURE VARIABLE TRANSDUCER (BVT)

The BVT controls the vacuum input to the EGR valve based on the engine operating condition.

Testing

1. Make sure all vacuum hoses are correctly routed and securely attached. Replace cracked, crimped or broken hoses.
2. Make sure there is no vacuum to the EGR valve at idle with the engine at normal operating temperature.
3. Connect a suitable tachometer.
4. Disconnect the idle air bypass valve electrical connector.
5. Remove the vacuum supply hose from the EGR valve nipple and plug the hose.
6. Start the engine and let it idle with the transaxle selector lever in neutral. Check the engine idle speed and adjust to the proper specification, if necessary.
7. Slowly apply 5–10 in. Hg of vacuum to the EGR valve vacuum nipple using a suitable hand vacuum pump.
8. When vacuum is fully applied to the EGR valve, check for the following:
    a. If idle speed drops more than 100 rpm or if the engine stalls, perform the next step. Otherwise, for a vacuum leak at the EGR valve, replace the valve.
    b. If the EGR passages are blocked, clean the EGR valve using a suitable cleaner.
    c. Remove the vacuum from the EGR valve. If the idle speed does not return to normal, ± 25 rpm, check for contamination; clean the valve.

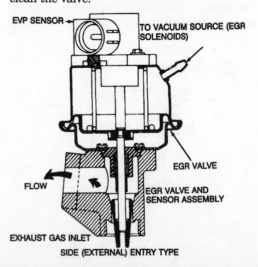

Crossectional view of an electronic EGR valve assembly

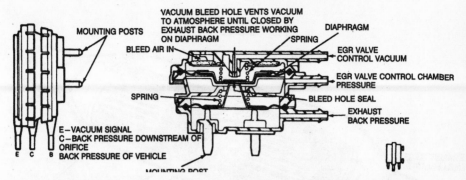

VACUUM BLEED HOLE VENTS VACUUM
TO ATMOSPHERE UNTIL CLOSED BY
EXHAUST BACK PRESSURE WORKING
ON DIAPHRAGM

MOUNTING POSTS

BLEED AIR IN

DIAPHRAGM

SPRING

EGR VALVE
CONTROL VACUUM

EGR VALVE CONTROL CHAMBER
PRESSURE

SPRING

BLEED HOLE SEAL

EXHAUST
BACK PRESSURE

E—VACUUM SIGNAL
C—BACK PRESSURE DOWNSTREAM OF
ORIFICE
B—BACK PRESSURE OF VEHICLE

E C B

MOUNTING POST

Crossectional view of a back pressure variable transducer EGR valve assembly

d. If the symptom still exists, replace the EGR valve.

9. Reconnect the idle air bypass valve electrical connector.

10. Unplug and reconnect the EGR vacuum supply hose.

11. Disconnect the vacuum connection at the BVT.

12. Gently blow into the hose to port C until the relief valve closes and at the same time apply 5–10 in. Hg of vacuum to port E with the hand vacuum pump. Port E should hold vacuum as long as there is pressure on port C.

13. Apply a minimum of 5–10 in. Hg of vacuum to ports B and C using the hand vacuum pump. Ports B and C should hold vacuum.

14. Replace the BVT if any of the ports do not hold vacuum.

15. Reconnect the vacuum at the BVT.

16. If neither the EGR valve nor the BVT were replaced, the system is okay.

Removal and Installation

1. Disconnect the negative battery cable.

2. Disconnect the vacuum lines from the BVT.

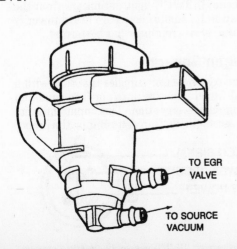

TO EGR
VALVE

TO SOURCE
VACUUM

EGR vacuum regulator assembly

3. Remove the BVT from it's mounting position and remove it from the vehicle.

4. Installation is the reverse of the removal procedure.

EGR VACUUM REGULATOR (EVR)

The EVR is an electromagnetic device which controls vacuum output to the EGR valve. The EVR replaces the EGR solenoid vacuum vent valve assembly. An electric current in the coil induces a magnetic field in the armature. The magnetic field pulls the disk closed, closing the vent and increasing the vacuum level. The vacuum source is either manifold or vacuum. As the duty cycle is increased, an increased vacuum signal goes to the EGR valve.

Removal and Installation

1. Disconnect the negative battery cable.

2. Disconnect the electrical connector and the vacuum lines from the regulator.

3. Remove the regulator mounting bolts and remove the regulator.

4. Installation is the reverse of the removal procedure.

Catalytic Converters

Engine exhaust consists mainly of Nitrogen (N_2), however, it also contains Carbon Monoxide (CO), Carbon Dioxide (CO_2), Water Vapor (H_2O), Oxygen (O_2), Nitrogen Oxides (NOx) and Hydrogen, as well as various, unburned Hydrocarbons (HC). Three of these exhaust components, CO, NOx and HC, are major air pollutants, so their emission to the atmosphere has to be controlled.

The catalytic converter, mounted in the engine exhaust stream, plays a major role in the emission control system. The converter works as a gas reactor and it's catalytic function is to speed up the heat producing chemical reaction between the exhaust gas components in order to reduce the air pollutants in the engine exhaust. The catalyst material, contained inside the converter, is made of a ce-

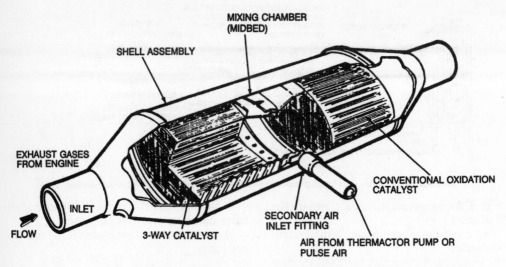

MIXING CHAMBER (MIDBED)

SHELL ASSEMBLY

EXHAUST GASES FROM ENGINE

INLET

FLOW

3-WAY CATALYST

SECONDARY AIR INLET FITTING

AIR FROM THERMACTOR PUMP OR PULSE AIR

CONVENTIONAL OXIDATION CATALYST

Crossectional view of a typical catalytic converter assembly

ramic substrate that is coated with a high surface area alumina and impregnated with catalytically active, precious metals.

CATALYTIC CONVERTER

All vehicles use a 3-way catalyst and some also use this in conjunction with a conventional oxidation catalyst. The conventional oxidation catalyst, containing Platinum (Pt) and Palladium (Pd), is effective for catalyzing the oxidation reactions of HC and CO. The 3-way catalyst, containing Platinum (Pt) and Rhodium (RH) or Palladium (Pd) and Rhodium (RH), is not only effective for catalyzing the oxidation reactions of HC and CO, but it also catalyzes the reduction of NOx.

The catalytic converter assembly consists of a structured shell containing a monolithic substrate—a ceramic, honeycomb construction. In order to maintain the converter's exhaust oxygen content at a high level to obtain the maximum oxidation for producing the heated chemical reaction, the oxidation catalyst usually requires the use of a secondary air source. This is provided by the pulse air or thermactor air injection systems.

The catalytic converter is protected by several devices that block out the air supply from the air injection system when the engine is laboring under 1 or more of the following conditions:

• Cold engine operation with rich choke mixture.

• Abnormally high engine coolant temperatures above 225°F (107°C), which may result from a condition such as an extended, hot idle on a hot day.

• Wide-open throttle.
• Engine deceleration.
• Extended idle operation.

Service Interval Reminder Lights

RESETTING

Every 5000 or 7,500 miles (approximately, depending on engine application) the word SERVICE will appear on the electronic display for the first 1.5 miles to remind the driver that is is time for the regular vehicle service interval maintenance (i.e. oil change).

To reset the service interval reminder light for another interval proceed as follows. With the engine running, press the ODO SEL and TRIP RESET buttons. Hold the buttons down until the SERVICE light disappears from the display and 3 audible beeps are heard to verify that the service reminder has been reset.

Oxygen Sensor

The oxygen sensor supplies the ECU with a signal which indicates a rich or lean condition during engine operation. This input information assists the ECU in determining the proper

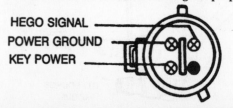

HEGO SIGNAL

POWER GROUND

KEY POWER

Oxygen sensor (HEGO) assembly electrical connector

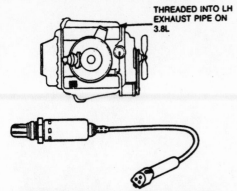

THREADED INTO LH EXHAUST PIPE ON 3.8L

THREADED INTO Y-PIPE JUNCTURE OF CATALYST INLET ON 3.0L EFI

Oxygen sensor (HEGO) assembly

air/fuel ratio. The oxygen sensor is threaded into the exhaust manifold on all vehicles.

TESTING

Except Engines Equipped With MAF Sensor

1. Disconnect the oxygen sensor from the vehicle harness.

2. Connect a voltmeter between the HEGO signal terminal of the oxygen sensor connector and the negative battery terminal.

3. Disconnect and plug the vacuum line at the MAP sensor and set the voltmeter on the 20 volt scale.

4. Apply 10–14 in. Hg of vacuum to the MAP sensor.

5. Start the engine and run it at approximately 2000 rpm for 2 minutes.

6. If the voltmeter does not indicate greater than 0.5 volts within 2 minutes, replace the sensor.

REMOVAL AND INSTALLATION

1. Disconnect the negative battery cable.

2. Disconnect the oxygen sensor connector.

3. Remove the sensor from the exhaust manifold.

4. Installation is the reverse of the removal procedure.

Fuel System

5

FUEL INJECTION SYSTEM

General Description

CENTRAL FUEL INJECTION SYSTEM (CFI)

The Ford Central Fuel Injection (CFI) System is a single point, pulse time modulated injection system. Fuel is metered into the air intake stream according to engine demands by one or two solenoid injection valves, mounted in a throttle body on the intake manifold. Fuel is supplied from the fuel tank by a single low-pressure pump. The fuel is filtered, and sent to the air throttle body where a regulator keeps the fuel delivery pressure at a constant 39 psi (269 kPa) on high-pressure systems, or 14.5 psi (100kPa) on low-pressure systems. One or two injector nozzles are mounted vertically above the throttle plates and connected in parallel with the fuel pressure regulator. Excess fuel supplied by the pump but not needed by the engine is returned to the fuel tank by a steel fuel return line.

Fuel Delivery System

FUEL CHARGING ASSEMBLY

The fuel charging assembly controls air/fuel ratio. It consists of a typical carburetor throttle body. It has one or two bores without venturis. The throttle shaft and valves control engine air flow based on driver demand. The throttle body attaches to the intake manifold mounting pad.

A throttle position sensor is attached to the throttle shaft. It includes a potentiometer (or rheostat) that electrically senses throttle opening. A throttle kicker solenoid fastens opposite the throttle position sensor. During air conditioning operation, the solenoid extends to slightly increase engine idle speed.

Cold engine speed is controlled by an auto-

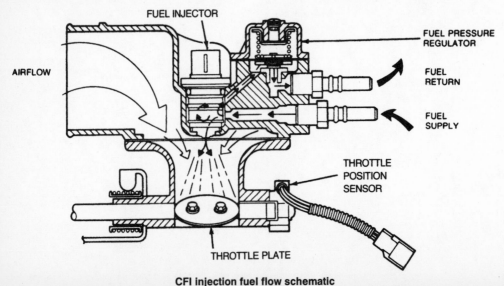

CFI injection fuel flow schematic

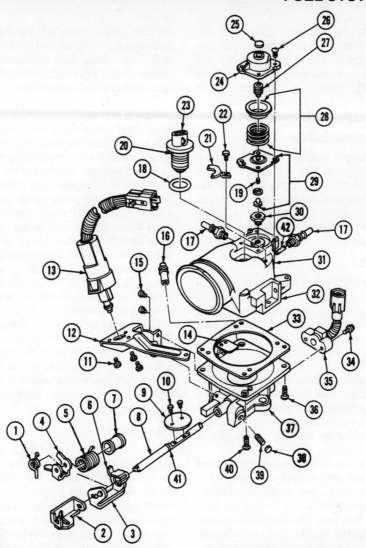

ITEM	PART NO.	PART NAME
1.	9C531-A	Spring—engine idle speed-up control actuator
2.	9G542-A	Lever—carb. transmission linkage
3.	9E551-A	Ball—carb. throttle lever
4.	9D549-A	Lever—carb. idle speed-up control
5.	9B569-A	Spring—carb. throttle return
6.	9583-AA	Lever—carb. throttle
7.	9C834-A	Bearing—throttle control linkage
8.	9E951-A	Shaft—air intake charge throttle
9.	9E950-A	Plate—air intake charge throttle
10.	903076-S100	Screw—M4 × .7 × 8.0
11.	384755-S2	Screw—M4.2 × 1.41 × 15.9 (self tapping)
12.	9S555-A	Bracket—engine throttle positioner
13.	9N825-A	Actuator Assy—throttle control
14.	9F553-A	Plate—engine air distribution
15.	N603253-S100	Screw—M5 × .8 × 14.0
16.	6B608-B	Tube—carb. emission inlet
17.	9F681-A	Connector—quick connect fuel injection (5/16 × 1/4 NPTF)
18.	87021-S100	O-ring—20.4 ID × 1.78 wide
19.	9D920-A	Spring—fuel pressure reg. valve
20.	87049-S100	O-ring—18.6 ID × 3.50 wide
21.	9C976-A	Retainer—fuel injector
22.	N603078-S100	Screw—M4 × .7 × 12.0
23.	9F593-A	Injector assy—fuel
24.	9D911-B	Cover—fuel pressure regulator
25.	383191-S	Plug—expansion
26.	N603245-S100	Screw—M4 × .7 × 16.0
27.	9D932-A	Screw—fuel pressure regulator adjusting
28.	9D923	Cup and spring assy—fuel pressure regulator
29.	9D919	Diaphragm assy—fuel pressure regulator
30.	9D909-A	Tube—fuel press reg. outlet
31.	9C974-B	Body assy—fuel charging main
32.	9C973-A	Body—fuel charging main
33.	9C983-B	Gasket—fuel charging body
34.	N800885-S	Screw—M4 × .7 × 22.0
35.	9B989-B	Potentiometer assy—carburetor throttle
36.	N603256-S100	Screw—M5 × .8 × 25.0
37.	9C981-A	Body—fuel charging throttle
39.	NN800545-S52	Screw—M5 × .8 × 19.0
40.	N603257-S100	Screw—M5 × .8 × 30.0
41.	9F791-A	Seal—fuel charging shaft
42.	9F525-AA	Screen—fuel inlet

CFI injection components

matic kick-down vacuum motor. There is also an all-electric, bimetal coil spring which controls cold idle speed. The bimetal electric coil operates like a conventional carburetor choke coil, but the electronic fuel injection system uses no choke. Fuel enrichment for cold starts is controlled by the computer and injectors.

FUEL PRESSURE REGULATOR

The fuel pressure regulator controls critical injector fuel pressure. The regulator receives fuel from the electric fuel pump and then adjusts the fuel pressure for uniform fuel injection. The regulator sets fuel pressure at 39 psi on high pressure systems, or 14.5 psi on low pressure systems.

FUEL MANIFOLD

The fuel manifold (or fuel rail) evenly distributes fuel to each injector. Its main purpose is to equalize the fuel flow. One end of the fuel rail contains a relief valve for testing fuel pressure during engine operation.

FUEL INJECTORS

The fuel injectors are electromechanical devices. The electrical solenoid operates a pindle or ball metering valve which always travels the same distance from closed to open to closed. Injection is controlled by varying the length of time the valve is open.

The computer, based on voltage inputs from the crank position sensor, operates each injector solenoid two times per engine revolution. When the injector metering valve unseats, fuel is sprayed in a fine mist into the intake manifold. The computer varies fuel enrichment based on voltage inputs from the exhaust gas oxygen sensor, barometric pressure sensor, manifold absolute pressure sensor, etc., by calculating how long to hold the injectors open. The longer the injectors remain open, the richer the mixture. This injector ON time is called pulse duration.

ELECTRONIC FUEL INJECTION (EFI)

The EFI fuel subsystem include a high pressure (30-45 psi) tank mounted electric fuel pump, fuel charging manifold, pressure regulator, fuel filter and both solid and flexible fuel lines. The fuel charging manifold includes six electronically controlled fuel injectors, each mounted directly above an intake port in the lower intake manifold. The Electronic Engine Control computer outputs a command to the fuel injectors to meter the appropriate quantity of fuel.

The fuel pressure regulator maintains a constant pressure drop across the injector nozzles. The regulator is referenced to intake manifold

vacuum and is connected parallel to the fuel injectors and positioned on the far end of the fuel rail. Any excess fuel supplied by the pump passes through the regulator and is returned to the fuel tank via a return line.

The fuel pressure regulator is a diaphragm operated relief valve in which one side of the diaphragm senses fuel pressure and the other side senses manifold vacuum. Normal fuel pressure is established by a spring preload applied to the diaphragm. Control of the fuel system is maintained through the EEC (Electronic Engine Control) power relay and the EEC IV control unit, although electrical power is routed through the fuel pump relay and an inertia switch. The fuel pump relay is normally located on a bracket somewhere above the Electronic Control Assembly (ECA) and the Inertia Switch is located in the trunk. Tank-mounted pumps can be either high or low-pressure, depending on the model.

The inertia switch opens the power circuit to the fuel pump in the event of a collision. Once tripped, the switch must be reset manually by pushing the reset button on the assembly. Check that the inertia switch is reset before diagnosing power supply problems to the fuel pump circuit.

Fuel Injectors

The fuel injectors used with the EFI system are electromechanical (solenoid) type designed to meter and atomize fuel delivered to the intake ports of the engine. The injectors are mounted in the lower intake manifold and positioned so that their spray nozzles direct the fuel charge in front of the intake valves. The injector body consists of a solenoid actuated pindle and needle valve assembly. The control unit sends an electrical impulse that activates the solenoid, causing the pindle to move inward off the seat and allow the fuel to flow. The amount of fuel delivered is controlled by the length of time the injector is energized (pulse width), since the fuel flow orifice is fixed and the fuel pressure drop across the injector tip is constant. Correct atomization is achieved by contouring the pindle at the point where the fuel enters the pindle chamber.

NOTE: *Exercise care when handling fuel injectors during service. Be careful not to lose the pindle cap and replace O-rings to assure a tight seal. Never apply direct battery voltage to test a fuel injector.*

The injectors receive high pressure fuel from the fuel manifold (fuel rail) assembly. The complete assembly includes a single, preformed tube with six injector connectors, mounting flange for the pressure regulator, mounting attachments to locate the manifold and provide

CHILTON'S
FUEL ECONOMY & TUNE-UP TIPS

Tune-up • Spark Plug Diagnosis • Emission Controls

Fuel System • Cooling System • Tires and Wheels

General Maintenance

CHILTON'S FUEL ECONOMY & TUNE-UP TIPS

Fuel economy is important to everyone, no matter what kind of vehicle you drive. The maintenance-minded motorist can save both money and fuel using these tips and the periodic maintenance and tune-up procedures in this Repair and Tune-Up Guide.

There are more than 130,000,000 cars and trucks registered for private use in the United States. Each travels an average of 10-12,000 miles per year, and, and in total they consume close to 70 billion gallons of fuel each year. This represents nearly ⅔ of the oil imported by the United States each year. The Federal government's goal is to reduce consumption 10% by 1985. A variety of methods are either already in use or under serious consideration, and they all affect you driving and the cars you will drive. In addition to "down-sizing", the auto industry is using or investigating the use of electronic fuel delivery, electronic engine controls and alternative engines for use in smaller and lighter vehicles, among other alternatives to meet the federally mandated Corporate Average Fuel Economy (CAFE) of 27.5 mpg by 1985. The government, for its part, is considering rationing, mandatory driving curtailments and tax increases on motor vehicle fuel in an effort to reduce consumption. The government's goal of a 10% reduction could be realized — and further government regulation avoided — if every private vehicle could use just 1 less gallon of fuel per week.

How Much Can You Save?

Tests have proven that almost anyone can make at least a 10% reduction in fuel consumption through regular maintenance and tune-ups. When a major manufacturer of spark plugs sur-

TUNE-UP

1. Check the cylinder compression to be sure the engine will really benefit from a tune-up and that it is capable of producing good fuel economy. A tune-up will be wasted on an engine in poor mechanical condition.

2. Replace spark plugs regularly. New spark plugs alone can increase fuel economy 3%.

3. Be sure the spark plugs are the correct type (heat range) for your vehicle. See the Tune-Up Specifications.

Heat range refers to the spark plug's ability to conduct heat away from the firing end. It must conduct the heat away in an even pattern to avoid becoming a source of pre-ignition, yet it must also operate hot enough to burn off conductive deposits that could cause misfiring.

The heat range is usually indicated by a number on the spark plug, part of the manufacturer's designation for each individual spark plug. The numbers in bold-face indicate the heat range in each manufacturer's identification system.

Periodically, check the spark plugs to be sure they are firing efficiently. They are excellent indicators of the internal condition of your engine.

Manufacturer	Typical Designation
AC	R **45** TS
Bosch (old)	WA **145** T30
Bosch (new)	HR **8** Y
Champion	RBL **15** Y
Fram/Autolite	4**15**
Mopar	P-**62** PR
Motorcraft	BRF-**42**
NGK	BP **5** ES-15
Nippondenso	W **16** EP
Prestolite	14GR **5** 2A

On AC, Bosch (new), Champion, Fram/Autolite, Mopar, Motorcraft and Prestolite, a higher number indicates a hotter plug. On Bosch (old), NGK and Nippondenso, a higher number indicates a colder plug.

4. Make sure the spark plugs are properly gapped. See the Tune-Up Specifications in this book.

5. Be sure the spark plugs are firing efficiently. The illustrations on the next 2 pages show you how to "read" the firing end of the spark plug.

6. Check the ignition timing and set it to specifications. Tests show that almost all cars have incorrect ignition timing by more than 2°.

veyed over 6,000 cars nationwide, they found that a tune-up, on cars that needed one, increased fuel economy over 11%. Replacing worn plugs alone, accounted for a 3% increase. The same test also revealed that 8 out of every 10 vehicles will have some maintenance deficiency that will directly affect fuel economy, emissions or performance. Most of this mileage-robbing neglect could be prevented with regular maintenance.

Modern engines require that all of the functioning systems operate properly for maximum efficiency. A malfunction anywhere wastes fuel. You can keep your vehicle running as efficiently and economically as possible, by being aware of your vehicle's operating and performance characteristics. If your vehicle suddenly develops performance or fuel economy problems it could be due to one or more of the following:

PROBLEM	POSSIBLE CAUSE
Engine Idles Rough	Ignition timing, idle mixture, vacuum leak or something amiss in the emission control system.
Hesitates on Acceleration	Dirty carburetor or fuel filter, improper accelerator pump setting, ignition timing or fouled spark plugs.
Starts Hard or Fails to Start	Worn spark plugs, improperly set automatic choke, ice (or water) in fuel system.
Stalls Frequently	Automatic choke improperly adjusted and possible dirty air filter or fuel filter.
Performs Sluggishly	Worn spark plugs, dirty fuel or air filter, ignition timing or automatic choke out of adjustment.

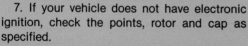

Check spark plug wires on conventional point type ignition for cracks by bending them in a loop around your finger.

Be sure that spark plug wires leading to adjacent cylinders do not run too close together. (Photo courtesy Champion Spark Plug Co.)

7. If your vehicle does not have electronic ignition, check the points, rotor and cap as specified.

8. Check the spark plug wires (used with conventional point-type ignitions) for cracks and burned or broken insulation by bending them in a loop around your finger. Cracked wires decrease fuel efficiency by failing to deliver full voltage to the spark plugs. One misfiring spark plug can cost you as much as 2 mpg.

9. Check the routing of the plug wires. Misfiring can be the result of spark plug leads to adjacent cylinders running parallel to each other and too close together. One wire tends to pick up voltage from the other causing it to fire "out of time".

10. Check all electrical and ignition circuits for voltage drop and resistance.

11. Check the distributor mechanical and/or vacuum advance mechanisms for proper functioning. The vacuum advance can be checked by twisting the distributor plate in the opposite direction of rotation. It should spring back when released.

12. Check and adjust the valve clearance on engines with mechanical lifters. The clearance should be slightly loose rather than too tight.

SPARK PLUG DIAGNOSIS

Normal

APPEARANCE: This plug is typical of one operating normally. The insulator nose varies from a light tan to grayish color with slight electrode wear. The presence of slight deposits is normal on used plugs and will have no adverse effect on engine performance. The spark plug heat range is correct for the engine and the engine is running normally.

CAUSE: Properly running engine.

RECOMMENDATION: Before reinstalling this plug, the electrodes should be cleaned and filed square. Set the gap to specifications. If the plug has been in service for more than 10-12,000 miles, the entire set should probably be replaced with a fresh set of the same heat range.

Oil Deposits

APPEARANCE: The firing end of the plug is covered with a wet, oily coating.

CAUSE: The problem is poor oil control. On high mileage engines, oil is leaking past the rings or valve guides into the combustion chamber. A common cause is also a plugged PCV valve, and a ruptured fuel pump diaphragm can also cause this condition. Oil fouled plugs such as these are often found in new or recently overhauled engines, before normal oil control is achieved, and can be cleaned and reinstalled.

RECOMMENDATION: A hotter spark plug may temporarily relieve the problem, but the engine is probably in need of work.

Incorrect Heat Range

APPEARANCE: The effects of high temperature on a spark plug are indicated by clean white, often blistered insulator. This can also be accompanied by excessive wear of the electrode, and the absence of deposits.

CAUSE: Check for the correct spark plug heat range. A plug which is too hot for the engine can result in overheating. A car operated mostly at high speeds can require a colder plug. Also check ignition timing, cooling system level, fuel mixture and leaking intake manifold.

RECOMMENDATION: If all ignition and engine adjustments are known to be correct, and no other malfunction exists, install spark plugs one heat range colder.

Carbon Deposits

APPEARANCE: Carbon fouling is easily identified by the presence of dry, soft, black, sooty deposits.

CAUSE: Changing the heat range can often lead to carbon fouling, as can prolonged slow, stop-and-start driving. If the heat range is correct, carbon fouling can be attributed to a rich fuel mixture, sticking choke, clogged air cleaner, worn breaker points, retarded timing or low compression. If only one or two plugs are carbon fouled, check for corroded or cracked wires on the affected plugs. Also look for cracks in the distributor cap between the towers of affected cylinders.

RECOMMENDATION: After the problem is corrected, these plugs can be cleaned and reinstalled if not worn severely.

MMT Fouled

APPEARANCE: Spark plugs fouled by MMT (Methycyclopentadienyl Maganese Tricarbonyl) have reddish, rusty appearance on the insulator and side electrode.

CAUSE: MMT is an anti-knock additive in gasoline used to replace lead. During the combustion process, the MMT leaves a reddish deposit on the insulator and side electrode.

RECOMMENDATION: No engine malfunction is indicated and the deposits will not affect plug performance any more than lead deposits (see Ash Deposits). MMT fouled plugs can be cleaned, regapped and reinstalled.

High Speed Glazing

APPEARANCE: Glazing appears as shiny coating on the plug, either yellow or tan in color.

CAUSE: During hard, fast acceleration, plug temperatures rise suddenly. Deposits from normal combustion have no chance to fluff-off; instead, they melt on the insulator forming an electrically conductive coating which causes misfiring.

RECOMMENDATION: Glazed plugs are not easily cleaned. They should be replaced with a fresh set of plugs of the correct heat range. If the condition recurs, using plugs with a heat range one step colder may cure the problem.

Ash (Lead) Deposits

APPEARANCE: Ash deposits are characterized by light brown or white colored deposits crusted on the side or center electrodes. In some cases it may give the plug a rusty appearance.

CAUSE: Ash deposits are normally derived from oil or fuel additives burned during normal combustion. Normally they are harmless, though excessive amounts can cause misfiring. If deposits are excessive in short mileage, the valve guides may be worn.

RECOMMENDATION: Ash-fouled plugs can be cleaned, gapped and reinstalled.

Detonation

APPEARANCE: Detonation is usually characterized by a broken plug insulator.

CAUSE: A portion of the fuel charge will begin to burn spontaneously, from the increased heat following ignition. The explosion that results applies extreme pressure to engine components, frequently damaging spark plugs and pistons.

Detonation can result by over-advanced ignition timing, inferior gasoline (low octane) lean air/fuel mixture, poor carburetion, engine lugging or an increase in compression ratio due to combustion chamber deposits or engine modification.

RECOMMENDATION: Replace the plugs after correcting the problem.

Photos Courtesy Champion Spark Plug Co.

EMISSION CONTROLS

13. Be aware of the general condition of the emission control system. It contributes to reduced pollution and should be serviced regularly to maintain efficient engine operation.

14. Check all vacuum lines for dried, cracked or brittle conditions. Something as simple as a leaking vacuum hose can cause poor performance and loss of economy.

15. Avoid tampering with the emission control system. Attempting to improve fuel econ-

FUEL SYSTEM

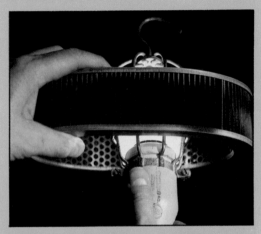

Check the air filter with a light behind it. If you can see light through the filter it can be reused.

Extremely clogged filters should be discarded and replaced with a new one.

18. Replace the air filter regularly. A dirty air filter richens the air/fuel mixture and can increase fuel consumption as much as 10%. Tests show that ⅓ of all vehicles have air filters in need of replacement.

19. Replace the fuel filter at least as often as recommended.

20. Set the idle speed and carburetor mixture to specifications.

21. Check the automatic choke. A sticking or malfunctioning choke wastes gas.

22. During the summer months, adjust the automatic choke for a leaner mixture which will produce faster engine warm-ups.

COOLING SYSTEM

29. Be sure all accessory drive belts are in good condition. Check for cracks or wear.

30. Adjust all accessory drive belts to proper tension.

31. Check all hoses for swollen areas, worn spots, or loose clamps.

32. Check coolant level in the radiator or expansion tank.

33. Be sure the thermostat is operating properly. A stuck thermostat delays engine warm-up and a cold engine uses nearly twice as much fuel as a warm engine.

34. Drain and replace the engine coolant at least as often as recommended. Rust and scale

TIRES & WHEELS

38. Check the tire pressure often with a pencil type gauge. Tests by a major tire manufacturer show that 90% of all vehicles have at least 1 tire improperly inflated. Better mileage can be achieved by over-inflating tires, but never exceed the maximum inflation pressure on the side of the tire.

39. If possible, install radial tires. Radial tires deliver as much as ½ mpg more than bias belted tires.

40. Avoid installing super-wide tires. They only create extra rolling resistance and decrease fuel mileage. Stick to the manufacturer's recommendations.

41. Have the wheels properly balanced.

omy by tampering with emission controls is more likely to worsen fuel economy than improve it. Emission control changes on modern engines are not readily reversible.

16. Clean (or replace) the EGR valve and lines as recommended.

17. Be sure that all vacuum lines and hoses are reconnected properly after working under the hood. An unconnected or misrouted vacuum line can wreak havoc with engine performance.

23. Check for fuel leaks at the carburetor, fuel pump, fuel lines and fuel tank. Be sure all lines and connections are tight.

24. Periodically check the tightness of the carburetor and intake manifold attaching nuts and bolts. These are a common place for vacuum leaks to occur.

25. Clean the carburetor periodically and lubricate the linkage.

26. The condition of the tailpipe can be an excellent indicator of proper engine combustion. After a long drive at highway speeds, the inside of the tailpipe should be a light grey in color. Black or soot on the insides indicates an overly rich mixture.

27. Check the fuel pump pressure. The fuel pump may be supplying more fuel than the engine needs.

28. Use the proper grade of gasoline for your engine. Don't try to compensate for knocking or "pinging" by advancing the ignition timing. This practice will only increase plug temperature and the chances of detonation or pre-ignition with relatively little performance gain.

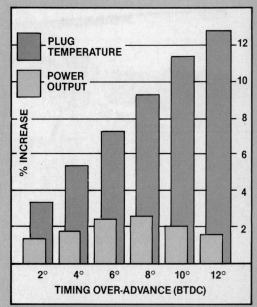

Increasing ignition timing past the specified setting results in a drastic increase in spark plug temperature with increased chance of detonation or preignition. Performance increase is considerably less. (Photo courtesy Champion Spark Plug Co.)

that form in the engine should be flushed out to allow the engine to operate at peak efficiency.

35. Clean the radiator of debris that can decrease cooling efficiency.

36. Install a flex-type or electric cooling fan, if you don't have a clutch type fan. Flex fans use curved plastic blades to push more air at low speeds when more cooling is needed; at high speeds the blades flatten out for less resistance. Electric fans only run when the engine temperature reaches a predetermined level.

37. Check the radiator cap for a worn or cracked gasket. If the cap does not seal properly, the cooling system will not function properly.

42. Be sure the front end is correctly aligned. A misaligned front end actually has wheels going in differed directions. The increased drag can reduce fuel economy by .3 mpg.

43. Correctly adjust the wheel bearings. Wheel bearings that are adjusted too tight increase rolling resistance.

Check tire pressures regularly with a reliable pocket type gauge. Be sure to check the pressure on a cold tire.

GENERAL MAINTENANCE

Check the fluid levels (particularly engine oil) on a regular basis. Be sure to check the oil for grit, water or other contamination.

A vacuum gauge is another excellent indicator of internal engine condition and can also be installed in the dash as a mileage indicator.

44. Periodically check the fluid levels in the engine, power steering pump, master cylinder, automatic transmission and drive axle.

45. Change the oil at the recommended interval and change the filter at every oil change. Dirty oil is thick and causes extra friction between moving parts, cutting efficiency and increasing wear. A worn engine requires more frequent tune-ups and gets progressively worse fuel economy. In general, use the lightest viscosity oil for the driving conditions you will encounter.

46. Use the recommended viscosity fluids in the transmission and axle.

47. Be sure the battery is fully charged for fast starts. A slow starting engine wastes fuel.

48. Be sure battery terminals are clean and tight.

49. Check the battery electrolyte level and add distilled water if necessary.

50. Check the exhaust system for crushed pipes, blockages and leaks.

51. Adjust the brakes. Dragging brakes or brakes that are not releasing create increased drag on the engine.

52. Install a vacuum gauge or miles-per-gallon gauge. These gauges visually indicate engine vacuum in the intake manifold. High vacuum = good mileage and low vacuum = poorer mileage. The gauge can also be an excellent indicator of internal engine conditions.

53. Be sure the clutch is properly adjusted. A slipping clutch wastes fuel.

54. Check and periodically lubricate the heat control valve in the exhaust manifold. A sticking or inoperative valve prevents engine warm-up and wastes gas.

55. Keep accurate records to check fuel economy over a period of time. A sudden drop in fuel economy may signal a need for tune-up or other maintenance.

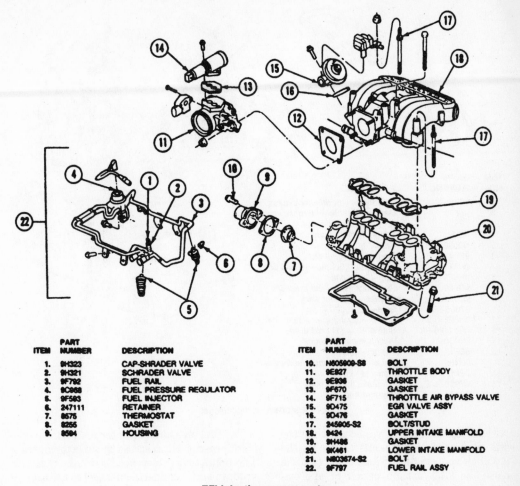

ITEM	PART NUMBER	DESCRIPTION
1.	9H323	CAP-SHRADER VALVE
2.	9H321	SCHRADER VALVE
3.	9F792	FUEL RAIL
4.	9C968	FUEL PRESSURE REGULATOR
5.	9F593	FUEL INJECTOR
6.	247111	RETAINER
7.	8575	THERMOSTAT
8.	8255	GASKET
9.	8504	HOUSING
10.	N605909-S8	BOLT
11.	9E927	THROTTLE BODY
12.	9E936	GASKET
13.	9F670	GASKET
14.	9F715	THROTTLE AIR BYPASS VALVE
15.	9D475	EGR VALVE ASSY
16.	9D476	GASKET
17.	245905-S2	BOLT/STUD
18.	9424	UPPER INTAKE MANIFOLD
19.	9H486	GASKET
20.	9K461	LOWER INTAKE MANIFOLD
21.	N803574-S2	BOLT
22.	9F797	FUEL RAIL ASSY

EFI injection components

the fuel injector retainers and a Schrader® quick-disconnect fitting used to perform fuel pressure tests.

The fuel manifold is normally removed with fuel injectors and pressure regulator attached. Fuel injector electrical connectors are plastic and have locking tabs that must be released when disconnecting the wiring harness.

Air Subsystem

The air subsystem components include the air cleaner assembly, air flow (vane) meter, throttle air bypass valve and air ducts that connect the air system to the throttle body assembly. The throttle body regulates the air flow to the engine through a single butterfly-type throttle plate controlled by conventional accelerator linkage. The throttle body has an idle adjustment screw (throttle air bypass valve) to set the throttle plate position, a PCV fresh air source upstream of the throttle plate, individual vacuum taps for PCV and control signals and a throttle position sensor that provides a voltage signal for the EEC-IV control unit.

Throttle Air Bypass Valve

The throttle air bypass valve is an electro-mechanical (solenoid) device whose operation is controlled by the EEC IV control unit. A variable air metering valve controls both cold and warm idle air flow in response to commands from the control unit. The valve operates by bypassing a regulated amount of air around the throttle plate; the higher the voltage signal from the control unit, the more air is bypassed through the valve. In this manner, additional air can be added to the fuel mixture without moving the throttle plate. At curb idle, the valve provides smooth idle for various engine coolant temperatures, compensates for A/C load and compensates for transaxle load and no-load conditions. The valve also provides fast idle for start-up, replacing the fast idle cam, throttle kicker and anti-dieseling solenoid common to previous models.

There are no curb idle or fast idle adjustments. As in curb idle operation, the fast idle speed is proportional to engine coolant temper-

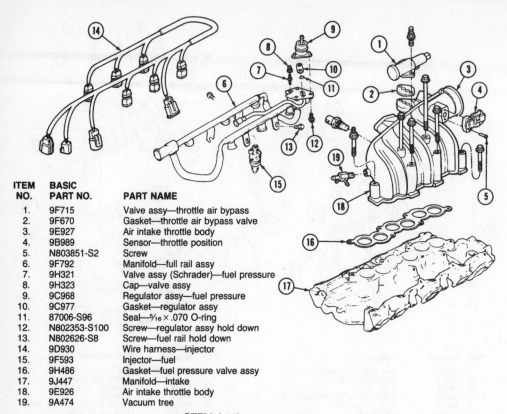

ITEM NO.	BASIC PART NO.	PART NAME
1.	9F715	Valve assy—throttle air bypass
2.	9F670	Gasket—throttle air bypass valve
3.	9E927	Air intake throttle body
4.	9B989	Sensor—throttle position
5.	N803851-S2	Screw
6.	9F792	Manifold—full rail assy
7.	9H321	Valve assy (Schrader)—fuel pressure
8.	9H323	Cap—valve assy
9.	9C968	Regulator assy—fuel pressure
10.	9C977	Gasket—regulator assy
11.	87006-S96	Seal—5/16 × .070 O-ring
12.	N802353-S100	Screw—regulator assy hold down
13.	N802626-S8	Screw—fuel rail hold down
14.	9D930	Wire harness—injector
15.	9F593	Injector—fuel
16.	9H486	Gasket—fuel pressure valve assy
17.	9J447	Manifold—intake
18.	9E926	Air intake throttle body
19.	9A474	Vacuum tree

SEFI injection components

ature. Fast idle kick-down will occur when the throttle is kicked. A time-out feature in the ECA will also automatically kick-down fast idle to curb idle after a time period of approximately 15-25 seconds; after coolant has reached approximately 71°C (160°F). The signal duty cycle from the ECA to the valve will be at 100% (maximum current) during the crank to provide maximum air flow to allow no touch starting at any time (engine cold or hot).

SEQUENTIAL ELECTRONIC FUEL INJECTION (SEFI)

The Sequential Electronic Fuel Injection system is classified as a multi-point, pulse time, speed density control fuel injection system. The fuel is metered into the intake manifold port in sequence in accordance with the engine demand through the six injectors mounted on a tuned intake manifold. The Electronic Engine Control (EEC) computer outputs a command to the fuel injectors to meter the appropriate quantity of fuel. The remainder of the fuel system is basically the same as the EFI system installed on the 3.0L and 3.8L engines.

The SEFI fuel subsystem include a high pressure (30-45 psi) tank mounted electric fuel pump, fuel charging manifold, pressure regulator, fuel filter and both solid and flexible fuel lines.

The fuel pressure regulator maintains a constant pressure drop across the injector nozzles. The regulator is referenced to intake manifold vacuum and is connected parallel to the fuel injectors and positioned on the far end of the fuel rail. Any excess fuel supplied by the pump passes through the regulator and is returned to the fuel tank via a return line.

The fuel pressure regulator is a diaphragm operated relief valve in which one side of the diaphragm senses fuel pressure and the other side senses manifold vacuum. Normal fuel pressure is established by a spring preload applied

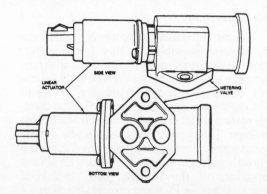

1 Air bypass valve — 3.0L and 3.8L engines

to the diaphragm. Control of the fuel system is maintained through the EEC (Electronic Engine Control) power relay and the EEC IV control unit, although electrical power is routed through the fuel pump relay and an inertia switch. The fuel pump relay is normally located on a bracket somewhere above the Electronic Control Assembly (ECA) and the Inertia Switch is located in the trunk. Tank mounted pumps can be either high or low pressure, depending on the model.

Fuel Injectors

The fuel injectors used with the SEFI system are electromechanical (solenoid) type designed to meter and atomize fuel delivered to the intake ports of the engine. The injectors are mounted in the lower intake manifold and positioned so that their spray nozzles direct the fuel charge in front of the intake valves. The injector body consists of a solenoid actuated pindle and needle valve assembly. The control unit sends an electrical impulse that activates the solenoid, causing the pindle to move inward off the seat and allow the fuel to flow. The amount of fuel delivered is controlled by the length of time the injector is energized (pulse width), since the fuel flow orifice is fixed and the fuel pressure drop across the injector tip is constant. Correct atomization is achieved by contouring the pindle at the point where the fuel enters the pindle chamber.

NOTE: *Exercise care when handling fuel injectors during service. Be careful not to lose the pindle cap and replace O-rings to assure a tight seal. Never apply direct battery voltage to test a fuel injector.*

The injectors receive high pressure fuel from the fuel manifold (fuel rail) assembly. The complete assembly includes a single, preformed tube with six injector connectors, mounting flange for the pressure regulator, mounting attachments to locate the manifold and provide the fuel injector retainers and a Schrader® quick-disconnect fitting used to perform fuel pressure tests.

The fuel manifold is normally removed with fuel injectors and pressure regulator attached. Fuel injector electrical connectors are plastic and have locking tabs that must be released when disconnecting the wiring harness.

Air Subsystem

The air subsystem components include the air cleaner assembly, air flow (vane) meter, throttle air bypass valve and air ducts that connect the air system to the throttle body assembly. The throttle body regulates the air flow to the engine through a single butterfly-type throttle plate controlled by conventional accelerator linkage. The throttle body has an idle adjustment screw (throttle air bypass valve) to set the throttle plate position, a PCV fresh air source upstream of the throttle plate, individual vacuum taps for PCV and control signals, and a throttle position sensor that provides a voltage signal for the EEC-IV control unit.

Throttle Air Bypass Valve

The throttle air bypass valve is an electromechanical (solenoid) device whose operation is controlled by the EEC IV control unit. A variable air metering valve controls both cold and warm idle air flow in response to commands from the control unit. The valve operates by bypassing a regulated amount of air around the throttle plate; the higher the voltage signal from the control unit, the more air is bypassed through the valve. In this manner, additional air can be added to the fuel mixture without moving the throttle plate. At curb idle, the valve provides smooth idle for various engine coolant temperatures, compensates for A/C load and compensates for transaxle load and no-load conditions. The valve also provides fast idle for start-up, replacing the fast idle cam, throttle kicker and anti-dieseling solenoid common to previous models.

There are no curb idle or fast idle adjustments. As in curb idle operation, the fast idle speed is proportional to engine coolant temperature. Fast idle kick-down will occur when the throttle is kicked. A time-out feature in the ECA will also automatically kick-down fast idle to curb idle after a time period of approximately 15-25 seconds; after coolant has reached approximately 71°C (160°F). The signal duty cycle from the ECA to the valve will be at 100% (maximum current) during the crank to provide maximum air flow to allow no touch starting at any time (engine cold or hot).

Fuel System Precautions

Safety is the most important factor when performing not only fuel system maintenance but any type of maintenance. Failure to conduct maintenance and repairs in a safe manner may result in serious personal injury or death. Maintenance and testing of the vehicle's fuel system components can be accomplished safely and effectively by adhering to the following rules and guidelines.

To avoid the possibility of fire and personal injury, always disconnect the negative battery cable unless the repair or test procedure requires that battery voltage be applied.

• Always relieve the fuel system pressure prior to disconnecting any fuel system component (injector, fuel rail, pressure regulator, etc.), fitting or fuel line connection. Exercise extreme caution whenever relieving fuel system pressure to avoid exposing skin, face and eyes to fuel spray. Please be advised that fuel under pressure may penetrate the skin or any part of the body that it contacts.

• Always place a shop towel or cloth around the fitting or connection prior to loosening to absorb any excess fuel due to spillage. Ensure that all fuel spillage (should it occur) is quickly removed from engine surfaces. Ensure that all fuel soaked cloths or towels are deposited into a suitable waste container.

• Always keep a dry chemical (Class B) fire extinguisher near the work area.

• Do not allow fuel spray or fuel vapors to come into contact with a spark or open flame.

• Always use a backup wrench when loosening and tightening fuel line connection fittings. This will prevent unnecessary stress and torsion to fuel line piping. Always follow the proper torque specifications.

• Always replace worn fuel fitting O-rings with new. Do not substitute fuel hose or equivalent where fuel pipe is installed.

Relieving Fuel System Pressure

PROCEDURE

1. The pressure in the fuel system must be released before attempting to disconnect any fuel lines.

2. A special valve is incorporated in the fuel rail assembly for the purpose of relieving the pressure in the fuel system.

3. Attach pressure gauge tool T80L–9974–A or equivalent, to the fuel pressure valve on the fuel rail assembly and release the pressure from the system into a suitable container.

Fuel Filter

REMOVAL AND INSTALLATION

1. Disconnect the negative battery cable. Relieve the fuel system pressure.

2. Remove the push connect fittings at both ends of the fuel filter. This is accomplished by removing the hairpin clips from the fittings. Remove the hairpin clips by first bending and then breaking the shipping tabs on the clips. Then spread the 2 clip legs approximately $1/8$ in. (3mm) to disengage the body and push the legs into the fitting. Pull on the triangular end of the clip and work it clear of the fitting.

3. Remove the filter from the mounting bracket by loosening the worm gear mounting clamp enough to allow the filter to pass through.

To install:

4. Install the filter in the mounting

bracket, ensuring that the flow direction arrow is pointing forward. Locate the fuel filter against the tab at the lower end of the bracket.

5. Insert a new hairpin clip into any 2 adjacent openings on each push connect fitting, with the triangular portion of the clip pointing away from the fitting opening. Install the clip to fully engage the body of the fitting. This is indicated by the legs of the hairpin clip being locked on the outside of the fitting body. Apply a light coat of engine oil to the ends of the fuel filter and then push the fittings onto the ends of the fuel filter. When the fittings are engaged, a definite click will be heard. Pull on the fittings to ensure that they are fully engaged.

6. Tighten the worm gear mounting clamp to 15–25 inch lbs. (1.7–2.8 Nm).

7. Start the engine and check for leaks.

Electric Fuel Pump

REMOVAL AND INSTALLATION

1. Disconnect the negative battery cable.

2. Relieve the fuel system pressure.

3. Remove the fuel tank from the vehicle and place it on a work bench. Remove any dirt around the fuel pump attaching flange.

4. Turn the fuel pump locking ring counterclockwise and remove the lock ring.

5. Remove the fuel pump from the fuel tank and discard the flange gasket.

To install:

6. Clean the fuel pump mounting flange and fuel tank mounting surface and seal ring groove.

7. Put a light coating of grease on the new seal gasket to hold it in place during assembly and install it in the fuel ring groove.

8. Install the fuel pump and sender assembly. Make sure the locating keys are in the keyways and the seal gasket remains in place.

9. Hold the assembly in place and install the lock ring making sure all locking tabs are under the tank lock ring tabs. Tighten the lock ring by turning it clockwise until it is up against the stops.

10. Install the fuel tank.

11. Fill the tank with a minimum of 10 gal-

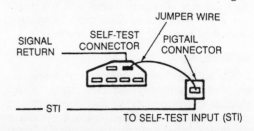

Jumper wire terminal test connection point locations — 2.5L engine with CFI

lons of fuel and check for leaks.

12. Connect a suitable fuel pressure gauge. Turn the ignition switch to the **ON** position 5–10 times, leaving it on for 3 seconds at a time, until the pressure gauge reads at least 30 psi. Check for leaks at the fittings.

13. Remove the pressure gauge, start the engine and recheck for leaks.

TESTING

1. Ground the fuel pump lead of the self-test connector through a jumper wire at the FP lead.

2. Connect a suitable fuel pressure tester to the fuel pump outlet.

3. Turn the ignition key to the **RUN** position to operate the fuel pump.

4. The fuel pressure should be 35–45 psi for all engines except the 2.5L engine. On the 1986–90 2.5L CFI engine, the fuel pressure should be 13–17 psi. On the 1991 2.5L SEFI engine, the fuel pressure should be 45–60 psi.

NOTE: *A safety inertia switch is installed to shut off the electric fuel pump in case of collision. The switch is located on the left hand side (driver's side) of the car, behind the rear most seat side trim panel, or inside the rear quarter shock tower access door. If the pump shuts off, or if the vehicle has been hit and will not start, check for leaks first then reset the switch. The switch is reset by pushing down on the button provided.*

Push Connect Fittings

Push connect fittings are designed with two different retaining clips. The fittings used with 8mm diameter tubing use a hairpin clip. The fittings used with 6mm and 12.7mm diameter tubing use a "duck bill" clip. Each type of fitting requires different procedures for service.

Push connect fitting disassembly must be accomplished prior to fuel component removal (filter, pump, etc.) except for the fuel tank

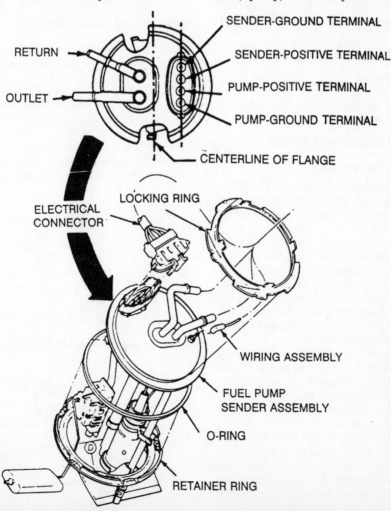

Electric fuel pump assembly and terminal location

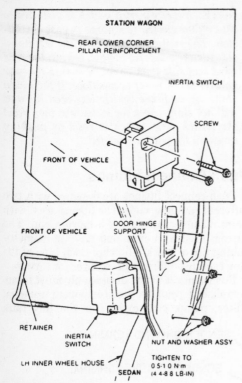

Inertia switch location

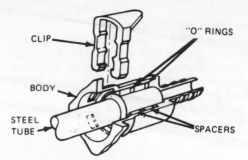

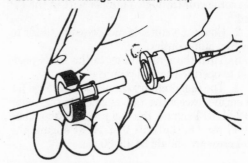

Push connect fittings with hairpin clip

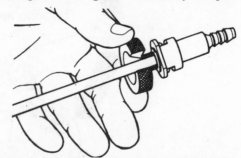

Pulling off push connect fitting

where removal is necessary for access to the push connects.

REMOVAL AND INSTALLATION

5/16 in. Fittings (Hairpin Clip)

1. Inspect the internal portion of the fitting for dirt accumulation. If more than a light coating of dust is present, clean the fitting before disassembly.

2. Remove the hairpin type clip from the fitting. This is done (using hands only) by spreading the two clip legs about 3mm each to disengage the body and pushing the legs into the fitting. Complete removal is accomplished by lightly pulling from the triangular end of the clip and working it clear of the tube and fitting. NOTE: *Do not use any tools.*

3. Grasp the fitting and hose assembly and pull in an axial direction to remove the fitting from the steel tube. Adhesion between sealing surfaces may occur. A slight twist of the fitting may be required to break this adhesion and permit effortless removal.

4. When the fitting is removed from the tube end, inspect clip to ensure it has not been damaged. If damaged, replace the clip. If undamaged, immediately reinstall the clip, insert the clip into any two adjacent openings with the triangular portion pointing away from the fitting opening. Install the clip to fully engage the

body (legs of hairpin clip locked on outside of body). Piloting with an index finger is necessary.

5. Before installing the fitting on the tube, wipe the tube end with a clean cloth. Inspect the inside of the fitting to ensure it is free of dirt and/or obstructions.

6. To reinstall the fitting onto the tube, lubricate the sealing O-rings with clean engine oil, align the fitting and tube axially and push

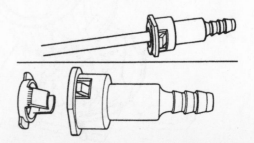

Removing push connect with proper removal tool

Push connect fittings with duck bill clip

the fitting onto the tube end. When the fitting is engaged, a definite click will be heard. Pull on the fitting to ensure it is fully engaged.

1/2 in. and 1/4 in. Fittings (Duck Bill Clip)

The fitting consists of a body, spacers, O-rings and a duck bill retaining clip. The clip maintains the fitting to the steel tube juncture. When disassembly is required for service, one of the two following methods are to be followed:

1/4 in. FITTINGS

To disengage the tube from the fitting, align the slot on the push connect disassembly Tool T82L-9500-AH or equivalent with either tab on the clip (90° from slots on side of fitting) and insert the tool. This disengages the duck bill from the tube. Holding the tool and the tube with one hand, pull fitting away from the tube.

NOTE: *Only moderate effort is required if the tube has been properly disengaged. Use hands only. After disassembly, inspect and clean the tube sealing surface. Also inspect the inside of the fitting for damage to the retaining clip. If the retaining clip appears to be damaged, replace it. Some fuel tubes have a secondary bead which aligns with the outer surface of the clip. These beads can make tool insertion difficult. If there is extreme difficulty, use the disassembly method following.*

1/2 in. FITTING AND ALTERNATE METHOD FOR 1/4 in. FITTING

This method of disassembly disengages the retaining clip from the fitting body.

Use a pair of narrow pliers, (6 in. [153mm] locking pliers are ideal). The pliers must have a jaw width of 5mm or less.

Align the jaws of the pliers with the openings in the side of the fitting case and compress the portion of the retaining clip that engages the fitting case. This disengages the retaining clip from the case (often one side of the clip will disengage before the other. It is necessary to disengage the clip from both openings). Pull the fitting off the tube.

NOTE: *Only moderate effort is required if the retaining clip has been properly disengaged. Use hands only.*

The retaining clip will remain on the tube. Disengage the clip from the tube bead and remove. Replace the retaining clip if it appears to be damaged.

NOTE: *Slight ovality of the ring of the clip will usually occur. If there are no visible cracks and the ring will pinch back to its circular configuration, it is not damaged. If there is any doubt, replace the clip.*

Install the clip into the body by inserting one of the retaining clip serrated edges on the duck bill portion into one of the window openings. Push on the other side until the clip snaps into place. Lubricate the O-rings with clean engine oil and slide the fuel line back into the clip.

Fuel Charging Assembly

REMOVAL AND INSTALLATION

CFI Injection

1986–90

1. Disconnect the negative battery cable. Remove the air cleaner.
2. Release pressure from the fuel system at the diagnostic (pressure relief) valve on the fuel charging assembly by carefully depressing the pin and discharging fuel into the throttle body.
3. Disconnect the throttle cable and transmission throttle valve lever.
4. Disconnect fuel, vacuum and electrical connections.

NOTE: *Either the multi or single ten pin connectors may be used on the system. To disconnect electrical ten pin connectors, push in or squeeze on the right side lower locking tab while pulling up on the connection. Multi connectors disconnect by pulling apart. The ISC (Idle Speed Control) connector tab must be moved out while pulling apart.*

5. Remove fuel charging assembly retaining nuts, then, remove fuel charging assembly.
6. Remove mounting gasket from intake manifold. Always use a new gasket for installation.

To install:

1. Clean gasket mounting surfaces of spacer and fuel charging assembly.
2. Place spacer between two new gaskets and place spacer and gaskets on the intake manifold. Position the charging assembly on the spacer and gasket.
3. Secure fuel charging assembly with attaching nuts.

NOTE: *To prevent leakage, distortion or damage to the fuel charging assembly body flange, snug the nuts; then, alternately tighten each nut in a criss-cross pattern. Tighten to 10 ft. lbs.*

4. Connect the fuel line, electrical connectors, throttle cable and all emission lines.
5. Start the engine, check for leaks. Adjust engine idle speed if necessary. Refer to the Engine/Emission Control Decal for idle speed specifications.

1991

1. Disconnect the negative battery cable. Properly relieve fuel system pressure. Disconnect the air bypass connector from the EEC-IV harness. Disconnect the spring lock coupling. Remove the engine air cleaner outlet tube.

2. Disconnect and remove the accelerator and speed control cables from the accelerator mounting bracket and the throttle lever.

3. Disconnect the top manifold vacuum fitting by disconnecting the rear vacuum line to dash panel vacuum tee, the vacuum line at the intake manifold, the MAP sensor vacuum line and the fuel pressure regulator vacuum line.

4. Disconnect the PCV system hoses. Disconnect the EGR vacuum line at the EGR valve.

5. Disconnect the EGR tube from the upper intake manifold by supporting the connector while loosening the compression nut.

6. Disconnect the upper support manifold bracket by removing only the top bolt. Leave the bottom bolts attached.

7. Disconnect the electrical connectors at the main engine harness.

8. Remove the fuel supply and return lines. Remove the eight manifold retaining bolts.

9. Disconnect the lower support manifold bracket by removing only the top bolt. Leave the bottom bolts attached.

10. Remove the manifold along with the wiring harness and gasket.

To install:

11. Clean and inspect the mounting surfaces. Install a new gasket.

12. Install the manifold assembly and finger tighten the retaining bolts at this time.

13. Install the fuel return line. Tighten the manifold retaining bolts to 15–22 ft. lbs.

14. Connect the upper and lower manifold support brackets. Torque the retaining bolts to 15–22 ft. lbs.

15. Install the EGR tube. Install the PCV system. Connect the rear manifold connections.

16. Connect the accelerator and speed control linkages. Connect the electrical wiring harness.

17. Connect the fuel supply line. Connect the fuel return line. Install the spring lock coupling.

18. Use the EEC-IV self test connector to check that the EEC-IV sensor is functioning properly.

19. Start the engine and check for fuel leaks.

Adjust the idle speed, as required.

EFI Injection

EXCEPT 3.8L ENGINE

1. With the ignition OFF, disconnect the negative (–) battery cable.

2. Remove the fuel cap and release the pressure at the pressure relief valve on the fuel rail assembly using a Fuel Pressure Gauge part No. T80L-9974-B.

3. Disconnect electrical connectors at air bypass valve, throttle position sensor, EGR sensor and air charge temperature sensor (ACT).

4. Disconnect the fuel supply and return lines using a Fuel Line Disconnect Tool part No. D87L-9280-A or equivalent.

5. Disconnect the wiring connectors from the fuel injectors.

6. Remove snow/ice shield to expose throttle linkage. Disconnect throttle cable from ball stud.

7. Remove the engine air cleaner outlet

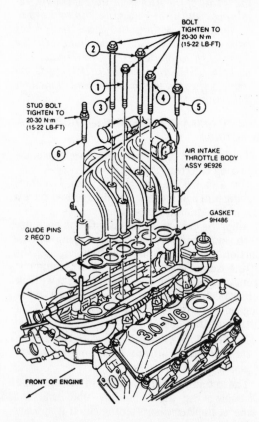

Fuel charging assembly – 3.0L engine

tube between air cleaner and air throttle body by loosening the two clamps.

8. Disconnect and remove the accelerator and speed control cables, if so equipped, from the throttle lever.

9. Remove the transaxle TV (throttle valve) linkage from the throttle lever (automatic only).

10. Loosen bolt which retains A/C line at the upper rear of the upper manifold and disengage retainer.

11. Remove the six retaining bolts and lift air intake throttle body assembly from the lower intake manifold assembly.

12. Clean and inspect mounting faces of the lower and upper intake manifold.

To install:

1. Position new gasket on lower intake mounting face. The use of alignment studs may be helpful.

2. Install upper intake manifold and throttle body assembly to lower manifold making sure gasket remains in place (if alignment studs aren't used). Align EGR tube in valve.

3. Install six upper intake manifold retaining bolts. Tighten to 15-22 ft. lbs. in sequence as shown in the fuel charging assembly diagram in this Chapter.

4. Engage A/C line retainer cup and tighten bolt to specification.

5. Tighten EGR tube and flare fitting. Tighten lower retainer nut at the exhaust manifold.

6. Install canister purge line to fitting.

7. Connect PCV vacuum hose to bottom of upper manifold and PCV closure hose to throttle body.

8. Connect vacuum lines to vacuum tree, EGR valve, and fuel pressure regulator.

9. Connect throttle cable to throttle body and install snow/ice shield.

10. Connect electrical connector at air bypass valve, TPS sensor, EGR sensor, and ACT sensor.

11. Install the fuel cap, start the engine and idle, and check for vacuum, fuel, or coolant leaks.

12. The transaxle TV (throttle valve) linkage has to be readjusted after the fuel charging assembly has been serviced:

   a. With the ignition key OFF and shift selector in PARK.

   b. Reset the automatic transaxle TV linkage by holding the ratchet in the released position and pushing the cable fitting toward the accelerator control bracket.

   c. At the throttle body, reset the TV cable by rotating the throttle linkage to wide-open throttle position by hand and release.

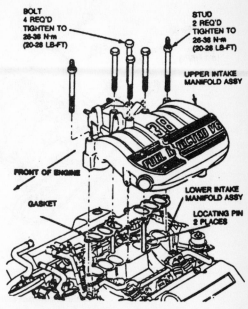

Fuel charging assembly — 3.8L engine

NOTE: *If lower intake manifold was removed, fill and bleed the cooling system.*

3.8L ENGINE

1. Disconnect the battery negative (–) cable.

2. Drain cooling system

3. Remove the fuel cap at the tank.

4. Release the fuel pressure by attaching a Fuel Pressure Gauge part No. T80L-9974-B or equivalent to the pressure relief valve on the fuel rail assembly.

5. Disconnect the electrical connectors at the air bypass valve, throttle position sensor, and EGR position sensor.

6. Disconnect the throttle linkage at the throttle ball and transaxle linkage from the throttle body.

7. Position the throttle and speed control linkage out of the way.

8. Disconnect the upper intake manifold vacuum fittings at the vacuum tree.

9. Remove the six upper intake manifold retaining bolts.

10. Remove the upper intake and throttle body assembly from the lower intake.

To install:

1. Clean and inspect the mounting surfaces of the upper and lower intake manifolds. Be careful not to damage the mounting surfaces.

2. Install the new gasket and upper intake into position using the alignment studs. If alignment studs are not used, make sure the gasket stays in place.

3. Install the six manifold retaining bolts

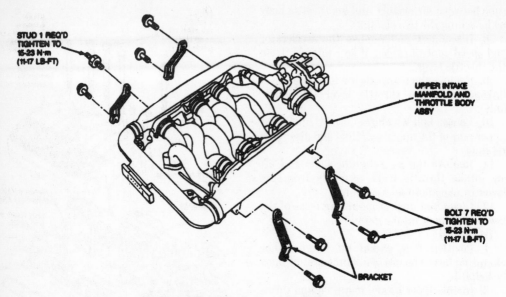

STUD 1 REQ'D
TIGHTEN TO
15-23 N·m
(11-17 LB-FT)

UPPER INTAKE
MANIFOLD AND
THROTTLE BODY
ASSY

BOLT 7 REQ'D
TIGHTEN TO
15-23 N·m
(11-17 LB-FT)

BRACKET

Intake manifold brackets — 3.0L SHO engine

and torque to 20-28 ft. lbs.

4. Install the canister purge lines, PCV hose, and vacuum lines to the vacuum tree.

5. Install the throttle and speed control, if so equipped, to the upper intake manifold. Connect the TV cable to the throttle body.

6. The transaxle TV (throttle valve) linkage has to be readjusted after the fuel charging assembly has been serviced

a. With the ignition key OFF and shift selector in PARK

b. Reset the automatic transaxle TV linkage by holding the ratchet in the released position and pushing the cable fitting toward the accelerator control bracket.

c. At the throttle body, reset the TV cable by rotating the throttle linkage to wide-open throttle position by hand and release.

7. Refill the engine with coolant. Start the engine and check for fuel, vacuum, and coolant leaks.

SEFI Injection

NOTE: *The fuel charging assembly consists of the air throttle body, and the upper and lower intake manifolds. Prior to service or removal of the fuel charging assembly, the following procedures must be taken.*

a. Open the hood and install protective fender covers.

b. Disconnect the negative (–) battery cable.

c. Remove the fuel cap at the tank.

d. Release the fuel pressure from the fuel system. Depressurize the fuel system by connecting a Fuel Pressure Gauge part No.

T80L-9974-B or equivalent to the pressure relief valve on the fuel rail assembly.

1. Remove the intake air boot from the throttle body and airflow sensor and disconnect the throttle cable.

2. Disconnect the vacuum and electrical connectors from the throttle body.

3. Disconnect the coolant bypass hoses at the throttle body.

CAUTION: *The cooling system may be under pressure. Release the pressure at the radiator cap before removing the hoses. Also, allow the engine to cool down before performing any service.*

4. Disconnect the EGR pipe from the EGR valve, if so equipped.

5. Remove the eight bolts at the intake manifold support brackets and remove the brackets.

6. Remove the bolt retaining the coolant hose bracket and disconnect the PCV hoses, if so equipped.

7. Remove the intake and throttle body assembly.

To install:

1. Clean and inspect the manifold mounting surfaces.

2. Position new intake manifold gaskets and install the manifold assembly onto the cylinder heads.

3. Install the 12 intake-to-head attaching bolts and torque to 11-17 ft. lbs.

4. Install the intake manifold support brackets and coolant hose bracket.

5. Connect all the coolant and vacuum hoses.

6. Connect the electrical connectors at the

DIS module, vacuum switching valve, throttle position sensor, and the air bypass valve.

7. Install the throttle cable and intake air boot.

8. Connect the negative (–) battery cable. Start the engine and check for fuel and coolant leaks.

Air Bypass Valve

REMOVAL AND INSTALLATION

2.5L Engine

1991

1. Disconnect the negative battery cable. Properly relieve the fuel system pressure, as required.

2. Disconnect the air bypass valve assembly connector from the wiring harness.

3. Remove the air bypass valve and gasket.
To install:

4. If scraping is necessary be careful not to damage the air bypass valve or throttle body gasket surfaces. Also, do not allow gasket material to drop into the throttle body.

5. Install the gasket on the intake manifold surface. Mount the air bypass valve to its mounting. Torque the retaining bolts to 71–97 inch lbs.

6. Connect the electrical connector.

3.0L Engine Except SHO

1. Disconnect the negative battery cable. Properly relieve the fuel system pressure, as required.

2. Disconnect the air bypass valve assembly connector from the wiring harness.

3. Remove the air bypass valve retaining bolts. Remove the valve and gasket.

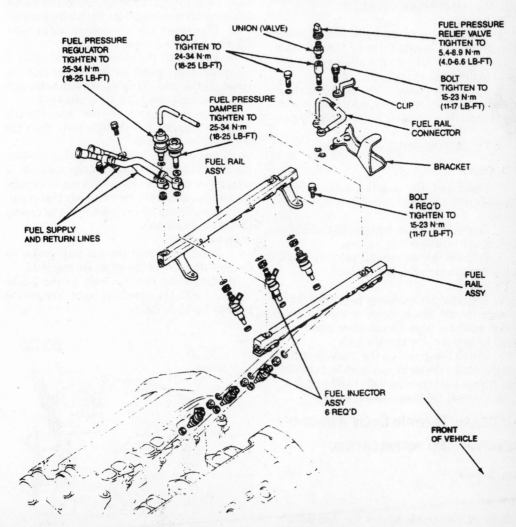

Fuel rail assemblies — 3.0L SHO engine

To install:

4. If scraping is necessary be careful not to damage the air bypass valve or throttle body gasket surfaces. Also, do not allow gasket material to drop into the throttle body.

5. Install the gasket on the intake manifold surface. Mount the air bypass valve to its mounting. Torque the retaining bolts to 84 inch lbs.

6. Connect the electrical connector.

3.0L SHO Engine

1. Disconnect the negative battery cable. Properly relieve the fuel system pressure, as required.

2. Disconnect the air bypass valve assembly connector from the wiring harness.

3. Remove the air bypass valve retaining bolts. Remove the top retaining bolt first and swing the valve upward to provide working clearance in order to remove the lower retaining bolt. Remove the valve and gasket.

To install:

4. If scraping is necessary be careful not to damage the air bypass valve or throttle body gasket surfaces. Also, do not allow gasket material to drop into the throttle body.

5. Install the gasket on the intake manifold surface. Mount the air bypass valve to its mounting. Torque the retaining bolts to 63–97 inch lbs.

6. Connect the electrical connector.

3.8L Engine

1. Disconnect the negative battery cable. Properly relieve the fuel system pressure, as required.

2. Disconnect the air bypass valve assembly connector from the wiring harness.

3. Remove the air bypass valve retaining bolts. Remove the valve and gasket.

To install:

4. If scraping is necessary be careful not to damage the air bypass valve or throttle body gasket surfaces. Also, do not allow gasket material to drop into the throttle body.

5. Install the gasket on the intake manifold surface. Mount the air bypass valve to its mounting. Torque the retaining bolts to 87 inch lbs.

6. Connect the electrical connector.

Air Intake/Throttle Body Assembly

REMOVAL AND INSTALLATION

2.5L Engine

1986–90

Refer to the above figures for disassembly and assembly information. To remove the TPS sensor and the ISC motor procede as follows.

1. Remove the throttle position sensor retaining screws. Remove the throttle position sensor from the throttle body.

2. Remove the idle speed control motor retaining screws. Remove the idle speed control motor from the throttle body assembly.

3. Installation is the reverse of the removal procedure.

4. Position the TPS sensor with the connector facing up toward the main body. Rotate the assembly in the counterclockwise position only and align the screw holes. Failure to properly install this sensor will result in excessive idle speeds.

1991

1. Disconnect the negative battery cable. Remove the air cleaner assembly.

2. Remove the throttle valve body retaining bolts. Be sure that the TPS electrical connector has been disconnected from the wiring harness.

3. Disconnect the air cleaner outlet tube. Disconnect the air bypass hose.

4. Disconnect the throttle control cable. If equipped with speed control, disconnect the speed control cable. If equipped with automatic transaxle, disconnect the TV control rod.

5. Disconnect and remove the throttle bracket. Separate the throttle body from the upper intake manifold.

6. Remove and discard the gasket between the throttle body and upper intake manifold. If scraping is necessary be careful not to damage the air bypass valve or throttle body gasket surfaces. Also, do not allow gasket material to drop into the throttle body.

To install:

7. Install the upper throttle body gasket on the two studs of the upper intake manifold.

8. Retain the throttle body to the intake manifold with the attaching bolts. Torque the bolts to 12–15 ft. lbs.

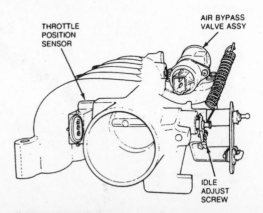

Throttle body assembly — 3.0L engine

9. Install the throttle body bracket. Connect the TPS electrical connector. Connect the engine air cleaner outlet tube.

10. Connect the throttle control cable, speed control cable and transaxle TV control rod, as required.

3.0L Engine Except SHO

1. Disconnect the negative battery cable. Loosen the air cleaner duct hose retaining clamps and remove the hose.

2. Remove the idle speed control solenoid shield. Disconnect the throttle and TV cable from the throttle body linkage.

3. Mark the location and remove the vacuum hoses from the vacuum tee.

4. Loosen the EGR tube nuts, if equipped at the EGR valve and exhaust manifold fitting. Remove or rotate the tube to the side.

5. Remove the PCV valve hose from under the throttle body. Disconnect the electrical connectors for the ACT, ISC and TPS sensors.

6. Remove the retaining bolts from the alternator brace. Remove the brace.

7. Loosen and remove the six throttle body retaining bolts, record bolt location to air in reinstallation.

8. Lift and remove the throttle body assembly from the manifold. Discard the gasket.

To install:

9. Clean and inspect all gasket surfaces. When cleaning aluminum parts be careful not ot gouge the surfaces. Coat all bolts with clean engine oil prior to installation.

10. If available inatall guide pins to guide the

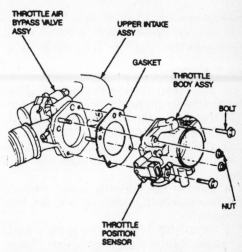

Throttle body assembly — 3.0L SHO engine

assembly onto its mounting. Place a new gasket on the manifold surface.

11. Install the throttle body onto the manifold. Torque the retaining bolts to 19 ft. lbs.

12. Install the alternator brace. Connect the PCV hose. Install the EGR tube to the EGR valve.

13. Connect the vacuum hoses. Connect the required electrical connectors to there proper locations.

14. Connect the throttle cable, speed control cable and TV cable, as required. Connect the air cleaner assembly to its mounting.

15. Connect the negative battery cable. Start the engine and check for vacuum leaks.

16. Check and adjust the engine idle speed

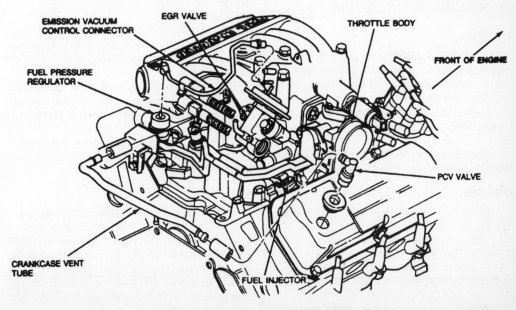

Throttle body assembly — 3.8L engine

as necessary. Adjust the transaxle TV cable. Install the idle speed control solenoid shield. Torque the retaining bolts to 13 inch lb.

3.0L SHO Engine

1. Disconnect the negative battery cables. Remove the air intake tube and throttle cables.
2. Disconnect the electrical connectorsa at the TPS and air bypass valve.
3. Drain the engine coolant. Remove the coolant bypass hoses. Disconnect the PCV hoses.
4. Remove the throttle body retaining bolts. Remove the throttle body assembly from its mounting.
5. Installation is the reverse of the removal procedure. Be sure to use a new gasket. Torque the retaining bolts 11–17 ft. lbs.

3.8L Engine

1. Disconnect the negative battery cable. Disconnect the TPS sensor and air bypass valve electrical connectors.
2. Remove the four throttle body retaining bolts. Remove the throttle body assembly.
3. Remove and discard the gasket. If scraping is necessary be careful not to damage the air bypass valve or throttle body gasket surfaces. Also, do not allow gasket meterial to drop into the throttle body.
4. Installation is the reverse of the removal procedure. Be sure to use a new gasket. Torque the retaining bolts to 19 ft. lbs.

Pressure Relief Valve

REMOVAL AND INSTALLATION

CFI Engine

1. If the fuel charging assembly is mounted to the engine, remove the fuel tank gas cap.
2. Properly release the fuel system pressure, using the proper tools.
3. Using the proper wrench, remove the pressure relief valve from the fuel injection manifold.
4. Installation is the reverse of the removal procedure. Tighten the valve 4–6 inch lbs.

EFI Engine

1. If the fuel charging assembly is mounted to the engine, remove the fuel tank gas cap.
2. Properly release the fuel system pressure, using the proper tools.
3. Using the proper wrench, remove the pressure relief valve from the fuel injection manifold.
4. Installation is the reverse of the removal procedure. Tighten the valve 5.5 inch lbs.

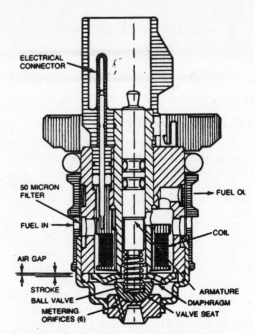

Fuel injector assembly — 2.5L engine with CFI

Fuel Injector

REMOVAL AND INSTALLATION

2.5L Engine

1986–90

1. Disconnect the negative battery cable.
2. Relieve the fuel system pressure.
3. Remove the fuel injector retaining screw and retainer.
4. Remove the injector and lower O-ring. Discard the O-ring.
   To install:
5. Lubricate a new lower O-ring and the injector seat area with clean engine oil; do not use transmission fluid. Install the lower O-ring on the injector.
6. Lubricate the upper O-ring and install the injector by centering and applying a steady downward pressure with a slight rotational force.
7. Install the injector retainer and retaining screw. Tighten the screw to 18–22 inch lbs. (2.0–2.5 Nm).

1991

1. Disconnect the negative battery cable.
2. Relieve the fuel pressure in the system.
3. Disconnect the engine air cleaner outlet tube from the air intake throttle body and the TP sensor from the wiring harness.
4. Disconnect the vacuum lines from the upper manifold and disconnect the EGR tube at the manifold connection.
5. Disconnect the air bypass valve connec-

tor, remove the accelerator and, if equipped, speed control cables and remove the manifold upper support bracket top bolt.

6. Remove the fuel supply manifold shield and the 4 upper manifold retaining bolts and 1 retaining shoulder stud.

7. Remove the upper manifold assembly and gasket and set it aside.

8. Disconnect the fuel supply and return lines and the vacuum line at the pressure regulator.

9. Disconnect the fuel injector wiring harness and disconnect the connectors from the injectors.

10. Remove the fuel supply manifold retaining bolts and remove the fuel supply manifold.

11. Grasping the injector body, pull up while gently rocking the injector from side-to-side.

12. Inspect the injector O-rings, the injector plastic hat and washer for signs of deterioration. Replace as necessary. If the hat is missing, look for it in the intake manifold.

To install:

13. Before installation, lubricate new O-rings with light engine oil and install on the injectors prior to installation.

14. Install the injectors.

15. Install the fuel supply manifold. Tighten the fuel supply manifold retaining bolts and the upper intake manifold retaining bolts to 15–22 ft. lbs. (20–30 Nm).

16. Install the fuel injector wiring harness. Connect the fuel supply and return lines and the vacuum line at the pressure regulator.

17. Connect the fuel supply manifold shield and the 4 upper manifold retaining bolts and 1 retaining shoulder stud.

18. Connect the air bypass valve connector, accelerator and, if equipped, speed control cables.

19. Connect the vacuum lines from the upper manifold and connect the EGR tube at the manifold connection.

20. Connect the engine air cleaner outlet tube to the air intake throttle body and the TP sensor to the wiring harness.

21. Connect the battery cable. Start the engine and check for leaks, correct as required.

3.0L Engine Except SHO

1. Disconnect the negative battery cable.

2. Relieve the fuel system pressure. Remove the air intake throttle body.

3. On the 1992 engine, the distributor must be raised to allow the crossover tube to clear the distributor housing and lower intake manifold assembly.

4. Disconnect the fuel supply and fuel return lines.

5. Disconnect the wiring harness from the injectors.

6. Disconnect the vacuum line from the fuel pressure regulator valve.

7. Remove the 4 fuel injector manifold retaining bolts.

8. Carefully disengage the fuel rail assembly from the fuel injectors by lifting and gently rocking the rail.

9. Remove the injectors by lifting while gently rocking from side to side.

To install:

10. Lubricate new O-rings with engine oil and install 2 on each injector.

11. Make sure the injector cups are clean and undamaged.

12. Install the injectors in the fuel rail using a light twisting-pushing motion.

13. Carefully install the rail assembly and injectors into the lower intake manifold, 1 side at a time. Make sure the O-rings are seated by pushing down on the fuel rail.

14. While holding the fuel rail assembly in place, install the 2 retaining bolts and tighten to 7 ft. lbs. (10 Nm).

15. Connect the fuel supply and fuel return lines.

16. Before connecting the fuel injector harness, turn the ignition switch to the **ON** position. This will pressurize the fuel system.

17. Using a clean paper towel. check for leaks where the injector connects to the fuel rail.

18. Install the air intake throttle body and connect the vacuum line to the fuel pressure regulator valve.

19. Connect the fuel injector harness, start the engine and let it idle for 2 minutes.

20. Using a clean paper towel, check for leaks where the injector is installed into the intake manifold.

3.0L SHO Engine

1. Disconnect the negative battery cable.

2. Relieve the fuel system pressure.

3. Remove the intake manifold as follows:

   a. Drain the cooling system.

   b. Remove the intake air tube from the throttle body and MAF sensor. Disconnect the throttle cables.

   c. Disconnect the electrical connectors at the TP sensor, air bypass valve, vacuum switching valve and DIS module.

   d. Disconnect the coolant bypass hoses and vacuum lines.

   e. Disconnect the EGR pipe from the EGR valve.

   f. Remove the 8 bolts at the intake manifold support brackets and remove the brackets.

   g. Remove the bolt retaining the coolant

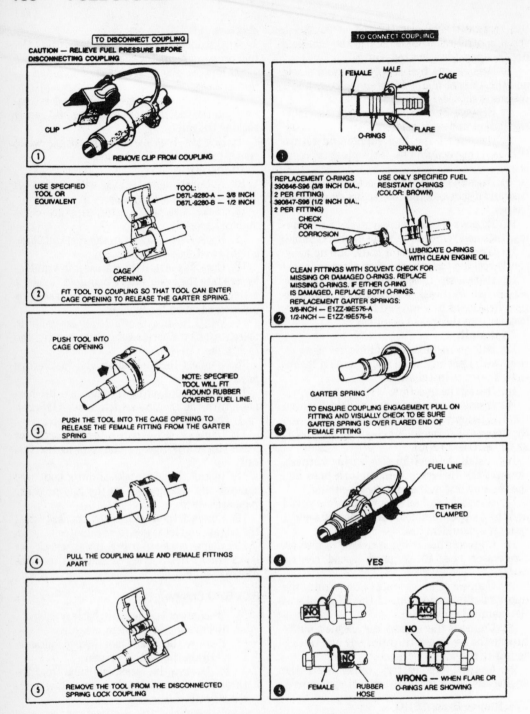

Fuel line disconnect points — 3.0L SHO engine

hose bracket and disconnect the PCV hoses.

h. Remove the 12 manifold retaining bolts and remove the intake manifold and throttle body assembly.

4. Disconnect the electrical connectors at the fuel injectors.

5. Remove the fuel rail retaining bolts.

6. Raise and slightly rotate the fuel rail assembly and remove the injectors.

To install:

7. Lubricate new O-rings with engine oil and install them on the fuel injectors.

8. Install the injectors in the fuel rail by lightly twisting and pushing the injectors into position.

9. Install the fuel rail, making sure the injectors seat properly in the cylinder head.

10. Install the fuel rail retaining bolts and tighten to 11–17 ft. lbs. (15–23 Nm).

11. Connect the electrical connectors at the injectors. Install the intake manifold by reversing the removal procedure.

12. Run the engine and check for leaks.

3.8L Engine

1. Disconnect the negative battery cable.

2. Remove the fuel cap at the tank and release the pressure.

3. Relieve the pressure from the fuel system.

4. Remove the upper intake manifold and the fuel supply manifold as follows:

a. Disconnect the electrical connectors at the air bypass valve, TP sensor and EGR position sensor.

b. Disconnect the throttle linkage at the throttle ball and the transmission linkage from the throttle body. Remove the 2 bolts securing the bracket to the intake manifold and position the bracket with the cables aside.

c. Disconnect the upper intake manifold vacuum fitting connections by disconnecting all vacuum lines to the vacuum tree, EGR valve and pressure regulator.

d. Disconnect the PCV hose and remove the nut retaining the EGR transducer to the upper intake manifold.

e. Loosen the EGR tube at the exhaust manifold and disconnect at the EGR valve.

f. Remove 2 bolts retaining the EGR valve to the upper intake manifold and remove the EGR valve and EGR transducer as an assembly.

g. Remove the 2 canister purge lines from the fittings on the throttle body and remove the 6 upper intake manifold retaining bolts.

h. Remove 2 retaining bolts on the front and rear edges of the upper intake manifold

where the manifold support brackets are located.

i. Remove the nut retaining the alternator bracket to the upper intake manifold and the 2 bolts retaining the alternator bracket to the water pump and alternator.

j. Remove the upper intake manifold and throttle body as an assembly.

k. Disconnect the fuel supply and return lines from the fuel rail assembly.

l. Remove the fuel rail assembly retaining bolts, carefully disengage the fuel rail from the fuel injectors and remove the fuel rail.

5. Remove the injector retaining clips.

6. Remove the electrical connectors from the fuel injectors.

7. To remove the injector, pull it up while gently rocking it from side-to-side.

8. Inspect the injector pintle protection cap (plastic hat) and washer for deterioration and replace, as required.

To install:

9. Lubricate new engine O-rings with engine oil and install 2 on each injector.

10. Install the injectors, using a light, twisting, pushing motion to install them.

11. Reconnect the injector retaining clips.

12. Install the fuel rail assembly.

13. Install the electrical harness connectors to the injectors.

14. Install the upper intake manifold by reversing the removal procedure.

15. Install the fuel cap at the tank.

16. Connect the negative battery cable.

17. Turn the ignition switch from **ON** to **OFF** position several times without starting the engine to check for fuel leaks.

Fuel Pressure Regulator

REMOVAL AND INSTALLATION

1. Depressurize the fuel system by connecting a Fuel Pressure Gauge part No. T80L-9974-B or equivalent to the pressure relief valve on the fuel rail assembly.

2. If equipped remove the fuel supply line. Remove the vacuum line at the pressure regulator.

3. Remove the three Allen retaining screws from the regulator housing.

4. Remove the pressure regulator assembly, gasket and O-ring. Discard the gasket and check the O-ring for signs of cracks or deterioration.

To install:

5. Clean the gasket mating surfaces. If scraping is necessary, be careful not to damage the fuel pressure regulator or supply line gasket mating surfaces.

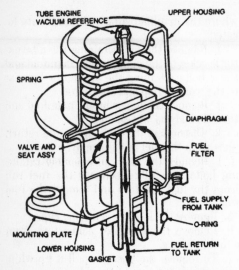

Fuel pressure regulator — 3.0L and 3.8L engines

6. Lubricate the pressure regulator O-ring with with light engine oil. Do not use silicone grease; it will clog the injectors.

7. Install the O-ring and a new gasket on the pressure regulator.

8. Install the pressure regulator on the fuel manifold and tighten the retaining screws to 27-40 inch lbs. If equipped install the fuel supply shield.

9. Install the vacuum line at the pressure regulator. Build up fuel pressure by turning the ignition switch on and off at least six times, leaving the ignition on for at least five seconds each time. Check for fuel leaks.

Throttle Position Sensor

REMOVAL AND INSTALLATION

1. Disconnect the TP sensor from wiring harness

2. Scribe a reference mark across the edge of the sensor and to the throttle body to ensure correct position during installation.

3. Remove the two TP sensor retaining screws and sensor.

To install:

4. Place the TP sensor in the same position

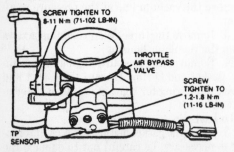

Throttle position sensor assembly

as it was removed. Install the two retaining screws and torque to 11-16 inch lbs.

Idle Speed

ADJUSTMENT

2.5L Engine *1986–90*

1. Apply the parking brake, block the drive wheels and place the vehicle in **P** or **N**.

2. Start the engine and let it run until it reaches normal operating temperature, then turn the engine **OFF**. Disconnect the negative battery cable for 5 minutes minimum, then reconnect it.

3. Start the engine and let it run at idle for 2 minutes. The idle rpm should now return to the specified idle speed. The idle specifications can be found on the calibration sticker located under the hood. Now lightly step on and off the accelerator. The engine rpm should return to the specified idle speed. If the engine does not idle properly, proceed to Step 4.

4. Shut the engine **OFF** and remove the air cleaner. Locate the self-test connector and self-test input connector in the engine compartment.

5. Connect a jumper wire between the self-test input connector and the signal return pin, the top right terminal on the self-test connector.

6. Place the ignition key in the **RUN** position but do not start the engine. The ISC

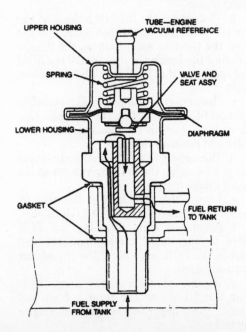

Fuel pressure regulator — 3.0L SHO engine

plunger will retract, so wait approximately 10–15 seconds until the ISC plunger is fully retracted.

7. Turn the ignition key to the **OFF** position. Remove the jumper wire and unplug the ISC motor from the wire harness.

8. Start the engine and check the idle speed. On automatic transaxle vehicles, it should be 50 rpm less than that specified on the calibration sticker. On manual transaxle vehicles, it should be 100 rpm less than that specified on the calibration sticker. If not proceed to Step 9.

9. Remove the CFI assembly from the vehicle.

10. Use a small punch or equivalent, to punch through and remove the aluminum plug which covers the throttle stop adjusting screw.

11. Remove and replace the throttle stop screw. Reinstall the CFI assembly onto the vehicle.

12. Start the engine and allow to the idle to stabilize. Set the idle rpm to the specification listed in Step 8. 13. Turn **OFF** the engine. Reconnect the ISC motor wire harness, remove all test equipment and reinstall the air cleaner assembly.

3.0L Engine Except SHO

1986–90

1. Apply the parking brake, turn the air conditioning control selector **OFF** and block the wheels.

2. Connect a tachometer and an inductive timing light to the engine. Start the engine and allow it to reach normal operating temperatures.

3. Unplug the spout line at the distributor, then check and/or adjust the ignition timing to the specification listed on the underhood emission calibration decal.

4. Stop the engine and remove the PCV hose at the PCV valve. Install a 0.200 in. (5mm) diameter orifice, tool T86P-9600–A or equivalent.

5. Disconnect the idle speed control/air bypass solenoid.

6. Start the engine and run at 2000 rpm for 30 seconds.

7. If equipped with an automatic transaxle, place the selector in **D**. If equipped with a manual transaxle, place the selector in neutral.

8. Check and/or adjust, the idle speed to 760 ± 20 rpm by turning the throttle plate stop screw.

9. After adjusting the idle speed, stop the engine and disconnect the battery for 5 minutes minimum.

10. Stop the engine and remove all test equip-

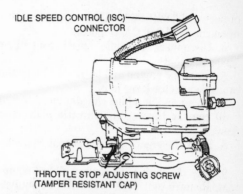

Throttle stop adjusting screw — 2.5L engine with CFI

ment. Reconnect the spout line and remove the orifice from the PCV hose. Reconnect the idle speed control/air bypass solenoid.

11. Make sure the throttle is not stuck in the bore and the linkage is not preventing the throttle from closing.

3.0L SHO Engine

1989–90

1. Apply the parking brake, turn the air conditioning control selector **OFF** and block the wheels.

2. Connect a tachometer and an inductive timing light to the engine. Start the engine and allow it to reach normal operating temperatures.

3. Unplug the spout line at the distributor, then check and/or adjust the ignition timing to the specification listed on the underhood emission calibration decal.

4. Stop the engine and disconnect and plug the PCV hose at the intake manifold. Remove the CANP hose from the intake manifold and

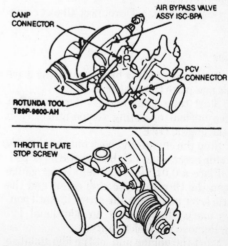

Engine throttle plate stop adjusting screw — 3.0L SHO engine

connect tool T89P–9600–AH or equivalent, between the PCV and CANP ports.

5. Disconnect the idle speed control/air bypass solenoid.

6. Start the engine and let it idle. Place the transaxle selector lever in **N**.

7. Check and/or adjust the idle speed to 800 ± 30 rpm by turning the throttle plate stop screw.

8. Shut the engine off and repeat Steps 6–8.

9. Stop the engine and remove all test equipment. Remove tool T89P–9600–AH or equivalent, and unplug the PCV hose. Connect the PCV and CANP hoses. Reconnect the idle speed control/air bypass solenoid.

10. Make sure the throttle is not stuck in the bore and the linkage is not preventing the throttle from closing.

3.8L Engine

1988

1. Apply the parking brake, block the drive wheels and place the vehicle in **P** or **N**.

2. Start the engine and let it run until it reaches normal operating temperature, then turn the engine **OFF**. Connect a suitable tachometer.

3. Start the engine and run the engine at 2500 rpm for 30 seconds.

4. Allow the engine idle to stabilize.

5. Place the automatic transaxle in **D** or the manual transaxle in neutral.

6. Adjust the engine idle rpm to the specification shown on the vehicle emission control label by adjusting the throttle stop screw.

7. After the idle speed is within specification, repeat Steps 3–6 to ensure that the adjustment is correct.

8. Stop the engine. Disconnect all test equipment.

1989–90

1. Apply the parking brake, block the drive wheels and place the vehicle in **P**.

2. Start the engine and let it run until it reaches normal operating temperature, then turn the engine **OFF**.

3. Stop the engine and back out the throttle plate stop screw clear off the throttle lever pad.

4. Place a 0.010 in. (0.25mm) feeler gauge between the throttle plate stop screw and the throttle lever pad. Turn the screw in until contact is made, then turn it an additional 1¹/₂ turns. Remove the feeler gauge.

5. Start the engine and let the idle stabilize for 2 minutes. Lightly depress and release the accelerator. Let the engine idle.

2.5L, 3.0L and 3.8L Engines

1991–92

The idle speed on these engines is preset at the factory and is not adjustable in the field. In the event that adjustment is necessary, STAR tester 007–00028 or equivalent, must be used.

Idle Mixture

ADJUSTMENT

Idle mixture is controlled by the electronic control unit. No adjustment is possible.

FUEL TANK

REMOVAL AND INSTALLATION

1. Disconnect the negative battery cable.

2. Relieve the fuel system pressure.

3. Siphon or pump the fuel from the fuel tank, through the filler neck, into a suitable container.

NOTE: *There are reservoirs inside the fuel tank to maintain fuel near the fuel pickup during cornering and under low fuel operating conditions. These reservoirs could block siphon tubes or hoses from reaching the bottom of the tank. A few repeated attempts using different hose orientations can overcome this situation.*

4. Raise and safely support the vehicle.

5. Loosen the filler pipe and vent hose clamps at the tank and remove the hoses from the tank.

6. Place a safety support under the fuel tank and remove the bolts from the rear of the fuel tank straps. The straps are hinged at the front and will swing aside.

7. Partially remove the tank. Remove the hairpin clips from the push connect fitting and disconnect the fuel lines. Disconnect the electrical connector from the fuel sender/pump assembly.

8. Remove the fuel tank.

To install:

9. Raise the fuel tank into position. Connect the fuel lines and the electrical connector.

10. Bring the fuel tank straps around the tank and start the retaining bolt. Align the tank as far forward in the vehicle as possible while securing the retaining bolts.

NOTE: *If equipped with a heat shield, make sure it is installed with the straps and positioned correctly on the tank.*

11. Check the hoses and wiring mounted on the tank top, to make sure they are correctly

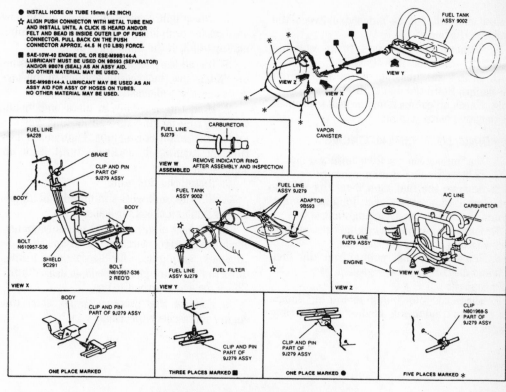

- INSTALL HOSE ON TUBE 15mm (.62 INCH)
- ☆ ALIGN PUSH CONNECTOR WITH METAL TUBE END AND INSTALL UNTIL A CLICK IS HEARD AND/OR FELT AND BEAD IS INSIDE OUTER LIP OF PUSH CONNECTOR. PULL BACK ON THE PUSH CONNECTOR APPROX. 44.5 N (10 LBS) FORCE.
- ■ SAE-10W-40 ENGINE OIL OR ESE-M99B144-A LUBRICANT MUST BE USED ON 9B593 (SEPARATOR) AND/OR 9B076 (SEAL) AS AN ASSY AID. NO OTHER MATERIAL MAY BE USED.

  ESE-M99B144-A LUBRICANT MAY BE USED AS AN ASSY AID FOR ASSY OF HOSES ON TUBES. NO OTHER MATERIAL MAY BE USED.

Fuel tank, lines and related components

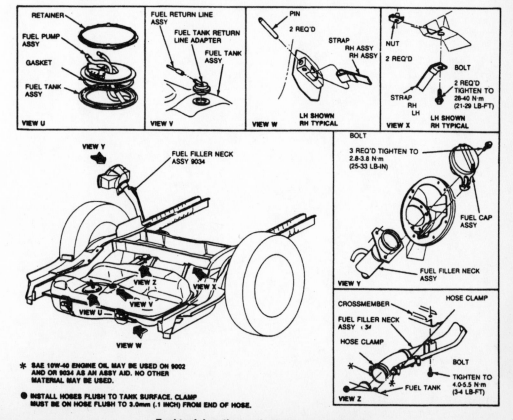

* SAE 10W-40 ENGINE OIL MAY BE USED ON 9002 AND OR 9034 AS AN ASSY AID. NO OTHER MATERIAL MAY BE USED.

● INSTALL HOSES FLUSH TO TANK SURFACE. CLAMP MUST BE ON HOSE FLUSH TO 3.0mm (.1 INCH) FROM END OF HOSE.

Fuel tank location and related components

routed and will not be pinched between the tank and the body.

12. Tighten the fuel tank strap retaining bolts to 21–29 ft. lbs. (28–40 Nm).

13. Install the fuel filler hoses and tighten the clamps. Refill the fuel tank.

14. Check all connections for leaks. Connect the negative battery cable.

SENDING UNIT REPLACEMENT

1. Disconnect the negative battery cable.

2. Relieve the fuel system pressure.

3. Remove the fuel tank from the vehicle and place it on a work bench. Remove any dirt around the fuel pump attaching flange.

4. Turn the fuel pump locking ring counterclockwise and remove the lock ring.

5. Remove the fuel pump from the fuel tank and discard the flange gasket.

To install:

6. Clean the fuel pump mounting flange and fuel tank mounting surface and seal ring groove.

7. Put a light coating of grease on the new seal gasket to hold it in place during assembly and install it in the fuel ring groove.

8. Install the fuel pump and sender assembly. Make sure the locating keys are in the keyways and the seal gasket remains in place.

9. Hold the assembly in place and install the lock ring making sure all locking tabs are under the tank lock ring tabs. Tighten the lock ring by turning it clockwise until it is up against the stops.

10. Install the fuel tank.

11. Fill the tank with a minimum of 10 gallons of fuel and check for leaks.

12. Connect a suitable fuel pressure gauge. Turn the ignition switch to the **ON** position 5–10 times, leaving it on for 3 seconds at a time, until the pressure gauge reads at least 30 psi. Check for leaks at the fittings.

13. Remove the pressure gauge, start the engine and recheck for leaks.

Chassis Electrical

HEATING AND AIR CONDITIONING

Blower Motor

REMOVAL AND INSTALLATION

1. Disconnect the negative battery cable.
2. Open the glove compartment door, release the door retainers and lower the door.
3. Remove the screw attaching the recirculation duct support bracket to the instrument panel cowl.

4. Remove the vacuum connection to the recirculation door vacuum motor. Remove the screws attaching the recirculation duct to the heater assembly.
5. Remove the recirculation duct from the heater assembly, lowering the duct from between the instrument panel and the heater case.
6. Disconnect the blower motor electrical lead. Remove the blower motor wheel clip and remove the blower motor wheel.
7. Remove the blower motor mounting plate screws and remove the blower motor from the evaporator case.

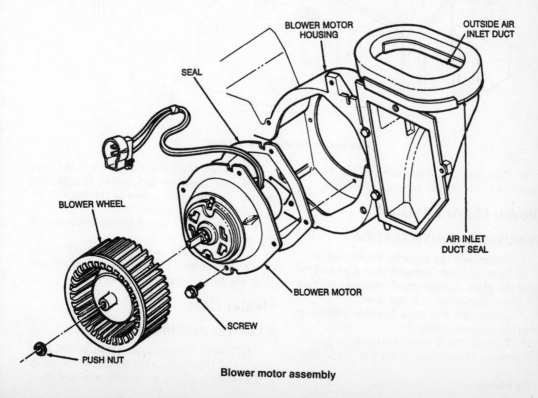

Blower motor assembly

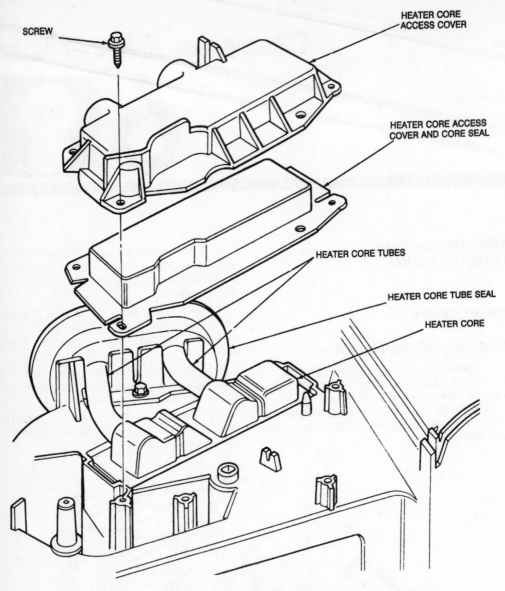

SCREW

HEATER CORE ACCESS COVER

HEATER CORE ACCESS COVER AND CORE SEAL

HEATER CORE TUBES

HEATER CORE TUBE SEAL

HEATER CORE

Heater core access cover location

8. Complete the installation of the blower motor by reversing the removal procedure.

Blower Motor Resistor

REMOVAL AND INSTALLATION

1. Disconnect the negative battery cable.
2. Open the glove compartment door and release the glove compartment retainers so that the glove compartment hangs down.
3. Disconnect the wire harness connector from the resistor assembly.
4. Remove the 2 resistor attaching screws and remove the resistor from the evaporator case.

To install:

5. Position the resistor assembly in the evaporator case opening and install 2 attaching screws. Do not apply sealer to the resistor assembly mounting surface.
6. Connect the wire harness connector to the resistor.
7. Connect the negative battery cable, check the operation of the blower motor and close the glove compartment door.

Heater Core

REMOVAL AND INSTALLATION

CAUTION: *When draining the coolant, keep in mind that cats and dogs are attracted by the ethylene glycol antifreeze, and are quite*

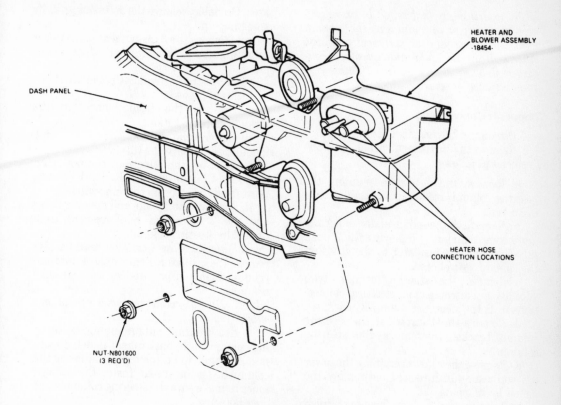

DASH PANEL

HEATER AND
BLOWER ASSEMBLY
-18454-

HEATER HOSE
CONNECTION LOCATIONS

NUT-N801600
(3 REQ'D)

Heater case assembly

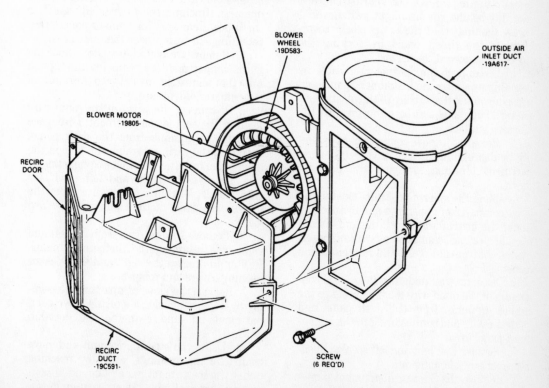

BLOWER
WHEEL
-19D583-

OUTSIDE AIR
INLET DUCT
-19A617-

BLOWER MOTOR
-19805-

RECIRC
DOOR

RECIRC
DUCT
-19C591-

SCREW
(6 REQ'D)

Recirc duct to heater assembly

likely to drink any that is left in an uncovered container or in puddles on the ground. This will prove fatal in sufficient quantity. Always drain the coolant into a sealable container. Coolant should be reused unless it is contaminated or several years old.

Without Air Conditioning

1. Disconnect the negative battery cable.
2. Remove the instrument panel on 1986–89 vehicles as follows:

    a. Remove the 4 screws retaining the steering column opening cover and remove the cover.

    b. Remove the sound insulator under the glove compartment by removing the 2 push nuts securing the insulator to the studs on the climate control case.

    c. Remove the steering column trim shrouds and disconnect all electrical connections from the steering column switches.

    d. Remove the 4 screws at the steering column bracket to remove the steering column.

    e. Remove the screws retaining the lower left and radio finish panels and remove the panels by snapping out.

    f. Remove the cluster opening finish panel retaining screws. On Taurus remove 1 jam nut behind the headlight switch and 1 screw behind the clock or clock cover. Remove the finish panel by rocking the upper edge toward the driver.

    g. Disconnect the speedometer cable by reaching up under the instrument panel and pressing on the flat surface of the plastic connector. The panel can be removed with the cluster installed.

    h. Release the glove compartment assembly by depressing the side of the glove compartment bin and swinging the door/bin down.

    i. Using the steering column, cluster and glove compartment openings and by reaching under the instrument panel, tag and disconnect all electrical connections, vacuum hoses, heater control cables and the radio antenna cable.

    j. Disconnect all underhood electrical connectors of the main wire loom. Disengage the rubber grommet from the dash panel and push the wire and connectors into the instrument panel area.

    k. Remove the right and left speaker opening covers by snapping out.

    l. Remove the 2 lower instrument panel-to-cowl side retaining screws from the right and left side. Remove the 1 instrument panel brace retaining screw from under the radio area. On Sable, remove the defroster grille by snapping out.

    m. Remove the 3 instrument panel upper retaining screws and remove the instrument panel.

3. Remove the instrument panel on 1990–92 vehicles as follows:

    a. Position the front wheels in the straight-ahead position.

    b. Remove the ignition lock cylinder and, if equipped, remove the tilt lever.

    c. Remove the steering column trim shrouds. Disconnect all electrical connections from the steering column switches.

    d. Remove the 4 bolts and opening cover and the 2 bolts and reinforcement from under the steering column.

    e. Disengage the insulator retainer and remove the insulator. Remove the 4 nuts and reinforcement from under the steering column.

NOTE: *Do not rotate the steering column shaft.*

    f. Remove the 4 nuts retaining the steering column to the instrument panel, disconnect the shift indicator cable and lower the column on the front seat. Install the lock cylinder to make sure the steering column shaft does not turn.

    g. Remove 1 bolt at the steering column opening attaching the instrument panel to the brace. Remove 1 instrument panel brace retaining bolt from under the radio area.

    h. Remove the sound insulator under the glove compartment by removing the 2 push nuts that secure the insulator to the studs on the climate control case.

    i. Disconnect the wires of the main wire loom in the engine compartment. Disengage the rubber grommet from the dash panel, then feed the wiring through the hole in the dash panel into the passenger compartment.

    j. Remove the right and left cowl side trim panels. Disconnect the wires from the instrument panel at the right and left cowl sides.

    k. Remove 1 screw each from the left and right side retaining the instrument panel. Pull up to unsnap the right and left speaker opening covers and remove.

    l. Release the glove compartment assembly by depressing the side of the glove compartment bin and swinging the door/bin down.

    m. Using the steering column and glove compartment openings and by reaching under the instrument panel, tag and disconnect all electrical connections, vacuum hoses, heater control cables, speedometer cable and radio antenna cable.

n. Close the glove compartment door, support the panel and remove the 3 screws attaching the top of the instrument panel to the cowl top and disconnect any remaining wires. Remove the panel from the vehicle.

4. Drain the coolant from the radiator.

5. Disconnect and plug the heater hoses at the heater core. Plug the heater core tubes.

6. Disconnect the vacuum supply hose from the inline vacuum check valve in the engine compartment. Remove the screw holding the instrument panel shake brace to the heater case and remove the shake brace.

7. Remove the floor register and rear floor ducts from the bottom of the heater case. Remove the 3 nuts attaching the heater case to the dash panel in the engine compartment.

8. Remove the 2 screws attaching the brackets to the cowl top panel. Pull the heater case assembly away from the dash panel and remove from the vehicle.

9. Remove the vacuum source line from the heater core tube seal and remove the seal from the heater core tubes.

10. Remove the 4 heater core access cover attaching screws and remove the access cover from the heater case. Lift the heater core and seals from the heater case.

To install:

11. Transfer the 3 foam core seals to the new heater core. Install the heater core and seals into the heater case.

12. Position the heater case access cover on the case and install the 4 screws.

13. Install the seal on the heater core tubes and install the vacuum source line through the seal.

14. Position the heater case assembly to the dash panel and cowl top panel at the air inlet opening. Install the 2 screws to attach the support brackets to the cowl top panel.

15. Install the 3 nuts in the engine compartment to attach the heater case to the dash panel. Install the floor register and rear floor ducts on the bottom of the heater case.

16. Install the instrument panel shake brace and screw to the heater case. Install the instrument panel by reversing the removal procedure.

17. Connect the heater hoses to the heater core. Connect the black vacuum supply hose to the vacuum check valve in the engine compartment.

18. Fill the radiator and bleed the cooling system.

19. Connect the negative battery cable and check the system for proper operation.

With Air Conditioning

NOTE: *It is necessary to remove the evaporator case in order to remove the heater core. Whenever an evaporator case is removed, it will be necessary to replace the suction accumulator/drier.*

1. Disconnect the negative battery cable.

2. Remove the instrument panel on 1986–89 vehicles as follows:

a. Remove the 4 screws retaining the steering column opening cover and remove the cover.

b. Remove the sound insulator under the glove compartment by removing the 2 push nuts securing the insulator to the studs on the climate control case.

c. Remove the steering column trim shrouds and disconnect all electrical connections from the steering column switches.

d. Remove the 4 screws at the steering column bracket to remove the steering column.

e. Remove the screws retaining the lower left and radio finish panels and remove the panels by snapping out.

f. Remove the cluster opening finish panel retaining screws. On Taurus remove 1 jam nut behind the headlight switch and 1 screw behind the clock or clock cover. Remove the finish panel by rocking the upper edge toward the driver.

g. Disconnect the speedometer cable by reaching up under the instrument panel and pressing on the flat surface of the plastic connector. The panel can be removed with the cluster installed.

h. Release the glove compartment assembly by depressing the side of the glove compartment bin and swinging the door/bin down.

i. Using the steering column, cluster and glove compartment openings and by reaching under the instrument panel, tag and disconnect all electrical connections, vacuum hoses, heater/air conditioner control cables and the radio antenna cable.

j. Disconnect all underhood electrical connectors of the main wire loom. Disengage the rubber grommet from the dash panel and push the wire and connectors into the instrument panel area.

k. Remove the right and left speaker opening covers by snapping out.

l. Remove the 2 lower instrument panel-to-cowl side retaining screws from the right and left side. Remove the 1 instrument panel brace retaining screw from under the radio area. On Sable, remove the defroster grille by snapping out.

m. Remove the 3 instrument panel upper retaining screws and remove the instrument panel.

3. Remove the instrument panel on 1990–92 vehicles as follows:

a. Position the front wheels in the straight-ahead position.

b. Remove the ignition lock cylinder and, if equipped, remove the tilt lever.

c. Remove the steering column trim shrouds. Disconnect all electrical connections from the steering column switches.

d. Remove the 4 bolts and opening cover and the 2 bolts and reinforcement from under the steering column.

e. Disengage the insulator retainer and remove the insulator. Remove the 4 nuts and reinforcement from under the steering column.

NOTE: *Do not rotate the steering column shaft.*

f. Remove the 4 nuts retaining the steering column to the instrument panel, disconnect the shift indicator cable and lower the column on the front seat. Install the lock cylinder to make sure the steering column shaft does not turn.

g. Remove 1 bolt at the steering column opening attaching the instrument panel to the brace. Remove 1 instrument panel brace retaining bolt from under the radio area.

h. Remove the sound insulator under the glove compartment by removing the 2 push nuts that secure the insulator to the studs on the climate control case.

i. Disconnect the wires of the main wire loom in the engine compartment. Disengage the rubber grommet from the dash panel, then feed the wiring through the hole in the dash panel into the passenger compartment.

j. Remove the right and left cowl side trim panels. Disconnect the wires from the instrument panel at the right and left cowl sides.

k. Remove 1 screw each from the left and right side retaining the instrument panel. Pull up to unsnap the right and left speaker opening covers and remove.

l. Release the glove compartment assembly by depressing the side of the glove compartment bin and swinging the door/bin down.

m. Using the steering column and glove compartment openings and by reaching under the instrument panel, tag and disconnect all electrical connections, vacuum hoses, heater/air conditioner control cables, speedometer cable and radio antenna cable.

n. Close the glove compartment door, support the panel and remove the 3 screws attaching the top of the instrument panel to the cowl top and disconnect any remaining wires. Remove the panel from the vehicle.

4. Drain the coolant from the radiator. Properly discharge the air conditioning system.

5. Disconnect and plug the heater hoses at the heater core. Plug the heater core tubes.

6. Disconnect the vacuum supply hose from the inline vacuum check valve in the engine compartment.

7. Disconnect the air conditioning lines from the evaporator core at the dash panel. Cap the lines and the core to prevent entrance of dirt and moisture.

8. Remove the screw holding the instrument panel shake brace to the evaporator case and remove the shake brace.

9. Remove the 2 screws attaching the floor register and rear seat duct to the bottom of the evaporator case. Remove the 3 nuts attaching the evaporator case to the dash panel in the engine compartment.

10. Remove the 2 screws attaching the support brackets to the cowl top panel. Carefully pull the evaporator assembly away from the dash panel and remove the evaporator case from the vehicle.

11. Remove the vacuum source line from the heater core tube seal and remove the seal from the heater core tubes.

12. If equipped with automatic temperature control, remove the 3 screws attaching the blend door actuator to the evaporator case and remove the actuator.

13. Remove the 4 heater core access cover attaching screws and remove the access cover and seal from the evaporator case. Lift the heater core and seals from the evaporator case.

To install:

14. Transfer the seal to the new hater core. Install the heater core into the evaporator case.

15. Position the heater core access cover on the evaporator case and install the 4 attaching screws. If equipped with automatic temperature control, position the blend door actuator to the blend door shaft and install the 3 attaching screws.

16. Install the seal on the heater core tubes and install the vacuum source line through the seal.

17. Position the evaporator case assembly to the dash panel and cowl top panel at the air inlet opening. Install the 2 screws attaching the support brackets to the cowl top panel.

18. Install the 3 nuts in the engine compartment attaching the evaporator case to the dash panel. Install the floor register and rear seat duct to the evaporator case and tighten the 2 attaching screws.

19. Install the instrument panel shake brace

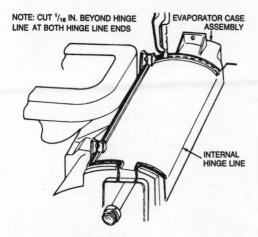

NOTE: CUT 1/16 IN. BEYOND HINGE LINE AT BOTH HINGE LINE ENDS

EVAPORATOR CASE ASSEMBLY

INTERNAL HINGE LINE

Evaporator case cutting

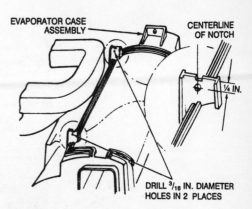

EVAPORATOR CASE ASSEMBLY

CENTERLINE OF NOTCH

1/4 IN.

DRILL 3/16 IN. DIAMETER HOLES IN 2 PLACES

Drilling holes in evaporator case tabs

and screw to the evaporator case. Install the instrument panel in the reverse order of removal.

20. Connect the air conditioning lines to the evaporator core and the heater hoses to the heater core.

21. Connect the black vacuum supply hose to the vacuum check valve in the engine compartment.

22. Fill and bleed the cooling system. Connect the negative battery cable.

23. Leak test, evacuate and charge the air conditioning system. Observe all safety precautions.

24. Check the system for proper operation.

Evaporator Core

NOTE: *Refer to CHAPTER 1 for air conditioning system discharging information.*

REMOVAL AND INSTALLATION

CAUTION: *When draining the coolant, keep in mind that cats and dogs are attracted by the ethylene glycol antifreeze, and are quite likely to drink any that is left in an uncovered container or in puddles on the ground. This will prove fatal in sufficient quantity. Always drain the coolant into a sealable container. Coolant should be reused unless it is contaminated or several years old.*

NOTE: *Whenever an evaporator is removed, it will be necessary to replace the accumulator/drier.*

1. Disconnect the negative battery cable.

2. Drain the coolant from the radiator into a clean container.

3. Properly discharge the refrigerant from the air conditioning system.

4. Disconnect the heater hoses from the heater core. Plug the heater core tubes.

5. Disconnect the vacuum supply hose from

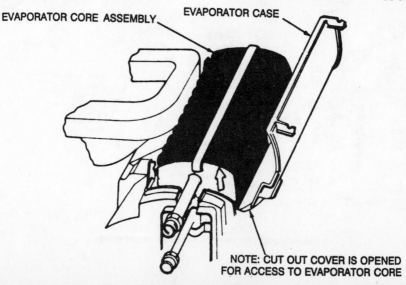

EVAPORATOR CORE ASSEMBLY

EVAPORATOR CASE

NOTE: CUT OUT COVER IS OPENED FOR ACCESS TO EVAPORATOR CORE

Evaporator core removal

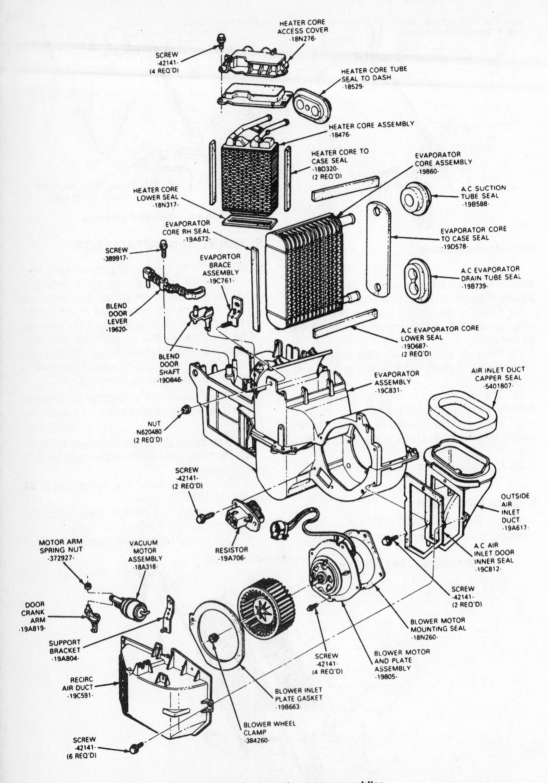

SCREW
-42141-
(4 REQ'D)

HEATER CORE
ACCESS COVER
-18N276-

HEATER CORE TUBE
SEAL TO DASH
-18529-

HEATER CORE ASSEMBLY
-18476-

HEATER CORE TO
CASE SEAL
-18D320-
(2 REQ'D)

EVAPORATOR
CORE ASSEMBLY
-19860-

A.C SUCTION
TUBE SEAL
-19B588-

HEATER CORE
LOWER SEAL
-18N317-

EVAPORATOR CORE
TO CASE SEAL
-19D578-

EVAPORATOR
CORE RH SEAL
-19A672-

SCREW
-389917-

EVAPORTOR
BRACE
ASSEMBLY
-19C761-

A.C EVAPORATOR
DRAIN TUBE SEAL
-19B739-

BLEND
DOOR
LEVER
-19620-

A.C EVAPORATOR CORE
LOWER SEAL
-19D687-
(2 REQ'D)

BLEND
DOOR
SHAFT
-19D846-

EVAPORATOR
ASSEMBLY
-19C831-

AIR INLET DUCT
CAPPER SEAL
-5401807-

NUT
N620480
(2 REQ'D)

SCREW
-42141-
(2 REQ'D)

OUTSIDE
AIR
INLET
DUCT
-19A617-

MOTOR ARM
SPRING NUT
-372927-

VACUUM
MOTOR
ASSEMBLY
-18A318-

RESISTOR
-19A706-

A C AIR
INLET DOOR
INNER SEAL
-19C812-

SCREW
-42141-
(2 REQ'D)

DOOR
CRANK
ARM
-19A819-

BLOWER MOTOR
MOUNTING SEAL
-18N260-

SUPPORT
BRACKET
-19A804-

BLOWER MOTOR
AND PLATE
ASSEMBLY
-19805-

RECIRC
AIR DUCT
-19C591-

SCREW
-42141-
(4 REQ'D)

BLOWER INLET
PLATE GASKET
-19B663-

BLOWER WHEEL
CLAMP
-384260-

SCREW
-42141-
(6 REQ'D)

Heater case and evaporator case assemblies

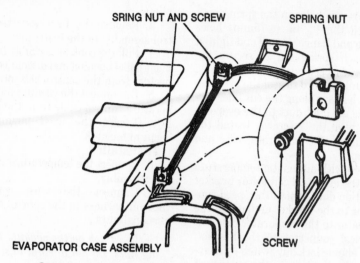

SRING NUT AND SCREW   SPRING NUT

EVAPORATOR CASE ASSEMBLY   SCREW

Securing cutout evaporator case cover in closed position

the in-line vacuum check valve in the engine compartment.

6. Disconnect the liquid line and the accumulator from the evaporator core at the dash panel. Cap the refrigerant lines and evaporator core to prevent entrance of dirt and moisture.

7. Remove the instrument panel and place it on the front seat.

8. Remove the screw holding the instrument panel shake brace to the evaporator case and remove the instrument panel shake brace.

9. Remove the 2 screws attaching the floor register and rear seat duct to the bottom of the evaporator case.

10. Disconnect the vacuum line, electrical connections and aspirator hose from the evaporator case.

11. Remove the 3 nuts attaching the evaporator case to the dash panel in the engine compartment. Remove the 2 screws attaching the support brackets to the cowl top panel.

12. Carefully pull the evaporator assembly away from the dash panel and remove the evaporator case from the vehicle.

13. Disconnect and remove the vacuum harness.

14. Remove the 6 screws attaching the recirculation duct and remove the duct from the evaporator case.

15. Remove the 2 screws from the air inlet duct and remove the duct from the evaporator case.

16. Remove the support bracket from the evaporator case.

17. If equipped with automatic temperature control, remove the screws holding the electronic connector bracket to the recirculation duct and remove the blend door actuator and cold engine lock out switch, which is held on by

spring tension at the outermost heater core tube.

18. Remove the moulded seals from the evaporator core tubes.

19. Drill a $\frac{3}{16}$ in. (4.75mm) hole in both upright tabs on top of the evaporator case.

20. Using a suitable tool, cut the top of the evaporator case between the raised outline. Fold the cutout cover back from the opening and lift the evaporator core from the case.

To install:

NOTE: *Add 3 oz. (90 ml) of clean refrigerant oil to a new replacement evaporator core to maintain total system refrigerant oil requirements.*

21. Transfer the foam core seals to the new evaporator core.

22. Position the evaporator core in the case and close the cutout cover.

23. Install a spring nut on each of the 2 upright tabs with 2 holes drilled in the front

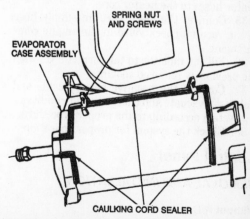

SPRING NUT
AND SCREWS

EVAPORATOR
CASE ASSEMBLY

CAULKING CORD SEALER

Caulking cord installation on evaporator case

flange. Make sure the holes in the spring nuts are aligned with the $\frac{3}{16}$ in. (4.75mm) holes drilled in the tab and flange. Install and tighten the screw in each spring nut to secure the cutout cover in the closed position.

24. Install caulking cord to seal the evaporator case against leakage along the cut line.

25. Install the air inlet duct to the evaporator case and tighten the 2 screws. Install the recirculation duct to the evaporator case and tighten 6 screws.

26. If equipped with automatic temperature control, install the electrical connector bracket to the recirculation duct, install the speed controller connector to the bracket and attach the blend door actuator to the evaporator case. Install the electrical connector to the bracket. Attach the cold engine lock out switch by snapping the spring clip in place on the outermost heater core tube.

27. Install the vacuum harness to the evaporator case and install the foam seals over the evaporator tubes. Assemble the support bracket to the evaporator case.

28. Position the evaporator case assembly to the dash panel and cowl top panel at the air inlet opening. Install the 2 screws attaching the support brackets to the top cowl panel.

29. Install the 3 nuts in the engine compartment attaching the evaporator case to the dash panel.

30. Connect the vacuum line, electrical connections and aspirator hose at the evaporator case.

31. Install the floor register and rear seat duct to the evaporator case and tighten the 2 attaching screws.

32. Install the instrument panel shake brace and screw to the evaporator case.

33. Install the instrument panel.

34. Connect the liquid line and accumulator/drier to the evaporator core and connect the heater hoses to the heater core.

35. Connect the black vacuum supply hose to the vacuum check valve in the engine compartment.

36. Fill the radiator to the correct level with the previously removed coolant.

37. Connect the negative battery cable and leak test, evacuate and charge the air conditioning system according to the proper procedure.

38. Check the system for proper operation.

Control Panel

REMOVAL AND INSTALLATION

Without A/C

1. Disconnect the negative battery cable.
2. Remove the instrument panel finish applique.
3. Remove the 4 screws attaching the control assembly to the instrument panel.
4. Pull the control assembly from the instrument panel opening and disconnect the wire connectors from the control assembly.
5. Disconnect the vacuum harness and temperature control cable from the control assembly. Discard the used pushnut from the vacuum harness.

To install:

6. Connect the temperature cable to the control assembly.
7. Connect the wire connectors and vacuum harness to the control assembly using new pushnuts.

NOTE: *Push on the vacuum harness retaining nuts. Do not attempt to screw them onto the post.*

8. Position the control assembly to the instrument panel opening and install 4 attaching screws.
9. Install the instrument panel finish applique.
10. Connect the negative battery cable and check the system for proper operation.

With A/C

MANUAL CONTROL

1. Disconnect the negative battery cable.
2. Remove the instrument panel finish applique.
3. Remove the 4 screws attaching the control assembly to the instrument panel.
4. Pull the control assembly from the instrument panel opening and disconnect the wire connectors from the control assembly.
5. Disconnect the vacuum harness and temperature control cable from the control assembly. Discard the used pushnut from the vacuum harness.

To install:

6. Connect the temperature cable to the control assembly.
7. Connect the wire connectors and vacuum harness to the control assembly using new pushnuts.

NOTE: *Push on the vacuum harness retaining nuts. Do not attempt to screw them onto the post.*

8. Position the control assembly to the instrument panel opening and install 4 attaching screws.
9. Install the instrument panel finish applique.
10. Connect the negative battery cable and check the system for proper operation.

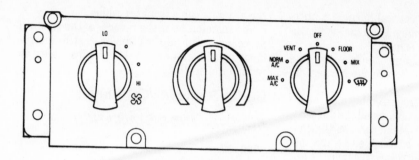

FRONT VIEW

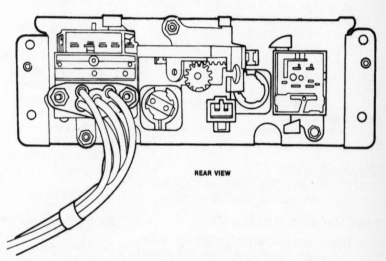

REAR VIEW

Control head assembly — manual air conditioning

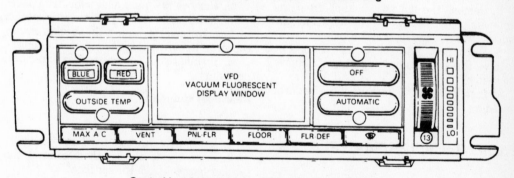

Control head assembly — electronic air conditioning

ELECTRONIC CONTROL

1. Disconnect the negative battery cable.
2. Perform the following:

    a. Pull out the lower left and lower right instrument panel snap-on finish panel inserts. Remove the 8 screws retaining the upper finish panel.

    b. Pull the lower edge of the upper finish panel away from the instrument panel. It is best to grasp the finish panel from the lower left corner and pull the panel away by walking the hands around the panel in a clockwise direction.

3. Remove the 4 Torx® head screws retaining the control assembly. Pull the control assembly away from the instrument panel into a position which provides access to the rear connections.

4. Disconnect the 2 harness connectors from the control assembly by depressing the latches at the top of the connectors and pulling.

5. Remove the nuts retaining the vacuum harness to the control assembly.

6. Connect the 2 electrical harness connectors to the control assembly. Push the keyed connectors in until a click is heard.

7. Attach the vacuum harness to the vacuum port assembly. Secure the harness by tightening the 2 nuts.

8. Position the control assembly into the instrument panel opening and install the 4 attaching Torx® head screws. Make sure, as the control is positioned, the locating posts are correctly aligned with their respective holes.

9. Carefully place the instrument panel applique into it's assembly position. Make sure the spring clips are aligned with their proper holes. Press the applique into place. Make sure all spring clips and screws are secure.

10. Install the 8 screws retaining the upper finish panel. Insert the lower left and lower right instrument panel snap-on finish panel inserts.

11. If removed install the left and right shelf mouldings.

12. Connect the negative battery cable and check the system operation.

Blower Switch

NOTE: *Refer to CHAPTER 1 for air conditioning system discharging information.*

REMOVAL AND INSTALLATION

1. Disconnect the negative battery cable. Remove the control assembly from the instrument panel.

2. Remove the fan switch knob from the fan switch. Remove the screws attaching the control switch to the instrument panel.

3. Disconnect the electrical connector. Remove the switch retaining screw. Remove the switch.

4. Installation is the reverse of the removal procedure.

RADIO RECIEVER/TAPE PLAYER

REMOVAL AND INSTALLATION

1986–89

1. Disconnect the negative (–) battery cable.

2. Remove the trim panel-to-center instrument panel.

3. Remove the radio/bracket-to-instrument panel screws.

4. Push the radio toward the front, then raise the rear of the radio slightly so that the rear support bracket clears the clip in the instrument panel. Slowly, pull the radio from the instrument panel.

5. Disconnect the electrical connectors and the antenna cable from the radio.

6. Installation is the reverse of the removal procedures. Torque the radio/bracket-to-instrument panel screws to 14–16 inch lbs. Test the radio for operation.

Radio Reciever/CD Player

REMOVAL AND INSTALLATION

1990–92

1. Disconnect the negative battery cable.

2. Install radio removal tool T87P–19061–A into the radio assembly face plate. Push the tool in about 1 in. (25mm) in order to release the retaining clips.

NOTE: *Do not use excessive force when installing the special tool as this will cause damage to the retaining clips.*

3. Apply a light spreading force to the tool and pull the aasembly from the dash.

4. Disconnect the electrical connectors and the antenna wire from the assembly and remove it from the vehicle.

5. Installation is the reverse of the removal procedure.

Speakers

REMOVAL AND INSTALLATION

Door Mounted

1. Disconnect the negative battery cable.

2. Remove the inner door panel trim panel.

3. Remove the screws retaining the speaker to its mounting. Disconnect the speaker electrical wires. Remove the speaker from the vehicle.

4. Installation is the reverse of the removal procedure.

Rear Seat Mounted

STANDARD SPEAKER

1. Disconnect the negative battery cable.

2. From inside the trunk disconnect the speaker harness from the speaker.

3. Remove the speaker cover. Pull the retaining strap to disengage the speaker and remove it from the vehicle.

4. Installation is the reverse of the removal procedure.

OPTIONAL SPEAKER

1. Disconnect the negative battery cable.

2. Remove the speaker grille from the package tray. Remove the speaker retaining screws.

3. Pull the speaker forward and diaconnect the electrical connector. Remove the speaker from the vehicle.

4. Installation is the reverse of the removal

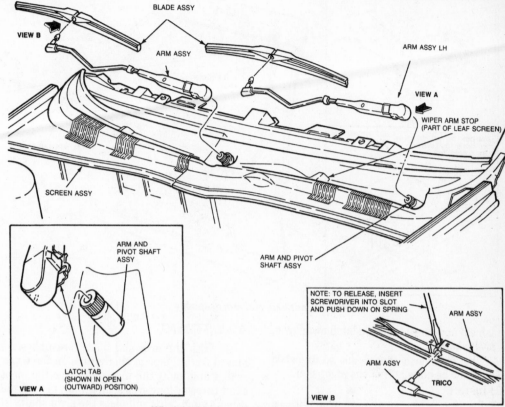

Windshield wiper blade and arm assembly

procedure.

Station Wagon

1. Disconnect the negative battery cable.
2. Remove the rear corner of the upper finish panel.
3. Remove the speaker retaining screws.
3. Pull the speaker forward and diaconnect the electrical connector. Remove the speaker from the vehicle.
4. Installation is the reverse of the removal procedure.

WINDSHIELD WIPERS AND WASH ERS

Windshield Wiper Blade And Arm

REMOVAL AND INSTALLATION

1. Turn the ignition switch to the ACC position. Turn the wiper switch ON. Allow the motor to move the pivot shafts 3 or 4 cycles, then turn off the switch.
2. This operation will place the pivot shafts

in the PARK position. Turn the ignition switch to the OFF position. Disconnect the negative battery cable.

3. Raise the blade end of the arm off the

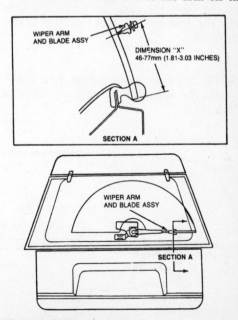

Rear wiper arm positioning

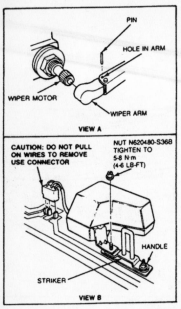

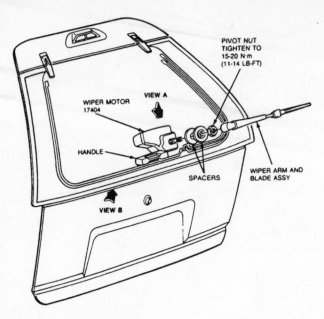

Rear wiper blade and arm assembly

windshield and move the slide latch away from the pivot shaft.

4. The wiper arm should not be unlocked and can now be pulled off of the pivot shaft.

To install:

5. Position the auxiliary arm (if so equipped) over the pivot pin, hold it down and push the main arm head over the pivot shaft. Make sure the pivot shaft is in the park position.

6. Hold the main arm head on the pivot shaft while raising the blade end of the wiper arm and push the slide latch into the lock under the pivot shaft. Lower the blade to the windshield.

NOTE: *If the blade does not touch the windshield, the slide latch is not completely in place.*

ADJUSTMENT

1. With the arm and blade assemblies removed from the pivot shafts turn on the wiper switch and allow the motor to move the pivot shaft three or four cycles, and then turn off the wiper switch. This will place the pivot shafts in the park position.

2. Install the arm and blade assemblies on the pivot shafts to the correct distance between the windshield lower molding or weatherstrip and the blade saddle centerline.

Rear Window Wiper Blade And Arm

REMOVAL AND INSTALLATION

1. Raise the arm away from the glass. Insert a 0.062 in. (1.6mm) pin into the holes in the retainer arm.

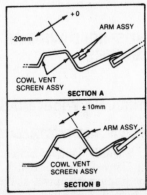

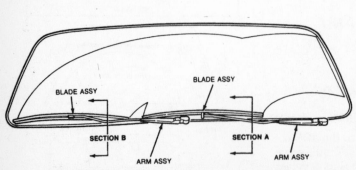

Windshield wiper arm positioning

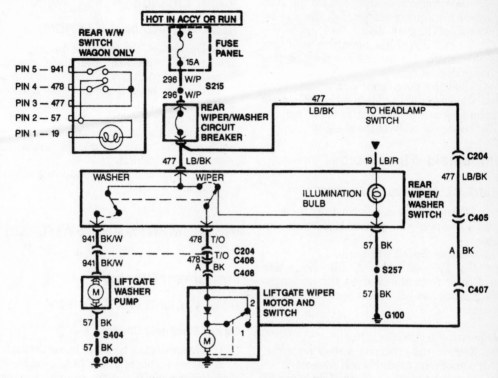

Rear wiper motor electrical circuit schematic

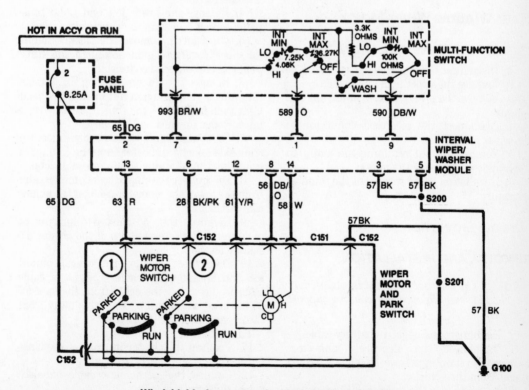

Windshield wiper motor electrical circuit schematic

2. Allow the arm to move toward the glass to relieve arm spring tension. Lift the arm assembly off of the pivot shaft.

3. To install push the main arm head over the pivot shaft. Be sure that the pivot shaft is in the park position.

4. Hold the main arm head on the pivot shaft while raising the blade end of the wiper arm and remove the 0.062 in. (1.6mm) pin.

5. Lower the blade to the glass.

Windshield Wiper Motor

REMOVAL AND INSTALLATION

1. Disconnect the negative battery cable.
2. Disconnect the power lead from the motor.
3. Remove the left wiper arm.
4. On 1991–92 vehicles, lift the water shield cover from the cowl on the passenger side. Remove the left cowl screen on 1986–90 vehicles.
5. Remove the linkage retaining clip from the operating arm on the motor.
6. Remove the attaching screws from the motor and bracket assembly and remove.
7. Installation is the reverse of the removal procedure.

Rear Window Wiper Motor

REMOVAL AND INSTALLATION

1. Disconnect the negative battery cable.
2. Remove the wiper arm and blade.
3. Remove the pivot shaft retaining nut and spacers.
4. Disconnect the electrical connector to the wiper motor.
5. Remove the nut retaining the motor to the handle and remove the motor.
6. Installation is the reverse of the removal procedure.

Internal Governor

REMOVAL AND INSTALLATION

NOTE: *The internal governor is mounted on a bracket near the steering column support bracket.*

1. Disconnect the negative battery cable.
2. Disconnect the electrical connector. Remove the retaining screws. Remove the component from the vehicle.
3. Installation is the reverse of the removal procedure. Check wiper system for proper operation.

Wiper Linkage

REMOVAL AND INSTALLATION

1. Disconnect the negative battery cable. Remove the wiper arm and blade assembly from the pivot shafts.

2. Remove both the right and left cowl screens. Disconnect the linkage drive arm from the motor crank pin after removing the clip.

3. Remove the screws retaining the pivot assemblies to the cowl. Remove the linkage and pivots from the vehicle.

4. Installation is the reverse of the removal procedure.

INSTRUMENTS AND SWITCHES

Instrument Cluster

REMOVAL AND INSTALLATION

Except Electronic Cluster

1. Disconnect the negative battery cable.
2. Remove the ignition lock cylinder to allow removal of the steering column shrouds.
3. Remove the steering column trim shrouds.
4. Remove the lower left and radio finish panel screws and snap the panels out.
5. On Taurus, remove the clock assembly (or clock cover) to gain access to the finish panel screw behind the clock.
6. Remove the cluster opening finish panel retaining screws and jam nut behind the headlight switch. Remove the finish panel by rocking the edge upward and outward.
7. On column shift vehicles, disconnect the transaxle selector indicator from the column by removing the retaining screw and cable loop.
8. Disconnect the upper speedometer cable from the lower speedometer cable in the engine compartment.
9. Remove the 4 cluster-to-instrument panel retaining screws and pull the cluster assembly forward.
10. Disconnect the cluster electrical connector and speedometer cable. Press the cable latch to disengage the cable from the speedometer head while pulling the cable away from the cluster. Remove the cluster.

To install:
11. Position the cluster in front of the cluster opening.
12. Connect the speedometer cable and electrical connectors.
13. Install the cluster and the 4 cluster-to-instrument panel retaining screws.

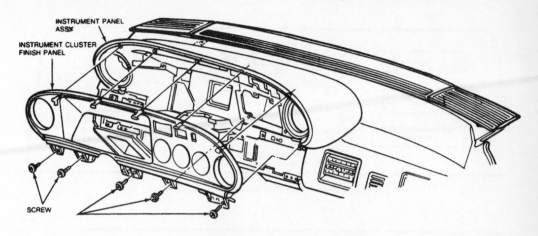

Sable instrument cluster removal points

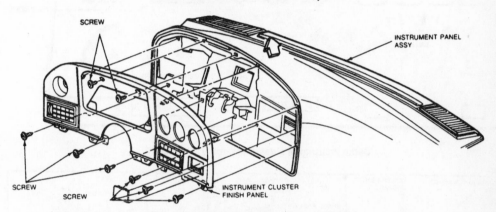

Taurus instrument cluster removal points

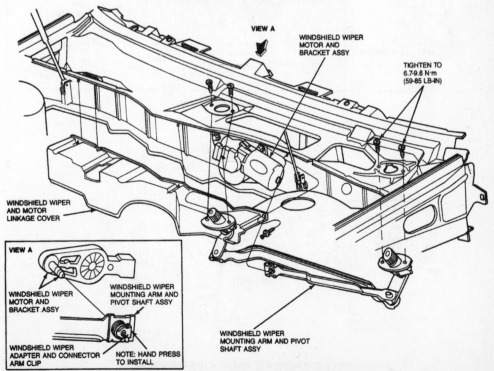

Windshield wiper linkage and related components

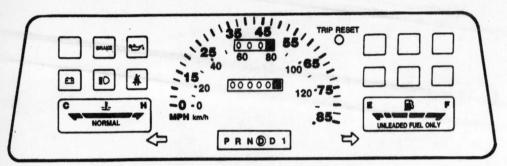

Taurus instrument cluster assembly — 1986–89

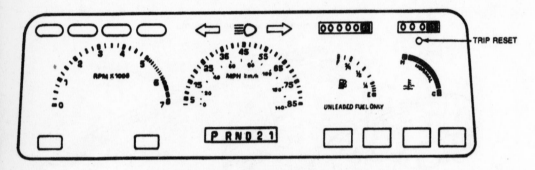

Sable instrument cluster assembly — 1986–89

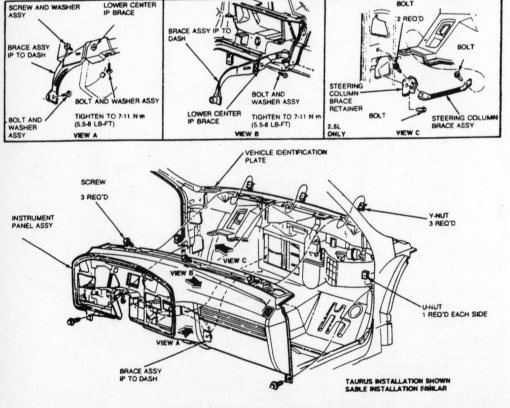

Instrument panel assembly and related components

14. Connect the upper speedometer cable to the lower speedometer cable in the engine compartment.

15. On column shift vehicles, connect the transaxle selector indicator.

16. Install the cluster opening finish panel.

17. On Taurus vehicles, install the clock assembly or clock cover.

18. Install the lower left and radio finish panels.

19. Install the steering column trim shrouds.

20. Install the ignition lock cylinder and connect the negative battery cable.

Electronic Cluster

1. Disconnect the negative battery cable.
2. Remove the lower trim covers.

3. Remove the steering column cover and disconnect the shift indicator cable from the cluster by removing the retaining screws.

4. Disconnect the switch module and remove the cluster trim panel.

5. Remove the cluster mounting screws and pull the bottom of the cluster toward the steering wheel.

6. Reach behind and under the cluster, disconnect the 3 electrical connectors.

7. Swing the bottom of the cluster out to clear the top of the cluster from the crash pad and remove.

To install:

8. Insert the top of the cluster under the crash pad, leaving the bottom out.

9. Connect the 3 connectors.

10. Properly seat the cluster and install the

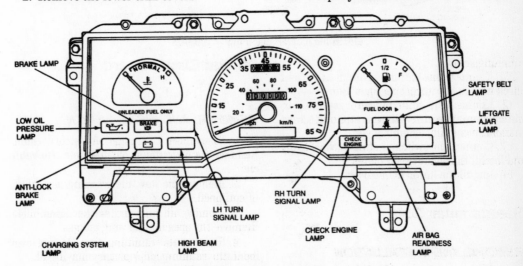

Standard instrument cluster assembly — 1990–92

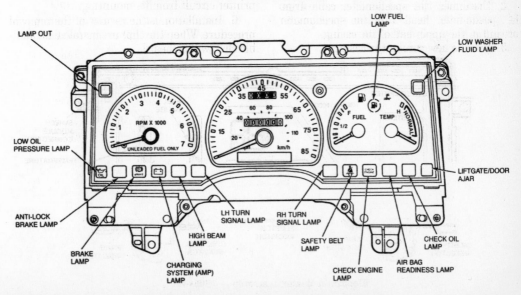

Optional instrument cluster assembly — 1990-92

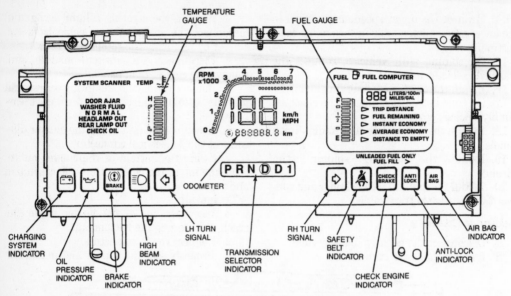

Electronic cluster assembly — 1990–92

retaining screws.

11. Connect the battery ground cable and check the cluster for proper operation.

12. Connect the shift indicator assembly to the cluster and secure with the retaining screw. Install the steering column cover.

13. Connect the switch module to the cluster and install the cluster trim panel.

14. Install the lower trim covers.

Speedometer Core

REMOVAL AND INSTALLATION

1. Disconnect the negative battery cable.

2. Disconnect the speedometer cable from the speedometer head. Pull the speedometer core out of the upper end of the casing.

3. Installa new core in the casing.

Printed Circuit Board

REMOVAL AND INSTALLATION

1. Disconnect the negative battery cable. Remove the instrument cluster from the vehicle.

2. Remove the low fuel warning assembly, if equipped.

3. Remove all bulb and socket assemblies. Remove the speedometer and gauges.

4. Remove the retaining clips. Do not over bend the retaining clips as they may break.

5. After the clips are removed remove the printer circuit from its mounting.

6. Installation is the reverse of the removal procedure. When the clips are installed an audible click will be heard.

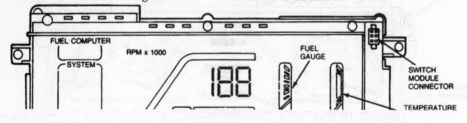

Electronic cluster assembly — 1986–89

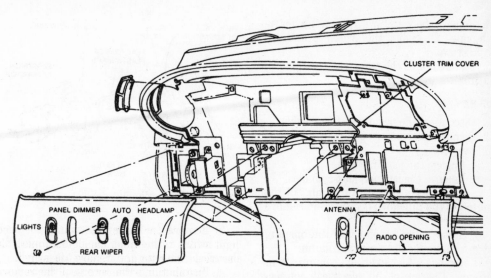

Sable headlight switch location — 1986–89

Windshield Wiper Switch

REMOVAL AND INSTALLATION

The front wiper switch is a function of the combination switch refer to the proper CHAPTER for detailed information.

Rear Window Wiper Switch

REMOVAL AND INSTALLATION

1986–89

1. Disconnect the negative battery cable.
2. Remove the 4 cluster opening finish panel retaining screws. Remove the finish panel by rocking the upper edge toward the driver.
3. Disconnect the wiring connector from the rear wiper switch.

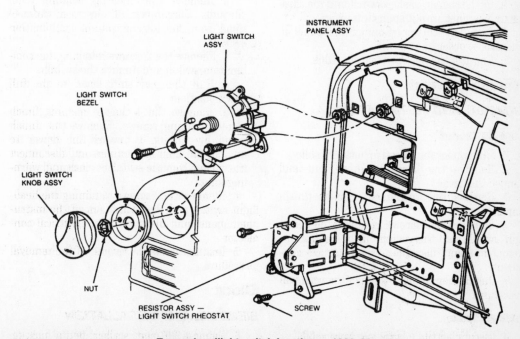

Taurus headlight switch location — 1986–89

4. Remove the wiper switch from the instrument panel. On Sable, the switch is retained with 2 screws.

5. Installation is the reverse of the removal procedure.

1990–92

1. Disconnect the negative battery cable.
2. Remove the cluster opening finish panel as follows:

  a. Engage the parking brake.

  b. Remove the ignition lock cylinder.

  c. If equipped with a tilt column, tilt the column to the full down position and remove the tilt lever.

  d. Remove the 4 bolts and the opening cover from under the steering column.

  e. Remove the steering column trim shrouds. Disconnect all electrical connections from the combination switch.

  f. Remove the 2 screws retaining the combination switch and remove the switch.

  g. Pull the gear shift lever to the full down position.

  h. Remove the 4 cluster opening finish panel retaining screws and the light switch knob and retaining nut.

  i. Remove the finish panel by pulling it toward the driver to unsnap the snap-in retainers and disconnect the wiring from the switches, clock and warning lights.

3. Remove the washer switch from the cluster opening finish panel.

To install:

4. Push the rear washer switch into the cluster finish panel until it snaps into place.

5. Install the cluster opening finish panel in the reverse order of removal.

6. Connect the negative battery cable.

Headlight Switch

REMOVAL AND INSTALLATION

1986–89 Taurus

1. Disconnect the negative battery cable.
2. Remove the bezel retaining nut and remove the bezel.
3. Remove the instrument cluster finish panel.
4. Remove the 2 screws retaining the headlight switch, pull the switch out of the instrument panel and disconnect the electrical connector.
5. Installation is the reverse of the removal procedure.

1988–89 Sable

1. Disconnect the negative battery cable.
2. Remove the lower left finish panel.

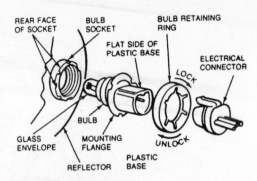

Headlight bulb assembly

3. Remove the 2 screws retaining the headlight switch to the finish panel, disconnect the electrical connector and remove the switch.

4. Installation is the reverse of the removal procedure.

1990–92 Taurus and Sable

1. Disconnect the negative battery cable.
2. Pull off the headlight switch knob and remove the retaining nut.
3. Remove the instrument cluster finish panel as follows:

  a. Apply the parking brake.

  b. Remove the ignition lock cylinder.

  c. If equipped with a tilt column, tilt the column to the most downward position and remove the tilt lever.

  d. Remove the 4 bolts and opening cover from under the steering column.

  e. Remove the steering column trim shrouds. Disconnect all electrical connections from the steering column combination switch.

  f. Remove the 2 screws retaining the combination switch and remove the switch.

  g. Pull the gear shift lever to the full down position.

  h. Remove the 4 cluster opening finish panel retaining screws. Remove the finish panel by pulling it toward the driver to unsnap the snap-in retainers and disconnect the wiring from the switches, clock and warning lights.

4. Remove the 2 screws retaining the headlight switch, pull the switch out of the instrument panel and disconnect the electrical connector.

5. Installation is the reverse of the removal procedure.

Clock

REMOVAL AND INSTALLATION

1. Using a 90° bent scriber, dental pick or similar hardened tool, insert the bent end of

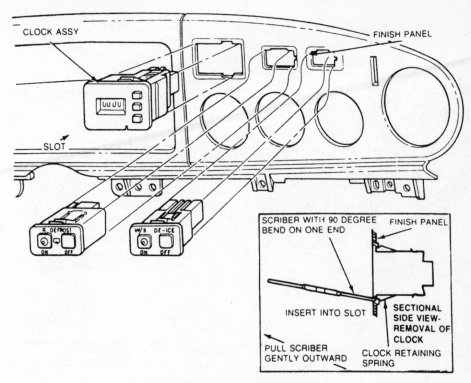

Clock location and removal points

the tool into the slot at the bottom center of the clock.

2. Gently pull the scriber tool outward until the bottom clock retaining spring releases.

3. Grasp the clock and pull it outward to remove.

4. Disconnect the electrical connector.

5. To install connect the electrical connector and snap the clock back into position.

LIGHTING

Headlights

REMOVAL AND INSTALLATION

Bulb Replacement

CAUTION: *The replaceable Halogen headlamp bulb contains gas under pressure. The bulb may shatter if the glass envelope is scratched or the bulb is dropped. Handle the bulb carefully. Grasp the bulb ONLY by its*

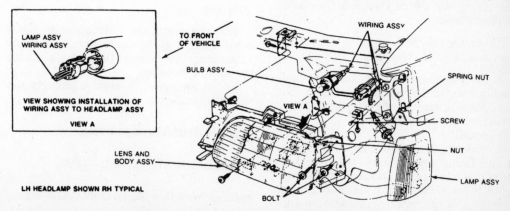

Taurus front light assembly and related components

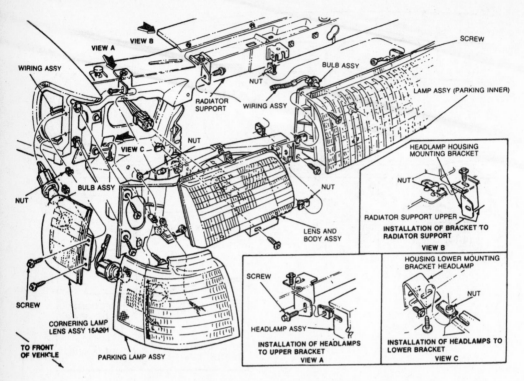

VIEW B

VIEW A

SCREW

WIRING ASSY

BULB ASSY

NUT

LAMP ASSY (PARKING INNER)

RADIATOR SUPPORT

WIRING ASSY

NUT

HEADLAMP HOUSING MOUNTING BRACKET

VIEW C

NUT

NUT

BULB ASSY

NUT

RADIATOR SUPPORT UPPER

NUT

LENS AND BODY ASSY

INSTALLATION OF BRACKET TO RADIATOR SUPPORT

VIEW B

HOUSING LOWER MOUNTING BRACKET HEADLAMP

SCREW

NUT

SCREW

CORNERING LAMP LENS ASSY 15A201

HEADLAMP ASSY

TO FRONT OF VEHICLE

PARKING LAMP ASSY

INSTALLATION OF HEADLAMPS TO UPPER BRACKET

VIEW A

INSTALLATION OF HEADLAMPS TO LOWER BRACKET

VIEW C

Sable front light assembly and related components

plastic base. Avoid touching the glass envelope because the finger prints from your hand may cause the bulb to burst when turned on. Keep the bulb out of the reach of children.

1. Check to see that the headlight switch is in the OFF position.
2. Raise the hood and locate the bulb installed in the rear of the headlight body.
3. Remove the electrical connector from the bulb by grasping the wires firmly and snapping the connector rearward.
4. Remove the bulb retaining ring by rotating it counterclockwise (when viewed from the rear) about $1/8$ of a turn, then slide the ring off the plastic base.

NOTE: *Keep the bulb retaining ring, it will be reused with the new bulb.*

5. Carefully remove the headlight bulb from its socket in the reflector by gently pulling it straight backward out of the socket. DO NOT rotate the bulb during removal.

To install:
6. With the flat side of the plastic base of the bulb facing upward, insert the glass envelope of the bulb into the socket. Turn the base slightly to the left or right, if necessary to align the grooves in the forward part of the plastic base with the corresponding locating tabs inside the socket. When the grooves are

aligned, push the bulb firmly into the socket until the mounting flange on the base contacts the rear face of the socket.

7. Slip the bulb retaining ring over the rear of the plastic base against the mounting flange. Lock the ring into the socket by rotating the ring counterclockwise. A stop will be felt when the retaining ring is fully engaged.

8. Push the electrical connector into the rear of the plastic until it snaps and locks into position.

9. Turn the headlights on and check for proper operation.

AIMING

All adjustments should be made with at least a half tank of gas in the fuel tank, an empty trunk except for the spare tire and jack and the correct tire pressures.

Special equipment is used to properly aim the front headlights.

Signal And Marker Lights

REMOVAL AND INSTALLATION

Parking/Front Turn Signal Light Combination

The parking and turn signal lights share the same dual filament bulb.

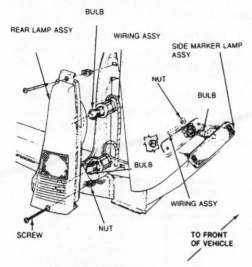

RH SHOWN LH SYMMETRICALLY OPPOSITE

Taurus and Sable rear light assembly and related components — wagon

TAURUS

1. Using the access hole in the radiator support, rotate the bulb socket counterclockwise to disengage it from the light housing and remove the bulb.

2. To install reverse the removal procedure. Rotate the bulb socket clockwise to engage the socket into the housing.

SABLE

1. Remove the two screws attaching the parking lamp assembly and pull it forward.

2. Remove the bulb socket by twisting and then remove the bulb.

3. Install the bulb in the socket, and install the socket in the lamp assembly by twisting.

4. Position the parking lamp in place and install the screws.

Side Marker Lights

TAURUS

1. Remove one nut and washer from the attaching stud at the top of the lamp assembly.

2. Rotate the top outboard until the stud tip has cleared the slot in the housing.

3. Lift the lamp to clear the two lower tabs (on the headlamp) from the headlamp housing.

4. Remove the bulb socket by twisting it counterclockwise and pull the bulb from the socket.

To install:

5. Install the bulb into the socket, and install the socket by twisting it counterclockwise.

6. Position the lamp in place by lowering

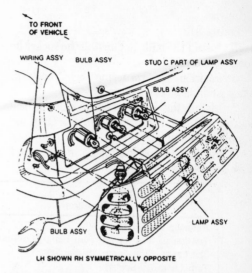

LH SHOWN RH SYMMETRICALLY OPPOSITE

Taurus rear light assembly and related components — except wagon

the two tabs on the lamp into the two slots on the headlamp housing.

7. Rotate the lamp inboard to allow the stud to enter the upper slot in the housing.

8. Install the nut and washer to the attaching stud, and secure them.

Cornering Lights

SABLE

1. Remove the two screws attaching the parking lamp assembly and pull it forward.

2. Remove the bulb socket by twisting and then remove the bulb.

3. Remove the two screws attaching the cornering lamp assembly and lift it out.

4. Remove the bulb by twisting it counter-

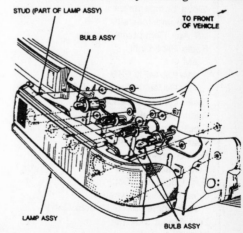

RH SHOWN LH SYMMETRICALLY OPPOSITE

Sable rear light assembly and related components — except wagon

clockwise.

To install:

5. Install the bulb, and install the socket by turning it clockwise.

6. Position the cornering light back in place, and install the two screws.

7. Install the parking lamp bulb in the socket, and install the socket in the lamp assembly by twisting.

8. Position the parking lamp in place and install the screws.

1990–92 TAURUS

1. Disconnect the negative battery cable.

2. Remove the cornering lamp retaining nuts. Lift the cornering lamp from its mounting.

3. Remove the bulb and socket assembly. Remove the cornering lamp from the vehicle.

4. Installation is the reverse of the removal procedure.

Function	Number of Bulbs	Trade Number
Exterior Illumination		
Tail Lamp, Stop Lamp, Turn Lamp (Lo-Series)	2	1157
Tail Lamp, Stop Lamp, (Hi-Series)	2	1157
Turn Lamp (Hi-Series)	2	1156
Back-up Lamp	2	1156
Rear Side Marker Lamp	2	194
Front Park, Turn Lamp	2	2357
Headlamp	2	9004
Cornering	2	1156
Front Side Marker Lamp	2	194
License Plate Lamp	2	194
Hi-Mount Stop Lamp (Sedan)	2	912
(Station Wagon)	2	921
Interior Illumination		
Cargo Lamp (Opt.)	1	906
Dome Lamp	1	906
Dome/Map Lamp (Opt.)		
Dome	1	912
Map	2	105
Visor Vanity Map (Opt.)	4	168
Door Courtesy Lamp	2	194
Engine Compartment Lamp	1	168
Floor Console	1	168
Luggage Compartment Lamp	1	906
Instrument Panel Illumination		
Glove Compartment	1	194
High Beam Indicator	1	194
I/P Ash Receptacle Lamp	1	1892
Radio Pilot Light		
AM	1	37
AM/FM/MPX ESR	6	7152
AM/FM/MPX Cassette ESR	6	7152
Radio Dial Illumination	1	936
Radio General Illumination	6	7152
Clock	1	ENW-2
Warning Lamps (All)	1 each	194
Fuel Gauge	2	194
Temperature Gauge	2	194
Fuel Computer (Opt.)	1	882
Odometer/Speedometer/ Tachometer (MT5 Models Only)	2	882
Turn Signal Indicator	2	194
"PRNDL" Bulb	1	194
Heater or Heater-A/C (Opt.)	2	161
Automatic Climate Control (Opt.)	5	37

Light bulb usage information – 1986–87

Function	Number of Bulbs	Trade Number
Exterior Illumination		
Tail Lamp, Stop Lamp, Turn Lamp (Lo-Series)	2	2458
Tail Lamp, Stop Lamp, (Hi-Series)	2	2458
Tail Lamp, Stop Lamp, Turn Lamp (Wagons)	2	2458
Turn Lamp (Hi-Series)	2	1156
Back-up Lamp	2	2456
Rear Side Marker Lamp	2	194
Front Park, Turn Lamp	2	2458
Headlamp	2	9004
Cornering	2	2456
Front Side Marker Lamp	2	194
License Plate Lamp	2	194
Hi-Mount Stop Lamp (Sedan)	2	912
(Station Wagon)	2	921
Interior Illumination		
Cargo Lamp (Opt.)	1	562
Cargo Lamp (Wagon)	2	214-2
Dome Lamp	1	562
Dome/Map Lamp (Opt.)		
Dome	1	563
Map	2	561
Visor Vanity Map (Opt.)	4	74-194
Door Courtesy Lamp	2	168
Engine Compartment Lamp	1	906
Floor Console	1	906
Luggage Compartment Lamp	1	906
Instrument Panel Illumination		
Glove Compartment	1	194
High Beam Indicator	1	194
I/P Ash Receptacle Lamp	1	194
Radio Pilot Light		
AM	1	37
AM/FM/MPX Search	6	7152
AM/FM/MPX Cassette EPC	6	7152
Radio Stereo Light	1	936
Clock	1	ENW-2
Warning Lamps (All)	1 each	194
Fuel Gauge	2	194
Temperature Gauge	2	194
Fuel Computer (Opt.)	1	882
Odometer/Speedometer/ Tachometer (MT5 Models Only)	2	882
Turn Signal Indicator	2	194
"PRNDL" Bulb	1	194
Heater or Heater-A/C (Opt.)	2	161
Automatic Climate Control (Opt.)	5	37

Light bulb usage information — 1988–92

Auxiliary Headlight Assembly

TAURUS SHO

1. Disconnect the negative battery cable. Remove the headlight assembly.

2. Remove the two screws attaching the auxiliary headlight to the headlight assembly.

3. Installation is the reverse of the removal procedure.

Rear Turn Signal/Brake Lights

1. Bulbs can be serviced from the inside of the luggage compartment by removing the lug-

gage compartment rear trim panel, if so equipped.

2. Remove the socket(s) from the lamp body and replace the bulb(s).

3. Install the socket(s) in the lamp body and install the trim panel.

High Mount Brake Light

1. Disconnect the negative battery cable.

2. On the sedan remove the two covers and screws that retain the lamp assembly to the retainer.

3. On the wagon remove the lamp assembly trim cover at the top of the liftgate frame. Remove the four retaining nuts retaining the lamp trim cover.

4. Remove the lamp assembly from its mounting.

5. Installation is the reverse of the removal procedure.

Dome Light

EXCEPT w/MOONROOF

1. Carefully squeeze the lense inward to release the locking tabs.

2. Remove the lense from the lamp body. Replace the defective bulb.

3. Installation is the reverse of the removal procedure.

WITH MOONROOF

1. Use a thin bladed tool and carefully pry out and unsnap the lense.

2. Replace the defective bulb.

3. Installation is the reverse of the removal procedure.

License Plate Lights

1. Remove the two lamp body plastic retaining rivits.

2. Remove the lamp assembly.

3. Remove the scoket and bulb assembly from the rear of the lamp assembly. Replace the defective bulb.

4. Installation is the reverse of the removal procedure.

Fog/Driving Lights

REMOVAL AND INSTALLATION

1. Disconnect the negative battery cable.

2. From inside the front fascia remove the two nuts, retaining springs and lamp mounting brackets.

3. Disconnect the electrical connector. Slide the fog lamp assembly off its mounting studs and remove it from the vehicle.

4. Installation is the reverse of the removal procedure.

TRAILER WIRING

Wiring the car for towing is fairly easy. There are a number of good wiring kits available and these should be used, rather than trying to design your own. All trailers will need brake lights and turn signals as well as tail lights and side marker lights. Most states require extra marker lights for overly wide trailers. Also, most states have recently required back-up lights for trailers, and most trailer manufacturers have been building trailers with back-up lights for several years.

Additionally, some Class I, most Class II and just about all Class III trailers will have electric brakes.

Add to this number an accessories wire, to operate trailer internal equipment or to charge the trailer's battery, and you can have as many as seven wires in the harness.

Determine the equipment on your trailer and buy the wiring kit necessary. The kit will contain all the wires needed, plus a plug adapter set which included the female plug, mounted on the bumper or hitch, and the male plug, wired into, or plugged into the trailer harness.

When installing the kit, follow the manufacturer's instructions. The color coding of the wires is standard throughout the industry.

One point to note: some vehicles, have separate turn signals. On most vehicles, the brake lights and rear turn signals operate with the same bulb. For those vehicles with separate turn signals, you can purchase an isolation unit so that the brake lights won't blink whenever the turn signals are operated, or, you can go to your local electronics supply house and buy four diodes to wire in series with the brake and turn signal bulbs. Diodes will isolate the brake and turn signals. The choice is yours. The isolation units are simple and quick to install, but far more expensive than the diodes. The diodes, however, require more work to install properly, since they require the cutting of each bulb's wire and soldering in place of the diode.

One final point, the best kits are those with a spring loaded cover on the vehicle mounted socket. This cover prevents dirt and moisture from corroding the terminals. Never let the vehicle socket hang loosely; always mount it securely to the bumper or hitch.

CIRCUIT PROTECTION

Fuses

REPLACEMENT

All vehicles have a fuse panel located under the left side of the instrument panel.

Fuses are a one-time circuit protection. If a circuit is overloaded or shorts, the fuse will blow thus protecting the circuit. A fuse will continue to blow until the circuit is repaired.

Fusible Links

REPLACEMENT

Fusible links are used to prevent major wire harness damage in the event of a short circuit or an overload condition in the wiring circuits that are normally not fused, due to carrying

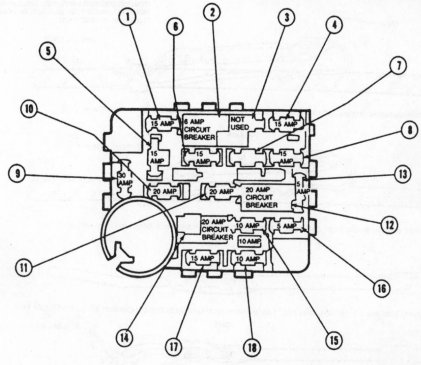

CAVITY NUMBER	CIRCUIT PROTECTED
1	HI-MOUNT STOPLAMP, STOPLAMPS, FRONT AND REAR TURN SIGNALS, INSTRUMENT PANEL TURN INDICATOR LAMPS
2	WINDSHIELD WIPER MOTOR, INTERMITTENT WIPER MODULE, WINDSHIELD WASHER MOTOR
3	NOT USED
4	FRONT PARK, SIDE MARKER AND TAIL LAMPS, "HEADLAMPS-ON" WARNING BUZZER/CHIME, FRONT LASER LAMP (SABLE).
5	ELECTRONIC CLUSTER, HEATED BACKLIGHT SWITCH, ELECTRONIC FLASHER, BACKUP LAMPS, HEATED E G O, ILLUMINATED/KEYLESS ENTRY MODULE
6	REAR WINDOW WIPER AND WASHER MOTORS (WAGONS), DIAGNOSTIC WARNING LAMP MODULE, WARNING CHIME, HEADLAMP SWITCH ILLUMINATION (SABLE), CLOCK ILLUMINATION, RADIO ILLUMINATION, EATC CONTROL ILLUMINATION, POWER WINDOW RELAY
7	NOT USED
8	CLOCK, RADIO MEMORY, GLOVE COMPT. LAMP, LUGGAGE COMPT. LAMP, INST. PANEL COURTESY LAMPS, INTERIOR LAMPS, ILLUMINATED/KEYLESS ENTRY MODULE, POWER MIRRORS
9	BLOWER MOTOR, BLOWER SPEED CONTROLLER (EATC)
10	FLASH-TO-PASS, HIGH BEAM HEADLAMPS AND INDICATOR LAMP
11	RADIO, PREMIUM SOUND AMPLIFIER, POWER ANTENNA MOTOR
12	CIGAR LIGHTERS, HORN RELAY, HORNS
13	CLUSTER ILLUMINATION, RADIO DISPLAY, ASH TRAY ILLUM., EATC CONTROL DISPLAY, HEATED BACKLIGHT SWITCH ILLUM., HEATED WINDSHIELD SWITCH ILLUM., REAR WIPER SWITCH ILLUM., HEADLAMP SWITCH ILLUM., CLOCK DISPLAY, P R N D L ILLUMINATION
14	NOT USED
15	LICENSE LAMPS, SIDE MARKER AND TAIL LAMPS
16	ELECTRONIC CLUSTER EATC CONTROL SWITCH
17	EATC COMPRESSOR CLUTCH, EATC BLEND DOOR ACTUATOR, A/C COMPRESSOR CLUTCH
18	AUTOLAMP MODULE, CLUSTER WARNING LAMPS, LOW OIL LEVEL RELAY, BUZZER/CHIME

Fuse locations

high amperage loads or because of their locations within the wiring harness. Each fusible link is of a fixed value for a specific electrical load and should a fusible link fail, the cause of the failure must be determined and repaired prior to installing a new fusible link of the same value. Please be advised that the color coding of replacement fusible links may vary from the production color coding that is outlined in the text that follows.

Taurus and Sable

Gray 12 Gauge Wire – located in left side of engine compartment at starter relay; used to protect battery to alternator circuit on all except 3.0L SHO engine.

Green 14 Gauge Wire – located in left side of engine compartment at starter relay; used to protect battery to alternator circuit if with 3.0L SHO engine.

Green 14 Gauge Wire – located in left

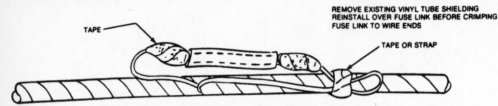

REMOVE EXISTING VINYL TUBE SHIELDING
REINSTALL OVER FUSE LINK BEFORE CRIMPING
FUSE LINK TO WIRE ENDS

TAPE

TAPE OR STRAP

TYPICAL REPAIR USING THE SPECIAL #17 GA. (9.00" LONG-YELLOW) FUSE LINK REQUIRED FOR THE AIR/COND. CIRCUITS

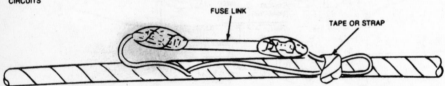

FUSE LINK

TAPE OR STRAP

TYPICAL REPAIR FOR ANY IN-LINE FUSE LINK USING THE SPECIFIED GAUGE FUSE LINK FOR THE SPECIFIC CIRCUIT

TAPE

TYPICAL REPAIR USING THE EYELET TERMINAL FUSE LINK OF THE SPECIFIED GAUGE FOR ATTACHMENT TO A CIRCUIT WIRE END

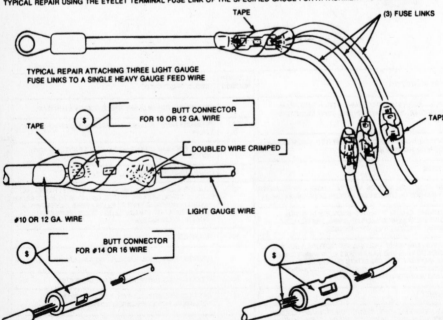

TAPE

(3) FUSE LINKS

TYPICAL REPAIR ATTACHING THREE LIGHT GAUGE FUSE LINKS TO A SINGLE HEAVY GAUGE FEED WIRE

TAPE

BUTT CONNECTOR FOR 10 OR 12 GA. WIRE

DOUBLED WIRE CRIMPED

TAPE

#10 OR 12 GA. WIRE

LIGHT GAUGE WIRE

BUTT CONNECTOR FOR #14 OR 16 WIRE

FUSIBLE LINK REPAIR PROCEDURE

General fuse link repair procedures

side of engine compartment at starter relay; used to protect anti-lock brake system power relay circuit.

Black 16 Gauge Wire – located on the left shock tower; used to protect the battery feed to headlight switch and fuse panel circuits.

Black 16 Gauge Wire – located on the left shock tower; used to protect the battery feed to ignition switch and fuse panel circuits.

Black 16 Gauge Wire – located in left side of engine compartment at starter relay; used to protect rear window defrost circuit on 1986–90 vehicles and 1991–92 2.5L engine vehicles.

Brown 18 Gauge Wire – located in left side of engine compartment at starter relay; used to protect rear window defrost circuit on 1991–92 vehicles, except 2.5L engine.

Brown 18 Gauge Wire – located in right front of engine compartment at alternator output control relay; used to protect the alternator output control relay to heated windshield circuit.

Blue 20 Gauge Wire – located on the left shock tower; used to protect the ignition coil, ignition module and cooling fan controller circuits.

Blue 20 Gauge Wire – located in left rear of engine compartment; used to protect ignition switch to anti-lock brake system circuit.

Circuit Breakers

REPLACEMENT

Circuit breakers protect electrical circuits by interupting the current flow. A circuit breaker conducts current through an arm made of 2 types of metal bonded together. If the arm starts to carry too much current, it heats up. As 1 metal expands faster than the other the arm bends, opening the contacts and interupting the current flow.

Taurus and Sable

Station Wagon Rear Window/Washer – One 4.5 amp circuit breaker located on the instrument panel brace, on the left side of the steering column on Taurus or on the left instrument panel end panel on Sable.

Windshield Wipers and Washer Pump – One 6 amp circuit breaker located on the fuse panel, on 1988 vehicles.

Windshield Wipers and Washer Pump – One 8.25 amp circuit breaker located on the fuse panel, on 1989–92 vehicles.

Cigar Lighters, Horn Relay and Horns – One 20 amp circuit breaker located on the fuse panel.

Power Windows, Power Locks and Power Seats – One 20 amp circuit breaker

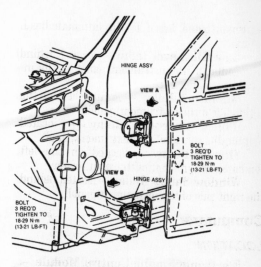

Fuse amperage values

located near the starter relay, on 1986–89 vehicles.

Power Windows, Power Locks and Power Seats – One 20 amp circuit breaker located on the fuse panel, on 1990–92 vehicles.

Headlights – One 22 amp circuit breaker incorporated in the headlight switch.

Relays

REPLACEMENT

Various relays are used in conjunction with the vehicle's electrical components. If a relay should fail it must be replaced with one of equal value

Taurus and Sable

Alternator Output Control Relay – located between the right front inner fender and fender splash shield, if with 3.0L or 3.8L engines and heated windshield.

Anti-lock Motor Relay – located in lower left front of engine compartment, if with anti-lock brakes.

Anti-lock Power Relay – located in left rear corner of engine compartment, if with anti-lock brakes.

Autolight Dual Coil Relay – located behind the center of the instrument panel on the instrument panel brace, if with automatic headlights.

Fog Light Relay – located behind the center of the instrument panel on the instrument panel brace.

Horn Relay – located behind the center of the instrument panel on the instrument panel brace.

LCD Dimming Relay – located behind the center of the instrument panel on the instrument panel brace, if with automatic head-lights.

Low Oil Level Relay — located behind the center of the instrument panel on the instrument panel brace.

Moonroof Relay — located behind the right side of the instrument panel.

Police Accessory Relay — located behind the center of the instrument panel.

Starter Relay — located on the left fender apron, in front of the strut tower.

Window Safety Relay — located behind the right side of the instrument panel.

Computers

LOCATION

Electronic Engine Control Module — located on the passenger side of the firewall.

Anti-lock Brake Control Module — located at the front of the engine compartment next to the passenger side fender, except on Taurus SHO where it is located at the front of the engine compartment on the driver's side.

Automatic Temperature Control Module — located behind the center of the instrument panel.

Heated Windshield Control Module — located behind the left side of the instrument panel, to the right of the steering column.

Integrated Control Module — located at the front of the engine compartment, on the upper radiator support.

Air Bag Diagnostic Module — located behind the right side of the instrument panel, above the glove box.

Flashers

REPLACEMENT

An electronic combination turn signal and emergency warning flasher is attached to the lower left instrument panel reinforcement above the fuse panel.

The turn signal unit is located on the LH side of the instrument panel. The combination turn signal and hazard flasher can be removed by pressing the plastic retaining clip and pulling straight rearward. One phillips® head screw has to be removed from the retaining bracket.

MANUAL TRANSAXLE

Identification

Your Taurus/Sable uses a front wheel drivetransmission called a transaxle.

A 5-speed fully synchronized manual transaxle is available on the 2.5L and 3.0L SHO Taurus/Sable models. An internally gated shift mechanism and a single rail shift linkage eliminate the need for periodic shift linkage adjustments. The MTX transaxle is designed to use Type F or Dexron®II automatic transmission fluid as a lubricant. Never use gear oil (GL) in the place of Type F or Dexron®II.

Adjustments

The manual shift mechanism and cables incorporate no adjustable features, therefore adjustments are neither possible or necessary.

Shift Linkage

REMOVAL AND INSTALLATION

1. Disconnect the negative battery cable. Remove the console, shift knob and boot.
2. Fold the carpet back from the dash panel to expose the shift cables and cable sealing grommets.
3. Remove the rear seat heating duct. Loosen the two screws and remove the cable bracket.
4. Pull the cable sealing grommets loose from the floorpan and dash panel.
5. Raise and support the vehicle safely.
6. Remove the two retaining screws that retain the cables to the bracket assembly.
7. Pry the cable sockets off the clamp assembly pivot balls and slide the cable insulators out of the bracket slots.

8. Loosen the two bolts retaining the bracket assembly to the transaxle case. Remove the bracket assembly.
9. Lower the vehicle. From inside the vehicle pull the shift cables through the sheet metal holes and remove them from the vehicle.

To install:

10. From inside the vehicle push the shift cables through the sheet metal holes. The crossover cable goes through the dash panel hole and the selector cable goes through the tunnel hole.
11. Seat the cable grommets in the sheet metal holes. Install the cable bracket. Torque the retaining screws to 17–22 inch lbs.
12. Make sure the crossover cable is secured under the hook on the bracket. A white alignment mark on the cable will assist in where to clip the cable under the hook.
13. Install the rear seat heat duct. Fold back the carpet over the cables.
14. Install the shifter, shift knob, boot and console.
15. Raise and support the vehicle safely. Install the clamp assembly onto the transaxle input shift shaft. Torque the retaining nut to 6–10 ft. lbs.
16. Install the bracket assembly to the transaxle case. Torque the M12 retaining bolt to 22–35 ft. lbs. and the M10 bolt to 16–24 ft. lbs.
17. Feed the shift cables into the slots of the bracket assembly. Retain the cables with two retainers and four bolts. Tighten the bolts 6–10 ft. lbs.
18. Snap the crossover cable socket onto the clamp assembly piviot ball. Position the selector cable rod end with the yellow painted side down. Snap the rod end onto the clamp assembly post.

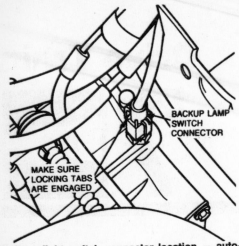

Back up light switch connector location — automatic transaxle

Shift Handle

REMOVAL AND INSTALLATION

1. Disconnect the negative battery cable. Remove the leather wrapped knob, by rotating the knob counterclockwise.

2. Remove the console trim surrounding the shift boot in order to expose the four screws which connect the boot to the top of the console. Slide the boot assembly off the shift lever.

3. Remove the console to expose the shifter assembly. Remove the four bolts retaining the shifter to the floorpan.

4. Pry the two clips holding the shift cables to control assembly and pry the cable sockets off the control assembly pivot balls.

5. Do not bend or kink the cable core rods.

To install:

6. Feed the loose ends of the cables into the control assembly slots. A green painted mark on the shifter and crossover cable will aid in proper alignment.

7. Attach the control assembly to the floorpan J-nuts with four bolts. Torque the bolts to 49–70 inch lbs.

8. Seat the cable insulators into the shifter slots. Install new U-clips. Snap the cable sockets onto the shifter pivot balls. Install the console.

9. Slide the boot assembly over the shift lever. Attach it to the console and tighten the retaining screws to 14–21 inch lbs.

10. Attach the shift knob to the shift lever.

Back-Up Light Switch

REMOVAL AND INSTALLATION

1. The back-up lamp switch is located on the top left side of the transaxle.

2. Disconnect the negative (–) battery cable.

3. Disconnect the switch electrical connector.

4. Using a 22mm wrench, remove the switch.

To install:

5. Apply Pipe Sealant with Teflon® part No. D8AZ–19554–A or equivalent to the threads of the switch. Turn the switch into the transaxle case clockwise and torque to 14–18 ft. lbs, and connect the electrical connector.

6. There is no adjustment needed on the back-up lamp switch.

Transaxle

REMOVAL AND INSTALLATION

1986–88

1. Disconnect the negative battery cable. Wedge a wood block approximately 7 in. (178mm) long under the clutch pedal to hold the pedal up slightly beyond its normal position. Grasp the clutch cable and pull forward, disconnecting it from the clutch release shaft assembly. Remove the clutch casing from the rib on the top surface of the transaxle case.

2. Remove the 2 top transaxle-to-engine mounting bolts.

3. Raise the vehicle and support safely.

4. Remove the nut and bolt that secures the lower control arm ball joint to the steering knuckle assembly. Discard the nut and bolt. Repeat this procedure on the opposite side.

5. Using a large prybar, pry the lower control arm away from the knuckle.

NOTE: *Exercise care not to damage or cut the ball joint boot. Prybar must not contact the lower arm.*

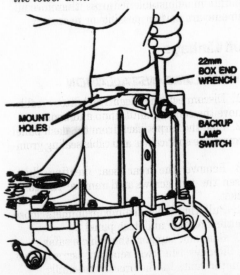

Back up light assembly — manual transaxle

6. Using a large prybar, pry the left inboard CV-joint assembly from the transaxle.

NOTE: *Plug the seal opening to prevent lubricant leakage.*

7. Remove the inboard CV-joint from the transaxle by grasping the left-hand steering knuckle and swinging the knuckle and halfshaft outward from the transaxle. If the CV-joint assembly cannot be pried from the transaxle, insert differential rotator tool T81P-4026–A or equivalent, through the left side and tap the joint out. Tool can be used from either side of transaxle.

8. Wire the halfshaft assembly in a near level position to prevent damage to the assembly during the remaining operations. Repeat this procedure on the opposite side.

9. Disengage the locking tabs and remove the backup light switch connector from the transaxle backup light switch.

10. Remove the starter stud bolts.

11. Remove the shift mechanism to shift shaft attaching nut and bolt and control selector indicator switch arm. Remove from the shift shaft.

12. Remove the bolts attaching the shift cable and bracket assembly to the transaxle.

13. Remove the speedometer cable from the transaxle.

14. Remove the stiffener brace attaching bolts from the lower position of the clutch housing.

15. Remove the sub-frame.

16. Position a suitable jack under the transaxle.

17. Lower the transaxle support jack.

18. Remove the lower engine to transaxle attaching bolts.

19. Remove the transaxle from the rear face of the engine and lower it from the vehicle.

To install:

20. Raise the transaxle into position with the support jack. Engage the input shaft spline into the clutch disc and work the transaxle onto the dowel sleeves. Make sure the transaxle assembly is flush with the rear face of the engine prior to installation of the attaching bolts.

21. Install the lower engine to transaxle attaching bolts and tighten them to 28–31 ft. lbs. (38–42 Nm).

22. Install the speedometer cable.

23. Install the 10M and 12M bolts attaching the the shift cable and bracket to the transaxle. Tighten the 10M bolt to 16–22 ft. lbs. (22–30 Nm) and the 12M bolt to 22–35 ft. lbs. (31–48 Nm).

24. Install the bolt attaching the shift mechanism-to-shift shaft and tighten to 7–10 ft. lbs. (9–13 Nm).

25. Install the 2 bolts that attach the stiffener brace to the lower portion of the clutch housing and tighten to 15–21 ft. lbs. (21–28 Nm).

26. Install the starter stud bolts and tighten to 30–40 ft. lbs. (41–54 Nm).

27. Install the backup light switch connector to the transaxle switch.

28. Remove the seal plugs and install the inner CV-joints into the transaxle.

29. Install the center bearing to the bracket on the right side halfahaft.

NOTE: *New circlips are required on both inner CV-joints prior to installation. Make sure both CV-joints are seated in the transaxle.*

30. Attach the sub-frame and the lower ball joint to the steering knuckle. Insert a new service pinch bolt and a new nut. Tighten the nut to 37–44 ft. lbs. (50–60 Nm) but do not tighten the bolt.

31. Fill the transaxle with the proper type and quantity of transmission fluid.

32. Install the top transaxle to engine mounting bolts and tighten to 28–31 ft. lbs. (38–42 Nm).

33. Connect the clutch cable to the clutch release shaft assembly.

34. Remove the wood block from under the clutch pedal. Prior to starting the engine, set the hand brake and pump the clutch pedal a minimum of 2 times to ensure proper clutch adjustment.

1989–92

1. Disconnect the negative battery cable.

2. Wedge a 7 in. (178mm) block of wood under the clutch pedal to hold the pedal up beyond it's normal position.

3. Remove the air cleaner hose.

4. Grasp the clutch cable and pull it forward, disconnecting it from the clutch release shaft assembly.

5. Disconnect the clutch cable casing from the rib on top of the transaxle case.

6. Install engine lifting eyes.

7. Tie up the wiring harness and power steering cooler hoses.

8. Disconnect the speedometer cable and speed sensor wire.

9. Support the engine using a suitable engine support fixture.

10. Raise the vehicle and support it safely. Remove the wheel and tire assemblies.

11. Remove the nut and bolt retaining the lower control arm ball joint to the steering knuckle assembly. Discard the removed nut and bolt. Repeat the procedure on the opposite side.

12. Using a suitable halfshaft remover, pry

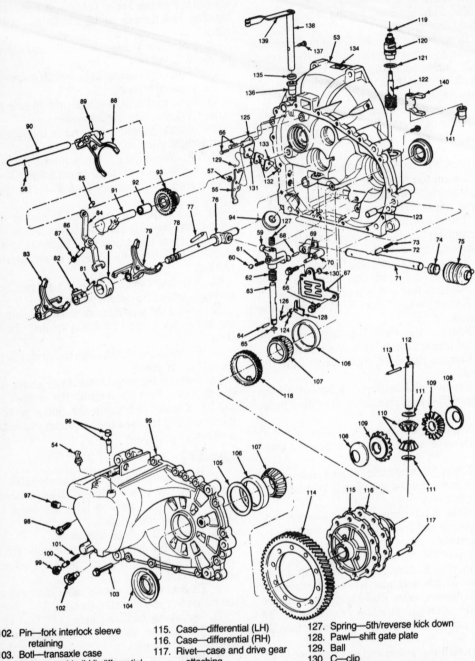

102. Pin—fork interlock sleeve
     retaining
103. Botl—transaxle case
104. Seal assembly (LH) differential
105. Shim differential bearing preload
106. Cup—differential bearing
107. Bearing assembly—differential
108. Washer—side gear thrust
109. Gear—side
110. Gear—pinion
111. Washer—pinion gear thrust
112. Shaft—pinion gear
113. Pin—pinion gear shaft retaining
114. Gear—final drive

115. Case—differential (LH)
116. Case—differential (RH)
117. Rivet—case and drive gear
     attaching
118. Gear—speedo drive
119. Seal—5.16mm x 1.6 O-ring
120. Retainer—speedo gear
121. Seal—speedo retainer-to-case
122. Gear—speedo driven
123. Dowel—case-to-clutch housing
124. Spring—shift gate pawl
125. Bracket—reverse shift relay
     lever support
126. Pin—reverse lockout pawl pivot

127. Spring—5th/reverse kick down
128. Pawl—shift gate plate
129. Ball
130. C—clip
131. Ball 8.731mm
132. Spring—trans reverse shift relay lever
133. Spring—trans reverse shift
     relay lever ret
134. Plug—trans timing window
135. Washer—flat (felt)
136. Bushing—clutch release shaft—upper
137. Pin—clutch release lever
138. Shaft—clutch release
139. Lever—clutch release

Manual transaxle — exploded view

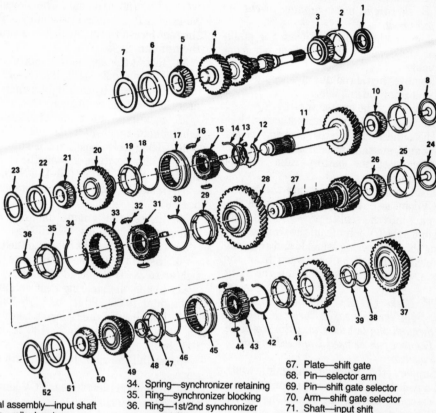

Legend:

1. Seal assembly—input shaft
2. Cup—roller bearing
3. Bearing—input shaft front
4. Shaft—input cluster
5. Bearing input shaft rear
6. Cup—roller bearing
7. Shim—bearing preload
8. Funnel—5th gear
9. Cup—roller bearing
10. Bearing—5th gear shaft—front
11. Shaft—5th gear drive
12. Retainer—synchronizer insert
13. Spacer—synchronizer retaining
14. Spring—synchronizer retaining
15. Hub—5th synchronizer
16. Insert—synchronizer hub 5th
17. Sleeve—5th synchronizer
18. Spring—synchronizer retaining
19. Ring—synchronizer blocking
20. Gear—5th speed
21. Bearing—5th gear shaft—rear
22. Cup—roller bearing
23. Shim—bearing preload
24. Funnel—mainshaft
25. Cup—roller bearing
26. Bearing—mainshaft front
27. Shaft—main
28. Gear—1st speed
29. Ring—synchronizer blocking
30. Spring—synchronizer retaining
31. Hub—1st/2nd synchronizer
32. Insert—synchronizer hub 1st/2nd
33. Gear—reverse sliding

34. Spring—synchronizer retaining
35. Ring—synchronizer blocking
36. Ring—1st/2nd synchronizer retaining
37. Gear—2nd speed
38. Ring—2nd/3rd thrust washer retaining
39. Washer—2nd/3rd thrust
40. Gear—3rd speed
41. Ring—synchronizer blocking
42. Spring—synchronizer retaining
43. Hub—3rd/4th synchronizer
44. Insert—synchronizer hub 3rd/4th
45. Sleeve—3rd/4th synchronizer
46. Spring—synchronizer retaining
47. Ring—synchronizer blocking
48. Ring—3rd/4th synchronizer
49. Gear—4th speed
50. Bearing—main shaft rear
51. Cup—roller bearing
52. Shim—bearing preload
53. Case—clutch housing
54. Switch assembly backup lamps
55. Lever—reverse relay
56. Pin—reverse relay lever pivot
57. Ring—external retaining
58. Pin—shift gate selector
59. Lever—shift
60. Ball—10.319 mm
61. Spring—5th/reverse inhibitor
62. Spring—3rd/4th shift bias
63. Shaft—shift lever
64. Pin—shift lever
65. Seal—shift lever shaft
66. Bolts—shift gate attaching

67. Plate—shift gate
68. Pin—selector arm
69. Pin—shift gate selector
70. Arm—shift gate selector
71. Shaft—input shift
72. Plunger—shift shaft detent
73. Spring—shift shaft detent
74. Seal—assembly—shift shaft—oil
75. Boot—shift shaft
76. Block—trans input fork control shaft
77. Spring pin—reverse relay lever actuating
78. Shaft—main shift fork control
79. Fork—1st/2nd
80. Sleeve—fork interlock
81. Pin—spring
82. Arm—fork selector
83. Fork—3rd/4th
84. Lever—5th shift relay
85. Pin—reverse shift relay lever
86. Pin—5th relay lever pivot
87. Ring—external retaining
88. Fork—5th
89. Fork—5th fork retaining
90. Shaft—5th fork control
91. Shaft—reverse idler gear
92. Bushing—reverse idler gear
93. Gear—reverse idler
94. Magnet—case
95. Case—transaxle
96. Vent assembly
97. Plug—fill
98. Bolt—reverse shaft retaining
99. Screw—detent plunger retaining
100. Plunger—shift shaft detent
101. Spring—shift shaft detent

Manual transaxle gear set — exploded view

the lower control arm away from the knuckle.

NOTE: *Be careful not to damage or cut the ball joint boot.*

13. Remove the upper nut from the stabilizer bar and separate the stabilizer bar from the knuckle.

14. Remove the tie rod nut and separate the tie rod end from the knuckle.

15. Disconnect the oxygen sensor.

16. Remove the exhaust catalyst assembly.

17. Disconnect the power steering cooler from the subframe and place it aside.

18. Disconnect the battery cable bracket from the subframe.

19. Using a suitable prybar, pry the left inboard CV-joint assembly from the transaxle. Install a plug into the seal to prevent fluid leakage. Remove the CV-joint from the transaxle by grasping the left steering knuckle and swinging the knuckle and halfshaft outward from the transaxle. Repeat the procedure on the right side.

NOTE: *If the CV-joint assembly cannot be pried from the transaxle, insert a suitable tool through the left side and tap the joint out. The tool can be used from either side of the transaxle.*

20. Support the halfshaft assembly with wire in a near level position to prevent damage to the assembly during the remaining operations. Repeat the procedure on the opposite side.

21. Remove the retaining bolts from the center support bearing and remove the right halfshaft from the transaxle.

22. Remove the 2 steering gear retaining nuts from the sub-frame. Support the steering gear by wiring up the tie rod ends to the coil springs.

23. Remove the transaxle to engine retaining bolts.

24. Disconnect the 2 shift cables from the transaxle.

25. Remove the engine mount bolts.

26. Position jacks under the body mount positions and remove the 4 bolts, lower the subframe and position it aside.

27. Remove the starter motor assembly.

28. Remove the left engine vibration dampener lower bracket.

29. Remove the backup light switch connector from the transaxle backup light switch, located on top of the transaxle and remove the backup light switch.

30. Position a suitable support jack under the transaxle.

31. Lower the transaxle, remove it from the engine and lower it from the vehicle.

To install:

32. Raise the transaxle into position. Engage the input shaft spline into the clutch disc and work the transaxle onto the dowel sleeves. Make sure the transaxle assembly is flush with the rear face of the engine before installation of the retaining bolts.

33. Install the engine to transaxle retaining bolts. Tighten to 28–31 ft. lbs. (38–42 Nm).

34. Install the backup light switch and connect the electrical connector.

35. Install the starter motor. Tighten the retaining bolts to 30–40 ft. lbs. (41–54 Nm).

36. Using jacks, position the sub-frame and raise it into position. Install the 4 bolts and tighten to 65–85 ft. lbs. (90–115 Nm).

37. Install the left vibration dampener lower bracket.

38. Install the engine mount bolts and tighten to 40–55 ft. lbs. (54–75 Nm).

39. Connect the shift cables to the transaxle.

40. Install the engine to transaxle bolts and tighten to 28–31 ft. lbs. (38–42 Nm).

41. Install the steering gear retaining nuts and tighten to 85–100 ft. lbs. (115–135 Nm).

42. Install the center support bearing retaining bolts and tighten to 85–100 ft. lbs. (115–135 Nm).

43. Install the right halfshaft into the transaxle.

44. Install the left inboard CV-joint assembly into the transaxle.

45. Connect the battery cable bracket to the sub-frame.

46. Connect the power steering cooler to the subframe.

47. Install the exhaust catalyst retaining bolts and tighten to 25–34 ft. lbs. (34–47 Nm).

48. Connect the oxygen sensor.

49. Install the tie rod in the knuckle and the tie rod retaining nut. Tighten to 35–47 ft. lbs. (47–64 Nm).

50. Position the stabilizer bar to the knuckle and install the nut.

51. Install the lower control arm ball joint to steering knuckle assembly. Install and tighten a new retaining nut and bolt to 37–44 ft. lbs. (50–60 Nm).

52. Install the wheel and tire assemblies.

53. Check the transaxle fluid level.

54. Lower the vehicle.

55. Remove the engine support tool.

56. Install the speedometer cable. Connect the speedometer cable and speed sensor wire.

57. Remove the engine lifting eyes.

58. Connect the clutch cable to the transaxle.

59. Install the air cleaner hose and remove the wood block from the clutch pedal.

60. Connect the negative battery cable and check the transaxle for fluid leaks.

Halfshafts

When removing both the left and right halfshafts, install suitable shipping plugs to prevent dislocation of the differential side gears. Should the gears become misaligned, the differential will have to be removed from the transaxle to re-align the side gears.

REMOVAL AND INSTALLATION

1. Disconnect the negative battery cable. Remove the wheel cover/hub cover from the wheel and tire assembly and loosen the wheel nuts.

2. Raise the vehicle and support safely. Remove the wheel assembly, remove the hub nut and washer. Discard the old hub nut. Remove the nut from the ball joint to steering knuckle attaching bolts.

3. Drive the bolt out of the steering knuckle using a punch and hammer. Discard this bolt and nut after removal.

4. If equipped with anti-lock brakes, remove the anti-lock brake sensor and position aside. If equipped with air suspension, remove the height sensor bracket retaining bolt and wire sensor bracket to inner fender. Position the sensor link aside.

5. Separate the ball joint from the steering knuckle using a suitable prybar. Position the end of the prybar outside of the bushing pocket to avoid damage to the bushing. Use care to prevent damage to the ball joint boot. Remove the stabilizer bar link at the stabilizer bar.

6. To remove the right halfshaft perform the following:

a. Remove the bolts attaching the bearing support to the bracket. Slide the link shaft out of the transaxle. Support the end of the shaft by suspending it from a convenient

underbody component with a piece of wire. Do not allow the shaft to hang unsupported, damage to the outboard CV-joint may occur.

b. Separate the outboard CV-joint from the hub using front hub remover tool T81P-1104-C or equivalent and metric adapter tools T83-P-1104-BH, T86P-1104-Al and T81P-1104-A or equivalent.

NOTE: *Never use a hammer to separate the outboard CV-joint stub shaft from the hub. Damage to the CV-joint threads and internal components may result. The right side link shaft and halfshaft assembly is removed as a complete unit.*

7. To remove the left halfshaft perform the following:

a. Install the CV-joint puller tool T86P-3514-A1 or equivalent, between CV-joint and transaxle case. Turn the steering hub and/or wire strut assembly aside.

b. Screw extension tool T86P-3514-A2 or equivalent, into the CV-joint puller and hand tighten. Screw an impact slide hammer onto the extension and remove the CV-joint.

c. Support the end of the shaft by suspending it from a convenient underbody component with a piece of wire. Do not allow the shaft to hang un-supported, damage to the outboard CV-joint may occur.

d. Separate the outboard CV-joint from the hub using front hub remover tool T81P-1104-C or equivalent and metric adapter tools T83-P-1104-BH, T86P-1104-Al and T81P-1104-A or equivalent.

e. Remove the halfshaft assembly from the vehicle.

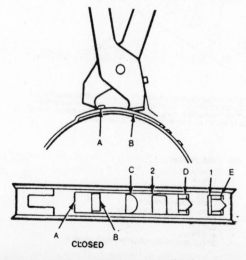

Inboard CV-joint boot clamp attachment

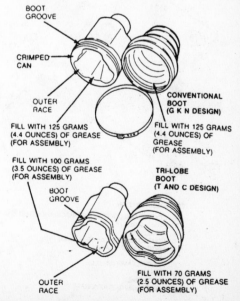

Conventional and Tri-lobe style CV-joints

To install:

8. Install a new circlip on the inboard CV-joint stub shaft and/or link shaft. The outboard CV-joint does not have a circlip. When installing the circlip, start one end in the groove and work the circlip over the stub shaft end into the groove. This will avoid over expanding the circlip.

NOTE: *The circlip must not be re-used. A new circlip must be installed each time the inboard CV-joint is installed into the transaxle differential.*

9. Carefully align the splines of the inboard CV-joint stub shaft with the splines in the differential. Exerting some force, push the CV-joint into the differential until the circlip is felt to seat in the differential side gear. Use care to prevent damage to the differential oil seal. If equipped, torque the link shaft bearing to 16–23 ft. lbs.

NOTE: *A non-metallic mallet may be used to aid in seating the circlip into the differential side gear groove. If a mallet is necessary, tap only on the outboard CV-joint stub shaft.*

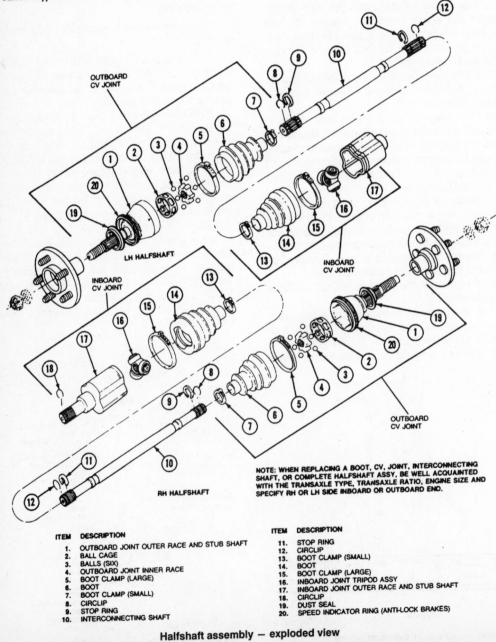

NOTE: WHEN REPLACING A BOOT, CV, JOINT, INTERCONNECTING SHAFT, OR COMPLETE HALFSHAFT ASSY, BE WELL ACQUAINTED WITH THE TRANSAXLE TYPE, TRANSAXLE RATIO, ENGINE SIZE AND SPECIFY RH OR LH SIDE INBOARD OR OUTBOARD END.

ITEM	DESCRIPTION
1.	OUTBOARD JOINT OUTER RACE AND STUB SHAFT
2.	BALL CAGE
3.	BALLS (SIX)
4.	OUTBOARD JOINT INNER RACE
5.	BOOT CLAMP (LARGE)
6.	BOOT
7.	BOOT CLAMP (SMALL)
8.	CIRCLIP
9.	STOP RING
10.	INTERCONNECTING SHAFT

ITEM	DESCRIPTION
11.	STOP RING
12.	CIRCLIP
13.	BOOT CLAMP (SMALL)
14.	BOOT
15.	BOOT CLAMP (LARGE)
16.	INBOARD JOINT TRIPOD ASSY
17.	INBOARD JOINT OUTER RACE AND STUB SHAFT
18.	CIRCLIP
19.	DUST SEAL
20.	SPEED INDICATOR RING (ANTI-LOCK BRAKES)

Halfshaft assembly — exploded view

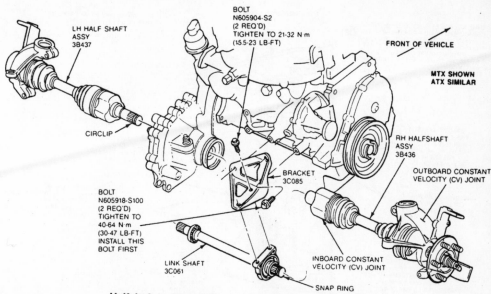

Halfshaft and linkshaft assemblies — manual transaxle

10. Carefully align the splines of the outboard CV-joint stub shaft with the splines in the hub and push the shaft into the hub as far as possible.

11. Temporarily fasten the rotor to the hub with washers and 2 wheel lug nuts. Insert a steel rod into the rotor and rotate clockwise to contact the knuckle to prevent the rotor from turning during the CV-joint installation.

12. Install the hub nut washer and a new hub nut. Manually thread the retainer onto the CV-joint as far as possible.

13. Connect the control arm to the steering knuckle and install a new nut and bolt. Tighten the nut to 40–55 ft. lbs. (54–74 Nm). A new bolt must be installed also.

14. Install the anti-lock brake sensor and/or the ride height sensor bracket, if equipped.

15. Connect the stabilizer link to the stabilizer bar. Tighten to 35–48 ft. lbs. (47–65 Nm).

16. Tighten the hub retainer nut to 180–200 ft. lbs. (245–270 Nm). Remove the steel rod.

17. Install the wheel and tire assembly and lower the vehicle. Tighten the wheel nuts to 80–105 ft. lbs. Fill the transaxle to the proper level with the specified fluid.

CLUTCH

CAUTION: *The clutch driven disc contains asbestos, which has been determined to be a cancer causing agent. Never clean clutch surfaces with compressed air! Avoid inhaling any dust from any clutch surface! When clean-*

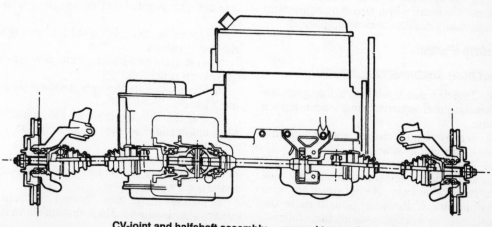

CV-joint and halfshaft assembly — manual transaxle

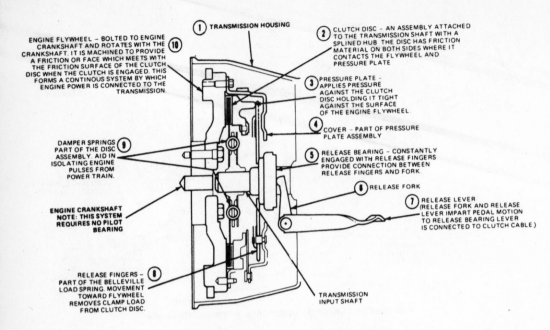

ENGINE FLYWHEEL – BOLTED TO ENGINE CRANKSHAFT AND ROTATES WITH THE CRANKSHAFT. IT IS MACHINED TO PROVIDE A FRICTION OR FACE WHICH MEETS WITH THE FRICTION SURFACE OF THE CLUTCH DISC WHEN THE CLUTCH IS ENGAGED. THIS FORMS A CONTINOUS SYSTEM BY WHICH ENGINE POWER IS CONNECTED TO THE TRANSMISSION.

① TRANSMISSION HOUSING

② CLUTCH DISC – AN ASSEMBLY ATTACHED TO THE TRANSMISSION SHAFT WITH A SPLINED HUB. THE DISC HAS FRICTION MATERIAL ON BOTH SIDES WHERE IT CONTACTS THE FLYWHEEL AND PRESSURE PLATE.

③ PRESSURE PLATE – APPLIES PRESSURE AGAINST THE CLUTCH DISC HOLDING IT TIGHT AGAINST THE SURFACE OF THE ENGINE FLYWHEEL.

④ COVER – PART OF PRESSURE PLATE ASSEMBLY.

⑤ RELEASE BEARING – CONSTANTLY ENGAGED WITH RELEASE FINGERS PROVIDE CONNECTION BETWEEN RELEASE FINGERS AND FORK.

⑥ RELEASE FORK

⑦ RELEASE LEVER (RELEASE FORK AND RELEASE LEVER IMPART PEDAL MOTION TO RELEASE BEARING LEVER IS CONNECTED TO CLUTCH CABLE)

DAMPER SPRINGS ⑨ PART OF THE DISC ASSEMBLY. AID IN ISOLATING ENGINE PULSES FROM POWER TRAIN.

ENGINE CRANKSHAFT NOTE: THIS SYSTEM REQUIRES NO PILOT BEARING

RELEASE FINGERS – ⑧ PART OF THE BELLEVILLE LOAD SPRING. MOVEMENT TOWARD FLYWHEEL REMOVES CLAMP LOAD FROM CLUTCH DISC.

TRANSMISSION INPUT SHAFT

Clutch assembly and operational information

ing clutch surfaces, use a commercially available brake cleaning fluid

Adjustments

PEDAL HEIGHT/FREE PLAY

The free-play in the clutch is adjusted by a built in mechanism that allows the clutch controls to be self-adjusted during normal operation. The self-adjusting feature should be checked every 5000 miles (8,000km). This is accomplished by insuring that the clutch pedal travels to the top of its upward position. Grasp the clutch pedal by hand or put a foot under the clutch pedal; pull up on the pedal until it stops. Very little effort is required (about 10 lbs.). During the application of upward pressure, a click may be heard which means an adjustment was necessary and has been accomplished.

Clutch Pedal

REMOVAL AND INSTALLATION

1. Prop the clutch pedal up to disengage the automatic clutch adjuster using tape or a piece of wire.
2. Remove the air cleaner assembly to gain access to the clutch cable.
3. Grasp the extended tip of the clutch cable with a pair of pliers and unlock the cable from the release lever. Do not grasp the wire strand portion of the inner cable because the strands may be damaged causing cable failure.
4. Position the clutch shield away from the mounting plate.

5. Pull the cable out through the recess between the pedal and gear quadrant.
6. Unseat the cable from the insulator at the clutch pedal stop bracket. Disconnect the clutch switches.
7. Remove the mounting plate and the clutch pedal assembly from the brake pedal support by removing the two nuts from the brake booster studs and two screws from the pedal support.
8. Remove the pedal stop bracket-to-mounting and remove the pedal.

To install:

1. Lubricate the quadrant pivot bore, pawl pivot bore, quadrant pivot pin, and quadrant pivot sleeve.
2. Insert the pawl, spring, and the pivot pin into the clutch pedal and secure the retainer clip.
3. Assemble the gear quadrant spring to the gear quadrant.
4. Install the two bushings and pivot sleeve into clutch pedal.
5. Place the bolt through the pivot sleeve and torque to 25–30 ft. lbs.
6. Position the assembly on the mounting plate and install the three nuts, torque to 15–25 ft. lbs.
7. Secure the clutch pedal assembly and mounting plate to the brake booster studs and brake pedal support.
8. Pull the clutch cable through the insulator and gear quadrant. Hook the cable into the gear quadrant.
9. Install the clutch switch electrical connec-

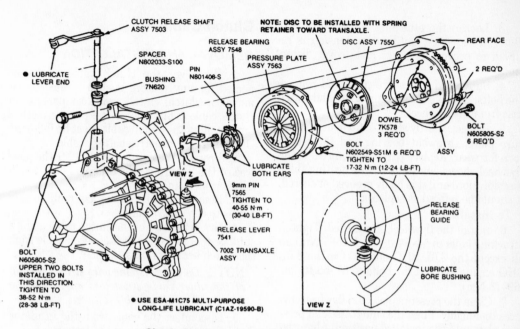

Clutch disc, pressure plate and release bearing

tors, clutch shield, and make sure all the fasteners are torqued properly.

10. Using a piece of wire or tape, secure the clutch pedal in its upright position. Hook the clutch cable into the release lever in the engine compartment.

11. Adjust the clutch by depressing the clutch pedal up against its stop several times. Install the air cleaner and start engine to check clutch operation.

Driven Disc and Pressure Plate

REMOVAL AND INSTALLATION

1. Disconnect the negative battery cable. Raise the vehicle and support it safely. Remove the transaxle.

2. Mark the pressure plate assembly and the flywheel so they can be assembled in the same position.

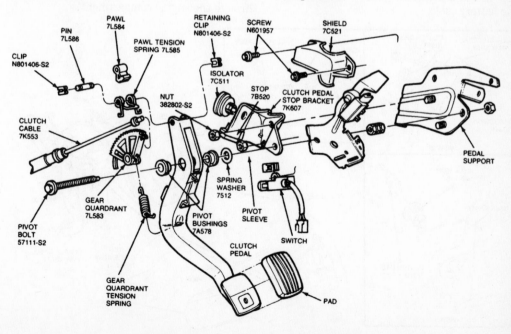

Clutch mechanism and related components

3. Loosen the attaching bolts 1 turn at a time, in sequence, until spring tension is relieved to prevent pressure plate cover distortion.

4. Support the pressure plate and remove the bolts. Remove the pressure plate and clutch disc from the flywheel.

5. Inspect the flywheel, clutch disc, pressure plate, throwout bearing and the clutch fork for wear. Replace parts as required. If the flywheel shows any signs of overheating (blue discoloration) or if it is badly grooved or scored, it should be refaced or replaced.

To install:

6. Install the flywheel, if removed. Tighten attaching bolts to 54–64 ft. lbs. (73–87 Nm) on all except the 3.0L SHO engine. On the 3.0L SHO engine, tighten the bolts to 51–58 ft. lbs. (69–78 Nm).

7. Clean the pressure plate and flywheel surfaces thoroughly. Place the clutch disc and pressure plate into the installed position. Align the marks made during the removal procedure if components are being reused. Support the clutch disc and pressure plate with a suitable dummy shaft or clutch aligning tool.

8. Install the pressure plate-to-flywheel bolts. Tighten them gradually in a cross pattern to 12–24 ft. lbs. (17–32 Nm). Remove the alignment tool.

9. Lubricate the release bearing and install it in the fork.

10. Install the transaxle and connect the negative battery cable.

Clutch Cable

REMOVAL AND INSTALLATION

1. Whenever the clutch cable is disconnected for any reason, such as transaxle removal or clutch, clutch pedal components or clutch cable replacement, the proper method for installing the clutch cable must be followed. Disconnect the negative battery cable.

2. Prop up the clutch pedal to lift the pawl free of the quadrant which is part of the self-adjuster mechanism.

3. Remove the air cleaner assembly to gain access to the clutch cable.

4. Grasp the end of the clutch cable using a suitable tool and unhook the clutch cable from the clutch bearing release lever.

NOTE: *Do not grasp the wire strand portion of the inner cable since this might cut the wires and result in cable failure.*

5. Disconnect the cable from the insulator that is located on the rib of the transaxle.

6. Position the clutch shield away from the mounting plate bracket by removing the rear retaining screw. Loosen the front retaining screw located near the toe board and rotate the shield aside.

7. With the clutch pedal lifted up to release the pawl, rotate the gear quadrant forward. Unhook the clutch cable from the gear quadrant. Let the quadrant swing rearward but do not let it snap back.

8. Remove the cable by withdrawing it through the engine compartment.

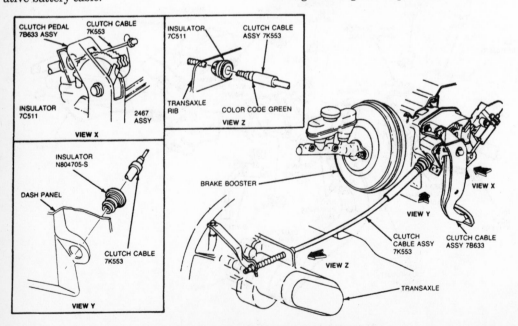

Clutch cable and related components

To install:

NOTE: *The clutch pedal must be lifted to disengage the adjusting mechanism during cable installation. Failure to do so will result in damage to the self adjuster mechanism. A prying instrument must never be used to install the cable into the quadrant.*

9. Insert the clutch cable assembly from the engine or passenger compartment through the dash panel and dash panel grommet. Make sure the cable is routed inboard of the brake lines and not trapped at the spring tower by the brake lines.

10. Push the clutch cable through the insulator on the stop bracket and through the recess between the pedal and the gear quadrant.

11. With the clutch pedal lifted up to release the pawl, rotate the gear quadrant forward. Hook the cable into the gear quadrant.

12. Secure the clutch shield on the clutch mounting plate.

13. Using a suitable device, secure the pedal in the upper most position.

14. Install the clutch cable in the insulator on the rib of the transaxle.

15. Hook the cable into the clutch release lever in the engine compartment.

16. Remove the device that was used to temporarily secure the pedal against it's stop.

17. Adjust the clutch by depressing the clutch pedal several times.

18. Install the air cleaner and connect the negative battery cable.

Clutch/Starter Interlock Switch

REMOVAL AND INSTALLATION

1. Disconnect the negative battery cable. Disconnect the electrical connector.

2. Remove the clutch/starter interlock retaining screw and hairpin clip. Remove the component from the vehicle.

3. Installation is the reverse of the removal procedure.

4. Always install the switch with the self adjusting clip about 1 in. (25mm) from the end of the rod. Be sure that the clutch pedal is in the full up position or the switch will be improperly adjusted.

AUTOMATIC TRANSAXLE

Identification

Two automatic transaxle units are available, the ATX (automatic transaxle) model which is used with the 2.5L engine, and the AXOD (automatic transaxle overdrive) which is used with the 3.0L and 3.8L engine. Beginning in 1991 some vehicles were equipped with the AXOD-E transaxle which is basically the same as the AXOD with the addition of electronic transaxle controls.

The ATX automatic transaxle is a 3-speed unit. A unique feature is a patented split path torque converter. The engine torque in second and third gears is divided, so that part of the engine torque is transmitted hydrokinetically through the torque converter, and part is transmitted mechanically by direct connection of the engine and transaxle. In the third gear, 93% of the torque is transmitted mechanically, making the ATX highly efficient. Torque splitting is accomplished through a splitter gear set. A conventional compound gear set is also used.

Only one band is used in the ATX. In service fluid additions, or fluid changes may be made with **Motorcraft Type H** automatic transmission fluid.

The AXOD and the AXOD-E automatic transaxle is a 4-speed unit. This unit has two planetary gear sets and a combination planetary/differential gear set. Four multiple plate clutches, two band assemblies, and two one-way clutches act together for proper operation of the planetary gear sets.

A lockup torque converter is coupled to the engine crankshaft and transmits engine power to the gear train by means of a drive link assembly (chain) that connects the drive and the driven sprockets. The application of the converter clutch is controlled through an electronic control integrated in the on-board EEC-IV system computer. These controls, along with the hydraulic controls in the valve body, operate a piston plate clutch in the torque converter to provide improved fuel economy by eliminating converter slip when applied.

In service fluid additions, or fluid changes may be made with **Motorcraft Type H** automatic transmission fluid.

The AXOD-E uses a turbine speed sensor in conjunction with a vehicle electronic control system. These components send operational signals to the EEC-IV microprocessor.

Fluid Pan

REMOVAL AND INSTALLATION

In normal service it should not be necessaryor required to drain and refill the automatic transaxle. However, under severe operation or dusty conditions the fluid should be changed every 20 months or 20,000 miles.

1. Raise the car and safely support it on jackstands. If the pan is equipped with a drain plug, drain the fluid into a suitable conatiner.

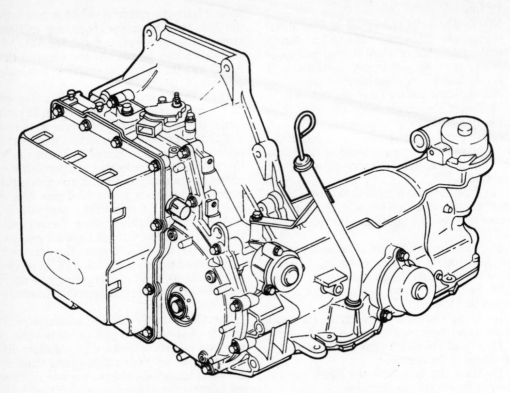

Automatic transaxle assembly — AXOD shown

2. If the pan does not have a drain plug, place a suitable drain pan underneath the transaxle oil pan. Loosen the oil pan mounting bolts and allow the fluid to drain until it reaches the level of the pan flange. Remove the attaching bolts, leaving one end attached so that the pan will tip and the rest of the fluid will drain.

3. Remove the oil pan. Thoroughly clean the pan. Remove the old gasket. Make sure that the gasket mounting surfaces are clean.

4. Remove the transaxle filter screen retaining bolt. Remove the screen.

5. Install a new filter screen and O-ring. Place a new gasket on the pan and install the pan to the transaxle. Torque the transaxle pan to 15–19 ft. lbs.

6. Fill the transaxle to the correct level. Remove the jackstands and lower the car to the ground.

Adjustments

SHIFT CABLE

AXOD and AXOD-E Transaxle

1. Position the selector lever in the **OD** position against the rearward stop. The shift lever must be held in the rearward position using a constant force of 3 lbs. (1.4 Kg) while the linkage is being adjusted.

2. Loosen the manual lever-to-control cable retaining nut.

3. Move the transaxle manual lever to the **OD** position, second detent from the most rearward position.

4. Tighten the retaining nut to 11–19 ft. lbs. (14–27 Nm).

5. Check the operation of the transaxle in each selector lever position. Make sure the park and neutral start switch are functioning properly.

ATX Transaxle

1. Position the selector lever in the **D** position against the drive stop. The shift lever must be held in the **D** position while the linkage is being adjusted.

2. Loosen the transaxle manual lever-to-control cable adjustment trunnion bolt.

3. Move the transaxle manual lever to the **D** position, second detent from the most rearward position.

4. Tighten the adjustment trunnion bolt to 12–20 ft. lbs. (16–27 Nm).

5. Check the operation of the transaxle in each selector lever position. Make sure the neu-

tral start switch functions properly in **P** and **N** and the back-up lights are on in **R**.

THROTTLE CABLE

NOTE: *Transaxle downshift control is controlled through the throttle position switch on 1991–92 vehicles equipped with the electronic automatic overdrive transaxle.*

1986–90 3.0L and 3.8L Engines

The Throttle Valve (TV) cable normally does not need adjustment. The cable should be adjusted only if one of the following components is removed for service or replacement:
- Main control assembly
- Throttle valve cable
- Throttle valve cable engine mounting bracket
- Throttle control lever link or lever assembly
- Engine throttle body
- Transaxle assembly

1. Connect the TV cable eye to the transaxle throttle control lever link and attach the cable boot to the chain cover.

2. If equipped with the 3.0L engine, with the TV cable mounted in the engine bracket, make sure the threaded shank is fully retracted. To retract the shank, pull up on the spring rest with the index fingers and wiggle the top of the thread shank while pressing the shank through the spring with the thumbs.

3. If equipped with the 3.8L engine, the TV cable must be unclipped from the right intake manifold clip. To retract the shank, span the crack between the two 180 degree segments of the adjuster spring rest with a suitable tool. Compress the spring by pushing the rod toward the throttle body with the right hand. While the spring is compressed, push the threaded shank toward the spring with the index and middle fingers of the left hand. Do not pull on the cable sheath.

4. Attach the end of the TV cable to the throttle body.

5. If equipped with the 3.8L engine, rotate the throttle body primary lever by hand, the lever to which the TV-driving nailhead is attached, to the wide-open-throttle position. The white adjuster shank must be seen to advance. If not, look for cable sheath/foam hang-up on engine/body components. Attach the TV cable into the top position of the right intake manifold clip.

NOTE: *The threaded shank must show movement or "ratchet" out of the grip jaws. If there is no movement, inspect the TV cable system for broken or disconnected components and repeat the procedure.*

THROTTLE VALVE CONTROL LINKAGE

ATX Transaxle

The Throttle Valve (TV) Control Linkage System consists of a lever on the throttle body of the injection unit, linkage shaft assembly, mounting bracket assembly, control rod assembly, a control lever on the transaxle and a lever return spring.

The coupling lever follows the movement of throttle lever and has an adjustment screw that is used for setting TV linkage adjustment when a line pressure gauge is used. If a pressure gauge is not available, a manual adjustment can be made.

A number of shift troubles can occur if the throttle valve linkage is not in adjustment. Some are:

1. **Symptom:** Excessively early and/or soft upshift with or without slip-bump feel. No forced downshift (kickdown) function at appropriate speeds. **Cause:** TV control linkage is set too short. **Remedy:** Adjust linkage.

2. **Symptom:** Extremely delayed or harsh upshifts and harsh idle engagement. **Cause:** TV control linkage is set too long. **Remedy:** Adjust linkage.

3. **Symptom:** Harsh idle engagement after the engine is warmed up. Shift clunk when throttle is backed off after full or heavy throttle acceleration. Harsh coasting downshifts (automatic 3–2, 2–1 shift in D range). Delayed upshift at light acceleration. **Cause:** Interference due to hoses, wires, etc. prevents return of

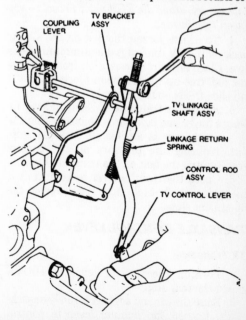

Throttle valve linkage — ATX transaxle

TV control rod or TV linkage shaft. Excessive friction caused by binding grommets prevents the TV control linkage to return to its proper location. **Remedy:** Correct the interference area, check for bent or twisted rods, levers. or damaged grommets. Repair or replace whatever is necessary. Check and adjust linkage is necessary.

4. **Symptom:** Erratic/delayed upshifts, possibly no kickdown, harsh engagement. **Cause:** Clamping bolt on trunnion at the upper end of the TV control rod is loose. **Remedy:** Reset TV control linkage.

5. **Symptom:** No upshift and harsh engagements. **Cause:** TV control rod is disconnected or the linkage return spring is broken or disconnected. **Remedy:** Reconnect TV control rod, check and replace the connecting grommet if necessary, reconnect or replace the TV return spring.

The TV control linkage is adjusted at the sliding trunnion block.

1. Operate the engine until normal operating temperature is reached. Adjust the curb idle speed to specification.

2. After the curb idle speed has been set, shut off the engine. Make sure the choke is completely opened. Check the throttle lever to make sure it is against the hot engine curb idle stop.

3. Set the coupling lever adjustment screw at its approximate midrange. Make sure the TV linkage shaft assembly is fully seated upward into the coupling lever.

CAUTION: *If adjustment of the linkage is necessary, allow the EGR valve to cool so you won't get burned.*

4. To adjust, loosen the bolt on the sliding block on the TV control rod a minimum of one turn. Clean any dirt or corrosion from the control rod, free-up the trunnion block so that it will slide freely on the control rod.

5. Rotate the transaxle TV control lever up using a finger and light force, to insure that the TV control lever is against its internal stop. With reducing the pressure on the control lever, tighten the bolt on the trunnion block.

6. Check the throttle lever to be sure it is still against the hot idle stop. If not, repeat the adjustment steps.

TRANSAXLE CONTROL LEVER

ATX Transaxle

1. Position the selector lever in DRIVE against the rear stop.

2. Raise the car and support it safely on jackstands. Loosen the manual lever to control lever nut.

3. Move the transaxle lever to the Drive po-

sition, second detent from the rear most position. Tighten the attaching nut. Check the operation of the transaxle in each selector position. Readjust if necessary. Lower the car.

AXOD and AXOD-E Transaxles

1. Position the selector lever in the OVERDRIVE position against the rearward stop.

2. If the vehicle is equipped with a floor shift selector the shift lever must be held in the rearward position using a constant force of about 3 lbs. as the linkage is being adjusted.

3. Loosen the manual lever to control cable retaining nut. Be sure that the transaxle lever is in the OVERDRIVE position. Tighten the retaining nut to 11–19 ft. lbs.

4. Check operation of the transaxle in each range. Be sure that the park switch and neutral safety switch are working properly.

Neutral Safety Switch/Back-Up Light Switch

The neutral start and backup switch are one unit mounted on the top left end of the transaxle. The neutral start portion of the switch allows electrical current to travel to the ignition system when the shift selector is in park or neutral only. The vehicle will not start when the selector is in any other gear. The backup portion operates the rear backup lamps when selector is in the reverse gear.

REMOVAL AND INSTALLATION

1. Place the shift selector in the Park position and apply the emergency brake.

2. Disconnect the negative (–) battery cable.

3. Disconnect the neutral start switch electrical connector and remove the shift control lever on top of the switch.

4. Remove the two neutral switch attaching bolts and remove the switch.

5. Installation is the reverse of the removal procedure.

ADJUSTMENT

1. Loosely install the two switch attaching bolts and washers, insert a No. 43 drill bit through the hole provided in the switch.

2. Torque the two attaching bolts to 84–108 inch lbs.

3. Check the neutral start switch for proper operation.

Shift Lever Cable

REMOVAL AND INSTALLATION

1. Remove the shift knob, locknut, console, bezel assembly, control cable clip and cable retaining pin.

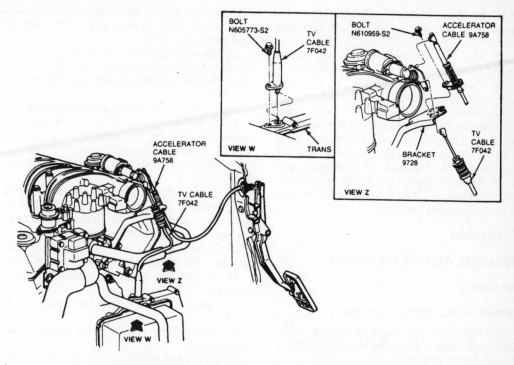

Accelerator and throttle valve cables — automatic transaxle

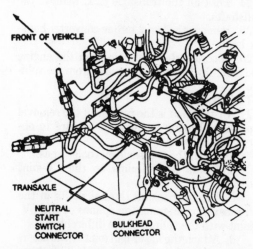

Neutral safety switch and back up switch location — automatic transaxle

2. Disengage the rubber grommet from the floor pan by pushing it into the engine compartment.

3. Raise the car and safely support it on jackstands.

4. Remove the retaining nut and control cable assembly from the transaxle lever.

5. Remove the control cable bracket bolts. Pull the cable through the floor.

6. To install the cable, feed the round end through the floor board. Press the rubber grommet into its mounting hole.

7. Position the control cable assembly in the selector lever housing and install the spring clip.

8. Install the bushing and control cable assembly on the selector lever and housing assembly shaft and secure it with the retaining pin.

9. Install the bezel assembly, console, locknut and shift knob.

10. Position the selector lever in the Drive position. The selector lever must be held in this position while attaching the other end of the control cable.

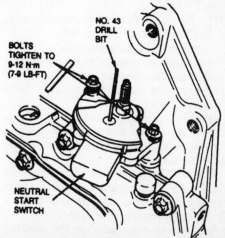

Neutral safety switch adjustment — automatic transaxle

11. Position the control cable bracket on the retainer bracket and secure the tow mounting bolts.

12. Shift the control lever into the second detent from full rearward (Drive position).

13. Place the cable end on the transaxle lever stud. Align the flats on the stud with the slot in the cable. Make sure the transaxle selector lever has not moved from the second detent position and tighten the retaining nut.

14. Lower the car to the ground. Check the operation of the transaxle selector in all positions. Make sure the neutral safety switch is operating properly. The engine should start only in park or neutral position.

Transaxle

REMOVAL AND INSTALLATION

1986–90

EXCEPT TAURUS WITH 2.5L ENGINE

1. Disconnect the negative battery cable. Raise and support the vehicle safely. Remove the air cleaner assembly.

2. Remove the bolt retaining the shift cable and bracket assembly to the transaxle.

NOTE: *Hold the bracket with a prybar in the slot to prevent the bracket from moving.*

3. Remove the shift cable bracket bolts and bracket from the transaxle. Disconnect the electrical connector from the neutral safety switch.

4. Disconnect the electrical bulkhead connector from the rear of the transaxle. Remove the dipstick. If with 3.8L engines, remove the throttle valve cable cover. Unsnap the throttle valve cable from the throttle body lever. Remove the throttle valve cable from the transaxle case.

5. Carefully pull up on the throttle valve cable and disconnect the throttle valve cable from the TV link.

NOTE: *Pulling to hard on the throttle valve may bend the internal TV bracket.*

6. Install engine lifting brackets.

7. Disconnect the power steering pump pressure and return line bracket.

8. Remove the converter housing bolts from the top of the transaxle.

9. Install a suitable engine support fixture.

10. Raise the vehicle and support it safely.

11. Remove both front wheels. Remove the left outer tie rod end.

12. Remove the lower ball joint attaching nuts and bolts. Remove the lower ball joints and remove the lower control arms from each spindle. Remove stabilizer bar bolts.

13. Remove the nuts securing the steering rack to the sub-frame.

14. If equipped with 3.8L engine, disconnect the oxygen sensor electrical connection and remove the exhaust pipe, converter assembly and mounting bracket.

15. Remove the two 15mm bolts from the transaxle mount. Remove the four 15mm bolts from the left engine support and remove the bracket.

16. Position the sub-frame removal tool.

17. Remove the steering gear from the sub-frame and secure to the rear of the engine compartment. Remove the sub-frame.

18. Remove the dust cover and the starter assembly.

19. Rotate the engine by the crankshaft pulley bolt to align the torque converter bolts with the starter drive hole. Remove the torque converter-to-flywheel retaining nuts.

20. Remove the transaxle cooler line retaining clips. Disconnect the transaxle cooler lines.

21. Remove the engine to transaxle retaining bolts.

22. Remove the speedometer sensor heat shield.

23. Remove the vehicle speed sensor from the transaxle.

NOTE: *Vehicles with electronic instrument clusters do not use a speedometer cable.*

24. Position the transaxle jack. Remove the halfshafts.

25. Remove the last 2 torque converter housing bolts.

26. Seperate the transaxle from the engine and carefully lower the transaxle from the vehicle.

To install:

27. Installation is the reverse of the removal procedure. During installation be sure to observe the following:

a. Clean the transaxle oil cooler lines.

b. Install new circlips on the CV-joint seals.

c. Carefully install the halfshafts in the transaxle by aligning the splines of the CV-joint with the splines of the differential.

d. Attach the lower ball joint to the steering knuckle with a new nut and bolt. Tighten the nut to 37–44 ft. lbs.

e. When installing the transaxle to the engine, verify that the converter-to-transaxle engagement is maintained. Prevent the converter from moving forward and disengaging during installation.

f. Adjust the TV and manual linkages. Check the transaxle fluid level.

g. Tighten the following bolts to the torque specifications listed:
- Transaxle-to-engine bolts: 41–50 ft. lbs. (55–68 Nm)
- Control arm-to-knuckle bolts: 36–44 ft. lbs. (50–60 Nm)

• Stabilizer U-clamp-to-bracket bolts: 60–70 ft. lbs. (81–95 Nm)

• Tie rod-to-knuckle nut: 23–35 ft. lbs. (31–47 Nm)

• Starter-to-transaxle bolts: 30–40 ft. lbs. (41–54 Nm)

• Converter-to-flywheel bolts: 23–39 ft. lbs. (31–53 Nm)

• Insulator-to-bracket bolts: 55–70 ft. lbs. (75–90 Nm)

TAURUS WITH 2.5L ENGINE

1. Disconnect the negative battery cable and remove the air cleaner assembly.

2. Position the engine control wiring harness away from the transaxle converter housing.

3. Disconnect the TV linkage and manual lever cable at the respective levers. Failure to disconnect the linkage during transaxle removal and allowing the transaxle to hang will fracture the throttle valve cam shaft joint, which is located under the transaxle cover.

4. Remove the power steering hose brackets.

5. Remove the upper transaxle-to-engine attaching bolts.

6. Install suitable engine lifting brackets to the right and left areas of the cylinder head and attach with bolts. Install 2 suitable engine support bars.

NOTE: *An engine support bar may be fabricated from a length of 4 × 4 wood cut to 57 in. (145cm).*

7. Place 1 of the engine support bars across the vehicle in front of each engine shock tower. Place another support bar across the vehicle approximately between the alternator and valve cover. Attach chains to the lifting brackets. Raise the vehicle and support safely. Remove the wheel and tire assemblies.

8. Remove the catalytic converter inlet pipe and disconnect the exhaust air hose assembly.

9. Remove each tie rod end from it's spindle. Separate the lower ball joints from the struts and remove the lower control arm from each spindle.

10. Disconnect the stabilizer bar by removing the retaining nuts.

11. Disconnect and remove the rack and pinion and auxiliary cooler from the sub-frame. Position the rack and pinion away from the sub-frame and secure with wire.

12. Remove the right front axle support and bearing assembly retaining bolts.

13. Remove the halfshaft and link shaft assembly out of the right side of the transaxle.

14. Disengage the left halfshaft from the differential side gear. Pull the halfshaft from the transaxle.

NOTE: *Support and secure the halfshaft from an underbody component with a length of wire. Do not allow the halfshafts to hang unsupported.*

15. Plug the seal holes.

16. Remove the front support insulator and position the left front splash shield aside.

17. Properly support the sub-frame and lower the vehicle onto the sub-frame support. Remove the sub-frame and disconnect the neutral start switch wire assembly.

18. Raise the vehicle after the sub-frame is removed. Disconnect the speedometer cable.

19. Disconnect and remove the shift cable from the transaxle.

20. Disconnect the oil cooler lines and remove the starter.

21. Remove the dust cover from the torque converter housing and remove the torque converter-to-flywheel housing nuts.

22. Position a suitable transaxle jack under the transaxle.

23. Remove the remaining transaxle-to-engine attaching bolts.

NOTE: *Before the transaxle can be lowered from the vehicle, the torque converter studs must be clear of the flywheel. Insert a suitable tool between the flywheel and converter and carefully guide the transaxle and converter away from the engine.*

24. Lower the transaxle from the engine.

To install:

25. Installation is the reverse of the removal procedure. During installation be sure to observe the following:

  a. Clean the transaxle oil cooler lines.

  b. Install new circlips on the CV-joint seals.

  c. Carefully install the halfshafts in the transaxle by aligning the splines of the CV-joint with the splines of the differential.

  d. Attach the lower ball joint to the steering knuckle with a new nut and bolt. Tighten the nut to 37–44 ft. lbs. Torquing of the bolt is not required.

  e. When installing the transaxle to the engine, verify that the converter-to-transaxle engagement is maintained. Prevent the converter from moving forward and disengaging during installation.

  f. Adjust the TV and manual linkages. Check the transaxle fluid level.

  g. Tighten the following bolts to the torque specifications listed:

• Transaxle-to-engine bolts: 25–33 ft. lbs. (34–45 Nm)

• Control arm-to-knuckle bolts: 36–44 ft. lbs. (50–60 Nm)

• Stabilizer U-clamp-to-bracket bolts: 60–70 ft. lbs. (81–95 Nm)

• Tie rod-to-knuckle nut: 23–35 ft. lbs. (31–47 Nm)

• Starter-to-transaxle bolts: 30–40 ft. lbs. (41–54 Nm)

• Converter-to-flywheel bolts: 23–39 ft. lbs. (31–53 Nm)

• Insulator-to-bracket bolts: 55–70 ft. lbs. (75–90 Nm)

1991–92

1. Disconnect the battery cables and removethe battery and battery tray.

2. Remove the air cleaner assembly, hoses and tubes.

3. Disconnect the electrical connectors from the engine and remove the bolt retaining the main wiring harness bracket.

4. Remove the shift lever. Remove the EGR bracket and throttle body bracket retaining bolts and install engine lifting eyes.

5. Secure the wiring harness aside and remove the radiator sight shield. Position a suitable engine support fixture.

6. If equipped with air suspension, turn the air suspension switch located in the luggage compartment to the **OFF** position.

7. Remove the dipstick and disconnect the power steering line bracket. Remove the 4 torque converter housing bolts from the top of the transaxle.

8. Raise and safely support the vehicle. Remove the front wheel and tire assemblies.

9. Disconnect the left outer tie rod end. Remove the suspension height sensor, if equipped. Disconnect the brake line support brackets.

10. Remove the retaining bolts from the front stabilizer bar assembly. Disconnect the right and left lower arm assemblies.

11. Remove the steering gear retaining nuts from the sub-frame. Remove the front oxygen sensor, exhaust pipe, converter assembly and mounting bracket.

12. Remove 2 bolts from the transaxle mount and the 4 bolts from the left engine support. Remove the engine support.

13. Position a suitable sub-frame removal tool. Remove the steering gear from the sub-frame and secure to the rear of the engine compartment. Remove the sub-frame-to-body bolts and lower the sub-frame.

14. Remove the starter and the dust cover.

15. Rotate the engine at the crankshaft pulley to align the torque converter bolts with the starter drive hole. Remove the 4 torque converter-to-flywheel retaining nuts.

16. Disconnect the transaxle cooler lines. Remove the engine-to-transaxle retaining bolts.

17. Remove the speedometer sensor heat shield. Remove the vehicle speed sensor from the transaxle.

NOTE: *Vehicles with electronic instrument clusters do not use a speedometer cable.*

18. Position a suitable transaxle jack. Remove the halfshafts.

19. Remove the last 2 torque converter housing bolts, carefully separate the transaxle from the engine and lower out of the vehicle.

20. Installation is the reverse of the removal procedure. During installation be sure to observe the following:

a. Clean the transaxle oil cooler lines.

b. Install new circlips on the CV-joint seals.

c. Carefully install the halfshafts in the transaxle by aligning the splines of the CV-joint with the splines of the differential.

d. Attach the lower ball joint to the steering knuckle with a new nut and bolt. Tighten the nut to 37–44 ft. lbs.

e. When installing the transaxle to the engine, verify that the converter-to-transaxle engagement is maintained. Prevent the converter from moving forward and disengaging during installation.

f. Adjust the TV and manual linkages. Check the transaxle fluid level.

g. Tighten the following bolts to the torque specifications listed:

• Transaxle-to-engine bolts: 41–50 ft. lbs. (55–68 Nm)

• Control arm-to-knuckle bolts: 36–44 ft. lbs. (50–60 Nm)

• Stabilizer U-clamp-to-bracket bolts: 60–70 ft. lbs. (81–95 Nm)

• Tie rod-to-knuckle nut: 23–35 ft. lbs. (31–47 Nm)

• Starter-to-transaxle bolts: 30–40 ft. lbs. (41–54 Nm)

• Converter-to-flywheel bolts: 23–39 ft. lbs. (31–53 Nm)

• Insulator-to-bracket bolts: 55–70 ft. lbs. (75–90 Nm)

Halfshafts

When removing both the left and right halfshafts, install suitable shipping plugs to prevent dislocation of the differential side gears. Should the gears become misaligned, the differential will have to be removed from the transaxle to re-align the side gears.

NOTE: *Due to the automatic transaxle case configuration, the right halfshaft assembly must be removed first. Differential Rotator T81P–4026–A or equivalent, is then inserted into the transaxle to drive the left inboard CV-joint assembly from the transaxle. If only the left halfshaft assembly is to be removed for*

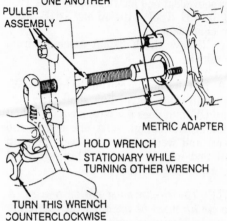

MAKE SURE THE ADAPTERS ARE FULLY
THREADED ONTO THE HUB STUDS AND
THAT THEY ARE POSITIONED OPPOSITE
ONE ANOTHER

PULLER
ASSEMBLY

METRIC ADAPTER

HOLD WRENCH
STATIONARY WHILE
TURNING OTHER WRENCH

TURN THIS WRENCH
COUNTERCLOCKWISE

Removing the stub shaft from the hub assembly

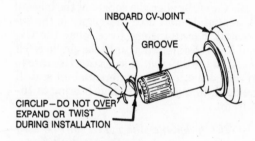

INBOARD CV-JOINT

GROOVE

CIRCLIP—DO NOT OVER
EXPAND OR TWIST
DURING INSTALLATION

Stub shaft circlip installation

*service, remove only the right halfshaft assem-
bly from the transaxle. After removal, support it with a length of wire. Then drive the
left halfshaft assembly from the transaxle.*

REMOVAL AND INSTALLATION

1. Disconnect the negative battery cable.
Remove the wheel cover/hub cover from the

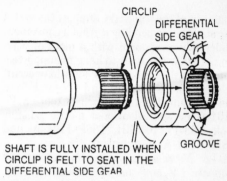

CIRCLIP

DIFFERENTIAL
SIDE GEAR

GROOVE

SHAFT IS FULLY INSTALLED WHEN
CIRCLIP IS FELT TO SEAT IN THE
DIFFERENTIAL SIDE GEAR

**Seating the circlip in the transaxle differential side
gear**

wheel and tire assembly and loosen the wheel
nuts.

2. Raise the vehicle and support safely.
Remove the wheel assembly, remove the hub
nut and washer. Discard the old hub nut.
Remove the nut from the ball joint to steering
knuckle attaching bolts.

3. Drive the bolt out of the steering knuckle
using a punch and hammer. Discard this bolt
and nut after removal.

4. If equipped with anti-lock brakes,
remove the anti-lock brake sensor and position
aside. If equipped with air suspension, remove
the height sensor bracket retaining bolt and
wire sensor bracket to inner fender. Position
the sensor link aside.

5. Separate the ball joint from the steering
knuckle using a suitable prybar. Position the
end of the prybar outside of the bushing pocket
to avoid damage to the bushing. Use care to prevent damage to the ball joint boot. Remove the
stabilizer bar link at the stabilizer bar.

6. The following removal procedure applies
to the right side halfshaft/link shaft for the
1986–90 2.5L engine Taurus. For all other automatic transaxles, proceed to Step 7:

a. Remove the bolts attaching the bearing support to the bracket. Slide the link

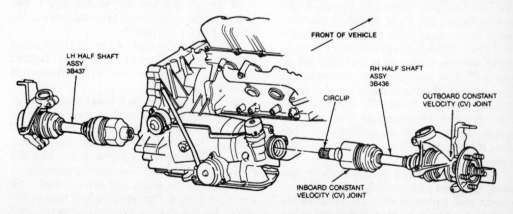

FRONT OF VEHICLE

LH HALF SHAFT
ASSY
3B437

RH HALF SHAFT
ASSY
3B436

CIRCLIP

OUTBOARD CONSTANT
VELOCITY (CV) JOINT

INBOARD CONSTANT
VELOCITY (CV) JOINT

Halfshaft assembly — AXOD automatic transaxle

shaft out of the transaxle. Support the end of the shaft by suspending it from a convenient underbody component with a piece of wire. Do not allow the shaft to hang unsupported, damage to the outboard CV-joint may occur.

b. Separate the outboard CV-joint from the hub using front hub remover tool T81P–1104–C or equivalent and metric adapter tools T83–P–1104–BH, T86P–1104–Al and T81P–1104–A or equivalent.

NOTE: *Never use a hammer to separate the outboard CV-joint stub shaft from the hub. Damage to the CV-joint threads and internal components may result. The right side link shaft and halfshaft assembly is removed as a complete unit.*

7. The following removal procedure applies to the right and left side halfshafts for the automatic transaxle, except 1986–90 2.5L engine Taurus.

a. Install the CV-joint puller tool T86P–3514–A1 or equivalent, between CV-joint and transaxle case. Turn the steering hub and/or wire strut assembly aside.

b. Screw extension tool T86P–3514–A2 or equivalent, into the CV-joint puller and hand tighten. Screw an impact slide hammer onto the extension and remove the CV-joint.

c. Support the end of the shaft by suspending it from a convenient underbody component with a piece of wire. Do not allow the shaft to hang un-supported, damage to the outboard CV-joint may occur.

d. Separate the outboard CV-joint from the hub using front hub remover tool T81P–1104–C or equivalent and metric adapter tools T83–P–1104–BH, T86P–1104–Al and T81P–1104–A or equivalent.

e. Remove the halfshaft assembly from the vehicle.

8. The following removal procedure applies to the left side halfshaft for the 1986–90 Taurus with 2.5L engine automatic transaxle:

NOTE: *Due to the automatic transaxle case configuration, the right halfshaft assembly must be removed first. Differential rotator tool T81P–4026–A or equivalent, is then inserted into the transaxle to drive the left inboard CV-joint assembly from the transaxle. If only the left halfshaft assembly is to be removed for service, remove the right halfshaft assembly from the transaxle first. After removal, support it with a length of wire. Then drive the left halfshaft assembly from the transaxle.*

a. Support the end of the shaft by suspending it from a convenient underbody component with a piece of wire. Do not allow the shaft to hang unsupported as damage to the outboard CV-joint may occur.

b. Separate the outboard CV-joint from the hub front hub remover tool T81P–1104–C or equivalent and metric adapter tools T83–P–1104–BH, T86P–1104–Al and T81P–1104–A or equivalent.

c. Remove the halfshaft assembly from the vehicle.

To install:

9. Install a new circlip on the inboard CV-joint stub shaft and/or link shaft. The outboard CV-joint does not have a circlip. When installing the circlip, start one end in the groove and work the circlip over the stub shaft end into the groove. This will avoid over expanding the circlip.

NOTE: *The circlip must not be re-used. A new circlip must be installed each time the inboard CV-joint is installed into the transaxle differential.*

10. Carefully align the splines of the inboard CV-joint stub shaft with the splines in the differential. Exerting some force, push the CV-joint into the differential until the circlip is felt to seat in the differential side gear. Use care to prevent damage to the differential oil seal. If equipped, torque the link shaft bearing to 16–23 ft. lbs.

NOTE: *A non-metallic mallet may be used to aid in seating the circlip into the differential side gear groove. If a mallet is necessary, tap only on the outboard CV-joint stub shaft.*

11. Carefully align the splines of the outboard CV-joint stub shaft with the splines in the hub and push the shaft into the hub as far as possible.

12. Temporarily fasten the rotor to the hub with washers and 2 wheel lug nuts. Insert a steel rod into the rotor and rotate clockwise to contact the knuckle to prevent the rotor from turning during the CV-joint installation.

13. Install the hub nut washer and a new hub nut. Manually thread the retainer onto the CV-joint as far as possible.

14. Connect the control arm to the steering knuckle and install a new nut and bolt. Tighten the nut to 40–55 ft. lbs. (54–74 Nm). A new bolt must be installed also.

15. Install the anti-lock brake sensor and/or the ride height sensor bracket, if equipped.

16. Connect the stabilizer link to the stabilizer bar. Tighten to 35–48 ft. lbs. (47–65 Nm).

17. Tighten the hub retainer nut to 180–200 ft. lbs. (245–270 Nm). Remove the steel rod.

18. Install the wheel and tire assembly and lower the vehicle. Tighten the wheel nuts to 80–105 ft. lbs. Fill the transaxle to the proper level with the specified fluid.

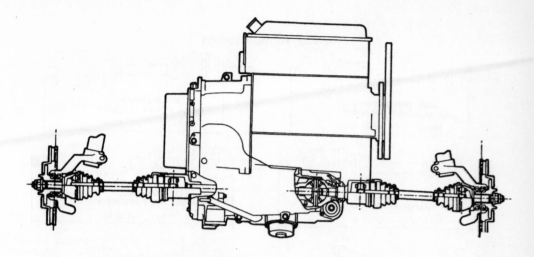

CV-joint and halfshaft assembly — automatic transaxle

CV-Boot

REMOVAL AND INSTALLATION

Outboard CV-Joint Boot

1. Disconnect the negative battery cable. Raise and safely support the vehicle.

2. Remove the halfshaft assembly from the vehicle.

3. Clamp the halfshaft in a vise that is equipped with soft jaw covers. Do not allow the vise jaws to contact the boot or boot clamp.

4. Cut the large boot clamp with a pair of side cutters and peel the clamp away from the boot. Roll the boot back over the shaft after the clamp has been removed.

5. Clamp the interconnecting shaft in a soft jawed vise with the CV-joint pointing downward so the inner bearing race is exposed.

6. Use a brass drift and hammer, give a sharp tap to the inner bearing race to dislodge the internal snapring and separate the CV-joint

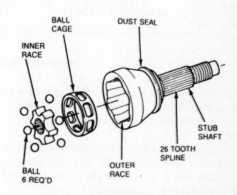

Outboard CV-joint assembly

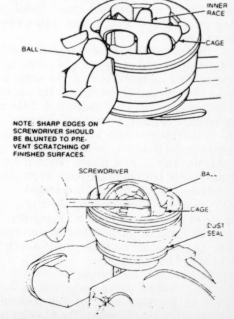

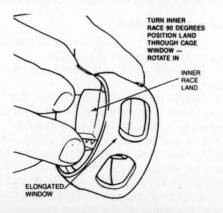

Removing the inner race land from the cage

Removing the cage balls from the cage

HALFSHAFT ASSEMBLED LENGTHS

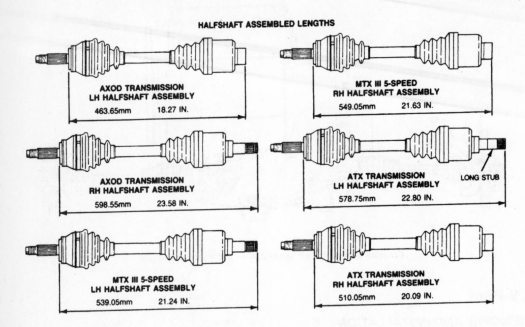

AXOD TRANSMISSION
LH HALFSHAFT ASSEMBLY
463.65mm   18.27 IN.

MTX III 5-SPEED
RH HALFSHAFT ASSEMBLY
549.05mm   21.63 IN.

AXOD TRANSMISSION
RH HALFSHAFT ASSEMBLY
598.55mm   23.58 IN.

ATX TRANSMISSION
LH HALFSHAFT ASSEMBLY
578.75mm   22.80 IN.   LONG STUB

MTX III 5-SPEED
LH HALFSHAFT ASSEMBLY
539.05mm   21.24 IN.

ATX TRANSMISSION
RH HALFSHAFT ASSEMBLY
510.05mm   20.09 IN.

Halfshaft overall length dimensions

from the interconnecting shaft. Take care to secure the CV-joint so it does not drop after separation. Remove the clamp and boot from the shaft.

7. Remove and discard the circlip at the end of the interconnecting shaft. The stop ring, located just below the circlip should be removed and replaced only if damaged or worn.

To install:

8. Clean the joint and repack with fresh grease. Do not reuse the old grease Install a new boot or reinstall the old boot with a new clamp.

9. The left and right interconnecting shafts are different, depending on year and vehicle application. The outboard end of the shaft is shorter from the end of the shaft to the end of the boot groove than the inboard end. Take a measurement to insure correct installation.

10. Install the new boot. Make sure the boot is seated in the mounting groove and secure it in position with a new clamp. Tighten the clamp securely, but not to the point where the clamp bridge is cut or the boot is damaged.

11. Clean the interconnecting shaft splines and install a new circlip and stop ring if removed. To install the circlip correctly, start one end in the groove and work the circlip over the shaft end and into the groove.

12. Pack the boot with grease.

13. With the boot peeled back, position the CV-joint on the shaft and tap into position using a plastic tipped hammer. The CV-joint is fully seated when the circlip locks into the

groove cut into the CV-joint inner bearing race. Check for seating by attempting to pull the joint away from the shaft.

14. Remove all excess grease form the CV-joint external surface and position the boot over the joint.

15. Before installing the boot clamp, make sure all air pressure that may have built up in the boot is removed. Pry up on the boot lip to allow the air to escape.

16. The large end clamp should be installed after making sure of the correct shaft length and that the boot is seated in its groove. Tighten the clamp securely, but not to the point where the clamp bridge is cut or the boot is damaged.

17. Install the halfshaft assembly and lower the vehicle. Connect the negative battery cable.

Inboard CV-Joint Boot

1. Disconnect the negative battery cable. Raise and safely support the vehicle.

2. Remove the halfshaft assembly from the vehicle.

3. Clamp the halfshaft in a vise that is equipped with soft jaw covers. Do not allow the vise jaws to contact the boot or boot clamp.

4. Cut and remove both boot clamps and slide the boot back on the shaft. Remove the clamp by engaging the pincer jaws of boot clamp pliers D87P–1090–A or equivalent, in the closing hooks on the clamp and draw together. Disengage the windows and locking hooks and remove the clamp.

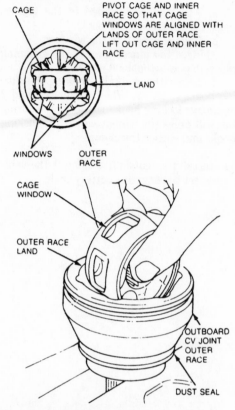

Removing the cage from the outer race land

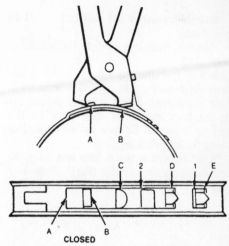

Inboard CV-joint boot clamp attachment

5. Mark the position of the outer race in relation to the shaft and remove the outer race.

6. Move the stop ring back on the shaft using snapring pliers. Move the tripod assembly back on the shaft to allow access to the circlip.

7. Remove the circlip from the shaft. Mark the position of the tripod on the shaft and remove the tripod assembly. Remove the boot.

8. Check the CV-joint grease for contamination. If the CV-joints are operating properly and the grease is not contaminated, add grease and replace the boot. If the grease appears contaminated, disassemble the CV-joint and clean or replace, as necessary.

To install:

9. Install the CV-joint boot. Make sure the boot is seated in the boot groove on the shaft. Tighten the clamp using crimping pliers, but do not tighten to the point where the clamp bridge is cut or the boot is damaged.

10. Install the tripod assembly with chamfered side toward the stop ring. If the tripod is being reused, align the marks that were made during the removal procedure.

11. Install a new circlip. Compress the circlip and slide the tripod assembly forward over the circlip to expose the stop ring groove.

12. Move the stop ring into the groove using snapring pliers, making sure it is fully seated in the groove.

13. Fill the CV-joint outer race and CV-boot with grease. Install the outer race over the tripod assembly, aligning the marks made during the removal procedure.

14. Remove all excess grease from the CV-joint external surfaces and mating boot surface. Position the boot over the CV-joint making sure the boot is seated in the groove. Move the CV-joint in and out, as necessary, to adjust the length to the following specifications:

• Automatic transaxle left halfshaft, except 1986–90 2.5L engine Taurus – 18.27 in. (464mm)

• Automatic transaxle right halfshaft, except 1986–90 2.5L engine Taurus – 23.58 in. (599mm)

• Automatic transaxle left halfshaft, 1986–90 2.5L engine Taurus – 22.80 in. (579mm)

• Automatic transaxle right halfshaft, 1986–90 2.5L engine Taurus – 20.09 in. (510mm)

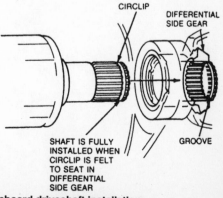

Inboard driveshaft installation

• Manual transaxle left halfshaft — 21.24 in. (539.5mm)

• Manual transaxle right halfshaft — 21.63 in. (549.5mm)

15. Before installing the boot clamp, make sure any air pressure that may have built up in the boot is relieved. Insert a small prybar between the boot and outer race to allow the trapped air to escape. Release the air only after adjusting the length dimension.

16. Seat the boot in the groove and clamp in position using crimping pliers D87P–1098–A or equivalent. Install the clamp as follows:

a. With the boot seated in the groove, place the clamp over the boot.

b. Engage hook C in the window.

c. Place the pincer jaws of the crimping pliers in closing hooks A and B.

d. Secure the clamp by drawing the closing hooks together. When windows 1 and 2 are above locking hooks D and E, the spring tab will press the windows over the locking hooks and engage the clamp.

17. Install the halfshaft and lower the vehicle. Connect the negative battery cable.

8

WHEELS

Wheels

REMOVAL AND INSTALLATION

1. Position the vehicle on a level surface. Apply the emergency brake.

2. If equipped with automatic transaxle be sure that the selector lever is in the PARK position.

3. If equipped with manual transaxle be sure that the selector lever is gear.

4. Remove the hub cap from the wheel and tire assembly.

5. Using the proper size lug nut wrench, loosen but do not remove the lug nuts from the wheel and tire assembly.

6. Raise and properly support the vehicle. Loosen and remove the lug nuts from the wheel and tire assembly.

7. Remove the wheel and tire assembly from its mounting.

To install:

8. Install the tire and wheel assembly to the brake rotor or drum.

9. Install the lug nuts finger tight. Lower the vehicle to the ground.

10. Torque the lug nuts to specification using the proper tool. Install the hub cap.

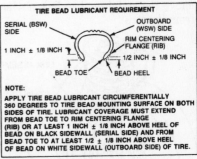

TIRE BEAD LUBRICANT REQUIREMENT

SERIAL (BSW) SIDE — OUTBOARD (WSW) SIDE
RIM CENTERING FLANGE (RIB)
1 INCH ± 1/8 INCH — 1/2 INCH ± 1/8 INCH
BEAD TOE — BEAD HEEL

NOTE:
APPLY TIRE BEAD LUBRICANT CIRCUMFERENTIALLY 360 DEGREES TO TIRE BEAD MOUNTING SURFACE ON BOTH SIDES OF TIRE. LUBRICANT COVERAGE MUST EXTEND FROM BEAD TOE TO RIM CENTERING FLANGE (RIB) OR AT LEAST 1 INCH ± 1/8 INCH ABOVE HEEL OF BEAD ON BLACK SIDEWALL (SERIAL SIDE) AND FROM BEAD TOE TO AT LEAST 1/2 ± 1/8 INCH ABOVE HEEL OF BEAD ON WHITE SIDEWALL (OUTBOARD SIDE) OF TIRE.

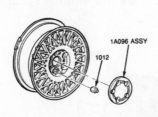

1A096 ASSY
1012

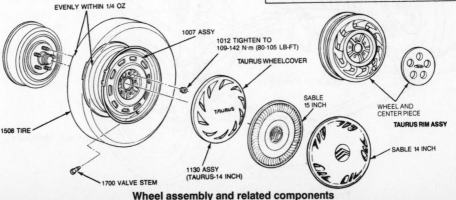

EVENLY WITHIN 1/4 OZ

1007 ASSY

1012 TIGHTEN TO 109-142 N·m (80-105 LB-FT)

TAURUS WHEELCOVER

SABLE 15 INCH

WHEEL AND CENTER PIECE

TAURUS RIM ASSY

TAURUS

SABLE 14 INCH

1508 TIRE

1130 ASSY (TAURUS-14 INCH)

1700 VALVE STEM

Wheel assembly and related components

INSPECTION

Replace wheels if they are bent, dented, heavily rusted, have air leaks, elongated bolt holes or excessive lateral and radial runout.

Also inspect wheel lug nuts and be sure that they are torqued to specification.

FRONT SUSPENSION

MacPherson Struts

REMOVAL AND INSTALLATION

1. Place the ignition switch in the **OFF** position and the steering column in the **UNLOCKED** position.

2. Remove the hub nut. Loosen the 3 top mount-to-shock tower nuts; do not remove the nuts at this time.

3. Raise and support the vehicle safely.

NOTE: *When raising the vehicle, do not lift by using the lower control arms.*

4. Remove the tire and wheel assembly. Remove the brake caliper, supporting it on a wire. Remove the rotor.

5. At the tie rod end, remove the cotter pin and the castle nut. Discard the cotter pin and nut and replace with new.

6. Using tie rod end remover tool 3290–D and the tie rod remover adapter tool T81P–3504–W or equivalents, separate the tie rod from the steering knuckle.

7. Remove the stabilizer bar link nut and the link from the strut.

8. Remove the lower arm-to-steering knuckle pinch bolt and nut; it may be necessary to use a drift punch to remove the bolt. Using a suitable tool, spread the knuckle-to-lower arm pinch joint and remove the lower-arm from the steering knuckle. Discard the pinch nut/bolt and replace with new.

9. Remove the halfshaft from the hub and support it on a wire.

NOTE: *When removing the halfshaft, do not allow it to move outward as the internal parts of the tripod CV-joint could separate, causing failure of the joint.*

10. Remove the strut-to-steering knuckle pinch bolt. Using a small prybar, spread the pinch bolt joint and separate the strut from the steering knuckle. Remove the steering knuckle/hub assembly from the strut.

11. Remove the 3 top mount-to-shock tower nuts and the strut assembly from the vehicle.

12. Compress the coil spring using a suitable spring compressor. Use a 10mm box end wrench to hold the top of the strut shaft while removing the nut with a 21mm 6-point crow foot wrench and ratchet.

13. Loosen the spring compressor, then remove the top mount bracket assembly, bearing plate assembly and spring.

To install:

14. Install the spring compressor. Install the spring, bearing plate assembly, lower washer and top mount bracket assembly.

15. Compress the spring. Install the upper washer and nut on the shock strut shaft. Tighten the nut with the 21mm 6-point crow

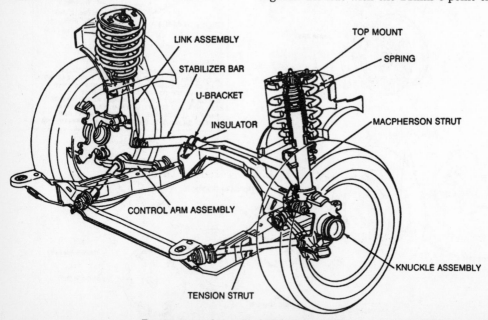

LINK ASSEMBLY

STABILIZER BAR

U-BRACKET

INSULATOR

TOP MOUNT

SPRING

MACPHERSON STRUT

CONTROL ARM ASSEMBLY

KNUCKLE ASSEMBLY

TENSION STRUT

Front suspension and related components

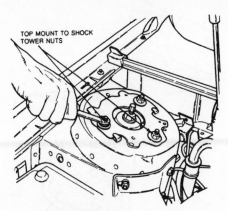

Upper strut mounting nuts

foot wrnch and ratchet while holding the shaft with the 10mm box end wrench.

16. Install the strut assembly and the 3 top mount-to-shock tower nuts.

17. Install the steering knuckle and hub assembly to the strut.

18. Install a new strut-to-steering knuckle pinch bolt. Tighten the bolt to 70–95 ft. lbs. (95–129 Nm).

19. Install the halfshaft into the hub.

20. Install the lower arm to the steering knuckle and install a new pinch bolt and nut. Tighten to 40–55 ft. lbs. (54–74 Nm).

21. Install the stabilizer link to the strut and install a new stabilizer bar link nut. Tighten to 55–75 ft. lbs. (75–101 Nm).

22. Install the tie rod end onto the knuckle using a new castle nut. Tighten the castle nut to 23–35 ft. lbs. (31–47 Nm). Retain the castle nut with a new cotter pin.

23. Install the disc brake rotor, caliper and tire and wheel assembly.

24. Tighten the 3 top mount-to-shock tower nuts to 20–30 ft. lbs. (27–40 Nm).

25. Lower the vehicle and tighten the hub nut to 180–200 ft. lbs. (244–271 Nm).

26. Check the front end alignment.

OVERHAUL

1. The following procedure is performed with the strut assembly removed from the car.

2. A MacPherson Strut compression tool is required for the disassembly of the strut, a cage type tool such as the part No. D85P–7181–A or equivalent is required.

3. Never attempt to disassemble the spring or top mount without first compressing the spring using the strut compressor tool No. D85P–7178–A or equivalent.

4. Compress the spring with the coil spring compressor part No. D85P–7178–A or equivalent.

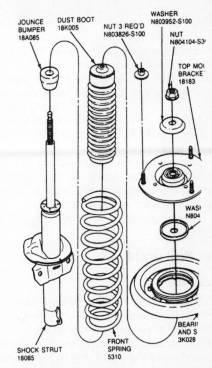

Exploded view of Macpherson strut assembly

5. Place a 10mm box wrench on top of the shock strut shaft and hold while removing the top shaft mounting nut with a 21mm 6-point crow foot wrench and ratchet.

NOTE: *It is important that the mounting nut be turned and the rod held still to prevent fracture of the rod at the base of the hex.*

6. Loosen the spring compressor tool, then remove the top mounting bracket assembly, bearing plate assembly and spring.

To assemble:

NOTE: *Ensure that the correct assembly sequence and proper positioning of the bearing and seat assembly are followed. The bearing and seat assembly is press-fit onto the upper*

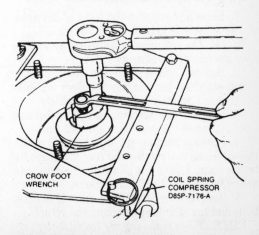

Removing the spring retaining nut

mount. *The mount washers must be installed with orientation.*

7. Install the spring compressor tool part No. D85P–7178–A or equivalent.

8. Install the spring, bearing plate assembly, lower washer and top mount bracket assembly.

9. Compress the spring with the coil spring compressor tool. Install the upper washer and nut on the shock strut shaft.

10. Place a 10mm box end wrench on the top of the shock strut shaft and hold while tightening the top shaft mounting nut with a 21mm 6-point crow foot wrench and a ratchet.

11. The strut assembly may now be installed in the vehicle.

Lower Ball Joint

INSPECTION

1. Disconnect the negative battery cable.

2. Raise the vehicle and safely support it so the wheels fall to the full-down position.

3. Have an assistant grasp the lower edge of the tire and move the wheel and tire assembly in and out.

4. Observe the lower end of the knuckle and the lower control arm as the wheel is being moved in and out. Any movement indicates abnormal ball joint wear.

5. If there is any movement, install a new lower control arm assembly.

6. Lower the vehicle.

REMOVAL AND INSTALLATION

Ball joints are integral parts of the lower control arms. If an inspection reveals an unsatisfactory ball joint, the entire lower control arm assembly must be replaced.

Stabilizer Bar

REMOVAL AND INSTALLATION

1. Raise and support the front of the vehicle on jackstands behind the subframe.

NOTE: *Do not raise or support the vehicle on the front control arms.*

2. Remove and discard the stabilizer bar link-to-stabilizer bar nut, the stabilizer bar link-to-strut nut and the link from the vehicle.

3. Remove the steering gear-to-subframe nuts and move the gear from the sub-frame.

4. Position another set of jackstands under the subframe and remove the rear subframe-to-frame bolts. Lower the subframe rear to gain access to the stabilizer bar brackets.

5. Remove the stabilizer bar U-bracket bolts and the stabilizer bar from the vehicle.

NOTE: *When removing the stabilizer bar, replace the insulators and the U-bracket bolts*

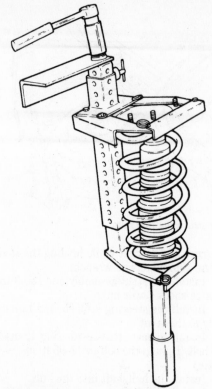

Compressing the coil spring using a strut spring compressor tool

with new ones.

To install:

6. To install, reverse the removal procedure. Tighten the bolts to the folowing torque specifications:

• U-bracket-to-subframe 21–32 ft. lbs. (28–43 Nm)

• Subframe-to-steering gear 85–100 ft. lbs. (115–135 Nm)

• Stabilizer bar-to-stabilizer bar link 35–48 ft. lbs. (47–65 Nm)

• Stabilizer bar-to-strut 55–75 ft. lbs. (75–101 Nm)

7. Prior to assembly, coat the inside diameter of the new insulators with No. E25Y–19553–A or equivalent lubricant. Do not use any mineral or petroleum base lubricants as they will cause deterioration of the rubber insulators.

Lower Control Arm

REMOVAL AND INSTALLATION

1. Disconnect the negative battery cable.

2. Raise and support the front of the vehicle safely. Remove the wheel and tire assembly.

3. Position the steering column in the unlocked position.

4. Remove the tension strut-to-control arm nut and the dished washer.

5. Remove and discard the control arm-to-

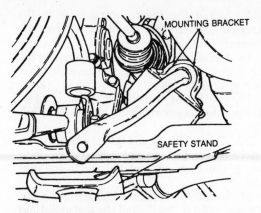

MOUNTING BRACKET

SAFETY STAND

Stabilizer bar removal

steering knuckle pinch bolt. Using a small prybar, spread the pinch joint and separate the control arm from the steering knuckle.

NOTE: *When separating the control arm from the steering knuckle, do not use a hammer. Be careful not to damage the ball joint boot seal.*

6. Remove the control arm-to-frame nut/bolt, then the control arm from the frame and the tension strut.

NOTE: *Do not allow the halfshaft to move outward or the tripod CV-joint internal parts could separate, causing failure of the joint.*

7. To install, use a new pinch nut/bolt and reverse the removal procedures. Tighten the bolts to the following torque specifications:

• Control arm-to-frame 70–95 ft. lbs. (95–129 Nm)

• Control arm-to-steering knuckle 40–55 ft. lbs. (54–74 Nm)

• Tension strut-to-control arm 70–95 ft. lbs. (95–129 Nm)

• Wheel lug nuts 80–105 ft. lbs. (109–142 Nm)

8. Check the front end alignment.

BUSHING REPLACEMENT

Inner Pivot Bushing

1. Remove the lower control arm from the vehicle.

2. Using bushing removal tools T86P–5493–A3 and T86P–5493–A2 and a C clamp assembly remove the old bushings from the control arm assembly.

To install:

3. Use the bushing removal tool and press new bushings in place on the lower control arm assembly.

4. Be sure that the bushing flange is at the front of the arm.

5. Install the lower control arm on the vehicle.

6. Check and adjust the front end alignment, as required.

Control Arm/Tension Strut Bushing

1. Remove the lower control arm from the vehicle.

2. Using bushing removal tools T86P–5493–A5 and T86P–5493–A and a C clamp assembly remove the old bushings from the control arm assembly. Be sure that the C clamp is positioned tightly in a bench vise.

To install:

3. Before install the new bushing saturate it in motor oil, this will aid in the installation process.

4. Use the bushing removal tool and install new bushings in place on the lower control arm assembly. Stop tightening the C clamp when the bushing pops in place.

5. Install the lower control arm on the vehicle.

6. Check and adjust the front end alignment, as required.

Tension Strut/Sub Frame Insulators

1. Remove the lower control arm from the vehicle.

2. Remove and discard the nut, washer and insulator from the front of the tension strut. Pull the strut rearward to remove it from the sub frame.

3. Remove and discard the insulator from the tension strut.

To install:

4. Install a new insulator on the tension strut end and insert it into the sub frame.

5. Install a new front insulator. Clean the tension strut threads. Install a new washer, and nut. Torque to 70–95 ft. lbs.

6. Install the lower control arm on the vehicle.

7. Check and adjust the front end alignment, as required.

Knuckle and Spindle

REMOVAL AND INSTALLATION

1. Turn the ignition switch to the OFF position. Position the steering wheel in the unlocked position.

2. Remove the hub nut. Raise and support the vehicle safely. Remove the tire and wheel assembly.

3. Remove the cotter pin from the tie rod end stud and remove the slotted nut. Discard the cotter pin and nut.

4. Using a tie rod end removal tool remove the tie rod end from the knuckle.

5. Remove the stabilizer bar link assembly from the strut.

6. Remove the brake caliper and wire it aside in order to gain working clearance.

7. Loosen, but do not remove, the three top retaining nuts from the top of the shock tower.

8. Remove and discard the lower arm to steering knuckle pinch bolt and nut. Using the proper tool spread the knuckle to lower arm pinch joint apart. Remove the lower arm from the steering knuckle.

NOTE: *Be sure that the steering column is in the unlocked position. Do not use a hammer to perform this operation. Use extreme care not to damage the boot seal.*

9. Remove the shock absorber strut to steering knuckle pinch bolt.

NOTE: *Do not allow the halfshaft to move outboard. Over extension of the CV joint could result in separation of internal parts, causing failure of the joint.*

10. Press the halfshaft from the hub. Wire the halfshaft body to maintain a level position. If equipped, remove the rotor splash shield.

11. Remove the steering knuckle and hub assembly from the shock absorber strut.

12. Position the assembly on the work bench and remove the hub retainer ring and bearing.

To install:

13. Install the rotor splash shield using new rivits, if equipped.

14. Install the bearing, retainer ring and hub. If required, replace the seal on the outboard CV joint.

15. Install the steering knuckle onto the shock absorber strut. Loosely install a new pinch bolt in the knuckle to retain the strut.

16. Install the steering knuckle and hub onto the halfshaft.

17. Install the lower control arm to the knuckle. Be sure that the ball stud groove is properly positioned.

18. Install a new nut and bolt. Torque to 40–55 ft. lbs. Tighten the strut to knuckle pinch bolt to 70–95 ft. lbs.

19. Install the rotor and brake caliper. Torque the caliper retaining pins to 18–25 ft. lbs.

20. Position the tie rod into the knuckle, install a new slotted nut and tighten to 23–35 ft. lbs. If necessary advance the nut to the next slot.

21. Install the stabilizer link bar assembly. Torque to 75 ft. lbs. Install the tire and wheel assembly.

22. Lower the vehicle. Install the three top mount retaining bolts. Torque to 20–30 ft. lbs.

23. Tighten the hub nut to 180–200 ft. lbs.

24. Pump the brake pedal prior to moving the vehicle, in order to reposition the brake linings.

Front Hub and Bearing

REMOVAL AND INSTALLATION

1. Remove the wheelcover/hub cover and loosen the wheel nuts.

2. Remove the hub nut retainer and washer by applying sufficient torque to the nut to overcome the prevailing torque feature of the crimp in the nut collar. Do not use an impact-type tool to remove the hub nut retainer. The hub nut retainer is not reusable and must be discarded after removal.

3. Raise the vehicle and support it safely. Remove the wheel.

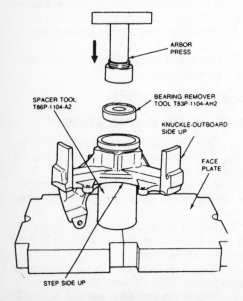

Pressing the bearing from the hub

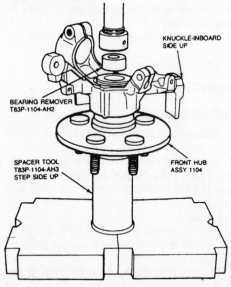

Seating the bearing in the knuckle

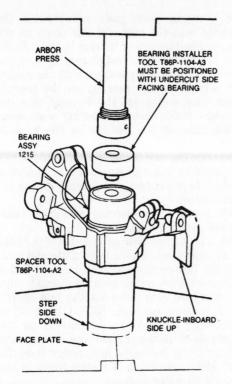

Pressing the bearing into the knuckle

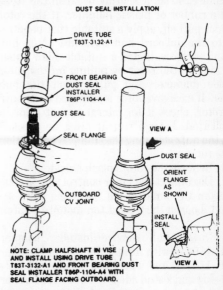

Bearing dust seal installation

4. Remove the brake caliper by loosening the caliper locating pins and rotating the caliper off of the rotor, starting from the lower end of the caliper and lifting upwards. Do not remove the caliper pins from the caliper assembly. Once the caliper is free of the rotor, support it with a length of wire. Do not allow the caliper to hang from the brake hose.

5. Remove the rotor from the hub by pulling it off of the hub bolts. If the rotor is difficult

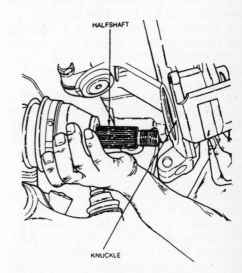

Installing the halfshaft into the knuckle

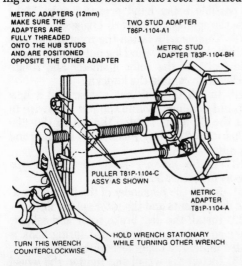

Removing the hub assembly

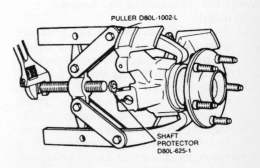

Removing the hub from the knuckle

to remove, strike it sharply between the studs with a rubber or plastic hammer. If the rotor will not pull off, apply a suitable rust penetrator to the inboard and outboard rotor hub mating surfaces. Install a suitable 3-jaw puller and remove the rotor by pulling on the rotor outside diameter and pushing on the hub center. If excessive force is required to remove the rotor, check it for lateral runout prior to installation. Lateral runout must be checked with the nuts clamping the stamped hat section of the rotor.

6. Remove the rotor splash shield.

7. Disconnect the lower control arm and tie rod from the knuckle but leave the strut attached. Loosen the 2 strut top mount-to-apron nuts.

8. Install hub remover/installer adapter T81P–1104–A with front hub remover/installer T81P–1104–C and wheel bolt adapters T83P–1104–BH and 2 stud adapter T86P–1104–A1 or equivalent, and remove the hub, bearing and knuckle assembly by pushing out the CV-joint outer shaft until it is free of the assembly.

9. Support the knuckle with a length of wire, remove the strut bolt and slide the hub/bearing/knuckle assembly off of the strut. Remove the support wire and carry the hub/bearing/knuckle assembly to a bench.

10. Install front hub puller D80L–1002–L and shaft protector D80L–625–1 or equivalent, with the jaws of the puller on the knuckle bosses. Make sure the shaft protector is centered, clears the bearing inside diameter and rests on the end face of the hub journal. Remove the hub.

11. Remove the snapring that retains the bearing in the knuckle assembly and discard.

12. Using a suitable hydraulic press, place front bearing spacer T86P–1104–A2 or equivalent, on the press plate with the step side facing up and position the knuckle with the outboard side up on the spacer. Install front bearing remover T83P–1104–AH2 or equivalent, centered on the bearing inner race and press the bearing out of the knuckle and discard.

To install:

13. Remove all foreign material from the knuckle bearing bore and hub bearing journal to ensure correct seating of the new bearing.

NOTE: *If the hub bearing journal is scored or damaged it must be replaced. The front wheel bearings are pregreased and sealed and require no scheduled maintenance. The bearings are preset and cannot be adjusted. If a bearing is disassembled for any reason, it must be replaced as a unit, as individual service seals, rollers and races are not available.*

14. Place front bearing spacer T86P–1104–A2 or equivalent, with the step side down on the hydraulic press plate and position the knuckle with the outboard side down on the spacer. Position a new bearing in the inboard side of the knuckle. Install bearing installer T86P–1104–A3 or equivalent, with the undercut side facing the bearing, on the bearing outer race and press the bearing into the knuckle. Make sure the bearing seats completely against the shoulder of the knuckle bore.

NOTE: *Bearing installer T86P–1104–A3 or equivalent, must be positioned as indicated above to prevent bearing damage during installation.*

15. Install a new snapring (part of the bearing kit) in the knuckle groove.

16. Place front bearing spacer T86P–1104–A2 or equivalent, on the press plate and position the hub on the tool with the lugs facing downward. Position the knuckle assembly with the outboard side down on the hub barrel. Place bearing remover T83P–1104–AH2 or equivalent, flat side down, centered on the inner race of the bearing and press down on the tool until the bearing is fully seated onto the hub. Make sure the hub rotates freely in the knuckle after installation.

17. Prior to hub/bearing/knuckle installation, replace the bearing dust seal on the outboard CV-joint with a new seal from the bearing kit. Make sure the seal flange faces outboard toward the bearing. Use drive tube T83T–3132–A1 and front bearing dust seal installer T86P–1104–A4 or equivalent.

18. Suspend the hub/bearing/knuckle assembly on the vehicle with wire and attach the strut loosely to the knuckle. Lubricate the CV-joint stub shaft with SAE 30 weight motor oil and insert the shaft into the hub splines as far as possible using hand pressure only. Make sure the splines are properly engaged.

19. Temporarily fasten the rotor to the hub with washers and 2 wheel lug nuts. Insert a suitable tool into the rotor diameter and rotate clockwise to contact the knuckle.

20. Install the hub nut washer and a new hub nut retainer. Rotate the nut clockwise to seat the CV-joint. Tighten the nut to 180–200 ft. lbs. (245–270 Nm). Remove the washers and lug nuts.

NOTE: *Do not use power or impact-type tools to tighten the hub nut.*

21. Install the remainder of the front suspension components and the rotor splash shield.

22. Install the disc brake rotor and caliper. Make sure the outer brake pad spring hook is seated under the upper arm of the knuckle.

23. Install the wheel and tighten the wheel nuts finger tight.

24. Lower the vehicle. Tighten the wheel

nuts to 85–105 ft. lbs. (115–142 Nm). Install the wheelcover/hub cover.

Upper Mount and Bearing Assembly

REMOVAL AND INSTALLATION

CAUTION: *When servicing the front suspension, brake shoes contain asbestos which has been determined to be a cancer causing agent. Never clean the brake surfaces with compressed air! Avoid inhaling any dust from any brake surface! When cleaning brake surfaces, use a commercially available brake cleaning fluid.*

1. Place the ignition switch to the OFF position and the steering column in the unlocked position.
2. Remove the hub nut. Loosen the strut-to-fender apron nuts; do not remove the nuts.
3. Raise and support the front of the vehicle on jackstands. Remove the wheels.

NOTE: *When raising the vehicle, do not lift it by using the lower control arms.*

4. Remove the brake caliper (support it on a wire) and the rotor.
5. At the tie rod end, remove the cotter pin and the castle nut.
6. Using the tie rod end remover tool No. 3290–C and the tie rod remover adapter tool No. T81P–3504–W, separate the tie rod from the steering knuckle.
7. Remove the stabilizer bar link nut and the link from the strut.
8. Remove the lower arm-to-steering knuckle pinch bolt and nut; it may be necessary to use a drift punch to remove the bolt. Using a small pry bar, spread the knuckle-to-lower arm pinch joint and remove the lower arm from the steering knuckle.
9. Remove the halfshaft from the hub and support it on a wire.

NOTE: *When removing the halfshaft, DO NOT allow it to move outward for the tripod CV-joint could separate from the internal parts, causing failure of the joint.*

10. Remove the strut-to-steering knuckle pinch bolt. Using a small pry bar, spread the pinch bolt joint and separate the strut from steering knuckle. Remove the steering knuckle/hub assembly from the strut assembly.
11. Remove the strut-to-fender apron nuts and the strut assembly from the vehicle.

CAUTION: *Never attempt to disassemble the spring or top mount without first compressing the spring using a Universal MacPherson Strut Spring Compressor*

D85P–7178–A or a Rotunda Spring Compressor 086–00029 or equivalent.

12. Place a 10mm box-end wrench on top of the shock strut shaft and hold while removing the top shaft mounting nut with a 21mm 6-point crow foot wrench and ratchet.
13. Loosen the MacPherson Strut Spring Compressor slowly. Remove the top mount bracket assembly, bearing plate, and spring.

NOTE: *When servicing the shock absorber strut, check the spring insulator for damage before assembly. If the outer metal splash shield is bent or damaged, it must be bent back carefully so that it does not touch the locator tabs on the bearing and seal assembly.*

To install:
14. Place the MacPherson Strut Spring Compressor on the base of the strut.
15. Install the upper mount and bearing assembly on top of the strut and tighten the spring compressor far enough to install the shaft mounting nut.
16. Install the washer and nut on the shock strut shaft and tighten with the 10mm box-end and the 21mm 6-point crow foot wrench and ratchet.
17. Refer to the "MacPherson Strut" installation procedure.

Front End Alignment

CASTER AND CAMBER

1. Caster and camber angles are preset at the factory and can only be adjusted by extensive upper strut modifications and are not included in this publication.
2. Measurement procedures that follow are for diagnostic purposes.
3. Caster measurements must be made on the left hand side by turning the left wheel through the prescribed angle of the sweep and on the right hand side by turning the right wheel through the prescribed angle of sweep.
4. When using the alignment equipment designed to measure the caster on both the right hand and left hand side, turning only one wheel will result in a significant error in the caster angle for the opposite side.

TOE IN

The toe-in is controlled by adjusting the tie rod ends. To adjust the toe-in setting, loosen the tie rod jam nuts. Rotate the tie rod as required to adjust the toe-in into specifications. Once the toe-in is set, re-tighten the tie rod jam nuts.

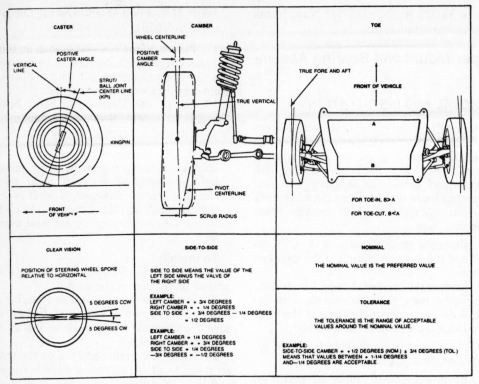

Front end wheel alignment reference points

REAR SUSPENSION

Coil Springs

REMOVAL AND INSTALLATION

Wagon

1. Raise the rear of the vehicle and support safely on the pads of the underbody forward of the tension strut bracket. Position a floor jack under the lower suspension arm and raise the lower arm to normal curb height.

2. Remove the wheel and tire assembly.

3. Locate the bracket retaining the flexible hose to the body. Remove the bracket retaining bolt and bracket from the body.

4. Remove the stabilizer bar U-bracket from the lower suspension arm.

5. Remove and discard the nuts attaching the shock absorber to the lower suspension arm.

6. Disconnect and remove the parking brake cable and clip from the lower suspension arm.

7. If equipped with rear disc brakes, remove the ABS cable from the clips on the lower suspension arm.

8. Remove and discard the bolt and nut at-

taching the tension strut to the lower suspension arm.

9. Suspend the spindle and upper suspension arms from the body with a piece of wire to prevent them from dropping.

10. Remove the nut, bolt, washer and adjusting cam that retain the lower suspension arm to the spindle. Discard the nut, bolt and washer and replace with new. Set the cam aside.

11. With the floor jack, slowly lower the suspension arm until the spring, lower and upper insulators can be removed. Replace the spring and insulators as required.

To install:

12. Position the lower insulator on the lower suspension arm and press the insulator downward into place. Make certain the insulator is properly seated.

13. Position the upper insulator on top of the spring. Install the spring on the lower suspension arm. Make certain the spring is properly seated.

14. With the floor jack, slowly raise the suspension arm. Guide the upper spring insultor onto the upper spring underbody seat.

15. Position the spindle in the lower suspension arm with a new bolt, nut washer, and the existing cam. Install the bolt with the head of the bolt toward the front of the vehicle. Do not tighten the bolt at this time.

16. Remove the wire supporting the spindle

WHEEL ALIGNMENT—Front

Year	Model	Caster Range (deg.)	Caster Preferred Setting (deg.)	Camber Range (deg.)	Camber Preferred Setting (deg.)	Toe-in (in.)	Steering Axis Inclination (deg.)
1986	Taurus	3P–6P①	4P	$1\frac{3}{32}$N–$\frac{3}{32}$P	$\frac{1}{2}$N	$\frac{7}{32}$–$\frac{1}{64}$	$15\frac{3}{8}$
	Sable	3P–6P①	4P	$1\frac{3}{32}$N–$\frac{3}{32}$P	$\frac{1}{2}$N	$\frac{7}{32}$–$\frac{1}{64}$	$15\frac{3}{8}$
1987	Taurus	3P–6P①	4P	$1\frac{3}{32}$N–$\frac{3}{32}$P	$\frac{1}{2}$N	$\frac{7}{32}$–$\frac{1}{64}$	$15\frac{3}{8}$
	Sable	3P–6P①	4P	$1\frac{3}{32}$N–$\frac{3}{32}$P	$\frac{1}{2}$N	$\frac{7}{32}$–$\frac{1}{64}$	$15\frac{3}{8}$
1988	Taurus	3P–6P①	4P	$1\frac{3}{32}$N–$\frac{3}{32}$P	$\frac{1}{2}$N	$\frac{7}{32}$–$\frac{1}{64}$	$15\frac{3}{8}$
	Sable	3P–6P①	4P	$1\frac{3}{32}$N–$\frac{3}{32}$P	$\frac{1}{2}$N	$\frac{7}{32}$–$\frac{1}{64}$	$15\frac{3}{8}$
1989	Taurus	3P–6P①	4P	$1\frac{3}{32}$N–$\frac{3}{32}$P	$\frac{1}{2}$N	$\frac{7}{32}$–$\frac{1}{64}$	$15\frac{3}{8}$
	Sable	3P–6P①	4P	$1\frac{3}{32}$N–$\frac{3}{32}$P	$\frac{1}{2}$N	$\frac{7}{32}$–$\frac{1}{64}$	$15\frac{3}{8}$
1990	Taurus Sedan	$2\frac{13}{16}$P–$5\frac{13}{16}$P①	$3\frac{13}{16}$P	$1\frac{3}{32}$N–$\frac{3}{32}$P	$\frac{1}{2}$N	$\frac{7}{32}$N–$\frac{1}{64}$P	$15\frac{1}{2}$
	Taurus Wagon	$2\frac{11}{16}$P–$5\frac{11}{16}$P①	$3\frac{11}{16}$P	$1\frac{3}{32}$N–$\frac{3}{32}$P	$\frac{1}{2}$N	$\frac{7}{32}$N–$\frac{1}{64}$P	$15\frac{1}{2}$
	Sable Sedan	$2\frac{13}{16}$P–$5\frac{13}{16}$P①	$3\frac{13}{16}$P	$1\frac{3}{32}$N–$\frac{3}{32}$P	$\frac{1}{2}$N	$\frac{7}{32}$N–$\frac{1}{64}$P	$15\frac{1}{2}$
	Sable Wagon	$2\frac{11}{16}$P–$5\frac{11}{16}$P①	$3\frac{11}{16}$P	$1\frac{3}{64}$N–$\frac{3}{32}$P	$\frac{1}{2}$N	$\frac{7}{32}$N–$\frac{1}{64}$P	$15\frac{1}{2}$
1991	Taurus Sedan	$2\frac{13}{16}$P–$5\frac{13}{16}$P①	$3\frac{13}{16}$P	$1\frac{3}{32}$N–$\frac{3}{32}$P	$\frac{1}{2}$N	$\frac{7}{32}$N–$\frac{1}{64}$P	$15\frac{1}{2}$
	Taurus Wagon	$2\frac{11}{16}$P–$5\frac{11}{16}$P①	$3\frac{11}{16}$P	$1\frac{3}{64}$N–$\frac{3}{32}$P	$\frac{1}{2}$N	$\frac{7}{32}$N–$\frac{1}{64}$P	$15\frac{1}{2}$
	Sable Sedan	$2\frac{13}{16}$P–$5\frac{13}{16}$P①	$3\frac{13}{16}$P	$1\frac{3}{32}$N–$\frac{3}{32}$P	$\frac{1}{2}$N	$\frac{7}{32}$N–$\frac{1}{64}$P	$15\frac{1}{2}$
	Sable Wagon	$2\frac{11}{16}$P–$5\frac{11}{16}$P①	$3\frac{11}{16}$P	$1\frac{3}{64}$N–$\frac{3}{32}$P	$\frac{1}{2}$N	$\frac{7}{32}$N–$\frac{1}{64}$P	$15\frac{1}{2}$
1992	Taurus Sedan	$2\frac{13}{16}$P–$5\frac{13}{16}$P①	$3\frac{13}{16}$P	$1\frac{3}{32}$N–$\frac{3}{32}$P	$\frac{1}{2}$N	$\frac{7}{32}$N–$\frac{1}{64}$P	$15\frac{1}{2}$
	Taurus Wagon	$2\frac{11}{16}$P–$5\frac{11}{16}$P①	$3\frac{11}{16}$P	$1\frac{3}{64}$N–$\frac{3}{32}$P	$\frac{1}{2}$N	$\frac{7}{32}$N–$\frac{1}{64}$P	$15\frac{1}{2}$
	Sable Sedan	$2\frac{11}{16}$P–$5\frac{11}{16}$P①	$3\frac{11}{16}$P	$1\frac{3}{32}$N–$\frac{3}{32}$P	$\frac{1}{2}$N	$\frac{7}{32}$N–$\frac{1}{64}$P	$15\frac{1}{2}$
	Sable Wagon	$2\frac{11}{16}$P–$5\frac{11}{16}$P①	$3\frac{11}{16}$P	$1\frac{3}{64}$N–$\frac{3}{32}$P	$\frac{1}{2}$N	$\frac{7}{32}$N–$\frac{1}{64}$P	$15\frac{1}{2}$

P—Positive
N—Negative
① The caster measurements are made by turning each individual wheel through the prescribed angle of sweep.

and suspension arms.

17. Install the tension strut in the lower suspension arm using a new nut and bolt; do not tighten at this time.

18. Attach the parking brake cable and clip to the lower suspension arm.

19. If equipped with rear disc brakes, install the ABS cable into the clips on the lower suspension arm.

20. Position the shock absorber on the lower suspension arm and install 2 new nuts. Torque the nuts to 13–20 ft. lbs. (17–27 Nm).

21. Attach the stabilizer U-bracket to the

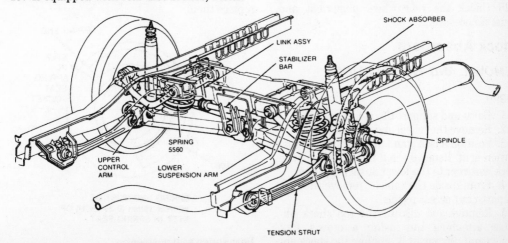

Rear suspension and related components — Wagon

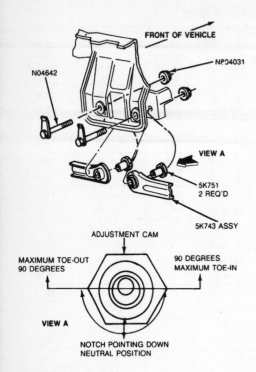

Rear spring positioning

lower suspension arm using a new bolt. Torque the bolt to 20–30 ft. lbs. (27–40 Nm).

22. Attach the flexible brake hose to the body and tighten the bolt to 8–12 ft. lbs. (11–16 Nm).

23. With the floor jack, raise the lower suspension to normal curb height. Torque the lower suspension arm to 40–55 ft. lbs. (54–74 Nm). Torque the bolt that attaches the tension strut to the body bracket to 40–55 ft. lbs. (54–74 Nm).

24. Install the wheel and tire assembly. Remove the floor jack and lower the vehicle.

25. Check the rear wheel alignment and adjust if necessary.

Shock Absorbers

REMOVAL AND INSTALLATION

Wagon

1. Raise and support the vehicle safely.
2. Remove the wheel and tire assembly.
3. Position a jack stand under the lower suspension arm. Remove the 2 nuts retaining the shock absorber to the lower suspension arm.
4. From inside the vehicle, remove the rear compartment access panels.
5. Remove and discard the top shock absorber attaching nut using a crow's foot wrench and ratchet while holding the shock ab-

sorber shaft stationary with an open end wrench.

NOTE: *If the shock absorber is to be reused, do not grip the shaft with pliers or vise grips. Gripping the shaft in this manner will damage the shaft surface finish and will result in severe oil leakage.*

6. Remove the rubber insulator from the shock and the shock from the vehicle.

NOTE: *The shocks are gas filled. It will require an effort to remove the shock from the lower arm.*

To install:

7. Install a new washer and insulator on the upper shock absorber rod.

8. Maneuver the upper part of the shock absorber into the shock tower opening in the body. Push slowly on the lower part of the shock absorber until the mounting studs are aligned with the mounting holes in the lower suspension arm.

9. Install new lower attaching nuts but do not tighten at this time.

10. Install a new insulator, washer and nut on top of the shock absorber. Torque the nut to 19–27 ft. lbs. (26–37 Nm.).

11. Install the rear compartment access panel.

12. Torque the 2 lower attaching nuts to 13–20 ft. lbs. (17–27 Nm).

13. Install the wheel and tire assembly. Remove the safety stand supporting the lower suspension arm and lower the vehicle.

TESTING

1. Visually inspect the shock absorber for signs of leakage.

2. If one shock absorber is leaking replace both shock absorbers.

3. Stand back and look at the vehicle if it sags on one end, check the shocks if defective replace them.

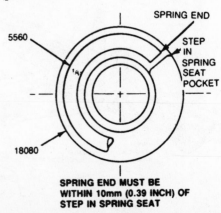

Rear spring seat positioning

4. Bounce the vehicle up and down a few times it the vehicle bounces more that twice the shocks could be defective and require replacement.

MacPherson Struts

REMOVAL AND INSTALLATION

Sedan

1. Raise and support the rear of the vehicle safely. Remove the wheel and tire.

NOTE: *Do not raise or support the vehicle using the tension struts.*

2. Raise the luggage compartment lid and loosen but do not remove, the upper strut-to-body nuts.

3. Remove the brake differential control valve-to-control arm bolt. Using a wire, secure the control arm to the body to ensure proper support leaving at least 6 in. (152mm) clearance to aid in the strut removal.

4. Remove the brake hose-to-strut bracket clip and move the hose aside.

5. If equipped, remove the stabilizer bar U-bracket from the vehicle.

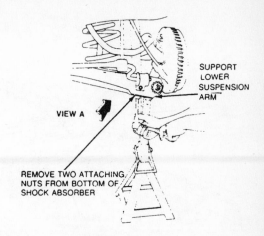

VIEW A

SUPPORT LOWER SUSPENSION ARM

REMOVE TWO ATTACHING NUTS FROM BOTTOM OF SHOCK ABSORBER

Lower shock absorber retaining bolts

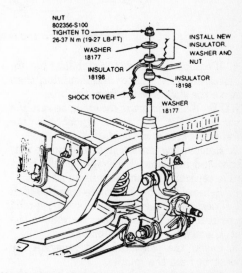

NUT 802356-S100 TIGHTEN TO 26-37 N·m (19-27 LB-FT)
WASHER 18177
INSULATOR 18198
SHOCK TOWER

INSTALL NEW INSULATOR, WASHER AND NUT
INSULATOR 18198
WASHER 18177

Upper shock absorber and related components

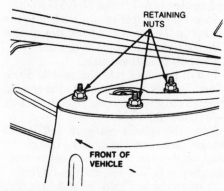

RETAINING NUTS

FRONT OF VEHICLE

Upper strut mounting nuts

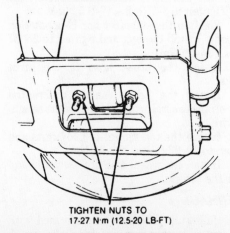

TIGHTEN NUTS TO 17-27 N·m (12.5-20 LB-FT)

Lower shock absorber retaining bolt locations

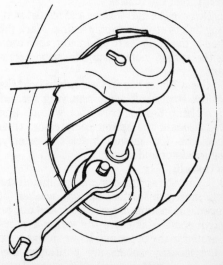

Upper shock absorber retaining bolts

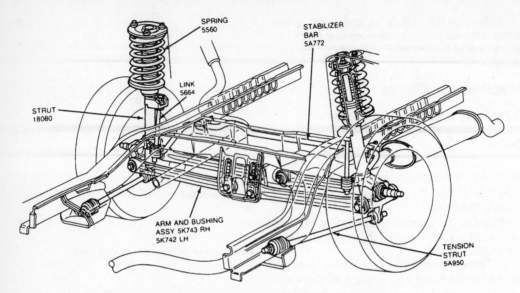

STRUT
18080

SPRING
5560

LINK
5664

STABILIZER
BAR
5A772

ARM AND BUSHING
ASSY 5K743 RH
5K742 LH

TENSION
STRUT
5A950

Rear suspension and related components — Sedan

6. If equipped, remove the stabilizer bar-to-stabilizer link nut, washer and insulator, then separate the stabilizer bar from the link.

NOTE: *When removing the strut, be sure the rear brake flex hose is not stretched or the steel brake tube is not bent.*

7. Remove the tension strut-to-spindle nut, washer and insulator. Move the spindle rearward to separate it from the tension strut.

8. Remove the shock strut-to-spindle pinch bolt. If necessary, use a medium prybar, spread the strut-to-spindle pinch joint to remove the strut. Discard the bolt and replace it.

9. Lower the jackstand and separate the shock strut from the spindle.

10. Support the shock strut, then loosen the top strut-to-body nuts completely and remove the strut from the vehicle.

11. Remove the nut, washer and insulator attaching link to strut and remove link. Mark the location of the insulator to top mount, then compress the spring, using a suitable spring compressor.

12. Use a 10mm box end wrench to hold the top of the strut shaft while removing the nut with a 21mm 6-point crow foot wrench and ratchet. Loosen the spring compressor, then remove the top mount bracket assembly, spring insulator and spring.

To install:

13. Using the spring compressor, install the spring, spring insulator, bottom washer, if equipped, top mount, upper washer and nut on the strut shaft. Make sure the spring is properly located in the upper and lower spring seats and the mount washers are positioned correctly.

14. Tighten the rod nut to 35–50 ft. lbs. (48–

68 Nm). Use a 21mm crow foot wrench to turn the nut and a 10mm box end wrench to hold the shaft. Do not use pliers or vise grips.

15. Position the stabilizer bar link in the strut bracket. Install the insulator, washer and nut and tighten to 5–7 ft. lbs. (7–9.5 Nm).

16. Insert the 3 upper mount studs into the strut tower in the apron and hand start 3 new nuts. Do not tighten the nuts at this time.

17. Partially raise the vehicle.

18. Install the strut into the spindle pinch joint. Install a new pinch bolt into the spindle and through the strut bracket. Tighten the bolt to 50–70 ft. lbs. (68–95 Nm).

19. Move the spindle rearward and install the tension strut into the spindle. Install the insulator, washer and nut on the tension strut. Tighten the nut to 35–50 ft. lbs. (48–68 Nm).

20. Position the link into the stabilizer bar. Install the insulator, washer and nut on the link. Tighten to 5–7 ft. lbs. (7–9.5 Nm).

21. Position the stabilizer bar U-bracket on the body. Install the bolt and tighten to 25–37 ft. lbs. (34–50 Nm).

22. Install the brake hose to the strut bracket.

23. Install the brake control differential valve on the control arm and remove the retaining wire.

24. Install the top mount-to-body nuts and tighten to 19–26 ft. lbs. (26–35 Nm).

25. Install the wheel and tire assembly and lower the vehicle.

OVERHAUL

The following procedure is performed with the strut assembly removed from the car. A MacPherson Strut compression tool is required

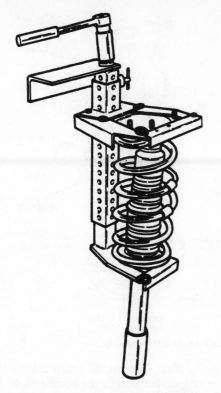

Compressing the strut using the proper tool

for the disassembly of the strut, a cage type tool such as the No. D85P–7181–A or equivalent is required.

CAUTION: *Never attempt to disassemble the spring or top mount without first compressing the spring using the strut compressor tool No. D85P–7178–A or equivalent. If a strut spring compressor is not used, the assembly will fly apart by the force of the spring tension!*

NOTE: *Before compressing the spring, mark the location of the insulator to the top mount using a grease pencil.*

1. Compress the spring with the coil spring compressor D85P–7178–A or equivalent.

2. Place a 10mm box wrench on top of the shock strut shaft and hold while removing the top shaft mounting nut with a 21mm 6-point crowfoot wrench and ratchet.

NOTE: *It is important that the mounting nut be turned and the rod held still to prevent fracture of the rod at the base of the hex.*

3. Loosen the spring compressor tool, then remove the top mounting bracket assembly, bearing plate assembly and spring.

To assemble:

NOTE: *Ensure that the correct assembly sequence and proper positioning of the bearing and seat assembly are followed. The bearing*

and seat assembly is press-fit onto the upper mount. The mount washers must be installed with orientation.

4. Inspect the spring to ensure the dampers, sleeves and clips are properly positioned.

5. Install the spring compressor tool No. D85P–7178–A or equivalent.

6. Install the spring, bearing plate assembly, lower washer and top mount bracket assembly.

7. Compress the spring with the coil spring compressor tool. Be certain the spring is properly located in the upper and lower spring seats and that the mount washers are oriented correctly.

8. Install the upper washer and nut on the shock strut shaft.

9. Place a 10mm box end wrench on the top of the shock strut shaft and hold while tightening the top shaft mounting nut with a 21mm 6-point crowfoot wrench and a ratchet. Torque the nut to 35–50 ft. lbs.

10. The strut assembly may now be installed in the vehicle.

Control Arms

REMOVAL AND INSTALLATION

Sedan

1. Raise the vehicle and support it safely. Do not raise the vehicle by the tension strut.

2. Disconnect the brake proportioning valve from the left side front arm.

3. Disconnect the parking brake cable from the front arms.

4. Remove and discard the arm-to-spindle bolt, washer and nut.

5. Remove and discard the arm-to-body bolt and nut.

6. Remove the arm from the vehicle.

To install:

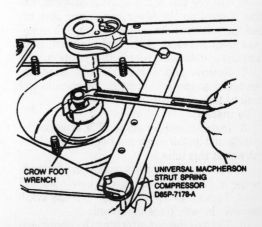

CROW FOOT WRENCH

UNIVERSAL MACPHERSON STRUT SPRING COMPRESSOR D85P-7178-A

Removing the spring retainer nut

NOTE: *When installing new control arms, the offset on all arms must face up. The arms are stamped "bottom" on the lower edge. The flange edge of the right side rear arm stamping must face the front of the vehicle. The other 3 must face the rear of the vehicle. The rear control arms have 2 adjustment cams that fit inside the bushings at the arm-to-body attachment. The cam is installed from the rear on the left arm and from the front on the right arm.*

7. Position the arm and cam where required, at the center of the vehicle. Insert a new bolt and nut but do not tighten at this time.

8. Move the arm end up to the spindle and insert a new bolt, washer and nut. Tighten the nut to 42–57 ft. lbs. (57–77 Nm).

9. Tighten the arm-to-body nut to 45–65 ft. lbs. (61–88 Nm).

10. Attach the parking brake cable to the front arms and the brake proportioning valve to the left side front arm.

11. Lower the vehicle and check the alignment.

Wagon

UPPER ARM

1. Raise the vehicle and support it with wood blocks on jackstands so the suspension is at normal curb height.

2. Remove the wheel and tire assembly.

3. Remove the brake line flexible hose bracket from the body.

4. Loosen, but do not remove the nuts attaching the spindle to the upper and lower suspension arms.

5. Remove and discard the nuts and bolts attaching the front and rear upper suspension arms to the body brackets. Make sure the spindle does not fall outward.

6. Tilt the top of the spindle outward, letting it pivot on the lower suspension arm attaching bolt until the ends of the upper suspension arms are clear of the body bracket. Support the spindle with wire in this position.

7. Remove and discard the nut attaching the upper suspension arms to the spindle and remove the arms from the vehicle.

To install:

8. Install the upper suspension arms on the spindle and install a new nut but do not tighten the nut at this time.

9. Position the upper suspension arm ends to the body bracket and install new nuts and bolts. Tighten to 70–95 ft. lbs. (95–129 Nm). Remove the wire from the spindle.

10. Tighten the nut attaching the upper suspension arms to the spindle to 150–190 ft. lbs.

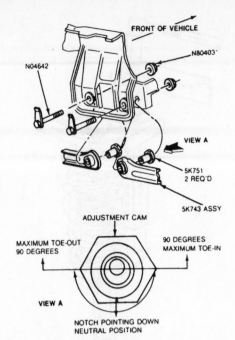

Rear control arm assembly

(204–257 Nm). Tighten the nut attaching the lower suspension arm to the spindle to 40–55 ft. lbs. (54–74 Nm).

11. Install the brake line bracket to the body.

12. Install the wheel and tire assembly, remove the jackstand and wood block and lower the vehicle.

13. Check the rear wheel alignment.

LOWER ARM

1. Raise and support the vehicle safely on the lifting pads on the underbody forward of the tension strut body bracket.

2. Remove the wheel and tire assembly.

3. Place a floor jack under the lower suspension arm.

4. Remove the bracket retaining the flexible brake hose to the body.

5. Remove the stabilizer bar U-bracket from the lower suspension arm.

6. Remove and discard the nuts attaching the shock absorber to the lower suspension arm.

7. Remove the parking brake cable and clip from the lower suspension arm.

8. Remove and discard the bolt and nut attaching the tension strut to the lower suspension arm.

9. Support the spindle and upper suspension arms by wiring them to the body, to prevent them from dropping down.

10. Remove the nut, bolt, washer and adjusting cam retaining the lower suspension arm to the spindle. Discard the nut, bolt and washer.

11. Lower the suspension arm with the floor jack until the spring can be removed.

12. Remove and discard the bolt and nut attaching the lower suspension arm to the center body bracket and remove the arm.

To install:

13. Position the lower suspension arm-to-center body bracket and install but do not tighten a new bolt and nut with the bolt head toward the front of the vehicle.

14. Position the lower insulator on the lower suspension arm and press the insulator downward into place. Make sure the insulator is properly seated.

15. Position the upper insulator on top of the spring. Install the spring on the lower suspension arm, making sure the spring is properly seated.

16. Raise the suspension arm with the floor jack and guide the upper spring insulator onto the upper spring seat on the underbody.

17. Position the spindle in the lower suspension arm and install, but do not tighten, a new bolt, nut, washer and the existing cam, with the bolt head toward the front of the vehicle.

18. Remove the wire from the spindle and suspension arms.

19. Install the tension strut in the lower suspension arm using a new bolt and nut but do not tighten at this time.

20. Install the parking brake cable and clip to the lower suspension arm.

21. Position the shock absorber on the lower suspension arm and install 2 new nuts. Tighten the nuts to 13–20 ft. lbs. (17–27 Nm).

22. Install the stabilizer bar and U-bracket to the lower suspension arm using a new bolt. Tighten the bolt to 20–30 ft. lbs. (27–40 Nm).

23. Install the flexible brake hose bracket to the body. Tighten the bolt to 8–12 ft. lbs. (11–16 Nm).

24. Using the floor jack, raise the lower suspension arm to normal curb height.

• Lower suspension arm-to-body bracket nut: 40–55 ft. lbs.

• Lower suspension arm-to-spindle nut: 40–55 ft. lbs.

• Tension strut-to-body bracket bolt: 40–55 ft. lbs.

25. Install the wheel and tire assembly and lower the vehicle.

26. Check the rear wheel alignment.

Rear Wheel Bearings

REPLACEMENT

Drum Brakes

1986–89

1. Raise the vehicle and support it safely. Remove the wheel from the hub and drum.

2. Remove the grease cap from the hub. Remove the cotter pin, nut retainer, adjusting nut and keyed flat washer from the spindle. Discard the cotter pin.

3. Pull the hub and drum assembly off of the spindle. Remove the outer bearing assembly.

4. Using seal remover tool 1175–AC or equivalent, remove and discard the grease seal. Remove the inner bearing assembly from the hub.

5. Wipe all lubricant from the spindle and inside of the hub. Cover the spindle with a clean cloth and vacuum all loose dust and dirt from the brake assembly. Carefully remove the cloth to prevent dirt from falling on the spindle.

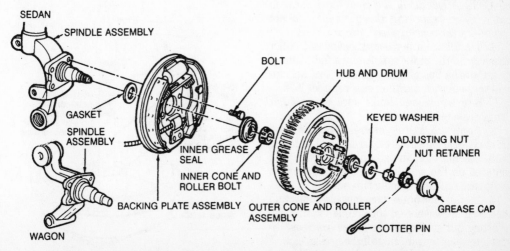

Rear wheel hub and bearing assembly — 1986–89 vehicles with drum brakes

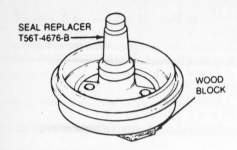

SEAL REPLACER
T56T-4676-B

WOOD BLOCK

Rear grease seal installation

6. Clean both bearing assemblies and cups using a suitable solvent. Inspect the bearing assemblies and cups for excessive wear, scratches, pits or other damage and replace as necessary.

7. If the cups are to be replaced, remove them with impact slide hammer T50T–100–A and bearing cup puller T77F–1102–A or equivalent.

To install:

8. If the inner and outer bearing cups were removed, install the replacement cups using driver handle T80T–4000–W and bearing cup replacers T73T–1217–A and T77F–1217–A or equivalent. Support the drum hub on a block of wood to prevent damage. Make sure the cups are properly seated in the hub.

NOTE: *Do not use the cone and roller assembly to install the cups. This will result in damage to the bearing cup and the cone and roller assembly.*

9. Make sure all of the spindle and bearing surfaces are clean.

10. Using a bearing packer, pack the bearing assemblies with a suitable wheel bearing grease. If a packer is not available, work in as much grease as possible between the rollers and cages. Grease the cup surfaces.

NOTE: *Allow all of the cleaning solvent to dry before repacking the bearings. Do not spin-dry the bearings with air pressure.*

11. Install the inner bearing cone and roller assembly in the inner cup. Apply a light film of grease to the lips of a new grease seal and install the seal with rear hub seal replacer T56T–4676–B or equivalent. Make sure the retainer flange is seated all around.

12. Apply a light film of grease on the spindle shaft bearing surfaces. Install the hub and drum assembly on the spindle. Keep the hub centered on the spindle to prevent damage to the grease seal and spindle threads.

13. Install the outer bearing assembly and the keyed flatwasher on the spindle. Install the adjusting nut and adjust the wheel bearings. Install a new cotter pin. Install the grease cap.

14. Install the wheel and tire assembly and ver the vehicle.

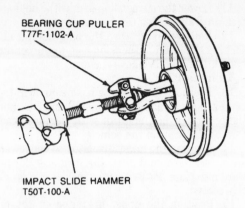

BEARING CUP PULLER
T77F-1102-A

IMPACT SLIDE HAMMER
T50T-100-A

Removing the bearing cups using a slide hammer

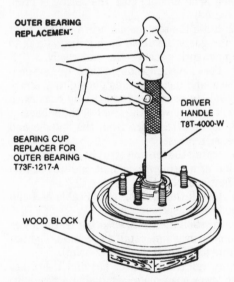

OUTER BEARING REPLACEMENT

DRIVER HANDLE
T8T-4000-W

BEARING CUP REPLACER FOR OUTER BEARING
T73F-1217-A

WOOD BLOCK

Driving the outer bearing cup into the hub

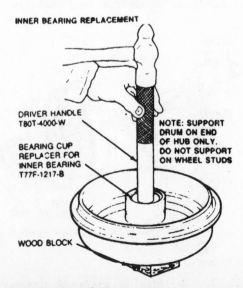

INNER BEARING REPLACEMENT

DRIVER HANDLE
T80T-4000-W

BEARING CUP REPLACER FOR INNER BEARING
T77F-1217-B

NOTE: SUPPORT DRUM ON END OF HUB ONLY. DO NOT SUPPORT ON WHEEL STUDS

WOOD BLOCK

Inner bearing installation

1990–92

1. Raise the vehicle and support it safely.
2. Remove the wheel.
3. Remove the 2 pushnuts retaining the drum to the hub and remove the drum.
4. Remove the grease cap from the bearing and hub assembly and discard it.
5. Remove the hub retaining nut and remove the bearing and hub assembly from the spindle.
6. Install in the reverse order of removal. Use coil remover T89P–19623–FH or equivalent, to install the new grease cap. Tap on the tool to make sure the grease cap is fully seated. Tighten the hub retaining nut to 188–254 ft. lbs. (255–345 Nm).

Disc Brakes

1986–89

1. Raise the vehicle and support it safely. Remove the tire and wheel assembly from the hub.
2. Remove the brake caliper by removing the 2 bolts that attach the caliper support to the cast iron brake adapter. Do not remove the caliper pins from the caliper assembly. Lift the caliper off of the rotor and support it with a length of wire. Do not allow the caliper assembly to hang from the brake hose.
3. Remove the rotor from the hub by pulling it off the hub bolts. If the rotor is difficult to remove, strike the rotor sharply between the studs with a rubber or plastic hammer.
4. Remove the grease cap from the hub. Remove the cotter pin, nut retainer, adjusting nut and keyed flat washer from the spindle. Discard the cotter pin.

5. Pull the hub assembly off of the spindle. Remove the outer bearing assembly.
6. Using seal remover tool 1175–AC or equivalent, remove and discard the grease seal. Remove the inner bearing assembly from the hub.
7. Wipe all of the lubricant from the spindle and inside of the hub. Cover the spindle with a clean cloth and vacuum all of the loose dust and dirt from the brake assembly. Carefully remove the cloth to prevent dirt from falling on the spindle.
8. Clean both bearing assemblies and cups using a suitable solvent. Inspect the bearing assemblies and cups for excessive wear, scratches, pits or other damage and replace as necessary.
9. If the cups are being replaced, remove them with impact slide hammer tool T50T–100–A and bearing cup puller tool T77F–1102–A or equivalent.
To install:
10. If the inner and outer bearing cups were removed, install the replacement cups using driver handle tool T80T–4000–W and bearing cup replacer tools T73F–1217–A and T77F–1217–B or equivalent. Support the hub on a block of wood to prevent damage. Make sure the cups are properly seated in the hub.

NOTE: *Do not use the cone and roller assembly to install the cups. This will result in damage to the bearing cup and the cone and roller assembly.*

11. Make sure all of the spindle and bearing surfaces are clean.
12. Pack the bearing assemblies with a suitable wheel bearing grease using a bearing packer. If a packer is not available, work in as

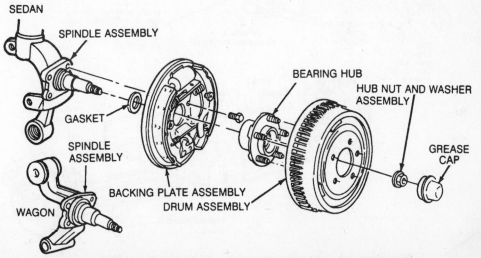

Rear wheel hub and bearing assembly – 1990–92 vehicles with drum brakes

much grease as possible between the rollers and the cages. Grease the cup surfaces.

NOTE: *Allow all of the cleaning solvent to dry before repacking the bearings. Do not spin-dry the bearings with air pressure.*

13. Place the inner bearing cone and roller assembly in the inner cup. Apply a light film of grease to the lips of a new grease seal and install the seal with rear hub seal replacer tool T56T–4676–B or equivalent. Make sure the retainer flange is seated all around.

14. Apply a light film of grease on the spindle shaft bearing surfaces. Install the hub assembly on the spindle. Keep the hub centered on the spindle to prevent damage to the grease seal and spindle threads.

15. Install the outer bearing assembly and keyed flat washer on the spindle. Install the adjusting nut and adjust the wheel bearings. Install a new cotter pin. Install the grease cap.

16. Install the disc brake rotor to the hub assembly. Install the disc brake caliper over the rotor.

17. Install the wheel and tire assembly and lower the vehicle.

1990–92

1. Raise the vehicle and support it safely.
2. Remove the wheel and tire assembly.
3. Remove the caliper assembly from the brake adapter. Support the caliper assembly with a length of wire.
4. Remove the push on nuts that retain the rotor to the hub and remove the rotor.
5. Remove the grease cap from the bearing and hub assembly and discard the grease cap.
6. Remove the bearing and hub assembly retaining nut and remove the bearing and hub assembly from the spindle.
7. Install in the reverse order of removal. Install a new grease cap using coil remover tool T89P–19623–FH or equivalent. Tap on the tool until the grease cap is fully seated. Tighten the hub retaining nut to 188–254 ft. lbs. (255–345 Nm).

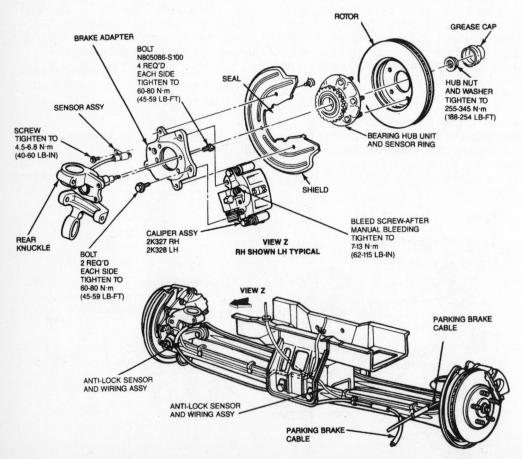

Rear wheel hub and bearing assembly — 1990–92 with disc brakes

WHEEL ALIGNMENT—Rear

Year	Model	Caster Range (deg.)	Caster Preferred Setting (deg.)	Camber Range (deg.)	Camber Preferred Setting (deg.)	Toe-in (in.)	Steering Axis Inclination (deg.)
1986	Taurus	—	—	$1^5/_8$N–$^1/_4$N	—	$^{13}/_{64}$N–$^{19}/_{64}$P ①	—
	Sable	—	—	$1^5/_8$N–$^1/_4$N	—	$^{13}/_{64}$N–$^{19}/_{64}$P ①	—
1987	Taurus	—	—	$1^5/_8$N–$^1/_4$N	—	$^{13}/_{64}$N–$^{19}/_{64}$P ①	—
	Sable	—	—	$1^5/_8$N–$^1/_4$N	—	$^{13}/_{64}$N–$^{19}/_{64}$P ①	—
1988	Taurus	—	—	$1^5/_8$N–$^1/_4$N	—	$^{13}/_{64}$N–$^{19}/_{64}$P ①	—
	Sable	—	—	$1^5/_8$N–$^1/_4$N	—	$^{13}/_{64}$N–$^{19}/_{64}$P ①	—
1989	Taurus	—	—	$1^5/_8$N–$^1/_4$N	—	$^{13}/_{64}$N–$^{19}/_{64}$P ①	—
	Sable	—	—	$1^5/_8$N–$^1/_4$N	—	$^{13}/_{64}$N–$^{19}/_{64}$P ①	—
1990	Taurus	—	—	$1^5/_8$N–$^1/_4$N	—	$^{13}/_{64}$N–$^{19}/_{64}$P ①	—
	Sable	—	—	$1^5/_8$N–$^1/_4$N	—	$^{13}/_{64}$N–$^{19}/_{64}$P ①	—
1991	Taurus	—	—	$1^5/_8$N–$^1/_4$N	—	$^{13}/_{64}$N–$^{19}/_{64}$P ①	—
	Sable	—	—	$1^5/_8$N–$^1/_4$N	—	$^{13}/_{64}$N–$^{19}/_{64}$P ①	—
1992	Taurus	—	—	$1^5/_8$N–$^1/_4$N	—	$^{13}/_{64}$N–$^{19}/_{64}$P ①	—
	Sable	—	—	$1^5/_8$N–$^1/_4$N	—	$^{13}/_{64}$N–$^{19}/_{64}$P ①	—

① Individual sides

ADJUSTMENT

The following procedure applies only to 1986–89 vehicles. Adjustment is not possible on 1990–92 vehicles. This procedure should be performed whenever the wheel is excessively loose on the spindle or it does not rotate freely.

NOTE: *The rear wheel uses a tapered roller bearing which may feel loose when properly adjusted; this condition should be considered normal.*

1. Raise and support the rear of the vehicle until tires clear the floor.
2. Remove the wheel cover or the ornament and nut covers. Remove the hub grease cap.

NOTE: *If the vehicle is equipped with styled steel or aluminum wheels, the wheel/tire assembly must be removed to remove the dust cover.*

3. Remove the cotter pin and the nut retainer.
4. Back off the hub nut 1 full turn.
5. While rotating the hub/drum assembly, tighten the adjusting nut to 17–25 ft. lbs. (23–24 Nm). Back off the adjusting nut $^1/_2$ turn, then retighten it to 24–28 inch lbs. (2.7–3.2 Nm).
6. Position the nut retainer over the adjusting nut so the slots are in line with cotter pin hole, without rotating the adjusting nut.
7. Install the cotter pin and bend the ends around the retainer flange.
8. Check the hub rotation. If the hub rotates freely, install the grease cap. If not, check

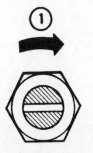

WITH WHEEL ROTATING TIGHTEN ADJUSTING NUT TO 23-34 N·m (17-25 LB-FT)

BACK ADJUSTING NUT OFF 1/2 TURN

TIGHTEN ADJUSTING NUT TO 1.1-1.4 N·m (10-12 LB-IN)

INSTALL THE RETAINER AND A NEW COTTER PIN

Rear wheel bearing adjustment

the bearings for damage and replace, as necessary.

9. Install the wheel and tire assembly and the wheel cover, if necessary. Lower the vehicle.

Rear Wheel Alignment

CASTER
Caster is pre set at the factory and not adjustable.

CAMBER

Camber is not adjustable on the Sedan. On the Wagon camber is adjustable but requires special equipment and procedures. If you suspect an alignment problem have it checked by a qualified repair shop.

TOE IN

Rear toe is adjustable but requires special equipment and procedures. If you suspect an alignment problem have it checked by a qualified repair shop.

STEERING

Steering Wheel

REMOVAL AND INSTALLATION

CAUTION: *If equipped with an air bag, the negative battery cable must be disconnected before working on the system. On 1990–92 vehicles, the backup power supply must also be disconnected. Failure to do so may result in deployment of the air bag and possible personal injury. Always wear safety glasses when servicing an air bag vehicle and when handling an air bag.*

1986–89

1. Disconnect the negative battery cable.
2. Remove the steering wheel horn pad cover by removing 2 screws from the back of the steering wheel. If equipped with cruise control, disconnect the connector from the slip ring terminal.
3. Remove and discard the steering wheel retaining bolt.
4. Remove the steering wheel from the upper shaft by grasping the rim of the steering wheel and pulling off. A steering wheel puller is not required.
To install:
5. Position the steering wheel on the end of the shaft. Align the mark on the steering wheel with the mark on the shaft to ensure the straight-ahead steering wheel position corresponds to the straight-ahead position of the front wheels.

NOTE: *The combination switch lever must be in the middle position before installing the steering wheel or damage to the switch cam may result.*

6. Install a new steering wheel retaining bolt and tighten to 23–33 ft. lbs. (31–45 Nm).
7. If equipped with cruise control, connect the connector to the slip ring terminal. Install the steering wheel horn pad cover with the 2 screws. Tighten to 5–10 inch lbs. (0.5–1.1 Nm).
8. Connect the negative battery cable.

1990–92

1. Center the front wheels in the straight-ahead position.
2. Disconnect the negative battery cable. Lower the glove compartment past it's stops and disconnect the air bag backup power supply..
3. Remove the 4 air bag module retaining nuts and lift the module from the wheel. Disconnect the air bag wire harness from the air bag module and remove the module from the wheel.

CAUTION: *When carrying a live air bag, make sure the bag and trim cover are pointed away from the body. In the unlikely event of an accidental deployment, the bag will then deploy with minimal chance of injury. In addition, when placing a live air bag on a bench or other surface, always face the bag and trim cover up, away from the surface. This will reduce the motion of the module if it is accidentally deployed.*

4. Disconnect the cruise control wire harness from the steering wheel. Remove and discard the steering wheel retaining bolt.
5. Install a suitable steering wheel puller and remove the steering wheel. Route the contact assembly wire harness through the steering wheel as the wheel is lifted off the shaft.
To install:
6. Make sure the vehicle's front wheels are in the straight-ahead position.
7. Route the contact assembly wire harness through the steering wheel opening at the 3 o'clock position and install the steering wheel on the shaft. The steering wheel and shaft alignment marks should be aligned. Make sure the air bag contact wire is not pinched.
8. Install a new steering wheel retaining bolt and tighten to 23–33 ft. lbs. (31–48 Nm).
9. Connect the cruise control wire harness to the wheel and snap the connector assembly into the steering wheel clip. Make sure the wiring does not get trapped between the steering wheel and contact assembly.

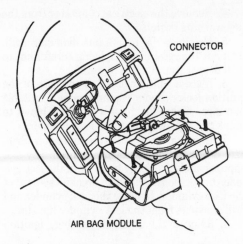

CONNECTOR

AIR BAG MODULE

Air bag module and steering wheel — 1990–92

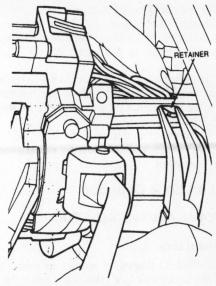

RETAINER

Ignition switch lock removal

10. Connect the air bag wire harness to the air bag module and install the module to the steering wheel. Tighten the module retaining nuts to 3–4 ft. lbs. (4–6 Nm).

11. Connect the air bag backup power supply and the negative battery cable. Verify the air bag warning indicator.

Combination Switch

The combination switch incorporates the turn signal, headlight dimmer, headlight flash-to-pass, hazard warning, cornering lights and windshield washer/wiper functions.

REMOVAL AND INSTALLATION

1. Disconnect the negative battery cable. If equipped with a tilt steering column, set the tilt

column to its lowest position and remove the tilt lever by removing the Allen head retaining screw.

2. Remove the ignition lock cylinder. Remove the steering column shroud screws and remove the upper and lower shrouds.

3. Remove the wiring harness retainer and disconnect the 3 electrical connectors.

4. Remove the self tapping screws attaching the switch to the steering column and disengage the switch from the steering column casting.

To install:

5. Align the turn signal switch mounting holes with the corresponding holes in the steering column and install self-tapping screws. Torque the screws to 17–26 inch lbs. (2–3 Nm).

6. Install the electrical connectors and in-

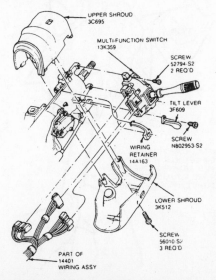

UPPER SHROUD
3C695

MULTI-FUNCTION SWITCH
13K359

SCREW
52794-S2
2 REQ'D

TILT LEVER
3F609

SCREW
N802953-S2

WIRING
RETAINER
14A163

LOWER SHROUD
3K512

SCREW
56010-S?
3 REQ'D

PART OF
14401
WIRING ASSY

Combination switch assembly

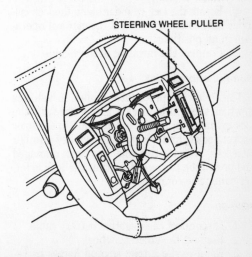

STEERING WHEEL PULLER

Steering wheel removal — 1990–92

stall the wiring harness retainer.

7. Install the upper and lower steering column shroud and shroud retaining screws, torque the screws to 6–10 inch lbs. (0.7–1.1 Nm).

8. Install the ignition lock cylinder. Attach the tilt lever, if removed and torque the tilt lever Allen head retaining screw to 6–9 inch lbs. (0.7–1.0 Nm).

9. Connect the negative battery cable. Check the switch and the steering column for proper operation.

Ignition Lock Cylinder

REMOVAL AND INSTALLATION

Functional Lock

The following procedure applies to vehicles that have functional lock cylinders. Lock cylinder keys are available for these vehicles or the lock cylinder key numbers are known and the proper key can be made.

1. Disconnect the negative battery cable.
2. Turn the lock cylinder key to the **RUN** position.
3. Using an $1/8$ in. (3mm) diameter wire pin or a small drift, depress the lock cylinder retaining pin through the access hole, while pulling out on the lock cylinder to remove it from the column.

To install:

4. Install the lock cylinder by turning it to the **RUN** position and depressing the retaining pin. Insert the lock cylinder into it's housing. Make sure the cylinder is fully seated and aligned in the interlocking washer before turning the key to the **OFF** position. This will permit the cylinder retaining pin to extend into the cylinder housing.

5. Rotate the lock cylinder using the lock cylinder key, to ensure correct mechanical operation in all positions.

6. Connect the negative battery cable.

Non-Functional Lock

The following procedure applies to vehicles in which the ignition lock is inoperative and the lock cylinder cannot be rotated due to a lost or broken lock cylinder key, unknown key number or a lock cylinder cap that has been damaged and/or broken to the extent that the lock cylinder cannot be rotated.

1986–90

1. Disconnect the negative battery cable.
2. Remove the steering wheel.
3. Remove the 2 trim shroud halves by removing the 3 attaching screws.

4. Remove the electrical connector from the key warning switch.

5. Using an $1/8$ in. (3mm) diameter drill, drill out the retaining pin, being careful not to drill deeper than $1/2$ in. (13mm).

6. Place a suitable chisel at the base of the ignition lock cylinder cap and using a suitable hammer, strike the chisel with sharp blows to break the cap away from the lock cylinder.

7. Using a $3/8$ in. (10mm) diameter drill, drill down the middle of the ignition key slot approximately $1^3/4$ in. (44mm) until the lock cylinder breaks loose from the breakaway base of the lock cylinder. Remove the lock cylinder and drill shavings from the lock cylinder housing.

8. Remove the retainer, washer, ignition

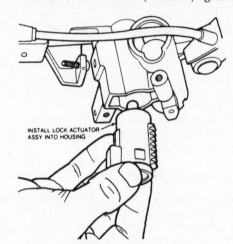

INSTALL LOCK ACTUATOR ASSY INTO HOUSING

Lock cylinder installation

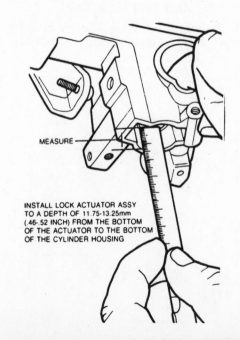

MEASURE

INSTALL LOCK ACTUATOR ASSY TO A DEPTH OF 11.75-13.25mm (.46-.52 INCH) FROM THE BOTTOM OF THE ACTUATOR TO THE BOTTOM OF THE CYLINDER HOUSING

Depth measurement

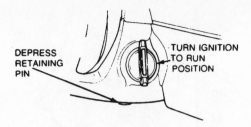

Combination switch electrical harness removal

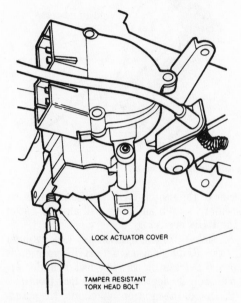

Lock actuator cover plate removal

switch and actuator. Thoroughly clean all the drill shavings from the casting.

9. Inspect the lock cylinder housing for damage from the removal operation.

To install:

10. Replace the lock cylinder housing if it was damaged.

11. Install the actuator and ignition switch.

12. Install the trim and electrical parts.

13. Install a new ignition lock cylinder.

14. Install the steering wheel.

15. Connect the negative battery cable.

16. Check the lock cylinder operation.

1991–92

1. Disconnect the negative battery cable.

2. Remove the steering wheel.

3. Using channel lock or vise grip pliers, twist the lock cylinder cap until it separates from the lock cylinder.

4. Using a ³/₈ in. (10mm) diameter drill bit, drill down the middle of the ignition lock key slot approximately 1³/₄ in. (44mm) until the lock cylinder breaks loose from the breakaway

base of the lock cylinder. Remove the lock cylinder and drill shavings from the lock cylinder housing.

5. Remove the retainer, washer, ignition switch and actuator. Thoroughly clean all drill shavings and other foreign materials from the casting.

6. Inspect the lock cylinder housing for damage from the removal operation. If the housing is damaged, it must be replaced.

To install:

7. Replace the lock cylinder housing, if damaged.

8. Install the actuator and ignition switch.

9. Install the trim and electrical parts.

10. Install the ignition lock cylinder.

11. Install the steering wheel.

12. Check the lock cylinder operation.

Ignition Switch

REMOVAL AND INSTALLATION

1986–89

1. Disconnect the negative battery cable.

2. Turn the ignition lock cylinder to the **RUN** position and depress the lock cylinder retaining pin through the access hole in the shroud with a ¹/₈ diameter punch.

3. Remove the lock cylinder. If equipped with tilt columns, remove the tilt release lever.

4. Remove the instrument panel lower cover and the steering column shroud.

5. Remove the 4 nuts attaching the steering column to the support bracket and lower the column.

6. Disconnect the ignition switch electrical connector.

7. Remove the lock actuator cover plate. The lock actuator assembly will slide freely out of the lock cylinder housing when the ignition switch is removed.

8. Remove the ignition switch and cover.

To install:

9. Make sure the ignition switch is in the **RUN** position by rotating the driveshaft fully clockwise to the **START** position and releasing.

10. Install the lock actuator assembly to a depth of 0.46–0.52 in. (11.75–13.25mm) from the bottom of the actuator assembly to the bottom of the lock cylinder housing.

11. While holding the actuator assembly at the proper depth, install the ignition switch. Install the ignition switch cover and tighten the retaining bolts to 30–48 inch lbs. (3.4–5.4 Nm).

12. Install the lock cylinder. Rotate the ignition lock cylinder to the **LOCK** position and measure the depth of the actuator assembly as in Step 10. The actuator assembly must be

0.92–1.00 in. (23.5–25.5mm) inside the lock cylinder housing. If the depth measured does not meet specification, the actuator assembly must be removed and installed again.

13. Install the lock actuator cover plate and tighten the bolts to 30–48 inch lbs. (3.4–5.4 Nm).

14. Install the ignition switch electrical connector.

15. Connect the negative battery cable. Check the ignition switch for proper function in all positions, including **START** and **ACC**.

16. Check the column function as follows:

a. With the column shift lever in the **P** position or with the floor shift key release button depressed and with the ignition lock cylinder in the **LOCK** position, make certain the steering column locks.

b. Position the column shift lever in the **D** position or the floor shift key release button fully extended and rotate the cylinder lock to the **RUN** position. Continue to rotate the cylinder toward the **LOCK** position until it stops. In this position, make certain the engine and all electrical accessories are **OFF** and that the steering shaft does not lock.

c. Turn the radio power button **ON**. Rotate the cylinder counterclockwise to the **ACC** position to verify that the radio is energized.

d. Place the shift lever in **P** and rotate the cylinder clockwise to the **START** position to verify that the starter energizes.

17. Remove the ignition lock cylinder.

18. Align the steering column mounting holes with the support bracket, center the steering column in the instrument panel opening and install the 4 nuts. Tighten the nuts to 15–25 ft. lbs. (20–34 Nm).

19. Install the column trim shrouds and the instrument panel lower cover. Install the tilt release lever, if equipped.

20. Install the ignition lock cylinder.

1990–92

1. Disconnect the negative battery cable.

2. Remove the steering column shroud by removing the self-tapping screws. Remove the tilt lever, if equipped.

3. Remove the instrument panel lower steering column cover.

4. Disconnect the ignition switch electrical connector.

5. Turn the ignition key lock cylinder to the **RUN** position.

6. Remove the 2 screws attaching the ignition switch and disengage the switch from the actuator pin.

To install:

7. Adjust the ignition switch by sliding the

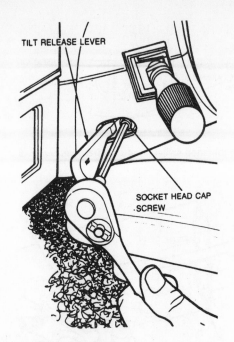

Tilt release lever removal

carrier to the switch **RUN** position. A new replacement switch assembly will already be set in the **RUN** position.

8. Make sure the ignition key lock cylinder is in the **RUN** position. The **RUN** position is achieved by rotating the key lock cylinder approximately 90 degrees from the lock position.

9. Install the ignition switch into the actuator pin. It may be necessary to move the switch slightly back and forth to align the switch mounting holes with the column lock housing threaded holes.

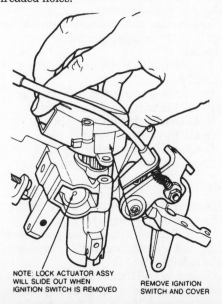

NOTE: LOCK ACTUATOR ASSY WILL SLIDE OUT WHEN IGNITION SWITCH IS REMOVED

REMOVE IGNITION SWITCH AND COVER

Ignition switch assembly removal

10. Install the attaching screws and tighten to 50–69 inch lbs. (5.6–7.9 Nm).

11. Connect the electrical connector to the ignition switch.

12. Connect the negative battery cable.

13. Check the ignition switch for proper function, including **START** and **ACC** positions. Make sure the column is locked with the switch in the **LOCK** position.

14. Install the instrument panel lower steering column cover, the steering column trim shrouds and the tilt lever, if equipped.

Steering Column

REMOVAL AND INSTALLATION

1986–89

1. Disconnect the negative battery cable.

2. Remove the 4 self-tapping screws and remove the steering column cover from the lower portion of the instrument panel.

3. Remove the retaining screw and the tilt release lever. Remove the ignition lock cylinder.

4. Remove the 3 self-tapping screws from the bottom of the lower shroud and remove the steering column trim shrouds. Remove the steering wheel.

5. If equipped with column shift, perform the following:

   a. Disconnect the shift position indicator cable from the lock cylinder housing by removing the retaining screw.

   b. Disconnect the shift position indicator cable from the shift socket.

   c. Remove the shift position indicator cable from the retaining hook on the bottom of the lock cylinder housing.

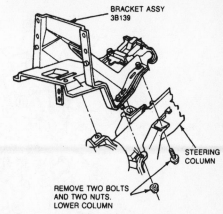

Steering column support bracket location

6. Using a punch, remove the shift lever-to-shift socket retaining pin and remove the shift lever.

7. Disconnect the cruise control/horn brush wiring connector from the main wiring harness.

8. Remove the combination switch wiring harness retainer from the lock cylinder housing by squeezing the end of the retainer and pushing out. Disconnect the combination switch connector and remove the 2 self-tapping retaining screws. Remove the combination switch.

9. Disconnect the key warning buzzer switch wiring connector from the main wiring harness and disconnect the wiring connector from the ignition switch.

10. Disconnect the steering shaft from the intermediate shaft by removing 2 nuts and 1 U-clamp. If equipped with an air bag, wire the lower end of the steering shaft to the column housing to prevent rotation of the steering shaft. Rotating the steering shaft could damage

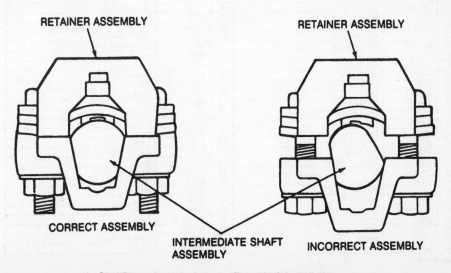

Steering column to intermediate shaft installation

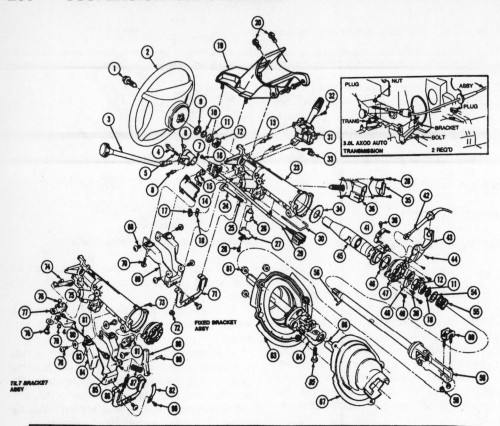

ITEM	PART NO.	DESCRIPTION	ITEM	PART NO.	DESCRIPTION
1	N805167	Bolt	45.	3K521	Tube and Bearing Assy.
2.	3600	Wheel	46.	3C708	Washer
3.	7202	Shift Lever	47.	3E736	Retainer
4.	7361	Plunger	48.	2B623	Parking Brake Rel. Switch
5.	7B071	Spring	49.	N804130	3 Screw Attach Retainer to Column
6.	7G357	Pin	54.	3D672	Spacer
7.	7228	Socket	55.	3C674	Spring
8.	380098	Rivet	56.	3E716	Pin
9.	3D640	Spacer	58.	3E729	Shaft Assy.
10.	3L539	Ring	59.	N620457	Nut — 2 Req'd.
11.	3517	Bearing Assy.	60.	3C068	Plate Assy.
12.	3518	Sleeve	61.	N804795-S2	Nut — 3 Req'd.
13.	3F643	Rivet Serviced	63.	3E735	Boot
*14.	3A573	Cover	64.		Intermediate Shaft
15.	3F643	Insert Serviced	65.	N803942	Bolt
16.	N804445-S2	Screw	66.		Steering Gear Input Shaft
17.	3F579	Retainer	67.	3E735	Boot
18.	3E700	Bearing	68.	N804086	Torx® Bolt — 5 Req'd. Also 2 Req'd.
19.		Not Used	69.	3E660	Fixed Bracket Assy.
20.	N605905	Bolt — 4 Req'd.	70.	N804140	Screw/Washer Assy. — 2 Req'd.
21.		Not Used	71.	3B632	Bracket
22.		Not Used	72.	N621939	Nut — 2 Req'd.
23.	3F643	Housing Assy.	73.	3F643	Pin Serviced
*24.	3F531	Key Release Knob	74.	N802953	Screw
*25.	3E696	Spring	75.	3F609	Handle Shank Assy.
26.	3E723	Actuator Assy.	76.	N804067	Bolt
27.	3E745	Actuator Cover	77.	3D544	Bracket
28.	N804089	Bolt — 3 Req'd.	78.	N804066	Bolt
29.	9C899	Brush Assy.	79.	N804064	Nut
*30.	3F526	Key Release Lever	80.	390345	Screw
31.	13K359	Turn Signal	81.	3F700	Bracket/Cable Assy.
32.	52794	Screw — 2 Req'd.	82.	3D655	Spring
33.	14A163	Wire Retainer	83.	N804065	Washer — 3 Req'd.
*34.	3K616	Bearing	84.	3E660	Tilt Bracket Assy.
35.		Not Used	85.	3D656	Bumper
36.	11572	Ignition Switch	86.	3D655	Spring
38.	N804444-S2	Screw — 3 Req'd.	87.	3D655	Spring
41.	2B624	Actuator	88.	3B662	Lever
42.	7E395	Cable	89.	N804090	Pin
43.	7E364	Bracket	90.	N804409	Screw — 7 Req'd.
44.	N605771	Screw — 2 Req'd.	91.	3F716	Locator

*Floor Shift only.

Steering column and related components — 1986–89

the air bag contact clockspring if the steering wheel is attached to the column.

11. If equipped with column shift, perform the following:

a. Remove the shift cable plastic terminal from the column selector lever pivot ball using a small prybar and prying between the plastic terminal and the selector lever. Be careful not to damage the cable during or after assembly.

b. Remove the shift cable bracket, with shift cable still attached, from the lock cylinder housing by removing the 2 retaining screws.

12. If equipped with an automatic parking brake release mechanism, remove the vacuum hoses from the parking brake release switch.

13. Remove the 2 nuts retaining the rear column assembly. Loosen the 2 nuts retaining the front column assembly to the end of the studs, but do not remove at this time.

14. Use a downward force to disengage the column assembly push-on clips from the rear attachments. Remove the remaining 2 nuts.

NOTE: *When forcing downward, care should be taken to avoid damaging the safety slip-clips on the steering column.*

15. Carefully lower the steering column assembly and remove from the vehicle.

To install:

16. Raise the steering column assembly into position and align the 4 mounting holes over the 4 support bracket studs. Hand start the 4 retaining nuts.

17. Center the column assembly in the instrument panel opening and tighten the 4 nuts to 15–25 ft. lbs. (21–33 Nm).

18. If equipped with an automatic parking brake release mechanism, install the vacuum hoses on the parking brake release switch.

19. If equipped with column shift, perform the following:

a. Attach the cable shift bracket, with the shift cable attached, to the lock cylinder housing and tighten the retaining screws to 5–7 ft. lbs. (7–9 Nm).

b. Snap the transaxle shift cable terminal to the selector lever pivot ball on the steering column.

20. Apply a generous amount of grease to the V-shaped steering shaft yoke. Connect the steering shaft to the intermediate shaft with 1 U-clamp and 2 hex nuts. When installing the steering column to the intermediate shaft, connect the intermediate shaft to the steering column with the retainer assembly and 2 nuts.

NOTE: *Make sure the V-angle of the intermediate shaft fits correctly into the V-angle of the mating steering column yoke. If the V-angle is mis-aligned and the retainer is tight-*

ened, the retainer plate will be bent and then must be replaced.

21. After correctly installing the steering column to the intermediate shaft, tighten the nuts to 15–25 ft. lbs. (21–33 Nm).

NOTE: *Tilt columns must be in the middle tilt position before the nuts are tightened.*

22. Connect the main wiring harness connector to the ignition switch and connect the key warning buzzer switch wiring connector to the main harness. Install the steering sensor wire connector to the sensor lead connector.

23. Install the combination switch and tighten the 2 self-tapping screws to 18–26 inch lbs. (2.0–2.9 Nm). Install the combination switch wiring harness retainer over the shroud mounting boss and snap it into the slot in the lock cylinder housing.

24. Connect the cruise control/horn brush wiring connector to the main wiring harness.

25. If equipped with column shift, install the shift position indicator cable into the retaining hook on the lock cylinder housing, connect the cable to the shift socket and loosely install the cable onto the lock cylinder housing with 1 screw. Adjust the shift position indicator cable as follows:

a. Place the shift lever in **D** on Taurus equipped with the 2.5L engine. On all others, place the shift lever in **OD**. A weight of 8 lbs. should be hung on the shift selector lever to make sure the lever is firmly against the **D** or **OD** drive detent.

b. Adjust the cable until the indicator pointer completely covers the **D** or **OD**, then tighten the screw to 18–30 inch lbs. (2.0–3.4 Nm).

c. Cycle the shift lever through all positions and check that the shift position idicator completely covers the proper letter or number in each position.

26. Install the shift lever into the shift lever socket and install a new shift lever retaining pin. Use care to avoid damaging the shift position indicator post on the shift socket.

27. Place the combination switch in the middle position and install the steering wheel.

28. Install the shrouds with the retaining screws. Tighten to 6–10 inch lbs. (0.7–1.1 Nm). If equipped with tilt column, install the tilt release lever and tighten the screw to 6.5–9.0 ft. lbs. (8.8–12 Nm).

29. Install the ignition lock cylinder. Install the steering column cover on lower portion of instrument panel with the 4 self-tapping screws.

30. Connect the negative battery cable. Check the column function as follows:

a. With the column shift lever in **P** position or the floor shift key release button de-

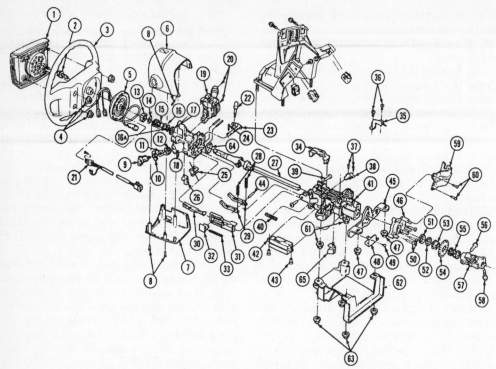

Steering column and related components (floor shift) — 1990–92

pressed, and with the ignition switch in the **LOCK** position; make sure the steering column locks.

b. With the column shift lever in **D** or with the floor shift key release button extended, and with the ignition switch in the **RUN** position; rotate the ignition switch toward the **LOCK** position until it stops. In this position, make sure engine electrical off has been achieved and that the steering shaft does not lock.

c. On tilt columns, check column tilt travel through it's entire range to make sure there is no interference between the column and instrument panel.

d. Cycle the combination switch through all of it's functions.

1990–92

1. Disconnect the negative battery cable. Lower the glove compartment past it's stops and disconnect the air bag backup power supply.

2. Remove the steering wheel.

3. Remove the left and right lower mouldings from the instrument panel by pulling up and snapping out of the retainers.

4. Remove the instrument panel lower trim cover and the lower steering column shroud.

5. Disconnect the air bag clockspring contact assembly wire harness. Apply 2 strips of tape across the contact assembly stator and

rotor to prevent accidental rotation. Remove the 3 contact assembly retaining screws and pull the contact assembly off the steering column shaft.

6. Remove the tilt lever by unscrewing it from the columnn.

7. Rotate the ignition lock cylinder to the **RUN** position. Using an $1/8$ in. (3mm) drift, depress the lock cylinder retaining pin through the access hole and remove the lock cylinder.

8. Remove the 4 retaining screws from the lower shroud and remove the steering column shrouds.

9. Remove the 2 instrument panel reinforcement brace retaining bolts and remove the reinforcement.

10. If equipped with column shift, disconnect the shift position indicator cable from the actuator housing by removing 1 screw and disconnect the cable loop from the shift tube hook. If equipped with console shift, remove the interlock cable retaining screws and remove the cable.

11. Remove the 2 combination switch retaining screws and set the switch aside.

12. Remove the pinch bolt from the steering shaft flex coupling.

13. Disconnect the shift cable from the selector lever pivot. Remove the shift cable and bracket from the lower column mounting. Remove the column skid plate.

14. While supporting the column assembly,

Item	Description	Part No.	Item	Description	Part No.
1	Air Bag Module	—	34	Shield	14A099
2	Steering Wheel Bolt	N804385-S100	35	Trans Control Selector Position Insert	7A216
3	Steering Wheel	—	36	Screws	N805858
4	Air Bag Module Retaining Nuts	—	37	Screws	390345-S36
5	Air Bag Clockspring Contact Assy	14A664	38	Parking Brake Vacuum Release Switch	2B623
6	Upper Column Shroud	3530	39	Tilt Pivot Screws	N805865
7	Lower Column Shroud	3533	40	Spring — Steering Column Position Lock	3D655
8	Shroud Retaining Screws	55929	41	Actuator Housing	3F723
9	Ignition Lock Cylinder Assy	11572	42	Ignition Switch	—
10	Retainer	3F579	43	Screws	N805858
11	Bearing	3E700	44	Pin — Pivot Lever	3F530
12	Gear — Steering Lock	3E717	45	Lower Column Bracket	3B632
13	Turn Signal Cancelling Cam	13318	46	Lower Bearing Housing Retainer	3E738
14	Snap Ring	3C610	47	Lower Column Mounting Nuts	N801555
15	Spring — Upper Bearing	3520	48	Bracket	14A206
16	Sleeve	3518	49	Screw	N804409
16A	Ring	3L539	50	Lower Bearing Housing Retaining Screws	805859
17	Bearing — Upper (Small)	3517	51	Lower Column Bearing Sleeve	3A649
18	Lock Cylinder Housing	3F642	52	Lower Column Bearing	3517
19	Multi-Function Switch	13K359	53	Tolerance Ring — Lower	36539
20	Screws	390345-S36	54	Sensor Ring	3C131
21	Horn Brush Assy	9C899	55	Spring	3C674
22	Tilt Release Lever	3F527	56	Bolt — Flange Yoke	N803942
23	Tilt Actuator Lever	3D544	57	Steering Shaft U — Joint Assy	3N725
24	Tilt Actuator Lever Pin	3F530	58	Bolt	N803942
25	Cam Steering Column Lock	3E695	59	Shift Cable Bracket	7E364
26	Clip Wiring — Upper	14A163	60	Shift Cable Bracket Mounting Screws	805858
27	Steering Shaft Assy	3E729 3D657	61	Upper Column Mounting Nuts	N801555
28	Spring Lock Lever	3C732	62	Absorber — Steering Column Impact	3E645
29	Lever Steering Column Lock	3B662 — RH 3D653 — LH	63	Nuts	N801555
30	Lock Actuator Assy — Upper	3E723	64	Bearing — Upper (Large)	3517
31	Lock Actuator Assy — Lower	3E715	65	Clip Wiring — Lower	14A163
32	Pawl — Steering Column Lock (Shaft)	3E691			
33	Spring — Steering Column Lock (Shaft)	3E696			

Steering column and related components (floor shift) — 1990–92 continued

remove the 4 column assembly retaining nuts. Lower the column and disconnect the vacuum hoses at the parking brake release switch or remove the vacuum release assembly.

15. Remove the column from the vehicle.

To install:

16. Align the column lower universal joint to the lower shaft. Install 1 bolt and tighten to 29–41 ft. lbs. (40–56 Nm). Connect the parking brake release vacuum hoses.

17. Support the column assembly to the column support bracket. Install the 4 retaining nuts and tighten to 10–14 ft. lbs. (13–19 Nm).

18. Position the shift cable bracket, with the shift cable attached, to the lower 2 screws of the column. Tighten to 5–8 ft. lbs. (7–11 Nm). Snap the shift cable onto the shift selector pivot ball.

19. If equipped with automatic console shift, position the interlock cable and install the 2 retaining screws.

20. Position the combination switch and install the 2 retaining screws. Tighten to 18–26 inch lbs. (2–3 Nm). Connect all electrical connectors.

21. If equipped with column shift, attach the shift position indicator cable loop on the shift selector hook and install the cable bracket to the actuator housing. Install the retaining screw and tighten to 5–8 ft. lbs. (7–11 Nm).

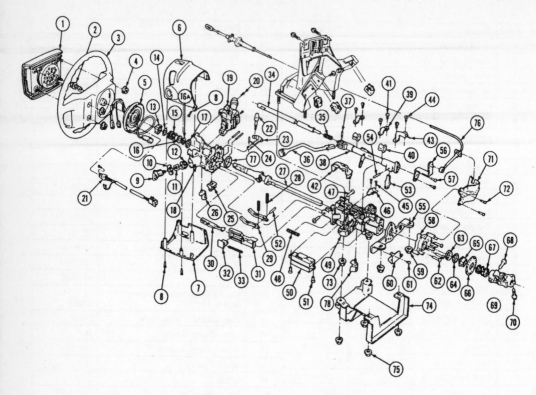

Steering column and related components (column shift) — 1990–92

22. Install the steering column skid plate and tighten the retaining nuts to 15–25 ft. lbs. (20–34 Nm).

23. Install the upper and lower column shrouds and the instrument panel reinforcement brace.

24. Install the lower instrument panel cover. Snap the right and left lower instrument panel mouldings into place.

25. Install the lock cylinder assembly and the tilt lever.

26. Install the air bag clockspring contact assembly screws and tighten to 18–26 inch lbs. (2–3 Nm). Route the contact assembly down the column and connect to the wire harness.

NOTE: *If a new contact assembly is being installed, remove the plastic lock mechanism after the contact assembly is secured to the column.*

27. Install the steering wheel with a new bolt. Tighten to 23–33 ft. lbs. (31–48 Nm). Position the air bag module to the steering wheel. Install the 4 retaining nuts and tighten to 3–4 ft. lbs. (4–6 Nm).

28. Connect the air bag backup power supply and the negative battery cable. Verify the air bag warning indicator.

Steering Linkage

REMOVAL AND INSTALLATION

Tie Rod Ends

1. Remove and discard the cotter pin and nut from the worn tie rod end ball stud.

2. Disconnect the tie rod end from the steering spindle, using tie rod remover tool 3290–D or equivalent.

3. Hold the tie rod end with a wrench and loosen the tie rod jam nut.

4. Note the depth to which the tie rod is located, then grip the tie rod with a pair of suitable pliers and remove the tie rod end assembly from the tie rod.

To install:

5. Clean the tie rod threads. Thread the new tie rod end into the tie rod to the same depth as the removed tie rod end.

6. Place the tie rod end stud into the steering spindle. Make sure the front wheels are pointed straight-ahead before connecting the stud to the spindle.

7. Install a new nut on the tie rod end stud. Tighten the nut to 35 ft. lbs. (48 Nm) and continue tightening until the next castellation on

Item	Description	Part No.	Item	Description	Part No.
1	Air Bag Module	—	40	Bushings	7335
2	Steering Wheel Bolt	N804385-S100	41	Screws	N805858
3	Steering Wheel	—	42	Shield	14A099
4	Air Bag Module Retaining Nuts	—	43	Trans Control Selector Position Insert	7A216
5	Air Bag Clockspring Contact Assy	14A664	44	Screws	N805858
6	Upper Column Shroud	3530	45	Screws	390345-S36
7	Lower Column Shroud	3533	46	Parking Brake Vacuum Release Switch	2B623
8	Shroud Retaining Screws	55929	47	Tilt Pivot Screws	N805865
9	Ignition Lock Cylinder Assy	11572	48	Spring — Steering Column Position Lock	3D655
10	Retainer	3F579	49	Actuator Housing	3F723
11	Bearing	3E700	50	Ignition Switch	—
12	Gear — Steering Lock	3E717	51	Screws	N805858
13	Turn Signal Cancelling Cam	13318	52	Pin — Pivot Lever	3F530
14	Snap Ring	3C610	53	Pawl Steering Column Lock Shifter	3E691
15	Spring — Upper Bearing	3520	54	Pin — Steering Column Lock Shifter	3B663
16	Sleeve	3518	55	Lower Column Bracket	3B632
16A	Ring	3L539	56	Trans Control Selector Lower Lever	7D282
17	Bearing — Upper (Small)	3517	57	Screws	805858
18	Lock Cylinder Housing	3F642	58	Lower Bearing Housing Retainer	3E738
19	Multi — Function Switch	13K359	59	Lower Column Mounting Nuts	N801555
20	Screws	390345-S36	60	Bracket	14A206
21	Horn Brush Assy	9C899	61	Screw	N804409
22	Tilt Release Lever	3F527	62	Lower Bearing Housing Retaining Screws	805859
23	Tilt Actuator Lever	3D544	63	Lower Column Bearing Sleeve	3A649
24	Tilt Actuator Lever Pin	3F530	64	Lower Column Bearing	3517
25	Cam Steering Column Lock	3E695	65	Tolerance Ring — Lower	3L539
26	Clip Wiring — Upper	14A163	66	Sensor Ring	3C131
27	Steering Shaft Assy	3E729 3D657	67	Spring	3C674
28	Spring Lock Lever	3C732	68	Bolt — Flange Yoke	N803942
29	Lever Steering Column Lock	3B662 — RH 3D653 — LH	69	Steering Shaft U — Joint Assy	3N725
30	Lock Actuator Assy — Upper	3E723	70	Bolt	N803942
31	Lock Actuator Assy — Lower	3E715	71	Shift Cable Bracket	7E364
32	Pawl — Steering Column Lock (Shaft)	3E691	72	Shift Cable Bracket Mounting Screws	805858
33	Spring — Steering Column Lock (Shaft)	3E696	73	Upper Column Mounting Nuts	N801555
34	Plunger Trans Control Select	7361	74	Absorber — Steering Column Impact	3E645
35	Spring — Trans Control Selector Return	7B071	75	Nuts	N801555
36	Shift Lever	7302	76	Shift Cable Assembly	7E395
37	Shift Lever Pin	7W441	77	Bearing — Upper (Large)	3517
38	Trans Selector Control Tube	7215	78	Clip Wiring — Lower	14A163
39	Trans Gear Shift Tube Clamps	7E400			

Steering column and related components (column shift) — 1990–92 continued

the nut is aligned with the cotter pin hole in the stud. Install a new cotter pin.

8. Set the toe to specification. Tighten the jam nut to 35–50 ft. lbs. (47–68 Nm).

Power Steering Rack

ADJUSTMENTS

Integral Power Rack and Pinion Except 1990–92
Taurus LX and Sable with 3.8L Engine

RACK YOKE PLUG CLEARANCE

NOTE: *The rack yoke clearance adjustment is not a normal service adjustment. It is only required when the input shaft and valve assembly is removed.*

1. Remove the steering gear from the vehicle. Clean the exterior of the steering gear thoroughly.

2. Install the steering gear in a suitable holding fixture. Do not remove the external transfer tubes unless they are leaking or damaged. If

these lines are removed, they must be replaced with new ones.

3. Drain the power steering fluid by rotating the input shaft lock-to-lock twice, using a suitable tool. Cover the ports on the valve housing with a shop cloth while draining the gear to avoid possible oil spray.

4. Insert an inch pound torque wrench with a maximum capacity of 60 inch lbs. (6.77 Nm) into pinion shaft torque adapter T74P–3504–R or equivalent. Position the adapter and wrench on the input shaft splines.

5. Loosen the yoke plug locknut and then the yoke plug.

6. With the rack at the center of travel, tighten the yoke plug to 45–50 inch lbs. (5–5.6 Nm). Clean the threads of the yoke plug prior to tightening to prevent a false reading.

7. Back off the yoke plug approximately $1/8$ turn, 44 degrees minimum to 54 degrees maximum, until the torque required to initiate and sustain rotation of the input shaft is 7–18 inch lbs. (0.78–2.03 Nm).

8. Place a suitable wrench on the yoke plug locknut. While holding the yoke plug, tighten the locknut to 44–66 ft. lbs. (60–89 Nm). Do not allow the yoke plug to move while tightening or preload will be affected. Check the input shaft torque as in Step 7 after tightening the locknut.

9. Install the steering gear.

REMOVAL AND INSTALLATION

Integral Power Rack and Pinion Except 1990–92 Taurus LX and Sable with 3.8L Engine

1. Disconnect the negative battery cable. Working from inside the vehicle, remove the nuts retaining the steering shaft weather boot to the dash panel.

2. Remove the bolts retaining the intermediate shaft to the steering column shaft. Set the weather boot aside.

3. Remove the pinch bolt at the steering gear input shaft and remove the intermediate shaft. Raise the vehicle and support safely.

4. Remove the left front wheel and tire assembly. Remove the heat shield. Cut the bundling strap retaining the lines to the gear.

5. Remove the tie rod ends from the spindles. Place a drain pan under the vehicle and remove the hydraulic pressure and return lines from the steering gear.

NOTE: *The pressure and return lines are on the front of the housing. Do not confuse them*

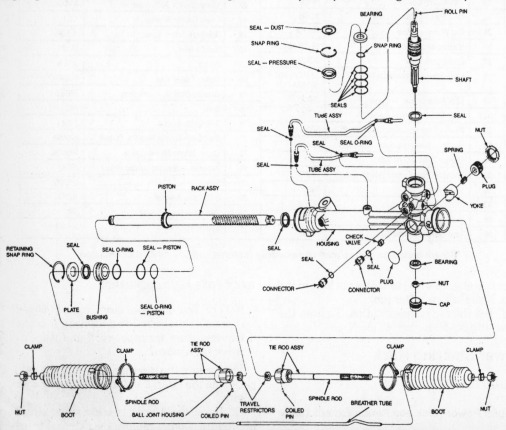

Power steering gear assembly except VAPS system and SHO vehicles

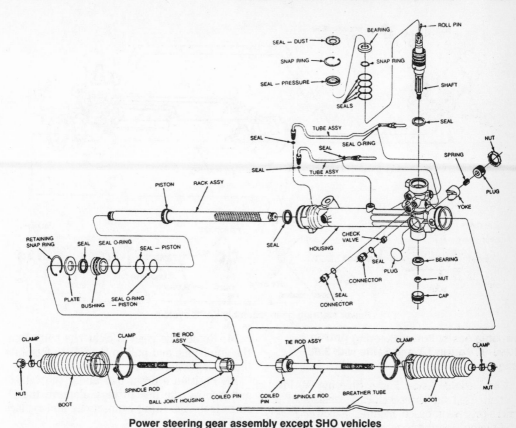

Power steering gear assembly except SHO vehicles

with the transfer lines on the side of the valve.

6. Remove the nuts from the gear mounting bolts. The bolts are pressed into the gear housing and should not be removed during gear removal.

7. Push the weather boot end into the vehicle and lift the gear out of the mounting holes. Rotate the gear so the input shaft will pass between the brake booster and the floor pan. Carefully start working the steering gear out through the left fender apron opening.

8. Rotate the input shaft so it clears the left fender apron opening and complete the removal of the steering gear. If the steering gear seems to be stuck, check the right tie rod to ensure the stud is not caught on anything.

To install:

9. Install new plastic seals on the hydraulic line fittings.

10. Insert the steering gear through the left fender apron. Rotate the input shaft forward to completely clear the fender apron opening.

11. To allow the gear to pass between the brake booster and the floorpan, rotate the input shaft rearward. Align the steering gear bolts to the bolt holes. Install the mounting nuts and torque them to 85–100 ft. lbs. (115–135 Nm). Lower the vehicle.

12. From inside the engine compartment, install the hydraulic pressure and return lines. Tighten the pressure line to 20–25 ft. lbs. (28–33Nm) and the return line to 15–20 ft. lbs. (20–28 Nm). Swivel movement of the lines is normal when the fittings are properly tightened.

13. Raise the vehicle and support safely. Secure the pressure and return lines to the transfer tube with the bundle strap. Install the heat shield.

14. Install the tie rod ends to spindles. Torque the castle nuts to 35 ft. lbs. (48 Nm) and if necessary, torque the nuts a little bit more to align the slot in the nut for the cotter pin. Install the cotter pin.

15. Install the left front wheel and tire assembly and lower the vehicle. Working from inside the vehicle, pull the weather boot end out of the vehicle and install it over the valve housing. Install the intermediate shaft to the steering gear input shaft. Install the the inner weather boot to the floor pan.

16. Install the intermediate shaft to the steering column shaft. Fill the power steering system.

17. Check the system for leaks and proper operation. Adjust the toe setting as necessary.

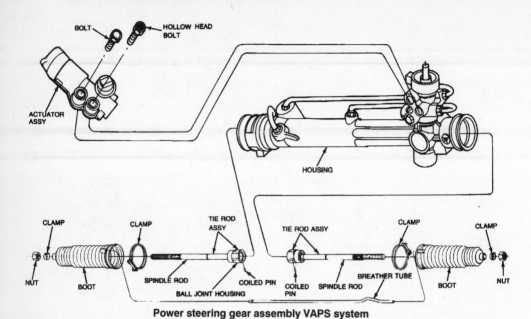

Power steering gear assembly VAPS system

Variable Assist Power Steering (VAPS)
1990–92 Taurus LX and Sable with 3.8L
Engine

The Variable Assist Power Steering (VAPS) system used on these vehicles consists of a micro-processor based module, a power rack and pinion steering gear, an actuator valve assembly, hose assemblies and a high efficiency power steering pump.

1. Disconnect the negative battery cable. Remove the primary steering column boot attachments.

2. Remove the intermediate shaft retaining bolts and remove the intermediate shaft.

3. From inside the passenger compartment, remove the secondary steering column boot.

4. Raise the vehicle and support safely. Remove the front wheels. Support the vehicle under the rear edge of the sub-frame.

5. Remove the tie rod cotter pins and nuts. Remove the tie rod ends from the spindle.

6. Remove the tie rod ends from the shaft.

7. Mark the position of the jam nut to maintain the alignment.

8. Remove the nuts from the gear-to-sub-frame attaching bolts.

9. Remove the rear sub-frame-to-body attaching bolts.

10. Remove the exhaust pipe-to-catalytic converter attachment.

11. Lower the vehicle carefully until the subframe separates from the body; approximately 4 in. (102mm).

12. Remove the heat shield band and fold the shield down.

13. Disconnect the VAPS electrical connector from the actuator assembly.

14. Rotate the gear to clear the bolts from the sub-frame and pull to the left to facilitate line fitting removal.

15. Position a drain pan under the vehicle and remove the line fittings. Remove the O-rings from the fiting connections and replace with new.

16. Remove the left sway bar link.

17. Remove the steering gear assembly through the left wheel well.

To install:

18. Install new O-rings into the line fittings.

19. Place the gear attachment bolts in the gear housing.

20. Install the steering gear assembly through the left wheel well.

21. Connect and tighten the line fittings to the steering gear assembly.

22. Connect the VAPS electrical connector.

23. Position the steering gear into the sub-frame.

24. Install the tie rod ends onto the shaft.

25. Install the heat shield band.

26. Attach the tie rod ends onto the spindle. Install the nuts and secure with new cotter pins.

27. Attach the sway bar link.

28. Raise the vehicle until the sub-frame contacts the body. Install the sub-frame attaching bolts.

29. Install the gear-to-sub-frame nuts and torque to 85–100 ft. lbs. (115–135 Nm).

30. Attach the exhaust pipe to the catalytic converter.

31. Install the wheels and lower the vehicle.

32. Fill the power steering system.

33. Install the secondary steering column boot and attach the intermediate shaft to the

steering gear. Tighten the bolt to 30–38 ft. lbs. (41–51 Nm).

34. Install the primary steering column boot and attach the intermediate shaft to the steering column.

35. Bleed the system and align the front end.

Power Steering Pump

REMOVAL AND INSTALLATION

2.5L and 3.8L Engines

1. Disconnect the negative battery cable. Loosen the tensioner pulley attaching bolts and using the ¹/₂ in. drive hole provided in the tensioner pulley, rotate the tensioner pulley clockwise and remove the belt from the alternator and power steering pulley.

2. Position a drain pan under the power steering pump from underneath the vehicle. Disconnect the hydraulic pressure and return lines.

3. Remove the pulley from the pump shaft using hub puller T69L–10300–B or equivalent. Remove the bolts retaining pump to bracket and remove the power steering pump.

4. Installation is the reverse of the removal procedure. Fill the pump with fluid and check the system for proper operation.

NOTE: *To install the power steering pump pulley, use steering pump pulley replacer T65P–3A733–C or equivalent. When using this tool, the small diameter threads must be fully engaged in the pump shaft before pressing on the pulley. Hold the head screw and turn the nut to install the pulley. Install the pulley face flush with the pump shaft within ± 0.100 in. (0.25mm).*

3.0L Except SHO Engine

1. Disconnect the negative battery cable. Loosen the idler pulley and remove the power steering belt.

2. Remove the radiator overflow bottle in order to gain access to the 3 screws attaching the pulleys to the pulley hub.

3. Matchmark both pulley to hub positions.

4. Remove the pulleys from the pulley hub.

5. Remove the return line from the pump. Be prepared to catch any spilled fluid in a suitable container.

6. Back off the pressure line attaching nut completely. The line will separate from the pump connection when the pump is removed.

7. Remove the pump mounting bolts and remove the pump.

8. Installation is the reverse of the removal procedure. Fill the pump with fluid and check for proper operation.

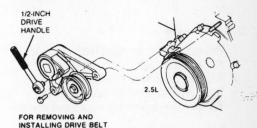

Drive belt assembly — 2.5L engine

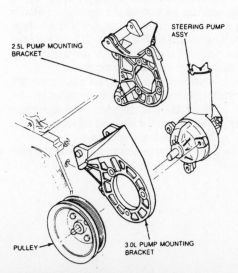

Power steering pump and brackets

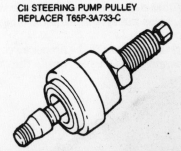

Power steering pump pulley tools

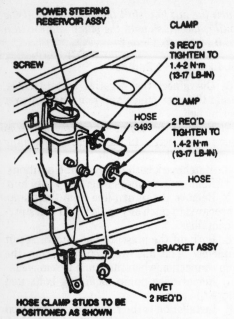

POWER STEERING
RESERVOIR ASSY

SCREW

CLAMP

3 REQ'D
TIGHTEN TO
1.4-2 N·m
(13-17 LB-IN)

CLAMP

HOSE
3493

2 REQ'D
TIGHTEN TO
1.4-2 N·m
(13-17 LB-IN)

HOSE

BRACKET ASSY

RIVET
2 REQ'D

HOSE CLAMP STUDS TO BE
POSITIONED AS SHOWN

Remote power steering pump reservoir — 3.0L SHO engine

3.0L SHO Engine

1. Disconnect the negative battery cable.
2. Remove the engine damper strut.
3. Remove the power steering belt.
4. Raise and support the vehicle safely.
5. Remove the right front wheel and tire assembly.
6. Position a jack under the engine and remove the right rear engine mount.
7. Remove the power steering pump pulley.
8. Place a drain pan under the pump and remove the pressure and return lines from the pump.
9. Remove the 4 pump retaining bolts and remove the pump.
10. Installation is the reverse of the removal procedure. Tighten the pump retaining bolts to 15–24 ft. lbs. (20–33 Nm).

BLEEDING

If air bubbles are present in the power steering fluid, bleed the system by performing the following:

1. Fill the reservoir to the proper level.
2. Operate the engine until the fluid reaches normal operating temperature of 165–175°F (74–79°C).
3. Turn the steering wheel all the way to the left then all the way to the right several times. Do not hold the steering wheel in the far left or far right position stops.
4. Check the fluid level and recheck the fluid for the presence of trapped air. If apparent that air is still in the system, fabricate or obtain a vacuum tester and purge the system as follows:

   a. Remove the pump dipstick cap assembly.
   b. Check and fill the pump reservoir with fluid to the **COLD FULL** mark on the dipstick.
   c. Disconnect the ignition wire and raise the front of the vehicle and support safely.
   d. Crank the engine with the starter and check the fluid level. Do not turn the steering wheel at this time.
   e. Fill the pump reservoir to the **COLD FULL** mark on the dipstick. Crank the engine with the starter while cycling the steering wheel lock-to-lock. Check the fluid level.
   f. Tightly insert a suitable size rubber stopper and air evacuator pump into the reservoir fill neck. Connect the ignition coil wire.
   g. With the engine idling, apply a 15 in. Hg vacuum to the reservoir for 3 minutes. As air is purged from the system, the vacuum will drop off. Maintain the vacuum on the system as required throughout the 3 minutes.
   h. Remove the vacuum source. Fill the reservoir to the **COLD FULL** mark on the dipstick.
   i. With the engine idling, re-apply 15 in. Hg vacuum source to the reservoir. Slowly cycle the steering wheel to lock-to-lock stops for approximately 5 minutes. Do not hold the steering wheel on the stops during cycling. Maintain the vacuum as required.
   j. Release the vacuum and disconnect the vacuum source. Add fluid as required.
   k. Start the engine and cycle the wheel slowly and check for leaks at all connections.
   l. Lower the front wheels.
5. In cases of severe aeration, repeat the procedure.

BRAKE OPERATING SYSTEM

Adjustments

DRUM BRAKES

The rear drum brakes, on your car, are self-adjusting. The only adjustment necessary should be an initial one after new brake shoes have been installed or some type of service work has been done on the rear brake system.

NOTE: *After any brake service, obtain a firm brake pedal before moving the car. Adjusted brakes must not drag. The wheel must turn freely. Be sure the parking brake cables are not too tightly adjusted.*

A special brake shoe gauge is necessary for making an accurate adjustment after installing new brake shoes. The special gauge measures both the drum diameter and the brake shoe setting.

Since no adjustment is necessary except when service work is done on the rear brakes, we will assume that the car is jacked up and safely supported by jackstands, and that the rear drums have been removed.

Measure and set the special brake gauge to the inside diameter of the brake drum. Lift the adjuster lever from the starwheel teeth. Turn the starwheel until the brake shoes are adjusted out to the shoe setting fingers of the brake gauge. Install the hub and drum.

NOTE: *Complete the adjustment by applying the brakes several times. After the brakes have been properly adjusted, check their operation by making several stops from varying forward speeds.*

DISC BRAKES

Front disc brakes require no adjustment. Hydraulic pressure maintains the proper pad-to-disc contact at all times.

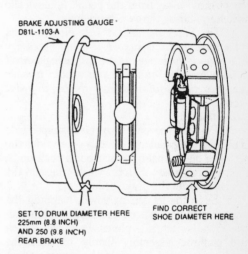

BRAKE ADJUSTING GAUGE
D81L-1103-A

SET TO DRUM DIAMETER HERE
225mm (8.8 INCH)
AND 250 (9.8 INCH)
REAR BRAKE

FIND CORRECT
SHOE DIAMETER HERE

Measuring brake drum diameter for shoe adjustment

On vehicles equipped with rear disc brakes, the main difference is that the rear caliper houses the emergency brake actuator. The rear disc brakes are self-adjusting. Hydraulic pressure maintains the proper pad-to-disc at all times.

BRAKE PEDAL FREE HEIGHT

1. Insert a slender sharp pointed prod through the carpet and sound deadener to dash panel metal.

2. Measure the distance to the center on top of the brake pedal pad.

3. If the position of the pedal is not within specification, check the pedal for worn bushings, missing bushings and loose retaining bolts.

4. Repair defective components as required. Proper specification should be minimum 161mm (6.34 in.) pedal free height to maximum 180mm (7.09 in.) and maximum 59.4mm (2.34 in.) pedal travel.

5. If still not within specification check the brake pedal booster for proper adjustment.

Brake Light Switch

REMOVAL AND INSTALLATION

The mechanical stoplight switch assembly is installed on the pin of the brake pedal arm, so it straddles the master cylinder pushrod.

1. Disconnect the negative battery cable.
2. Disconnect the wire harness at the connector from the switch.

NOTE: *The locking tab must be lifted before the connector can be removed.*

3. Remove the hairpin retainer and white nylon washer. Slide the stoplight switch and the pushrod away from the pedal. Remove the switch by sliding the switch up/down.

NOTE: *Since the switch side plate nearest the brake pedal is slotted, it is not necessary to remove the brake master cylinder pushrod black bushing and 1 white spacer washer nearest the pedal arm from the brake pedal pin.*

To install:

4. Position the switch so the U-shaped side is nearest the pedal and directly over/under the pin. The black bushing must be in position in the push rod eyelet with the washer face on the side away from the brake pedal arm.
5. Slide the switch up/down, trapping the master cylinder pushrod and black bushing between the switch side plates. Push the switch and pushrod assembly firmly towards the brake pedal arm. Assemble the outside white plastic washer to pin and install the hairpin retainer to trap the whole assembly.

NOTE: *Do not substitute other types of pin retainer. Replace only with production hairpin retainer.*

6. Connect the wire harness connector to the switch.
7. Check the stoplight switch for proper operation. Stoplights should illuminate with less than 6 lbs. applied to the brake pedal at the pad.

NOTE: *The stoplight switch wire harness must have sufficient length to travel with the switch during full stroke at the pedal.*

Master Cylinder

REMOVAL AND INSTALLATION

1. Disconnect the negative battery cable.
2. Disconnect the brake lines from the primary and secondary outlet ports of the master cylinder and the pressure control valve.
3. Remove the nuts attaching the master cylinder to the brake booster assembly. Disconnect the brake warning light wire.

4. Slide the master cylinder forward and upward from the vehicle.

To install:

5. Before installation, bench bleed the new master cylinder as follows:

   a. Mount the new master cylinder in a holding fixture. Be careful not to damage the housing.

   b. Fill the master cylinder reservoir with brake fluid.

   c. Using a suitable tool inserted into the booster pushrod cavity, push the master cylinder piston in slowly. Place a suitable container under the master cylinder to catch the fluid being expelled from the outlet ports.

   d. Place a finger tightly over each outlet port and allow the master cylinder piston to return.

   e. Repeat the procedure until clear fluid only is expelled from the master cylinder. Plug the outlet ports and remove the master cylinder from the holding fixture.

6. Mount the master cylinder on the booster. Attach the brake fluid lines to the master cylinder.
7. Install the brake warning light wire.
8. Bleed the system. Operate the brakes several times, then check for external hydraulic leaks.

Power Brake Booster

REMOVAL AND INSTALLATION

1. Disconnect the battery ground cable and remove the brake lines from the master cylinder.
2. Disconnect the manifold vacuum hose and the warning indicator. Remove the retaining nuts and the master cylinder.
3. From under the instrument panel, remove the stoplight switch wiring connector from the switch. Remove the pushrod retainer and outer nylon washer from the brake pin, slide the stoplight switch along the brake pedal pin, far enough for the outer hole to clear the pin.
4. Remove the switch by sliding it upward. Remove the booster to dash panel retaining nuts. Slide the booster pushrod and pushrod bushing off the brake pedal pin.
5. Remove the screws and position the vacuum fitting at the dash panel aside. Position the wire harness aside. Remove the transaxle shift cable and bracket.
6. Move the booster forward until the booster studs clear the dash panel and remove the booster.
7. Installation is the reverse of the removal procedure. Bleed the brake system. Torque the master cylinder to brake booster retaining bolts

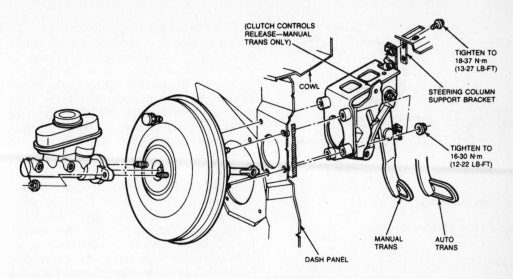

(CLUTCH CONTROLS RELEASE—MANUAL TRANS ONLY)

COWL

TIGHTEN TO 18-37 N·m (13-27 LB-FT)

STEERING COLUMN SUPPORT BRACKET

TIGHTEN TO 16-30 N·m (12-22 LB-FT)

MANUAL TRANS

AUTO TRANS

DASH PANEL

Master cylinder and vacuum booster mounting — except ABS

to 13–25 ft. lbs. (18–34 Nm). Torque the brake booster to fire wall retaining nuts to 12–22 ft. lbs. (16–30 Nm). Torque the brake pedal pivot shaft nut to 10–20 fT. lbs. (14–27 Nm).

NOTE: *If equipped with speed control, the vacuum dump valve must be adjusted if the brake booster has been removed.*

ADJUSTMENT

1. Without disconnecting the brake lines, disconnect the master cylinder and set it away from the booster power unit.

NOTE: *The master cylinder must be supported to prevent damaging the brake lines.*

2. With the engine running, check and adjust the pushrod length as shown in the illus-tration. A force of approximately 5 lbs. applied to the pushrod with the gauge will confirm that the pushrod is seated within the power booster. If adjustment is necessary, grip the rod only by the knurled area.

3. Install the master cylinder on the power booster. Gradually and alternately tighten the retaining nuts to 13–25 ft. lbs.

Proportioning Valve

REMOVAL AND INSTALLATION

The valve for the sedan is mounted to the floorpan near the left rear wheel. The valve for the station wagon are screwed into the master cylinder.

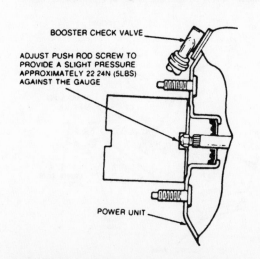

BOOSTER CHECK VALVE

ADJUST PUSH ROD SCREW TO PROVIDE A SLIGHT PRESSURE APPROXIMATELY 22 24N (5LBS) AGAINST THE GAUGE

POWER UNIT

Power brake booster pushrod adjustment

GAUGE DIMENSIONS

76.2 mm (3-INCHES)

31.75 mm (1.25-INCHES)

12.7 mm (0.5-INCH)

5.84 mm (0.23-INCH)

MINIMUM

76.2 mm (3-INCHES)

6.223 mm (0.254-INCH)

MAXIMUM

Power booster adjustment gauge

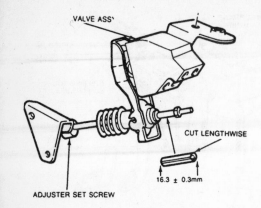

Control valve adjustment — Sedan

Sedan

1. Raise the vehicle and support it safely.
2. Disconnect the brake lines from the valve assembly and note their position.
3. Remove the screw retaining the valve bracket to the lower suspension arm. Remove the 2 screws retaining the valve bracket to the underbody and remove the assembly.

NOTE: *The service replacement valve will have a red plastic gauge clip on the valve and must not be removed until it is installed on the vehicle.*

To install:

4. Make sure the rear suspension is in the full rebound position.
5. Make sure the red plastic gauge clip is in position on the valve and that the operating rod lower adjustment screw is loose.
6. Position the valve lower mounting bracket to the lower suspension arm. Install 1 retaining screw. Make sure the valve adjuster is resting on the lower bracket and tighten the set screw.
7. Connect the brake lines in the same position as removed. Bleed the rear brakes.
8. Remove the red plastic gauge clip and lower the vehicle.

Station Wagon

1. Disconnect the primary or secondary brake line from the master cylinder, as necessary.
2. Loosen and remove the valve from the master cylinder housing.
3. Installation is the reverse of the removal procedure. Fill and bleed the brake system.

Bleeding

PROCEDURE

1. Clean all dirt from the master cylinder filler cap.

2. If the master cylinder is known or suspected to have air in the bore, it must be bled before any of the wheel cylinders or calipers. To bleed the master cylinder, loosen the upper secondary left front outlet fitting approximately ³/₄ turn. Have an assistant depress the brake pedal slowly through it's full travel. Close the outlet fitting and let the pedal return slowly to the fully released position. Wait 5 seconds and then repeat the operation until all air bubbles disappear.
3. Repeat Step 2 with the right-hand front outlet fitting.
4. Continue to bleed the brake system by removing the rubber dust cap from the wheel cylinder bleeder fitting or caliper fitting at the right-hand rear of the vehicle. Place a suitable box wrench on the bleeder fitting and attach a rubber drain tube to the fitting. The end of the tube should fit snugly around the bleeder fitting. Submerge the other end of the tube in a container partially filled with clean brake fluid and loosen the fitting ³/₄ turn.
5. Have an assistant push the brake pedal down slowly through it's full travel. Close the bleeder fitting and allow the pedal to slowly return to it's full release position. Wait 5 seconds and repeat the procedure until no bubbles appear at the submerged end of the bleeder tube. Secure the bleeder fitting and remove the bleeder tube. Install the rubber dust cap on the bleeder fitting.
6. Repeat the procedure in Steps 4 and 5 in the following sequence: left front, left rear and right front. Refill the master cylinder reservoir after each wheel cylinder or caliper has been bled and install the master cylinder cover and gasket. When brake bleeding is completed, the

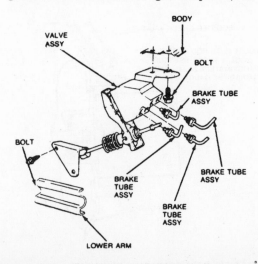

Control valve replacement — Sedan

fluid level should be filled to the maximum level indicated on the reservoir.

7. Always make sure the disc brake pistons are returned to their normal positions by depressing the brake pedal several times until normal pedal travel is established. If the pedal feels spongy, repeat the bleeding procedure.

Rear Brake Bleeding
ABS Systems with a Fully Charged Accumu lator

1. Remove the dust cap from the right rear caliper bleeder fitting. Attach a rubber drain tube to the fitting, making sure the tube fits snugly.

2. Turn the ignition switch to the **RUN** position. This will turn on the electric pump to charge the accumulator, as required.

3. Have an assistant hold the brake pedal in the applied position. Open the bleeder fitting for 10 seconds at a time until an air-free stream of brake fluid flow is observed.

CAUTION: *To prevent possible injury, care must be used when opening the bleeder screws due to the high pressures available from a fully charged accumulator.*

4. Repeat the procedure at the left rear caliper.

5. Pump the brake pedal several times to complete the bleeding procedure.

6. Adjust the fluid level in the reservoir to the MAX mark with a fully charged accumulator.

NOTE: *If the pump motor is allowed to run continuously for approximately 20 minutes, a thermal safety switch inside the motor may shut the motor off to prevent it from overheating. If that happens, a 2–10 minute cool down period is typically required before normal operation can resume.*

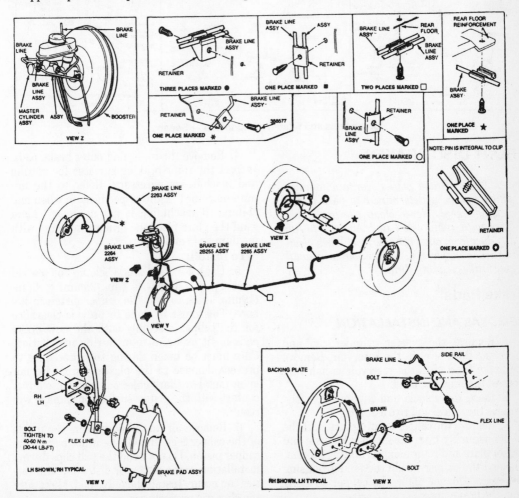

Brake lines and related components — Wagon

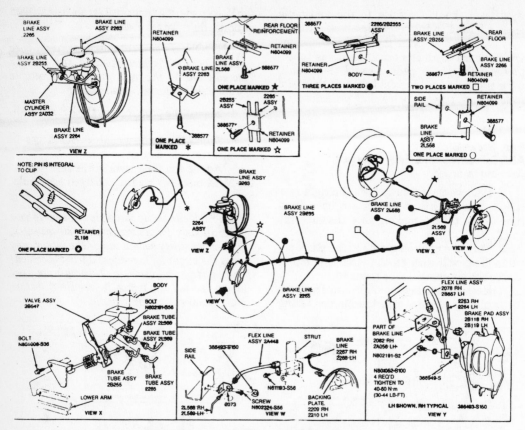

Brake lines and related components — Sedan

FRONT DISC BRAKES

CAUTION: *Brake shoes contain abestos, which has been determined to be a cancer causing agent. Never clean the brake surfaces with compressed air! Avoid inhaling any dust from and brake surface! When cleaning brake surfaces, use a commercially available brake cleaning fluid.*

Brake Pads

REMOVAL AND INSTALLATION

1. Remove the master cylinder cap and check the fluid level in the reservoir. Remove the brake fluid until the reservoir is half full. Discard the removed fluid.

2. Raise the vehicle and support it safely. Remove the wheel and tire assembly.

3. Remove the caliper locating pins. Lift the caliper assembly from the integral knuckle and anchor plate and rotor using a rotating motion. Suspend the caliper inside the fender housing with wire. Do not allow the caliper to hang from the brake hose.

NOTE: *Do not pry directly against the plastic piston or damage will result.*

4. Remove the inner and outer brake pads. Inspect the rotor braking surfaces for scoring and machine as necessary. Refer to the mimimum rotor thickness specification when machining. If machining is not necessary, hand sand the glaze from the braking surfaces with medium grit sand paper.

To install:

5. Use a 4 in. (102mm) C-clamp and a wood block 2 3/4 in. (70mm) × 1 in. (25mm) × 3/4 in. (19mm) thick to seat the caliper piston in it's bore. This must be done to provide clearance for the caliper assembly with the new brake pads to fit over the rotor during installation. Care must be taken during this procedure to prevent damage to the plastic piston. Do not allow metal or sharp objects to come into direct contact with the piston surface or damage will result.

6. Remove all rust buildup from the inside of the caliper legs. Install the inner pad in the caliper piston. Do not bend the pad clips during installation in the piston or distortion and rattles can occur. Install the outer pad. Make sure the clips are properly seated.

7. Install the caliper over the rotor and install the wheel. Lower the vehicle.

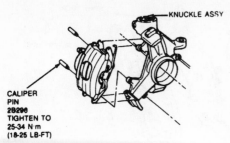

Caliper mounting pin locations

CALIPER
PIN
28296
TIGHTEN TO
25-34 N·m
(18-25 LB-FT)

8. Pump the brake pedal prior to moving the vehicle to position the brake linings. Refill the master cylinder.

INSPECTION

1. Remove the pads from the caliper.
2. Check both the primary and secondary pad for excessive wear.
3. If only one pad is found to be defective, replace both of them not just the defective one.

Brake Caliper

REMOVAL AND INSTALLATION

1. Raise and support the vehicle safely.
2. Remove the wheel and tire assembly. Mark the caliper to ensure that it is reinstalled on the correct knuckle.
3. Disconnect the flexible brake hose from the caliper. Remove the hollow retaining bolt that connects the hose fitting to the caliper.

Remove the hose assembly from the caliper and plug the hose.

4. Remove the caliper locating pins.
5. Lift the caliper off of the rotor, integral knuckle and anchor plate using a rotating motion.

NOTE: *Do not pry directly against the plastic piston or damage to the piston will result.*

To install:

6. Retract the piston fully in the piston bore. Position the caliper assembly above the rotor with the anti-rattle spring under the upper arm of the knuckle. Install the caliper over the rotor with a rotating motion. Make sure the inner and outer shoes are properly positioned and the outer anti-rattle spring is properly positioned. Make sure the correct caliper assembly, as marked during removal, is installed on the correct knuckle. The caliper bleed screw should be positioned on top of the caliper when assembled on the vehicle.

7. Lubricate the locating pins and the inside of the insulators with silicone grease. Install the locating pins through the caliper insulators and hand start the threads into the knuckle attaching holes. Tighten the locating pins to 18–25 ft. lbs. (24–34 Nm).

8. Remove the plug and install the brake hose on the caliper with a new copper washer on each side of the fitting outlet. Insert the attaching bolt through the washers and fittings and tighten to 30–45 ft. lbs. (40–60 Nm).

9. Bleed the brake system, filling the master cylinder as required.

10. Install the wheel and lower the vehicle.

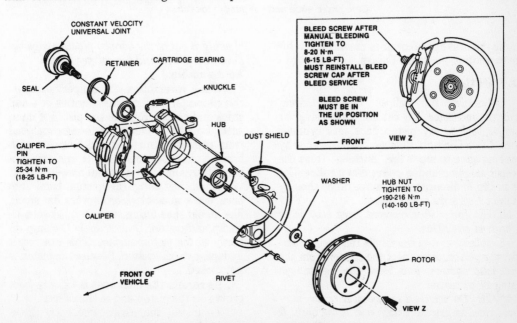

Front disc brake components

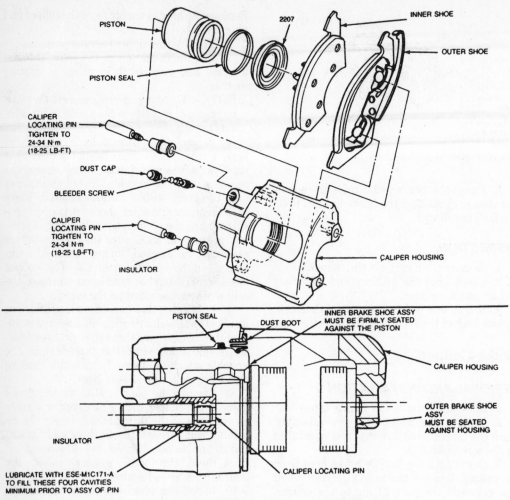

PISTON
2207
INNER SHOE
PISTON SEAL
OUTER SHOE
CALIPER LOCATING PIN TIGHTEN TO 24-34 N·m (18-25 LB-FT)
DUST CAP
BLEEDER SCREW
CALIPER LOCATING PIN TIGHTEN TO 24-34 N·m (18-25 LB-FT)
INSULATOR
CALIPER HOUSING

PISTON SEAL
DUST BOOT
INNER BRAKE SHOE ASSY MUST BE FIRMLY SEATED AGAINST THE PISTON
CALIPER HOUSING
OUTER BRAKE SHOE ASSY MUST BE SEATED AGAINST HOUSING
INSULATOR
LUBRICATE WITH ESE-M1C171-A TO FILL THESE FOUR CAVITIES MINIMUM PRIOR TO ASSY OF PIN
CALIPER LOCATING PIN

Disc brake shoe and caliper pin locations

Pump the brake pedal prior to moving the vehicle to position the brake linings.

OVERHAUL

1. Remove the caliper assembly from knuckle and rotor. Do not use screwdriver or similar tool to pry piston back into cylinder bore. Use a C-clamp. Remove the outer shoe by pushing shoe to move the "buttons" from the caliper housing and slipping down caliper leg until clip is disengaged. Remove inner shoe by pulling it straight out of piston.

NOTE: *Inner shoe removal force may be as high as 10–20 lbs.*

2. If further disassembly is required to service the piston, disconnect the caliper from the hydraulic system, and blow the piston out using air pressure.

NOTE: *Do not use a screwdriver or any similar tool to pry the piston out of the bore. It will result in damage to the piston. Cushion the piston's impact against the caliper when*

blowing it out of the bore by placing rags between the piston and the caliper bridge.

To assemble:

1. When assembling the caliper, examine the piston for surface irregularities or small chips and cracks. Replace the piston if damaged. Be sure to clean the foreign material from the piston surfaces and lubricate with brake fluid before inserting it into the caliper. Always install a new seal and dust boot.

2. When installing the piston back into bore, use a wood block or another flat stock, like an old shoe lining assembly, between C-clamp and piston. Do not apply C-clamp directly to the piston surface. This can result in damage to the piston. Be sure the piston is not cocked.

3. Be certain the dust boot is tight in boot groove on the piston and in the caliper.

4. To install the inner shoe with three-finger clip attached to the shoe into piston, grab each end of shoe, making it square with

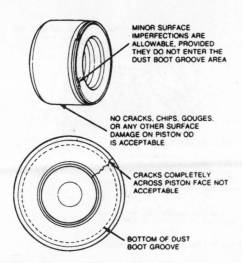

MINOR SURFACE IMPERFECTIONS ARE ALLOWABLE, PROVIDED THEY DO NOT ENTER THE DUST BOOT GROOVE AREA

NO CRACKS, CHIPS, GOUGES, OR ANY OTHER SURFACE DAMAGE ON PISTON OD IS ACCEPTABLE

CRACKS COMPLETELY ACROSS PISTON FACE NOT ACCEPTABLE

BOTTOM OF DUST BOOT GROOVE

Caliper piston inspection

piston. Push firmly until the shoe clip snaps into the piston. Do not allow the shoe or the clip tangs to cock during installation.

Brake Rotor

REMOVAL AND INSTALLATION

1. Raise the vehicle and support it safely.
2. Remove the wheel and tire assembly.
3. Remove the caliper assembly from the rotor. Position the caliper aside and support it with a length of wire. Do not allow the caliper to hang by the brake hose.
4. Remove the rotor from the hub assembly by pulling it off the hub studs. If additional force is required to remove the rotor, apply rust penetrator on the front and rear rotor/hub mating surfaces and then strike the rotor between the studs with a plastic hammer. If this does not work, attach a 3-jaw puller and remove the rotor.

NOTE: *If excessive force must be used to remove the rotor, it should be checked for lateral runout before installation.*

5. Check the rotor for scoring and/or other wear. Machine or replace, as necessary. If machining, observe the minimum thickness specification.
6. Install the rotor in the reverse order of removal.

INSPECTION

Using a micrometer measure the thickness of the rotor in four different places. If the rotor is not within specification either have it cut, if possible, or replace it.

REAR DRUM BRAKES

CAUTION: *Brake shoes contain abestos, which has been determined to be a cancer causing agent. Never clean the brake surfaces with compressed air! Avoid inhaling any dust from and brake surface! When cleaning brake surfaces, use a commercially available brake cleaning fluid.*

Brake Drums

REMOVAL AND INSTALLATION

1986–89

1. Raise and safely support the vehicle.
2. Remove the wheelcover and nut covers, as required. Remove the wheel and tire assembly.
3. Remove the grease cap from the hub. Remove the cotter pin, nut lock, adjusting nut and keyed flatwasher from the spindle. Remove the outer bearing and discard the cotter pin.
4. Remove the hub/drum assembly as a unit. Be careful not to damage the grease seal and inner bearing during removal.

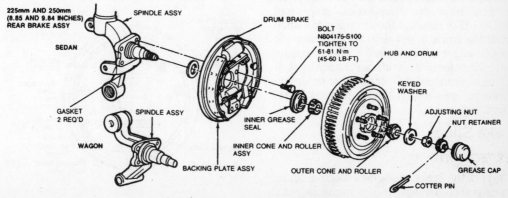

225mm AND 250mm (8.85 AND 9.84 INCHES) REAR BRAKE ASSY

SPINDLE ASSY

DRUM BRAKE

SEDAN

BOLT N804175-S100 TIGHTEN TO 61-81 N·m (45-60 LB-FT)

HUB AND DRUM

KEYED WASHER

GASKET 2 REQ'D

SPINDLE ASSY

INNER GREASE SEAL

ADJUSTING NUT

NUT RETAINER

WAGON

INNER CONE AND ROLLER ASSY

BACKING PLATE ASSY

OUTER CONE AND ROLLER

GREASE CAP

COTTER PIN

Rear brake drum and lining assembly

5. Inspect the drum for scoring and/or other wear. Machine or replace, as necessary. If machining, observe the maximum permissible drum diameter specification.

To install:

6. Inspect and lubricate the bearings, as necessary. Replace the grease seal if any damage is visible.

7. Clean the spindle stem and apply a thin coat of wheel bearing grease.

8. Install the hub and drum assembly on the spindle. Install the outer bearing, keyed flat washer and adjusting nut. Tighten the nut finger-tight.

9. Adjust the wheel bearings. Install the nut retainer and a new cotter pin. Install the grease cap.

10. Install the wheel and tire assembly. Install the wheel cover and nut covers, as required. Lower the vehicle.

1990–92

1. Raise the vehicle and support it safely.

2. Remove the wheel cover.

3. Remove the lugnuts and the wheel and tire assembly.

4. Remove the 2 drum retaining nuts and the drum.

NOTE: *If the drum will not come off, pry the rubber plug from the backing plate inspection hole. Remove the brake line-to-axle retention bracket. This will allow sufficient room to insert suitable brake tools through the inspection hole to disengage the adjusting lever and back off the adjusting screw.*

5. Inspect the drum for scoring and/or other wear. Machine or replace, as necessary. If machining, observe the maximum permissible drum diameter specification.

6. Installation is the reverse of the removal procedure.

INSPECTION

Inspect the brake drums for excessive wear. Using a brake drum inspection gauge tool D81L–1103–A measure the drum inside diameter. If the drum is not within specification it must be either cut or replaced. The maximum inside diameter of the drum is stamped on it. If this number exceeds the drum wear or the refinishing specification the drum must be replaced.

Brake Shoes

INSPECTION

Inspect the brake shoes for excessive lining wear or shoe damage. If the lining is worn below $\frac{1}{32}$ in. (0.8mm) replace both shoes. Re-

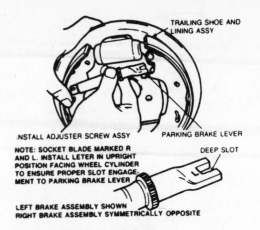

NOTE: SOCKET BLADE MARKED R AND L. INSTALL LETER IN UPRIGHT POSITION FACING WHEEL CYLINDER TO ENSURE PROPER SLOT ENGAGEMENT TO PARKING BRAKE LEVER

LEFT BRAKE ASSEMBLY SHOWN
RIGHT BRAKE ASSEMBLY SYMMETRICALLY OPPOSITE

Rear brake adjuster installation

place lining that has become contaminated with brake fluid, oil or grease.

REMOVAL AND INSTALLATION

1. Raise the vehicle and support it safely.

2. Remove the wheel and tire assembly and the brake drum.

3. Remove the 2 shoe hold-down springs and pins.

4. Lift the brake shoes, springs and adjuster assembly off the backing plate and wheel cylinder assembly. When removing the assembly, be careful not to bend the adjusting lever.

5. Remove the parking brake cable from the parking brake lever.

6. Remove the retracting springs from the lower brake attachments and upper shoe-to-adjusting lever attachment points. This will seperate the brake shoes and disengage the adjuster mechanism.

7. Remove the horse shoe retaining clip and spring washer and slide the lever off the parking brake lever pin on the trailing shoe.

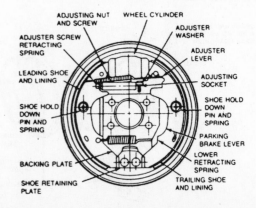

Rear brake lining components

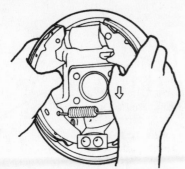

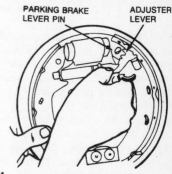

STEP 1

A. ASSEMBLE PARKING BRAKE CABLE TO TRAILING SHOE AND PARKING BRAKE LEVER.

B. INSTALL LOWER RETRACTING SPRING TO LEADING-TRAILING SHOES.

C. INSTALL THIS ASSY TO BACKING PLATE.

LEADING SHOE AND LINING ASSY

STEP 2

INSTALL ADJUSTER SCREW ASSY.

NOTE: SOCKET BLADE MARKED R AND L. INSTALL LETTER IN UPRIGHT POSITION TO ENSURE PROPER SLOT ENGAGEMENT TO PARKING BRAKE LEVER.

PARKING BRAKE LEVER PIN   ADJUSTER LEVER

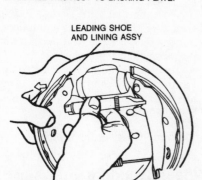

STEP 3

INSTALL ADJUSTER SCREW TO LEADING SHOE AND LINING ASSY.

LEADING SHOE AND LINING ASSY SLOT

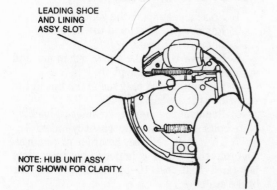

NOTE: HUB UNIT ASSY NOT SHOWN FOR CLARITY.

STEP 4

INSTALL THE ADJUSTER LEVER IN GROOVE OF PARKING BRAKE LEVER PIN.

STEP 5

A. INTALL SHOE HOLD-DOWN SPRINGS AND PINS.

B. INSTALL UPPER RETRACTING SPRING TO LEADING SHOE SLOT- STRETCH SPRING TO INSTALL TO TRAILING SHOE. IF ADJUSTER LEVER DOES NOT CONTACT STAR WHEEL AFTER SPRING INSTALLATION CHECK ADJUSTER SOCKET INSTALLATION.

Drum brake replacement procedure

To install:

8. Apply a light coating of disc brake caliper slide grease at the points where the brake shoes contact the backing plate.

9. Apply a thin coat of lubricant to the adjuster screw threads and socket end of the adjusting screw. Install the stainless steel washer over the socket end of the adjusting screw and install the socket. Turn the adjusting screw into the adjusting pivot nut to the limit of the threads and then back off 1/2 turn.

10. Assemble the parking brake lever to the trailing shoe by installing the spring washer and a new horse shoe retaining clip. Crimp the clip until it retains the lever to the shoe securely.

11. Attach the parking brake cable to the parking brake lever.

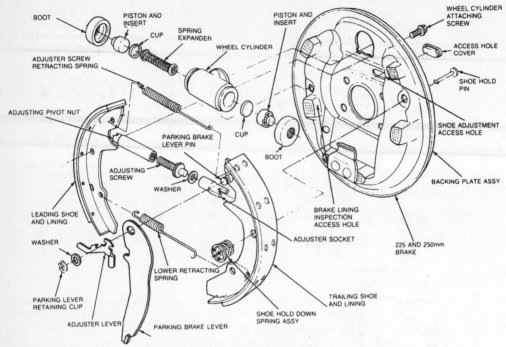

Rear brake assembly and related components

12. Attach the lower shoe retracting spring to the leading and trailing shoe and install to the backing plate. It will be necessary to stretch the retracting spring as the shoes are installed downward over the anchor plate to the inside of the shoe retaining plate.

13. Install the adjuster screw assembly between the leading shoe slot and the slot in the trailing shoe and parking brake lever. The adjuster socket end slot must fit into the trailing shoe and parking brake lever.

14. Assemble the adjuster lever in the groove located in the parking brake lever pin and into the slot of the adjuster socket that fits into the trailing shoe web.

15. Attach the upper retracting spring to the leading shoe slot. Using a suitable spring tool, stretch the other end of the spring into the notch on the adjuster lever. If the adjuster lever does not contact the star wheel after installing the spring, it is possible that the adjuster socket is installed incorrectly.

NOTE: *The adjuster socket blade is marked R for the right-hand or L for the left-hand brake assemblies. The R or L adjuster blade must be installed with the letter R or L in the upright position, facing the wheel cylinder, on the correct side to ensure that the deeper of the 2 slots in the adjuster sockets fits into the parking brake lever.*

16. Adjust the brake shoes.

17. Install the brake drum and wheel and tire assembly. Lower the vehicle.

Wheel Cylinders

REMOVAL AND INSTALLATION

1. Raise and support the vehicle safely.
2. Remove the wheel and tire assembly.
3. Remove the brake drum.
4. Remove the brake shoes, retainers and springs from the backing plate.
5. Disconnect and plug the brake line at the rear-side of the wheel cylinder.
6. Remove the wheel cylinder-to-backing plate bolts and remove the wheel cylinder.
7. To install, reverse the order of removal. Tighten the wheel cylinder-to-backing plate bolts to 8–10 ft. lbs. (10–14 Nm). Bleed the rear brake system.

REAR DISC BRAKES

CAUTION: *Brake shoes contain asbestos, which has been determined to be a cancer causing agent. Never clean the brake surfaces with compressed air! Avoid inhaling any dust from and brake surface! When cleaning brake surfaces, use a commercially available brake cleaning fluid.*

Brake Pads

REMOVAL AND INSTALLATION

1. Remove the master cylinder cap and check the fluid level in the reservoir. Remove the brake fluid until the reservoir is half full. Discard the removed fluid.

2. Raise the vehicle and support it safely.

3. Remove the wheel and tire assembly.

4. Remove the screw retaining the brake hose bracket to the shock absorber bracket. Remove the retaining clip from the parking brake cable at the caliper. Remove the cable end from the parking brake lever.

5. Hold the slider pin hex-heads with an open-end wrench. Remove the upper pinch bolt. Rotate the caliper away from the rotor.

6. Remove the brake pads.

To install:

7. Using a brake piston turning tool, rotate the piston clockwise until it is fully seated. Make sure 1 of the 2 slots in the piston face is positioned so it will engage the nib on the brake pad.

8. Install the brake pads in the anchor plate. Rotate the caliper assembly over the rotor into position on the anchor plate. Make sure the brake pads are installed correctly.

9. Remove the residue from the pinch bolt threads and apply 1 drop of threadlock and sealer. Install and tighten the pinch bolts to 23–26 ft. lbs. (31–35 Nm) while holding the slider pins with an open-end wrench.

10. Attach the cable end to the parking brake lever. Install the cable retaining clip on the caliper assembly. Position the brake flex hose and bracket assembly to the shock absorber bracket and install the retaining screw. Tighten the screw to 8–11 ft. lbs. (11–16 Nm).

11. Install the wheel and tire assembly and lower the vehicle. Pump the brake pedal prior to moving the vehicle to position the brake linings. Refill the master cylinder.

INSPECTION

The rear disc brakes can be inspected through an oval hole in the back of the brake caliper. Raise the rear of the vehicle and remove the wheel and tire assembly to inspect the brake pads. If the brake lining thickness is

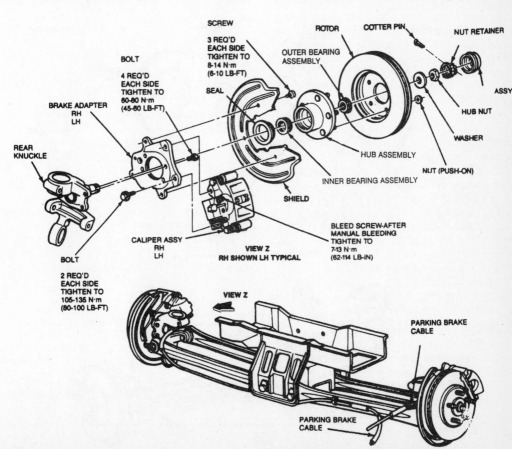

Rear disc brake assembly and related components — except ABS

less than 3mm the brake pads will have to be replaced.

Brake Caliper

REMOVAL AND INSTALLATION

1. Raise and support the vehicle safely.
2. Remove the wheel and tire assembly.
3. Remove the brake flex hose from the caliper assembly.
4. Remove the retaining clip from the parking brake at the caliper. Disengage the parking brake cable end from the lever arm.
5. Hold the slider pin hex-heads with an open-end wrench and remove the pinch bolts. Lift the caliper assembly away from the anchor plate. Remove the slider pins and boots from the anchor plate.

To install:

6. Apply silicone dielectric compound to the inside of the slider pin boots and to the slider pins.
7. Position the slider pins and boots in the anchor plate. Position the caliper assembly on the anchor plate. Make sure the brake pads are installed correctly.

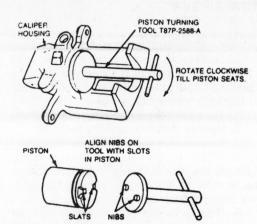

Turning the caliper piston into the bore

8. Remove the residue from the pich bolt threads and apply 1 drop of threadlock and sealer. Install the pinch bolts and tighten to 23–26 ft. lbs. (31–35 Nm) while holding the slider pins with an open-end wrench.
9. Attach the cable end to the parking

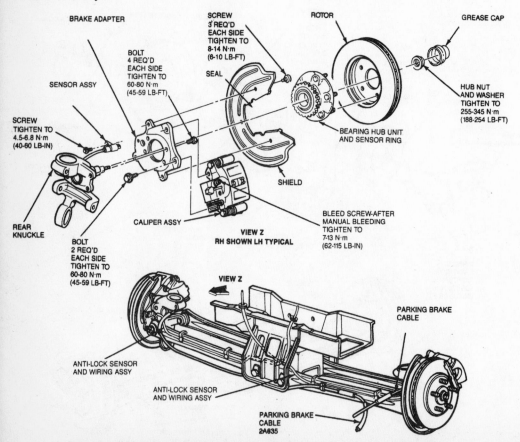

Rear disc brake assembly and related components — ABS except 1992 Wagon

brake lever. Install the cable retaining clip on the caliper assembly.

10. Using new washers, connect the brake flex hose to the caliper. Tighten the retaining bolt to 8–11 ft. lbs. (11–16 Nm).

11. Bleed the brake system, filling the master cylinder as required.

12. Install the wheel and lower the vehicle. Pump the brake pedal prior to moving the vehicle to position the brake pads.

OVERHAUL

1. Remove the caliper assembly from the vehicle.

2. Mount the caliper in a vise. Using a Brake Piston Turning Tool T75P-2588-B or equivalent and turn the piston counterclockwise to remove the piston from the bore.

3. Using a snapring pliers, remove the snapring retaining the pushrod from the caliper.

CAUTION: *The snapring and spring cover are under spring load. Be careful when removing the snapring.*

4. Remove the spring cover, spring, washer, key plate, and pull out the pushrod strut pin from the piston bore.

5. Remove the parking brake lever return

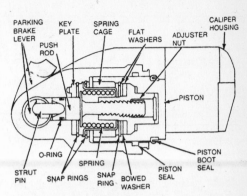

Rear caliper cross-section

spring, unscrew the parking brake lever stop bolt and pull the parking brake lever out of the caliper housing.

6. Clean all medal parts with isopropyl alcohol. Use clean dry compressed air to clean the grooves and passages. Inspect the caliper bores for damage or excessive wear. If the piston is pitted, scratched, or scored replace the piston.

To assemble:

1. Lightly grease the parking brake lever bore and the lever shaft seal with Silicone Die-

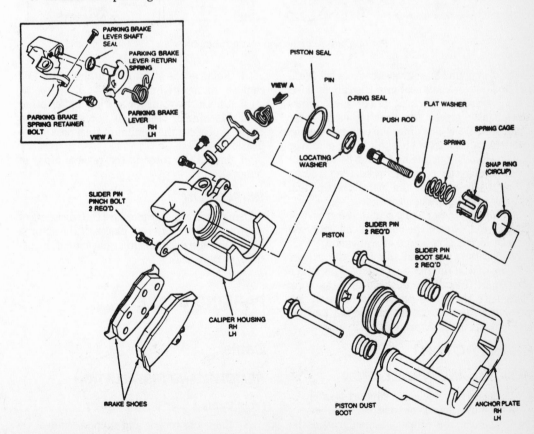

Rear brake caliper — exploded view

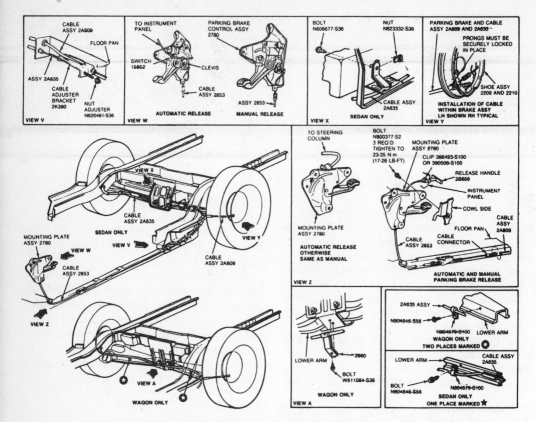

Parking brake cables and related components

lectric Compound or equivalent. Press the parking brake lever shaft seal into the caliper bore.

2. Grease the parking brake shaft recess and slightly grease the parking brake lever shaft. Install the shaft into the caliper housing.

3. Install the lever stop bolt into the caliper housing and torque the bolt to 60–84 inch lbs.

4. Attach the parking brake lever return spring to the stop bolt and install the free end into the parking brake lever slot.

5. Install a new O-ring seal in the groove of the pushrod. Grease the pushrod end with Silicone Dielectric Compound or equivalent.

6. Position the strut pin into the caliper housing and in the recess of the parking brake lever shaft. Install the pushrod into the bore. Make sure the pin is positioned correctly between the shaft recess. Install the flat washer, pushrod, spring and spring cover in order.

BRAKE ROTOR

REMOVAL AND INSTALLATION

1. Raise the vehicle and support it safely.
2. Remove the wheel and tire assembly.
3. Remove the caliper assembly from the rotor and support it with a length of wire. Do not let the caliper hang from the brake line.

4. Remove the 2 rotor retaining nuts and remove the rotor from the hub.

5. Check the rotor for scoring and/or other wear. Machine or replace, as necessary. If machining, observe the minimum thickness specification.

6. Install the rotor in the reverse order of removal.

INSPECTION

Using a micrometer measure the thickness of the rotor in four different places. If the rotor is not within specification either have it cut, if possible, or replace it.

PARKING BRAKE

Cable

REMOVAL AND INSTALLATION

Front Cable

1. Raise the vehicle and support safely.
2. Loosen the adjuster nut at the cable adjuster bracket.

3. Lower the vehicle.

4. Disconnect the cable from the control assembly at the clevis.

5. Raise the vehicle and support safely.

6. At the cable connector, disconnect the front cable from the rear cable.

7. Remove the cable and push-in prong retainer from the cable bracket, using a 13mm box end wrench to depress the retaining prongs. Allow the cable to hang.

8. Push the grommet up through the floor pan and lower the vehicle.

9. Remove the left cowl side panel. Pull the carpet away from the cowl panel.

10. From inside the vehicle, remove the cable end from the clevis and remove the conduit retainer from the control assembly.

11. Pull the cable assembly through the floorpan hole.

To install:

12. Position the cable assembly through the floorpan hole.

13. From inside the vehicle, install the cable end from the clevis and install the conduit retainer to the control assembly.

14. Install the left cowl side panel. Reposition the carpet at the cowl panel.

15. Push the grommet up through the floor pan and raise the vehicle.

16. Install the cable and push-in prong retainer from the cable bracket.

17. At the cable connector, connect the front cable to the rear cable.

18. Lower the vehicle. Connect the cable from the control assembly at the clevis.

19. Raise the vehicle and support it safely. Tighten the adjuster nut at the cable adjuster bracket. Lower the vehicle.

Rear Cable

LEFT SIDE

1. Raise the vehicle and support safely.

2. Remove the parking brake cable adjusting nut.

3. Remove the rear cable end fitting from the front cable connector.

4. Remove the wheel and drum assembly if equipped with drum brakes.

5. Disconnect the brake cable from the parking brake actuating lever. On drum brake vehicles, use a 13mm box end wrench to depress the conduit retaining prongs and remove the cable end pronged fitting from the backing plate. On disc brake vehicles, remove the E-clip from the conduit end of the fitting at the caliper.

6. Push the plastic snap-in grommet rearward to disconnect it from the side rail bracket.

7. Remove the pronged connector from the

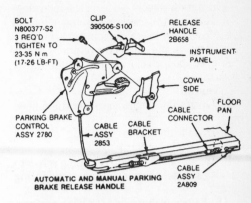

Parking brake cable release mechanism

parking park adjuster bracket. Remove the cable assembly.

To install:

8. Install the pronged connector to the parking park adjuster bracket. Install the cable assembly.

9. Push the plastic snap-in grommet forward to connect it from the side rail bracket.

10. Connect the brake cable to the parking brake actuating lever.

11. Install the wheel and drum assembly if equipped with drum brakes.

12. Install the rear cable end fitting to the front cable connector. Install the parking brake cable adjusting nut. Lower the vehicle.

RIGHT SIDE

1. Raise the vehicle and support it safely.

2. Remove the parking brake cable adjuster nut.

3. Use a 13mm box wrench to remove the conduit retainer prongs and remove the cable from the frame side rail bracket.

4. Remove the rear wheel and drum assembly if equipped with drum brakes.

5. Disconnect the brake cable from the parking brake actuating lever. On drum brake vehicles, use a 13mm box end wrench to depress the conduit retaining prongs and remove the cable end pronged fitting from the backing plate. On disc brake vehicles, remove the E-clip from the conduit end of the fitting at the caliper.

6. On Taurus/Sable sedan vehicles, perform the following:

    a. Remove the brake pressure control valve bracket at the control arm.

    b. Remove the cable retaining screw and clip from the lower suspension arm.

    c. Remove one screw from the cable bracket at the crossmember.

    d. Remove the entire right cable assembly.

7. On station wagon, perform the following:

a. Remove the cable retaining clip and screw from each lower suspension arm.

b. Remove the cable clip retaining screw from lower suspension arm inner mounting bracket.

To install:

8. On station wagon, perform the following:

a. Install the cable retaining clip and screw to each lower suspension arm.

b. Install the cable clip retaining screw to the lower suspension arm inner mounting bracket.

9. On Taurus/Sable sedan vehicles, perform the following:

a. Install the brake pressure control valve bracket at the control arm.

b. Install the cable retaining screw and clip to the lower suspension arm.

c. Install one screw to the cable bracket at the crossmember.

d. Install the right cable assembly.

10. Connect the brake cable to the parking brake actuating lever.

11. Install the rear wheel and drum assembly if equipped with drum brakes. Install the parking brake cable adjuster nut.

12. Lower the vehicle and support it safely. Ensure the pronged fitting is securely locked in place. Adjust the parking brake.

ADJUSTMENT

Except Taurus SHO

1. Make sure the parking brake is fully released. Place the transaxle in the **N** position.

2. Raise the vehicle and support it safely. Working in front of the left rear wheel, tighten the adjusting nut against the cable equalizer causing a rear wheel brake drag. Then loosen the adjusting nut until the rear brakes are fully released. There should be no brake drag.

3. If the brake cables were replaced, stroke the parking brake several times, then release control and repeat Step 2.

4. Check for operation of the parking brake with the vehicle supported and the parking brake fully released. If there is any slack in the cables or if the rear brakes drag when the wheels are turned, adjust as required.

5. Lower the vehicle.

Taurus SHO

1. Make sure the parking brake is fully released.

2. Raise and safely support the vehicle.

3. Tighten the adjusting nut against the cable adjuster bracket until there is a slight,

less than $\frac{1}{16}$ in. (1.6mm), movement of either rear parking brake lever at the caliper.

4. If the brake cables were replaced, stroke the parking brake several times, then release the control and repeat Step 3.

5. Lower the vehicle.

ANTI-LOCK BRAKE SYSTEM

Description And Operation

The Taurus and Sable except with the 2.5L engine offers ABS as an option. The system is standard on the Taurus SHO. The system prevents wheel lockup by automatically modulating the brake pressure during emergency stopping. The system controls each front brake separately and the rear brakes as an axle set. During ABS operation the driver will sense brake pedal pulsation this is normal.

Troubleshooting

Due to the numerous diagnostic charts and need for special tools, diagnosis of the anti-lock

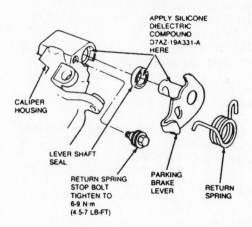

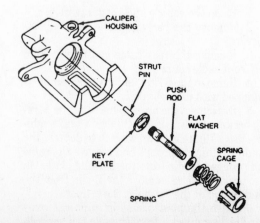

Rear brake caliper and parking brake assembly

brake systems, fall outside the confines of this manual. For diagnosis of anti-lock brakes, please refer to the Ford Taurus/Mercury Sable Total Car Care Manual, Part No. 8251.

Anti-Lock Brake System Service

PRECAUTIONS

Failure to observe the following precautions may result in system damage.
• Before servicing any high pressure component, be sure to discharge the hydraulic pressure from the system.
• Do not allow the brake fluid to contact any of the electrical connectors.
• Use care when opening the bleeder screws due to the high pressures available from the accumulator.

RELIEVING SYSTEM PRESSURE

Before servicing any components which contain high pressure, it is mandatory that the hydraulic pressure in the system be discharged. To discharge the system, turn the ignition **OFF** and pump the brake pedal a minimum of 20 times until an increase in pedal force is clearly felt.

Hydraulic Control Unit (HCU)

REMOVAL AND INSTALLATION

1. On all vehicles, except Taurus SHO, disconnect the battery cables and remove the battery from the vehicle. Remove the battery tray. Remove the 3 plastic push pins holding the acid shield to the HCU mounting bracket and remove the acid shield. On Taurus SHO, it is only necessary to disconnect the negative battery cable and remove the electronic control unit and it's mounting bracket from the top of the HCU mounting bracket.
2. Disconnect the 19-pin connector from the HCU to the wiring harness and disconnect the 4-pin connector from the HCU to the pump motor relay.
3. Remove the 2 lines from the inlet ports and the 4 lines from the outlet ports of the HCU. Plug each port to prevent brake fluid from spilling onto the paint and wiring.
4. Remove the 3 nuts retaining the HCU assembly to the mounting bracket and remove the assembly from the vehicle. The nut on the front of the HCU also retains the relay mounting bracket.
5. Install in the reverse order of removal. Tighten the 3 retaining nuts to 12–18 ft. lbs. (16–24 Nm) and the brake lines to 10–18 ft. lbs. (14–24 Nm). Bleed the brake system and check for fluid leaks.

Wheel Sensors

REMOVAL AND INSTALLATION

Front

1. Disconnect the sensor connector located in the engine compartment.
2. For the right front sensor, remove the 2 plastic push studs to loosen the front section of the splash shield in the wheel well. For the left front sensor, remove the 2 plastic push studs to loosen the rear section of the splash shield.
3. Thread the sensor wires through the holes in the fender apron. For the right front sensor, remove the 2 retaining clips behind the splash shield.
4. Raise and support the vehicle safely. Remove the wheel.
5. Disengage the sensor wire grommets at the height sensor bracket and from the retainer clip on shock strut above the spindle.
6. Loosen the sensor retaining screw and remove the sensor assembly from the front knuckle.
7. Install in the reverse order of removal. Tighten the sensor retaining screws to 40–60 inch lbs. (4.5–6.8 Nm).

Rear

EXCEPT WAGON

1. Remove the rear seat and seat back insulation.
2. Disconnect the sensor from the harness and tie the sensor connector to the rear seat sheet metal bracket with wire or string.
3. Push the sensor wire grommet and connector through the floorpan drawing the string or wire with the sensor connector.
4. Disconnect the string or wire from the sensor from underneath the vehicle. Raise and support the vehicle safely.
5. Disconnect the routing clips from the suspension arms and remove the sensor retaining bolts from the rear brake adapters.
6. Install in the reverse order of removal. Use string or wire to pull the new sensor connector through the hole in the floorpan. Tighten the sensor retaining bolt to 40–60 inch lbs. (4.6–6.8 Nm).

STATION WAGON

1. Raise and support the vehicle safely.
2. Remove the sensor wire with the attached grommet from the hole in the floorpan.
3. Disconnect the sensor from the harness.
4. Remove the routing clips. Remove the sensor retaining bolt. Remove the sensor.
5. Installation is the reverse of the removal procedure.

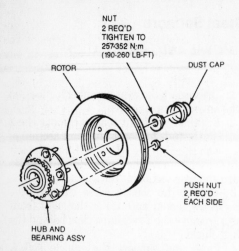

NUT
2 REQ'D
TIGHTEN TO
257-352 N·m
(190-260 LB-FT)

ROTOR

DUST CAP

PUSH NUT
2 REQ'D
EACH SIDE

HUB AND
BEARING ASSY

Rear speed indicator ring location

Rear Speed Indicator Ring

REMOVAL AND INSTALLATION

1. Raise and support the vehicle safely. Remove the tire and wheel assembly.
2. Remove the caliper. Remove the rotor.
3. Remove the rear hub assemby.
4. Position the hub assembly in an arbor pressand press the hub out of the speed sensor ring.
5. Installation is the reverse of the removal procedure.

Front Speed Indicator Ring

REMOVAL AND INSTALLATION

1. Raise and support the vehicle safely.
2. Remove the outboard CV joint.
3. Position the speed sensor removal tool

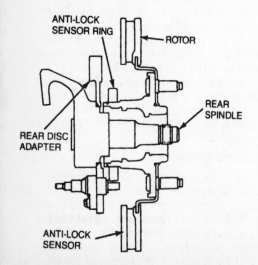

ANTI-LOCK
SENSOR RING

ROTOR

REAR
SPINDLE

REAR DISC
ADAPTER

ANTI-LOCK
SENSOR

Rear wheel speed sensor

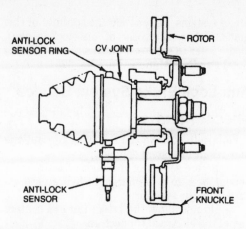

ANTI-LOCK
SENSOR RING

CV JOINT

ROTOR

ANTI-LOCK
SENSOR

FRONT
KNUCKLE

Front wheel speed sensor

T88P–20202–A in a press. Position the CV joint on the tool.

4. Remove the speed sensor ring from the CV joint.
5. Installation is the reverse of the removal procedure.

Pedal Travel Switch

REMOVAL AND INSTALLATION

1. Disconnect the wiring harness lead at the switch.
2. Unsnap the switch hook from the pin on the dump valve adapter bracket.
3. Remove the switch from its mounting.
4. Installation is the reverse of the removal procedure.

Electronic Control Unit (ECU)

REMOVAL AND INSTALLATION

The ECU is located on the front right side of the engine compartment next to the washer bottle, except on Taurus SHO. On Taurus SHO it is mounted on the left side on top of the HCU mounting bracket.

1. Disconnect the negative battery cable.
2. Disconnect the 55-pin connector from the ECU. Unlock the connector by completely pulling up the lever. Move the top of the connector away from the ECU until all terminals are clear, then pull the connector up out of the slots in the ECU.
3. Remove the screws attaching the ECU and remove the ECU.
4. Install in the reverse order of removal. Connect the 55-pin connector by installing the bottom part of the connector into the slots in the ECU and pushing the top portion of the connector into the ECU. Then pull the locking lever completely down to ensure proper installation. Tighten the retaining screws to 15–20 inch lbs. (1.7–2.3 Nm).

Bleeding

PROCEDURE

The anti-lock brake system must be bled in 2 steps.

1. The master cylinder and hydraulic control unit must be bled using the Rotunda Anti-Lock Brake Breakout Box/Bleeding Adapter tool No. T90P–50–ALA or equivalent. If this procedure is not followed, air will be trapped in the hydraulic control unit which will eventually lead to a spongy brake pedal. To bleed the master cylinder and the hydraulic control unit, disconnect the 55-pin plug from the electronic control unit and install the Anti-Lock Brake Breakout Box/Bleeding Adapter to the wire harness 55-pin plug.

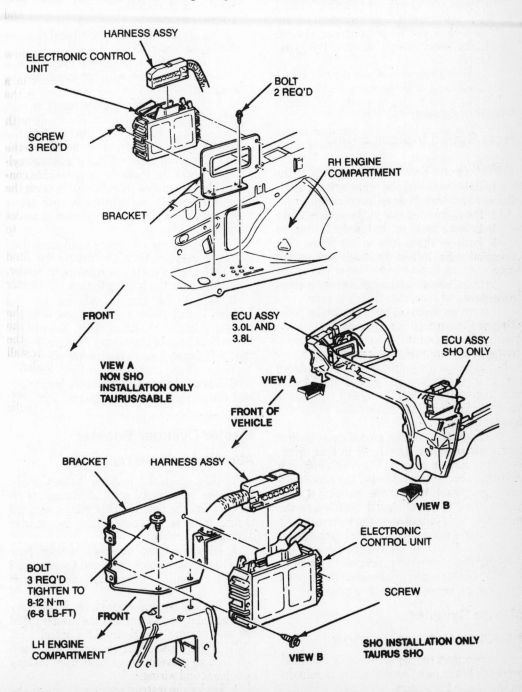

ECU unit location and related components

a. Place the Bleed/Harness switch in the **BLEED** position.

b. Turn the ignition to the **ON** position. At this point the red off light should come ON.

c. Push the motor button on the adapter down to start the pump motor. The red OFF light will turn OFF and the green ON light will turn ON. The pump motor will run for 60 seconds after the motor button is pushed. If the pump motor is to be turned off for any reason before the 60 seconds has elapsed, push the abort button to turn the pump motor off.

d. After 20 seconds of pump motor operation, push and hold the valve button down. Hold the valve button down for 20 seconds and then release it.

e. The pump motor will continue to run for an additional 20 seconds after the valve button is released.

2. The brake lines can now be bled in the normal fashion. Bleed the brake system by removing the rubber dust cap from the caliper fitting at the right-hand rear of the vehicle. Place a suitable box wrench on the bleeder fitting and attach a rubber drain tube to the fitting. The end of the tube should fit snugly around the bleeder fitting. Submerge the other end of the tube in a container partially filled with clean brake fluid and loosen the fitting ³/₄ turn.

3. Have an assistant push the brake pedal down slowly through it's full travel. Close the bleeder fitting and allow the pedal to slowly return to it's full release position. Wait 5 seconds and repeat the procedure until no bubbles appear at the submerged end of the bleeder tube. Secure the bleeder fitting and remove the bleeder tube. Install the rubber dust cap on the bleeder fitting.

4. Repeat the bleeding procedure at the left front, left rear and right front in that order. Refill the master cylinder reservoir after each caliper has been bled and install the master cylinder and gasket. When brake bleeding is completed, the fluid level should be filled to the maximum level indicated on the reservoir.

5. Always make sure the disc brake pistons are returned to their normal positions by depressing the brake pedal several times until normal pedal travel is established. If the pedal feels spongy, repeat the bleeding procedure.

Master Cylinder

REMOVAL AND INSTALLATION

1. Disconnect the negative battery cable. Depress the brake pedal several times to exhaust all vacuum in the system.

2. Disconnect the brake lines from the primary and secondary outlet ports of the master cylinder and the pressure control valve.

3. Remove the nuts attaching the master cylinder to the brake booster assembly. Disconnect the brake warning light wire. Disconnect the Hydraulic Control Unit (HCU) supply hose at the master cylinder and secure in a position to prevent loss of brake fluid.

4. Slide the master cylinder forward and upward from the vehicle.

To install:

5. Before installation, bench bleed the new master cylinder as follows:

a. Mount the new master cylinder in a holding fixture. Be careful not to damage the housing.

b. Fill the master cylinder reservoir with brake fluid.

c. Using a suitable tool inserted into the booster pushrod cavity, push the master cylinder piston in slowly. Place a suitable container under the master cylinder to catch the fluid being expelled from the outlet ports.

d. Place a finger tightly over each outlet port and allow the master cylinder piston to return.

e. Repeat the procedure until clear fluid only is expelled from the master cylinder. Plug the outlet ports and remove the master cylinder from the holding fixture.

6. Mount the master cylinder on the booster. Install a new seal in the groove in the master cylinder mounting face. Attach the brake fluid lines to the master cylinder. Install the HCU supply hose to the master cylinder.

7. Install the brake warning light wire.

8. Bleed the system. Operate the brakes several times, then check for external hydraulic leaks.

Master Cylinder Booster

REMOVAL AND INSTALLATION

1. Disconnect the negative battery cable. Pump the brake pedal until all vacuum is removed from the booster. This will prevent the O-ring from being sucked into the booster during disassembly.

2. Disconnect the manifold vacuum hose from the booster check valve and the electrical connector from the master cylinder reservoir cap.

3. Remove the brake lines from the primary and secondary outlet ports of the master cylinder and remove the Hydraulic Control Unit (HCU) supply hose. Plug the ports and reservoir feed to prevent brake fluid from leaking onto paint and wiring.

4. Under the instrument panel, remove the stoplight switch wiring connector from the

switch. Disengage the pedal position switch from the stud. Remove the hairpin retainer and outer nylon washer from the pedal pin. Slide the stoplight switch off the brake pedal just far enough for the outer arm to clear the pin. Remove the switch.

5. Remove the booster to dash panel attaching nuts. Slide the bushing and booster pushrod off the brake pedal pin.

6. Move the booster forward until the booster studs clear the dash panel. Remove the booster and master cylinder assembly.

7. Place the booster and master cylinder assembly on a bench. Remove the 2 nuts attaching the master cylinder to the booster and remove the master cylinder.

To install:

8. Slide the master cylinder onto the booster studs. Make sure the O-ring is in place in the groove on the master cylinder and install the 2 attaching nuts. Tighten the nuts to 13–25 ft. lbs. (18–34 Nm).

9. Under the instrument panel, install the booster pushrod and bushing on the brake pedal pin. Fasten the booster to the dash panel with self-locking nuts. Tighten the nuts to 13–25 ft. lbs. (18–34 Nm).

10. Position the stoplight switch so it straddles the booster pushrod with the switch slot towards the pedal blade and hole just clearing the pin. Slide the switch completely onto the pin.

11. Install the outer nylon washer on the pin and secure all parts to the pin with the hairpin retainer. Make sure the retainer is fully installed and locked over the pedal pin. Install the stoplight switch wiring connector.

12. Install the pedal travel switch. To adjust the switch, push the switch plunger fully into the switch housing. This zeros out the switch adjustment so it can be automatically reset to the correct dimension during the following steps:

  a. Slowly pull the arm back out of the switch housing past the detent point. At this point it should be impossible to reattach the arm to the pin unless the brake pedal is forced down.

  b. Depress the brake pedal until the switch hook can be snapped onto the pin. Snap the hook onto the pin and pull the brake pedal back up to it's normal at rest position. This automatically sets the switch to the proper adjustment.

13. Connect the brake lines to the master cylinder and tighten to 10–18 ft. lbs. (14–24 Nm). Connect the HCU supply hose to the resorvoir.

14. Connect the manifold vacuum hose to the booster check valve and the electrical connector to the master cylinder reservoir cap.

15. Connect the negative battery cable and bleed the brake system.

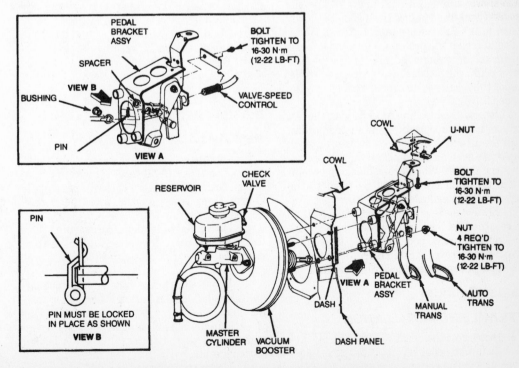

ABS power brake booster and related components

BRAKE SPECIFICATIONS

All measurements in inches unless noted

Year	Model	Master Cylinder Bore	Brake Disc			Brake Drum Diameter			Minimum Lining Thickness	
			Original Thickness	Minimum Thickness	Maximum Runout	Original Inside Diameter	Max. Wear Limit	Maximum Machine Diameter	Front	Rear
1986	Taurus	0.875	1.024	0.974	0.003	8.86⑥	0.60	0.059	0.125	0.030
	Sable	0.875	1.024	0.974	0.003	8.86⑥	0.60	0.059	0.125	0.030
1987	Taurus	0.875	1.024	0.974	0.003	8.86⑥	0.60	0.059	0.125	0.030
	Sable	0.875	1.024	0.974	0.003	8.86⑥	0.60	0.059	0.125	0.030
1988	Taurus	0.875	1.024	0.974	0.003	8.86⑥	0.60	0.059	0.125	0.030
	Sable	0.875	1.024	0.974	0.003	8.86⑥	0.60	0.059	0.125	0.030
1989	Taurus	0.875	1.024	0.974	0.003	8.86⑥	0.60	0.059	0.125	0.030
	Taurus SHO	0.875	1.024⑤	0.974①	③	8.86⑥	0.60	0.059	0.125	0.123
	Sable	0.875	1.024	0.974	0.003	8.86⑥	0.60	0.059	0.125	0.030
1990	Taurus	0.875	1.024	0.974	0.003	8.86⑥	0.60	0.059	0.125	0.030
	Taurus SHO	0.875	1.024⑤	0.974①	③	8.86⑥	0.60	0.059	0.125	0.123
	Sable	0.875	1.024	0.974	0.003	8.86⑥	0.60	0.059	0.125	0.030
1991	Taurus	0.875	1.024	0.974	0.003	8.86⑥	0.60	0.059	0.125	0.030
	Taurus SHO	0.875	1.024⑤	0.974①	③	8.86⑥	0.60	0.059	0.125	0.123
	Sable	0.875	1.024	0.974	0.003	8.86⑥	0.60	0.059	0.125	0.030
1992	Taurus	0.875	1.024⑤	0.974②	③	8.86⑥	0.60	0.059	0.125	0.030④
	Taurus SHO	0.875	1.024⑤	0.974②	③	8.86⑥	0.60	0.059	0.125	④
	Sable	0.875	1.024⑤	0.974②	③	8.86⑥	0.60	0.059	0.125	0.030④

① Front and Rear
② Rear—0.900
③ Front—0.003
　Rear—0.002
④ Rear disc—0.123
⑤ Rear disc—1.02
⑥ Optional—9.84

Body

10

EXTERIOR

Doors

REMOVAL AND INSTALLATION

Front

1. Support the door using padded jack or other suitable tool.
2. Remove the hinge attaching bolts and nuts from the door and remove the door.

3. Disconnect the wiring harness connectors, if so equipped.
4. If the door is to be replaced, transfer the following components to the new door if they are in usable condition: trim panel, watershield, outside moldings, clips, window regulators and the door latch components.

To install:

5. Position the door hinges and partially tighten the bolts.
6. Align the door and tighten the bolts securely to 13–21 ft. lbs.

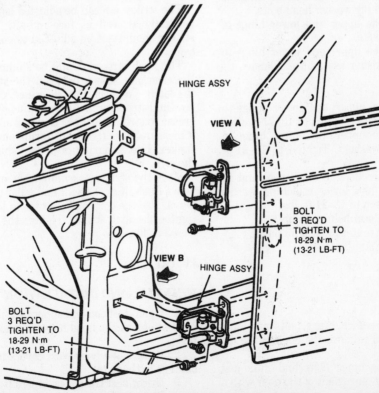

Front door hinges and related components

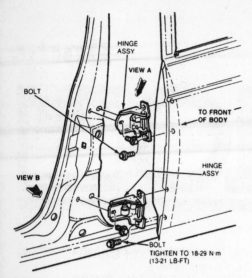

Rear door hinges and related components

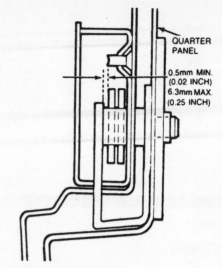

Front and rear door latches

Rear

1. Remove the scuff plate.
2. Remove the center pillar trim panel.
3. Remove the seat belt assembly.
4. Open the door and support it with a padded jack or other suitable tool.
5. Scribe the hinge location to the door for a reference point when reinstalling.
6. Remove the upper and lower hinge-to-door hinge attaching washer head bolts.
7. Remove the upper and lower hinge-to-body attaching bolts.
8. Remove the upper and lower hinge-to-body nut and washer assemblies. Remove the hinges.

To install:

9. Install the upper and lower hinge-to-body attaching bolts. Tighten to 13–21 ft. lbs.
10. Install the upper and lower hinge-to-body nuts and washers. Tighten to 13–21 ft. lbs.
11. Position the door to the hinges and install the upper and lower attaching washer head bolts. Tighten to 13–21 ft. lbs.
12. Install the seat belt assembly.
13. Install the center pillar trim panel.
14. Install the scruff plate.

ADJUSTMENT

Door Alignment

1. Determine which hinge bolts and nuts must be loosened to move the door in the desired direction.
2. Loosen the hinge bolts and nuts just enough to permit movement of the door with a padded pry bar.
3. Move the door the distance estimated to

be necessary. Tighten the hinge bolts and nuts to 13–21 ft. lbs., and check the door fit to ensure there is no bind or interference with the adjacent panel.

4. Repeat the operation until the desired fit is obtained, and check the striker plate alignment for proper door closing.

Door Latch Striker

The striker pin can be adjusted laterally and vertically as well as fore-and-aft. The latch striker should not be adjusted to correct door sag.

The latch striker should be shimmed to get the clearance shown between the striker and the latch. To check this clearance, clean latch jaws and striker area. Apply a thin layer of dark grease to striker. As door is closed and opened, a measurable pattern will result on the latch striker. Use a maximum of two shims under the striker.

Move the striker assembly in or out to provide a flush fit at the door and pillar or quarter panel. Use the correct Torx® bit to loosen and tighten the latch striker. Tighten the striker to 24–33 ft. lbs.

Hood

REMOVAL AND INSTALLATION

1. Open the hood and support it in the open position. Mark the hood hinge locations on the hood.
2. Protect the body with covers to prevent damage to the paint.
3. Disconnect the gas cylinders from hood.
4. Place thick rags under the corners of the hood. Remove the two bolts attaching each

hinge to the hood, taking care not to let the hood slip when bolts are removed.

5. Remove the hood from the vehicle.

To install:

6. Position the hood-to-hood hinges. Install the attaching bolts.

7. Adjust the hood for even fit between the fenders and for a flush fit with the front of the fenders.

8. Adjust the hood for a flush fit with the top of the cowl and the fenders.

9. Adjust the hood latch, if necessary. Remove the protective fender covers.

10. Attach the gas cylinder to the hood.

ADJUSTMENT

Hood

The hood can be adjusted fore-and-aft and side-to-side by loosening two hood-to-hinge attaching bolts at each hinge. Then, reposition hood as required and tighten the hood-to-hinge attaching bolts. Always use protective fender covers.

To raise or lower the rear of the hood, loosen the hood hinge pivot nut. The pivot can now move up or down. Raise or lower hood as necessary to obtain a flush condition at the rear of the hood with the fenders. Then, tighten the hood hinge pivot nut to 16–25 ft. lbs.

Hood Latch

Before adjusting hood latch mechanism, make certain that the hood is properly aligned. The hood latch can be moved from side-to-side to align with the opening in the hood inner panel.

Adjust latch up and down to obtain a flush fit with front fenders.

1. Loosen the hood latch attaching bolts in the radiator support until they are just loose enough to move the latch from side-to-side.

2. Move the latch from side-to-side to align it with the opening in the hood.

3. Loosen the locknuts on the two hood bumpers. Lower the bumpers.

4. Move the hood latch up and down as required to obtain a flush fit between the top of hood and the fenders when upward pressure is applied to the front of the hood. Then, tighten the hood latch attaching screw to 7–10 ft. lbs.

5. Raise the two hood bumpers to eliminate any looseness at the front of hood when closed. Then, tighten the hood bumper locknuts.

6. Open and close the hood several times to check its operation.

Hood Latch Control Cable

REMOVAL AND INSTALLATION

1. From inside the vehicle, release the hood.

2. Remove the two bolts retaining the latch to the upper radiator support.

3. Remove the screw retaining the cable end retainer to the latch assembly.

4. Disengage the cable by rotating it out of the latch return spring.

5. To facilitate installing the cable, fasten a length of fishing line about 8 ft. long to latch the end of the cable.

6. From the inside vehicle, unseat the sealing grommet from the cowl side, remove the cable mounting bracket attaching screws and carefully pull the cable assembly out. Do not pull the "fish line" out.

To install:

7. Using the previously installed fish line, pull the new cable assembly through the retaining wall, seat the grommet securely, and install the cable mounting bracket attaching screws.

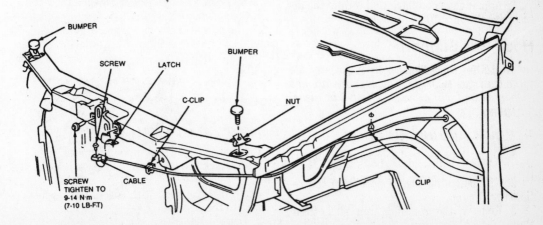

Hood latch and control cable mounting—exterior

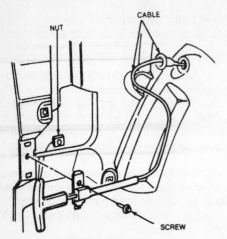

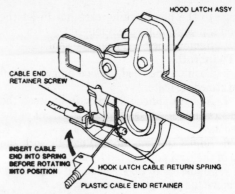

Hood latch and control cable mounting — interior

8. Thread the terminal end of cable into the hood latch return spring.

9. Route the cable through the V-slot on the latch and install the cable end retaining screw.

10. Check the hood latch cable release operation before the closing hood. Adjust if necessary.

Hood latch

REMOVAL AND INSTALLATION

1. From inside the vehicle release the hood.

2. Remove the two bolts retaining the latch to the upper radiator support.

3. Remove the two bolts retaining the hood latch assembly-to-radiator support and remove the latch.

To install:

1. Engage the hood latch to the control cable and position the hood latch to the radiator support.

2. Install the two attaching bolts.

3. Adjust the hood latch and torque the attaching bolts to 7–10 ft. lbs.

Hood Gas Support

CAUTION: *Do not heat or try to disassemble the hood gas supports. The supports are gas charged and will explode if heated or disassembled.*

REMOVAL AND INSTALLATION

1. Open the hood and temporarily support it.

2. Disengage the gas support from the retainer at the top.

3. Remove the retaining pin at bottom. Remove the gas support.

To install:

Hood latch assembly

4. Position the gas support. Install the retaining pin at the bottom.

5. Engage the gas support to the retainer at top.

6. Remove the temporary support and close the hood.

Tailgate

REMOVAL AND INSTALLATION

NOTE: *The liftgate removal and install is a two person operation and should not be attempted alone.*

1. Before removing the hinge-to-roof frame attachments at both hinges, scribe the location of each hinge on roof frame and bolt locations.

2. Remove the hinge-to-roof frame screw and washer assembly at each hinge.

3. Remove the liftgate from the vehicle.

To install:

4. Position the hinges to the scribe marks on the roof frame and reverse the removal pro-

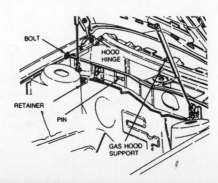

Gas hood support hinges and related components

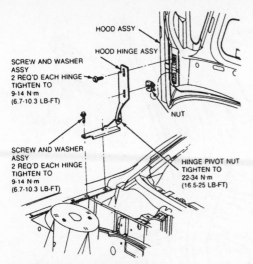

HOOD ASSY

HOOD HINGE ASSY

SCREW AND WASHER
ASSY
2 REQ'D EACH HINGE
TIGHTEN TO
9-14 N·m
(6.7-10.3 LB-FT)

NUT

SCREW AND WASHER
ASSY
2 REQ'D EACH HINGE
TIGHTEN TO
9-14 N·m
(6.7-10.3 LB-FT)

HINGE PIVOT NUT
TIGHTEN TO
22-34 N·m
(16.5-25 LB-FT)

Hood hinge adjustment location

cedures. Torque the hinge-to-roof screw and washer assemblies to 16–25 ft. lbs.

ALIGNMENT

The wagon liftgate latch has double-bolt construction, designed to be equivalent in function and load capacity to side door latches. The latch is non-adjustable. All movement for adjustment is accomplished in the striker which has a 5.5mm radial range. This latch system has a two-position latching system. The closing latch cycle consists of a secondary position which latches the liftgate but does not seal the door to the liftgate weatherstrip. The primary position holds the liftgate door firmly into the weatherstrip. Water leaks and rattles may occur because the liftgate appears closed. However, it may only be closed to the secondary (first) position. Be sure that positive primary engagement of the liftgate latch is achieved upon closing. To check it, use the following procedure:

LATCH FUNCTION TEST

1. Close the liftgate to an assumed primary condition.
2. Insert the key into the key cylinder. Place your left hand on the liftgate glass above and left of the key cylinder. Press firmly on the glass with your left hand and slowly turn the key until the latch is released. Return the key and release your left hand pressure. The liftgate should be in the secondary position.
3. If while performing the above test shows that the liftgate will not close to primary the position, adjust the striker rearward (to rear of vehicle) so that a positive primary engagement is obtained upon closing the liftgate.

Liftgate Support Cylinder

REMOVAL AND INSTALLATION

1. Open the liftgate and temporarily support it.
2. The lift cylinder end fitting is a spring-clip design and removal is accomplished by sliding a small screwdriver under it and prying up to remove it from the ball stud.
3. Remove the support cylinder.
To install:
4. Install each cylinder to the C-pillar and the liftgate bracket ball socket by pushing the cylinder's locking wedge onto the socket.
5. Close the liftgate. Check the support cylinder operation.

Trunk Lid

REMOVAL AND INSTALLATION

NOTE: *The trunk lid removal and install is a two person operation and should not be attempted alone.*

1. Remove the four hinge-to-trunk lid screws and remove the trunk lid.
2. To install, position the trunk lid to the

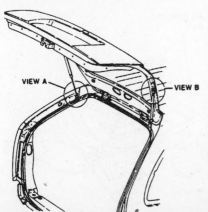

VIEW A

VIEW B

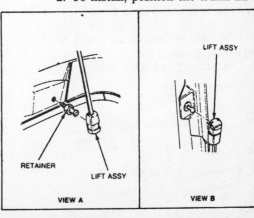

LIFT ASSY

RETAINER

LIFT ASSY

VIEW A

VIEW B

Liftgate support-cylinder location

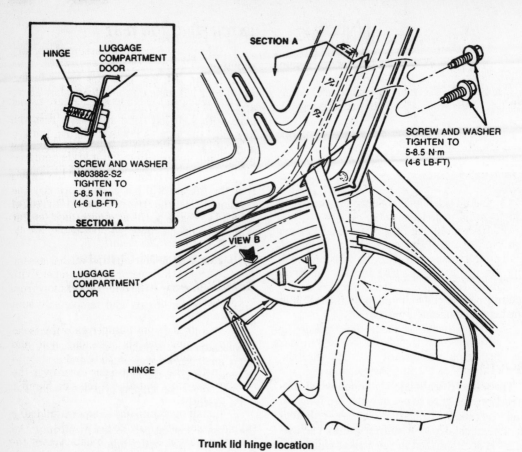

Trunk lid hinge location

hinges and install the four hinge-to-trunk lid retaining bolts.

3. Adjust for fit as outlined below.

4. Torque the retaining bolts to 16–25 ft. lbs.

ALIGNMENT

The trunk lid door can be shifted fore and aft and from side to side on all models.

The trunk lid door should be adjusted for an even and parallel fit with the door opening. The door should also be adjusted up and down for a flush fit with the surrounding panels. Care should be taken not to damage the trunk lid door or surrounding body panel.

Fore-and-aft and up-and-down adjustment of the trunk lid is achieved by loosening the hinge-to-trunk lid attaching screw, shifting the trunk lid to the proper fit and tightening the attaching screw to 7–10 ft. lbs.

TRUNK LID TORSION BAR LOADING

1. Locally obtain the following materials.

a. A round flexible cable, 6mm in diameter by 1220mm long.

b. One 1/4 in. (6mm) cable clamp.

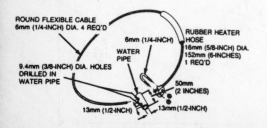

Trunk lid torsion bar adjusting tool

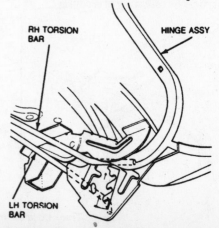

Trunk lid torsion bar positioning

c. A water pipe, $^1/_2$ in. (12.7mm) diameter by 2 in. (51mm) long.

d. A piece of heater hose, $^5/_8$ in. (16mm) diameter and 6 in. (153mm) long.

2. Properly assembly the materials. Safety glasses **MUST** be worn when performing this operation

3. Install the torsion bar by inserting one end into the hole provided in the luggage compartment door hinge and resting the other end in the upper groove of the opposite hinge support.

4. Install the home made tool on the end of the torsion bar to be loaded.

5. With an assistant, place a long flat pry bar over the top of the torsion bar to be loaded. Pull on the torsion bar with the assistant holding the pry bar, guide the torsion bar down along the rear edge of the support into the lower groove of the hinge support and lock it in the lowest adjustment notch.

6. Using the home made tool, install the tool into the end of the torsion bar and unlock the bar by pulling toward you with the tool. Work the torsion bar into the second notch and release. If further adjustment is needed proceed to step 7.

7. Using a $^3/_8$ in. drive, $^1/_2$ in. deep well socket and a 6 in. (153mm) extension. Position the socket over the end of the torsion bar and unlock the bar. Reposition the torsion bar up the hinge support to the top notch and release.

Front Bumper

REMOVAL AND INSTALLATION

1. Remove the four screws attaching the front bumper to the fenders. There are two on each side. Disconnect the cornering light electrical connectors, if equipped.

2. Remove the four bolts attaching the front bumper cover-to-radiator grille reinforcement assembly and remove the front bumper cover.

CAUTION: *Never apply heat to the bumper energy absorbers! The heat may cause the material inside to expand and flow out of the absorbers or crack the metal!*

3. Remove the four nut and washer assemblies attaching the isolator to the bumper. With an assistant remove the bumper assembly from the vehicle.

To install:

1. Install the front bumper onto the isolator and torque the six attaching bolt and washer assemblies to 12.5–20 ft. lbs.

2. Install the front bumper cover over the bumper assembly and attach the side bumper cover supports.

3. Install the four front bumper-to-radiator support bolts and torque to 6–10 ft. lbs.

4. Install the four front bumper cover-to-fender attaching bolts and torque to 9–12 inch lbs.

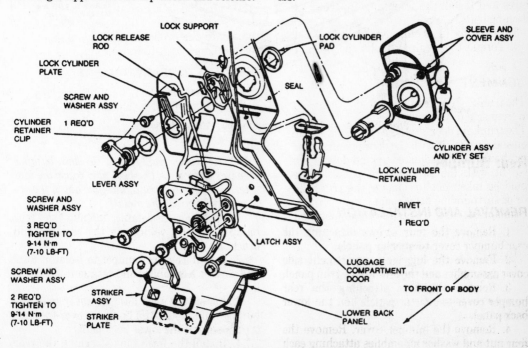

Trunk lid latch and lock assembly

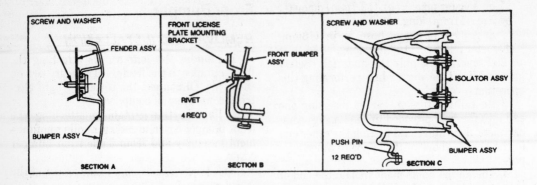

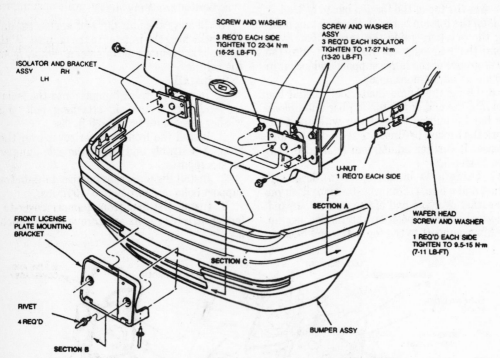

Front bumper and related components—1986–91 Taurus

Rear Bumper

REMOVAL AND INSTALLATION

1. Remove the four screws attaching the rear bumper cover-to-quarter panels.

2. Remove the luggage compartment side cover assemblies and the lower back trim panel.

3. Remove the nuts attaching the rear bumper cover-to-quarter panels and the lower back panel.

4. Remove the bumper cover. Remove the four nut and washer assemblies attaching each isolator to the rear bumper. With an assistant remove the rear bumper.

To install:

NOTE: *Never apply heat to the bumper energy absorbers! The heat may cause the material inside to expand and flow out of the absorbers or crack the metal!*

1. With an assistant, install the rear bumper on the vehicle at the isolator and bracket.

2. Install the six bumper-to-isolator nuts and washer assemblies and torque to 33–51 ft. lbs.

3. Install the rear bumper cover over the bumper and install the bumper cover-to-quarter panels and the lower back panel.

4. Install the push pins attaching the rear bumper cover to the rear bumper.

5. Install the luggage compartment side cover and lower trim panels.

6. Install the four screws attaching the rear bumper cover-to-quarter panels and torque the screws to 6–10 ft. lbs.

Grille

REMOVAL AND INSTALLATION

Except 1992 Sable

1. Raise and support the hood.
2. Remove the two plastic retainers at the top corners with a cross-recessed pry bar.
3. Depress the tabs on the spring clips attached to the grille at both lower corners and pull the grille assembly from the vehicle.

To install:

1. Position the bottom of the spring tabs in the slots in the grille opening reinforcement.
2. Rotate the top of the grille toward the rear of the vehicle until the upper tab slots line up with the holes in the grille opening.
3. Install the two plastic retainers through the holes in the grille and grille opening. Retainers can be tapped in.

1992 Sable

1. Remove the front bumper.
2. Remove the four nuts retaining the stone deflector ends to the front fender.
3. Remove the two screws retaining the stone deflector end bracket to the fender at the wheel opening.
4. Remove the nine shoulder screws retaining the stone deflector to the grille opening reinforcement panel. Remove the grille. Remove the stone deflector.
5. Installation is the reverse of the removal procedure.

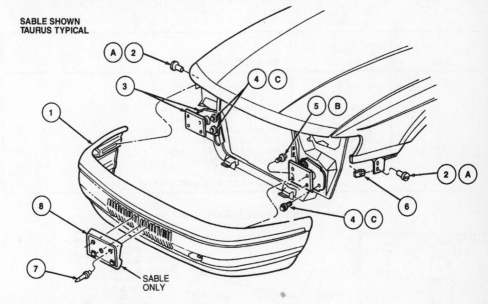

SABLE SHOWN
TAURUS TYPICAL

SABLE ONLY

Item	Part Number	Description
1	17750	Front Bumper Assy
2A	N804984-S100	Screw and Washer (1 Req'd Each Side)
3	17D809	Isolator and Bracket Assy
4C	N606689-S2	Screw and Washer Assy (3 Req'd Each Isolator)
5B	N805433-S54	Screw and Washer (3 Req'd Each Side)
6	N800538-S101	U-Nut (1 Req'd Each Side)
7	N805150-S	Rivet (3 Req'd) (Sable Only)
8	17N397	Bracket Assy (Sable Only)
A		Tighten to 9-21 N·m (7-15 Lb-Ft)
B		Tighten to 22-34 N·m (17-25 Lb-Ft)
C		Tighten to 17-27 N·m (13-19 Lb-Ft)

Front bumper and related components—1992 Taurus except SHO

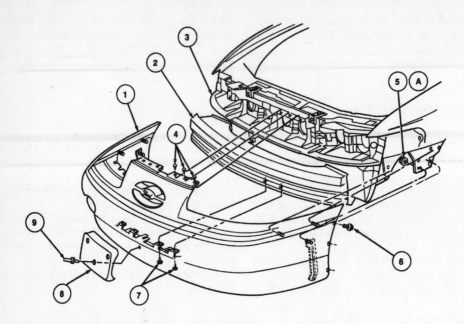

Item	Part Number	Description
1	17D957	Front Bumper Cover
2	—	Front Bumper Assy
3	8A164	Grille Opening Reinforcement
4	388577-S	Push Pin (3 Req'd each side)
5A	N621906-S36	Nut and Washer (2 Req'd each side)
6	388577-S	Push Pin (1 Req'd each side)
7	388577-S	Push Pin (2 Req'd each side)
8	17A385	Front L / Plate Bracket
9	N803043-S	Rivet (3 Req'd)
A		Tighten to 4.5-6.9 N·m (40-61 Lb-In)

Front bumper and related components – 1992 Taurus SHO

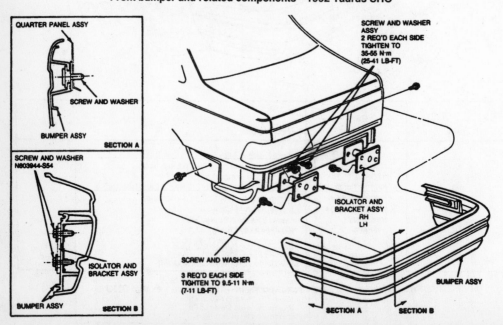

Rear bumper and related components – 1986–91 except wagon

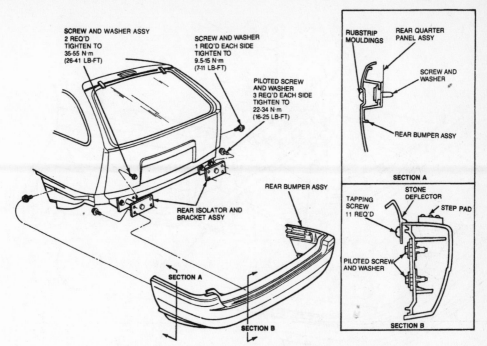

SCREW AND WASHER ASSY
2 REQ'D
TIGHTEN TO
35-55 N·m
(26-41 LB-FT)

SCREW AND WASHER
1 REQ'D EACH SIDE
TIGHTEN TO
9.5-15 N·m
(7-11 LB-FT)

PILOTED SCREW
AND WASHER
3 REQ'D EACH SIDE
TIGHTEN TO
22-34 N·m
(16-25 LB-FT)

REAR ISOLATOR AND
BRACKET ASSY

REAR BUMPER ASSY

SECTION A

SECTION B

RUBSTRIP
MOULDINGS

REAR QUARTER
PANEL ASSY

SCREW AND
WASHER

REAR BUMPER ASSY

SECTION A

TAPPING
SCREW
11 REQ'D

STONE
DEFLECTOR

STEP PAD

PILOTED SCREW
AND WASHER

SECTION B

Rear bumper and related components — 1986–92 wagon

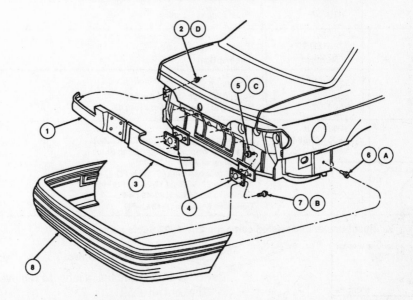

Item	Part Number	Description
1	42A341	LH Lower Back Finish Panel Assy
2D	N621926-S36	Nut and Washer (10 Req'd)
3	42A340	RH Lower Back Finish Panel Assy
4	17D788 RH	Isolator and Bracket Assy
	17D864 LH	
5C	N606702-S2	Screw and Washer (2 Req'd Each Side)
6A	N804984-S100	Screw and Washer (1 Req'd Each Side)
7B	N805433-S54	Screw and Washer (3 Req'd Each Side)
8	17775	Rear Bumper Assy
	17D780	Bumper and Cover Assy (Taurus SHO Only)
A		Tighten to 9.5-15 N·m (8-11 Lb-Ft)
B		Tighten to 22-34 N·m (17-25 Lb-Ft)
C		Tighten to 35-55 N·m (26-40 Lb-Ft)
D		Tighten to 9-14 N·m (7-10 Lb-Ft)

Rear bumper and related components — 1992 Taurus except wagon

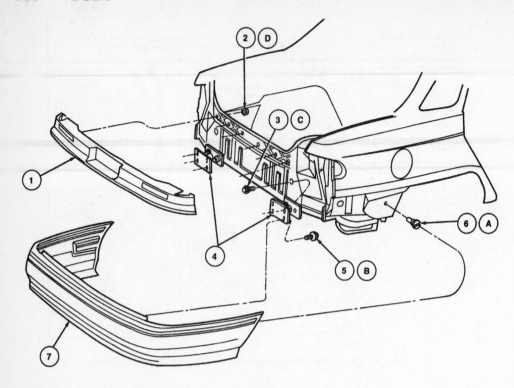

Item	Part Number	Description
1	17805	Deflector Assy
2D	N621927	Nut and Washer Assy (6 Req'd)
3C	N606702-S2	Screw and Washer Assy (2 Req'd)
4	17D788 RH	Isolator and Bracket Assy
	17D864 LH	
5B	N805433-S54	Screw and Washer (2 Req'd Each Side)
6A	N804984-S100	Screw and Washer (1 Req'd Each Side)
7	17775	Rear Bumper Assy
A		Tighten to 9.5-15 N·m (8-11 Lb-Ft)
B		Tighten to 22-34 N·m (17-25 Lb-Ft)
C		Tighten to 35-55 N·m (26-40 Lb-Ft)
D		Tighten to 9-14 N·m (7-10 Lb-Ft)

Rear bumper and related components—1992 Sable except wagon

Outside Mirror

REMOVAL AND INSTALLATION

Standard Manual Type
Right Hand Only

1. Remove the inside sail cover.
2. Remove the nut and washer assemblies and lift the mirror off the door.

To install:

3. Install the mirror on door.
4. Install and tighten the nut and washer assemblies.
5. Install the inside sail cover.

Left Hand Remote Control

1. Pull the nob assembly to remove it from the control shaft.
2. Remove the interior sail cover retainer screw and remove the cover.
3. Loosen the setscrew retaining control assembly to the sail cover.
4. Remove the mirror attaching nuts, washers and grommet. Remove the mirror and the control assembly.

To install:

5. Seat the grommet in the outer door panel and position the mirror to the door. Install the attaching nuts and washer and tighten to 25–39 inch lbs.
6. Route the control mechanism through

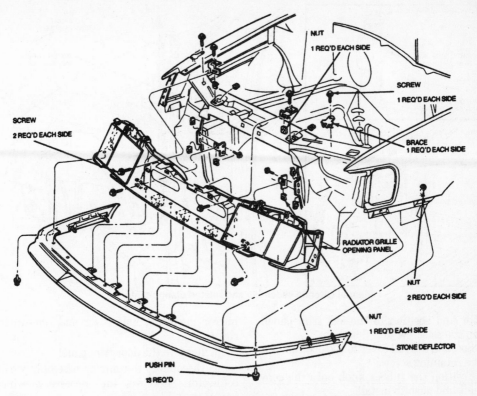

NUT
1 REQ'D EACH SIDE

SCREW
1 REQ'D EACH SIDE

BRACE
1 REQ'D EACH SIDE

SCREW
2 REQ'D EACH SIDE

RADIATOR GRILLE
OPENING PANEL

NUT
2 REQ'D EACH SIDE

NUT
1 REQ'D EACH SIDE

STONE DEFLECTOR

PUSH PIN
13 REQ'D

Front grille assembly and related components — Sable

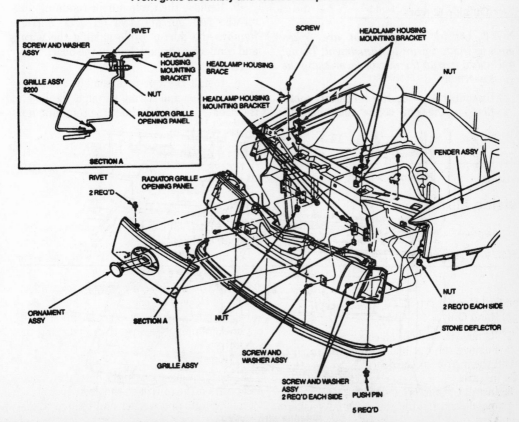

SCREW AND WASHER
ASSY

RIVET

HEADLAMP
HOUSING
MOUNTING
BRACKET

GRILLE ASSY
8200

NUT

RADIATOR GRILLE
OPENING PANEL

SECTION A

SCREW

HEADLAMP HOUSING
BRACE

HEADLAMP HOUSING
MOUNTING BRACKET

HEADLAMP HOUSING
MOUNTING BRACKET

NUT

FENDER ASSY

RIVET
2 REQ'D

RADIATOR GRILLE
OPENING PANEL

ORNAMENT
ASSY

SECTION A

NUT

GRILLE ASSY

SCREW AND
WASHER ASSY

SCREW AND WASHER
ASSY
2 REQ'D EACH SIDE

NUT

STONE DEFLECTOR

NUT
2 REQ'D EACH SIDE

PUSH PIN
5 REQ'D

Front grille assembly and related components — Taurus

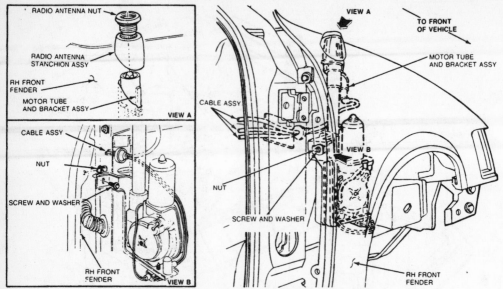

Manual antenna assembly and related components

the door and position to the sail trim panel. Tighten the setscrew to 2–6 inch lbs.

7. Position the sail cover to the door and install the retaining screw.

8. Position the rubber knob onto the control shaft and push to install.

Power Outside Mirrors

NOTE: *Outside mirrors that are frozen must be thawed prior to adjustment. Do not attempt to free-up the mirror by pressing the glass assembly.*

1. Disconnect the negative (–) battery cable.
2. Remove the one screw retaining the

mirror mounting hole cover and remove the cover.

3. Remove the door trim panel.

4. Disconnect the mirror assembly wiring connector. Remove the necessary wiring guides.

5. Remove the three mirror retaining nuts on the sail mirrors, two on door mirrors. Remove the mirror while guiding the wiring and connector through hole in the door.

To install:

6. Install the mirror assembly by routing the connector and wiring through the hole in the door. Attach with the three retaining nuts

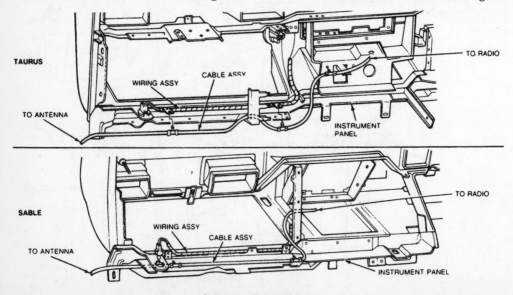

Antenna wire routing

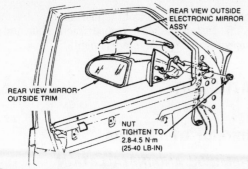

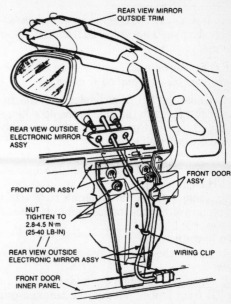

REAR VIEW OUTSIDE
ELECTRONIC MIRROR
ASSY

REAR VIEW MIRROR
OUTSIDE TRIM

NUT
TIGHTEN TO
2.8-4.5 N·m
(25-40 LB-IN)

Power remote control mirror assembly—sail mounted

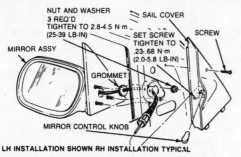

NUT AND WASHER
3 REQ'D
TIGHTEN TO 2.8-4.5 N·m
(25-39 LB-IN)

SAIL COVER

SET SCREW
TIGHTEN TO
.23-.68 N·m
(2.0-5.8 LB-IN)

SCREW

MIRROR ASSY

GROMMET

MIRROR CONTROL KNOB

LH INSTALLATION SHOWN RH INSTALLATION TYPICAL

Manual remote control mirror assembly

REAR VIEW OUTSIDE
ELECTRONIC MIRROR
ASSY

FRONT DOOR ASSY

NUT
TIGHTEN TO
2.8-4.5 N·m
(25-40 LB-IN)

REAR VIEW OUTSIDE
ELECTRONIC MIRROR ASSY

FRONT DOOR
INNER PANEL

FRONT DOOR
ASSY

WIRING CLIP

Power remote control mirror assembly—door mounted

Antenna

REMOVAL AND INSTALLATION

on the sail mirrors, two on the door mirrors. Tighten the retaining nuts.

7. Connect the mirror wiring connector and install the wiring guides.

8. Replace the mirror mounting hole cover and install one screw.

9. Replace the door trim panel.

10. Connect the negative (–) battery cable.

1. Push in on the sides of glove compartment door and place the door in the hinged downward position.

2. Disconnect the antenna lead from the RH rear of the radio and remove the cable from the heater or the A/C cable retaining clips.

3. Remove the RH front fender liner. Unplug the coaxial cable from the power an-

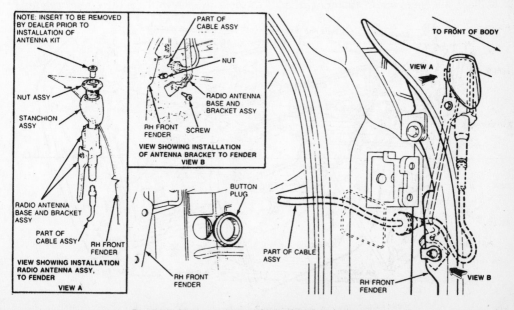

NOTE: INSERT TO BE REMOVED BY DEALER PRIOR TO INSTALLATION OF ANTENNA KIT

NUT ASSY

STANCHION
ASSY

RADIO ANTENNA
BASE AND BRACKET
ASSY

PART OF
CABLE ASSY

RH FRONT
FENDER

**VIEW SHOWING INSTALLATION
RADIO ANTENNA ASSY,
TO FENDER**
VIEW A

PART OF
CABLE ASSY

NUT

RADIO ANTENNA
BASE AND
BRACKET ASSY

RH FRONT
FENDER

SCREW

**VIEW SHOWING INSTALLATION
OF ANTENNA BRACKET TO FENDER**
VIEW B

BUTTON
PLUG

RH FRONT
FENDER

TO FRONT OF BODY

VIEW A

PART OF CABLE
ASSY

RH FRONT
FENDER

VIEW B

Power antenna assembly and related components

tenna assembly or the manual antenna base assembly. Unplug the power lead from the power antenna.

NOTE: *The manual antenna mast is detachable from the base and cable assembly.*

4. Under the RH front fender, pull the antenna cable through the hole in the door hinge pillar and remove the antenna cable assembly from the wheel well area.

5. To remove the manual or power antenna base, remove the antenna nut and stanchion on the RH front fender.

6. Remove the lower antenna base screw and remove either the manual antenna base or the power antenna.

To install:

1. Install the antenna assembly and base screw.

2. Install the antenna nut and stanchion on the RH front fender. Torgue the antenna nut to 4 inch lbs.

3. Pull the antenna cable through the hole in the door hinge pillar. Attach the antenna cable lead to the RH rear of the radio.

4. Attach the cable to the heater and A/C

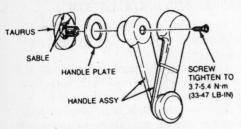

Manual door handle removal tool

housing. Install the front fender liner.

5. Install the glove compartment door and reposition the glove compartment.

INTERIOR

Interior Trim Panels

REMOVAL AND INSTALLATION

1986–88

1. Remove the window regulator handle by unsnapping the handle cover from the base and expose the attaching screw. Remove the screw, handle and the wearplate.

2. Remove the door pull handle retaining screws and cover. Remove the handle.

3. Remove the upper trim panel retaining screws and remove the panel.

4. On Taurus vehicles, remove the trim panel opening panel.

5. Remove the exterior rearview mirror

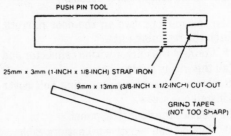

Door panel removal tool

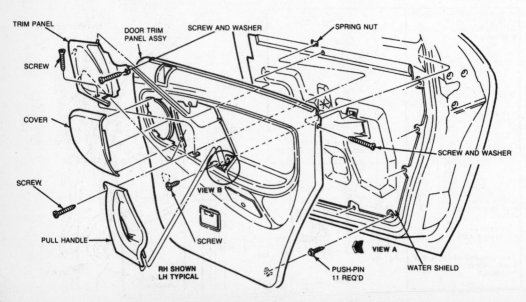

Rear door panel and related components – 1986–88 Taurus

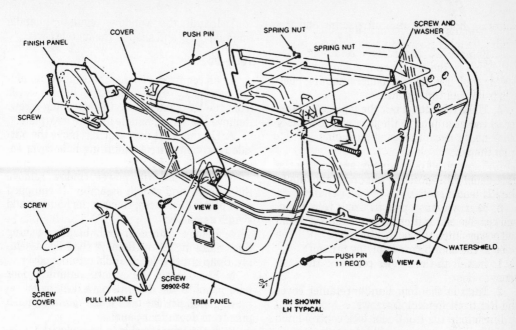

Rear door panel and related components—1986–88 Sable

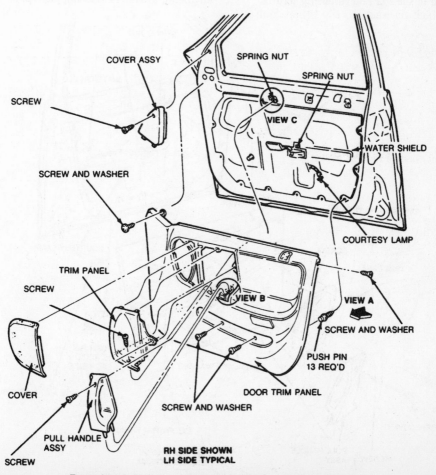

Front door panel and related components—1986–88 Taurus

mounting hole cover retaining screw and the cover.

6. Remove all the screws retaining door trim panel to the door, using a door panel removing tool, pry the trim panel retaining push pins from door inner panel.

7. If the trim panel is to be replaced, transfer all the push pins to the new panel. Replace any bend, broken or missing push pins.

To install:

1. Connect all door wiring and install the trim panel into position ensuring the upper ridge is seated properly in the door channel.

2. Snap the push pins in using your hand. Start at the top and move down the sides and make sure that the push pins align with the holes in the door before applying pressure.

3. Install all the screws retaining the trim panel-to-door.

4. Snap in the door handle retainer cover and install the retaining screws.

5. Snap in the front door lock control knob plate.

6. Install the outside rearview mirror mounting hole cover and retaining screws.

7. Install the window regulator handle (manual only) and snap in the handle cover.

1989–92

1. As required, remove the window regulator handle by unsnapping the handle cover from the base and expose the attaching screw. Remove the screw, handle and the wearplate.

2. On the front door panel, remove the outside rear view mirror mounting hole cover retaining screw and cover.

3. If equipped with power window, remove the housing and switch assembly. If equipped with power door locks, remove the housing and switch assembly.

4. Remove the door pull handle opening filler retaining screw. Remove the filler assembly. Snap out the door handle retainer cover.

5. Remove all the screws retaining door trim panel to the door, using a door panel removing tool, pry the trim panel retaining push pins from door inner panel.

6. If the trim panel is to be replaced, transfer all the push pins to the new panel. Replace any bend, broken or missing push pins.

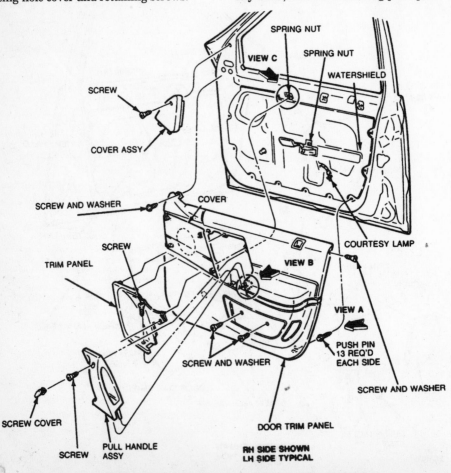

Front door panel and related components – 1986–88 Sable

8 Check to be sure that trim pieces that will be installed later will fit exactly. Sand the area with 40-grit paper.

9 If you wind up with low spots, you may have to apply another layer of filler.

10 Knock the high spots off with 40-grit paper. When you are satisfied with the contours of the repair, apply a thin coat of filler to cover pin holes and scratches.

11 Block sand the area with 40-grit paper to a smooth finish. Pay particular attention to body lines and ridges that must be well-defined.

12 Sand the area with 400 paper and then finish with a scuff pad. The finished repair is ready for priming and painting (see Painting Tips).

Materials and photos courtesy of Ritt Jones Auto Body, Prospect Park, PA.

REPAIRING RUST HOLES

There are many ways to repair rust holes. The fiberglass cloth kit shown here is one of the most cost efficient for the owner because it provides a strong repair that resists cracking and moisture and is relatively easy to use. It can be used on large and small holes (with or without backing) and can be applied over contoured areas. Remember, however, that short of replacing an entire panel, no repair is a guarantee that the rust will not return.

1 Remove any trim that will be in the way. Clean away all loose debris. Cut away all the rusted metal. But be sure to leave enough metal to retain the contour or body shape.

2 Grind away all traces of rust with a 24-grit grinding disc. Be sure to grind back 3-4 inches from the edge of the hole down to bare metal and be sure all traces of paint, primer and rust are removed.

3 Block sand the area with 80 or 100 grit sandpaper to get a clear, shiny surface and feathered paint edge. Tap the edges of the hole inward with a ball peen hammer.

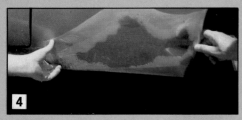

4 If you are going to use release film, cut a piece about 2-3" larger than the area you have sanded. Place the film over the repair and mark the sanded area on the film. Avoid any unnecessary wrinkling of the film.

5 Cut 2 pieces of fiberglass matte to match the shape of the repair. One piece should be about 1" smaller than the sanded area and the second piece should be 1" smaller than the first. Mix enough filler and hardener to saturate the fiberglass material (see Body Repair Tips).

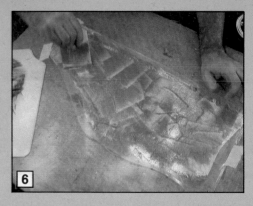

6 Lay the release sheet on a flat surface and spread an even layer of filler, large enough to cover the repair. Lay the smaller piece of fiberglass cloth in the center of the sheet and spread another layer of filler over the fiberglass cloth. Repeat the operation for the larger piece of cloth.

7 Place the repair material over the repair area, with the release film facing outward. Use a spreader and work from the center outward to smooth the material, following the body contours. Be sure to remove all air bubbles.

8 Wait until the repair has dried tack-free and peel off the release sheet. The ideal working temperature is 60°-90° F. Cooler or warmer temperatures or high humidity may require additional curing time. Wait longer, if in doubt.

9

9 Sand and feather-edge the entire area. The initial sanding can be done with a sanding disc on an electric drill if care is used. Finish the sanding with a block sander. Low spots can be filled with body filler; this may require several applications.

10

10 When the filler can just be scratched with a fingernail, knock the high spots down with a body file and smooth the entire area with 80-grit. Feather the filled areas into the surrounding areas.

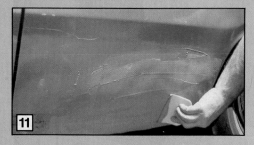

11

11 When the area is sanded smooth, mix some topcoat and hardener and apply it directly with a spreader. This will give a smooth finish and prevent the glass matte from showing through the paint.

12

12 Block sand the topcoat smooth with finishing sandpaper (200 grit), and 400 grit. The repair is ready for masking, priming and painting (see Painting Tips).

Materials and photos courtesy Marson Corporation, Chelsea, Massachusetts

PAINTING TIPS

Preparation

1 SANDING — Use a 400 or 600 grit wet or dry sandpaper. Wet-sand the area with a 1/4 sheet of sandpaper soaked in clean water. Keep the paper wet while sanding. Sand the area until the repaired area tapers into the original finish.

2 CLEANING — Wash the area to be painted thoroughly with water and a clean rag. Rinse it thoroughly and wipe the surface dry until you're sure it's completely free of dirt, dust, fingerprints, wax, detergent or other foreign matter.

3 MASKING — Protect any areas you don't want to overspray by covering them with masking tape and newspaper. Be careful not get fingerprints on the area to be painted.

4 PRIMING — All exposed metal should be primed before painting. Primer protects the metal and provides an excellent surface for paint adhesion. When the primer is dry, wet-sand the area again with 600 grit wet-sandpaper. Clean the area again after sanding.

4

Painting Techniques

P aint applied from either a spray gun or a spray can (for small areas) will provide good results. Experiment on an old piece of metal to get the right combination before you begin painting.

SPRAYING VISCOSITY (SPRAY GUN ONLY) — Paint should be thinned to spraying viscosity according to the directions on the can. Use only the recommended thinner or reducer and the same amount of reduction regardless of temperature.

AIR PRESSURE (SPRAY GUN ONLY) — This is extremely important. Be sure you are using the proper recommended pressure.

TEMPERATURE — The surface to be painted should be approximately the same temperature as the surrounding air. Applying warm paint to a cold surface, or vice versa, will completely upset the paint characteristics.

THICKNESS — Spray with smooth strokes. In general, the thicker the coat of paint, the longer the drying time. Apply several thin coats about 30 seconds apart. The paint should remain wet long enough to flow out and no longer; heavier coats will only produce sags or wrinkles. Spray a light (fog) coat, followed by heavier color coats.

DISTANCE — The ideal spraying distance is 8"-12" from the gun or can to the surface. Shorter distances will produce ripples, while greater distances will result in orange peel, dry film and poor color match and loss of material due to overspray.

OVERLAPPING — The gun or can should be kept at right angles to the surface at all times. Work to a wet edge at an even speed, using a 50% overlap and direct the center of the spray at the lower or nearest edge of the previous stroke.

RUBBING OUT (BLENDING) FRESH PAINT — Let the paint dry thoroughly. Runs or imperfections can be sanded out, primed and repainted.

Don't be in too big a hurry to remove the masking. This only produces paint ridges. When the finish has dried for at least a week, apply a small amount of fine grade rubbing compound with a clean, wet cloth. Use lots of water and blend the new paint with the surrounding area.

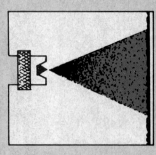  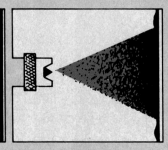

WRONG	CORRECT	WRONG
Thin coat. Stroke too fast, not enough overlap, gun too far away.	*Medium coat. Proper distance, good stroke, proper overlap.*	*Heavy coat. Stroke too slow, too much overlap, gun too close.*

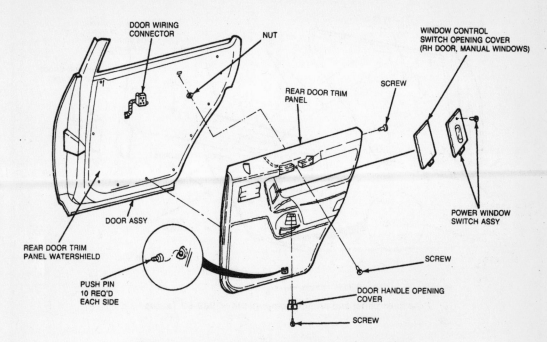

DOOR WIRING
CONNECTOR

NUT

REAR DOOR TRIM
PANEL

SCREW

WINDOW CONTROL
SWITCH OPENING COVER
(RH DOOR, MANUAL WINDOWS)

POWER WINDOW
SWITCH ASSY

DOOR ASSY

REAR DOOR TRIM
PANEL WATERSHIELD

PUSH PIN
10 REQ'D
EACH SIDE

SCREW

DOOR HANDLE OPENING
COVER

SCREW

Rear door panel and related components — 1989–92 Sable

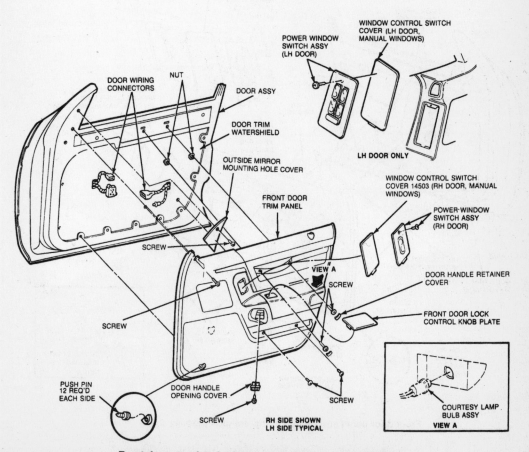

DOOR WIRING
CONNECTORS

NUT

DOOR ASSY

DOOR TRIM
WATERSHIELD

OUTSIDE MIRROR
MOUNTING HOLE COVER

FRONT DOOR
TRIM PANEL

SCREW

SCREW

PUSH PIN
12 REQ'D
EACH SIDE

DOOR HANDLE
OPENING COVER

SCREW

RH SIDE SHOWN
LH SIDE TYPICAL

SCREW

POWER WINDOW
SWITCH ASSY
(LH DOOR)

WINDOW CONTROL SWITCH
COVER (LH DOOR,
MANUAL WINDOWS)

LH DOOR ONLY

WINDOW CONTROL SWITCH
COVER 14503 (RH DOOR, MANUAL
WINDOWS)

POWER WINDOW
SWITCH ASSY
(RH DOOR)

VIEW A

SCREW

DOOR HANDLE RETAINER
COVER

FRONT DOOR LOCK
CONTROL KNOB PLATE

COURTESY LAMP
BULB ASSY

VIEW A

Front door panel and related components — 1989–92 Taurus

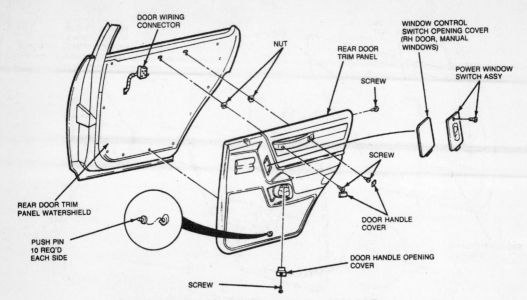

Rear door panel and related components — 1989–92 Taurus

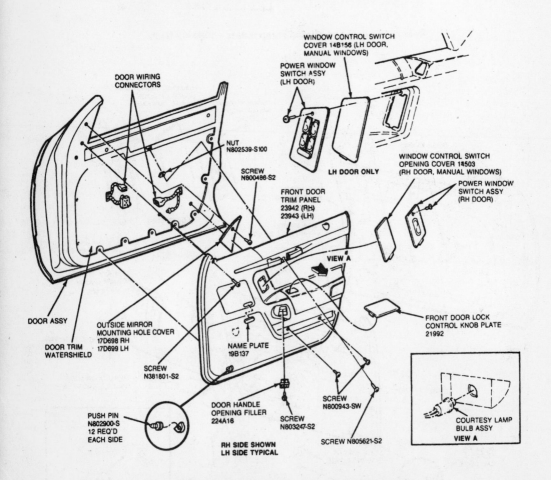

Front door panel and related components — 1989–92 Sable

To install:

7. Connect all door wiring and install the trim panel into position ensuring the upper ridge is seated properly in the door channel.

8. Snap the push pins in using your hand. Start at the top and move down the sides and make sure that the push pins align with the holes in the door before applying pressure.

9. Install all the screws retaining the trim panel-to-door. Snap in the door handle retainer cover and install the retaining screws.

10. If equipped with power window, install the housing and switch assembly. If equipped with power door locks, install the housing and switch assembly.

11. On the front door panel, install the outside rear view mirror mounting hole cover retaining screw and cover.

12. As required, install the window regulator handle by unsnapping the handle cover from the base and expose the attaching screw. Remove the screw, handle and the wearplate.

Power Door Lock Actuator

REMOVAL AND INSTALLATION

1. Remove the door trim panel and watershield.

2. Using a letter **X** and 1/4 in. (6mm) diameter drill bit, drill out the pop-rivet attaching the actuator motor to the door. Disconnect the wiring at the connector and the actuator rod at the latch assembly.

3. To install, attach the actuator motor rod to the door latch and connect the wire to the actuator connector.

4. Install the door actuator motor to the door with a pop-rivet or equivalent.

Front Door Latch

REMOVAL AND INSTALLATION

1. Remove the door trim panel and the watershield.

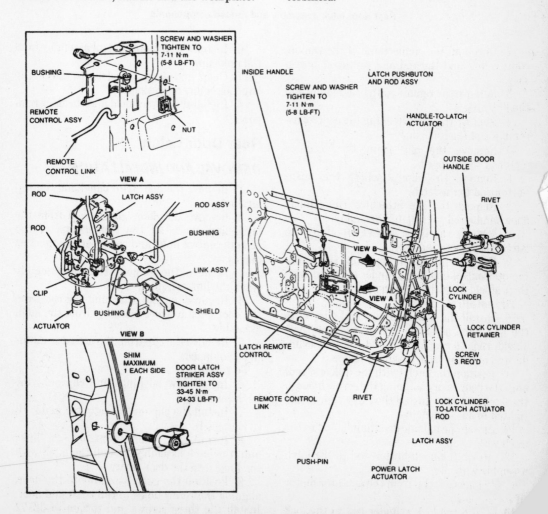

Front door latch assembly and related components

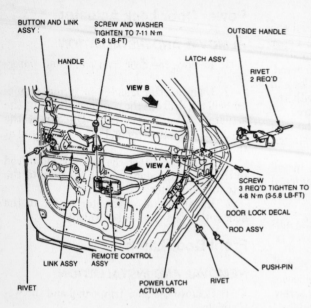

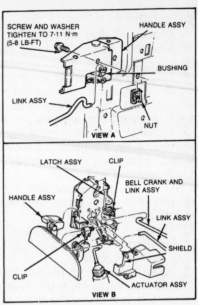

Rear door latch assembly and related components

2. Check all the connections of the remote control link and the rod and service if necessary.

3. Remove the remote control assembly and the link clip.

4. Remove the clip attaching the control assembly and the link clip.

5. Remove the clip from the actuator otor, if so equipped.

6. Remove the clip attaching the push-button rod to the latch.

7. Remove the clip attaching the outside door handle rod to the latch assembly.

8. Remove the three screws attaching the latch assembly to the door.

9. Remove the latch assembly (with the remote control link lock cylinder rod) and anti-theft shield from the door cavity.

To install:

10. Install the new bushings and clips onto the new latch assembly. Install the anti-theft shield, remote control link and the lock cylinder rod onto the latch assembly levers.

11. Position the latch (with the link and rod) onto the door cavity, aligning the screw holes in the latch and door. Install the three screws and tighten to 36–72 inch lbs.

12. Attach the outside door handle rod to the latch with a clip.

13. Attach the push-button rod to the latch assembly with clip.

ve the clip from the actuator motor
ed).

h the lock cylinder rod to the lock
h clip.

16. Install the remote control assembly (and the link clip).

17. Open and close the door to check the latch assembly operation.

18. Install the watershield and the door trim panel.

Rear Door Latch

REMOVAL AND INSTALLATION

1. Remove the door trim panel and the watershield.

2. Remove the door latch shield from the latch and check all the connections of the remote control links and rods. Service them as necessary.

3. Remove the remote control assembly (with the link retaining clip).

4. Remove the clip attaching the rod from the door latch bracket assembly from the latch assembly.

5. Remove the clip from the actuator motor (if so equipped).

To install:

6. Install new bushings and clip onto the latch assembly.

7. Install the clip on the actuator motor (if so equipped).

8. Install the remote control slide links onto the latch assembly. Install the latch with the links into the door cavity.

9. Position the latch assembly to the door, aligning the screw holes in the latch and door. Install the three screws and torque to 36–72 inch lbs.

10. Install the door latch shield.

11. Install the bellcrank to the inner door panel. Install the bellcrank attaching rivet.

12. Open and close the door to check the latch component operation.

13. Install the watershield and door trim panel.

Door Lock Assembly

REMOVAL AND INSTALLATION

NOTE: *When a lock cylinder must be replaced, replace both sides in a set to avoid carrying an extra set of keys.*

1. Remove the door trim panel and watershield.

2. Remove the clip attaching the lock cylinder rod-to-lock cylinder.

3. Pry the lock cylinder out of the slot in the door.

To install:

1. Work the lock cylinder assembly into the outer door panel.

2. Install the cylinder retainer into the slot and push the retainer onto the lock cylinder.

3. Connect the lock cylinder rod to the lock cylinder and install the clip. Lock and unlock the door to check for proper operation.

4. Install the watershield and door trim panel.

Tailgate Lock

REMOVAL AND INSTALLATION

1. Remove the liftgate interior trim panel. Remove the latch rod from the control assembly lever.

2. Remove the screws retaining the latch assembly to the liftgate. Disengage the lock cylinder rod at the latch lever.

3. Remove the latch assembly from the liftgate.

4. Installation is the reverse of the removal procedure. Tighten the liftgate retaining screws to 5–8 inch lbs.

Trunk Lid Lock

REMOVAL AND INSTALLATION

1. Remove the latch retaining screws. Remove the latch.

2. Remove the retainer clip and the lock support.

3. Remove the pop revir retining the lock cylinder retainer.

4. Remove the lock cylinder retainer as you remove the lock cylinder.

5. Installation is the reverse of the removal procedure. Torque the retaining screws 7–10 ft. lbs.

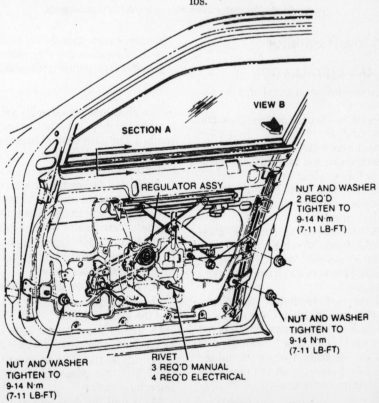

Front window regulator assembly and related components

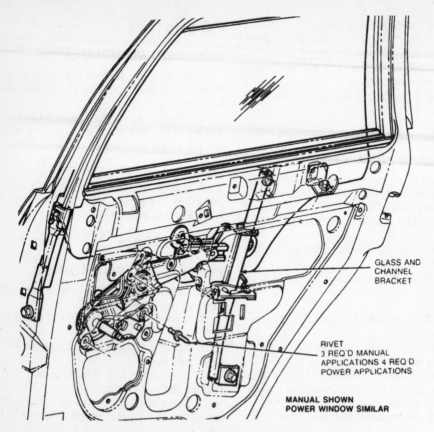

GLASS AND
CHANNEL
BRACKET

RIVET
3 REQ'D MANUAL
APPLICATIONS 4 REQ D
POWER APPLICATIONS

MANUAL SHOWN
POWER WINDOW SIMILAR

Rear window regulator assembly and related components

Front Window Regulator

REMOVAL AND INSTALLATION

1. Remove the door trim panel and the watershield.

2. Remove the inside door belt weatherstrip and the glass stabilizer.

3. Remove the door glass.

4. Remove the two nut and washer assemblies attaching the equalizer bracket.

5. Remove the three rivets (manual) or the four rivets (power) attaching the regulator base plate to the door inner panel.

6. Remove the regulator and the glass bracket assembly from the vehicle.

7. Working on a bench, carefully bend the tab flat to remove the arm slides from the glass bracket C-channel.

8. Install the new regulator arm plastic guides into the glass bracket C-channel and bend the tab back to 90° (use care not to break the tab, if the tab is cracked or broken, replace the glass bracket assembly. Ensure the rubber _____ is installed properly on the new glass _____ placement is made.

_____ the regulator counterbalance _____ t be removed or replaced for any

reason, ensure that the regulator arms are in a fixed position prior to removal to prevent possible injury during C-spring unwind.

The glass bracket assembly and regulator assembly are installed into the vehicle as one assembly. The glass bracket assembly may be disassembled from the regulator.

To install:

9. Install the regulator with the preassembled glass bracket into the vehicle. Set the regulator base plate to the door inner panel using the base plate locator tab as a guide.

10. Install the three (manual) or four (power) rivets (385189–S100) to attach the regulator to door inner panel.

11. Install the equalizer bracket.

12. Install the inside door belt weatherstrip and the glass stabilizer.

13. Lower the regulator arms to access holes in the door inner panel. Install the door glass.

14. Adjust the glass to ensure proper alignment with the glass run. Cycle the glass for smooth operation.

15. Install the door trim panel and the watershield.

Rear Window Regulator

REMOVAL AND INSTALLATION

1. Remove the door trim panel and the watershield.

2. Prop the glass in the full-up position.

3. Remove the three rivets (manual applications) or four rivets (power windows) attaching the regulator mounting plate assembly to the door inner panel.

4. Slide the regulator arm plastic guides out of the C-channel and disconnect the power wiring connector lift.

5. Remove the window regulator from door.

NOTE: *Use the access hole in the door inner panel for removal and installation.*

To install:

6. Install the window regulator through the access hole in the rear door and slide the regulator arm plastic guides into the glass bracket C-channel.

7. Install the rivets part No. 385189–S100 using Heavy Duty Riveter D80L–23200–A or equivalent, or $1/4$–20 x $1/2$ in. screw and washer assemblies to secure regulator mounting plate to door inner panel.

8. Cycle the glass to check for smooth operation.

9. Install the watershield and the door trim panel.

Electric Window Motor

REMOVAL AND INSTALLATION

1. Raise the window to the full up position, if possible. If glass cannot be raised and is in a partially down or in the full down position, it must be supported so that it will not fall into door well during the motor removal.

2. Disconnect the negative (–) battery cable.

3. Remove the door trim panel and watershield.

4. Remove the two forward regulator mounting plate attaching rivets. Use a $1/4$ in. (6mm) drill bit and drill out the attaching rivets.

NOTE: *Prior to motor drive assembly removal, ensure that the regulator arm is in a fixed position to prevent dangerous counterbalance spring unwind!*

5. Remove the three window motor mounting screws.

6. Push the regulator mounting plate outboard sufficiently to remove the power window motor.

To install:

7. Install the new motor and drive assembly. Tighten the three motor mounting screws to 50–85 inch lbs.

8. Install the two regulator mounting plate

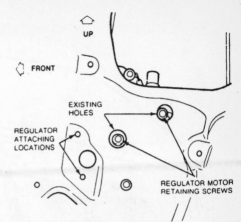

Power window motor template

rivets part No. 385189–S100 using a Heavy Duty Riveter No. D80L–23200–A or equivalent. A $1/4$–20 × $1/2$ in. screw and washer assembly may be used to secure the motor to the drive assembly.

9. Connect the window motor wiring leads.

10. Connect the negative (–) battery cable.

11. Check the power window for proper operation.

12. Install the door trim panel and the watershield.

NOTE: *Verify that all the drain holes at bottom of doors are open to prevent water accumulation over the motor.*

Front Door Glass

REMOVAL AND INSTALLATION

1. Remove the door trim panel and the watershield.

2. Remove the inside door belt weatherstrip assembly.

3. Lower the glass to access the holes in the door inner panel. Remove the two rivets retaining the glass to glass bracket.

NOTE: *Prior to removing the center pins from the rivets, it is recommended that a suitable block support be inserted between the door outer panel and glass bracket to stabilizer glass during rivet removal. Remove the center pin from each rivet using a drift punch. Using a $1/4$ in. (6mm) diameter drill, drill out the remaining rivets. Use care when drilling out the rivets to prevent enlarging the bracket and spacer holes and damaging the retainer.*

4. Loosen the nut and washer retaining the door glass stabilizer.

5. Remove the glass by tipping it forward then removing it from between the door belt opening to the outboard side of door.

6. Remove the drilling and pins the from bottom of door.

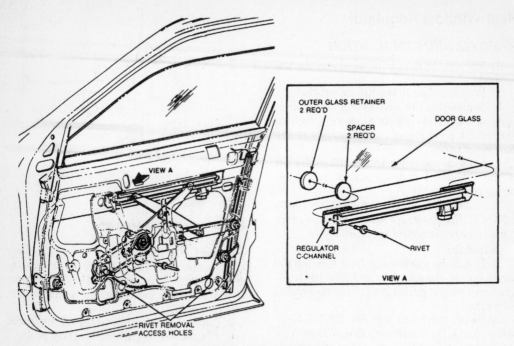

Front door glass replacement

To install:

7. Snap the plastic retainer and spacer into the two glass retainer holes. Ensure that the metal washer within the retainer assembly is on the outboard side of glass.

8. Install the glass into the door at belt. Ensure that the glass is set within the front and rear glass run retainers.

9. Position the glass to the glass bracket. Install the two rivets to secure the glass to glass bracket.

NOTE: *Two 1/4-20 x 1 in. bolts and two 1/4-20 nuts and washer assemblies may be used as alternates for glass retention. However, torque must not exceed 36–61 inch lbs. Equivalent metric retainers may be used.*

10. Install the inside door belt weatherstrip assembly.

11. Raise the glass to within 75mm of the full–up position and adjust glass as outlined below.

12. Install the door trim panel and watershield.

ADJUSTMENT

1. Remove the door trim panel and the watershield.

2. Lower the door glass approximately 75mm from the full-up position.

3. Loosen the nut and washer assemblies **A**
   ̲ ̲ining the equalizer bracket to the
   ̲ ̲ panel. Refer to the following door
   ̲ ̲tment illustration.

4. Loosen the nut and washer assembly **C** retaining the door glass stabilizer.

5. With the door open, place your hands on each side of the glass and pull the glass fully into the door glass run assembly at the B-pillar.

6. Tighten the nut and washer **A**, then apply a downward pressure on the equalizer bracket and tighten the nut and washer **B** to 5–8 ft. lbs.

7. Set the door glass stabilizer so that it is slightly touching the glass and tighten the nut and washer assembly to 5–8 ft. lbs.

8. Cycle the door glass to ensure proper function and door fit.

Rear Door Glass

REMOVAL AND INSTALLATION

1. Remove the door trim panel and the watershield.

2. Remove the inner door belt weatherstrip by gently pulling the weatherstrip from the door flange.

3. Remove the glass-to-glass bracket attaching rivets.

NOTE: *Prior to removing rivet center pins, a suitable block support should be inserted between the door outer panel and glass to stabilizer the glass during rivet pin removal. Use a 1/4 in. (6mm) diameter drill to drill out remainder of rivet, using care not to enlarge sheet metal holes and damage the plastic retainer and spacer.*

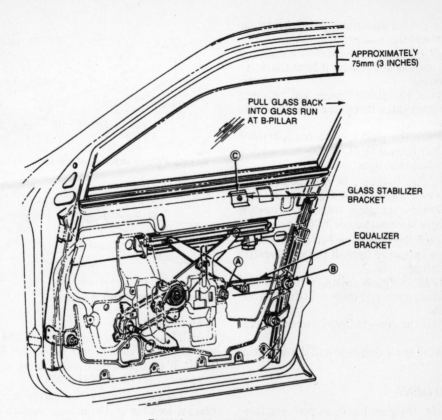

APPROXIMATELY
75mm (3 INCHES)

PULL GLASS BACK
INTO GLASS RUN
AT B-PILLAR

GLASS STABILIZER
BRACKET

EQUALIZER
BRACKET

Front door glass adjustment

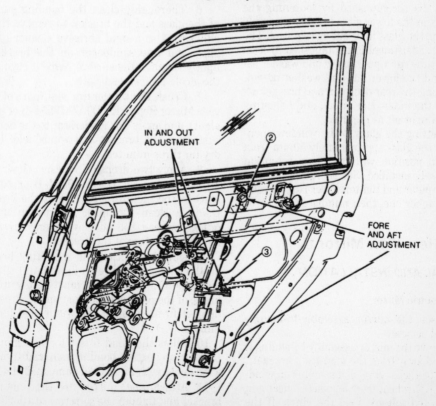

IN AND OUT
ADJUSTMENT

FORE
AND AFT
ADJUSTMENT

Rear door glass adjustment

4. Remove the glass stabilizer bracket retaining screw and the washer and bracket.

5. Lift the glass up between the door belt molding opening and remove it from the door.

To install:

6. Install the plastic spacer and retainers into the main glass. Install the main glass into the door.

7. Secure the glass-to-glass bracket using Heavy Duty Riveter D80L–23200–A or equivalent to install two rivets.

NOTE: *Two $^1/4$–20 x 1 in. bolts and two $^1/4$–20 nut and washer assemblies may be used as alternates for glass retention. However, the torque must not exceed 36–61 inch lbs.*

8. Install the inner door belt weatherstrip, using hand pressure to push the weatherstrip onto door flange.

9. Install the glass stabilizer bracket and the retaining screw and washer. Tighten to 36–61 inch lbs.

10. Cycle the glass to insure smooth operation.

11. Install the watershield and the door trim panel.

ADJUSTMENT

The rear door glass has in-and-out and fore-and-aft adjustments. The in-and-out adjustment may be accomplished by loosening the two screws in the lower glass bracket assembly and moving the glass in or out as required. The fore-and-aft adjustment is accomplished by loosening the tube run upper screw and washer assembly, and the lower nut and washer assembly attaching the rear door run and bracket assembly to the inner door panel, and adjusting the glass fore or aft as required.

When setting the glass to the window opening, lower the glass approximately 50mm from the full-up position with the four retention points loosely installed. Set the glass forward into the B-pillar and tighten lower run nut and washer number one, then numbers two, three and four.

Inside Rear View Mirror

REMOVAL AND INSTALLATION

Except Electric Mirror

1. Loosen the mirror assembly-to-mounting bracket setscrew.

2. Remove the mirror assembly by sliding it upward and away from the mounting bracket.

[...] acket vinyl pad remains on wind-[...] w heat from an electric heat gun [...] l softens. Peel the vinyl off the [...] d discard.

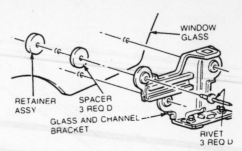

Reardoor glass attachment points

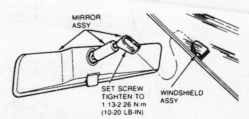

Interior rear view mirror mounting

To install:

4. Make the sure glass, bracket, and adhesive kit, (Rear view Mirror Repair Kit D9AZ–19554–B or equivalent) are at least at room temperature of 65–75°F (18–24°C).

5. Locate and mark the mirror mounting bracket location on the outside surface of the windshield with a wax pencil.

6. Thoroughly clean the bonding surfaces of the glass and the bracket to remove the old adhesive. Use a mild abrasive cleaner on the glass and fine sandpaper on the bracket to lightly roughen the surface. Wipe it clean with the alcohol-moistened cloth.

7. Crush the accelerator vial (part of Rear view Mirror Repair Kit D9AZ–19554–B or equivalent), and apply the accelerator to the bonding surface of the bracket and windshield. Let it dry for three minutes.

8. Apply two drops of adhesive (Rear view Mirror Repair Kit D9AZ–19554–B or equivalent) to the mounting surface of the bracket. Using a clean toothpick or wooden match, quickly spread the adhesive evenly over the mounting surface of the bracket.

9. Quickly position the mounting bracket on the windshield. The $^3/8$ in. (10mm) circular depression in the bracket must be toward the inside of the passenger compartment. Press the bracket firmly against the windshield for one minute.

10. Allow the bond to set for five minutes. Remove any excess bonding material from the windshield with an alcohol dampened cloth.

11. Attach the mirror to the mounting bracket and tighten the setscrew to 10–20 inch lbs.

Electric Mirror

1. Remove the grommet from the garnish moulding above the mirror assembly.

2. Pull the wire assembly away from the garnish moulding opening until the connector is exposed and disconnect the wire.

3. Loosen the mirror assembly-to-mounting bracket setscrew and remove the mirror by sliding upward away from the bracket.

To install:

1. If the mounting bracket on the windshield has to be serviced, refer to the following procedures.

2. If the bracket vinyl pad remains on windshield, apply low heat from an electric heat gun until the vinyl softens. Peel the vinyl off the windshield and discard.

3. Make the sure glass, bracket, and adhesive kit, (Rear view Mirror Repair Kit D9AZ–19554–B or equivalent) are at least at room temperature of 65–75°F (18–24°C).

4. Locate and mark the mirror mounting bracket location on the outside surface of the windshield with a wax pencil.

5. Thoroughly clean the bonding surfaces of the glass and the bracket to remove the old adhesive. Use a mild abrasive cleaner on the glass and fine sandpaper on the bracket to lightly roughen the surface. Wipe it clean with the alcohol-moistened cloth.

6. Crush the accelerator vial (part of Rear view Mirror Repair Kit D9AZ–19554–B or equiv-

alent), and apply the accelerator to the bonding surface of the bracket and windshield. Let it dry for three minutes.

7. Apply two drops of adhesive (Rear view Mirror Repair Kit D9AZ–19554–B or equivalent) to the mounting surface of the bracket. Using a clean toothpick or wooden match, quickly spread the adhesive evenly over the mounting surface of the bracket.

8. Quickly position the mounting bracket on the windshield. The $3/8$ in. (10mm) circular depression in the bracket must be toward the inside of the passenger compartment. Press the bracket firmly against the windshield for one minute.

9. Allow the bond to set for five minutes. Remove any excess bonding material from the windshield with an alcohol dampened cloth.

10. Position the mirror assembly over the mounting bracket after it has dryed.

11. Tighten the mounting bracket setscrew to 10–20 inch lbs.

12. Connect the wire connector and push the wire back into the garnish moulding. Install the grommet to the garnish moulding.

Manual Front Seats

REMOVAL AND INSTALLATION

1. Remove the plastic shield retaining screws and remove the shield.

2. Remove the bolts and nut and washer as-

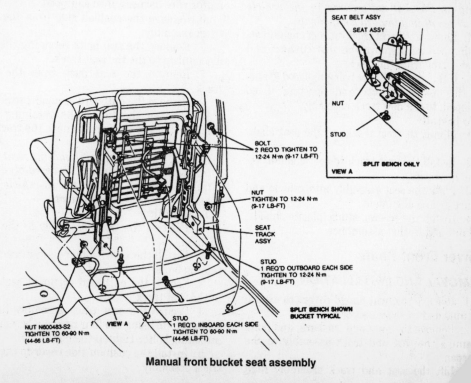

Manual front bucket seat assembly

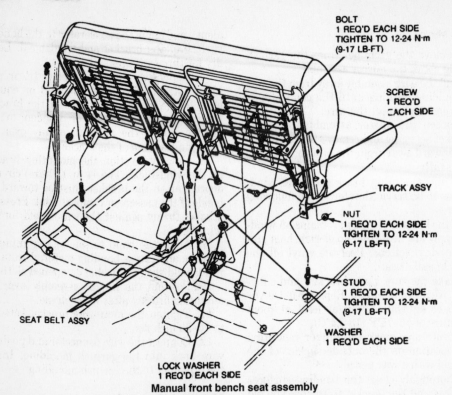

BOLT
1 REQ'D EACH SIDE
TIGHTEN TO 12-24 N·m
(9-17 LB-FT)

SCREW
1 REQ'D
EACH SIDE

TRACK ASSY

NUT
1 REQ'D EACH SIDE
TIGHTEN TO 12-24 N·m
(9-17 LB-FT)

STUD
1 REQ'D EACH SIDE
TIGHTEN TO 12-24 N·m
(9-17 LB-FT)

WASHER
1 REQ'D EACH SIDE

SEAT BELT ASSY

LOCK WASHER
1 REQ'D EACH SIDE

Manual front bench seat assembly

semblies retaining the seat tracks to the floor.

3. Remove the seat and track assembly from the vehicle and place on a clean working area.

NOTE: *Use care when handling seat and track assembly. Dropping the assembly or sitting on the seat not secured in the vehicle may result in damaged components.*

4. Remove the seat track-to-seat cushion attaching screws. Remove the seat cushion and assist spring from the tracks.

5. If the seat tracks are being replaced, transfer the assist springs and spacers, if so equipped, to the new track assembly.

To install:

1. Mount the seat tracks to the seat cushion.

2. Install the seat track-to-seat cushion retaining screws.

3. Place the seat assembly into vehicle and ensure proper alignment.

4. Install the screws, studs, plastic shields, and nut and washer assemblies.

Power Front Seats

REMOVAL AND INSTALLATION

1. Remove the heat shield covers to expose the nuts and washers and/or bolts.

2. [Remo]ve the nuts and washers, and bolts [and th]e seat and track assembly to the

[Rais]e the seat and track assembly high

enough to disconnect the wire harness. Remove the seat and track assembly from the vehicle.

4. Place the seat upside down on a clean bench. Remove the center occupant seat belt, if so equipped.

5. Disconnect the power seat switch-to-motor wire harness, if so equipped.

6. Remove the cushion side from the seat track assembly.

7. Remove the two bolts retaining the clip mechanism to the the seat track.

8. Remove the seat back from the seat track.

9. Remove the outboard occupant seat belt.

10. Remove the four bolts retaining seat track to the seat cushion. Remove the track assembly.

NOTE: *Use care when handling seat and track assembly. Dropping the assembly or sitting on the seat not secured in vehicle may result in damaged components.*

To install:

1. Position the track assembly to the seat cushion.

2. Install the seat recliner-to-seat track retaining bolts.

3. Secure the outboard occupant seat belt to the seat track.

4. Secure the seat track assembly to the seat cushion using the four previously removed attaching bolts. Tighten the bolts.

5. Install the cushion side cover to the seat track assembly.

6. Connect the power seat switch to motor wire harness, if so equipped.

7. Install the center occupant seat belt to seat track.

8. Position the seat and track assembly in vehicle.

9. Lift the seat and track assembly high enough to permit the connection of the wire harness, then, connect wires.

10. Install the seat track-to-floorpan attaching nuts and washer and/or bolts. Tighten the bolts.

11. Install the heat shield covers.

12. Install the seat belt-to-floorpan attaching bolts.

13. Check the seat tracks for proper operation.

Rear Seats

REMOVAL AND INSTALLATION

Seat Cushion

1. Apply knee pressure to the lower portion of the rear seat cushion. Push rearward to disengage the seat cushion from the retainer brackets.

NOTE: *The armrest is an integral part of the quarter trim panel. Its removal is not required to remove rear seat cushion or back.*

To install:

2. Position the seat cushion assembly into the vehicle.

3. Place the seat belts on top of the cushion.

4. Apply knee pressure to the lower portion of the seat cushion assembly. Push rearward and down to lock the seat cushion into position.

5. Pull the rear seat cushion forward to be certain it is secured into its floor retainer.

Seat Back Rest

1. Remove the rear seat cushion.

2. Remove the seat back bracket attaching bolts.

NOTE: *The seat belt bolts do not secure seat back to the vehicle.*

3. Grasp the seat back assembly at the bottom and lift it up to disengage the hanger wire from the retainer brackets.

To install:

4. Position the seat back in the vehicle so that the hanger wires are engaged with the retaining brackets.

5. Install the seat back bolts and tighten to 5–7 ft. lbs.

6. Install the rear seat cushion.

Split Folding Rear Seat Back

1. Remove the rear seat cushion.

2. Remove the seat back side pads by removing the attaching screws (one each) and sliding the pad upward.

3. Remove the four bolts (two each seat

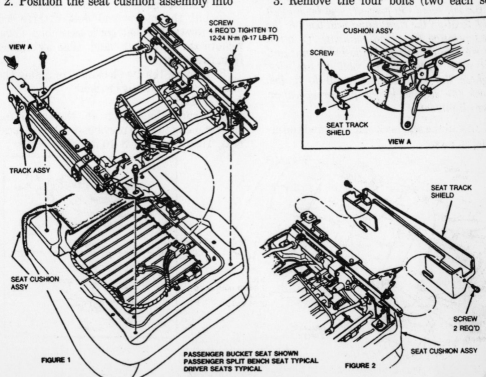

Power seat motor assembly

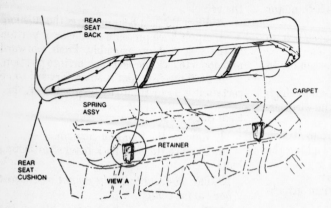

Rear seat cushion assembly

back) retaining the seat back assembly to the floorpan.

4. Remove the seat back from the inboard pivot pin by sliding the seat back toward the outboard side of the vehicle.

To install:

5. Position the seat back onto the inboard pivot pin in the full-up position.

6. Install the seat back-to-floorpan retaining bolts (two each side).

7. Check the seat back latch for proper operation.

NOTE: *A nut and bolt have been provided on the left hand (40 percent) seat back latch only, to align the right hand seat back to the fixed position (± 2° adjustment). To align the right hand seat back, loosen the nut and bolt and reposition the bolt in its slot. Tighten the bolt and nut to 30–40 ft. lbs. Check the seat backs for proper operation after alignment.*

8. Install the seat back side pads and the attaching screws.

Power Seat Motor

REMOVAL AND INSTALLATION

1. Remove the seat and track assembly from the vehicle.

2. Remove the seat recliner mechanism and seat back from seat track.

3. Remove the seat belt.

4. Remove the seat track from the seat cushion.

5. Identify the cables and their respective locations.

6. Remove the motor bracket screw.

7. Lift the motor and deflect three left cables toward the left track assembly. Then, remove the three left hand cable assemblies from the motor.

8. Remove the two locknuts retaining the motor to the mounting brackets.

To install:

1. Secure the motor to the mounting bracket using the two previously removed locknuts. Tighten nuts to 8–10 inch lbs.

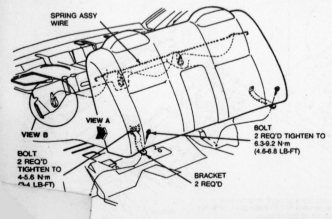

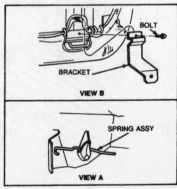

Rear seat back assembly

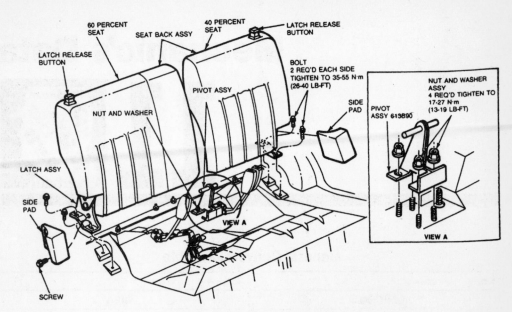

Rear split seat back assembly

2. Lower the motor in place.

3. Position the three left hand drive cables to the motor, being sure to fully engage the square ends of cables into the motor armature.

4. Align the right hand drive cable ends with the motor armatures.

5. With the three left hand cables engaged in the motor, lift the motor. Insert the right hand cable into the motor being sure to fully engage the square end of cable into the motor armature. Lower the motor into place.

6. Install the screw used to retain the motor bracket to the seat track. Tighten the screw to 54–70 inch lbs.

7. Install the seat track assembly to the seat cushion.

8. Install the seat recliner and the seat back to the seat track.

9. Install the seat belts.

10. Install the seat and track assembly in the vehicle.

Mechanic's Data

1":254mm
TAX 10.16mm Liter Parts Overhaul

General Conversion Table

Multiply By	To Convert	To	
LENGTH			
2.54	Inches	Centimeters	.3937
25.4	Inches	Millimeters	.03937
30.48	Feet	Centimeters	.0328
.304	Feet	Meters	3.28
.914	Yards	Meters	1.094
1.609	Miles	Kilometers	.621
VOLUME			
.473	Pints	Liters	2.11
.946	Quarts	Liters	1.06
3.785	Gallons	Liters	.264
.164	Cubic inches	Liters	61.02
16.39	Cubic inches	Cubic cms.	.061
28.32	Cubic feet	Liters	.0353
MASS (Weight)			
28.35	Ounces	Grams	.035
.4536	Pounds	Kilograms	2.20
—	To obtain	From	Multiply by

Multiply By	To Convert	To	
AREA			
6.45	Square inches	Square cms.	.155
.836	Square yds.	Square meters	1.196
FORCE			
4.448	Pounds	Newtons	.225
.138	Ft. lbs.	Kilogram/meters	7.23
1.356	Ft. lbs.	Newton-meters	.737
.113	In. lbs.	Newton-meters	8.844
PRESSURE			
.068	Psi	Atmospheres	14.7
6.89	Psi	Kilopascals	.145
OTHER			
1.104	Horsepower (DIN)	Horsepower (SAE)	.9861
.746	Horsepower (SAE)	Kilowatts (KW)	1.34
1.609	Mph	Km/h	.621
.425	Mpg	Km/L	2.35
—	To obtain	From	Multiply by

Tap Drill Sizes

National Coarse or U.S.S.

Screw & Tap Size	Threads Per Inch	Use Drill Number
No. 5	.40	.39
No. 6	.32	.36
No. 8	.32	.29
No. 10	.24	.25
No. 12	.24	.17
1/4	.20	8
5/16	.18	F
3/8	.16	5/16
7/16	.14	U
1/2	.13	27/64
9/16	.12	31/64
5/8	.11	17/32
	.10	21/32
	9	49/64

National Coarse or U.S.S.

Screw & Tap Size	Threads Per Inch	Use Drill Number
1	8	7/8
1 1/8	7	63/64
1 1/4	7	1 7/64
1 1/2	6	1 11/32

National Fine or S.A.E.

Screw & Tap Size	Threads Per Inch	Use Drill Number
No. 5	.44	.37
No. 6	.40	.33
No. 8	.36	.29
No. 10	.32	.21

National Fine or S.A.E.

Screw & Tap Size	Threads Per Inch	Use Drill Number
No. 12	.28	.15
1/4	.28	3
6/16	.24	1
3/8	.28	Q
7/16	.20	W
1/2	.20	29/64
9/16	.18	33/64
5/8	.18	37/64
3/4	.16	11/16
7/8	.14	13/16
1 1/8	.12	1 3/64
1 1/4	.12	1 11/64
1 1/2	.12	1 27/64

Drill Sizes In Decimal Equivalents

Inch	Decimal	Wire	mm	Inch	Decimal	Wire	mm	Inch	Decimal	Wire & Letter	mm	Inch	Decimal	Letter	mm	Inch	Decimal	mm
1/64	.0156		.39		.0730	49			.1614		4.1		.2717		6.9		.4331	11.0
	.0157		.4		.0748		1.9		.1654		4.2		.2720	I		7/16	.4375	11.11
	.0160	78			.0760	48			.1660	19			.2756		7.0		.4528	11.5
	.0165		.42		.0768		1.95		.1673		4.25		.2770	J		29/64	.4531	11.51
	.0173		.44	5/64	.0781		1.98		.1693		4.3		.2795		7.1	15/32	.4688	11.90
	.0177		.45		.0785	47			.1695	18			.2810	K			.4724	12.0
	.0180	77			.0787		2.0	11/64	.1719		4.36	9/32	.2812		7.14	31/64	.4844	12.30
	.0181		.46		.0807		2.05		.1730	17			.2835		7.2		.4921	12.5
	.0189		.48		.0810	46			.1732		4.4		.2854		7.25	1/2	.5000	12.70
	.0197		.5		.0820	45			.1770	16			.2874		7.3		.5118	13.0
	.0200	76			.0827		2.1		.1772		4.5		.2900	L		33/64	.5156	13.09
	.0210	75			.0846		2.15		.1800	15			.2913		7.4	17/32	.5312	13.49
	.0217		.55		.0860	44			.1811		4.6		.2950	M			.5315	13.5
	.0225	74			.0866		2.2		.1820	14			.2953		7.5	35/64	.5469	13.89
	.0236		.6		.0886		2.25		.1850	13		19/64	.2969		7.54		.5512	14.0
	.0240	73			.0890	43			.1850		4.7		.2992		7.6	9/16	.5625	14.28
	.0250	72			.0906		2.3		.1870		4.75		.3020	N			.5709	14.5
	.0256		.65		.0925		2.35	3/16	.1875		4.76		.3031		7.7	37/64	.5781	14.68
	.0260	71			.0935	42			.1890		4.8		.3051		7.75		.5906	15.0
	.0276		.7	3/32	.0938		2.38		.1890	12			.3071		7.8	19/32	.5938	15.08
	.0280	70			.0945		2.4		.1910	11			.3110		7.9	39/64	.6094	15.47
	.0292	69			.0960	41			.1929		4.9	5/16	.3125		7.93		.6102	15.5
	.0295		.75		.0965		2.45		.1935	10			.3150		8.0	5/8	.6250	15.87
	.0310	68			.0980	40			.1960	9			.3160	O			.6299	16.0
1/32	.0312		.79		.0981		2.5		.1969		5.0		.3189		8.1	41/64	.6406	16.27
	.0315		.8		.0995	39			.1990	8			.3228		8.2		.6496	16.5
	.0320	67			.1015	38			.2008		5.1		.3230	P		21/32	.6562	16.66
	.0330	66			.1024		2.6		.2010	7			.3248		8.25		.6693	17.0
	.0335		.85		.1040	37		13/64	.2031		5.16		.3268		8.3	43/64	.6719	17.06
	.0350	65			.1063		2.7		.2040	6		21/64	.3281		8.33	11/16	.6875	17.46
	.0354		.9		.1065	36			.2047		5.2		.3307		8.4		.6890	17.5
	.0360	64			.1083		2.75		.2055	5			.3320	Q		45/64	.7031	17.85
	.0370	63		7/64	.1094		2.77		.2067		5.25		.3346		8.5		.7087	18.0
	.0374		.95		.1100	35			.2087		5.3		.3386		8.6	23/32	.7188	18.25
	.0380	62			.1102		2.8		.2090	4			.3390	R			.7283	18.5
	.0390	61			.1110	34			.2126		5.4		.3425		8.7	47/64	.7344	18.65
	.0394		1.0		.1130	33			.2130	3		11/32	.3438		8.73		.7480	19.0
	.0400	60			.1142		2.9		.2165		5.5		.3445		8.75	3/4	.7500	19.05
	.0410	59			.1160	32		7/32	.2188		5.55		.3465		8.8	49/64	.7656	19.44
	.0413		1.05		.1181		3.0		.2205		5.6		.3480	S			.7677	19.5
	.0420	58			.1200	31			.2210	2			.3504		8.9	25/32	.7812	19.84
	.0430	57			.1220		3.1		.2244		5.7		.3543		9.0		.7874	20.0
	.0433		1.1	1/8	.1250		3.17		.2264		5.75		.3580	T		51/64	.7969	20.24
	.0453		1.15		.1260		3.2		.2280	1			.3583		9.1		.8071	20.5
	.0465	56			.1280		3.25		.2283		5.8	23/64	.3594		9.12	13/16	.8125	20.63
3/64	.0469		1.19		.1285	30			.2323		5.9		.3622		9.2		.8268	21.0
	.0472		1.2		.1299		3.3		.2340	A			.3642		9.25	53/64	.8281	21.03
	.0492		1.25		.1339		3.4	15/64	.2344		5.95		.3661		9.3	27/32	.8438	21.43
	.0512		1.3		.1360	29			.2362		6.0		.3680	U			.8465	21.5
	.0520	55			.1378		3.5		.2380	B			.3701		9.4	55/64	.8594	21.82
	.0531		1.35		.1405	28			.2402		6.1		.3740		9.5		.8661	22.0
	.0550	54		9/64	.1406		3.57		.2420	C		3/8	.3750		9.52	7/8	.8750	22.22
	.0551		1.4		.1417		3.6		.2441		6.2		.3770	V			.8858	22.5
	.0571		1.45		.1440	27			.2460	D			.3780		9.6	57/64	.8906	22.62
	.0591		1.5		.1457		3.7		.2461		6.25		.3819		9.7		.9055	23.0
	.0595	53			.1470	26			.2480		6.3		.3839		9.75	29/32	.9062	23.01
	.0610		1.55		.1476		3.75	1/4	.2500	E	6.35		.3858		9.8	59/64	.9219	23.41
1/16	.0625		1.59		.1495	25			.2520		6.		.3860	W			.9252	23.5
	.0630		1.6		.1496		3.8		.2559		6.5		.3898		9.9	15/16	.9375	23.81
	.0635	52			.1520	24			.2570	F		25/64	.3906		9.92		.9449	24.0
	.0650		1.65		.1535		3.9		.2598		6.6		.3937		10.0	61/64	.9531	24.2
	.0669		1.7		.1540	23			.2610	G			.3970	X			.9646	24.5
	.0670	51		5/32	.1562		3.96		.2638		6.7		.4040	Y		31/32	.9688	24.6
	.0689		1.75		.1570	22		17/64	.2656		6.74	13/32	.4062		10.31		.9843	25.0
	.0700	50			.1575		4.0		.2657		6.75		.4130	Z		63/64	.9844	25.0
	.0709		1.8		.1590	21			.2660	H			.4134		10.5	1	1.0000	25.4
	.0728		1.85		.1610	20			.2677		6.8	27/64	.4219		10.71			

AIR/FUEL RATIO: The ratio of air to gasoline by weight in the fuel mixture drawn into the engine.

AIR INJECTION: One method of reducing harmful exhaust emissions by injecting air into each of the exhaust ports of an engine. The fresh air entering the hot exhaust manifold causes any remaining fuel to be burned before it can exit the tailpipe.

ALTERNATOR: A device used for converting mechanical energy into electrical energy.

AMMETER: An instrument, calibrated in amperes, used to measure the flow of an electrical current in a circuit. Ammeters are always connected in series with the circuit being tested.

AMPERE: The rate of flow of electrical current present when one volt of electrical pressure is applied against one ohm of electrical resistance.

ANALOG COMPUTER: Any microprocessor that uses similar (analogous) electrical signals to make its calculations.

ARMATURE: A laminated, soft iron core wrapped by a wire that converts electrical energy to mechanical energy as in a motor or relay. When rotated in a magnetic field, it changes mechanical energy into electrical energy as in a generator.

ATMOSPHERIC PRESSURE: The pressure on the Earth's surface caused by the weight of the air in the atmosphere. At sea level, this pressure is 14.7 psi at 32°F (101 kPa at 0°C).

ATOMIZATION: The breaking down of a liquid into a fine mist that can be suspended in air.

AXIAL PLAY: Movement parallel to a shaft or bearing bore.

BACKFIRE: The sudden combustion of gases in the intake or exhaust system that results in a loud explosion.

BACKLASH: The clearance or play between two parts, such as meshed gears.

|SURE: Restrictions in the exthat slow the exit of exhaust he combustion chamber.

BAKELITE: A heat resistant, plastic insulator material commonly used in printed circuit boards and transistorized components.

BALL BEARING: A bearing made up of hardened inner and outer races between which hardened steel balls roll.

BALLAST RESISTOR: A resistor in the primary ignition circuit that lowers voltage after the engine is started to reduce wear on ignition components.

BEARING: A friction reducing, supportive device usually located between a stationary part and a moving part.

BIMETAL TEMPERATURE SENSOR: Any sensor or switch made of two dissimilar types of metal that bend when heated or cooled due to the different expansion rates of the alloys. These types of sensors usually function as an on/off switch.

BLOWBY: Combustion gases, composed of water vapor and unburned fuel, that leak past the piston rings into the crankcase during normal engine operation. These gases are removed by the PCV system to prevent the buildup of harmful acids in the crankcase.

BRAKE PAD: A brake shoe and lining assembly used with disc brakes.

BRAKE SHOE: The backing for the brake lining. The term is, however, usually applied to the assembly of the brake backing and lining.

BUSHING: A liner, usually removable, for a bearing; an anti-friction liner used in place of a bearing.

BYPASS: System used to bypass ballast resistor during engine cranking to increase voltage supplied to the coil.

CALIPER: A hydraulically activated device in a disc brake system, which is mounted straddling the brake rotor (disc). The caliper contains at least one piston and two brake pads. Hydraulic pressure on the piston(s) forces the pads against the rotor.

CAMSHAFT: A shaft in the engine on which are the lobes (cams) which operate the valves. The camshaft is driven by the crankshaft, via a belt, chain or gears, at one half the crankshaft speed.

CAPACITOR: A device which stores an electrical charge.

CARBON MONOXIDE (CO): A colorless, odorless gas given off as a normal byproduct of combustion. It is poisonous and extremely dangerous in confined areas, building up slowly to toxic levels without warning if adequate ventilation is not available.

CARBURETOR: A device, usually mounted on the intake manifold of an engine, which mixes the air and fuel in the proper proportion to allow even combustion.

CATALYTIC CONVERTER: A device installed in the exhaust system, like a muffler, that converts harmful byproducts of combustion into carbon dioxide and water vapor by means of a heat-producing chemical reaction.

CENTRIFUGAL ADVANCE: A mechanical method of advancing the spark timing by using fly weights in the distributor that react to centrifugal force generated by the distributor shaft rotation.

CHECK VALVE: Any one-way valve installed to permit the flow of air, fuel or vacuum in one direction only.

CHOKE: A device, usually a movable valve, placed in the intake path of a carburetor to restrict the flow of air.

CIRCUIT: Any unbroken path through which an electrical current can flow. Also used to describe fuel flow in some instances.

CIRCUIT BREAKER: A switch which protects an electrical circuit from overload by opening the circuit when the current flow exceeds a predetermined level. Some circuit breakers must be reset manually, while most reset automatically

COIL (IGNITION): A transformer in the ignition circuit which steps up the voltage provided to the spark plugs.

COMBINATION MANIFOLD: An assembly which includes both the intake and exhaust manifolds in one casting.

COMBINATION VALVE: A device used in some fuel systems that routes fuel vapors to a charcoal storage canister instead of venting

them into the atmosphere. The valve relieves fuel tank pressure and allows fresh air into the tank as the fuel level drops to prevent a vapor lock situation.

COMPRESSION RATIO: The comparison of the total volume of the cylinder and combustion chamber with the piston at BDC and the piston at TDC.

CONDENSER: 1. An electrical device which acts to store an electrical charge, preventing voltage surges.
2. A radiator-like device in the air conditioning system in which refrigerant gas condenses into a liquid, giving off heat.

CONDUCTOR: Any material through which an electrical current can be transmitted easily.

CONTINUITY: Continuous or complete circuit. Can be checked with an ohmmeter.

COUNTERSHAFT: An intermediate shaft which is rotated by a mainshaft and transmits, in turn, that rotation to a working part.

CRANKCASE: The lower part of an engine in which the crankshaft and related parts operate.

CRANKSHAFT: The main driving shaft of an engine which receives reciprocating motion from the pistons and converts it to rotary motion.

CYLINDER: In an engine, the round hole in the engine block in which the piston(s) ride.

CYLINDER BLOCK: The main structural member of an engine in which is found the cylinders, crankshaft and other principal parts.

CYLINDER HEAD: The detachable portion of the engine, fastened, usually, to the top of the cylinder block, containing all or most of the combustion chambers. On overhead valve engines, it contains the valves and their operating parts. On overhead cam engines, it contains the camshaft as well.

DEAD CENTER: The extreme top or bottom of the piston stroke.

DETONATION: An unwanted explosion of the air/fuel mixture in the combustion chamber caused by excess heat and compression, advanced timing, or an overly lean mixture. Also referred to as "ping".

DIAPHRAGM: A thin, flexible wall separating two cavities, such as in a vacuum advance unit.

DIESELING: A condition in which hot spots in the combustion chamber cause the engine to run on after the key is turned off.

DIFFERENTIAL: A geared assembly which allows the transmission of motion between drive axles, giving one axle the ability to turn faster than the other.

DIODE: An electrical device that will allow current to flow in one direction only.

DISC BRAKE: A hydraulic braking assembly consisting of a brake disc, or rotor, mounted on an axle, and a caliper assembly containing, usually two brake pads which are activated by hydraulic pressure. The pads are forced against the sides of the disc, creating friction which slows the vehicle.

DISTRIBUTOR: A mechanically driven device on an engine which is responsible for electrically firing the spark plug at a predetermined point of the piston stroke.

DOWEL PIN: A pin, inserted in mating holes in two different parts allowing those parts to maintain a fixed relationship.

DRUM BRAKE: A braking system which consists of two brake shoes and one or two wheel cylinders, mounted on a fixed backing plate, and a brake drum, mounted on an axle, which revolves around the assembly. Hydraulic action applied to the wheel cylinders forces the shoes outward against the drum, creating friction, slowing the vehicle.

DWELL: The rate, measured in degrees of shaft rotation, at which an electrical circuit cycles on and off.

ELECTRONIC CONTROL UNIT (ECU): Ignition module, amplifier or igniter. See Module for definition.

ELECTRONIC IGNITION: A system in which the timing and firing of the spark plugs is controlled by an electronic control unit, usu-̀ll·· called a module. These systems have no ̀denser.

̀: The measured amount of axial ̀n a shaft.

ENGINE: A device that converts heat into mechanical energy.

EXHAUST MANIFOLD: A set of cast passages or pipes which conduct exhaust gases from the engine.

FEELER GAUGE: A blade, usually metal, of precisely predetermined thickness, used to measure the clearance between two parts. These blades usually are available in sets of assorted thicknesses.

F-HEAD: An engine configuration in which the intake valves are in the cylinder head, while the camshaft and exhaust valves are located in the cylinder block. The camshaft operates the intake valves via lifters and pushrods, while it operates the exhaust valves directly.

FIRING ORDER: The order in which combustion occurs in the cylinders of an engine. Also the order in which spark is distributed to the plugs by the distributor.

FLATHEAD: An engine configuration in which the camshaft and all the valves are located in the cylinder block.

FLOODING: The presence of too much fuel in the intake manifold and combustion chamber which prevents the air/fuel mixture from firing, thereby causing a no-start situation.

FLYWHEEL: A disc shaped part bolted to the rear end of the crankshaft. Around the outer perimeter is affixed the ring gear. The starter drive engages the ring gear, turning the flywheel, which rotates the crankshaft, imparting the initial starting motion to the engine.

FOOT POUND (ft.lb. or sometimes, ft. lbs.): The amount of energy or work needed to raise an item weighing one pound, a distance of one foot.

FUSE: A protective device in a circuit which prevents circuit overload by breaking the circuit when a specific amperage is present. The device is constructed around a strip or wire of a lower amperage rating than the circuit it is designed to protect. When an amperage higher than that stamped on the fuse is present in the circuit, the strip or wire melts, opening the circuit.

GEAR RATIO: The ratio between the number of teeth on meshing gears.

GENERATOR: A device which converts mechanical energy into electrical energy.

HEAT RANGE: The measure of a spark plug's ability to dissipate heat from its firing end. The higher the heat range, the hotter the plug fires. **HUB:** The center part of a wheel or gear.

HYDROCARBON (HC): Any chemical compound made up of hydrogen and carbon. A major pollutant formed by the engine as a byproduct of combustion.

HYDROMETER: An instrument used to measure the specific gravity of a solution.

INCH POUND (in.lb. or sometimes, in. lbs.): One twelfth of a foot pound.

INDUCTION: A means of transferring electrical energy in the form of a magnetic field. Principle used in the ignition coil to increase voltage.

INJECTION PUMP: A device, usually mechanically operated, which meters and delivers fuel under pressure to the fuel injector.

INJECTOR: A device which receives metered fuel under relatively low pressure and is activated to inject the fuel into the engine under relatively high pressure at a predetermined time.

INPUT SHAFT: The shaft to which torque is applied, usually carrying the driving gear or gears.

INTAKE MANIFOLD: A casting of passages or pipes used to conduct air or a fuel/air mixture to the cylinders.

JOURNAL: The bearing surface within which a shaft operates.

KEY: A small block usually fitted in a notch between a shaft and a hub to prevent slippage of the two parts.

MANIFOLD: A casting of passages or set of pipes which connect the cylinders to an inlet or outlet source.

MANIFOLD VACUUM: Low pressure in an engine intake manifold formed just below the throttle plates. Manifold vacuum is highest at idle and drops under acceleration.

MASTER CYLINDER: The primary fluid pressurizing device in a hydraulic system. In automotive use, it is found in brake and hydraulic clutch systems and is pedal activated, either directly or, in a power brake system, through the power booster.

MODULE: Electronic control unit, amplifier or igniter of solid state or integrated design which controls the current flow in the ignition primary circuit based on input from the pickup coil. When the module opens the primary circuit, the high secondary voltage is induced in the coil.

NEEDLE BEARING: A bearing which consists of a number (usually a large number) of long, thin rollers.

OHM:(Ω) The unit used to measure the resistance of conductor to electrical flow. One ohm is the amount of resistance that limits current flow to one ampere in a circuit with one volt of pressure.

OHMMETER: An instrument used for measuring the resistance, in ohms, in an electrical circuit.

OUTPUT SHAFT: The shaft which transmits torque from a device, such as a transmission.

OVERDRIVE: A gear assembly which produces more shaft revolutions than that transmitted to it.

OVERHEAD CAMSHAFT (OHC): An engine configuration in which the camshaft is mounted on top of the cylinder head and operates the valves either directly or by means of rocker arms.

OVERHEAD VALVE (OHV): An engine configuration in which all of the valves are located in the cylinder head and the camshaft is located in the cylinder block. The camshaft operates the valves via lifters and pushrods.

OXIDES OF NITROGEN (NOx): Chemical compounds of nitrogen produced as a byproduct of combustion. They combine with hydrocarbons to produce smog.

OXYGEN SENSOR: Used with the feedback system to sense the presence of oxygen in the exhaust gas and signal the computer which can reference the voltage signal to an air/fuel ratio.

PINION: The smaller of two meshing gears

PISTON RING: An open ended ring which fits into a groove on the outer diameter of the piston. Its chief function is to form a seal between the piston and cylinder wall. Most automotive pistons have three rings: two for compression sealing; one for oil sealing.

PRELOAD: A predetermined load placed on a bearing during assembly or by adjustment.

PRIMARY CIRCUIT: Is the low voltage side of the ignition system which consists of the ignition switch, ballast resistor or resistance wire, bypass, coil, electronic control unit and pick-up coil as well as the connecting wires and harnesses.

PRESS FIT: The mating of two parts under pressure, due to the inner diameter of one being smaller than the outer diameter of the other, or vice versa; an interference fit.

RACE: The surface on the inner or outer ring of a bearing on which the balls, needles or rollers move.

REGULATOR: A device which maintains the amperage and/or voltage levels of a circuit at predetermined values.

RELAY: A switch which automatically opens and/or closes a circuit.

RESISTANCE: The opposition to the flow of current through a circuit or electrical device, and is measured in ohms. Resistance is equal to the voltage divided by the amperage.

RESISTOR: A device, usually made of wire, which offers a preset amount of resistance in an electrical circuit.

RING GEAR: The name given to a ring-shaped gear attached to a differential case, or affixed to a flywheel or as part a planetary gear set.

ROLLER BEARING: A bearing made up of hardened inner and outer races between which hardened steel rollers move.

ROTOR: 1. The disc-shaped part of a disc brake assembly, upon which the brake pads bear; also called, brake disc.
2. The device mounted atop the distributor which passes current to the distributor ꞏacts.

ꞏꞏY CIRCUIT: The high voltage ignition system, usually above 20,000 volts. The secondary includes the ignition coil, coil wire, distributor cap and rotor, spark plug wires and spark plugs.

SENDING UNIT: A mechanical, electrical, hydraulic or electromagnetic device which transmits information to a gauge.

SENSOR: Any device designed to measure engine operating conditions or ambient pressures and temperatures. Usually electronic in nature and designed to send a voltage signal to an on-board computer, some sensors may operate as a simple on/off switch or they may provide a variable voltage signal (like a potentiometer) as conditions or measured parameters change.

SHIM: Spacers of precise, predetermined thickness used between parts to establish a proper working relationship.

SLAVE CYLINDER: In automotive use, a device in the hydraulic clutch system which is activated by hydraulic force, disengaging the clutch.

SOLENOID: A coil used to produce a magnetic field, the effect of which is to produce work.

SPARK PLUG: A device screwed into the combustion chamber of a spark ignition engine. The basic construction is a conductive core inside of a ceramic insulator, mounted in an outer conductive base. An electrical charge from the spark plug wire travels along the conductive core and jumps a preset air gap to a grounding point or points at the end of the conductive base. The resultant spark ignites the fuel/air mixture in the combustion chamber.

SPLINES: Ridges machined or cast onto the outer diameter of a shaft or inner diameter of a bore to enable parts to mate without rotation.

TACHOMETER: A device used to measure the rotary speed of an engine, shaft, gear, etc., usually in rotations per minute.

THERMOSTAT: A valve, located in the cooling system of an engine, which is closed when cold and opens gradually in response to engine heating, controlling the temperature of the coolant and rate of coolant flow.

TOP DEAD CENTER (TDC): The point at which the piston reaches the top of its travel on the compression stroke.

TORQUE: The twisting force applied to an object.

TORQUE CONVERTER: A turbine used to transmit power from a driving member to a driven member via hydraulic action, providing changes in drive ratio and torque. In automotive use, it links the driveplate at the rear of the engine to the automatic transmission.

TRANSDUCER: A device used to change a force into an electrical signal.

TRANSISTOR: A semi-conductor component which can be actuated by a small voltage to perform an electrical switching function.

TUNE-UP: A regular maintenance function, usually associated with the replacement and adjustment of parts and components in the electrical and fuel systems of a vehicle for the purpose of attaining optimum performance.

TURBOCHARGER: An exhaust driven pump which compresses intake air and forces it into the combustion chambers at higher than atmospheric pressures. The increased air pressure allows more fuel to be burned and results in increased horsepower being produced.

VACUUM ADVANCE: A device which advances the ignition timing in response to increased engine vacuum.

VACUUM GAUGE: An instrument used to measure the presence of vacuum in a chamber.

VALVE: A device which control the pressure, direction of flow or rate of flow of a liquid or gas.

VALVE CLEARANCE: The measured gap between the end of the valve stem and the rocker arm, cam lobe or follower that activates the valve.

VISCOSITY: The rating of a liquid's internal resistance to flow.

VOLTMETER: An instrument used for measuring electrical force in units called volts. Voltmeters are always connected parallel with the circuit being tested.

WHEEL CYLINDER: Found in the automotive drum brake assembly, it is a device, actuated by hydraulic pressure, which, through internal pistons, pushes the brake shoes outward against the drums.

A: Ampere

AC: Alternating current

A/C: Air conditioning

A–h: Amper hour

AT: Automatic transmission

ATDC: After top dead center

μA: Microampere

bbl: Barrel

BDC: Bottom dead center

bhp: Brake horsepower

BTDC: Before top dead center

BTU: British thermal unit

C: Celsius (Centigrade)

CCA: Cold cranking amps

cd: Candela

cm^2: Square centimeter

cm^3, cc: Cubic centimeter

CO: Carbon monoxide

CO_2: Carbon dioxide

cu.in., in^3: Cubic inch

CV: Constant velocity

Cyl.: Cylinder

DC: Direct current

ECM: Electronic control module

EFE: Early fuel evaporation

EFI: Electronic fuel injection

~~GR: Ex~~haust gas recirculation

~~haust~~

~~heit~~

F: Farad

pF: Picofarad

μF: Microfarad

FI: Fuel injection

ft.lb., ft. lb., ft. lbs.: foot pound(s)

gal: Gallon

g: Gram

HC: Hydrocarbon

HEI: High energy ignition

HO: High output

hp: Horsepower

Hyd: Hydraulic

Hz: Hertz

ID: Inside diameter

in.lb; in. lbs.; in. lbs.: inch pound(s)

Int: Intake

K: Kelvin

kg: Kilogram

kHz: Kilohertz

km: Kilometer

km/h: Kilometers per hour

kΩ: Kilohm

kPa: Kilopascal

kV: Kilovolt

kW: Kilowatt

l: Liter

l/s: Liters per second

m: Meter

mA: Milliampere

mg: Milligram

mHz: Megahertz

mm: Millimeter

mm^2: Square millimeter

m^3: Cubic meter

MΩ: Megohm

m/s: Meters per second

MT: Manual transmission

mV: Millivolt

μm: Micrometer

N: Newton

N–m: Newton meter

NOx: Nitrous oxide

OD: Outside diameter

OHC: Over head camshaft

OHV: Over head valve

Ω: Ohm

PCV: Positive crankcase ventilation

psi: Pounds per square inch

pts: Pints

qts: Quarts

rpm: Rotations per minute

rps: Rotations per second

R–12: refrigerant gas (Freon)

SAE: Society of Automotive Engineers

SO$_2$: Sulfur dioxide

T: Ton

t: Megagram

TBI: Throttle Body Injection

TPS: Throttle Position Sensor

V: 1. Volt; 2. Venturi

μV: Microvolt

W: Watt

∞: Infinity

‹: Less than

›: Greater than

A

Abbreviations and Symbols   356
Air cleaner   7
Air conditioning
    Blower   195
    Control panel   204
    General service   26
    Refrigerant level   28
    Safety inspection   28
Alternator
    Alternator precautions   70
    Removal and installation   71
    Specifications   77
Alignment, wheel
    Camber   261, 274
    Caster   261, 274
    Toe   261, 274
Ammeter
Antenna   329
Anti-lock brake system   308
Automatic transaxle   35
    Adjustments   240
    Back-up light switch   242
    Filter change   35
    Fluid change   35
    Linkage adjustments   240
    Neutral safety switch   242
    Pan removal   239
    Removal and installation   244

B

Back-up light switch
    Automatic transaxle   242
    Manual transaxle   228
Balance shaft   137
Ball joints
    Inspection   256
    Removal and installation   256
Battery
    Fluid level and maintenance   15
    Jump starting   17
    Removal and installation   71
Bearings
    Engine   140-141
    Wheel   39
Belts   18
Blower motor   196
Boot (CV Joint)
    Replacement   249
Brakes
    Anti-lock brake system   308
    Bleeding   294
    light switch   292
    kes (Front)
    r   297
    296

Rotor (Disc)   299
Disc brakes (Rear)
    Caliper   304
    Pads   303
    Rotor (Disc)   306
Drum brakes (Rear)
    Adjustment   291
    Drum   299
    Shoes   300
    Wheel cylinder   302
Fluid level   37
Master cylinder   37, 292
Parking brake
    Adjustment   308
    Removal and installation   306
Power booster   292
Proportioning valve   293
Specifications   314
Bulbs   221
Bumpers   321-322

C

Calipers
    Overhaul   298, 305
    Removal and installation   297, 304
Camber   261
Camshaft and bearings
    Service   133
    Specifications   78
Camshaft sensor   57
Capacities Chart   48
Caster   261
Catalytic converter   150, 167
Charging system   70
Chassis electrical system
    Circuit protection   222
    Heater and air conditioning   195
    Instrument cluster   210
    Lighting   217
    Windshield wipers   29, 207, 214
Circuit breakers   225
Circuit protection   222
Clock   216
Clutch
    Adjustment   236
    Cable   238
    Pedal   236
    Removal and installation   237
Coil (ignition)   55, 65
Coil pack   57
Combination switch   275
Connecting rods and bearings
    Service   138-140
    Specifications   79
Constant velocity (CV) joints   249
Control arm
    Lower   256, 267

Upper 267
Cooling system 35, 98
CV-boot 249
Crankcase ventilation valve 13, 153
Crankshaft
  Service 141
  Specifications 79
Crankshaft sensor 57
Cylinder head 110
Cylinders 139

D

Disc brakes 296, 303
Distributor 67
Door glass 339
Door locks 337
Doors
  Glass 339
  Locks 337
  Removal and installation 315
Door trim panel 330
Dome light 222
Drive Train 227
Drum brakes 299

E

EGR valve 164
Electrical
  Chassis
    Battery 15, 71
    Bulbs 220-221
    Circuit breakers 225
    Fuses 222
    Fusible links 222
    Heater and air conditioning 195
    Jump starting 17
    Spark plug wires 53
  Engine
    Alternator 70
    Coil 55, 57, 65
    Distributor 67
    Ignition module 57, 66, 69
    Starter 72
Electronic Ignition 54
Emission controls
  Catalytic converter 167
  Exhaust Gas Recirculation 164
  Evaporative Emission Controls 154
  Exhaust Emission Controls 156
  Thermactor Air Injection System 158
  PCV valve 153
  Pulse Air Injection System 162
  Oxygen (O_2) sensor 168
Engine

Balance shaft 137
Camshaft 133
Connecting rods and bearings 138-140
Crankshaft 141
Cylinder head 110
Cylinders 139
Exhaust manifold 103
Fluids and lubricants 15
Flywheel 148
Front (timing) cover 124, 131
Front seal 127, 131
Identification 7
Intake manifold 98
Main bearings 141
Mounts 91
Oil pan 120
Oil pump 123
Overhaul tips 72
Piston pin 140
Pistons 138
Rear main seal 141
Removal and installation 75
Rings 140
Rocker arms 94
Rocker cover 93
Spark plug wires 53
Specifications 77-82
Thermostat 96
Timing belt 132
Timing chain and gears 128
Tools 73
Valve guides 118
Valve lifters 118
Valves 116
Valve seats 118
Valve springs 116
Valve stem oil seals 117
Water pump 108
Evaporative canister 13, 154
Evaporator core 201
Exhaust Manifold 103
Exhaust system 150

F

Fan 107
Filters
  Air 7
  Fuel 12
  Oil 33
Firing orders 53
Flashers 226
Flex plate 148
Fluids and lubricants
  Automatic transaxle 35
  Battery 15
  Coolant 35
  Engine oil 33

Fuel 33
Manual transaxle 34
Master cylinder
  Brake 37
  Power steering pump 37
Flywheel and ring gear 148
Fog lights 222
Front bumper 321
Front brakes 296
Front hubs 258
Front suspension
  Ball joints 256
  Knuckles 257
  Lower control arm 256
  Spindles 257
  Stabilizer bar 256
  Struts 254
  Wheel alignment 261
Front wheel bearings 258
Fuel injection
  Air bypass valve 183
  Fuel charging assembly 179
  Fuel pressure regulator 189
  Fuel pump 176
  Idle speed 190
  Injectors 186
  Operation 170
  Push connect fittings 177
  Pressure relief valve 186
  Relieving fuel system pressure 176
  Throttle body 184
  Throttle position sensor 190
Fuel filter 12, 176
Fuel pump
  Electric 176
Fuel system 170
Fuel tank 192
Fuses and circuit breakers 222-225
Fusible links 222

G

Gearshift handle 228
Gearshift linkage
  Adjustment
    Automatic 240
    Manual 227
Generator (see alternator)
Glass
  Door 339
Glossary 350
Grille 323

233, 246
sher 226
s 217

Blower 195
Control panel 204
Core 196
High mount brake light 222
Hoisting 44
Hood 316
Hoses
  Coolant 22
How to Use This Book 1
Hubs 258

I

Identification
  Engine 7
  Serial number 5
  Transaxle 7
  Vehicle 5
Idle speed and mixture adjustment 190
Ignition
  Coil 55, 57, 65
  Electronic 53
  Lock cylinder 276
  Module 57, 66, 69
  Switch 277
  Timing 58
Injectors, fuel 186
Instrument cluster 210
Instrument panel
  Cluster 210
  Radio 206
  Speedometer cable 214
Intake manifold 98
Interior lights 222

J

Jacking points 44
Jump starting 17

K

Knuckles 257

L

Light bulb chart 220-221
Lighting
  Dome light 222
  Fog/driving lights 222
  Headlights 217
  Signal and marker lights 218
Liftgate 318
Liftgate lock 337

Lower ball joint 256
Lubrication
  Automatic transaxle 35
  Engine 33
  Manual transaxle 34

M

MacPherson struts 254
Main bearings 141
Maintenance intervals 46
Manifolds
  Intake 98
  Exhaust 103
Manual transaxle
  Linkage adjustment 227
  Removal and installation 228
Marker lights 218
Master cylinder
  Brake 37, 292
Mechanic's data 348
Mirrors 326, 342
Model identification 5
Module (ignition) 57, 66, 69
Mounts (engine) 91
Muffler
Multi-function switch 275

N

Neutral safety switch 242

O

Oil and fuel recommendations 33
Oil and filter change (engine) 33
Oil level check
  Engine 33
  Transaxle
    Automatic 35
    Manual 34
Oil pan 120
Oil pump 123
Oxygen (O$_2$) sensor 168

P

Parking brake 306
Piston pin 140
Pistons 138
Pivot pins 140
PCV valve 13, 153
Power brake booster 292
Power seat motor 346

Power steering rack
  Removal and installation 284
Power steering pump
  Fluid level 37
  Removal and installation 288
Power windows 339
Preventive Maintenance Charts 49
Printed circuit board 214
Pushing 44

R

Radiator 107
Radiator cap 36
Radio 206
Rear brakes 294, 303
Rear bumper 322
Rear main oil seal 141
Rear suspension
  Alignment 274
  Control arms 267
  Shock absorbers 264
  Springs 262
  Struts 265
Rear wheel bearings 269
Receiver-drier
Regulator (voltage) 71
Rings 140
Rocker arm cover 93
Rocker arms 94
Rotor (Brake disc) 299, 306
Routine maintenance 7

S

Safety notice 1
Seats 343
Serial number location 5
Shock absorbers 264
Spark plugs 50
Spark plug wires 53
Special tools 4
Specifications Charts
  Brakes 314
  Camshaft 78
  Capacities 48
  Crankshaft and connecting rod 79
  Engine identification 8
  General engine 77
  Light bulbs 221
  Piston and ring 81
  Preventive Maintenance 49
  Torque 82
  Tune-up 51
  Valves 80
  Wheel alignment 263

Speakers 206
Speedometer cable 214
Spindles 257
Springs 262
Stabilizer bar 256
Stain removal 348
Starter 72
Steering column 279
Steering gear
    Power 284
Steering knuckles 257
Steering linkage
    Tie rod ends 284
Steering rack 39, 284
Stripped threads 74
Suspension 254
Switches
    Back-up light 228, 242
    Blower 206
    Brake light 292
    Headlight 216
    Ignition switch 277
    Multi-function switch 275
    Rear window wiper 215
    Windshield wiper 214

T

Tailpipe 150
Thermostat 96
Throttle body 184
Tie rod ends 284
Timing (ignition) 58
Timing belt 132
Timing chain and gears 128
Timing gear cover 124, 131
Tires
    Design 29
    Rotation 29
    Storage 29
    Inflation 29
Toe-in 261
Tools 2
Torque specifications 82
Towing 44
Trailer towing 43
Transaxle
    Automatic 239

Manual 227
Routine maintenance 34-35
Trunk lid 319
Tune-up
    Idle speed 62
    Ignition timing 58
    Procedures 50
    Spark plugs and wires 50-53
    Specifications 51
Turn signal flasher 226
Turn signal switch 275

V

Valve guides 118
Valve lash adjustment 60
Valve seats 118
Valve service 116
Valve specifications 80
Valve springs 116
Vehicle identification 5

W

Water pump 108
Wheel alignment
    Adjustment 261, 274
    Specifications 263, 273
Wheel bearings
    Front wheel 258
    Rear wheel 39, 269
Wheel cylinders 302
Wheels 253
Window glass 339
Window regulator 338
Windshield wipers
    Arm 207-208
    Blade assembly 207-208
    Linkage 210
    Motor 210
    Rear window wiper 210
    Rear window wiper switch 215
    Windshield wiper switch 214
Wiring
    Spark plug 53

Chilton's Repair & Tune-Up Guides

The Complete line covers domestic cars, imports, trucks, vans, RV's and 4-wheel drive vehicles.

RTUG Title	Part No.	RTUG Title	Part No.
AMC 1975-82 Covers all U.S. and Canadian models	7199	**Corvair 1960-69** Covers all U.S. and Canadian models	6691
Aspen/Volare 1976-80 Covers all U.S. and Canadian models	6637	**Corvette 1953-62** Covers all U.S. and Canadian models	6576
Audi 1970-73 Covers all U.S. and Canadian models.	5902	**Corvette 1963-84** Covers all U.S. and Canadian models	6843
Audi 4000/5000 1978-81 Covers all U.S. and Canadian models including turbocharged and diesel engines	7028	**Cutlass 1970-85** Covers all U.S. and Canadian models	6933
Barracuda/Challenger 1965-72 Covers all U.S. and Canadian models	5807	**Dart/Demon 1968-76** Covers all U.S. and Canadian models	6324
Blazer/Jimmy 1969-82 Covers all U.S. and Canadian 2- and 4-wheel drive models, including diesel engines	6931	**Datsun 1961-72** Covers all U.S. and Canadian models of Nissan Patrol; 1500, 1600 and 2000 sports cars; Pick-Ups; 410, 411, 510, 1200 and 240Z	5790
BMW 1970-82 Covers all U.S. and Canadian models	6844	**Datsun 1973-80 Spanish**	7083
Buick/Olds/Pontiac 1975-85 Covers all U.S. and Canadian full size rear wheel drive models	7308	**Datsun/Nissan F-10, 310, Stanza, Pulsar 1977-86** Covers all U.S. and Canadian models	7196
Cadillac 1967-84 Covers all U.S. and Canadian rear wheel drive models	7462	**Datsun/Nissan Pick-Ups 1970-84** Covers all U.S and Canadian models	6816
Camaro 1967-81 Covers all U.S. and Canadian models	6735	**Datsun/Nissan Z & ZX 1970-86** Covers all U.S. and Canadian models	6932
Camaro 1982-85 Covers all U.S. and Canadian models	7317	**Datsun/Nissan 1200, 210, Sentra 1973-86** Covers all U.S. and Canadian models	7197
Capri 1970-77 Covers all U.S. and Canadian models	6695	**Datsun/Nissan 200SX, 510, 610, 710, 810, Maxima 1973-84** Covers all U.S. and Canadian models	7170
Caravan/Voyager 1984-85 Covers all U.S. and Canadian models	7482	**Dodge 1968-77** Covers all U.S. and Canadian models	6554
Century/Regal 1975-85 Covers all U.S. and Canadian rear wheel drive models, including turbocharged engines	7307	**Dodge Charger 1967-70** Covers all U.S. and Canadian models	6486
Champ/Arrow/Sapporo 1978-83 Covers all U.S. and Canadian models	7041	**Dodge/Plymouth Trucks 1967-84** Covers all $^1/_2$, $^3/_4$, and 1 ton 2- and 4-wheel drive U.S. and Canadian models, including diesel engines	7459
Chevette/1000 1976-86 Covers all U.S. and Canadian models	6836	**Dodge/Plymouth Vans 1967-84** Covers all $^1/_2$, $^3/_4$, and 1 ton U.S. and Canadian models of vans, cutaways and motor home chassis	6934
Chevrolet 1968-85 Covers all U.S. and Canadian models	7135	**D-50/Arrow Pick-Up 1979-81** Covers all U.S. and Canadian models	7032
Chevrolet 1968-79 Spanish	7082	**Fairlane/Torino 1962-75** Covers all U.S. and Canadian models	6320
Chevrolet/GMC Pick-Ups 1970-82 Spanish	7468	**Fairmont/Zephyr 1978-83** Covers all U.S. and Canadian models	6965
Chevrolet/GMC Pick-Ups and Suburban 1970-86 Covers all U.S. and Canadian $^1/_2$, $^3/_4$ and 1 ton models, including 4-wheel drive and diesel engines	6936	**Fiat 1969-81** Covers all U.S. and Canadian models	7042
Chevrolet LUV 1972-81 Covers all U.S. and Canadian models	6815	**Fiesta 1978-80** Covers all U.S. and Canadian models	6846
Chevrolet Mid-Size 1964-86 Covers all U.S. and Canadian models of 1964-77 Chevelle, Malibu and Malibu SS; 1974-77 Laguna; 1978-85 Malibu; 1970-86 Monte Carlo; 1964-84 El Camino, including diesel engines	6840	**Firebird 1967-81** Covers all U.S. and Canadian models	5996
		Firebird 1982-85 Covers all U.S. and Canadian models	7345
Chevrolet Nova 1986 Covers all U.S. and Canadian models	7658	**Ford 1968-79 Spanish**	7084
Chevy/GMC Vans 1967-84 Covers all U.S. and Canadian models of $^1/_2$, $^3/_4$, and 1 ton vans, cutaways, and motor home chassis, including diesel engines	6930	**Ford Bronco 1966-83** Covers all U.S. and Canadian models	7140
		Ford Bronco II 1984 Covers all U.S. and Canadian models	7408
Chevy S-10 Blazer/GMC S-15 Jimmy 1982-85 Covers all U.S. and Canadian models	7383	**Ford Courier 1972-82** Covers all U.S. and Canadian models	6983
Chevy S-10/GMC S-15 Pick-Ups 1982-85 Covers all U.S. and Canadian models	7310	**Ford/Mercury Front Wheel Drive 1981-85** Covers all U.S. and Canadian models Escort, EXP, Tempo, Lynx, LN-7 and Topaz	7055
Chevy II/Nova 1962-79 Covers all U.S. and Canadian models	6841	**Ford/Mercury/Lincoln 1968-85** Covers all U.S. and Canadian models of FORD Country Sedan, Country Squire, Crown Victoria, Custom, Custom 500, Galaxie 500, LTD through 1982, Ranch Wagon, and XL; MERCURY Colony Park, Commuter, Marquis through 1982, Gran Marquis, Monterey and Park Lane; LINCOLN Continental and Towne Car	6842
Chrysler K- and E-Car 1981-85 Covers all U.S. and Canadian front wheel drive models	7163		
Colt/Challenger/Vista/Conquest 1971-85 Covers all U.S. and Canadian models	7037		
Corolla/Carina/Tercel/Starlet 1970-85 Covers all U.S. and Canadian models	7036		
Corona/Cressida/Crown/Mk.II/Camry/Van 1970-84 Covers all U.S. and Canadian models	7044	**Ford/Mercury/Lincoln Mid-Size 1971-85** Covers all U.S. and Canadian models of FORD Elite, 1983-85 LTD, 1977-79 LTD II, Ranchero, Torino, Gran Torino, 1977-85 Thunderbird; MERCURY 1972-85 Cougar,	6696

continued on ne[xt]

RTUG Title	Part No.	RTUG Title	Part No.
1983-85 Marquis, Montego, 1980-85 XR-7; LINCOLN 1982-85 Continental, 1984-85 Mark VII, 1978-80 Versailles		Mercedes-Benz 1974-84 Covers all U.S. and Canadian models	6809
Ford Pick-Ups 1965-86 Covers all ½, ¾ and 1 ton, 2- and 4-wheel drive U.S. and Canadian pick-up, chassis cab and camper models, including diesel engines	6913	Mitsubishi, Cordia, Tredia, Starion, Galant 1983-85 Covers all U.S. and Canadian models	7583
		MG 1961-81 Covers all U.S. and Canadian models	6780
Ford Pick-Ups 1965-82 Spanish	7469	Mustang/Capri/Merkur 1979-85 Covers all U.S. and Canadian models	6963
Ford Ranger 1983-84 Covers all U.S. and Canadian models	7338	Mustang/Cougar 1965-73 Covers all U.S. and Canadian models	6542
Ford Vans 1961-86 Covers all U.S. and Canadian ½, ¾ and 1 ton van and cutaway chassis models, including diesel engines	6849	Mustang II 1974-78 Covers all U.S. and Canadian models	6812
		Omni/Horizon/Rampage 1978-84 Covers all U.S. and Canadian models of DODGE omni, Miser, 024, Charger 2.2; PLYMOUTH Horizon, Miser, TC3, TC3 Tourismo; Rampage	6845
GM A-Body 1982-85 Covers all front wheel drive U.S. and Canadian models of BUICK Century, CHEVROLET Celebrity, OLDSMOBILE Cutlass Ciera and PONTIAC 6000	7309		
		Opel 1971-75 Covers all U.S. and Canadian models	6575
GM C-Body 1985 Covers all front wheel drive U.S. and Canadian models of BUICK Electra Park Avenue and Electra T-Type, CADILLAC Fleetwood and deVille, OLDSMOBILE 98 Regency and Regency Brougham	7587	Peugeot 1970-74 Covers all U.S. and Canadian models	5982
		Pinto/Bobcat 1971-80	7027
		Plymouth 1968-76 Covers all U.S. and Canadian models	6552
		Pontiac Fiero 1984-85 Covers all U.S. and Canadian models	7571
GM J-Car 1982-85 Covers all U.S. and Canadian models of BUICK Skyhawk, CHEVROLET Cavalier, CADILLAC Cimarron, OLDSMOBILE Firenza and PONTIAC 2000 and Sunbird	7059	Pontiac Mid-Size 1974-83 Covers all U.S. and Canadian models of Ventura, Grand Am, LeMans, Grand LeMans, GTO, Phoenix, and Grand Prix	7346
		Porsche 924/928 1976-81 Covers all U.S. and Canadian models	7048
GM N-Body 1985-86 Covers all U.S. and Canadian models of front wheel drive BUICK Somerset and Skylark, OLDSMOBILE Calais, and PONTIAC Grand Am	7657	Renault 1975-85 Covers all U.S. and Canadian models	7165
		Roadrunner/Satellite/Belvedere/GTX 1968-73 Covers all U.S. and Canadian models	5821
GM X-Body 1980-85 Covers all U.S. and Canadian models of BUICK Skylark, CHEVROLET Citation, OLDSMOBILE Omega and PONTIAC Phoenix	7049	RX-7 1979-81 Covers all U.S. and Canadian models	7031
		SAAB 99 1969-75 Covers all U.S. and Canadian models	5988
GM Subcompact 1971-80 Covers all U.S. and Canadian models of BUICK Skyhawk (1975-80), CHEVROLET Vega and Monza, OLDSMOBILE Starfire, and PONTIAC Astre and 1975-80 Sunbird	6935	SAAB 900 1979-85 Covers all U.S. and Canadian models	7572
		Snowmobiles 1976-80 Covers Arctic Cat, John Deere, Kawasaki, Polaris, Ski-Doo and Yamaha	6978
Granada/Monarch 1975-82 Covers all U.S. and Canadian models	6937	Subaru 1970-84 Covers all U.S. and Canadian models	6962
Honda 1973-84 Covers all U.S. and Canadian models	6980	Tempest/GTO/LeMans 1968-73 Covers all U.S. and Canadian models	5905
International Scout 1967-73 Covers all U.S. and Canadian models	5912	Toyota 1966-70 Covers all U.S. and Canadian models of Corona, MkII, Corolla, Crown, Land Cruiser, Stout and Hi-Lux	5795
Jeep 1945-87 Covers all U.S. and Canadian CJ-2A, CJ-3A, CJ-3B, CJ-5, CJ-6, CJ-7, Scrambler and Wrangler models	6817	
		Toyota 1970-79 Spanish	7467
		Toyota Celica/Supra 1971-85 Covers all U.S. and Canadian models	7043
Jeep Wagoneer, Commando, Cherokee, Truck 1957-86 Covers all U.S. and Canadian models of Wagoneer, Cherokee, Grand Wagoneer, Jeepster, Jeepster Commando, J-100, J-200, J-300, J-10, J20, FC-150 and FC-170	6739	Toyota Trucks 1970-85 Covers all U.S. and Canadian models of pick-ups, Land Cruiser and 4Runner	7035
		Valiant/Duster 1968-76 Covers all U.S. and Canadian models	6326
Laser/Daytona 1984-85 Covers all U.S. and Canadian models	7563	Volvo 1956-69 Covers all U.S. and Canadian models	6529
Maverick/Comet 1970-77 Covers all U.S. and Canadian models	6634	Volvo 1970-83 Covers all U.S. and Canadian models	7040
Mazda 1971-84 Covers all U.S. and Canadian models of RX-2, RX-3, RX-4, 808, 1300, 1600, Cosmo, GLC and 626	6981	VW Front Wheel Drive 1974-85 Covers all U.S. and Canadian models	6962
		VW 1949-71 Covers all U.S. and Canadian models	5796
Mazda Pick-Ups 1972-86 Covers all U.S. and Canadian models	7659	VW 1970-79 Spanish	7081
Mercedes-Benz 1959-70 Covers all U.S. and Canadian models	6065	VW 1970-81 Covers all U.S. and Canadian Beetles, Karmann Ghia, Fastback, Squareback, Vans, 411 and 412	6837
Mercedes-Benz 1968-73 Covers all U.S. and Canadian models	5907		

Chilton's Repair Manuals are available at your local retailer or by mailing a check or money order for **$15.95** per book plus **$3.50** for 1st book and **$.50** for each additional book to cover postage and handling to:

**Chilton Book Company
Dept. DM
Radnor, PA 19089**

NOTE: When ordering be sure to include your name & address, book part No. & title.